VISUAL QUICKSTART GUIDE

MACROMEDIA
FLASH MX 2004

FOR WINDOWS AND MACINTOSH

Katherine Ulrich

 Pea

Visual QuickStart Guide
Macromedia Flash MX 2004 for Windows and Macintosh
Katherine Ulrich

Peachpit Press

1249 Eighth Street
Berkeley, CA 94710
510/524-2178
800/283-9444
510/524-2221 (fax)

Find us on the World Wide Web at: www.peachpit.com
To report errors, please send a note to errata@peachpit.com
Peachpit Press is a division of Pearson Education

Published in association with Macromedia Press
Copyright © 2004 by Katherine Ulrich

Editors: Suki Gear, Becky Morgan
Production Editor: Lupe Edgar
Copyeditor: Nancy Reinhardt
Technical Editor: Sharon Selden
Compositors: Owen Wolfson, Christi Payne
Indexer: Karin Arrigoni
Cover design: Peachpit Press
Cover production: Nathalie Valette

Notice of Rights

Notice of Liability

The information in this book is distributed on an "As Is" basis, without warranty. While every precaution has been taken in the preparation of the book, neither the author nor Peachpit Press shall have any liability to any person or entity with respect to any loss or damage caused or alleged to be caused directly or indirectly by the instructions contained in this book or by the computer software and hardware products described in it.

Trademarks

Visual QuickStart Guide is a registered trademark of Peachpit Press, a division of Pearson Education.

Macromedia is a registered trademark, and Flash and Macromedia Flash are trademarks of Macromedia, Inc., in the United States and/or other countries.

All other trademarks are the property of their respective owners.

Throughout this book, trademarks are used. Rather than put a trademark symbol with every occurrence of a trademarked name, we state that we are using the names in an editorial fashion only and to the benefit of the trademark owner with no intention of infringement of the trademark. No such use, or the use of any trade name, is intended to convey endorsement or other affiliation with this book.

ISBN 0-321-21344-0

9 8 7 6

Printed and bound in the United States of America

Dedication

To Perry Whittle, who continues to offer both moral and technical support, who helps me keep it all in perspective, and who downplays my failings and promotes my successes shamelessly.

Thank You:

Special thanks to the editors of this edition, Suki Gear and Becky Morgan, for shepherding this book through its various stages. A huge and heartfelt thank you to Sharon Selden, Flash Quality Assurance Engineer, Macromedia, who gave the manuscript a careful and thoughtful technical edit, and gave generously of her time to answer my numerous questions, guiding me through the murkier waters of Flash—even from halfway around the world. Thanks also to Wendy Sharp, Macromedia Press Editor, Peachpit Press; and James Talbot, Principal Instructor, Macromedia, for their technical assistance and advice. Kudos to copyeditor Nancy Reinhardt for catching my typos, lapses of grammar, and occasional half-finished thoughts; and to Production Editor Lupe Edgar and compositors Owen Wolfson and Christi Payne for making these pages clean and clear.

A tip of the hat to those whose various forms of assistance in past editions still echo in this one: Brad Bechtel, Lisa Brazieal, Erika Burback, Jeremy Clark, Cliff Colby, Peter Alan Davy, Jane DeKoven, Jonathan Duran, Victor Gavenda, Erica Norton, Janice Pearce, Kathy Simpson, Bentley Wolfe, and Lisa Young.

And finally, a grateful thank you to Marjorie Baer, Executive Acquisitions and Development Editor, Peachpit Press, for her supportive friendship and for bringing me to this project in the first place.

CONTENTS AT A GLANCE

TABLE OF CONTENTS

TABLE OF CONTENTS

TABLE OF CONTENTS

TABLE OF CONTENTS

INTRODUCTION

Vectors on the Web! That was the early promise and excitement of Flash, back when the Internet was expanding exponentially and suddenly everybody wanted a "Web presence, filled with color and motion." Macromedia Flash gave Web designers an efficient way to send artwork and animation over the limited-bandwidth connections that most viewers had. Plus it offered a full set of natural-style drawing tools for creating graphic content and animating it. Another Flash advantage was its assistive scripting feature, which made the process of adding interactivity easy even for those who know little about scripting.

Ultimately, Flash's efficiency at feeding graphics through the Internet's bandwidth constrictions also attracted Web-content developers seeking to create more complex interactive and data-driven sites, developers who were more knowledgeable about (and/or willing to invest more time in learning and working with) complex coding and scripting procedures. With each new generation of the product, as Web developers continually push the boundaries of Flash's interactive capabilities, Macromedia has responded by increasingly exposing the inner workings of Flash through ActionScript and, now in Flash MX 2004, through the JavaScript API. Today, ActionScript is a full-fledged scripting language, and Flash is a tool designed to address the needs not only of designers who want to create beautiful, low-bandwidth artwork and animation, but also of developers who want to create robust multimedia Internet applications quickly. To that end, the latest version of Flash is actually two versions: Macromedia Flash MX 2004 and Macromedia Flash MX 2004 Professional. While the standard version of Flash is still a tool for application development, it's safe to say that most of the additional new features found in the professional version target advanced application developers more than they target beginning Flash users, or developers who focus on creating artwork and animation. The audience for this Flash Visual QuickStart Guide, falls more into the second category of Flash users, and therefore, this book covers only the standard version of Flash.

What Is Streaming?

Most viewers lack the patience to wait for an entire site to download, especially one that has big bitmaps, sounds, or video. Flash streams the content of your Web site over the Internet. Streaming means that once some of the vector art of your site has downloaded, Flash can display it while the rest of your data continues to download. As Flash plays the first frames of your movie, subsequent frames keep coming into your viewer's computer, and Flash feeds them out at the specified frame rate. If you plan your movie right, the frames coming in never catch up to the frames being displayed, and your viewer sees only a continuous flow of images.

About Flash

Flash began life as Future Splash Animator, a nifty little program for creating and animating vector art. In 1997, Macromedia acquired Future Splash, changed the name to Flash, and promoted the program as a tool for creating graphic content for the World Wide Web. The early Flash excelled as a Web-site-design tool because it provided everything you needed to put together a visually inter-esting Web site (as opposed to a text-only one): tools for creating graphic elements; tools for animating those elements; tools for creating interface elements and interactivity; and tools for writing the HTML necessary to display those graphics, animations, and interface elements as a Web page via a browser. Today, in addition to those tools, Flash also includes ActionScript 2.0 for scripting com-plex interactivity, video-import tools, and data-handling components that allow creation of Web sites that give viewers an even richer experience.

With each new generation of Flash, Macromedia has added features and func-tions that expand the program's capabilities. Originally centered on creating vector art-work, animation, and basic interactivity, Flash has become a toolkit for creating what have come to be called Rich Internet Applications (RIAs). An RIA might be any-thing, from an on-line store to a corporate training module to a snazzy promotional piece describing this year's hottest new car, complete with customizable virtual test-drives. Yet the program still preserves the easy-to-use drawing and animation tools that made it so popular to begin with. And Flash continues to assist authors with differ-ing skill levels to create the interactivity their projects require.

Flash MX 2004 Updater 7.0.1

As this book goes to press, Macromedia has just announced that it is working on an update for Flash MX 2004. This release will solve some problems that have cropped up in the initial release. To learn about how this update affects the specific tasks described in the following chapters, check out Peachpit Press's com-panion Web site for this book, located at *http://www.peachpit.com/vqs/flashmx2004/*.

About Flash

Vectors Versus Bitmaps

The data that creates vector graphics and the data that creates bitmapped graphics are similar, in that they are both mathematical instructions to the computer about where and how to create images onscreen. Bitmaps, however, are lengthier and result in a less versatile graphic; vector graphics are compact and fully scaleable.

Bitmap instructions break a whole graphic into little dots and must tell the computer about each dot; vector instructions describe the graphic mathematically as a series of lines and arcs (**Figure i.1**). Picture a 1-inch black horizontal line on a field of white. For a bitmap, the instructions would go something like this: Make a white dot, make a white dot, make a black dot, make a black dot, make a black dot, make a black dot, and so on. These instructions would repeat until you'd strung together enough black dots to make a 1-inch line. Then the white-dot instructions would start again and continue until the rest of the screen was filled with white dots. The vector instructions would simply be a mathematical formula for a straight line, plus the coordinates that define the line's position onscreen.

Figure i.1 For a computer to draw a bitmapped graphic, it must receive a set of instructions for each dot (each bit of data) that makes up the image. Instructions for a vector graphic describe the lines and curves that make up the image mathematically. The bitmapped line (left) appears much rougher than the vector line (right). You can't enlarge the bitmapped line without losing quality. But you can make the vector line as big as you like; it retains its solid appearance.

What Makes Flash a Special Web-Design Tool?

Flash's early claim to fame was its ability to deliver vector images over the Web. What's the advantage of using vector graphics? Vectors keep file sizes down, and they are scaleable, which means that you can maintain control of what a Web site looks like when your viewer resizes the browser window, for example, making the whole thing stay in proportion as the window grows or shrinks.

Another advantage that Flash provides is streaming capability. Streaming allows some elements of a Web site to display immediately upon download while more information continues to arrive over the Internet. Both the use of vector images and the use of streaming enhance the viewer's experience.

Other facets of Flash's appeal include its ability to create original artwork with both Bézier and natural-style drawing tools; its ability to handle imported artwork, sound, and video; and its ability to assist designers and developers in creating animation and interactivity. Over time, Macromedia has enhanced Flash's tools for creating interactivity. Now, Flash contains a full-fledged object-oriented scripting language. ActionScript 2.0 is compliant with the ECMA-262 specification, making it much more like JavaScript. ActionScript 2.0 supports inheritance, strong typing, and the event model.

How Flash Animates

Flash uses standard animation techniques to create the illusion of movement. You create a series of still images, each slightly different from the next. By displaying the images rapidly, one after another, you simulate continuous movement. Flash's animation tools help you create, organize, and synchronize the animation of multiple graphic elements, sounds, and video clips.

Flash File Formats

Flash is both an authoring environment for creating content and a playback system for making that content viewable on a local computer or in a Web browser. You create artwork, animation, and interactivity in Flash-format files. These files have the extension .fla, and are often referred to as FLAs. To make that content viewable on the Web, you convert the .fla files to Flash Player format; Flash Player files have the extension .swf. Another name for the playable format is SWF (pronounced *swif*).

How Flash Delivers

Flash's publishing feature creates the necessary HTML code to display your Flash content in a Web browser. You can also choose alternate methods of delivering Flash content—as animated GIF images, for example, or as a QuickTime movie. Flash creates those alternate files during the publishing process.

WHAT MAKES FLASH A SPECIAL WEB-DESIGN TOOL?

Flash MX 2004: What's New?

Recognizing the enormous scope of the application, Macromedia has begun to divide Flash into two versions: Macromedia Flash 2004 and Macromedia Flash 2004 Professional. The two versions don't directly correlate to the divisions we often make about who uses Flash: designer versus developer, artist versus programmer, beginner/amateur versus experienced professional. The standard version of Flash is still a tool that lets both halves of those dualities create artistic, interactive, Web content. The professional version of Flash adds extra features designed to be of particular help to those who use Flash to develop Web applications. This book is really aimed at helping beginner-to-intermediate Flash users, focusing more on Flash's design and animation than on scripting. Therefore, the exercises in the chapters that follow cover the standard version of Flash only. The headings below list some of the new features of Flash MX 2004 that will be of particular interest to beginning and intermediate Flash creators.

Start Page

The Start page (**Figure i.2**) is an optional method for accessing files and information; it eliminates the need to go through menu commands and dialog boxes to open new or existing Flash Documents. The Start page contains links to the last ten Flash files you edited, links for creating new documents (from scratch or from templates), links to Macromedia's Web site for downloading updated Help content, to Macromedia Exchange to download extensions to Flash, or to Macromedia's online store.

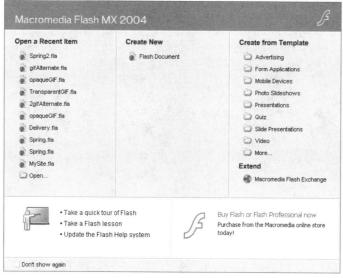

Figure i.2 The first time you launch Flash, you'll see the Start Page. You can configure Flash to display this page each time you launch, or to hide it.

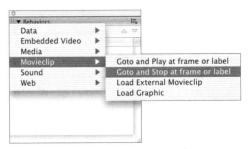

Figure i.3 The Behaviors that come standard with Flash appear in the Add Behavior menu in the Behaviors panel. After you apply Behaviors to a selected keyframe or object, the Behaviors panel lists those scripts whenever you select that keyframe or object.

Timeline Effects and Behaviors

To assist with the creation of animation and interactivity, Flash MX 2004 introduces Timeline Effects and Behaviors. Timeline Effects assist you in creating common animations, for example, moving or rotating graphic elements and text, creating wipes and fades, or creating exploding effects. To apply a Timeline Effect, you select a graphic element and choose a command from a menu. Similarly, Behaviors allow you to attach ActionScript to a selected keyframe or object to perform common actions, such as moving to a specified frame, or stopping and starting playback of movie clips, sounds, or video clips (**Figure i.3**).

Timeline Effects and Behaviors are both part of Flash's new extensibility. Anyone with knowledge of JavaScript can develop additional effects and behaviors and share them. Macromedia Exchange is one forum where such items may be available. Within larger design studios, where some workers specialize in developing Flash applications and scripting while others focus on design and animation, Flash's new extensibility features enable the scripting specialist to create effects and behaviors to streamline the work flow for their colleagues.

History Panel, Spelling Checker, Find and Replace, Help

Flash MX 2004 offers a number of new productivity utilities for Flash authors: a spelling checker for checking and correcting text anywhere in a Flash document; a find-and-replace feature that works on text strings, fonts, colors, symbols, sounds, video clips, and bitmap graphics (**Figure i.4**); a History panel that allows you to undo multiple steps in a single operation, to replay or repeat a series of steps, to apply a series of steps to various objects, to apply steps multiple times, and to save steps for future use. Documentation for Flash and ActionScript, tutorials, and reference guides are now integrated into a single Help panel. This panel can be updated as Macromedia makes changes to its documentation or offers new training materials.

PDF and EPS Import, Alias text

Flash now allows you to import high-quality artwork from .pdf, and .eps files. Flash has improved the way it renders small font sizes, and gives you more control over the antialiasing of text.

Enhanced Video Import

A new Video Import Wizard contains preset encoding profiles that help make the video clips you bring into Flash play back appropriately for your target viewers. The wizard also enables you to carry out some simple edits before importing video: trimming a video clip, dividing one large clip into a series of smaller clips, doing simple color correction, and cropping.

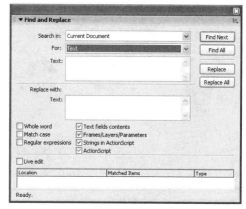

Figure i.4 Flash's Find and Replace feature enables you to search for and replace text strings, fonts, colors, symbols, sounds, video clips, and bitmap graphics.

A Word About Assistance for ActionScript

For Flash beginners, and those not yet ready to learn the ins and outs of scripting, a big change in MX 2004 is a reduction in the quantity and quality of assistance for using ActionScript. In previous versions of Flash, the Actions panel offered Normal mode, a feature that made scripting easy, walking you through all the requirements of each action statement and handling syntax for you. The Actions panel in MX 2004 offers no assisted-scripting mode. Instead, Flash implements a new panel: Behaviors. Behaviors create specific pre-set scripts for common simple actions (such as using gotoAndStop to make a navigation button). Although the Behaviors panel helps you to modify some aspects of these packaged scripts (for example, changing the mouse movements that trigger the button), Behaviors are less flexible than Normal mode, and the selection of Behaviors packaged with Flash is somewhat limited. On the plus side, however, Flash's new extensibility features, which make Behaviors possible, open the door to the creation of many more Behaviors in future. Ultimately, nonprogrammers may find plenty of scripting power is available thanks to third-party Behaviors.

Because a Visual QuickStart Guide cannot hope even to scratch the surface of what you need to know to really create scripts on your own with ActionScript, the exercises in this book focus on the kinds of scripting you can do with Flash's standard Behaviors.

Publish Settings Changes and Player Improvements

New publish settings options, notably a version-detection feature, help you to present your content to as wide an audience as possible. You can now create and save profiles for common combinations of publish settings options. Flash Player incorporates more strict security features. In addition, enhancements to the player make for faster delivery of Flash content to your audience.

ActionScript 2.0 and Other Advanced Features

Although they're not covered in this book, the following advanced features are all available in the standard version of Flash MX 2004. Flash is now much more extensible. Anyone who can use JavaScript can make new tools, new commands, new Timeline Effects, and new Behaviors through the JavaScript Application Programming Interface. Flash offers full support for Unicode, making it easier to publish localized versions of your content. A Strings panel that allows fast replacement of text strings will also help with localization. An updated version of ActionScript (2.0), which is compliant with the ECMA-262 specification and is more object oriented, will make creating interactivity easier for those already familiar with other scripting languages.

FLASH MX 2004: WHAT'S NEW?

Flash MX 2004 Professional: Overview

The Professional version of Flash contains all of the features found in the standard version, but has additional features that will be especially useful to those developing Web-based applications or sites that integrate a variety of data sources. There are also special features for collaborative workflows and for videographers.

The Professional version offers two new document types: Slide Presentation and Forms Application. Based on a screen metaphor instead of a Timeline, these documents let you organize material hierarchically, in separate pages, when time sequence is not the most relevant factor. Screens are designed for creating slide presentations or forms-based applications. Flash MX Professional also offers project-management and source-control features for shared workflow. Pro users, who incorporate lots of video into Flash, can download a plug-in that works with many of today's top rated video-editing packages, allowing them to export .flv files directly from a supported video-editor. The .flv files can then be linked for progressive download and playback with Flash content. The Pro version also allows Flash authors to open separate scripting documents for creating external ActionScript or JavaScript files, without leaving the Flash authoring environment.

The Mystery of Extensibility

In version 5, Macromedia broadened the scope of Flash's ActionScript language, allowing Flash authors to access some of Flash's internal programming commands to create graphics and interactivity for their audience at runtime (that is, when viewers watch or interact with a movie or application). Flash MX 2004 introduces a different way to access some of Flash's internal programming commands, this time to create graphics and animation within the Flash authoring environment. The feature that makes this possible is called the *JavaScript API.* Basically an API *(application programming interface)* runs interference between two different programs allowing the two to communicate in prescribed ways. In this case it allows a developer using JavaScript to tell Flash to do certain things that normally only the engineers who created Flash could tell it to do.

The JavaScript API allows developers to write instructions (scripts) in JavaScript that tell Flash to carry out certain operations within the authoring environment. The Extensibility API makes it possible to add commands to Flash menus, or add new tools to the Toolbar, for example one that draws 3-D cubes or graphs.

How to Use This Book

Like all Visual QuickStart Guides, this book seeks to take you out of the passive reading mode and help you get started working in the program. The exercises in the book teach you to use Flash's features. The book is suitable for beginners who are just starting to use Flash and for intermediate-level Flash designers. The initial chapters cover the basics of creating graphic elements by using Flash's unique set of drawing tools. Next, you learn how to turn graphic elements into animations. After that, you learn to create basic user-interface elements, such as rollover buttons. To make your content interactive, you'll use Behaviors to create basic ActionScript. There's also information about importing and working with various non-Flash content, artwork from other applications, sounds, and video clips. There's an overview of Flash's new authoring utilities. Finally, you learn to use Flash's Publish feature to create the HTML that you need to put your Flash creations on the Web.

Cross-Platform Issues

Macromedia designed Flash's authoring environment to have, as much as possible, the same interface on the Macintosh as it has on the Windows platform. Still, differences exist where the user interfaces of the platforms diverge. When these differences are substantial, this book describes the procedures for both platforms. Illustrations of dialog boxes come from both platforms, but generally, there is no special indication as to which platform is shown. If a given feature differs greatly between platforms, the variations are illustrated. If a feature is available only on one platform, that is noted in the text. Originally Macintosh computers required Macintosh keyboards and some key names were unique to that keyboard, for example, Return (instead of Enter) and Delete (instead of backspace). This book generally uses Enter and Delete for these two key names.

Keyboard Shortcuts

Most of Flash's menu-based commands have a keyboard equivalent. That equivalent appears in the menu next to the command name. When this book first introduces a command, it also describes the keyboard shortcut. In subsequent mentions of the command, however, the keyboard shortcut usually is omitted. You'll find a complete list of these commands on Peachpit Press's companion Web site for this book *http://www.peachpit.com/vqs/flashmx2004*.

Contextual Menus

Both the Macintosh and Windows platforms offer contextual menus. To access one of these contextual menus, Control-click (Mac) or right-click (Windows) an element in the Flash movie. You'll see a menu of commands that are appropriate for working with that element. For the most part, these commands duplicate commands in the main menu; therefore, this book does not generally note them as alternatives for the commands described in the book. The book does point out when using the contextual menu is particularly handy or when a contextual menu contains a command that is unavailable from the main menu bar.

The Artwork

The Flash graphics in this book are simple and easy to draw. In most cases, the examples are based on simple geometric shapes, which means that you can spend your time seeing the Flash features in action instead of re-creating fancy artwork. To make it even easier for you to follow along, Flash files containing the graphic elements that you need for each task are available on the Peachpit Press's companion Web site for this book, *http://www.peachpit.com/vqs/flashmx2004*.

System Requirements

You can create Flash MX 2004 content on the Macintosh and Windows platforms. As a Flash author, you must consider not only the requirements for creating and viewing Flash content on your own system, but also the requirements for viewers of your Flash content. The following sections list the system requirements for both activities.

To create and edit Flash MX 2004 content on a Macintosh:

◆ **Processor:** Power Macintosh

◆ **Operating system:** Mac OS X 10.2.6 or later

◆ **Free RAM:** 128 MB RAM (256 MB recommended)

◆ **Free disk space:** 215 MB

◆ **Monitor:** 16-bit (thousands of colors), 32-bit (millions of colors) recommended, 1024-by-768 resolution, or greater

To create and edit Flash MX 2004 content in Windows:

◆ **Processor:** 600 MHz Intel Pentium III (or equivalent)

◆ **Operating system:** Windows 98 SE; Windows 2000, or Windows XP

◆ **Free RAM:** 128 MB (256 MB recommended)

◆ **Free disk space:** 275 MB

◆ **Monitor:** 16-bit (thousands of colors), 32-bit (millions of colors) recommended, 1024-by-768 resolution, or greater

To view Flash MX 2004 content (in Flash Player 7) via browser:

◆ **For Macintosh OS 9.x:** Netscape 4.8 or Netscape 7.x, Microsoft Internet Explorer 5.1, or Opera 6

◆ **For Macintosh OS X 10.1.x:** Netscape 7.x, Microsoft Internet Explorer 5.2, Mozilla 1.x, AOL 7, or Opera 6.

◆ **For Macintosh OS X 10.2.x:** Any of the browsers for OS X 10.1.x or Safari 1.0

◆ **For Windows 98:** Netscape 4.7 or 7.x, Internet Explorer 5.x, Mozilla 1.x, AOL 8, or Opera 7.11

◆ **For Windows Me:** Netscape 4.7 or 7.x, Internet Explorer 5.5, Mozilla 1.x, AOL 8, or Opera 7.11

◆ **For Window 2000:** Any of the browsers for Windows 98 or CompuServe 7

◆ **For Windows XP:** Netscape 7.x, Internet Explorer 6.0, Mozilla 1.x, CompuServe 7, AOL 8, or Opera 7.11

About Flash Player

In Flash's early days, the need to use a player to view Flash content was considered to be a drawback to creating Web content with Flash. Designers feared that users would be reluctant to spend time downloading another helper application for their browsers. But Flash has become the de facto standard for delivering Web "rich-media" content, especially interactive vector art and animation on the Web, and Flash Player is now widely distributed. Macromedia estimates that 98 percent of machines that are being used to access the Internet already have some version of Flash Player installed.

THE FLASH AUTHORING TOOL

1

Before you get started creating projects in Macromedia Flash MX 2004, it's helpful to take a look around the authoring environment and begin to recognize and manipulate its components. When you open Flash, for the first time, you'll see the Flash Start page. This page acts as a gateway to many documents and operations in Flash. When you open a Flash Document, you enter the Flash authoring environment. Each Flash Document consists of four basic items: the Timeline, a record of every frame, layer, and scene in your movie; the Edit Bar, which displays identifying text and menus for choosing symbols and scenes to work on; the Stage, the actual area in which your movie displays; and the work area, a space that surrounds the Stage during authoring but doesn't appear in the final, published movie. The Stage and work area are always present when you work on a document. You can collapse or close the Timeline and hide the Edit Bar, and you can open any combination of other panels and tools that you need to work with your Flash content.

What does the Flash authoring environment look like? And how do you access tools and different views? This chapter presents a quick tour of the Flash authoring environment. Subsequent chapters explain in more detail what's what as you really get into using each element.

Understanding Flash Basics

For the most part, the way Flash works—in terms of installing the application, creating new documents, closing documents, and saving files—presents nothing unusual to the experienced computer user. The Flash installation software guides you through each step of the installation process. New in Flash MX 2004 is the requirement that you activate the product. Activation is a method that Macromedia has adopted to help guard against software piracy. You can activate Flash over the Internet or over the telephone. The procedures for launching the application and creating and saving documents are all standard. Because the Macintosh and Windows platforms offer users a variety of ways to organize their computers and workflow—such as using shortcuts (Windows), using aliases (Mac), and creating your own hierarchical setup for storing applications and data—it's impossible to cover all the ways you might set up and access files on your computer. But here are the basics of setting up Flash.

To begin installing Flash from a CD (Mac):

1. Insert the Flash MX 2004 CD.

   The Flash MX 2004 CD icon appears on the Desktop.

2. Double-click the CD icon.

   A window, containing the Flash MX 2004 installer icon, appears (**Figure 1.1**).

3. Double-click the installer icon.

   The installer window for Flash MX 2004 opens (**Figure 1.2**).

To begin installing Flash from a CD (Windows):

◆ Insert the Flash MX CD.

   The installer window for Flash MX 2004 opens (**Figure 1.3**).

Figure 1.1 The icon of the Flash MX 2004 installer on the Macintosh.

Figure 1.2 The opening screen of the Flash MX installer software on the Macintosh.

Figure 1.3 The opening screen of the Flash MX installer software on Windows.

Macintosh icon   *Windows icon*

Figure 1.4 Double-clicking the Flash MX 2004 application icon launches Flash.

To install and activate Flash:

1. Follow the steps appropriate to your system in the preceding exercises.

2. Click the Install button.

   The installation software walks you through all the necessary steps for installing and activating Flash. The installer asks you to read and accept a licensing agreement, to indicate where to place the working software on your system, to enter a serial number, and to activate the program. Keep that serial number in a safe place; you will have to reenter it should you ever need to reinstall Flash.

To launch Flash:

1. In the Finder (Mac), navigate to the Flash icon.

   or

   From the desktop (Windows), navigate to the Flash icon (**Figure 1.4**).

2. Double-click the icon.

   The first time Flash launches, it opens the Start page (see the "Touring the Start Page" sidebar). For subsequent launches Flash opens according to the settings in the General tab of the Preferences dialog.

UNDERSTANDING FLASH BASICS

The Mystery of Product Activation

Product activation is a method of verifying that someone installing software has purchased a legal copy of the software, has an appropriate serial number, and is not attempting to install the software on more computers than he or she is entitled to. If you have a live Internet connection, entering your serial number when asked during installation automatically carries out the activation procedure. If you do not have access to the Internet, after entering your serial number during installation, you have the option to call a toll-free number and activate Flash over the telephone. Flash's installer helps you find the correct phone number for your geographic location and provides you with a special verification number for phone activation. Punch in the activation number using your telephone's keypad or speak the number into the phone-activation's voice-recognition system.

You have 30 days to activate Flash MX 2004 after you install it. During that time, you are basically using a trial version of the software.

To set launch preferences:

1. From the Flash application menu (Mac) or Edit menu (Windows), choose Preferences.

   The Preferences dialog appears. The general tab is selected by default.

2. In the General tab, to set a launch option, *click any of the following radio buttons* (**Figure 1.5**):

   ▲ Show Start Page (the default setting). Flash displays the Start page at launch and any time you have closed all of the document windows during a work session.

   ▲ New Document. Flash opens a new document at launch.

   ▲ Last Documents Open. Flash opens the documents that were open when you ended the previous work session.

   ▲ No document. Flash's menu bar and panels appear at launch, but no document opens.

3. Click OK.

✔ Tip

■ To change launch preferences to the New Document option quickly, click the Don't Show Again button in the lower-left corner of the Start page. A dialog box appears to remind you that you must change the launch settings in the General tab of the Preferences dialog to see the Start page again. In Windows, you see the Start page immediately after choosing the Show Start Page option in the Preferences dialog; on the Mac, you see the Start page only after you quit and relaunch Flash.

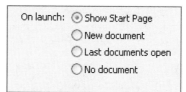

Figure 1.5 The On Launch options in the General tab of the Preferences dialog tell Flash what type of document(s), if any to open on start-up.

Touring the Start Page

Flash's default setting opens the Start page when you launch. The Start page contains active links that enable you to open documents quickly. You can open a new document, a document that you worked on recently, or a template document. You can link to Flash tutorials, or the Macromedia Flash Exchange site where you can download third-party extensions, such as new components, Timeline Effects, and Behaviors as they become available (**Figure 1.6**).

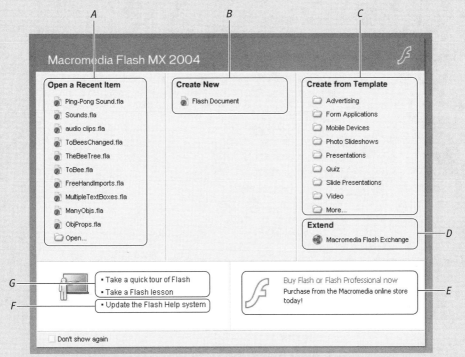

Figure 1.6 The Start page gathers together common operations you might want to carry out at the beginning of a work session: opening a document you worked on recently (A), creating a new Flash Document (B), or creating documents from Templates (C). There are also links for browsing the Macromedia Flash Exchange site, to find third-party extensions (D), visiting the Macromedia Online Store (E), and updating Flash's Help system (F). For new users there are links to the tutorials that come with Flash (G).

Working with Flash Documents

You have two ways to create new Flash documents: You can use a menu command, or choose a link from the Start page.

To create a new Flash Document:

◆ From the Start page, in the Create New section, click the Flash Document link.

Flash opens a new blank document.

or

1. From the File menu, choose New, or press ⌘-N (Mac) or Ctrl-N (Windows).

Flash opens the New Document dialog (**Figure 1.7**). This dialog offers two tabs, General and Templates. General is selected by default.

2. In the General tab, select Flash Document.

In Flash MX 2004, this is the only General-tab option and is therefore selected by default. In the Professional version of Flash, other document types appear in this tab.

3. Click OK.

Flash opens a new blank document.

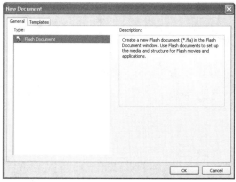

Figure 1.7 To create a new document in Flash, choose File > New. The New Document dialog opens, with the General tab and Flash Document selected by default. Click OK to create a new document.

Open a Recent Item

- Ping-Pong Sound.fla
- Sounds.fla
- audio clips.fla
- ToBeesChanged.fla
- TheBeeTree.fla
- ToBee.fla
- FreeHandImports.fla
- MultipleTextBoxes.fla
- ManyObjs.fla
- ObjProps.fla
- Open...

Figure 1.8 The Open a Recent Item section of the Start page allows you to view links to the last 10 documents you worked on. Clicking a filename opens the document.

To open an existing document:

◆ From the Start page, in the Open a Recent Item section, click the name of a recent file (**Figure 1.8**). Flash opens that file directly.

   or

1. From the Start page, in the Open a Recent Item section, click the Open link.

   or

   From the File menu, choose Open.

   The Open dialog appears.

2. Navigate to the file you want to open.

3. Select the file.

4. Click Open.

✔ Tip

■ In Windows, when you have multiple documents open and docked in the application window, the inactive documents appear in tabs above the top of the active document. Click a tab to bring that document to the front as the active document.

WORKING WITH FLASH DOCUMENTS

To close a document:

◆ In the top-left corner of the open document (Mac), click the close button.

or

◆ In the top-right corner of the document (Windows), click the close box (**Figure 1.9**).

To save changes to a document:

◆ From the File menu, choose Save.

Flash saves your changes to the file.

or

◆ From the File menu, choose Save As.

The Save As dialog appears, allowing you to name the file and place it in the location you desire on your hard drive. When you choose Save for a new document that has no name, the Save As dialog appears.

✔ Tips

■ When you've been working with a document for a while, making additions and deletions of graphic materials, sounds, video, and so on, the file size builds up because data about the deleted items remains in the file. Choosing File > Save and Compact reduces the file size. When you open the file and begin editing it, however, the file bulks up again pretty quickly. You may wish to compact the file only at the end of the authoring process or when file size is crucial, for example, if you need to e-mail the file to a colleague.

■ In the Macintosh operating system, you may experience a frustrating phenomenon with the Save As dialog. Any panels that you have open will float on top of the dialog. If you have sized a panel to take up a lot of room—as is often necessary with, for example, the Actions panel, or Movie Explorer—the Save As dialog may be completely hidden. To reveal it, just drag the open panels to the side.

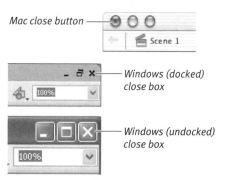

Mac close button

Windows (docked) close box

Windows (undocked) close box

Figure 1.9 Clicking the close button (Mac) or close box (Windows) closes a Flash document.

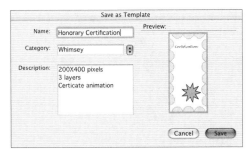

Figure 1.10 The Save As Template command allows you to save Flash documents for reuse. You can create your own template categories, and provide a brief description of the template file you are saving, in the Save As Template dialog.

✔ Tip

■ Once you've completed the basic template portions of the document, don't forget to close the document. You might think that after saving the document as a template you're now working in a copy made from the template, but you're not. You're still working on the master template document until the point that you close it.

Working with Template Documents

If you work repeatedly with one type of Flash Document—you create banner ads of a specific size with a consistent background or elements, for example—you can save that basic document as a template.

To create a template document:

1. Open the document that you want to turn into a template.

2. From the File menu, choose Save As Template.

   The Save As Template dialog appears, showing a preview of your document (**Figure 1.10**).

3. In the Name field, type a name for the template.

4. To specify a category; *do one of the following:*

   ▲ To select an existing category, from the Category pop-up menu, choose the desired category.

   ▲ To create a new category, in the Category field, type a name.

5. In the Description field, type a brief summary or reminder of what the template is for.

   Flash limits you to 255 words, but it's still a good idea to give some indication of the intended uses for the template or what its special features are.

6. Click Save.

   Flash saves the file as a master template document in a folder named Templates within the Configuration folder (see, "The Mystery of the Configuration Folder," later in this chapter).

To open a new document from a template document:

1. From the Start page, in the Create from Template section, click the name of a specific template folder or click the folder named More (**Figure 1.11**).

   The New from Template dialog appears.

   or

   From the File menu, choose New.

   The New Document/New From Template dialog appears (**Figure 1.12**). The New Document and New from Template dialogs are identical except for their names. Both display two tabs: General and Templates. The dialog's name changes to reflect the active tab. When you click a template folder in the Start page, the Templates tab is selected by default in the dialog.

2. From the Category list, choose the appropriate category.

3. From the Templates list, choose the template you want to use.

   The dialog previews the selected template's first frame and provides a brief description of the template, if one is available.

4. Click OK.

   Flash opens a new document with all the contents of the template.

Figure 1.11 Choose a template link in the Start page to access the New from Template dialog, or choose File > New to access the New Document dialog. The two dialogs are identical except for the name.

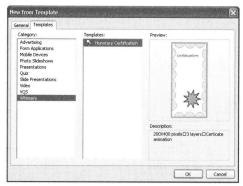

Figure 1.12 The Templates tab of the New from Template (or New Document) dialog, displays a preview and description (when available) for the item selected in the Category and Templates lists.

The Mystery of the Configuration Folder

The operating systems that run Flash MX 2004 can be configured for multiple users, storing each user's files and special settings separately. To deal with multiple users' customized settings, Flash uses two folders: One, called First Run, contains master files for all users; the other, Configuration, contains the files that each user has customized during work with the application. When you create a template document, for example, Flash stores it in a Templates folder inside the Configuration folder.

Every time you launch, Flash checks to make sure that all of the universal settings items from the First Run folder are covered by similar files in your Configuration folder. So, for example, with templates, Flash makes sure that Flash's default template folders and files are always available. If any items are missing, if you accidentally deleted the Quiz template folder from the Configuration folder, for example, Flash re-creates the missing folder and/or files in your Configuration folder. Flash ignores any additional customized files that you've created. They stay in your Configuration folder, just waiting for you.

To add, delete, or rename items in the Configuration folder manually, you must navigate the hierarchy of nested folders on your hard drive to open the folder. The first part of the folder hierarchy is slightly different in each operating system.

◆ **Windows 98:** `C:\WINDOWS\Application Data\`

◆ **Windows XP/2000:**
`C:\Documents and Settings\`*userName*`\Local Settings\Application Data\`

◆ **Mac OS X:** *HardDriveName*`:Users:`*userName*`:Library:Application Support:`

From there on, the hierarchy of folders is always the same. For those using the English version of Flash, it's: `Macromedia\Flash MX 2004\en\Configuration`. Users of localized versions will see their language code instead of `en` in the folder hierarchy.

Touring the Flash Authoring Environment

A Flash document consists of the Timeline, which holds the frames, layers, and scenes that make up your movie; the Stage, where the graphic content of the movie is displayed; the Edit Bar, which displays information about what you are currently editing, and provides access to other scenes and elements; and a work area, which extends beyond the Stage on all sides but remains outside the visible frame of the final movie as it plays (**Figure 1.13**).

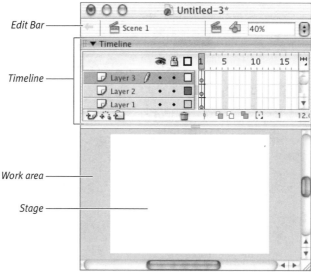

Edit Bar

Timeline

Work area

Stage

Figure 1.13 A new document opened in Flash consists of the Timeline, the Stage, the Edit Bar, and the work area.

About the Timeline

The Timeline is a visual representation of every frame, layer, and scene in your movie, in compressed form. Not only does the Timeline display the structure of your Flash creation, it is the framework on which you build your projects. The Timeline is a vital, complex organizational and navigational tool. You will use it extensively when you create animations. Then you'll need to go more deeply into its components. For now, you only need to understand the Timeline generally; you'll learn more about it in Chapter 8. **Figure 1.14** identifies the major Timeline elements. You can dock the Timeline to any side of a Flash window or float it as a separate window, collapse it, or hide it completely to get more room for working with elements on the Stage.

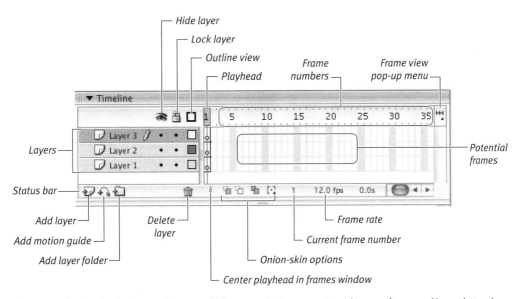

Figure 1.14 The Timeline is the complete record of your movie. It represents each scene, frame, and layer that make up the movie. Frames appear in chronological order. Clicking any frame in the Timeline takes you directly to that frame and displays its contents on the Stage.

To undock the Timeline window:

1. Position the pointer over the textured area on the left side of the title bar at the top of the Timeline.

   The pointer changes to the grabber hand (Mac) or move icon (Windows).

2. Click and drag away from the document window (**Figure 1.15**).

   A gray outline represents the Timeline window's position.

3. Release the mouse button where you want the Timeline to sit.

✔ Tip

- If you want to avoid accidentally redocking the Timeline, choose Edit > Preferences (Windows) or Flash > Preferences (Mac), then in the General tab of the Preferences dialog, select Disable Timeline Docking in the Timeline Options section.

To dock the Timeline:

1. Position the pointer over the title bar at the top of the Timeline window.

   The pointer changes to the grabber hand (Mac) or move icon (Windows).

2. Click and drag the Timeline to any of the four edges of the document window.

3. Release the mouse button when the pointer is at the edge of the window.

   The Timeline docks to that edge and resizes to fit the window.

Grab to drag for undocking

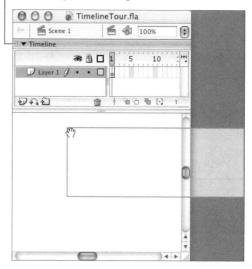

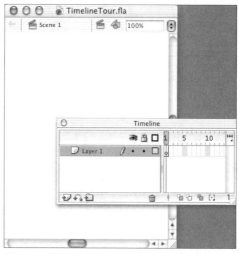

Figure 1.15 Drag the Timeline by the textured portion of its title bar (top) and then release the mouse button. The Timeline floats in its own window (bottom).

Click to collapse/expand

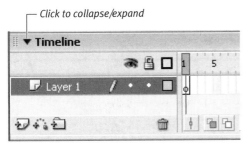

Figure 1.16 Click the triangle, the name, or anywhere to the right of the name in the title bar to collapse or expand the Timeline window.

The Mystery of the Timeline

If you think of your Flash movie as a book, the Timeline would be its interactive table of contents: Each scene is like a chapter; each frame is like a page. Imagine that you could point to Chapter 10 in the table of contents, and the book would flip open to the first page of that chapter. In Flash, when you click a frame in the Timeline (or when the playhead enters a frame), that frame appears in your document window.

A Flash movie is much more complex than a book, of course. Each movie "page" may actually be several transparent sheets stacked one on top of another. Flash keeps track of these "sheets" in what it calls *layers*. And the whole "book" appears to be in motion as you move through the table of contents, with some unseen hand flipping the pages.

✔ Tips

- Docking the Timeline vertically (at the left or right edge of the document window) gives you easy access to several layers at a time. Docking the Timeline horizontally increases the number of easily accessible frames.

- On a Mac, you can dock the Timeline to the left side of the Stage or undock it completely by positioning the pointer midway between the title bar and the first layer, in the gray area to the left of the eye icon. Click the left side of that area, up to about the letter *e* in *Timeline* to dock the Timeline to the left side of the Stage; click the right side to undock the Timeline.

- If you're having trouble redocking the Timeline, check that Disable Timeline Docking is not selected in the General tab of the Preferences dialog.

To hide the Timeline:

- From the Window menu, choose Timeline; or press Option-⌘-T (Mac) or Ctrl-Alt-T (Windows) to toggle between hiding and showing the Timeline.

✔ Tips

- To hide a floating Timeline quickly, simply click the close box (Windows) or the close button (Mac) to close the Timeline as you would any window.

- You can collapse the Timeline window. Clicking the arrow to the left of the name *Timeline*, or anywhere in the title bar toggles between the collapsed and expanded Timeline view (**Figure 1.16**).

ABOUT THE TIMELINE

15

About Document Properties

The Document Properties dialog defines the Stage (its dimensions, the color of the background on which your artwork appears, and the units of measure for rulers and grids) and sets a frame rate for playing your movie. You can also set some document properties in the Document Property Inspector. You'll learn more about using the Property Inspector later in this chapter.

The Stage is the area containing all the graphic elements that make up a Flash movie. Think of it as being the screen on which you will project your movie. At your local movie house, the screen is whatever size the management could afford to buy for the available space. In Flash, you control how big the screen is, and what color it is, through the Document Properties dialog.

Frames are the lifeblood of your animation, and the *frame rate* is the heart that keeps that blood flowing at a certain speed. Flash's default setting is 12 frames per second (fps)—a good setting for work viewed over the Web. (By comparison, the standard frame rate for film movies is double that speed.) Frame rate is another property that you set in the Document Properties dialog. You'll learn more about how frame rates affect animation in Chapter 8.

To open the Document Properties dialog:

Do one of the following:

◆ From the Modify menu, choose Document; or press ⌘-J (Mac) or Ctrl-J (Windows).

◆ In the Timeline's Status bar, double-click the frame-rate display (**Figure 1.17**). The Document Properties dialog appears (**Figure 1.18**).

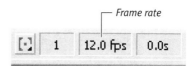

Frame rate

Figure 1.17 Double-clicking the frame-rate box in the Status bar is a quick way to access the Document Properties dialog.

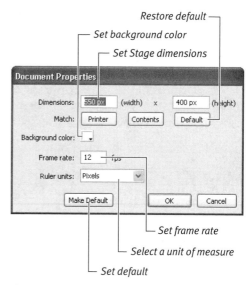

Restore default

Set background color

Set Stage dimensions

Set frame rate

Select a unit of measure

Set default

Figure 1.18 The Document Properties dialog is where you set all the parameters for viewing the Stage. Selecting a unit of measure for the rulers resets the unit measurement for all the Stage's parameters. Clicking the color box pops up the current set of colors and lets you choose one for the background. Clicking Save Default sets the parameters for all new documents you create.

✔ Tip

■ The Document Property Inspector also contains a shortcut to the Document Properties dialog. Just click the Size button. You'll learn more about the Property Inspector later in this chapter.

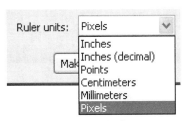

Figure 1.19 Choose a unit of measurement from the Ruler Units pop-up menu.

To set the units of measure:

1. In the Document Properties dialog, click the Ruler Units pop-up menu.

   A list of units appears (**Figure 1.19**).

2. Select the units you prefer to work in.

   Flash uses these units to calculate all measured items on the Stage: rulers, grid spacing, and dimensions.

3. Click OK.

✔ Tip

■ If you want a banner that's 1 inch tall and 5 inches wide but don't know what that size is in pixels (the standard units of measure used for working on the Web), Document Properties can figure it out for you. First, set Ruler Units to inches. Type 1 in the Width field and 5 in the Height field. Then return to Ruler Units and choose pixels. Flash does the math for you and sets the Stage dimensions. (Note that Flash uses screen pixels in its calculations, which means that an inch in your movie may differ from an inch in the real world, depending on the resolution of the monitor on which you view the Flash movie.)

ABOUT DOCUMENT PROPERTIES

To set the size of the Stage:

1. Open the Document Properties dialog and *do one of the following:*

   ▲ To set the Stage's dimensions, type values for Width and Height in the appropriate fields of the Dimensions section (**Figure 1.20**). Flash automatically assigns the units of measure currently selected in Ruler Units (see "To set the units of measure" earlier in this chapter).

   ▲ To create a Stage big enough to cover all the elements in your movie, in the Match section of the Document Properties dialog, click the Contents button (**Figure 1.21**). Flash calculates the minimum Stage size required to cover all the elements in the movie and enters those measurements in the Width and Height fields of the Dimensions section.

   ▲ To set the Stage size to the maximum print area currently available, in the Match section of the Document Properties dialog, click the Printer button. Flash gets the paper size from the Page Setup dialog, subtracts the current margins, and puts the resulting measurements in the Width and Height fields of the Dimensions section.

2. Click OK.

✔ Tip

■ If you've entered new dimensions either manually, or by clicking the Printer or Contents buttons, you can return to the default Stage dimensions by clicking the Default button.

Figure 1.20 To assign new proportions to your Stage, type a width and height in the Dimensions section of the Document Properties dialog.

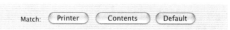

Figure 1.21 To make your Stage just big enough to enclose the objects in your movie, click the Contents button in the Match section of the Document Properties dialog.

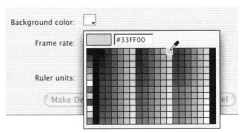

Figure 1.22 To assign your Stage a new color, choose one from the Background Color pop-up swatch set in the Document Properties dialog.

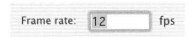

Figure 1.23 Typing a frame rate for your movie in the Frame Rate field of the Document Properties dialog sets Flash to display that number of frames in 1 second.

To set the background color:

1. Open the Document Properties dialog.

2. Click the Background Color box.

   The pointer changes to an eyedropper, and a set of swatches appears (**Figure 1.22**).

3. To select a background color, *do one of the following:*

   ▲ To select the color directly below the tip of the eyedropper, with the eyedropper pointer, click a swatch or an item on the Stage or elsewhere on the screen.

   ▲ In the hexadecimal-color field, type a value and press Enter.

   The selected color appears in the Background Color box in the Document Properties dialog.

4. Click OK.

   The Stage now appears in the color you selected.

✔ Tip

■ The Document Property Inspector also contains a color box pop-up for selecting the movie's background color. You'll learn more about the Property Inspector later in this chapter.

To set the frame rate:

1. Open the Document Properties dialog.

2. In the Frame Rate field, type the number of frames you want Flash to display in 1 second (**Figure 1.23**).

3. Click OK.

   The frame-rate setting appears in the Status bar of the current document.

To save your settings as the default:

◆ In the Document Properties dialog, click the Make Default button.

   The current settings in the Document Properties dialog become the defaults for any new documents.

Touring the Edit Bar

Another feature of the Flash document window is the Edit Bar, which lives at the top of the Stage. Its default position is above the Timeline docked to the top edge of the Stage. You can also position the Edit Bar below the top-docked Timeline. (When the Timeline is floating, or docked to the bottom or sides of the Stage, the Edit Bar is still located at the top of the Stage. You can even make the Edit Bar disappear entirely.

The Edit Bar lets you know what mode you are working in (editing your document, or editing a symbol or group within the movie). The Edit Bar's pop-up menus give you the power to switch scenes, to choose a symbol to edit and immediately switch to symbol-editing mode, and to change the magnification for viewing the Stage. When you are editing symbols or groups, the Edit Bar displays information about the elements you are editing (**Figure 1.24**). To learn about working with groups, see Chapter 4; for symbols, see Chapter 6; for scenes, see Chapter 10.

To reposition the Edit Bar, ⌘-Shift double-click (Mac) or Alt-Shift double-click (Windows) any blank area within the Edit Bar. If the Edit Bar was initially above the Timeline, double-clicking sends it down below the Timeline. If the Edit Bar started out in the low position, double-clicking sends it to the top. To hide the Edit Bar, choose Windows > Toolbars > Edit Bar. If you choose to hide the Edit Bar, however, you may find it more difficult to know when you are editing symbols within your document and when you are working on the Stage in the main document (see Chapter 6 for more information about symbol-editing mode).

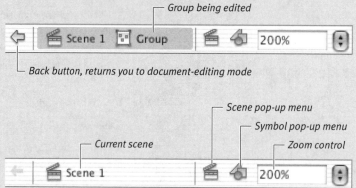

Figure 1.24 The Edit Bar is located above the Stage. You can use it to access symbols and scenes and to change magnification. In symbol-editing mode (top), the Edit Bar displays the name of the symbol you are editing. Clicking the Back button returns you to document-editing mode (bottom).

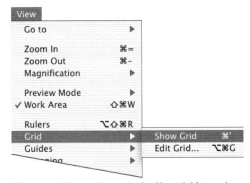

Figure 1.25 Choose View > Grid > Show Grid to make grid lines visible on the Stage during authoring.

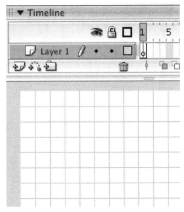

Figure 1.26 Visible grid lines help you position elements on the Stage during authoring.

Using Grids

A *grid* is a set of crisscrossing vertical and horizontal lines that acts as a guide for drawing and positioning elements, the way that graph paper functions in the nondigital world. Flash also uses the grid to align objects when you activate the Snap to Grid feature. The grid does not appear in your final movie.

To make grids visible:

Do one of the following:

◆ From the View menu, choose Grid > Show Grid (**Figure 1.25**).

◆ Press ⌘-apostrophe (') (Mac) or Ctrl-apostrophe (') (Windows).

A check indicates that this feature is on. Flash displays a set of crisscrossing lines as part of the Stage (**Figure 1.26**).

To set grid color:

1. From the View menu, choose Grid > Edit Grid, or press Option-⌘-G (Mac) or Ctrl-Alt-G (Windows).

   The Grid dialog appears (**Figure 1.27**).

2. Click the Color box.

   The pointer changes to an eyedropper, and a pop-up set of swatches appears (**Figure 1.28**).

3. To select a grid color, with the eyedropper, click a swatch or an item on the Stage.

   The selected color appears in the Color box in the Grid dialog. The grids on the Stage now appear in the color you selected.

4. Click OK.

To set grid spacing:

1. Follow step 1 of the preceding exercise to open the Grid dialog.

2. Type a value in the Width field.

3. Type a value in the Height field (**Figure 1.29**).

   The width and height values define the spacing of the grid. Note that the grid need not consist of perfect squares.

4. Click OK.

   The grid dimensions change on the Stage.

✔ Tips

■ In the Grid dialog, click the Save Default button to make your settings for grids the default for all new documents.

■ The Grids dialog contains a Snap Accuracy menu for setting the Snap Tolerance of grids, how close an item must get to the grid before Flash snaps the item to the grid.

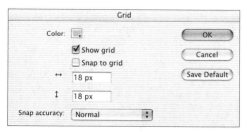

Figure 1.27 Choose View > Grid > Edit Grid to open the Grid dialog and change grid parameters.

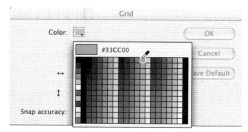

Figure 1.28 To select a new grid color, with the eyedropper pointer, click anywhere in the pop-up set of swatches or on the Stage. The pop-up color-swatch menu displays the currently selected color set.

Figure 1.29 Type values in the Width and Height fields to set grid spacing.

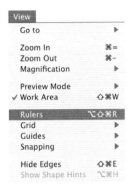

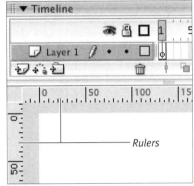

Figure 1.30 Choosing View > Rulers (top) makes rulers visible on the Stage (bottom).

Using Rulers and Guides

Rulers and guides aid you in drawing objects with precise sizes, shapes, and positions on the Stage.

To display rulers:

◆ From the View menu, choose Rulers, or press Option-Shift-⌘-R (Mac) or Ctrl-Alt-Shift-R (Windows).

Ruler bars appear on the left side and top of the Stage (**Figure 1.30**). To change ruler units, see "To set the units of measure" earlier in this chapter.

To hide rulers:

◆ With rulers visible on the Stage, choose View > Rulers, or press Option-Shift-⌘-R (Mac) or Ctrl-Alt-Shift-R (Windows).

To place a guide:

1. With rulers visible, position the pointer over the vertical or horizontal ruler bar.

   If you are using a tool other than the selection tool, the pointer changes to the selection arrow.

2. Click and drag the pointer onto the Stage.

   As you click, a small directional arrow appears next to the pointer, indicating which direction to drag (**Figure 1.31**).

3. Release the mouse button.

   Flash places a vertical or horizontal line on the Stage (**Figure 1.32**).

To reposition a guide:

1. From the Toolbar, select the selection tool.

2. On the Stage, position the selection tool over the guide you want to reposition.

   The direction arrow appears next to the pointer, indicating that the guide can be dragged.

3. Click and drag the guide to a new location.

4. Release the mouse button.

✔ Tips

■ To remove a guide, drag it completely off the Stage.

■ To avoid repositioning guides accidentally, choose View > Guides > Lock Guides, or press Option-Shift-semicolon (;) (Mac) or Ctrl-Shift-semicolon (;) (Windows). The directional arrow no longer appears next to the selection tool when you place it over a guideline, and the guides cannot be moved. To unlock the guides, choose View > Guides > Lock Guides or press the keyboard shortcut again.

Figure 1.31 As you drag a guideline from the ruler bar, a direction indicator appears next to the selection tool.

Figure 1.32 You can position individual vertical and horizontal guides anywhere you want on the Stage.

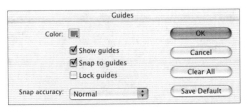

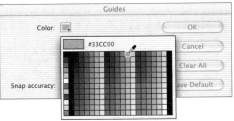

Figure 1.33 To choose the color for guides, in the Guides dialog (top), click the Color box to access swatches for the currently loaded color set. With the eyedropper pointer, select one of the swatches, or click an element on the Stage to sample its color (bottom).

To set guide color:

1. From the View menu, choose Guides > Edit Guides, or press Option-Shift-⌘-G (Mac) or Ctrl-Alt-Shift-G (Windows).

   The Guides dialog appears.

2. Click the Color box.

   The pointer changes to an eyedropper, and a set of pop-up swatches appears (**Figure 1.33**).

3. Using the eyedropper pointer, click a color swatch or an item on the Stage to select a new guide color.

4. Click OK.

   Flash applies that color to any existing guides and uses it for creating new guides.

✔ Tips

- If you've placed numerous guides in your document, dragging them from the Stage may get tedious. To remove them all at once, choose View > Guides > Clear All, or access the Guides dialog and click the Clear All button.

- You can lock or unlock guides and set their visibility and snapping property by selecting or deselecting check boxes in the Guides dialog.

USING RULERS AND GUIDES

25

Working with Snapping

Flash's five snapping features help you align objects as you position them on the Stage. Snap to Grid helps you position the edge or center of an object to sit directly on top of a user-defined grid. Snap to Guide does the same thing with objects and guidelines. Snap to Objects helps you position one object in relation to another. Snap to Pixels helps you position objects in relation to the intersections of a 1-pixel-by-1-pixel grid. Snap Align helps you align objects once you've dragged them within a user-definable distance from one another or from the edge of the Stage. By default Snap Align and Snap to Guides are active each time you launch Flash.

To snap objects to user-defined grids:

◆ From the View menu, choose Snapping > Snap to Grid, or press Shift-⌘-apostrophe (') (Mac) or Ctrl-Shift-apostrophe (') (Windows) (**Figure 1.34**).

    or

1. Choose View > Grid > Edit Grid, or press Option-⌘-G (Mac) or Ctrl-Alt-G (Windows).

    The Grid dialog appears.

2. Check the Snap to Grid check box (**Figure 1.35**).

Figure 1.34 Choose View > Snapping > Snap to Grid to get help aligning items to the grid as you move them around the Stage.

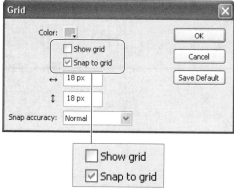

Figure 1.35 In the Grid dialog, checking the Snap to Grid check box turns on snapping.

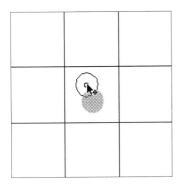

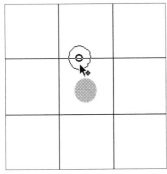

Figure 1.36 As you drag objects, the *snap ring,* a small circle, appears beneath the tip of the pointer (top). The snap ring grows larger when it moves over an item that you've chosen to snap to, such as a grid, a guide, or the edge or center of another object.

3. Click OK.

A check appears next to the Snap to Grid command in the menu.

As you drag an object, a circle, the *snap ring,* appears beneath the tip of the selection tool. As the object nears a grid line, Flash highlights potential snap points by enlarging the snap ring (**Figure 1.36**).

✔ Tip

■ The snap ring appears roughly in the place where the selection tool connects with the object you are dragging. Flash can snap an object only by its center point or a point on its perimeter, however. If you have trouble seeing the snap ring, try grabbing the object nearer to its center, an edge, or a corner.

To set parameters for snapping to the grid:

1. Choose View > Grid > Edit Grid.

2. In the Grid dialog, choose a parameter from the Snap Accuracy pop-up menu (**Figure 1.37**).

3. Click OK.

To snap objects to guides:

◆ From the View menu, choose Snapping > Snap to Guides, or press Shift-⌘-semicolon (;) (Mac) or Ctrl-Shift-semicolon (;) (Windows).

   or

1. Choose View > Guide > Edit Guides, or press Option-Shift-⌘-G (Mac) or Ctrl-Alt-Shift-G (Windows).
   The Guides dialog appears (**Figure 1.38**).

2. Check the Snap to Guides check box.

3. Click OK.

To set parameters for snapping to guides:

1. Choose View > Guides > Edit Guides.

2. In the Guides dialog, choose a parameter from the Snap Accuracy pop-up menu.

3. Click OK.

To snap objects to objects:

◆ From the View menu, choose Snapping > Snap to Objects, or press Shift-⌘-/ (Mac) or Ctrl-Shift-/.

   or

◆ With the selection, oval, rectangle, polystar, free-transform, or fill-transform tool selected, in the options section of the Toolbar, click the magnet icon.

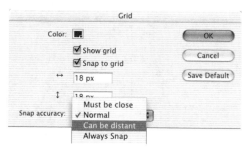

Figure 1.37 Choose a Snap Accuracy setting to determine how close an object must be to the grid before Flash snaps the object to the grid line. Choosing Always Snap forces the edge or center of an object to lie directly on a grid line.

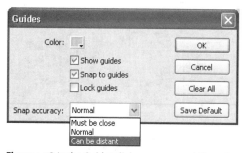

Figure 1.38 In the Guides dialog, you can set the color and visibility of guides, their status as locked or unlocked, and how close items must be before they will snap to the guides.

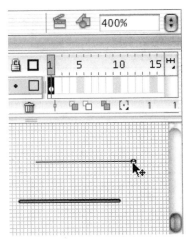

Figure 1.39 At magnifications of 400 percent or greater, the pixel grid used by Flash's Snap to Pixels feature becomes visible. You can use this mode for precise positioning of graphic elements.

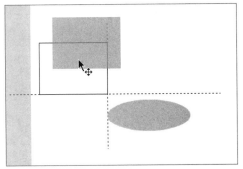

Figure 1.40 Flash's Snap Align feature displays a dotted guideline whenever an object comes within the user-specified distance from another object or the edge of the Stage. You can also set Snap Align to display the dotted guideline for aligning to the centers of objects.

To snap objects to pixels:

◆ From the View menu, choose Snapping > Snap to Pixels.

Flash creates a grid whose squares measure 1 pixel by 1 pixel. To see the grid, you must set the Stage's magnification to at least 400 percent (**Figure 1.39**). You'll learn more about magnified views in "Viewing Graphics at Various Magnifications" later in this chapter.

To turn on Snap Align:

◆ From the View menu, choose Snapping > Snap Align.

With Snap Align active, as you drag objects on the Stage, Flash displays a dotted line whenever the object gets within a user-specified distance from another object's edge, its center, or the edge of the Stage (**Figure 1.40**).

To set Snap Align tolerances:

◆ From the View menu, choose Snapping >
Edit Snap Align.

The Snap Align dialog appears
(**Figure 1.41**).

To turn off snapping:

◆ From the View > Snapping menu,
choose the snapping option that you
want to turn off.

The items with check marks are currently
turned on. You can only select one item at
a time from the menu. To turn off multiple snapping features, repeat this step.

✔ Tip

■ You can turn off snapping for grids and
guides from within the dialogs where
you set their parameters. Choose View >
Grid > Edit Grid (or View > Guides >
Edit Guides); in the dialog that appears,
deselect the Snap to Grids (or Snap to
Guides) check box.

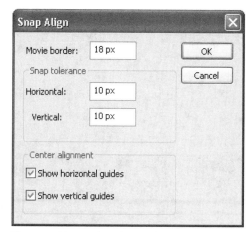

Figure 1.41 You set the tolerance for Snap Align in
the Snap Align dialog. Flash's default settings are
shown here.

WORKING WITH SNAPPING

Figure 1.42 To access Flash's drawing tools, choose Window > Tools (left). The Toolbar window appears on your desktop (right).

About the Toolbar

The Toolbar (also sometimes referred to as the *Tools panel*) contains Flash's drawing tools and other tools you'll need to create and manipulate graphics for animation. The Mac and Windows operating systems handle the Toolbar slightly differently. In Windows, you can dock the Toolbar on either side of the application window. In the Mac OS, the Toolbar always floats as a separate window. In addition, in Windows you can place a subset of the Toolbar tools into another toolbar (called the *Main toolbar*) at the top of the application window.

To view the Toolbar:

◆ From the Window menu, choose Tools or choose ⌘-F2 (Mac) or Ctrl-F2 (Windows).

A check indicates that the Toolbar window is open. The Toolbar window appears on the desktop (**Figure 1.42**).

To hide the Toolbar:

With the Toolbar open, *do one of the following:*

◆ From the Window menu, choose Tools. This menu command toggles the Toolbar, closing or opening it depending on its original state.

◆ Click the close button (Mac) or close box (Windows, when you have undocked the Toolbar from the application window).

To relocate the Toolbar:

1. Click the bar (Mac) or the textured area (Windows) at the top of the Toolbar, and hold down the mouse button.

2. Drag the Toolbar to the desired location. On Windows, you can use this technique to undock the Toolbar from the application window.

✔ Tip

■ If you have undocked the Toolbar in Windows, double-clicking the title bar of the floating Toolbar automatically docks it to the side of the window where it was last docked.

To turn on tool tips:

1. From the Edit menu (Windows) or Flash menu (Mac), choose Preferences.

2. In the Preferences dialog, select the General tab.

3. Check the Show Tooltips check box (**Figure 1.43**).

When the tool tips feature is active (as it is by default), Flash pops up an identifying label whenever you position the pointer over a tool icon and don't click it (**Figure 1.44**).

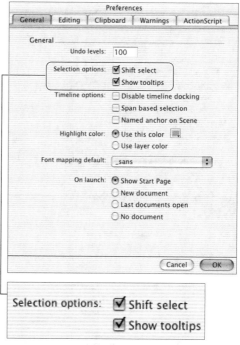

Figure 1.43 Turn on tool tips by checking Show Tooltips in the General tab of the Preferences dialog.

Figure 1.44 When the tool tips feature is active, a label appears whenever the pointer rests over an icon for a few seconds.

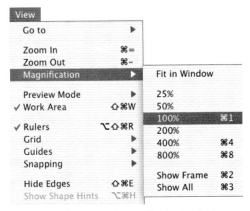

Figure 1.45 Choose 100% magnification to display graphics at the size they will be in the final movie.

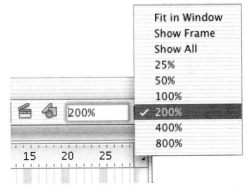

Figure 1.46 Enter a percentage greater than 100 in the Zoom Control field to magnify objects on the Stage. The pop-up menu to the right of the field offers several common magnification levels.

Viewing Graphics at Various Magnifications

Flash offers several ways to adjust the magnification of elements on the Stage.

To view objects at actual size:

◆ From the View menu, choose Magnification > 100% (**Figure 1.45**), or press ⌘-1 (Mac) or Ctrl-1 (Windows).

or

◆ In the Zoom Control field at the right side of the Stage's Edit Bar, type 100%. Press Enter.

At 100%, Flash displays objects as close as possible to the size they will be in the final movie. (Some monitors and video cards may display slightly different sizes.)

To zoom in or out on the Stage:

1. In the Zoom Control field, type the desired percentage of magnification and press Enter.

   To zoom in, type a percentage larger than 100. To zoom out, type a percentage smaller than 100 (**Figure 1.46**).

2. Press Enter.

✔ Tip

■ Click the scroll button next to the Zoom Control field to open a menu that duplicates the View > Magnification submenu. Choose a percentage from this menu to change magnification immediately. This menu also lets you choose Fit in Window (to display the full Stage area in the current window, without scroll bars), Show Frame (to display the full Stage area in the current window, with scroll bars), and Show All (to scale the Stage so that all elements on the Stage and in the work area appear in the current window).

To zoom in on specific areas of the Stage:

1. In the Toolbar, select the zoom tool (or press M or Z on the keyboard).

   The pointer changes to a magnifying glass.

2. Choose the Enlarge modifier.

3. Move the pointer over the Stage, and *select the area to magnify in one of two ways:*

   ▲ Click the area or element you want to enlarge.

   Flash doubles the percentage of magnification in the Zoom Control field and places the spot you clicked at the center of the viewing window.

   ▲ Click and drag to create a selection rectangle that encloses the element you want to view.

   Flash fills the window with your selected area (**Figure 1.47**).

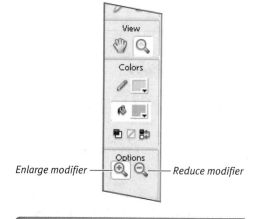

Enlarge modifier —— Reduce modifier

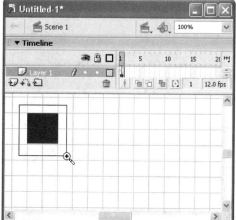

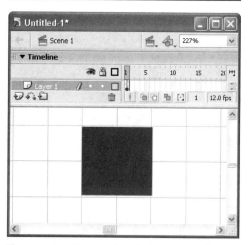

Figure 1.47 Use the zoom tool (top) to draw a selection rectangle around an element (middle). Flash places the element at the center of the enlarged view (bottom).

To zoom out:

1. In the Toolbar, select the zoom tool.

2. Choose the Reduce modifier.

3. Move the pointer over the Stage, and click the element or the area you want to see more of (or view at a smaller size).

Flash halves the percentage of magnification specified in the Zoom Control field.

✔ Tips

■ When you have the zoom tool selected, you can switch temporarily from Enlarge to Reduce, and vice versa, by holding down the Option (Mac) or Alt (Windows) key.

■ In Reduce mode, dragging a selection rectangle creates a magnified view.

■ To access the zoom tool in Enlarge mode temporarily while using another tool, press ⌘-spacebar (Mac) or Ctrl-spacebar (Windows). To access the tool in Reduce mode, press ⌘-Shift-spacebar (Mac) or Ctrl-Shift-spacebar (Windows).

VIEWING GRAPHICS AT VARIOUS MAGNIFICATIONS

About Panels

In addition to the Toolbar, Flash puts a number of authoring tools in *panels*—windows that can stay open on the desktop for quick access as you work. Some panels, such as the Color Mixer, let you set attributes to be used in creating new elements or modifying existing elements. Others, such as the Movie Explorer and Scenes panels, help you organize and navigate your Flash document. One crucial panel, the Property Inspector, lets you get information about selected elements and modify them. You'll learn to use individual panels in later chapters of this book. For now, you will learn general features of panels and how to manage the panel environment.

To open a panel window:

1. From the Window menu, choose a panel category—for example, Design Panels.

2. From the category submenu, choose the desired panel—for example, Color Mixer (**Figure 1.48**).

   Flash opens a window containing that panel (**Figure 1.49**).

✔ Tip

- The preceding technique works to open a panel that is not open, expand a panel if it is collapsed, or bring an open panel forward if other panels in front are obscuring it. If a panel is already open, expanded, and front-most in the panel stack, using this technique closes the panel.

Figure 1.48 The Window menu contains a list of panel categories and panels.

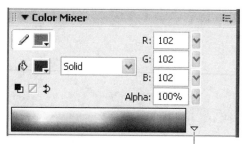

Click to view additional panel info

Figure 1.49 This panel window contains the Color Mixer.

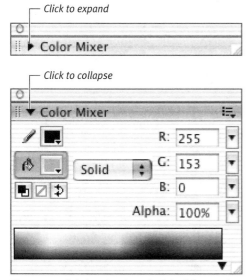

Click to expand

Click to collapse

Figure 1.50 Click the triangle to the left of the panel name to collapse and expand the panel window.

To close a panel window:

◆ Click the panel window's close button (Mac) or close box (Windows, for undocked panels).

or

◆ From the panel's Options menu, choose Close Panel.

or

◆ Control-click (Mac) or right-click (Windows) the panel's title bar, and choose Close Panel from the contextual menu.

✔ Tip

■ To hide all the open panels (including the Toolbar, Property Inspector, and any open Library windows), press F4. Press F4 again to show the panels.

To collapse or expand a panel window:

◆ Click the triangle to the left of the panel title (**Figure 1.50**).

To reposition a floating panel window:

◆ Click the bar at the top of the panel window, and drag the window to a new location.

On the Macintosh, panels (or panel groups) are always floating. In Windows, by default, panels are docked in the application window. To change a docked panel to a floating one, position the pointer over the textured area on the left side of the panel's title bar. Click and drag the panel away from the side of the application window.

✔ Tips

■ When you position one floating panel window so that one of its edges lies right next to the edge of another panel window, Flash snaps the two windows. It's not a permanent connection, but it ensures that the two take up as little space together as possible (**Figure 1.51**).

■ In the Windows operating system, you can more permanently dock panels at edges of the application window. Or, if you prefer free-floating panels and want to avoid accidentally docking them, choose Edit > Preferences, select the General tab of the Preferences dialog, and select Disable Panel Docking in the Panel Options section.

To resize a floating panel window:

◆ Click and drag the bottom-right corner of the window (Windows) or the resize handle (Mac).

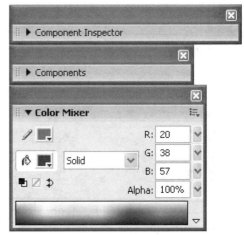

Figure 1.51 These floating panels snap together because of their proximity. They are still independent units. To join them more permanently, you must group them.

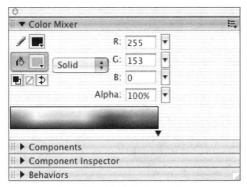

Figure 1.52 Part of Flash's default panel layout groups four panels—the Color Mixer, Components, Components Inspector, and Behaviors panels—in a single window on the right side of the desktop.

Working with Grouped Panels

You can group several panels in one window to save space on your desktop. Each panel within the window can be collapsed or expanded individually. Flash's default panel set groups the Color Mixer, Components, Components Inspector, and Behaviors panels.

To open the default panel set:

◆ From the Window menu, choose Panel Sets > Default Layout.

Flash opens the Toolbar and Property Inspector, plus one panel-group window containing four panels (**Figure 1.52**).

✔ Tip

■ The Training Layout panel set, which appears in the Panel Sets submenu, is specifically designed for use with the Tutorials that come with Flash. The Training Layout opens the Toolbar, Help panel, and Property Inspector. On the Mac, the Training Layout set comes in three versions for different monitor resolutions.

The Mysterious Persistence of Panel-Group Memory

If you have grouped panels, and you close the group by clicking the panel window's close box (Windows) or close button (Mac), the next time you choose any of the grouped panels from the Window menu, Flash opens the whole group together in its window. To see that one panel on its own, you'll need to drag it out of the group.

To separate panels:

1. Open the Default Layout panel set.

2. In the grouped-panel window, click the textured area at the left side of one panel's title bar.

   The pointer changes to the grabber hand (Mac) or move icon (Windows).

3. Drag the panel away from the grouped-panel window.

   Flash displays an outline of the panel as you drag.

4. Release the mouse button.

   The panel appears in its own window (**Figure 1.53**).

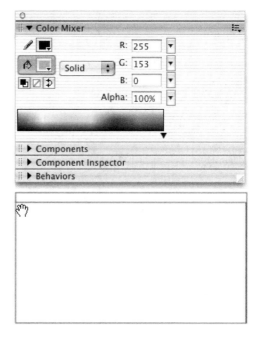

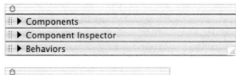

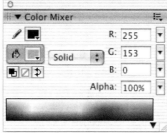

Figure 1.53 To separate one panel from a group, drag the panel's title bar away from the window until you see the outline of the panel (top); then release the mouse button to create a separate panel window (bottom).

— Highlighted target panel

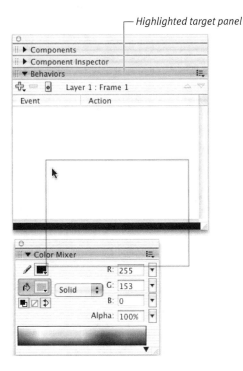

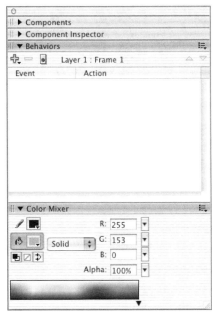

Figure 1.54 To group panels, drag one panel over another. When the target panel window highlights (top), release the mouse button. The new panel appears in the target window (bottom).

To combine panels in one window:

1. With two or more panel windows open on the desktop, click the textured area on the left side of the panel's title bar.

   The pointer changes to the grabber hand (Mac) or move icon (Windows).

2. Drag the panel on top of another open panel window.

   Flash highlights the target panel window with a thick black line.

3. Release the mouse button.

   The panel you dragged now appears in the destination window in expanded mode (**Figure 1.54**).

✔ Tips

■ You determine where in the target panel window Flash adds the new panel. Watch the way Flash highlights the target panel window. A thick black line indicates the spot where Flash will insert the added panel. Drag up or down in the target window to move the highlight line to the correct position.

■ To collapse and expand individual panels within the grouped-panel window, click the triangle to the left of the panel's title.

■ To expand one panel and collapse all the others in that panel window, choose Maximize Panel from the panel's Options menu. (To access the Options menu, you must have the panel in expanded mode.)

■ In Windows, when you have undocked a grouped set of panels so that they float in their own window, you can collapse or expand the whole group by double-clicking the bar at the top of the window.

Using Custom Panel Sets

Flash lets you save and restore any number
of customized panel configurations. A custom panel layout stores information about
which panels are open, which are grouped,
how large each panel or group window should
be, and where to place those windows on
the desktop.

To create a custom panel layout:

1. Open the panels you want to work with.

2. Group, resize, and reposition the panels
   as you desire.

3. From the Window menu, choose Save
   Panel Layout (**Figure 1.55**).

   The Save Panel Layout dialog appears.

4. Type a name for your layout
   (**Figure 1.56**).

5. Click OK.

   Flash saves the current panel configuration and makes it available in the Panel
   Sets submenu. Whenever you launch
   Flash, it opens the panel set that was
   active during your previous work session.

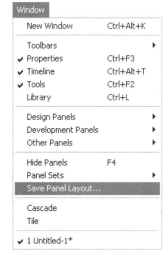

Figure 1.55 Choose Window >
Save Panel Layout to create a
custom panel set.

Figure 1.56 Type a name for your custom layout in the
Save Panel Layout dialog.

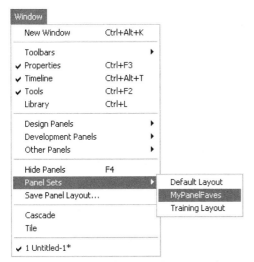

Figure 1.57 Choose Window > Panel Sets to invoke a custom panel configuration or to reestablish one of the panel layouts that come with Flash.

✔ Tips

- Assign a custom keyboard shortcut to the panel layouts you use most frequently (see "Customizing Keyboard Shortcuts" later in this chapter).

- If you discover a useful panel layout, you can share it with your friends and coworkers. Flash stores individual users' panel-set information in a folder named Panel Sets; each set is a separate text file. The location of the Panel Sets folder is slightly different in each operating system, but it's always found in the Configuration folder used for individual user settings (see "The Mystery of the Configuration Folder" earlier in this chapter).

- Should you ever need to delete (or rename) a custom panel set, navigate to the Panel Sets folder, select the file with your custom set, and delete (or rename) the file. (The Panel Sets folder is in the Configuration folder on your system, see "The Mystery of the Configuration Folder," earlier in this chapter.)

To invoke a custom panel set:

1. From the Window menu, choose Panel Sets.

   A submenu appears, listing the Default Layout, Training Layout(s), and any custom panel sets you have saved (**Figure 1.57**).

2. From the submenu, choose the desired custom set.

   Flash closes whatever panels you have open and configures your desktop with the custom panel set.

USING CUSTOM PANEL SETS

About the Property Inspector

The Property Inspector is a panel that displays information about the properties and attributes of tools and graphic elements (such as color, style, and font for the text tool). You can also use the Property Inspector to change the properties and attributes of a selected tool or graphic element. The Property Inspector is context-sensitive, changing constantly to reflect the particular element you have selected. You'll learn more about the many specific versions of the Property Inspector as they become relevant in later chapters. For now, just learn its general rules of operation.

To access the Property Inspector:

◆ From the Window menu, choose Properties or press ⌘-F3 (Mac) or Ctrl-F3 (Windows) (**Figure 1.58**).

Flash opens the Property Inspector. The panel displays information about whatever item you have selected in the Flash document (see "The Power of the Property Inspector").

✔ Tip

■ On a Mac, the Property Inspector always floats. In Windows, the Property Inspector docks to the bottom of the application window by default, but you can make it float as a separate panel by grabbing the textured area on the left side of the panel's title bar. Click and drag the panel away from the bottom of the application window.

Figure 1.58 To access the Property Inspector, choose Window > Properties.

ABOUT THE PROPERTY INSPECTOR

To hide or show the information area:

◆ To hide or show the lower half of the Property Inspector, click the triangle in the bottom-right corner of the panel (**Figure 1.59**).

For some elements, the lower half of the Property Inspector panel displays extra information. Hiding the information area gives you more room on your desktop.

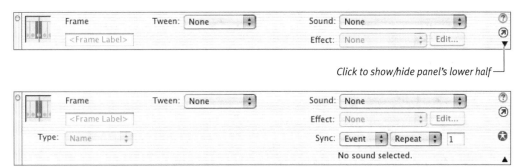

Click to show/hide panel's lower half

Figure 1.59 In some situations, the Property Inspector displays more information in the lower portion of the panel. Click the triangle in the lower-right corner of the panel to show or hide that information.

Entering Values in the Property Inspector

In many modes, the Property Inspector requires you to enter a value in a field to change a parameter. You can always type a new value. When modifying selected items, usually you must press Enter to apply the new value to selected items.

A small triangle to the right of an entry field indicates the presence of a pop-up slider for entering values quickly. Often, a slider previews new values interactively. The following methods work for most sliders:

◆ Click and drag. Click the small triangle, and hold down the mouse button; you can start dragging the slider's lever right away. Release the mouse button. Flash enters the current slider value in the field and—in most cases—applies that value to selected objects automatically.

◆ Click and click. Click the small triangle, and release the mouse button right away; the slider pops up and stays open. You can drag the slider's lever or click various locations on the slider to choose a new value. Flash enters the value in the field. To apply the value to selected items, you must click somewhere off the slider, click another entry field, click elsewhere on the panel, or click the Stage.

ABOUT THE PROPERTY INSPECTOR

To collapse or expand the Property Inspector (Windows):

◆ The docked Property Inspector collapses and expands vertically; click the triangle in the top-left corner of the panel to toggle between the collapsed and expanded modes (**Figure 1.60**).

or

◆ The floating Property Inspector collapses and expands horizontally; double-click the bar on the left side of the window to toggle between the collapsed and expanded modes.

To close the Property Inspector:

◆ When the Property Inspector is open, from the Window menu, choose Properties. Flash closes the Property Inspector panel.

or

◆ On the Mac, click the Close button; in Windows when the Property Inspector is floating, click the Close box.

or

◆ When the Property Inspector is docked (Windows), from the Options menu in the top-right corner, choose Close Panel (**Figure 1.61**).

Click to toggle vertical change

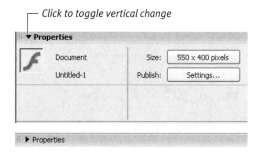

Double-click to toggle horizontal change

Figure 1.60 In Windows, you can collapse and expand the Property Inspector. The docked panel (top) collapses/expands vertically when you click the minimize/ maximize triangle. The floating panel (bottom) collapses/expands horizontally when you double-click the bar on the left side of the panel.

Figure 1.61 To close a docked Property Inspector, from the panel's Options menu, choose Close Panel.

The Power of the Property Inspector

Think of the Property Inspector as being a context-sensitive superpanel—a panel that changes to reflect whatever item you have selected. It displays information about the active Flash document, a selected tool, a selected graphic element (a shape, grouped shape, or symbol; a text block; a bitmap or video clip), or a selected frame.

The Property Inspector is also the place for setting many tools' parameters and for changing the attributes of selected elements.

Select the line tool, for example, and the Property Inspector becomes the Line Tool Property Inspector (**Figure 1.62**). In this incarnation, the Property Inspector presents all the line tool's parameters for you to set: color, thickness, and style. Select a line on the Stage, however, and the Property Inspector becomes the Shape Property Inspector. Because the selected shape is a line, the Property Inspector displays the same parameters as the Line Tool Property Inspector; change the parameters in the Property Inspector, and Flash changes the selected line to match.

Click a blank area of the Stage, and you'll see the Document Property Inspector, which gives you access to various document settings. Select a symbol instance on the Stage, and the Property Inspector reveals the instance's heritage (which master symbol it came from), as well as what its height, width, and Stage position are. Change those settings in the Property Inspector, and Flash makes those changes in the selected symbol instance.

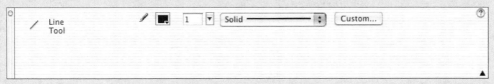

Figure 1.62 The Property Inspector displays information about selected items and allows you to modify them. In its Line Tool mode, for example, the Property Inspector lets you set the color, thickness, and style for lines that the line tool creates.

Using the Help Panel

In Flash MX 2004, Macromedia has consolidated all of the Help features into a single panel. The Help panel contains documentation of Flash's features and tutorial information for learning common tasks. The toolbar at the top of the Help panel gives you tools for navigating the Help content; viewing the Table of Contents pane; and searching, printing, and updating the Help content.

To access the Help panel:

◆ From the Help menu, choose Help.

Flash opens the Help panel (**Figure 1.63**). The panel has two tabs, organizing the information into two styles of assistance: documentation (Help) and tutorials (How Do I). There are also two panes for viewing information: the Table of Contents pane (on the left) shows a table of contents for the selected tab, the Documentation pane (on the right) contains the detailed text. Tools in the toolbar above the two panes allow you to navigate, search, print, and update the Help information.

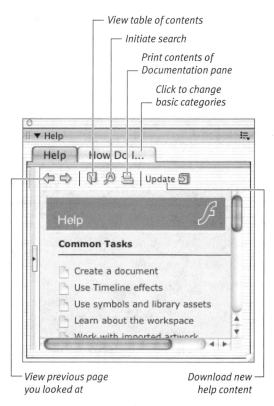

View table of contents
Initiate search
Print contents of Documentation pane
Click to change basic categories

View previous page you looked at

Download new help content

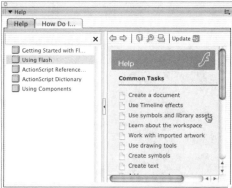

Figure 1.63 The Help panel offers a variety of ways to view Flash's documentation. By default on the Mac (and when the panel is undocked on Windows), the panel opens showing just one of its two panes (top). Reposition the pane divider and resize the panel to see the full range of the panel's information (bottom).

✔ Tips

- Due to a bug in the Help panel, on the Mac (or in Windows if you have undocked the panel), when you first open the panel, the Table of Contents pane is closed. You must reposition the pane divider to see the entries on the left. You can resize the Help panel as you would any other panel to see more content at one time. Just be aware that on the Mac (and Windows if the Help panel is floating) the Help panel has it's own ideas about how wide it must be to display both panes simultaneously. If you position the divider to make both panes visible and then you resize the panel, Flash may close down one of the panes for you. If this drives you wild, resize the window first, then position the divider.

- To view the Table of Contents pane quickly, click the book icon in the toolbar at the top of the Help panel.

- To close the Table of Contents pane quickly, click the *X* located above the scroll bar in the pane.

To view Help topics:

1. Access the Help panel.

2. To view main categories for each style of assistance, *do one of the following:*

▲ To view short tutorials, select the How Do I tab.

▲ To view the full documentation, select the Help tab.

When you first access the Help panel for a work session, the Documentation pane displays a list of tasks appropriate to the selected tab. The Table of Contents pane displays the table of contents entries for those tasks.

3. To view specific Help information, *do one of the following:*

▲ Click an entry in the Table of Contents pane.

▲ Click a task in the Documentation pane.

The Documentation pane changes to display the information or instructions associated with that entry or task (**Figure 1.64**). The Table of Contents entries appear in hierarchically nested "books" and sub-books, which act much like folders on a hard drive.

4. To view the contents of a book, or sub-book, double-click the book icon in the Table of Contents pane.

Individual topic entries appear as "pages."

5. To view a topic, click the page icon.

Flash displays the information for that topic in the Documentation pane.

Figure 1.64 Double-click a book (or sub-book) icon in the Table of Contents pane (the left-hand pane) to view the topics within that category. Click a page icon to view the specific topic in the Documentation pane (the right-hand pane).

USING THE HELP PANEL

Previous topic in documentation

Previous topic you selected

Next topic in documentation

Next topic you selected

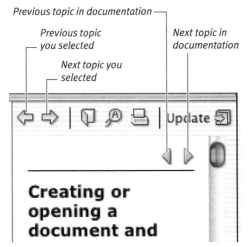

Figure 1.65 The scroll arrows in the Documentation pane move you through the documentation topics in strict order. Use the Forward and Back arrows in the Help panel's toolbar to navigate your own path through the documentation.

✔ Tips

■ When you view the text for a selected entry, scroll arrows appear inside the Documentation pane (**Figure 1.65**). Use the scroll arrows to navigate the hierarchy of documentation files. Click the scroll-forward arrow to move to the next topic; click the scroll-back arrow to move to the previous topic.

■ The Documentation pane often contains highlighted text links, which let you jump directly to related topics. You can also jump from topic to topic by clicking different entries in the Table of Contents pane. To move forward and backward along your own particular path through the documentation, use the Forward and Back arrows in the toolbar at the top of the Help panel. If, for example, in the Documentation pane for topic A, you click a text link to jump to topic G, clicking the Back arrow in the toolbar takes you back to topic A; clicking the scroll-back arrow in the Documentation pane takes you to topic F.

To search Help Topics:

1. Access the Help panel.

2. Click a tab to select a general Help-style category.

3. In the toolbar at the top of the Help panel, click the magnifying-glass icon.

   Flash clears the Table-of-Contents pane, and displays a Search field and Search button above the pane.

4. Type the text that you want to find into the Search field.

5. Click the Search button.

   Flash lists all the entries that contain the search text in the Table-of-Contents pane. Click an entry to see its full text in the Documentation pane (**Figure 1.66**).

✔ Tip

■ You cannot use the Search feature in the Help panel to find specific instances of the search text within the Documentation pane. If you are really having trouble finding the relevant spot, you can copy the text in the Help panel, paste the text into a text box on the Stage or in the Work area of your document, and use Flash's Find and Replace feature to locate the search text in the Help text. You'll learn to use Find and Replace in Chapter 13.

Figure 1.66 Click the magnifying glass icon in the Help panel's toolbar to start a search. Type text in the search field and click Search. The Table of Contents pane lists all topic entries that contain the search text.

Figure 1.67 Click the Update icon in the Help panel's toolbar (top). Flash connects to the Internet and downloads any new help materials. If no new Help content is available, Flash informs you of that fact with a dialog (bottom).

To update the Help panel:

1. Launch Flash and open an Internet connection.

2. Access the Help panel.

3. In the toolbar at the top of the Help panel, click the Update icon (**Figure 1.67**).

   Flash connects to the Macromedia site, checks for new information, and downloads any new Help material. If there is no new material, Flash informs you of that fact.

✔ Tip

■ You can also update the Help panel from the Start page. When Flash next opens to the Start page, click the Update the Flash Help System link in the lower-left section of the page.

Customizing Keyboard Shortcuts

Flash's default shortcut set (the Macromedia Standard set) lets you access the drawing tools and most menu commands from the keyboard quickly. But what if your favorite operation lacks a shortcut or uses a key combination that you find awkward? You can create your own set of combinations, add shortcuts to items that lack them, and change the assigned key commands. Flash comes with five additional shortcut sets that let you replicate the keyboard shortcuts of other popular graphics programs.

To switch among shortcut sets:

1. From the Edit menu (Windows) or the Flash menu (Mac), choose Keyboard Shortcuts.

   The Keyboard Shortcuts dialog appears.

2. From the Current Set pop-up menu, choose one of the listed shortcut sets (**Figure 1.68**).

3. Click OK.

   Flash loads the new shortcuts. The new key combinations appear in menus and tool tips.

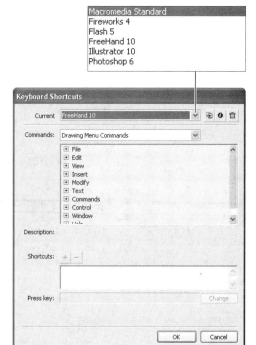

Figure 1.68 Use the Current Set pop-up menu in the Keyboard Shortcuts dialog to switch to a different set of shortcuts.

Figure 1.69 When creating custom shortcuts, you must work on a copy of one of the sets that comes with Flash. Click the Duplicate Set button to copy the set displayed in the Current Sets pop-up menu.

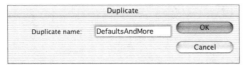

Figure 1.70 In the Duplicate dialog, type a name for your new shortcut set.

To create a custom shortcut set:

1. Follow the steps in the preceding exercise to select a set of keyboard shortcuts.

   The selected set forms the basis of your new set.

2. In the Keyboard Shortcuts dialog, click the Duplicate Set button in the top-right corner of the keyboard shortcuts dialog (**Figure 1.69**).

   The Duplicate dialog appears.

3. Type a name for your custom shortcut set (**Figure 1.70**).

4. Click OK.

   Flash makes the new set available in the Current Set list. Now you can add more shortcuts and delete or change existing ones.

To assign a new shortcut:

1. From the Edit menu (Windows) or the Flash menu (Mac), choose Keyboard Shortcuts.

   The Keyboard Shortcuts dialog appears.

2. From the Current Set pop-up menu, choose the set you created in the preceding exercise.

3. From the Commands pop-up menu, *choose one of the following options* (**Figure 1.71**):

   ▲ To modify a command used in Flash's authoring environment, choose Drawing Menu Commands.

   ▲ To modify a command that selects a drawing tool, choose Drawing Tools.

   ▲ To modify a command used in Flash's movie-testing environment, choose Test Movie Menu Commands.

   ▲ To modify commands for working with the Timeline, choose Timeline Commands.

   ▲ To modify commands for selecting panels and objects on the Stage during authoring, choose Workspace Accessibility Commands.

   ▲ To modify a command for use in creating scripts in ActionScript, Flash's scripting language, choose Actions Panel Commands.

   A scrolling list of the selected commands and their current assigned keyboard shortcuts appears in the Commands pane.

4. In the Commands pane, select the name of the command or tool you want to modify.

   An overview of the selected command appears in the Description area of the dialog (**Figure 1.72**). Any existing shortcuts for that item appear in the Shortcuts pane and in the Press Key field.

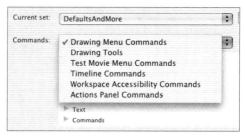

Figure 1.71 The Commands menu in the Keyboard Shortcuts dialog offers six categories of items to which you can assign keyboard shortcuts.

Figure 1.72 Menu-related commands appear in a hierarchical list. To expand or collapse entries in the list, click the triangle to the left of each menu name.

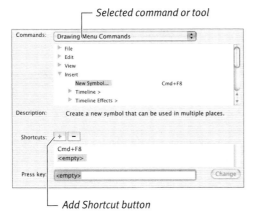

Selected command or tool

Add Shortcut button

Figure 1.73 Select a command or tool in the Commands pane to see its description. Click the Add Shortcut button to define a new shortcut. Flash replaces any existing shortcut in the Press Key field with the text <empty>.

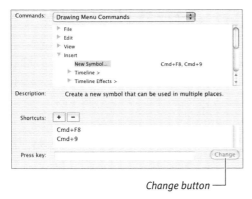

Change button

Figure 1.74 After entering a new shortcut, click the Change button to confirm the new key combination. Flash adds it to the list in the Shortcuts pane.

5. Click the Add Shortcut button.

Flash adds <empty> to the Shortcuts pane, and enters <empty> in the Press Key field (**Figure 1.73**).

6. On the keyboard, press the keys you want to use as a shortcut to access the item.

Flash enters the shortcut in the Press Key field.

7. Click the Change button to update the shortcut set.

Flash adds the new key combination in the Shortcuts and Commands panes (**Figure 1.74**).

✔ Tips

- Shortcut keys for menu commands must be function keys or must include the ⌘ character (Mac) or the Ctrl character (Windows).

- You can assign multiple shortcuts to a single command or tool.

- You cannot alter Flash's default shortcuts set (Macromedia Standard) directly. You must first duplicate the set named Macromedia Standard and then add and remove shortcuts in the duplicate set. You can alter the other shortcut sets, but it's a good idea to make a duplicate set before making changes to them as well. That way you can always get the standard set back, or use it as the basis for another custom set.

- Flash places the file of your custom keyboard shortcut set into a folder named Keyboard Shortcuts. That folder lives in the Configuration folder. For the precise pathname to that folder, see "The Mystery of the Configuration Folder," earlier in this chapter.

To remove a shortcut:

1. Follow steps 1 through 4 of the preceding exercise.

2. Click the Remove Shortcut button (**Figure 1.75**).

   Flash removes the shortcut from the Shortcuts and Commands panes.

✔ Tip

- To change an existing shortcut for a selected command or tool, select the shortcut name in the Shortcuts pane, select the shortcut characters in the Press Key field, enter a new key combination, and click the Change button.

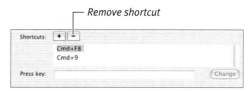

Figure 1.75 Clicking the Remove Shortcut button deletes a selected shortcut.

CREATING
SIMPLE GRAPHICS

This chapter teaches you to use Macromedia Flash MX 2004's drawing tools to create basic shapes from lines and areas of color—in Flash terminology, *strokes* and *fills*.

Flash also lets you import graphics from other programs. If you create graphics in a program such as Macromedia FreeHand or Adobe Illustrator, you can import them into Flash for animation (see Chapter 14).

Flash offers the option of using its original natural-style drawing tools or using a pen tool to create Bézier curves. Flash's natural drawing tools allow you to sketch freely with various levels of drawing assistance. Flash can help you, for example, by changing a basically straight line that bobbles a bit into one that's perfectly straight. Flash also can smooth curves so that they flow beautifully instead of in jaggy fits and starts. The pen tool works similarly to the Bézier tool featured in other graphics programs.

You can edit all shapes with the Bézier sub-selection tool—even those drawn with the natural drawing tools. You also can correct a shape by tugging on its outline. (To learn about editing shapes, see Chapter 3.)

Touring the Tools

The Flash MX 2004 Tools panel, also known as the Toolbar, holds all of the tools that you will need to create and modify graphic elements in Flash. The Toolbar has four sections for different types of tools: The Tools section contains tools for creating graphic elements; the View section contains tools for scrolling the Stage and for zooming in and out; the Colors section allows you to set colors for the elements you create, the Options section provides modifiers appropriate to whatever tool you have currently selected.

For the first time, in MX 2004, the tool bar is customizable and new tools are likely to become available through Flash's new extensibility features. The tools available in MX 2004 are the same as in the previous version of Flash, except for one new tool: the polystar tool (**Figure 2.1**).

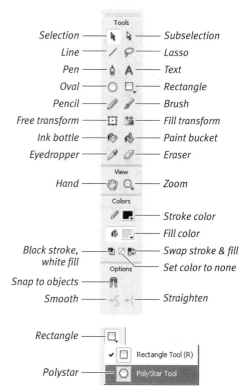

Figure 2.1 The Toolbar contains tools for drawing, editing, and manipulating graphic elements in Flash. The new polystar tool appears as a submenu item of the rectangle tool.

A Toolbar Is a Toolbox Is a Tool Panel

The panel that holds all the Flash drawing tools has undergone several changes of identity, from Toolbar to Toolbox and back again. The official name in Flash MX 2004 is the Tools panel. But you'll still find it referred to as the Toolbar in many places, including the hard copy documentation that comes with Flash. As Macromedia updates the electronic help files for the program, you'll see references to the Tools panel increase. For consistency, this book refers to the Toolbar.

Figure 2.2 Click the line icon in the Toolbar to select the line tool.

Using the Line Tool

Flash offers a tool that does nothing but draw perfectly straight line segments. By putting together several line segments, you can create a shape made of several straight sides, such as a pentagon or triangle.

To draw line segments:

1. In the Toolbar, select the line tool by clicking the line icon, or press N (**Figure 2.2**).

2. Move the pointer to the spot on the Stage where you want your line to begin.

   The pointer changes to a crosshair as it moves over the Stage area.

continues on next page

What Are Strokes and Fills?

Stroke and *fill* are two terms you will encounter often in graphics programs, and Flash is no exception. What do these terms mean? Basically, a stroke is an outline, and a fill is a solid shape. Picture a coloring book in pristine condition, with simple black lines creating the pictures: Those lines are strokes. When you fill in the areas outlined by strokes—say, with crayon—that colorful area is the fill. In a coloring book, you always start with an outline and create the fill inside it. In Flash, you can work the other way around—start with a solid shape and then create the outline around it as a separate object.

Flash's oval, rectangle, and polystar tools allow you to create an element that's just a stroke or just a fill, or to create the stroke and fill elements simultaneously. The line tool, as you might guess, creates only strokes. The pen tool can create both strokes and fills.

The concept of fills and strokes is a bit trickier to grasp in relation to the brush tool. This tool creates fills. Though these fills may look like lines or brush strokes, they are really shapes you can outline with a stroke. Flash provides special tools for adding, editing, and removing strokes and fills: the ink bottle, the paint bucket, and the faucet eraser. Chapter 3 discusses these tools in greater detail.

3. Click and drag to pull a line segment out from your starting point (**Figure 2.3**).

Flash displays an outline preview of the line—a simple form that doesn't show the line's color, style, and weight settings. A circle beneath the pointer indicates the line's endpoint.

4. Release the mouse button when the line is the right length and in the right position.

Flash draws a line segment on the Stage, using the current stroke-color, stroke-style, and stroke-height settings (see "Setting Stroke Attributes" later in this chapter).

✔ Tips

■ The line is not set until you release the mouse button. You can shorten, lengthen, and reorient the line's direction or angle by dragging until you release the mouse button.

■ Holding down the Shift key as you draw a line constrains it to the vertical, horizontal, or 45-degree angle position.

■ If you're using a narrow line thickness, you may need to zoom in to see it accurately onscreen. On screen, thin lines may look identical to slightly thicker lines unless you zoom in; they will print accurately, though.

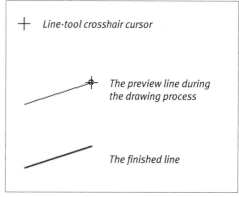

Figure 2.3 Click and drag with the line tool's crosshair cursor. Flash previews the line as you draw. Release the mouse button, and the line takes on the attributes currently assigned to strokes.

Figure 2.4 Choose Window > Properties (top) to display the Property Inspector (bottom).

Stroke color

Hexadecimal color

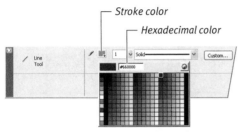

Figure 2.5 Clicking the stroke-color box in the Property Inspector opens a set of color swatches and provides an eyedropper pointer for selecting a new color.

Setting Stroke Attributes

A line has three attributes: color, thickness (also known as *weight* or, in Flash, *stroke height*), and style. You can set all three in the Property Inspector for any tool that creates or modifies strokes (the line, pen, oval, rectangle, polystar, and ink-bottle tools). In addition, you can set stroke color from the Toolbar or from the Color Mixer panel.

To access the Property Inspector:

◆ If the Property Inspector is not open, from the Window menu, choose Properties (**Figure 2.4**).

 The Property Inspector appears on the desktop. Note that the Property Inspector displays the attributes for lines only when you have selected a line-related tool in the Toolbar or you have selected lines on the Stage. (You learn to use line-related tools in the following exercises; you learn to use the Property Inspector with selections in Chapter 3.)

To set stroke properties:

1. With the Property Inspector open, choose the line tool.

 The Line Tool Property Inspector appears, showing the current settings for the three attributes for strokes.

2. In the Property Inspector, click the stroke-color box.

 The pointer changes to an eyedropper, and a set of swatches appears (**Figure 2.5**).

continues on next page

SETTING STROKE ATTRIBUTES

3. To select a stroke color, *do one of the following:*

▲ To select the color directly below the tip of the eyedropper, with the eyedropper pointer, click a swatch or an item on the Stage.

▲ In the hexadecimal-color field, enter a value.

The selected color appears in the stroke-color box in the Property Inspector, the Color Mixer, and the Toolbar.

4. To set the line's weight, in the stroke-height field, enter a number between 0.25 and 10 (**Figure 2.6**) or drag the slider next to the stroke-height field.

5. To set the line's style, click the Stroke Style pop-up menu (**Figure 2.7**).

A list of seven styles (hairline, solid, dashed, dotted, ragged, stippled, and hatched) appears.

6. Select a style.

A graphic representation of that style appears in the stroke-style menu.

Flash applies the color, weight, and style settings that are currently active in the Line Property Inspector to any lines you create using the line tool or any other tool that creates strokes.

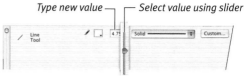

Type new value ⎯ ⎏ *Select value using slider*

Figure 2.6 Entering a new value in the stroke-height field sets the thickness for strokes created by tools that draw strokes.

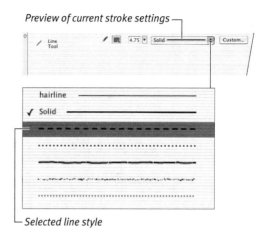

Preview of current stroke settings ⎯

⎣ *Selected line style*

Figure 2.7 Choose a line style from the pop-up menu in the Line Tool Property Inspector.

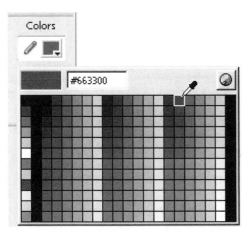

Figure 2.8 Click the stroke-color box in the Toolbar to open a set of color swatches similar to those available in the Property Inspector.

✔ Tips

■ You can also set stroke color in the Color Mixer panel. Choose Window > Design Panels > Color Mixer to open the Color Mixer panel, click the stroke-color box, and select a color as described in step 3 of the preceding exercise.

■ You can set stroke color without opening any panels. In the Toolbar, with any tool selected, click the stroke-color box. The eyedropper pointer and a set of swatches appear (**Figure 2.8**). Select a color; Flash updates all the stroke-color boxes, and tools that create strokes will use that color.

■ Use the trio of small buttons at the bottom of the Colors section of the Toolbar to set the stroke color (and fill color) to black, white, or no color quickly. To set stroke color to black (and fill color to white), with the stroke-color box selected, click the leftmost button of the trio: the Black and White button. Click the rightmost button to make the current stroke and fill colors change places. (The middle button lets you set fill or stroke to no color when you use the oval, rectangle, and polystar tools, which you'll learn about later in this chapter.)

■ In Flash, the hairline setting is considered to be a line style, not a line weight. (Use the Stroke Style pop-up menu to get the hairline setting.) In symbols, hairlines do not change thickness when you resize the symbol. Other lines in symbols grow thicker or thinner as you scale them up or down. (To learn about symbols, see Chapter 6.)

SETTING STROKE ATTRIBUTES

To customize a line style:

1. In the Line Tool Property Inspector, click the Custom button (**Figure 2.9**).

   The Stroke Style dialog appears.

2. From the Type menu, choose a style—for example, Dotted.

   The parameters appropriate to the currently selected stroke style appear in the dialog (**Figure 2.10**).

3. In the Dot Spacing box, enter a number between 1 and 20.

   This value specifies the amount of space (in points) that appears between the dots in the dotted line.

4. To select a thickness value, *do one of the following*:

   ▲ Enter a value from 1 to 10 in the Thickness field.

   ▲ Choose a value from the pop-up menu.

5. If you want Flash to place a dot at the tip of each corner when you draw a line, choose Sharp Corners.

6. Click OK.

   A preview of your custom dotted-line style appears in the Stroke Style menu in the Property Inspector. Any tools that create strokes are now set to use that style.

✔ Tips

■ Custom stroke-style settings remain in effect until you customize that style again or quit Flash. Define a custom dashed line that has really long dashes, and you'll get the same long dashes the next time you choose the dashed line from the Stroke Style menu in the Property Inspector.

■ Changing the stroke height doesn't affect other custom settings. To use your customized long dashes with a thinner line, just enter a new stroke-height value directly in the Property Inspector.

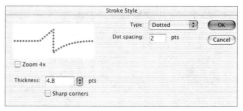

Figure 2.9 Click the Custom button in the Property Inspector to access the Stroke Style dialog.

Figure 2.10 The Stroke Style dialog contains a pop-up menu for selecting the type of line you want to customize. The dialog shown here is for dotted lines.

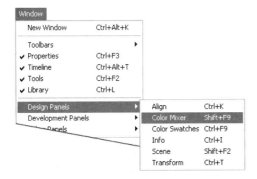

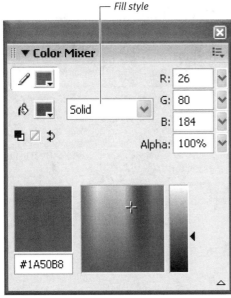

Fill style

#1A50B8

Figure 2.11 Choose Window > Design Panels > Color Mixer (top) to open the Color Mixer panel, where you can set fill attributes (bottom).

Setting Fill Attributes

Flash offers five fill styles: none, solid, linear gradient, radial gradient, and bitmap. You can set the fill style, color, and transparency in the Color Mixer panel. You can also choose some fills from the Toolbar and from fill-related Property Inspectors, such as the one that accompanies the rectangle tool. The following exercises deal with solid fills; you'll learn about gradients in Chapter 3 and about bitmaps in Chapter 14.

To access the Color Mixer panel:

◆ If the Color Mixer panel is not open, from the Window menu, choose Design Panels > Color Mixer.

The Color Mixer panel appears (**Figure 2.11**).

To select a fill style:

◆ From the Color Mixer panel's Fill Style menu, choose a fill type—Solid, for example.

The attributes for that fill appear in the panel.

To select a solid fill color from the Color Mixer panel:

1. In the Color Mixer panel, with Solid selected as the fill style, click the fill-color box.

The pointer changes to an eyedropper, and a set of swatches appears (**Figure 2.12**).

2. To select a color with the swatches pop-up menu open, *do one of the following:*

▲ To select the color directly below the tip of the eyedropper, click a swatch or an item on the Stage.

Enter hex values in the field above the swatches.

▲ To define a color that's not in the swatch set, click the color picker. (For more information on defining colors, see Chapter 3.)

The new color appears in the fill-color box and will be used by any of the tools that create fills.

3. To define a color without opening the swatches pop-up menu, enter values in the color RGB (or HSB) fields.

✔ Tip

■ You can set fill color without opening the Color Mixer panel. In the Toolbar, with any tool selected, click the fill-color box. The eyedropper pointer and a set of swatches appear. Select a color; Flash updates the fill-color box in the Toolbar, the Color Mixer panel, and the Property Inspector.

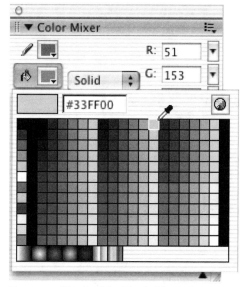

Figure 2.12 Click the Color Mixer's fill-color box to access the eyedropper pointer and swatches for selecting a new fill color. To define a color that's not in the swatch set, enter values in the RGB (or HSB) fields or click the color-picker.

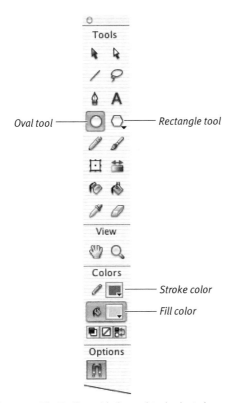

Oval tool — Rectangle tool

Stroke color

Fill color

Figure 2.13 The Toolbar with the oval tool selected.

Using the Geometric Shape Tools

Flash provides separate tools for drawing ovals, rectangles, and polygons or stars. The tools work quite similarly; all can draw a shape as an outline (just a stroke) or as a solid object (a fill). You can also create a geometric shape with a fill and a stroke simultaneously.

To draw an oval outline:

1. In the Toolbar, select the oval tool, or press O (**Figure 2.13**).

2. To activate the fill-color box, in the Colors section of the Toolbar, select the paint-bucket icon.

3. To set fill color to none, *do one of the following:*

   ▲ Click the fill-color box, and in the set of swatches that appears, click the No Color button (**Figure 2.14**).

   ▲ In the Colors section of the Toolbar, click the No Color button (**Figure 2.15**).

continues on next page

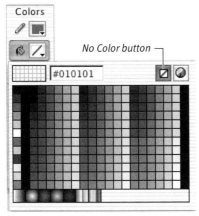

No Color button

Figure 2.14 The No Color button appears in the pop-up set of fill swatches. Choosing No Color as the fill color with the oval tool allows you to create oval outlines.

No Color button

Figure 2.15 When the fill-color box is selected in the Colors section of the Toolbar, clicking the No Color button allows whatever tool you select to create a shape with no fill.

4. Use the current stroke color and line weight or select new ones (see "Setting Stroke Attributes," earlier in this chapter).

5. Move the pointer over the Stage.

   The pointer turns into a crosshair.

6. Click and drag to create an oval of the size and proportions you want (**Figure 2.16**).

   Flash displays an outline preview of the oval as you drag.

7. Release the mouse button.

   Flash draws an oval outline.

✔ Tips

■ To draw a perfect circle, hold down the Shift key while you drag the crosshair cursor. Flash makes the oval grow with the proportions of a perfect circle.

■ To make a circle grow outward from the center point as you draw, position the pointer where you want the center of the circle to be, then hold down the Alt key (Windows) or Option key (Mac) while you drag.

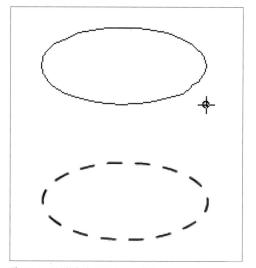

Figure 2.16 Click the Stage, and drag to create an oval. You see a preview outline of your shape (top). Release the mouse button, and Flash creates an oval outline, using the current color, thickness, and style settings. In this case, the oval tool is set to black stroke color, no fill, dashed line style, and a stroke height of 1 point (bottom).

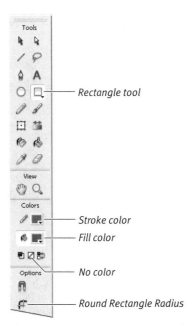

Rectangle tool

Stroke color

Fill color

No color

Round Rectangle Radius

Figure 2.17 Select the rectangle tool in the Toolbar; the Round Rectangle Radius modifier appears. Use the modifier to create rectangles with blunt corners.

Corner-radius value

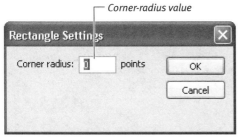

Figure 2.18 Enter a value of 0 in the Corner Radius field of the Rectangle Settings dialog to create a rectangle with sharp corners. Enter a larger value to round the corners of your rectangle.

To draw a rectangular fill:

1. In the Toolbar, select the rectangle tool, or press R (**Figure 2.17**).

2. To set a stroke color, in the Colors section of the Toolbar, click the pencil icon.

3. To set stroke color to none, *do one of the following*:

   ▲ Click the stroke-color box, and in the swatch window, click the No Color button.

   ▲ In the Colors section of the Toolbar, click the No Color button.

4. Use the current fill color or select a new one (see "Setting Fill Attributes," earlier in this chapter).

5. To open the Rectangle Settings dialog, *do one of the following*:

   ▲ In the Options section of the Toolbar, click the Round Rectangle Radius button.

   ▲ Double-click the rectangle tool.

   The Rectangle Settings dialog appears (**Figure 2.18**).

6. To define the types of corners for your rectangle, in the Corner Radius field, *enter one of the following*:

   ▲ To create a rectangle with 90-degree angles at the corners, enter a value of 0 points.

   ▲ To create a rectangle with rounded corners, enter a value of greater than 0 points.

7. Click OK to close the dialog.

8. Move the pointer over the Stage.

   The pointer changes to a crosshair.

   continues on next page

9. Click and drag to create a rectangle of the size and proportions you want.

   Flash displays an outline preview of the rectangle as you drag.

10. Release the mouse button.

    Flash draws a rectangular fill, using the currently selected fill color (**Figure 2.19**).

✔ Tips

■ To create a perfect square, hold down the Shift key as you draw your rectangle. Flash constrains the rectangle to the proportions of a perfect square.

■ Flash accepts corner-radius settings ranging from 0 to 999 points (integers only). This value equals the radius of the imaginary circle that creates the rounded corner. A larger value creates a more-rounded corner (**Figure 2.20**).

■ To reset the rectangle tool's corner radius to 0 quickly, Shift-double-click the rectangle tool or Shift-click the Round Rectangle Radius button.

■ You can change a rectangle's corner radius as you draw. Drag on the Stage with the rectangle tool to create your shape. Before releasing the mouse button, press the up-arrow key to reduce the corner-radius value; press the down-arrow key to increase it. The preview rectangle changes interactively as you press the arrow keys. Release the mouse button to complete your shape.

■ To make a rectangle grow outward from the center point as you draw, position the pointer where you want the center of the rectangle to be, then hold down the Alt key (Windows) or Option key (Mac) while you drag.

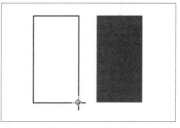

Figure 2.19 As you drag the rectangle tool, Flash creates an outline preview of a rectangle (left). To complete the fill shape, release the mouse button (right).

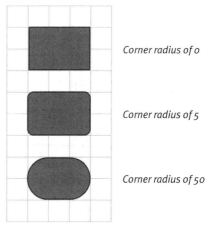

Corner radius of 0

Corner radius of 5

Corner radius of 50

Figure 2.20 With a higher corner radius setting, the rectangle tool creates a more-rounded corner.

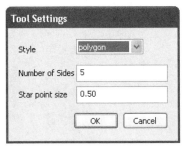

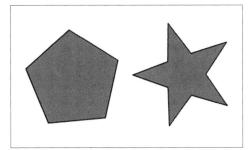

Figure 2.21 To set parameters for the polystar tool, click the Options button in the tool's Property Inspector (top). The Tool Settings dialog appears (middle). The Style menu allows you to choose multisided polygons (bottom, left) or multipointed stars (bottom, right).

To draw a polygon or star with fill and stroke:

1. In the Toolbar, click the rectangle tool.

   A submenu displaying the rectangle and polystar tools appears.

2. Select the polystar tool.

3. Access the Property Inspector for the polystar tool (**Figure 2.21**).

   If the Property Inspector is not open choose Window > Properties.

4. In the Property Inspector, click the Options button.

   The Tool Settings dialog appears. This dialog allows to choose the tool for drawing polygon shapes or stars.

5. From the Style menu, *choose one of the following:*

   ▲ To create polygon shapes, choose Polygon.

   ▲ To create star shapes, choose Star.

continues on next page

USING THE GEOMETRIC SHAPE TOOLS

6. In the Number of Sides field, enter a number between 3 and 32.

This value determines the number of sides in the polygon or the number of points in the star.

7. For stars, in the Star Point Size field, enter a number between 0 and 1.

This setting determines how sharp the points of the star are. Lower numbers translate to sharper points.

8. Click OK to close the dialog.

9. Make sure that you have selected a fill and stroke color other than No Color (see "Setting Stroke Attributes" and "Setting Fill Attributes" earlier in this chapter).

10. Click and drag on the Stage with the crosshair cursor to create a polygon or star.

11. Release the mouse button.

Flash creates a filled polygon or star, using the currently selected fill color, and gives the shape a stroke with the currently selected color, thickness, and style (Figure 2.21).

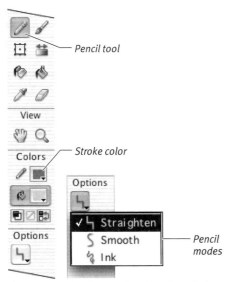

Figure 2.22 When the pencil tool is selected, the Toolbar displays a pop-up menu of pencil modes.

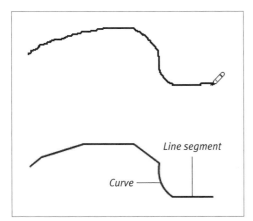

Figure 2.23 With the pencil in Straighten mode, when you draw a squiggle, Flash previews it for you. When you release the mouse button, Flash applies straightening, turning your rough squiggle (top) into a set of straight-line segments and smooth curves (bottom).

Using the Pencil Tool

Flash's pencil tool offers two freeform line-drawing modes—Straighten and Smooth—that help you draw smooth, neat shapes. For total freedom in drawing, the pencil's Ink mode leaves shapes exactly as you create them.

Straighten mode eliminates the small blips and tremors that can mar quick hand sketches. Straighten refines your line into straight-line segments and regular arcs. This mode also carries out what Flash calls shape recognition. In Straighten mode, Flash evaluates each rough shape you draw, and if the shape comes close enough to Flash's definition of an oval or rectangle, Flash turns your rough approximation into a version of the shape neat enough to please your high-school geometry teacher.

Smooth mode helps you by transforming your rough drawing into one composed of smooth, curved line segments. Note that Smooth mode does not recognize shapes or connect line segments; it simply smoothes out the curves you draw.

To use Straighten mode for freeform drawing:

1. In the Toolbar, select the pencil tool.

   The pencil-tool's modifiers appear at the bottom of the Toolbar (**Figure 2.22**).

2. From the Pencil Mode pop-up menu, choose Straighten.

3. Move the pointer over the Stage.

   The pointer turns into the pencil tool.

4. Click and draw a squiggle (**Figure 2.23**).

   Flash previews your rough line.

5. Release the mouse button.

   Flash recasts the line you've drawn, turning it into a set of straight-line segments and regular curves.

To use Straighten mode for drawing rectangles and ovals:

1. With the pencil tool in Straighten mode, click and quickly draw a rectangle or circle (**Figure 2.24**).

   You don't need to close the shape completely; leave a slight gap between the first and last points of your line.

2. Release the mouse button.

   Flash recognizes the shape and creates a perfect rectangle or oval, connecting the ends of your line and completing the shape for you.

✔ Tip

■ Tolerance settings are all-important here. You can set Flash to change almost anything ovoid into a circle and anything slightly more oblong into a rectangle. Take a little time to play around with the settings in the Editing tab of the Preferences dialog (see "Controlling Drawing Assistance" later in this chapter) to find the degree of accuracy that's right for you.

To draw smooth curves:

1. With the pencil tool selected, choose Smooth from the Pencil Mode pop-up menu.

2. Move the pointer over the Stage; then click and draw a wavy line.

3. Release the mouse button.

   Flash eliminates any vectors that aren't needed to define the basic shape (**Figure 2.25**).

   Notice that Flash turns your line into a set of smooth curved segments instead of straight-line segments.

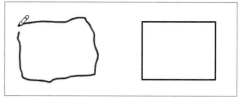

Figure 2.24 In the pencil tool's Straighten mode, when you draw a rough rectangle (left) and release the mouse button, Flash turns your shape into a rectangle with straight sides and sharp corners (right). You can also rough out oval shapes and have Flash fix them the same way.

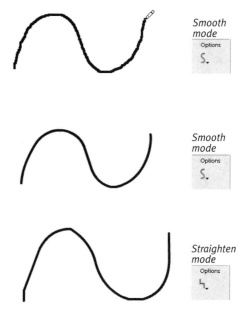

Figure 2.25 With the pencil in Smooth mode, when you draw a wavy line (top), Flash turns it into a series of smooth curves (middle). Compare a similar shape drawn with the pencil set to Straighten mode (bottom).

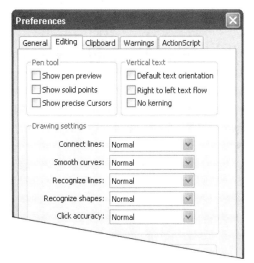

Figure 2.26 Choose Edit > Preferences (Windows) or Flash > Preferences (Mac), and select the Editing tab to set the amount of assistance Flash gives you in smoothing and recognizing shapes.

Figure 2.27 Connect Lines controls how close the beginning and ending points of an oval or rectangle must be before Flash closes them for you.

Figure 2.28 Smooth Curves determines how much Flash alters the curve you've drawn to make it smoother.

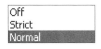

Figure 2.29 Recognize Lines determines how close to straight a line must be before Flash removes all curves and changes it to a straight-line segment.

Figure 2.30 Recognize Shapes determines how nearly ovoid or rectangular a shape must be for Flash to transform it to a perfect oval or rectangle.

Figure 2.31 Click Accuracy determines how close you must get to a line segment with the arrow pointer to select that segment.

Controlling drawing assistance

Flash helps you by straightening line segments, recognizing shapes, and smoothing curves as you draw them with the various pencil-tool modifiers discussed in the preceding sections. The degree of assistance depends on the settings in the Editing tab of the Preferences dialog. The settings are relative to the resolution of your monitor and the magnification level for the Stage. At 100 percent, with the setting Connect Lines > Can Be Distant, for example, Flash recognizes and closes an oval that has a gap of five pixels between its beginning and ending points. Bump the magnification to 400 percent, and Flash refuses to close a five-pixel gap. You must get the shape's end points within around one pixel of each other before Flash recognizes the gap and closes the shape for you.

To set the degree of assistance:

1. From the Edit menu (Windows) or from the Flash application menu (Mac), choose Preferences.

The Preferences dialog appears.

2. Choose the Editing tab of the Preferences dialog (**Figure 2.26**).

3. In the Drawing Settings section of the dialog, choose an option from each of the five pop-up menus (**Figure 2.27** through **Figure 2.31**).

Your choices range from turning off the feature to having Flash give you the highest degree of assistance.

✔ Tip

■ You can bypass Flash's drawing assistance entirely by choosing Ink mode for the pencil tool. In Ink mode, Flash creates a vector replica of your pencil line without doing much smoothing or straightening of curves and line segments.

USING THE PENCIL TOOL

Using the Pen Tool: Straight Lines

With most Flash tools, the math goes on behind the scenes. You draw a line or a shape, and Flash takes care of placing points that define the line segments and curves that make up that shape. The pen tool brings the process to center stage. The pen tool lets you place defining points (called *anchor points*) and adjust the curvature of the lines connecting them (using controllers called *Bézier handles*). You learn more about curves and handles in the following section of this chapter and in Chapter 3.

The *path*—the series of points and connecting lines created by the pen tool— is the skeleton of your object. When you've completed a path, Flash fleshes it out by applying a stroke to it.

For the following exercises, set the pen tool to show previews as you create your path. Choose Edit > Preferences (Windows) or Flash > Preferences (Mac) to open the Preferences dialog, select the Editing tab, and check the Show Pen Preview and Show Solid Points check boxes (**Figure 2.32**).

To draw straight-line segments with the pen tool:

1. In the Toolbar, select the pen tool, or press P (**Figure 2.33**).

2. Set the stroke attributes for your path.

3. Move the pointer over the Stage.

    The pen tool appears with a small *x* next to it (**Figure 2.34**). The *x* indicates that you are ready to place the first point of a path.

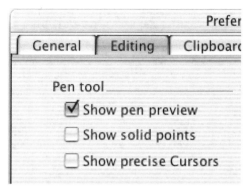

Figure 2.32 In its default mode, Flash's pen tool previews a curve segment only after you place both of the curve's defining anchor points. For these exercises, choose Edit > Preferences (Windows) or Flash > Preferences (Mac), select the Editing tab, and select the Show Pen Preview check box. This setting allows you to preview the curve as you position the pointer before clicking to set the second defining anchor point.

Figure 2.33 Select the pen tool to create paths.

Figure 2.34 The x next to the pen tool indicates that you are about to start a new path. Click to place the first anchor point.

First point previewed

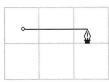

Preview line segment

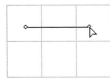

Click to place second point

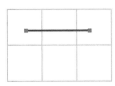

Completed line segment

Figure 2.35 Flash previews points as you place them (top) and it adds a stroke to the path as soon as you complete a segment (bottom).

4. Click where you want your line segment to begin.

The pointer changes to a hollow arrowhead; a small circle indicates the location of the anchor point on the Stage.

5. Reposition the pen tool where you want your line segment to end.

Flash extends a preview of the line segment from the first point to the tip of the pen as you move around the Stage.

6. Click.

Flash completes the line segment, using the selected stroke attributes. The anchor points appear as solid squares (**Figure 2.35**).

7. Repeat steps 5 and 6 to draw a series of connected line segments.

To end an open path:

To end a line segment or series of segments, *do one of the following*:

◆ Double-click the last point in your path.

◆ In the Toolbar, click the pen tool (or any other tool).

◆ From the Edit menu, choose Deselect All, or press ⌘-Shift-A (Mac) or Ctrl-Shift-A (Windows).

◆ On the Stage, ⌘-click (Mac) or Ctrl-click (Windows) away from your path.

To create a closed path:

1. With the pen tool selected, click three areas on the Stage to place three anchor points in a triangular layout.

    Flash completes two legs of your triangle with strokes.

2. Position the pointer over your first anchor point.

    Flash previews a line segment for the third side of the triangle. A small hollow circle appears next to the pen tool (**Figure 2.36**).

3. Click.

    Flash closes the shape, adding a stroke to the triangle's third side and filling the triangle with the currently selected fill color.

4. Move the pointer away from your anchor points.

    A small *x* appears next to the pen tool, indicating that you are free to place the first anchor point of a new path.

✔ Tip

- You don't have to close your shape directly on an anchor point. Position the pointer over the path and click to close the shape (**Figure 2.37**).

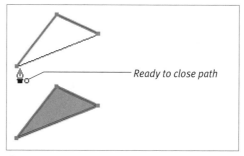

Figure 2.36 To close a path, position the pen tool over an existing anchor point (top). A circle next to the pen tool indicates that you are directly on top of the path. Click to complete the path (bottom).

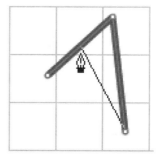

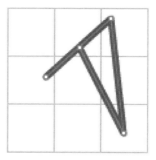

Figure 2.37 You can close a path by clicking between anchor points. Click once directly on the path (top) to create just a stroke. Double-click just inside the path to create a filled closed shape (bottom).

Using the Pen Tool: Curved Segments

In the preceding exercise, you clicked to lay down anchor points, and Flash created straight-line segments connecting those points. To create curved segments, you must activate the points' Bézier handles. Do this by clicking and dragging when you place a point. As you drag, the handles extend out from the anchor point. As you learn to create curves with the pen tool, it helps to have a grid visible on the Stage. To display the grid, choose View > Show Grid.

To draw an upward curve with the pen tool:

1. With the pen tool selected, move the pointer over the Stage.

   The pen icon appears with a small *x* next to it. The *x* indicates that you are ready to place the first point of a path.

2. Click the grid intersection where you want your curve segment to begin, and hold down the mouse button.

   Flash places a preview point on the Stage; the pointer changes to a hollow arrowhead.

3. Drag the pointer in the direction in which you want your curve to bulge.

   Two handles extend from the anchor point, growing in opposite directions as you drag.

continues on next page

4. Release the mouse button, and reposition the pointer to the right of your original point.

The pen tool returns, and Flash previews the curve you are drawing.

5. Click and drag in the opposite direction from the curve's bulge.

As you drag, the preview of the curve changes.

6. When the curve preview looks the way you want, release the mouse button.

Flash completes your curve segment with a stroke (**Figure 2.38**).

You can end the path here (as described in the preceding section) or repeat steps 2 through 6 to add more curves to your path.

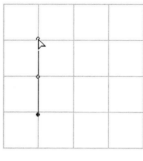

Click and drag upward—the direction in which the curve should bulge

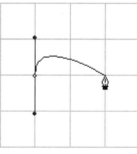

Preview of curve before placing second point

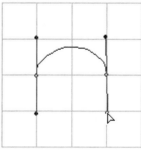

Click to place second point; drag away from the curve's bulge

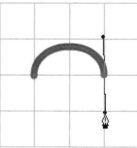

Completed line segment

Figure 2.38 To create an upward curve, when placing the first anchor point, click and drag toward the top of the Stage. Before you click and drag your second point, the preview looks lopsided. You adjust the curvature as you drag the Bézier handle. Drag toward the bottom of the Stage.

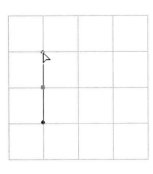

Click and drag upward—the direction in which the first half of the S curve should bulge

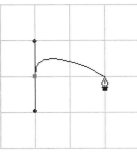

Preview of curve before placing second point

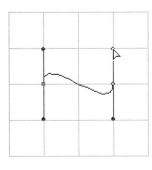

Click to place second point; drag in same direction as for first point

Completed curve segment

Figure 2.39 Click and drag your first point upward to start an S curve. Click and drag your second point in the same direction. Release the mouse button to finish the curve.

To draw an S curve with the pen tool:

1. Follow steps 1 and 2 of the preceding exercise.

2. Drag the pointer in the direction in which you want the left side of the curve to bulge.

3. Release the mouse button, and reposition the pointer to the right of your original point.

4. Click and drag in the same direction you went in step 2.

   Flash creates a horizontal S shape centered between the anchor points you placed (**Figure 2.39**).

✔ Tips

- When you create symmetrical curves, use grid lines to help position anchor points and Bézier handles.

- Don't worry about fine-tuning each curve as you draw; just get down the basic outlines. It's often easier to adjust points and curves when you have a rough version of the object to work on. You learn to modify paths in Chapter 3.

- One of the tricks of drawing with the pen tool is visualizing the way a shape's curves and lines must look before you place points and adjust handles. To get the hang of it, try creating paths that trace existing objects. Lock the layer that contains your template shapes. Add a new layer, and practice re-creating the shapes, using the locked layer as a guide. (You learn about using layers in Chapter 5.)

USING THE PEN TOOL: CURVED SEGMENTS

Using the Paint Bucket

The paint-bucket tool lets you fill the inside of a closed shape with a solid color. You can also use the paint bucket to change the color of an existing fill. The oval, rectangle, and polystar tools automatically create closed shapes that are easy to fill. If you draw a shape yourself, it may have some small gaps. You can have Flash ignore these gaps and fill the basic shape anyway.

In addition to filling with solid colors, the paint-bucket tool can fill shapes with gradients (see Chapter 3) or bitmapped patterns (see Chapter 14).

To fill an outline shape with a solid color:

1. In the Toolbar, select the paint-bucket tool by clicking the paint-bucket icon, or press K.

   The paint-bucket icon is highlighted in the Toolbar, and the Gap Size menu and Lock fill modifier appear in the Options section of the Toolbar (**Figure 2.40**).

2. From the Toolbar's fill-color box, the Color Mixer panel, or the Property Inspector, select a fill color.

3. Place the paint bucket's hot spot (the tip of the drip of paint) somewhere inside an outline shape, and click (**Figure 2.41**).

   The shape fills with the currently selected fill color (**Figure 2.42**).

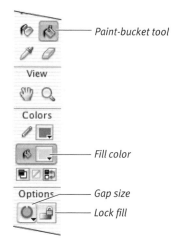

Figure 2.40 The paint-bucket tool and its modifiers.

Figure 2.41 The hot spot on the paint-bucket tool is the little drip at the end of the spilling paint. The hot spot changes to white when you move the paint bucket over a darker color.

Figure 2.42 Clicking inside an outline shape with the paint bucket (top) fills the shape with the currently selected color (bottom).

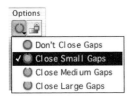

Figure 2.43 The Gap Size pop-up menu controls Flash's capability to fill shapes that aren't fully closed.

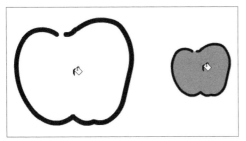

Figure 2.44 The paint bucket cannot fill this apple shape with the setting of Close Large Gaps and a magnification of 100 percent (left). But in a 50 percent view, the paint bucket with the same large-gap closure setting recognizes this shape as complete and fills it.

To set gap closure:

1. With the paint bucket selected, from the Gap Size menu in the Options section of the Toolbar, choose a setting (**Figure 2.43**).

   Flash presents four options for filling gaps.

2. Choose the amount of assistance you want.

   If you draw your shapes precisely, medium or small gap closure serves you best; you don't want Flash to fill areas that are not meant to be shapes. If your drawings are rougher, choose Close Large Gaps. This setting enables Flash to recognize less-complete shapes.

✔ Tips

- You may be unaware that your shape has any gaps. If nothing happens when you click inside a shape with the paint bucket, try changing the Gap Size setting.

- Gap-closure settings are relative to the amount of magnification you're using to view the Stage. If the paint bucket's largest gap-closure setting fails at your current magnification, try again after reducing magnification (**Figure 2.44**).

USING THE PAINT BUCKET

Using the Brush Tool in Normal Mode

Flash's brush tool offers a way to create free-flowing swashes of color. These shapes are actually freeform fills drawn without a stroke. The brush tool enables you to simulate the type of artwork you'd create in the real world with a paintbrush or marking pen. A variety of brush sizes and tip shapes helps you create a painterly look in your drawings.

If you have a pressure-sensitive drawing tablet, the brush can interact with it to create lines of varying thickness as you vary the pressure in your drawing stroke, simulating real-world brush work.

To create freeform fill shapes:

1. In the Toolbar, select the brush tool or press B.

   The various brush modifiers appear at the bottom of the Toolbar (**Figure 2.45**).

2. From the Toolbar's fill-color box, the Color Mixer panel, or the Property Inspector, select a fill color.

   Use the default settings for Brush Size and Brush Shape for now. You'll learn how to change them in the next task.

3. From the Brush Mode pop-up menu in the Options section of the Toolbar, choose Paint Normal (**Figure 2.46**).

   The other paint modes allow your paint strokes to interact in various ways with other lines and shapes on the Stage. You learn more about using these modes in Chapter 4.

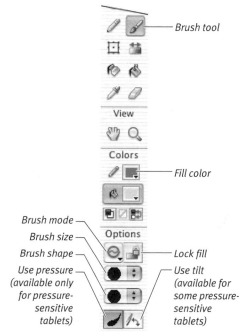

Figure 2.45 The brush tool and its modifiers.

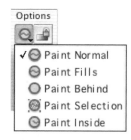

Figure 2.46 The Brush Mode pop-up menu with Paint Normal selected.

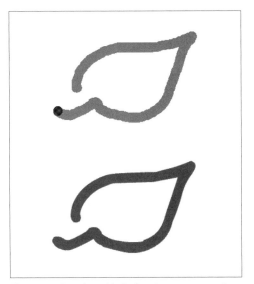

Figure 2.47 Drawing with the brush creates a preview of your shape (top); Flash recasts the shape as a vector graphic with the currently selected fill color.

4. Move the pointer over the Stage.

The pointer changes to reflect the current brush size and shape.

5. Click and draw on the Stage.

Flash previews your brushwork (**Figure 2.47**).

6. When you complete your shape, release the mouse button.

Flash creates the final shape in the currently selected fill color.

The Mystery of Brush Smoothness Settings

Flash MX 2004, gives you control over how your brush strokes translate into vector shapes. To access this control, in the Property Inspector for the brush tool, enter a value in the Smoothing field. The stroke-smoothness setting determines how closely Flash re-creates each movement of the brush as a separate vector segment; the setting ranges from 0 to 100; the default is 50. The lower the setting, the more faithfully Flash reproduces the shapes you draw. (It does this by using more vectors, which has an impact on the size of your final file.) With a higher setting, Flash re-creates your flourishes more roughly, using fewer vectors.

To see the difference most clearly, select the brush tool, assign a smoothing value of 1, and use the mouse (not a graphics pen) to draw a curvy line on the Stage. Now change the smoothing setting to 100. Draw a second curvy line. Using the subselection tool (you'll learn about using this tool in Chapter 3), select each shape. The line drawn with smoothing set to 1 displays many more points—that is, it contains many more vector segments.

To change the brush size and shape:

1. With the brush tool selected in the Toolbar, click the Brush Size pop-up menu.

   A set of circles representing various brush sizes appears (**Figure 2.48**).

2. Select the size you want.

   A circle the size you selected appears in the Brush Size box in the Toolbar. This circle represents what size brush tip Flash will use as you work with the brush tool.

3. In the Toolbar, click the Brush Shape pop-up menu.

   A list of nine tip shapes appears (**Figure 2.49**).

4. Select the shape you want.

   The shape you picked appears in the Brush Shape box in the Toolbar. This is the brush tip shape Flash will use as you work with the brush tool.

✔ Tip

■ You can change the size of your brush stroke by changing the magnification at which you view the Stage. To create a fat stroke without changing your brush-tip settings, set the Stage view to a small percentage. To switch to a thin stroke, zoom out to a higher percentage (**Figure 2.50**). Be sure to check your work in 100% view.

Figure 2.48 The Brush Size pop-up menu offers a variety of brush sizes.

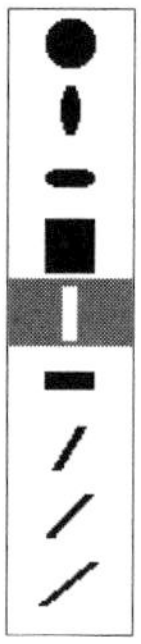

Figure 2.49 The Brush Shape pop-up menu.

Created with 200% magnification

Created with 100% magnification

Created with 50% magnification

Figure 2.50 Flash created these three brushstrokes with exactly the same brush size—only the magnification level of the Stage changed for each stroke.

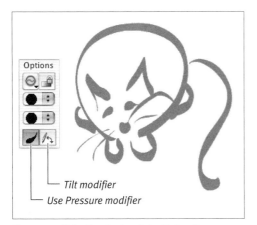

Tilt modifier
Use Pressure modifier

Figure 2.51 Selecting the brush tool's Use Pressure modifier activates the pressure-sensitive capabilities of a connected pressure-sensitive pen and graphics tablet. Then you can produce lively lines of varying thickness simply by applying more or less pressure as you draw. Flash created all the lines in this cat with a single brush size and shape.

If you have a Flash-compatible pressure-sensitive drawing tablet attached to your computer, the Toolbar displays two additional brush modifiers that let you take advantage of your tablet: Use Pressure and Tilt.

To use pressure sensitivity:

◆ With the brush tool selected in the Toolbar, click the Use Pressure modifier.

The modifier is highlighted. The pressure-sensitive capabilities of your pen are now active, and you can draw lines that vary in thickness according to the amount of pressure you use (**Figure 2.51**). Applying more pressure makes your brush stroke fatter; applying less pressure keeps the brush stroke thin. Note that Flash will not create a brush stroke fatter than the currently selected brush size.

To use tilt:

◆ With the brush tool selected in the Toolbar, click the Tilt modifier.

The modifier is highlighted. If your graphics tablet has tilt capability—the ability to measure the angle at which you are holding your pen—Flash will take advantage of that feature to control the way your pen creates shapes with the brush tool.

Using the Text Tool

The text tool creates blocks of editable text. You can set the text to read horizontally or vertically. You can also apply a variety of text attributes to text—including text and paragraph styles. Editable text can later be turned into raw shapes.

To create a single line of text for use as a graphic element:

1. In the Toolbar, select the text tool or press T (**Figure 2.52**).

    For this task, use the current settings for type and paragraph styles. You learn to change these settings in upcoming tasks.

2. Move the pointer over the Stage.

    The pointer turns into a crosshair with a letter *A* in the bottom-right corner (**Figure 2.53**).

3. Click the Stage at the spot where you want your text to start.

    Flash creates a text box with a round resize handle and a blinking insertion point, ready for you to enter text (**Figure 2.54**).

4. Start typing to enter your text.

    The text box grows to accommodate whatever you type (**Figure 2.55**).

5. When you finish typing, click elsewhere on the Stage or change tools.

    Flash hides the text box, leaving just the text visible. When you click this text with the selection tool, Flash selects the text box automatically so that you can reposition it or change the text's attributes directly.

— Text tool

Figure 2.52 Select the text tool in the Toolbar to start creating text boxes on the Stage.

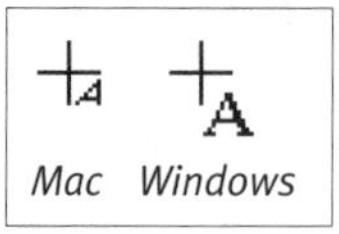

Mac   Windows

Figure 2.53 The text-tool pointer.

Figure 2.54 Click the Stage with the text tool to create a text box. The round resize handle indicates that the text box does not have word wrap turned on.

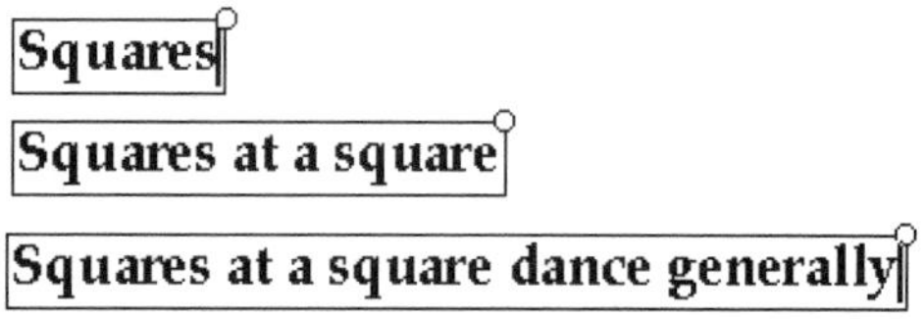

Squares

Squares at a square

Squares at a square dance generally

Figure 2.55 As you type, the box grows horizontally to accommodate your text. The text will not wrap.

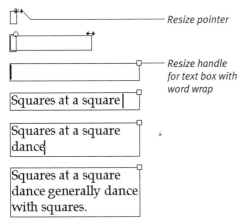

Resize pointer

Resize handle
for text box with
word wrap

Figure 2.56 Click and drag the resize handle to create a text box with a specific width. The handle changes to a square, indicating that the text you enter will wrap to fit the column width of the text box. The text box continues to grow in length—but not width—as you enter more text.

What Is Editable Text?

The term *editable text* has two meanings in Flash. First, you can modify text within the Flash authoring environment. As you create text elements for your movie, you can go back and change your font, pick a new text color, select another font size, fix typos—you name it. Flash calls this type of text *static text.*

Second, viewers of a movie playing in the Flash Player can modify text. Through ActionScript, you can retrieve user input and put it to work in various ways in your movie. Flash calls such text *input text.* Or you, the creator, can use editable text fields to update and display new information in a movie. Flash calls such text *dynamic text.*

In this chapter, you learn about using static text, which is strictly a graphic element in the final movie. The manipulation of input and dynamic text fields requires a more advanced form of ActionScripting than the scope of this book can cover.

To create a text box with set width and word wrap:

1. With the text tool selected in the Toolbar, click the Stage at the spot where you want your text to start.

   Flash creates a text box with a round resize handle.

2. Move the pointer over the resize handle.

   The pointer changes to a double-headed arrow.

3. Click and drag the handle until your text box is as wide as you want it (**Figure 2.56**).

   The resize handle changes to a square.

4. Release the mouse button.

   The blinking insertion point appears in the text box.

5. Enter your text.

   Flash wraps the text horizontally to fit inside the column that the text box defines. The box automatically grows longer (not wider) to accommodate your text.

✔ Tips

■ To reposition a text box with the text tool active, position the pointer along the edge of the text box. The pointer changes to the selection arrow. Now you can drag the text box to a new location.

■ If you enter so much text on one line that the end of the text box starts to disappear off the Stage, you can fix the problem. Either drag the text box to the left with the selection arrow or choose View > Work Area (Shift-⌘W [Mac], Ctrl-Shift-W [Windows]) and reduce magnification until you can see the resize handle. Then you can force the text to wrap by resizing the text box.

USING THE TEXT TOOL

Working with Vertical Text

Flash lets you create vertical text in static text boxes. You can create a single vertical column, or create text that flows automatically from column to column. You can set the columns to read left to right (as they do in English) or vice versa (as required for, say, Japanese text).

You set the text-flow direction in the Property Inspector.

To access the Property Inspector:

◆ If the Property Inspector is not open, from the Window menu, choose Properties.

To create vertical columns of text:

1. With the text tool selected and the Property Inspector open, in the Property Inspector, click the Change Direction of Text button (**Figure 2.57**).

    A pop-up menu of text directions appears.

2. To create a vertical text box, *do one of the following:*

    ▲ To make text columns read from the left side of the box to the right, choose Vertical, Left to Right.

    ▲ To make text columns read from the right side of the box to the left, choose Vertical, Right to Left.

3. Click the Stage at the spot where you want your text to start.

    Flash creates a vertical text box with a round resize handle. Notice that the blinking insertion pointer is lying on its side (**Figure 2.58**).

4. Click and drag the resize handle.

Figure 2.57 When you have selected the text tool or a text box, the Property Inspector displays a text-direction button. Clicking it opens a menu of options for setting the direction in which your text flows.

Figure 2.58 With text direction set to vertical, clicking the Stage with the text tool gives you an insertion point lying on its side (left). As you type, you enter a column of single characters (middle). The text box grows in length to accommodate all the text you enter (right).

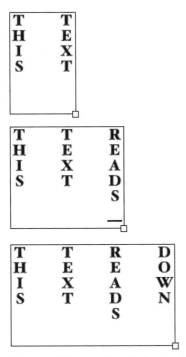

Figure 2.59 When text direction is set to Vertical, Left to Right, a fixed-height text box creates columns of downward-reading characters that flow from column to column automatically.

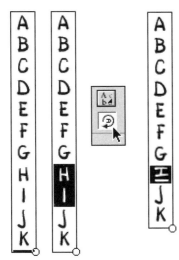

Figure 2.60 Select characters within a vertical text column (left); then click the Rotation button in the Property Inspector (middle) to rotate the characters and create a word that reads horizontally down (right).

5. When your text box is the desired height, release the mouse button.

The resize handle changes to the square word-wrap handle.

6. Enter your text.

Flash places one character below another till the text reaches the bottom edge of the box. Then text jumps to the next column and continues flowing vertically (**Figure 2.59**). You can force text to flow to the next column by adding a paragraph return.

7. When you finish typing, click elsewhere on the Stage or change tools.

✔ Tips

■ If you want to create a single column of vertical text, you can start typing as soon as you click the Stage to create the text box. As in the first task in the preceding exercise, the text box continues to grow in length as you type.

■ In some Asian languages whose text is set in vertical columns, it is common to set words borrowed from foreign languages in Latin characters so that they can be read as a unit instead of character by character. You can make any selected text characters read horizontally down as a unit by clicking the Rotation button in the Property Inspector (**Figure 2.60**).

■ If most of your text work demands vertical text columns, you can make that setting your default. From the Edit menu (Windows) or from the Flash menu (Mac), choose Preferences and click the Editing tab. The Vertical Text section offers defaults for vertical text orientation and for right-to-left text flow.

WORKING WITH VERTICAL TEXT

Setting Text Attributes

The Text Tool Property Inspector allows you to set the following attributes for your text: the typeface, font size, style, and spacing between letters. You can also define text as superscript or subscript, set line spacing, set text color, and create live links between text and URLs in this panel. Flash allows you to control *tracking*—the amount of space between letters and words in a chunk of selected text.

You can set character attributes in advance so that as you type, the text tool applies them automatically, or you can apply character attributes to existing text. The text tool always uses whatever settings currently appear in the Text Tool Property Inspector (**Figure 2.61**).

For the following exercises, keep the Text Tool Property Inspector open (choose Window > Properties if it's not already open).

✔ Tip

■ In addition to using the Text Tool Property Inspector's settings for text, you can set the font, size, style, paragraph alignment, and tracking from the Text menu. You can use the Text menu to change the properties of selected text or to load text properties into the Property Inspector.

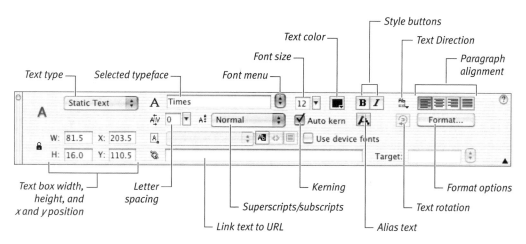

Figure 2.61 When you have selected the text tool in the Toolbar (or a text block on the Stage), the Property Inspector displays the type attributes to be created by the text tool (or applied to the current text selection).

To select text to apply character attributes:

Do one of the following:

◆ With the text tool selected, drag over existing text to highlight just a portion of text.

or

◆ With the selection tool active, click a text box to select all the text within it.

✔ Tip

■ You can select multiple text boxes with the selection tool and modify them at the same time. (You learn more about selections in Chapter 3.)

The Mystery of Device Fonts

Assigning an installed font to a static text box means that you want the text to look the same during playback as it does during authoring. Yet you have no way of knowing if your end users will have the font that you chose installed on their system. In order to re-create your static text box font accurately during playback, Flash saves information about the outlines of the letter forms with the published (.swf) file (you'll learn more about publishing files in Chapter 17). During playback, Flash Player uses those outlines to draw the letters correctly. Saving outline information increases the size of your .swf file. Device fonts allow you to eliminate that information. There are two ways to apply device fonts: Select one from a font menu, or click the Use Device Fonts button in the Property Inspector.

By choosing a device font from one of the font menus, you retain control over the style of type Flash displays but give up the use of a specific typeface. Three device fonts appear in the font menu in the Property Inspector and the Text > Font menu: _sans, _serif, and _typewriter. During movie playback of static text for which you chose a specific device font, Flash uses a font installed on the end user's machine that has the same type style. For static text set as _serif, Flash looks for a font with *serifs*, those little hooks and tails you see at the ends of some letters' strokes in typefaces such as Times Roman. For _sans (short for *sans serif*, or without serifs), Flash looks for a plainer font, one without hooks and tails; Helvetica or Arial are good examples. For _typewriter, Flash looks for a monospaced font (one in which each letter form takes up the same amount of space, like the letters on a typewriter); Courier is one example.

Choosing a specific font for your static text and then clicking the Use Device Fonts button in the Property Inspector gives Flash the greatest liberty in choosing a substitute font from the user's system. Flash looks for the closest match from the user's installed fonts, but there's no guarantee that the font Flash chooses will have the same style as the font you originally specified.

To choose an installed typeface:

1. Select the text you want to modify.

2. In the Text Tool Property Inspector, click the scroll arrow to the right of the Font field.

   A scrolling list of your installed fonts appears, together with a font-preview window (**Figure 2.62**).

3. Move the pointer over a font name.

   Flash highlights the font name and displays its preview.

4. Click to select the currently highlighted font and close the scrolling list.

   The selected font name appears in the Font field. Flash changes the selected text to the new font.

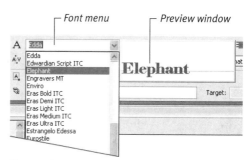

Figure 2.62 As you move the pointer through the font list in the Property Inspector, you see a preview of each font installed on your system.

✔ Tips

■ You can also enter a font by typing its name in the Property Inspector's Font field. The field is not case-sensitive, but you must type accurately. If you make a mistake in typing the name of an installed font, Flash assumes that it's dealing with a missing font and substitutes the system default font.

■ Another way to select a font is to choose it from the Text > Font menu.

■ If you want to reduce file size for your published movie and you don't need precise control over the look of your text in the movie as it plays, you can choose a device font instead of an installed font for your static text box (see the sidebar "The Mystery of Device Fonts").

■ You can allow end users to copy text from static text boxes. During authoring, select the text that you want users to be able to copy. In the Property Inspector, click the Selectable Text button (the button labeled with the letters *Ab*, just below the pop-up menu for creating superscripts and subscripts).

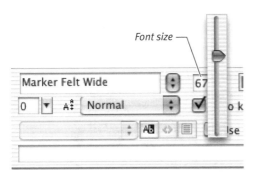

Font size

Figure 2.63 Drag the font-size slider to change the point size of selected text interactively on the Stage.

Windows   Mac

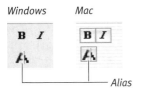

Alias

Figure 2.64 To turn off anti-aliasing, in the text Property Inspector, click the Alias button.

To set font size:

1. Select the text you want to modify.

2. In the Property Inspector, double-click (or click and drag) in the Font Size field to highlight the current value.

3. Enter the desired point size.

4. Press Enter.

or

1. Click the triangle to the right of the Font Size field.

   A slider pops open (**Figure 2.63**).

2. Drag the slider's lever to choose a value between 8 and 96 points.

   Flash previews the changes on the Stage as you drag the slider lever.

3. Click outside the slider to confirm the new font size.

✔ Tips

- For even quicker changes, just click and drag the slider triangle. When you release the slider's lever, Flash confirms the new font size automatically.

- To enter font sizes outside the slider's range, you must type the value in the Font Size field.

- Flash applies anti-aliasing to all text by default; this creates slightly blurred edges to the letter forms and making them smoother and, for large point sizes, easier to read. For smaller sizes, anti-aliasing can make text appear fuzzy and indistinct. To turn off anti-aliasing, in the Text Tool Property Inspector, click the Alias button (**Figure 2.64**). For very small text, however, (text smaller than 8-point), using aliasing can make the text too jaggy.

- You can also select a font size from the Text > Size menu.

SETTING TEXT ATTRIBUTES

To choose a text color:

1. Select the text you want to modify.

2. In the Text Tool Property Inspector, click the text-color box (note that text in Flash is considered to be a fill).

   The pointer changes to an eyedropper, and a set of swatches appears (**Figure 2.65**).

3. To select a color, *do one of the following:*

   ▲ To select the color directly below the tip of the eyedropper, with the eyedropper pointer, click a swatch or an item on the Stage.

   ▲ Enter a value in the hexadecimal color field.

   ▲ To define a new color using your system's color picker, click the Color Picker button (for more information on defining colors, see Chapter 3).

✔ Tips

■ Flash changes all the settings in the Text Tool Property Inspector to match the attributes of selected text, which means that by selecting text, you load the text tool with that text's attributes. Keep blocks of text with formatting you use often in the work area and just click to re-create their settings for the text tool.

■ Because Flash considers text to be a fill, you can also change text color by choosing a new fill color in the Toolbar or in the Color Mixer panel.

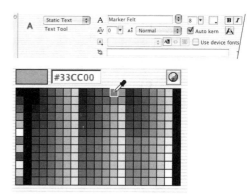

Figure 2.65 Choose a color for text created with the text tool from the Property Inspector's text (fill)-color box.

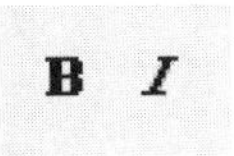

Figure 2.66 Access bold and italic styles by clicking the Bold (left) and Italic (right) buttons in the Text Tool Property Inspector.

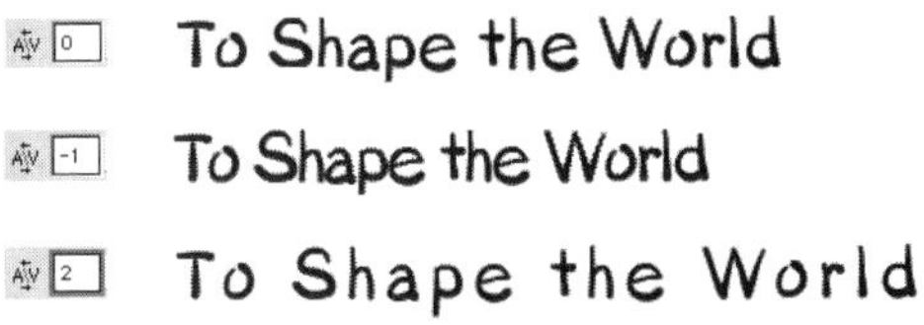

To Shape the World

To Shape the World

To Shape the World

Figure 2.67 Enter a negative tracking value to bring characters closer together. Enter a positive value to space characters out. Enter 0 to use a font's built-in tracking value.

To choose a type style:

1. Select the text you want to modify.

2. In the Property Inspector, *do one of the following:*

   ▲ To create boldface type, click the Bold button (**Figure 2.66**).

   ▲ To create italic type, click the Italic button.

   ▲ To create type that is both boldface and italic, click the Bold and Italic buttons.

   When creating bold and italic styles, Flash simply modifies the current typeface; Flash doesn't select a bold or italic typeface in the family of fonts you've chosen.

✔ Tip

■ You can also toggle boldface type by pressing Shift-⌘-B (Mac) or Ctrl-Shift-B (Windows). To toggle italic, press Shift-⌘-I (Mac) or Ctrl-Shift-I (Windows).

To apply tracking:

1. Within a text box in a Flash document, select the text to track.

2. In the Property Inspector's Character Spacing field, enter the desired point size.

   A negative value reduces the space between the letters; a positive value increases it (**Figure 2.67**).

3. Press Enter.

or

1. In the Property Inspector's Character Spacing field, click the triangle to the right of the field.

   A slider pops open.

continues on next page

SETTING TEXT ATTRIBUTES

2. Drag the slider's lever to a value between −59 and 59.

Flash previews the changes interactively on the Stage as you drag.

3. Click outside the slider to confirm the new spacing.

✔ Tips

■ For even quicker changes, just click and drag the slider triangle. When you release the slider's lever, Flash confirms the new tracking value; you don't need to press Enter.

■ You can increase tracking of selected text in 0.5-point increments by choosing Text > Tracking > Increase, or by pressing Option-⌘-right arrow (Mac) or Ctrl-Alt-right arrow (Windows). To decrease tracking, choose Text > Tracking > Decrease, or use the keyboard commands with the left arrow. Add the Shift key to the keyboard shortcuts for narrower and wider tracking; this method increases or decreases space in two-pixel increments.

■ You can also track interactively by using the keyboard shortcuts. The space between letters continues to expand or contract as long as you hold down the key combination.

■ To reset the font's original letter spacing, choose Text > Tracking > Reset or press Option-⌘-up arrow (Mac) or Alt-Ctrl-up arrow (Windows).

What Is Kerning?

While *tracking* affects the space between characters and words in an entire line or paragraph of text, *kerning* affects the space between a pair of letters. Because of the way fonts are constructed, with each letter being a separate element, some pairs of letters look oddly spaced when you type them. The space between a capital *T* and a lowercase *o*, for example, may seem too large because of the white space below the crossbar of the *T*. To make the characters look better, you can reduce the space between them, or *kern in* the pair. Some letters may seem to be too close together—say, a *t* and an *i*. You can *kern out* the pair so that it looks better.

Font designers often build into their fonts special information about how to space troublesome pairs of letters. Flash takes advantage of that embedded kerning information when you check the Auto Kern check box in the Text Tool Property Inspector. It's a good idea to turn kerning on to make your type look its best.

You can kern manually in Flash instead of using the embedded kerning or in addition to it. Select the character pair that you want to kern; then use Flash's Tracking feature to bring the letters closer together or move them farther apart.

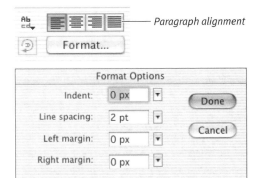

Paragraph alignment

Figure 2.68 In the Text Tool Property Inspector, click the format button (top) to access a dialog for setting text attributes, such as alignment, indents, margins, and space between lines of text (bottom).

Setting Paragraph Attributes

Flash allows you to work with paragraph formatting much as you would in a word processor. The Text Tool Property Inspector allows you to set right and left margins, a first-line indent, line spacing, and alignment (flush left, flush right, centered, or justified) (**Figure 2.68**). You can set paragraph attributes in advance so that as you type, the text tool applies them automatically. And you can apply paragraph attributes to existing text. The text tool uses whatever settings currently appear in the Property Inspector.

In the following exercises, you learn to modify existing text; keep the Property Inspector open. (Choose Window > Properties if it's not already open.)

To select paragraphs to modify:

Do one of the following:

- With the text tool, click within the paragraph you want to modify.

- With the text tool, click and drag to select multiple paragraphs within one text box.

- With the selection tool, click the text box to select all the paragraphs within the box.

SETTING PARAGRAPH ATTRIBUTES

To set paragraph alignment:

1. Select the paragraphs you want to modify.

2. In the Text Tool Property Inspector, *do one of the following* (**Figure 2.69**):

   ▲ To align horizontal text on the left (vertical text on the top), click the first alignment button.

   ▲ To center horizontal or vertical text, click the second alignment button.

   ▲ To align horizontal text on the right (vertical text on the bottom), click the third alignment button.

   ▲ To justify text (force all lines except the last line of a paragraph to fill the full column width), click the fourth alignment button.

✔ Tip

■ To select all the paragraphs within a text block, click with the text tool anywhere inside the text block; then choose Edit > Select All. Flash highlights the entire text block.

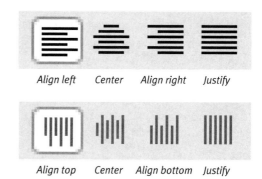

Align left   Center   Align right   Justify

Align top   Center   Align bottom   Justify

Figure 2.69 The paragraph-alignment buttons allow you to format the text of a paragraph in four ways. A graphic representation of the selected paragraph alignment style appears on each button in the Paragraph panel. The images on the buttons reflect whether the text box is set for horizontal (top) or vertical (bottom) text flow.

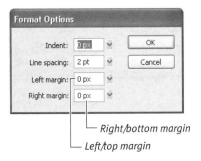

Right/bottom margin

Left/top margin

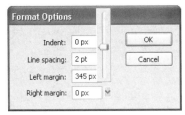

Figure 2.70 You can enter a value for right and left margins (horizontal text) or top and bottom margins (vertical text) directly in the appropriate box (top) or use the slider to select a value (bottom).

To set margins:

1. In the Text Tool Property Inspector, click the Format button.

   The Format Options dialog appears.

2. In the Left Margin or Right Margin field, enter the desired margin size.

   The units of measure used for the margin are the ones set in the Document Properties dialog (see Chapter 1).

3. Click OK (**Figure 2.70**).

   Flash uses the values that you enter to create margins from the left and right sides of the text box. Your audience will not see the margins unless you are creating text that they can edit, in which case you can make the border of the text box visible.

✔ Tips

- For easy entry of new values, click the triangle to the right of the Margin field. A slider pops open. Drag the slider's lever to choose a value between 0 and 720 pixels. Click the away from the slider to confirm the new margin value.

- Flash incorporates the current margin settings into text boxes as you create them. With margins set to the default (0 pixels), clicking the text tool on the Stage creates a small text box, just large enough for the blinking insertion point. If you get a longer text box than you expect when you click the Stage with the text tool, check your margin settings in the Property Inspector and adjust them as needed.

To set a first-line indent:

◆ In the Format Options dialog, in the Indent field, use the value-entry techniques described in the preceding exercise to enter a value for indenting the first line of text in the paragraph.

Flash calculates the indent from the left margin; when the left margin is set to 0, Flash measures the indent from the left edge of the text box.

To set line spacing:

◆ In the Format Options dialog, in the Line Spacing field, use the value-entry techniques described earlier in this chapter to enter a value for the amount of space you want between lines of text.

If your text contains various point sizes, Flash bases the spacing between two lines on the larger font (**Figure 2.71**).

✔ Tip

■ Points are the most common unit of measure for working with type, and regardless of what units you've set in the Document Properties dialog, Flash always enters the line-spacing value with the abbreviation pt (for points).

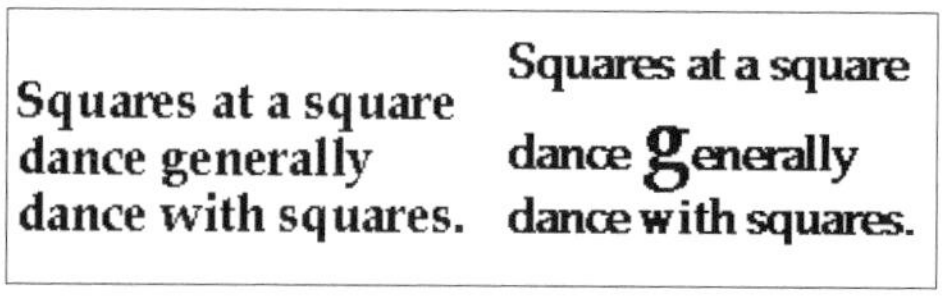

Figure 2.71 The line spacing for the text block on the left is set to 0 points. The space you see between lines is the space included as part of the font. Because the text is all one size, the spacing above and below the middle line of text is the same. In the text block on the right—with the same 0-point line spacing—one letter is a larger point size. Flash increases the space between lines to make room for the larger text.

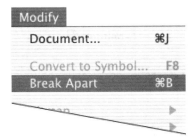

Figure 2.72 Choose Modify > Break Apart to place each letter of a text block in its own text box.

Breaking Apart Text

Flash allows you to *break apart* text—that is, divide one text block containing multiple editable characters into multiple blocks, each containing one editable character. This feature allows you to scale, reposition, or distort individual letters. (You learn to make these kinds of modifications to graphic elements in Chapter 3.) The ability to place letters in separate text boxes also comes in handy for animating text. (You learn more about animation techniques in chapters 7 through 10.)

To divide text blocks into single-letter text boxes:

1. Using the techniques from the preceding exercises, create a block of text.

2. While the text tool's blinking insertion point is still in the text box, choose Modify > Break Apart (**Figure 2.72**).

   Flash places each letter in its own text box and selects all the text boxes. Each text box is just wide enough to hold one letter. Each letter is fully editable on its own, though the group is no longer linked.

✔ Tip

■ You don't have to break text apart immediately after creating it. You can reactivate a text box by clicking it with the text tool. Or you can simply select the text box with the selection tool and then choose Modify > Break Apart.

To transform letters into raw shapes:

1. Follow the steps in the preceding exercise to place letters in individual text boxes.

2. From the Modify menu, choose Break Apart.

   This second Break Apart command transforms the editable letters into raw shapes on the Stage (**Figure 2.73**). You can edit them as you would any other fill, but you can no longer change their text attributes with the text tool.

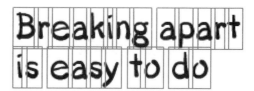

Figure 2.73 Applying the Break Apart command once transforms selected text (top) into single-letter text boxes (middle); applying the command again creates raw fill shapes out of the individual letters (bottom).

MODIFYING SIMPLE GRAPHICS

3

One way to modify Macromedia Flash MX 2004 graphics is to select one or more shapes and edit them by changing their attributes (such as color, size, and location) in the Property Inspector or in the appropriate panels.

You can also modify the shape of an element. Some operations—such as straightening lines, adjusting Bézier curves, and assigning new attributes—require that the element be selected. Other operations, such as reshaping a line segment or curve with the selection tool, require the element to be deselected. A few operations allow you to edit the element whether it is selected or not—using the paint-bucket tool to change a fill color, for example.

This chapter covers using the selection, lasso, and subselection tools to select and modify the elements you learned to make in Chapter 2. You also learn about using the Property Inspector and other panels to modify elements' attributes.

Setting Selection Preferences

Flash allows you to select elements in several ways. You can click an element with the selection tool or draw a selection outline. When you click to select an element using the selection tool, selecting an entire line can take several clicks because each segment and curve of a line is a separate element that you must select. Adding to a selection is a common operation, and Flash gives you two ways to do it: Shift selection and additive selection.

Flash's default setting has Shift Select turned on. (You set the selection method in the General tab of the Preferences dialog.) In Shift Select mode, you use the Shift key as a modifier while selecting an item to add it to any selection that is already active on the Stage. When you turn off Shift Select mode, selections become additive, which means that any new selections get added to current selections.

You always remove individual items from a selection by Shift-clicking.

To set a selection method for the selection tool:

1. From the Edit menu (Windows) or from the Flash application menu (Mac), choose Preferences.

   The Preferences dialog appears.

2. Choose the General tab (**Figure 3.1**).

3. In the Selection Options section, check or uncheck the Shift Select check box.

4. Click OK.

In Shift Select mode (Flash's default setting), you must Shift-click to add items to the current selection. With Shift Select turned off, each new item you click with the selection tool gets added to the current selection.

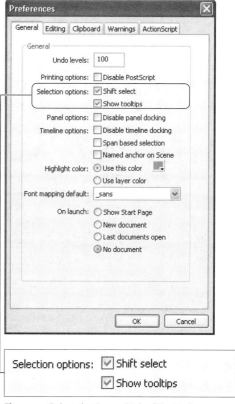

Figure 3.1 Select the General tab of the Preferences dialog to choose a selection method.

SETTING SELECTION PREFERENCES

Figure 3.2 As you prepare to select a line, Flash indicates what kind of point lies beneath the pointer.

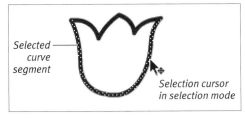

Figure 3.3 When you click a line to select it, Flash highlights that line segment (top). If you have the Property Inspector open, you can see information about your selected line, such as its color, thickness, and position on the Stage (bottom).

Selecting Lines with the Selection Tool

Using the selection tool to select lines and outline shapes may be a bit confusing at first. What you think of as being a single element—say, a swooping squiggly line or a square—may actually be several connected segments. Flash divides lines that you draw with the pencil tool into curves and segments that it defines as vectors. This means you may need to make multiple selections to select a single item with the selection tool.

Flash covers selections with a pattern of tiny dots. Make sure that all the parts of the line or outline you intend to select display this pattern.

To select a single line segment:

1. In the Toolbar, select the selection tool, or press V on the keyboard.

2. Move the pointer over a portion of the line (**Figure 3.2**).

   Flash appends a little arc or a little right-angle icon to the selection tool. These icons indicate that the tool is over a point in a line segment and show what type of point it is: a curve or a corner point. (For more information about points, see the sidebar, "About Curve and Corner Points" later in this chapter).

3. Click to select the line.

   Flash highlights the selected segment (**Figure 3.3**).

To select multiple line segments:

1. In the Toolbar, select the selection tool.

2. To select the segments you want to include, do one of the following:

   ▲ If you are using Flash's default selection style (Shift Select), Shift-click each segment you want to select. Flash adds each new segment to the highlighted selection (**Figure 3.4**).

   ▲ If you turned off the Shift Select option in the Preferences dialog, click each segment you want to include. Flash adds each new segment to the highlighted selection.

To select multiple connected line segments as a unit:

1. In the Toolbar, select the selection tool.

2. Double-click any segment in the series of connected line segments.

   Flash highlights all the segments (**Figure 3.5**).

✔ Tip

■ To switch to the selection tool temporarily while using another tool, press ⌘ (Mac) or Ctrl (Windows). The selection tool remains in effect as long as you hold down the modifier key.

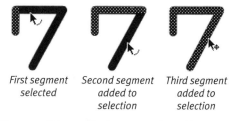

First segment selected   *Second segment added to selection*   *Third segment added to selection*

Figure 3.4 This graphic element consists of three segments. To select the entire element, you can Shift-click (or click, depending on your Preferences setting) each segment. Note that the line segments need not be connected, as they are in this example; they can be anywhere on the Stage.

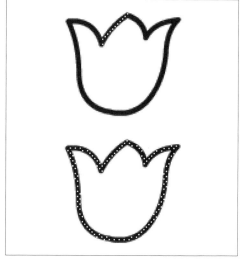

Figure 3.5 After single-clicking (top), you select one segment of this outline. After double-clicking (bottom), you select the entire shape.

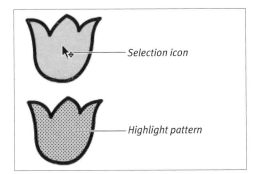

Figure 3.6 When the pointer sits above a filled area, it changes into the selection arrow. Click the fill to select it. A dot pattern in a contrasting color highlights the selected fill.

Edit	
Undo Double Click	Ctrl+Z
Redo	Ctrl+Y
Cut	Ctrl+X
Copy	Ctrl+C
Paste in Center	Ctrl+V
Paste in Place	Ctrl+Shift+V
Paste Special...	
Clear	Backspace
Duplicate	Ctrl+D
Select All	Ctrl+A
Deselect All	Ctrl+Shift+A
	Ctrl+F

Figure 3.7 Choose Edit > Select All, or press ⌘-A (Mac) or Ctrl-A (Windows), to select everything on the Stage.

Selecting Fills with the Selection Tool

You can select filled areas the same way you select lines.

To select multiple filled areas:

1. In the Toolbar, select the selection tool.

2. Position the pointer over the fill you want to select.

   The selection icon appears next to the selection pointer.

3. Click the fill.

   Flash highlights the selected fill with a dot pattern (**Figure 3.6**).

4. To select additional fills, do one of the following:

   ▲ If you are using Flash's default selection style (Shift Select), Shift-click each additional fill you want to select.

   ▲ If you turned off the Shift Select option in the Preferences dialog, click each fill you want to include.

   Flash adds each newly selected fill to the highlighted selection.

✔ Tip

■ To select everything that's currently on the Stage, from the Edit menu, choose Select All, or press ⌘-A (Mac) or Ctrl-A (Windows) (**Figure 3.7**).

Using a Selection Rectangle

Flash allows you to select several elements (or parts of elements) in a single operation by drawing a special rectangle around them. The rectangle is not a graphic element; it just defines the boundaries of your selection.

To create a selection rectangle:

1. In the Toolbar, select the selection tool.

2. Click and drag to pull out a selection rectangle (**Figure 3.8**).

3. Continue dragging until the rectangle encloses all the elements you want to select.

   Be sure to start dragging at a point that allows you to enclose the elements you want within a rectangle drawn from that point.

4. Release the mouse button.

   Flash highlights whatever falls inside the selection rectangle.

✔ Tip

■ If, as you drag out your selection rectangle, you realize that it won't include all the elements you want to select, and you don't want to add to the selection, drag back toward your starting point and release the mouse button when the rectangle encloses nothing. Then you can start over at a new point.

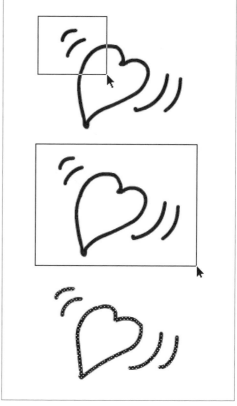

Figure 3.8 Clicking and dragging with the selection tool creates a selection rectangle (top). Be sure to start from a point that allows you to enclose all the elements you want to select within the rectangle (middle). Release the mouse button, and you've selected those elements (bottom).

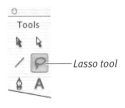

Tools

Lasso tool

Options

Polygon mode

Figure 3.9 Use the lasso tool to select an irregular area.

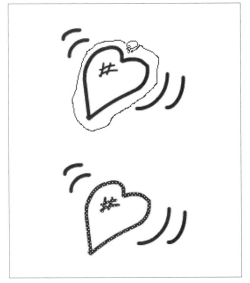

Figure 3.10 The lasso tool lets you select elements that are oddly shaped or too near other elements to allow use of the selection rectangle (top). Whatever falls within the area you outline with the lasso becomes highlighted and selected when you release the mouse button.

Using the Lasso Tool

If the lines or shapes you want to select are located close to other lines, you may have difficulty selecting just the items you want with a rectangle. The lasso tool lets you create an irregular selection outline.

To select elements with the lasso tool:

1. In the Toolbar, select the lasso tool, or press L (**Figure 3.9**).

2. Click and draw a freeform line around the elements you want to select (**Figure 3.10**).

3. Close the selection outline by bringing the lasso pointer back over the point where you began the selection line.

4. Release the mouse button.

   Flash highlights whatever falls inside the shape you drew with the lasso.

✔ Tips

- Flash draws a straight line between the starting point of your lasso line and the point at which you release the mouse button. You can skip the step of closing the shape if you're sure that Flash's closing will include the elements you want.

- The lasso's Polygon mode lets you define a selection area with a series of connected straight-line segments. With the lasso tool selected, click the polygon lasso button in the Options section of the Toolbar. Now you can click your way around the elements you want to select (**Figure 3.11**).

- You can combine the regular lasso tool with the polygon lasso in creating a single selection outline. To access Polygon mode temporarily, hold down Option (Mac) or Alt (Windows) as you click.

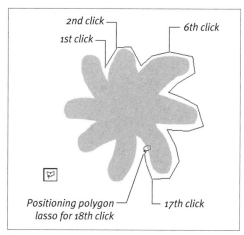

Figure 3.11 In Polygon mode, the lasso tool creates a series of connected line segments to outline whatever element you want to select. Double-clicking finishes the shape by drawing a line from the point where you double-clicked to the starting point.

USING THE LASSO TOOL

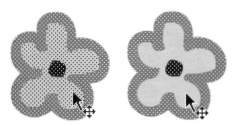

Figure 3.12 With the selection tool selected, position the pointer over the element you want to remove from the selection (left). Shift-click the item to deselect it (right). Repeat the process to deselect another item.

Edit	
Undo Selection Rect	Ctrl+Z
Repeat Select None	Ctrl+Y
Cut	Ctrl+X
Copy	Ctrl+C
Paste in Center	Ctrl+V
Paste in Place	Ctrl+Shift+V
Paste Special…	
Clear	Backspace
Duplicate	Ctrl+D
Select All	Ctrl+A
Deselect All	Ctrl+Shift+A
Find and Replace	Ctrl+F
	F3

Figure 3.13 Choose Edit > Deselect All to remove selection highlighting from all the graphic elements on the stage.

Deselecting Elements

No matter what method you use to select items, there is just one way to deselect individual elements when you have several selected: You must Shift-click with the selection tool to remove items from a selection.

To deselect individual items:

1. In the Toolbar, select the selection tool.

2. Hold down the Shift key.

3. Click any highlighted lines or fills you want to remove from the current selection.

   Flash removes the highlighting from the item you just clicked (**Figure 3.12**).

To deselect everything:

◆ From the Edit menu, choose Deselect All, or press Shift-⌘-A (Mac) or Ctrl-Shift-A (Windows) (**Figure 3.13**).

✔ Tip

■ To deselect all elements quickly, click the selection tool in an empty area of the Stage or work area.

Repositioning Elements Manually

If you aren't happy with the position of an element, you can always move it.

To reposition an element with the selection tool:

1. Position the selection tool over the element you want to move.

   The element doesn't need to be selected, although it can be. The selection tool displays the selection icon as it hovers over the element.

2. Click the element, and drag it to the desired location (**Figure 3.14**).

   An outline preview appears to help you position the element as you drag it.

3. Release the mouse button.

   The element is now selected and in its new location.

✔ Tips

- Turn on rulers (View > Rulers) to help you position your element. As you drag the element around the Stage, guide lines indicating the height and width of the element's bounding box (see the sidebar "How Flash Tracks Elements") appear in the ruler area (**Figure 3.15**).

- When Snap Align is active, as it is by default, Flash displays guidelines for aligning your selection with other objects on the Stage as you drag (**Figure 3.16**). To learn more about Snap settings, see Chapter 1.

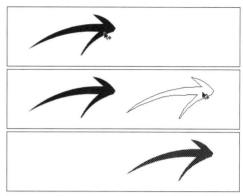

Figure 3.14 Use the selection tool to select and drag an element to a new location.

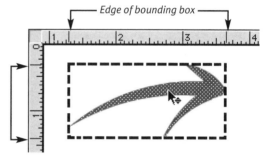

Figure 3.15 The longer lines in the ruler area indicate the edges of the element you are dragging.

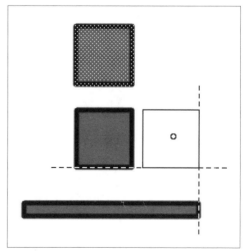

Figure 3.16 With Snap Align turned on, Flash displays guidelines as you drag a selection when you have more than one element on the Stage.

To reposition an element with the arrow keys:

1. In the Toolbar, select the selection tool.

2. Select the element you want to move.

3. Use one of the four arrow keys on the keyboard to move the element in 1-pixel increments.

The up-arrow key moves the element toward the top of the Stage. The down-arrow key moves the element toward the bottom of the Stage. The right-arrow key moves the element toward the right side of the Stage. The left-arrow key moves the element toward the left side of the Stage.

✔ Tip

■ To beef up the arrow keys' capability to move an element, hold down the Shift key. Each press of Shift-arrow moves a selected element 10 pixels.

How Flash Tracks Elements

To keep track of an element's size and position on the Stage, Flash encloses each element in a bounding box—an invisible rectangle just big enough to hold the element. Flash then treats the Stage as a giant graph, with the top-left corner of the Stage as the center of the x and y axis (**Figure 3.17**). Flash locates elements by means of x and y coordinates on that graph.

The units of measure for the graph are the ones currently selected in the Document Properties dialog (to learn more about document properties, see Chapter 1). The Shape Property Inspector and the Info panel show you the x and y coordinates for an element's current position and also display the height and width of the element's bounding box. Flash calculates an element's position on the Stage either from the top-left corner of the element's bounding box or from the element's center point (the point at the exact center of the bounding box).

By entering new x and y coordinates for Height and Width in the Shape Property Inspector or the Info panel, you can change an element's position and size. (For more information on resizing elements, see "Changing the Size of Graphic Elements" later in this chapter.)

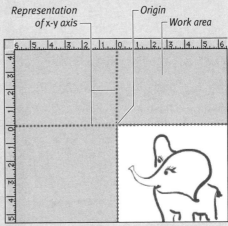

Figure 3.17 The dotted line here represents the *x-y* axis of the Stage. The origin—the o point both horizontally and vertically—is the top-left corner of the Stage.

Repositioning Elements Numerically

Flash allows you to reposition a selection numerically by specifying a precise Stage location in *x* and *y* coordinates. You can enter the *x* and *y* coordinates in either the Shape Property Inspector or the Info panel.

To reposition an element via the Shape Property Inspector:

1. With the Property Inspector open, on the Stage, select an element.

   The coordinates for the element's current position appear in the x and y fields of the Shape Property Inspector (**Figure 3.18**).

2. To position the element, do one, or both, of the following:

   ▲ Enter a new *x* coordinate for the element's position along the horizontal axis.

   ▲ Enter a new *y* coordinate for the element's position along the vertical axis.

3. Press Enter to confirm the last coordinate value you entered.

   Whenever you tab to or click another field, or press Enter, Flash confirms your change and the element moves to its new position (**Figure 3.19**).

✔ Tip

■ You can also position elements by entering *x* and *y* coordinates in the Info panel. To access the panel if it's not open, choose Window > Design Panels > Info. The set of nine squares in the middle of the Info panel (the coordinate grid) lets you choose what part of the element moves to the new coordinates. Click the top-left square to position the top-left corner of the element at the specified coordinates. Click the central square to position the element by its center point. Now enter values in the *x* and *y* fields and press Enter or click the Stage.

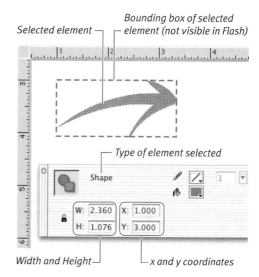

Selected element — Bounding box of selected element (not visible in Flash)

Type of element selected

Width and Height — x and y coordinates

Figure 3.18 With a shape selected on the Stage, the Property Inspector reveals attributes of that shape, including the x and y coordinates of the shape's bounding box. This element is located 1 inch to the right along the horizontal axis and 3 inches down the vertical axis.

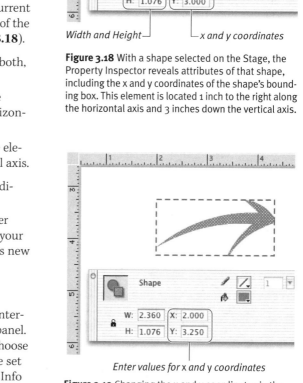

Enter values for x and y coordinates

Figure 3.19 Changing the x and y coordinates in the Shape Property Inspector changes the location of the selected element. This arrow is now located 2 inches to the right along the horizontal axis and 3.25 inches down the vertical axis.

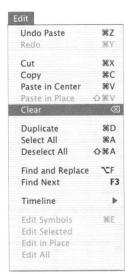

Figure 3.20
The Edit menu offers all the basic cut, copy, and paste commands, as well as some special ones for working with graphics and animations. Choose Clear or Cut to remove selected items on the Stage.

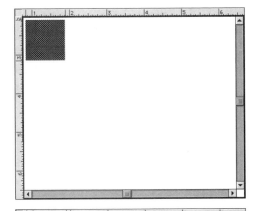

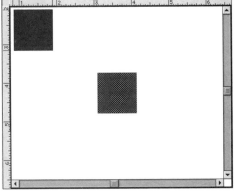

Figure 3.21 Copy a selected graphic element (top) and then choose the Paste in Center command. Flash pastes a copy of the element from the Clipboard to the center of the current view (bottom).

Basic Editing Tasks: Cut, Copy, Paste

Flash supports the standard cut, copy, and paste operations and also provides some special operations tailored for working with animated graphics.

To delete a selection:

1. Select the elements you want to remove.

2. From the Edit menu, choose Clear (**Figure 3.20**), or press the Delete key.
   Flash removes the selected items.

To cut a selection:

1. Select the elements you want to cut.

2. From the Edit menu, choose Cut, or press ⌘-X (Mac) or Ctrl-X (Windows).
   Flash copies the selected items to the Clipboard and removes them from the Stage.

To copy a selection:

1. Select the elements you want to copy.

2. From the Edit menu, choose Copy, or press ⌘-C (Mac) or Ctrl-C (Windows).
   Flash copies the selected items to the Clipboard.

   After you cut or copy an item, it resides on the Clipboard until your next cut or copy operation. You can retrieve the Clipboard's contents with the Paste command.

To paste the Clipboard's contents in the center of the window:

◆ From the Edit menu, choose Paste in Center, or press ⌘-V (Mac) or Ctrl-V (Windows).

   Flash pastes the Clipboard's contents in the center of the current view (**Figure 3.21**).

To paste Clipboard contents in their original location:

◆ From the Edit menu, choose Paste in Place, or press Shift-⌘-V (Mac) or Ctrl-Shift-V (Windows).

Flash pastes the Clipboard contents back into their original location on the Stage. The value of this command will become more apparent when you get into working with layers and animation, when it can be crucial to have elements appear in precisely the same spot but on a different layer or frame.

To duplicate a selection:

1. Select the elements you want to copy.

2. From the Edit menu, choose Duplicate, or press ⌘-D (Mac) or Ctrl-D (Windows).

Flash creates a copy of the selected items. The duplicate appears on the Stage, offset from the original item (**Figure 3.22**). The duplicate is selected so that it doesn't interact with the original. (For more information on interaction between elements, see Chapter 4.) The Duplicate command doesn't change the contents of the Clipboard.

✔ Tip

■ With the selection or lasso tool active, you can Option-click (Mac) or Ctrl-click (Windows) and drag any selected element to create a copy.

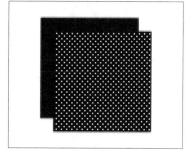

Figure 3.22 The Duplicate command (top) offsets a copy of the element from the original. The duplicate is the selected element (bottom).

BASIC EDITING TASKS: CUT, COPY, PASTE

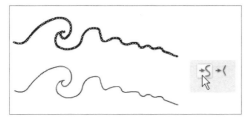

Figure 3.23 With your line selected on the Stage (top left) and the selection tool selected in the Toolbar, click the Smooth button (right). Flash smoothes the line (bottom left).

Figure 3.24 Choose Modify > Shape > Smooth to smooth curves selected on the Stage.

Editing Existing Elements with Assistance

Rather than have Flash assist you with everything you draw, you may prefer the flexibility of simply sketching with the pencil tool's freeform Ink mode. Flash can always recognize shapes and apply smoothing and straightening after you draw them.

To smooth an existing line:

1. Select the line with curves you want to smooth.

2. To smooth the curves, *do one of the following:*

   ▲ With the Selection tool selected, in the Toolbar, click the Smooth button (**Figure 3.23**).

   ▲ From the Modify menu, choose Shape > Smooth (**Figure 3.24**).

   Flash smoothes the curves in the selected line according to the tolerances currently set in the Editing tab of the Preferences dialog. With repeated clicking, you can smooth the curves further and ultimately reduce the number of curve segments in the line.

To straighten an existing line:

1. Select the line you want to straighten.

2. To straighten the line, *do one of the following:*

   ▲ With the selection tool selected, in the Toolbar, click the Straighten button (**Figure 3.25**).

   ▲ From the Modify menu, choose Shape > Straighten.

   Flash straightens the selected line according to the tolerances currently set in the Editing tab of the Preferences dialog (see Chapter 2).

✔ Tip

■ If the line still looks too rough after your first attempt, apply the Smooth or Straighten command again. Repeated smoothing eventually flattens your curves; repeated straightening eventually turns curve segments into straight-line segments (**Figure 3.26**).

To make Flash recognize existing shapes:

1. Select your rough version of an oval or rectangle.

2. To make Flash recognize your shape, *do one of the following:*

   ▲ With the selection tool selected, in the Toolbar, click the Straighten button.

   ▲ From the Modify menu, choose Shape > Straighten.

   If the shape is recognizable under the tolerances currently set in the Editing tab of the Preferences dialog (see Chapter 2), Flash recasts the shape as a perfect oval or rectangle.

✔ Tip

■ If at first Flash fails to recognize your rough shape, try again. Often, the newly straightened shape falls within the parameters Flash needs to recognize it (**Figure 3.27**).

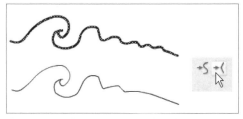

Figure 3.25 With your line selected on the Stage (top-left) and the selection tool selected, in the Toolbar, click the Straighten button (right). Flash straightens the line (bottom-left).

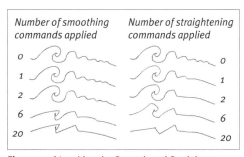

Figure 3.26 Invoking the Smooth and Straighten commands several times can change the appearance of a line dramatically.

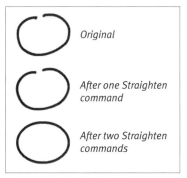

Figure 3.27 Use the Straighten command to recognize a shape.

EDITING EXISTING ELEMENTS WITH ASSISTANCE

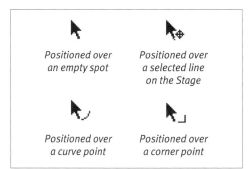

Figure 3.28 The small icons appearing with the selection pointer indicate what type of graphic element lies beneath the pointer.

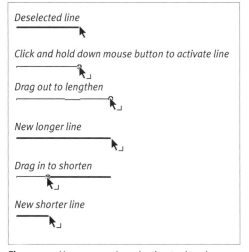

Figure 3.29 You can use the selection tool to change a line segment's length.

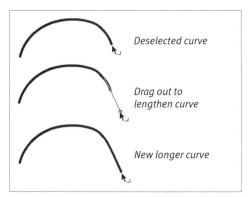

Figure 3.30 You can use the selection tool to change a curve's length.

Moving End Points with the Selection Tool

You can use the selection tool to change the length and direction of straight-line and curve segments. Simply grab and reposition a segment's end point. When you use the selection tool, the segment you want to modify must not be selected. If the segment is selected, the selection tool moves the segment as a unit. Always note what kind of icon the selection pointer is displaying as it hovers over the line you want to modify (**Figure 3.28**).

For the following exercises, make sure that the item you want to modify is deselected.

To reposition the end of a line segment with the selection tool:

1. Position the pointer over the end point of the line.

    The corner-point modifier appears.

2. Reposition the end point.

    The selection tool now operates like the straight-line tool (the line segment changes to preview mode). Dragging away from the existing line lengthens it; dragging toward the existing line shortens it (**Figure 3.29**). Dragging at an angle to the original line lets you pivot the line to a new position.

3. Release the mouse button.

    Flash redraws the line segment.

To reposition the end point of a curve with the selection tool:

1. Position the pointer over the end point of a curve.

    The corner-point modifier appears.

2. Click and drag the end point to the desired location.

3. Release the mouse button.

    Flash redraws the end of the curve (**Figure 3.30**).

Moving Points with the Subselection Tool

Figure 3.31 Use the subselection tool to modify the path of a line segment.

The subselection tool allows you to reveal and manipulate the anchor points that define a line segment or curve. Then you can grab and reposition these points to modify lines and curves.

Figure 3.32 When a solid square appears next to the subselection tool, the tool is ready to select the entire path (left). When a hollow square appears (right), the tool is ready to select and manipulate a single anchor point.

To view a path and anchor points:

1. In the Toolbar, choose the subselection tool (**Figure 3.31**).

   The pointer changes to a hollow arrow.

2. On the Stage, click the line or curve you want to modify.

   Flash selects and highlights the entire path. In Flash's default editing mode, anchor points appear as hollow squares in a contrasting highlight color.

To manipulate a particular point, you must select it directly.

To select an anchor point:

1. With the subselection tool active, position the pointer over the point you want to move.

   The anchor-point modifier (a small solid square) appears next to the hollow-arrow icon (**Figure 3.32**).

2. Click the anchor point.

   Flash highlights the selected point. At Flash's default setting, selected corner points appear as solid squares; selected curve points appear as solid circles with Bézier handles.

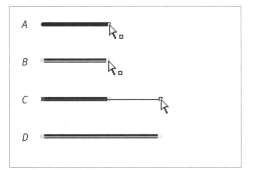

Figure 3.33 When you've selected an anchor point (A), Flash highlights the entire path (B). You can drag the anchor point to lengthen or shorten the path (C). The path and anchor points remain highlighted when you're done (D).

✔ Tips

■ If you know where a point is in your element, you can skip the step of clicking the path to highlight all the anchor points. To select the point directly, double-click it.

■ You can select multiple points on a path directly with the subselection tool. Draw a selection rectangle that includes the points you want to select. Flash highlights the entire path and selects any points that fall within the rectangle.

■ To view anchor points as hollow squares and selected points as solid, you need to change Flash's editing preferences. From the Edit menu (Windows) or the Flash menu (Mac), choose Preferences to open the Preferences dialog. Click the Editing tab, and uncheck the Show Solid Points check box.

To reposition anchor points with the subselection tool:

◆ With the subselection tool active, click and drag the desired anchor point to a new location.

Flash redraws the path (**Figure 3.33**).

About Curve and Corner Points

Flash's selection and pen/subselection tools let you modify an element's curves and lines. The subselection tool lets you do so by moving the curve and corner points that define the elements and by rearranging the curves' Bézier handles. When you highlight a path with the subselection tool, Flash reveals any curve points' Bézier handles. (Corner points have no handles.)

When you use the selection tool, Flash hides all the technical stuff. You simply pull on a line to reshape it. Still, the selection tool does have its own hidden version of curve and corner points, which are evident only in the changing icons that accompany the tool as it interacts with a line or curve.

For the selection tool, corner points appear at the end of a segment or at the point where two segments join to form a sharp angle. All those other in-between points—even if they fall in the middle of a line segment that happens to be completely flat—are curve points. When you tug on a curve point with the selection tool, you pull out a range of points in a tiny arc. When you tug on a corner point with the selection tool, you pull out a single point.

Reshaping Curves with the Selection Tool

You can reshape a curve, or change a straight-line segment into a curve, by using the selection tool to push and pull on the curve. You can also reshape curves by using the pen and subselection tools in combination (see "Reshaping Curves with the Subselection Tool" later in this chapter).

In the following exercises for the selection tool, make sure that the line or curve you want to reshape is deselected when you start each exercise.

To reposition the end of a curve with the selection tool:

1. Position the selection tool's pointer over the end point of the curve.

    The corner-point modifier appears.

2. Click and drag the end point to a new location.

    As you drag, the end of the line changes to a small circle, showing that the line is active for modifications. The last segment of the curve changes direction depending on where you locate the end point. Flash previews the new curve segment as you drag (**Figure 3.34**).

To reshape a curve with the selection tool:

1. Position the selection tool's pointer over the middle of a curve segment.

    The curve-point modifier appears.

2. Click and drag the curve to reshape it (**Figure 3.35**).

    Flash previews the curve you're drawing.

3. Release the mouse button.

    Flash redraws the curve.

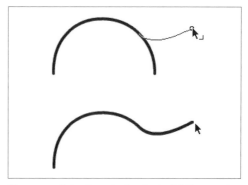

Figure 3.34 Using the selection tool, click the curve's end point and drag it to a new position. Flash reshapes the end of the curve.

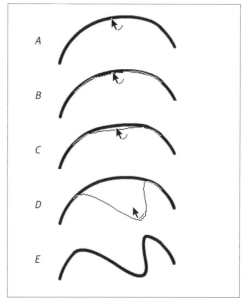

Figure 3.35 Click the middle of a curve (A). Flash activates the curve segment (B). Drag the curve to a new position (C, D). When you release the mouse button, Flash redraws the curve (E).

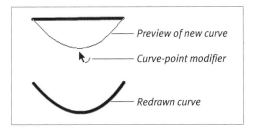

Figure 3.36 Although this line doesn't look curved (top), Flash considers all its middle points to be curve points. Drag one of those points to create a line that looks like a curve (bottom).

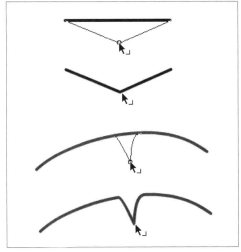

Figure 3.37 Option-click (Mac) or Ctrl-click (Windows) to create a new corner point for editing your line. Dragging a corner point from a straight-line segment creates a sharp V (top). Dragging a corner point from a curve creates a V with curving sides that comes to a sharp point (bottom).

To turn a straight-line segment into a curve segment with the selection tool:

1. Position the selection tool's pointer over the middle of a line segment.

   The curve-point modifier appears.

2. Click and drag the line to reshape it (**Figure 3.36**).

   Flash previews the curve that you're drawing.

3. Release the mouse button.

   Flash redraws the line, giving it the curve you defined.

To create new corner points with the selection tool:

1. Position the selection tool's pointer over the middle of a line or curve segment.

   The curve-point modifier appears.

2. Option-click (Mac) or Ctrl-click (Windows).

   After a brief pause, the selection tool's modifier changes to the corner-point modifier, and a circle appears where the pointer intersects the line. You are now activating a corner point.

3. Drag to modify the line or curve segment and add a new corner point (**Figure 3.37**).

Reshaping Curves with the Subselection Tool

The subselection tool lets you manipulate a point's Bézier handles to modify the slope and depth of the curve. You can add and delete points and convert existing curve points to corner points, or vice versa, with the pen tool (see "Converting, Removing, and Adding Points," later in this chapter).

One way to reshape a curve is to change the location of the anchor points that define the curve.

To move a curve point:

1. In the Toolbar, choose the subselection tool.

2. Click a path to select it.

   Flash highlights the entire path of the selected element.

3. Position the pointer over a curve point.

   The anchor-point modifier appears.

4. Click and drag the point to a new location.

   Flash previews the new curve as you drag (**Figure 3.38**).

   After you move a curve point, the path remains selected, and the Bézier control handles of the point you moved become active so that you can further manipulate the curve.

To reshape a curve with the Bézier handles:

1. With the subselection tool, click the curve you want to modify.

2. Click one of the anchor points that define the curve you want to modify.

   Bézier handles appear.

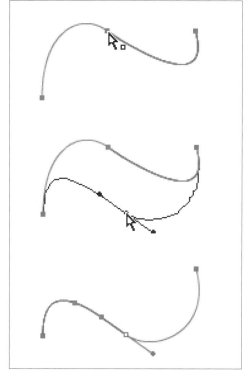

Figure 3.38 One way to modify a curved path is to reposition anchor points with the subselection tool.

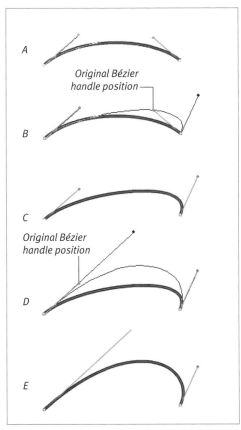

Figure 3.39 When you select anchor points, their Bézier handles appear (A). Leaning a Bézier handle away from a curve (B) makes that curve segment more pronounced (C). Leaning the handle toward the curve flattens that part of the curve. Dragging the Bézier handle away from its anchor point (D) makes the curve deeper (E); dragging the handle toward the anchor point makes the curve shallower.

3. Click and drag one of the Bézier handles. The pointer changes to an arrowhead.

4. To modify the curve, *do one or more of the following:*

▲ To make the curve more pronounced, position the Bézier handle farther from the curve in the direction in which the curve bulges.

▲ To make the curve flatter, position the Bézier handle closer to the curve.

▲ To make the curve bulge in the opposite direction, move the Bézier handle past the existing curve, in the opposite direction from the current bulge.

▲ To make the curve deeper, position the Bézier handle farther from the anchor point.

▲ To make the curve shallower, position the Bézier handle closer to the anchor point.

Flash previews the new curve as you manipulate the Bézier handle (**Figure 3.39**).

✔ Tips

■ To select an anchor point and activate its Bézier handles quickly, use the subselection tool to draw a selection rectangle around the curve you want to modify. Even if the path was not highlighted, Flash selects any anchor points that fall within the selection and activates their handles.

■ You can move selected anchor points with the arrow keys. To move in larger increments, press the Shift-arrow key.

RESHAPING CURVES WITH THE SUBSELECTION TOOL

129

Converting, Removing, and Adding Points

In some graphics programs, you select pen modifiers to convert, remove, and add points. In Flash, the pen tool automatically turns into a modifier as it hovers over a path or an anchor point. The subselection tool can change corner points to curve points. The pen tool can add new points between existing curve points; can reduce a curve point to a corner point; and can reduce a corner point to no point at all.

To convert corner points to curve points:

1. Using the subselection tool, click the path you want to modify.

   Flash highlights the path and its anchor points.

2. Position the hollow-arrow pointer over a corner point.

   The anchor-point modifier appears.

3. Click the anchor point to select it.

4. To pull Bézier handles out of the point, Option-drag (Mac) or Alt-drag (Windows) away from the selected corner point.

   Flash converts the corner point to a curve point (**Figure 3.40**).

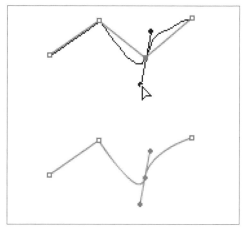

Figure 3.40 To change a corner point into a curve point (one with Bézier handles), use the subselection tool to Option-drag (Mac) or Alt-drag (Windows) a selected corner point (top). You actually pull a Bézier handle out of the point instead of relocating the point. When you release the mouse button, Flash redraws the curve (bottom).

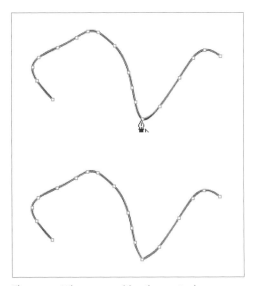

Figure 3.41 When you position the pen tool over a curve point, a small caret appears next to the pointer (top). With the caret modifier active, click the curve point to reduce it to a corner point (bottom). Flash redraws the path accordingly.

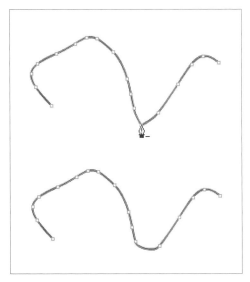

Figure 3.42 When you position the pen tool over a corner point, a small minus sign appears next to the pointer (top). With the minus-sign modifier active, click the corner point to reduce it to no point at all (bottom). Flash redraws the path accordingly.

To convert curve points to corner points:

1. With the path you want to modify selected, in the Toolbar, choose the pen tool.

2. Position the pen pointer over a curve point.

The convert-to-corner-point modifier (a small caret) appears next to the pen icon.

3. Click the curve point.

Flash converts the curve point to a corner point and flattens the curved path (**Figure 3.41**).

To delete anchor points:

1. With the path you want to modify selected, in the Toolbar, choose the pen tool.

2. Position the pen pointer over a corner point.

The remove-point modifier (a minus sign) appears next to the pen icon.

(Note that if the point you want to delete is currently a curve point, you must follow the steps in the preceding exercise to convert it to a corner point.)

3. Click the corner point.

Flash removes the anchor point and reshapes the path to connect the remaining points (**Figure 3.42**).

✔ Tip

■ You can also delete one or more anchor points by selecting them with the subselection tool and pressing Delete.

CONVERTING, REMOVING, AND ADDING POINTS

To add new anchor points to a curve segment:

1. With the path you want to modify selected, choose the pen tool from the Toolbar.

2. Position the pen pointer over the path between two curve points.

   The add-point modifier (a plus sign) appears next to the pen icon.

3. Click the path.

   Flash adds a new curve point (**Figure 3.43**).

✔ Tips

■ If you need to add points to a straight-line segment, first convert one of the corner points that define the segment to a curve point. Then you'll be able to add another curve point between them.

■ To add points to the end of an open path, position the pen pointer over the end of the path. When the x to the right of the pen pointer disappears, click the last anchor point and then continue clicking to add more points.

■ You can select an open path with the pen tool by clicking the anchor point at either end of the path. Flash won't convert or delete the end anchor point; it just highlights the path the same way that the subselection tool would.

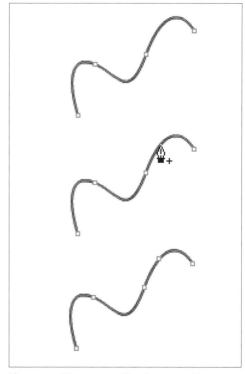

Figure 3.43 When you position the pen tool between existing curve points, a small plus sign appears next to the pointer (middle). With the plus-sign modifier active, click the curve to add a new curve point (bottom). Note that the pen tool cannot add points between corner points.

Figure 3.44 When you position the pointer over the edge of a fill shape, the selection tool displays either the curve-point or corner-point modifier. If you then click the edge of the fill, Flash activates part of the outline for reshaping.

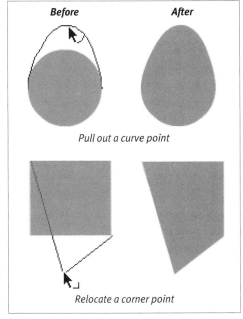

Before *After*

Pull out a curve point

Relocate a corner point

Figure 3.45 Take some time to play around with reshaping fills. You can pull points out to create protrusions or move points in to create indentations. You can reshape the fill pretty much any way you want.

Reshaping Fills

You can't see the outlines of filled shapes unless you give them a stroke, but fills do have outlines that act just like any other line. You can use the selection, pen, and subselection tools to reshape fills.

To reshape a fill with the selection tool:

1. With nothing selected, position the selection tool's pointer over the edge of your filled shape.

   The curve point or corner-point modifier appears (**Figure 3.44**).

2. Click and drag the curve point or corner point to reshape the fill (**Figure 3.45**).

   Flash previews the new outline.

3. Release the mouse button.

   Flash creates the new fill shape.

To reshape a fill with the subselection and pen tools:

1. In the Toolbar, choose the subselection tool.

2. Position the hollow-arrow pointer over the edge of your filled shape.

3. Click.

   Flash highlights the path and anchor points that define the fill shape (**Figure 3.46**).

4. Add, remove, and reposition anchor points and Bézier handles with the pen and subselection tools, as described earlier in this section.

✔ Tip

- To select an entire fill path quickly, use the subselection tool to drag a selection rectangle over any portion of the fill. Unlike the selection tool, the subselection tool selects the whole shape even if you include just a small portion of it within the selection rectangle. Any curve points that fall within the rectangle display their Bézier handles.

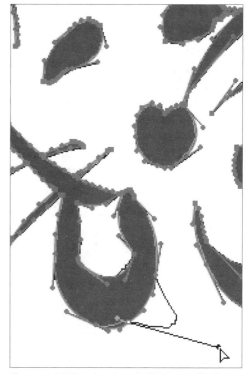

Figure 3.46 Select the edge of a fill shape with the subselection tool, and Flash highlights the path and anchor points that outline the shape. Reposition anchor points and Bézier handles to modify the fill shapes.

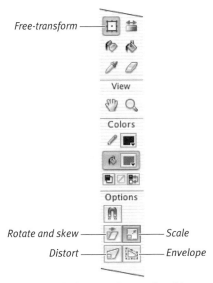

Free-transform

View

Colors

Options

Rotate and skew — Scale

Distort — Envelope

Figure 3.47 The free-transform tool enables you to select and scale elements interactively.

Changing the Size of Graphic Elements

Flash gives you several ways to resize, or scale, graphic elements. You can scale selected elements interactively on the Stage. You can also set specific scale percentages or dimensions for your element in the Transform panel, the Property Inspector, and the Info panel.

To resize a graphic element interactively:

1. In the Toolbar, select the free-transform tool (**Figure 3.47**).

2. On the Stage, click the element you want to resize.

   Flash selects and highlights the element, and places transformation handles on all four sides and at the corners of the element's bounding box.

3. In the Toolbar, choose the Scale modifier.

4. Position the pointer over a handle.

   The pointer changes to a double-headed arrow, indicating the direction in which the element will grow or shrink as you pull or push on the handles.

continues on next page

CHANGING THE SIZE OF GRAPHIC ELEMENTS

5. To resize the graphic element, *do one of the following:*

▲ To change the graphic element's width, click and drag one of the side handles.

▲ To change the element's height, click and drag the top or bottom handle.

▲ To change the size of the element proportionately, click and drag one of the corner handles.

Dragging toward the center of the element reduces it; dragging away enlarges it (**Figure 3.48**).

✔ Tips

■ If you have made a selection with the selection tool, you can activate transformational handles for the selection by choosing Modify > Transform > Scale. Flash chooses the free-transform tool and its Scale modifier in the Toolbar.

■ In the default scaling mode, the selection scales from the control point opposite the one you are dragging. To scale relative to the center of a selection, hold down the Option key (Mac) or Alt key (Winows) as you drag. The left- and right-side handles both move away from the center of the selection as you drag.

■ Do not use the subselection tool to select an element by its path when you want to scale it. Choosing the free-transform tool automatically deselects the selected path.

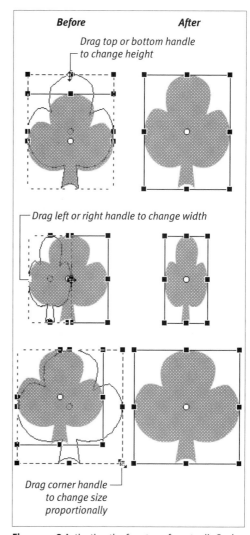

Figure 3.48 Activating the free-transform tool's Scale modifier places a set of handles around a selected element. Click and drag the handles to change the size of the element.

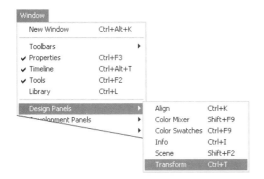

Check to scale proportionately

▼ Transform

100.0%   100.0%   ☑ Constrain

○ Rotate   ◿   0.0°

○ Skew   ▱   0.0°   ◹   0.0°

— Select to skew the element

Select to rotate the element

Copy and Apply button

Reset button undoes change

Figure 3.49 Choose Window > Design Panels > Transform (top) to access the Transform panel, where you can enter values for scaling, rotating, and skewing selected elements (bottom).

You can also resize elements by using the Transform panel.

To access the Transform panel:

◆ If the Transform panel is not open, from the Window menu, choose Design Panels > Transform.

The Transform panel appears (**Figure 3.49**).

To resize an element by using the Transform panel:

1. With the Transform panel open, on the Stage, select the element you want to resize.

   A value of 100% appears in the Width and Height fields of the Transform panel.

2. To resize the element, *do one of the following:*

   ▲ To resize proportionately, check the Constrain check box next to the Width and Height fields and enter a new value in either field.

   A value less than 100% shrinks the element; a value greater than 100% enlarges the element. As you enter the value in one field, Flash automatically updates the other field.

   or

   ▲ To allow the aspect ratio to change, in the Transform panel, uncheck the Constrain check box; enter new percentages in the Scale Width field and Scale Height field.

3. Press Enter.

   Flash resizes the element.

✔ Tips

■ As long as an element remains selected on the Stage, the Transform panel resizes the element on an absolute scale (always applying the percentage you enter into the panel to the element's original size). To make changes on a relative scale; for example, to shrink the element by 50 percent, and then shrink the shrunken element by 20 percent, you must deselect the element after the first transformation, then select it again and enter the percentage for the second transformation.

■ You can also enter specific width and height values for a selected element in the Shape Property Inspector (**Figure 3.50**) and the Info panel (**Figure 3.51**). To constrain proportions in the Property Inspector, click the lock button to the left of the Width and Height fields. The Info panel offers no option to constrain the width and height. To preserve the current aspect ratio, you'll have to do the math yourself. The Info panel does let you choose to change the element's size relative to the center of the object or the top-left corner of its bounding box. Click the appropriate point on the coordinate grid in the Info panel.

■ You can undo a transformation quickly— by clicking the Reset button in the bottom-right corner of the Transform panel—provided that you have not deselected the element.

■ You can scale several elements at the same time. Select all the elements and then use any of the scaling methods described earlier in this section. The bounding box that contains the elements scales relative to its center point, and the entire selection grows or shrinks to fit the new box.

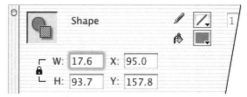

Figure 3.50 The Shape Property Inspector displays the width and height of the bounding box of the selected element. Enter new values to resize the element.

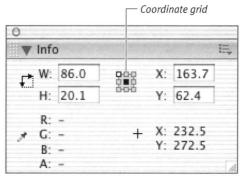

Figure 3.51 You can enter precise dimensions for an element's width and height in the Info panel. The coordinate grid shows whether changes will be relative to the center or to the top-left corner of the element's bounding box. To apply the values you entered in the panel to the selected graphic element, click the Stage or press Enter.

■ You can transform a copy of the element by clicking the Copy and Apply Transform button in the Transform panel. This feature can be tricky if you use it with raw shapes, however, because Flash doesn't offset the copy it makes. You must be sure to move the copy yourself before deselecting it.

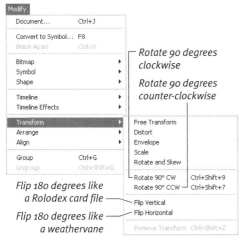

Figure 3.52 The Modify > Transform submenu offers commands for flipping graphic elements vertically and horizontally. It also offers commands for rotating an element in 90-degree increments, both clockwise and counterclockwise.

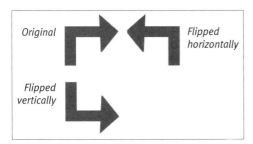

Figure 3.53 The results of flipping an element by using the Flip commands in the Modify > Transform submenu.

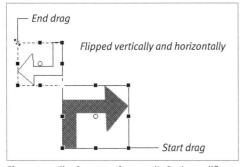

Figure 3.54 The free-transform tool's Scale modifier can flip and scale an element simultaneously. Here, the Scale modifier is flipping the element both vertically and horizontally.

Reorienting Graphic Elements

Flash lets you rotate, flip, and skew selected elements. You can either manipulate elements freely with the free-transform tool's Rotate and Skew modifier or use a variety of commands to do the job with more precision.

To flip a graphic element:

1. Select the element you want to flip.

2. To reorient the element so that it spins 180 degrees around its vertical central axis like a weathervane, choose Transform > Flip Horizontal from the Modify menu (**Figure 3.52**).

3. To reorient the element so that it spins 180 degrees around its horizontal central axis like a Rolodex file, choose Transform > Flip Vertical from the Modify menu.

   Figure 3.53 shows the results of the two types of flipping.

✔ Tip

■ You can flip and scale elements simultaneously by using the free-transform tool's Scale modifier. With the selected element in Scale mode, drag one handle all the way across the bounding box and past the handle on the other side. To flip a selected element vertically and horizontally, for example, drag the handle in the bottom-right corner diagonally upward, past the handle in the top-left corner (**Figure 3.54**). The flipped element starts small and grows as you continue to drag away from the element's top-left corner. Flash previews the flipped element; release the mouse button when the element is the size you want.

To rotate an element in 90-degree increments:

1. Select the element you want to rotate.

2. To rotate the element, *do one of the following:*

   ▲ To rotate the element counterclockwise 90 degrees, from the Modify menu, choose Transform > Rotate 90° CCW.

   ▲ To rotate the element clockwise 90 degrees, from the Modify menu, choose Transform > Rotate 90° CW.

   Flash rotates the element 90 degrees. You can repeat the command to rotate the element 180 and 270 degrees or back to its starting point.

To rotate an element by a user-specified amount:

1. Access the Transform panel (**Figure 3.55**).

   If the panel is not open, choose Window > Design Panels > Transform.

2. Click the Rotate radio button.

3. To specify the direction and amount of rotation, do one of the following:

   ▲ To rotate the element counterclockwise, enter a negative value (–1 to –360) in the Rotation field.

   ▲ To rotate the element clockwise, enter a positive value (1 to 360).

4. Press Enter.

   Flash rotates the selected element by the amount you specified.

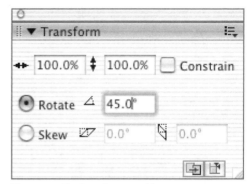

Figure 3.55 The Transform panel lets you rotate graphic elements in precise increments. Positive values rotate the element clockwise; negative values rotate it counterclockwise.

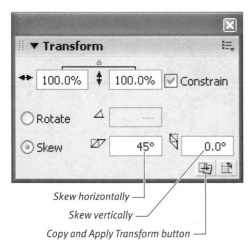

Skew horizontally

Skew vertically

Copy and Apply Transform button

Figure 3.56 Use the Transform panel to skew selected elements. You can set separate values for horizontal and vertical skewing.

Free transform

View

Colors

Options

Rotate and skew

Figure 3.57 Select the free-transform tool's Rotate and Skew modifier to access handles for rotating or skewing a selected element interactively.

To skew an element by a user-specified amount:

1. With the Transform panel open, select the element you want to skew.

2. In the Transform panel, choose Skew.

3. Enter the desired skew values in the horizontal and vertical fields (**Figure 3.56**).

4. To complete the transformation, press Enter.

✔ Tip

■ To skew a copy of the selected element, in the Transform panel, click the Copy and Apply Transform button.

To rotate or skew an element interactively:

1. Select the element you want to rotate or skew.

2. In the Toolbar, select the free-transform tool; then click the Rotate and Skew modifier (**Figure 3.57**).

   Solid square handles appear on all four sides and at the corners of the element's bounding box.

continues on next page

REORIENTING GRAPHIC ELEMENTS

3. To modify the selected element, *do one of the following:*

▲ To rotate the element, position the pointer over one of the corner handles.

The pointer changes to a circular arrow. Click and drag in the direction you want to rotate the element. Flash spins the element around its center point, previewing the rotation as you drag (**Figure 3.58**).

▲ To skew the element, position the pointer over one of the side handles of the element's bounding box.

The pointer changes to a two-way arrowhead. Click and drag the side handle in the direction you want to skew the element. Flash previews the skewing as you drag (Figure 3.58).

4. Release the mouse button.

Flash redraws the modified element.

✔ Tips

■ You can rotate an element around one of its corners instead of its center point by pressing Option (Mac) or Alt (Windows) while dragging. The handle diagonally across from the one you are manipulating becomes the point of rotation.

■ You don't have to choose the Scale modifier or the Rotate and Skew modifier to make those manipulations. You can just select an object with the free-transform tool and watch carefully as you move the pointer near the handles. If you pause directly on top of a corner handle, the icon changes to the double-headed arrow that allows you to scale the object. Move the pointer slightly away from the corner handle, and the icon changes to the rotation arrow. Click and drag to rotate the object. Position the pointer along the edge of the bounding box between handles and the icon changes to the opposing arrows. Click and drag in the direction you wish to skew the object.

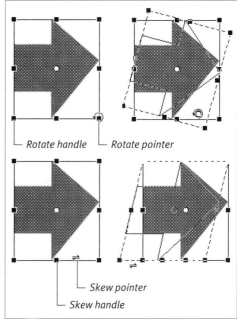

Figure 3.58 With the free-transform tool's Rotate and Skew modifier selected, you can drag one of the corner handles of a selected element's bounding box to rotate that element (top). Drag one of the side handles to skew the element (bottom).

■ To constrain rotation by 45-degree increments, hold down the Shift key while rotating.

■ The Rotate and Skew modifier creates a constrained skew. You can drag only in a straight line along the edge of the selected element. You can create a freeform skew by using the Distort modifier, which you learn about later in this chapter.

Free transform —

View

Colors

Options

Distort —

Figure 3.59 Choose the free-transform tool's Distort modifier to reposition the corner points of your selection independently.

Distorting Graphic Elements

The free-transform tool allows you to distort a graphic element by changing the shape of its bounding box. You can reposition one or more corners of the box individually; you can manipulate paired corner handles simultaneously to turn the rectangular box into a trapezoid; and you can stretch, shrink, and/or skew the box by moving the side handles of the bounding box. The selected element(s) stretch or shrink to fit the new bounding box. Distortion works only on raw shapes, not on grouped elements or symbols, which you'll learn about in Chapters 4 and 6.

To distort an element freely:

1. Using the free-transform tool, select the element you want to distort.

A bounding box with transformational handles appears.

2. In the Toolbar, select the Distort modifier (**Figure 3.59**).

continues on next page

Distorted Perspective

As beginning art students discover, it's not too hard to add depth to objects made up of rectangular shapes. You simply adjust the appropriate edges to align with imaginary "parallel" lines that converge at a distant point on the horizon—the vanishing point. This creates the illusion that the objects recede into the distance. Adding perspective to nonrectangular shapes takes a bit more experience and the ability to imagine the way that those shapes should look. The Distort modifier of Flash's free-transform tool helps you because it encloses your selected shape—circle, oval, or squiggle—within a rectangular bounding box. All you need to do is adjust that box as you would a rectangular shape.

Beginning art students learn about 1-point, 2-point, and 3-point perspective. The "points" here refer to the vanishing point—the spot in the distance where parallel lines seem to converge. By selecting elements in your artwork carefully, and by using the distort tools to make the edges of the bounding box seem to line up with those "converging" lines, you can add perspective to objects even if they do not contain the parallel lines that would make it easy for you to fake the depth perception you want.

DISTORTING GRAPHIC ELEMENTS

Note that the center point of your selection disappears, indicating that you are in Distort mode.

3. Position the pointer over one of the transformational handles.

The pointer changes to a hollow arrowhead.

4. To change the shape of the bounding box, *do one of the following*:

   ▲ To relocate one corner of the element's bounding box, position the pointer over one of the corner handles; then click and drag the handle to the desired location. You can position each of the four corner handles independently (**Figure 3.60**).

   ▲ To skew the element, position the pointer over one of the side handles; then drag the handle to the desired position. The element skews toward the direction you drag.

   ▲ To stretch the element as you skew it, move the selected side handle away from the element's center (**Figure 3.61**).

   ▲ To shrink the element as you skew it, move the selected side handle toward the element's center.

5. Release the mouse button.

Flash redraws the selection to fill the new bounding-box shape.

✔ Tip

■ You can use the free-transform tool to distort multiple graphic elements. Select the elements you want to modify. Then, using the Distort modifier of the free-transform tool, redefine the shape of the bounding box that surrounds the set of elements. The elements change as a unit.

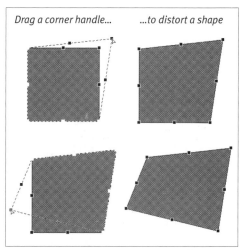

Figure 3.60 Use the free-transform tool's Distort modifier to redefine the shape of an element's bounding box. You can drag each corner handle separately.

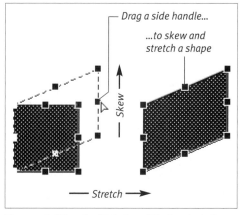

Figure 3.61 When the Distort modifier is selected, dragging the side handles of a selected element's bounding box skews the element. To enlarge (or shrink) the element at the same time, move the side handle away from (or in toward) the center of the original shape.

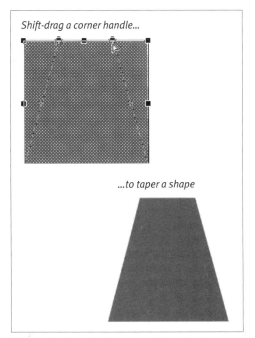

Shift-drag a corner handle...

...to taper a shape

Figure 3.62 Using the Distort modifier of the free-transform tool, Shift-click and drag a corner handle to taper selected elements.

To distort graphic elements symmetrically:

1. Follow steps 1 and 2 of the preceding exercise to prepare an element for distorting.

2. To taper the element, *do one of the following*:

   ▲ To make the top of the bounding box narrower than the bottom, Shift-click and drag the top-right corner handle toward the top-left corner handle, or vice versa (**Figure 3.62**).

   ▲ To make the top of the bounding box wider than the bottom, Shift-click and drag the top-right corner handle away from the top-left corner handle, or vice versa.

   As you drag, the two corner handles move in tandem, coming together if you drag in or moving apart if you drag out.

3. Release the mouse button.

   Flash redraws the bounding box and its contents. If you dragged in, the box appears to taper toward the top. If you dragged out, the box appears to taper toward the bottom. You can follow these procedures for the sides or bottom of the bounding box to taper the box in any direction.

✔ Tips

■ To access the Free Transform tool's hollow-arrowhead pointer temporarily without selecting the Distort modifier, press ⌘ (Mac) or Ctrl (Windows). Then you can drag or Shift-drag to distort selected elements.

■ If you make a mistake while distorting a graphic, and you choose Edit > Undo so you can fix it, your graphic will be selected with the Free Transform tool but the Distort modifier will not be active. You must reselect the Distort modifier in the Toolbar to continue your distortion.

DISTORTING GRAPHIC ELEMENTS

Changing the Envelope of Selected Elements

Earlier in this chapter, you learned to use the subselection tool to manipulate the anchor points and Bézier curves that make up the path of a selected element. The free-transform tool's Envelope modifier lets you manipulate the anchor points and Bézier curves that make up the path of the transformational bounding box of a selection. That selection could be one element or several, but it must contain raw shapes. The Envelope modifier does not work with grouped elements or symbols, which you'll learn about in Chapters 4 and 6.

To reshape a selection's bounding box by using Bézier curves:

1. Using the free-transform tool, select the element(s) you want to transform.

   A bounding box with transformational handles appears.

2. In the Toolbar, select the Envelope modifier (**Figure 3.63**).

   The center point of your selection disappears, and anchor points with Bézier handles appear on the bounding box, indicating that you are in Envelope mode (**Figure 3.64**).

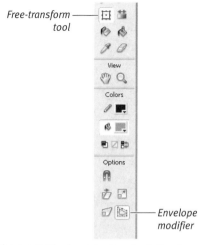

Free-transform tool

Envelope modifier

Figure 3.63 The free-transform tool's Envelope modifier allows you to reshape a selection by manipulating the Bézier curves that make up the selection's bounding box.

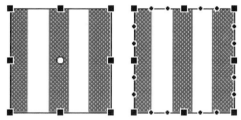

Figure 3.64 When you select multiple graphic elements with the free-transform tool, a single transformational bounding box surrounds all of them (left). Choosing the Envelope modifier hides the selection's center point and makes the box's Bézier handles available for manipulation (right).

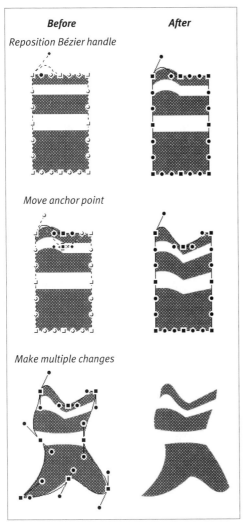

Before	*After*

Reposition Bézier handle

Move anchor point

Make multiple changes

Figure 3.65 You can use the free-transform tool in Envelope mode to reposition Bézier handles and move anchor points. All of the elements transform together.

3. To reshape the bounding box, *do one of the following:*

▲ Position the pointer over a Bézier handle. The hollow-arrowhead pointer appears. Then click and drag the handle to redefine the curve (**Figure 3.65**).

▲ Position the pointer over an anchor point. The hollow-arrowhead pointer appears. Then click and drag the anchor point to a new location.

For more details about modifying Bézier curves, see "Reshaping Curves with the Subselection Tools," earlier in this chapter.

4. Release the mouse button.

Flash redraws the curves, and all the selected elements transform together.

✔ Tip

■ If your selection consists of grouped elements or symbols, the Envelope modifier becomes inactive in the Toolbar, because Envelope doesn't work on groups or symbols. If your selection mixes raw shapes with groups or symbols, however, the Envelope modifier becomes available again. Selecting this modifier lets you see and manipulate a bounding box that includes the groups or symbols in your selection, but the changes you make have no effect on these items. The raw shapes are the only things that change.

CHANGING THE ENVELOPE OF SELECTED ELEMENTS

Modifying Strokes

Flash provides two methods for modifying the stroke of an existing element: You can select the element and change its stroke attributes in the Property Inspector, or you can use the ink-bottle tool to apply the current stroke settings to unselected elements. Certain modifications, however, you can make only with the ink bottle. To add a stroke to an element that currently lacks one, for example, you must use the ink bottle.

For the following exercises, keep the Property Inspector open (choose Window > Properties if it's not open).

To add a stroke to a shape:

1. In the Toolbar, select the ink-bottle tool or press S (**Figure 3.66**).

2. In the Property Inspector, *set any of the following attributes:*

   ▲ From the Stroke Style pop-up menu, choose a new style.

   ▲ In the stroke-height field, enter a value for the thickness of the stroke.

   ▲ Click the stroke-color box, and choose a new color from the swatch set.

   The stroke-color boxes in the Toolbar and Property Inspector display the selected color, and the ink-bottle tool is ready to apply the other stroke attributes you set in the Property Inspector. (For more details about setting stroke attributes, see Chapter 2.)

3. Move the pointer over the Stage.

   The pointer appears as a little ink bottle spilling ink.

Ink bottle

Figure 3.66 The ink-bottle tool applies all the stroke attributes currently set in the Ink Bottle Property Inspector.

MODIFYING STROKES

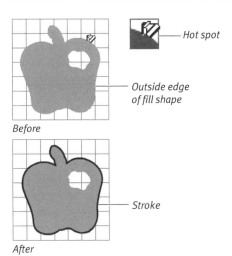

Hot spot

Outside edge
of fill shape

Before

Stroke

After

Figure 3.67 As you move the ink bottle over a filled shape, the hot spot appears as a white dot at the end of the ink drip that's spilling out of the bottle. To add a stroke around the outside edge of your fill shape, position the hot spot along that edge (top) and then click. Flash adds a stroke with the current attributes set in the Ink Bottle Property Inspector (bottom).

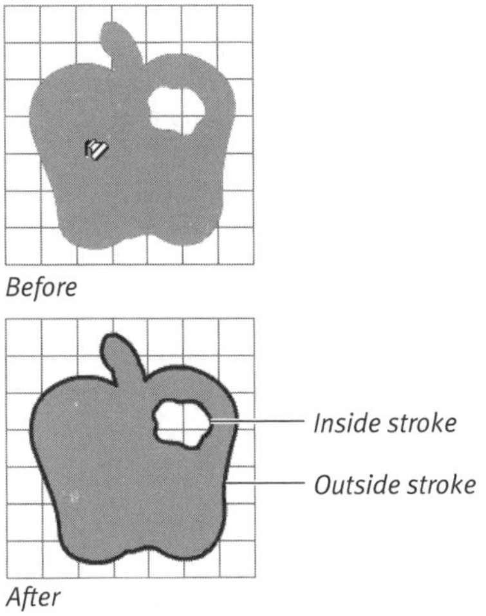

Before

Inside stroke

Outside stroke

After

Figure 3.68 Position the ink bottle's hot spot in the middle of your fill shape (top) and then click. Flash uses the current stroke attributes to add a stroke around the outside and inside of your shape (bottom).

4. With the ink bottle's hot spot, click the shape in one of the following ways:

▲ To add a stroke around the outside of your shape, click near the outside edge of the shape (**Figure 3.67**).

▲ To add a stroke around the inside of a shape that has a hole cut out of it, click near the inside edge of the shape.

▲ To outline both the outside of a shape and the hole inside the shape, click in the middle of the shape (**Figure 3.68**).

Flash adds strokes to the outside edge, inside edge, or both, using the Property Inspector's current settings for color, thickness, and style.

MODIFYING STROKES

To modify existing strokes with the ink bottle:

1. In the Toolbar, select the ink-bottle tool.

2. In the Property Inspector, set the attributes for color, stroke height, and stroke style.

3. Click the ink bottle's hot spot on the stroke you want to modify.

   When you click a stroke directly to modify it, the stroke can be selected or deselected.

✔ Tips

- If you leave an element fully deselected, or if you select the whole element (both fill and stroke), you won't need to position the ink bottle's hot spot so carefully. Clicking anywhere in the graphic element modifies its stroke. **Figure 3.69** shows the way that the ink bottle interacts with selections.

- To apply new attributes to the inside and outside strokes of a graphic element, click the middle of the shape with the ink bottle's hot spot.

- Remember that lines you've created with the straight-line tool and the pencil are also strokes. To change the attributes of an existing line, set the stroke attributes as described earlier in this section and then use the ink-bottle tool to click the line you want to modify. The line can be selected or deselected.

- You don't have to modify an entire stroke. You can select just a piece of a stroke and use the ink bottle to apply changes to just that piece.

With nothing selected, click stroke or fill

With fill and stroke selected, click stroke or fill

With just fill selected, click stroke

With part of stroke selected, click selection

Warning: Clicking a selected fill with unselected stroke does nothing

Figure 3.69 You don't have to select a stroke to change its attributes; just click the stroke or the unselected fill with the ink bottle. Warning: If you have the fill selected, you must click the stroke itself; you can't click the selected fill to change an unselected stroke.

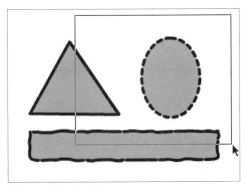

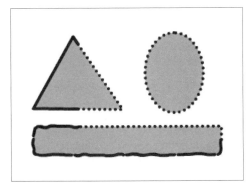

Figure 3.70 Select one or more strokes for modification (top). Set new attributes in the Property Inspector (middle). Flash applies the attributes to all the strokes in your selection (bottom).

To modify selected strokes by using the Property Inspector:

1. Use the selection tool to select one or more strokes on the Stage.

2. Set the attributes for color, stroke height, and stroke style in the Property Inspector.

Flash changes all selected strokes as you enter each new attribute in the Property Inspector (**Figure 3.70**).

✔ Tips

■ When a line is selected, it can be difficult to see certain line styles. The stipple and hatched styles, for example, are obscured by the selection highlighting. If you apply a new line style, but the line seems not to change, deselect it to see the new style in place. Or choose View > Hide Edges. Just don't forget to turn the feature off later; otherwise, you won't be able to see any selections.

■ You cannot modify the stroke attributes of a selected path (one selected with the subselection tool). You can, however, modify the stroke attributes of selections created with any other selection methods.

■ You can modify the color of a selected stroke without using the ink bottle or opening the Property Inspector. Click the stroke-color box in the Toolbar, and choose a new color. Any selected strokes update to the new color.

Using the Eraser Tool in Normal Mode

The eraser tool has five modes that interact with fills and strokes in a variety of ways. This chapter describes using the eraser in Erase Normal mode; the other modes will become more important when you handle complex graphics with multiple elements (see Chapter 4).

In Erase Normal mode, the eraser acts pretty much as you'd expect. When you click and drag it over the Stage, the tool removes any line or fill in its path.

To erase all strokes and fills (Erase Normal):

1. In the Toolbar, select the eraser tool, or press E (**Figure 3.71**).

   The eraser modifiers appear in the Options portion of the Toolbar.

2. From the Eraser Mode pop-up menu, choose Erase Normal.

   A check appears by that mode in the menu, and the Erase Normal icon appears in the Toolbar.

3. From the Eraser Shape pop-up menu, choose a size and shape for the eraser.

   The icon for the selected eraser shape appears in the Toolbar.

4. Move the pointer over the Stage.

   The pointer has the size and shape you selected.

5. Click and drag, or scrub back and forth as you would with an ordinary eraser (**Figure 3.72**).

   Flash removes all the lines and fills you erase.

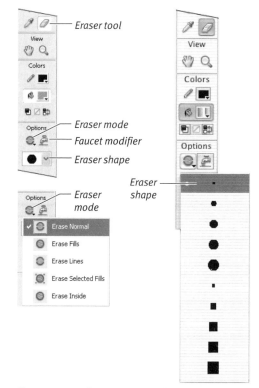

Figure 3.71 Use the eraser tool and its modifiers to remove all or part of strokes and fills.

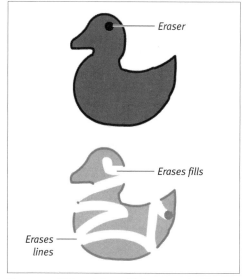

Figure 3.72 Click and drag with the eraser tool in Erase Normal mode to erase all lines and fills.

Faucet modifier

Figure 3.73 The eraser tool's faucet modifier lets you erase entire lines or fills with a single click.

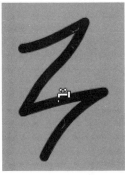

Figure 3.74 This squiggly line contains multiple curve segments, as the selection indicates (top). You can delete the whole line by using the eraser tool's faucet modifier. Click the hot spot of the water drip anywhere on the deselected line (middle); Flash deletes the entire line (bottom).

Using the Faucet Modifier

To speed the erasing of lines and fills, Flash provides the faucet modifier for the eraser tool. The faucet erases an entire fill shape or an entire line with a single click.

To erase a line:

1. In the Toolbar, with the eraser tool selected, click the faucet modifier (**Figure 3.73**).

   The pointer changes to a dripping-faucet icon.

2. Place the faucet's hot spot (the drop of water) over the line you want to remove (**Figure 3.74**).

   The line should not be selected.

3. Click.

   Flash deletes the entire line, even if it's made up of several line segments.

To erase a fill:

1. Select the eraser tool's faucet modifier.

2. Place the faucet's hot spot over the fill you want to remove.

3. Click.

   Flash deletes the fill.

✔ Tips

■ In the Toolbar, double-click the eraser tool to delete the entire contents of the Stage.

■ If you have multiple lines and/or fills selected, clicking any of the selected items with the eraser in Faucet mode deletes the entire selection.

Modifying Fill Colors

Flash provides two methods for modifying the color of an existing fill. You can use the paint-bucket tool to apply the current fill settings to an unselected fill shape, or you can select the fill shape on the Stage and then choose a new fill color via the fill-color box in the Color Mixer panel, the Toolbar, or the Property Inspector.

To change fill color with the paint-bucket tool and Color Mixer panel:

1. In the Toolbar, select the paint-bucket tool, or press K.

   Modifiers for fills appear in the Options section of the Toolbar (**Figure 3.75**).

2. In the Color Mixer panel, *set the following attributes:*

   ▲ From the Fill Style menu, choose Solid.

   ▲ Click the fill-color box, and choose a new color from the swatch set.

   The fill-color boxes in both the Color Mixer and the Toolbar display the selected color, and the paint bucket is ready to apply the new fill color.

3. Click the paint bucket's hot spot (the tip of the drip of paint) somewhere inside the fill you want to change.

   The shape fills with the new color (**Figure 3.76**).

✔ Tip

■ When you click the fill-color box once, the currently loaded set of color swatches pops up, and you can choose one with the eye-dropper tool. If you click the fill-color box and hold the mouse button down, you can move the eyedropper anywhere over your desktop, within Flash or outside it, to pick up a color. You could use this method to match colors with artwork you're creating in another graphics program.

Figure 3.75 The paint-bucket tool lets you modify fills without first selecting them.

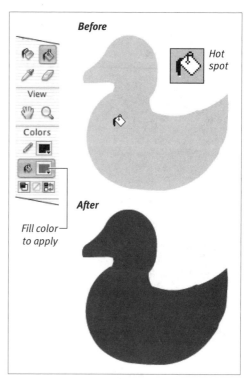

Figure 3.76 Clicking a fill with the paint bucket applies whatever color is selected in the fill-color box. Use this technique to change existing unselected fills.

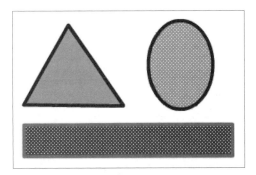

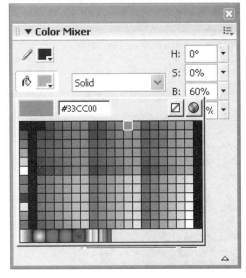

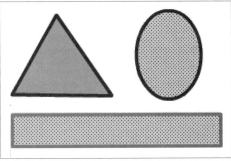

Figure 3.77 Select one or more fills for modification (top). Choose a new color from the Color Mixer panel's fill-color box (middle). Flash changes the color of all the fills in your selection (bottom).

To modify selected fills with the Color Mixer panel:

1. Using the selection tool, select one or more fills on the Stage.

2. In the Color Mixer panel, click the fill-color box, and choose a new color from the swatch set.

   Flash changes all selected fills to whatever color you chose in the Color Mixer panel (**Figure 3.77**).

✔ Tips

- The Color Mixer panel is not the only place where you can choose a new fill color. For either of the preceding methods of applying new colors to fill shapes, you can choose a new color from the fill-color box in the Toolbar or the Property Inspector. If the fill-color icon in any of these areas is selected, you can simply choose a new color from the Color Swatches panel.

- Note that changes made with the methods described in this section have no effect on selected strokes. You can safely include strokes in your selection even if you don't want to change them.

Creating Solid Colors: Color Mixer Panel

You can define new solid colors for fills and strokes in the Color Mixer panel. You can do so visually (by clicking a graphic representation of a color space—all the available colors in a given color-definition system) or numerically (by entering specific values for color components). Always choose the type of color—fill or stroke—before you start defining. Flash updates all the related color boxes with the new color. If you define a new fill color, for example, that color becomes the setting for all the tools that use fills. You can also set a color's transparency in the Color Mixer panel.

To access the Color Mixer panel:

◆ If the Color Mixer panel is not open, from the Window menu, choose Design Panels > Color Mixer (**Figure 3.78**) or press Shift-F9.

The Color Mixer panel appears.

To access solid-color attributes in the Color Mixer panel:

1. Open the Color Mixer panel.

2. From the Fill Style menu, choose Solid.

3. To choose a color space, from the panel's Options menu, do one of the following:

   ▲ To define colors as mixtures of red, green, and blue, choose RGB.

   ▲ To define colors by percentage of hue, saturation, and brightness, choose HSB (**Figure 3.79**).

4. To determine where Flash applies the new color, *do one of the following*:

   ▲ To set a new stroke color, click the pencil icon.

   ▲ To set a new fill color, click the paint-bucket icon.

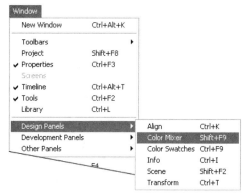

Figure 3.78 To access the Color Mixer panel, choose Window > Design Panels > Color Mixer.

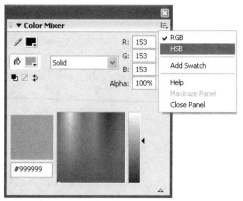

Figure 3.79 The Color Mixer panel lets you choose a color from the color-space bar or enter values directly to define a color in the RGB or HSB color space. Choose the desired color space from the Options pop-up menu.

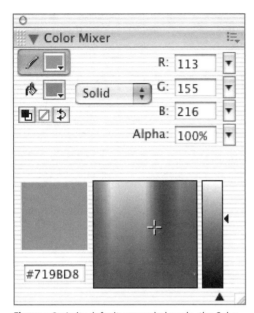

Figure 3.80 In its default, expanded mode, the Color Mixer panel displays a color-space window, a preview window for the new color, a luminosity/ lightness slider, and a text field for entering the precise hex value of a color. Click in the color-space window to choose a new color visually.

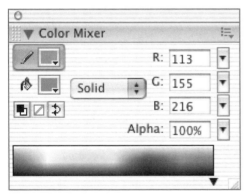

Figure 3.81 To save screen real estate, click the triangle in the Color Mixer's bottom right corner to collapse the color-space window. Dragging the cursor within the color-space bar displays new colors in the color chip for stroke or fill, whichever is currently selected. To expand the panel, click the triangle again.

To define a new color visually in the Color Mixer panel:

1. With the Color Mixer panel open, choose a color space.

2. Position the pointer over the desired hue in the color-space window.

3. Click.

   The crosshair cursor appears, and Flash selects the color within the crosshairs (**Figure 3.80**).

✔ Tips

- If you have trouble clicking exactly the right color, click and drag around within the color-space window. A preview of the new color appears along side the old color in the preview window. When the color you want appears, release the mouse button. Flash enters the values for that color in the appropriate fields.

- If you are mostly choosing colors from the pop-up swatches or by entering RGB/ HSB values, save some space on your desktop by collapsing the Color Mixer. Click the small triangle near the bottom-right corner of the panel; some of the color specification options disappear and small color-space bar replaces the full color-picker window (**Figure 3.81**).

- To match the color of something outside Flash, such as a color from an image file that's open on your desktop, pick up the color with the color box's eyedropper. In the Color Mixer, click the fill- or stroke-color box, and hold down the mouse button. Then position the eyedropper over the area that shows the color you want. Release the mouse button. Specs for that color appear in the Color Mixer panel.

To define a new color numerically in the Color Mixer panel:

1. With the Color Mixer panel open, choose a color space.

2. To define a new color, *do one of the following:*

   ▲ For RGB colors, enter values for red, green, and blue in the R, G, and B fields (**Figure 3.82**).

   ▲ For HSB, enter values for hue, saturation, and brightness in the H, S, and B fields.

To define a color's transparency:

1. With the Color Mixer panel open, define a color.

2. Enter a value in the Alpha field (**Figure 3.83**).

   A value of 100 (100 percent) results in a completely solid color; a value of 0 results in a completely transparent color.

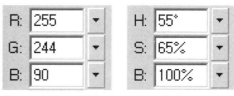

Figure 3.82 Enter RGB values to specify the amount of red, green, and blue that make up the color. Enter HSB values to specify the color by hue, saturation, and brightness. The new color appears in the selected color box.

Figure 3.83 Enter an Alpha value of less than 100 percent to define a transparent color.

About Using the System Color Pickers

In addition to creating colors in the Color Mixer panel, you can create colors in one of the System Color Pickers. These color pickers offer the advantage of letting you enter colors in a system that may be more to your liking than the RGB/HSB offered by the Color Mixer panel. The Windows System Color Picker allows you to specify colors according to Hue, Saturation, and Lightness values. The Macintosh OS actually offers five different System Color Pickers, including one with CMYK sliders.

To access the System Color Picker(s), click the Color Picker button in the upper-right corner of any fill-color or stroke-color box; for example, the ones on the Toolbar and Property Inspector. Whenever you select or specify a color that will dither, the color picker splits the preview window; half of the window shows the dithered color, and the other half shows the nearest Web-safe color.

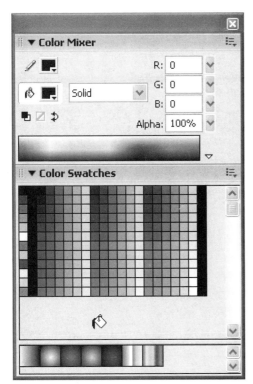

Figure 3.84 Positioning the pointer over the blank area in the Color Swatches panel brings up the paint-bucket icon. Click the blank area to add a swatch for whatever color is currently defined in the Color Mixer panel.

What Are Hex Colors?

The term *hex color* is short for hexadecimal color, which is a fancy way of saying "a color defined by a number written in base 16." Hexadecimal coding is the language of bits and bytes that computers speak; it's also the coding you use to specify color in HTML.

If you remember studying bases in high-school math, you'll recall that the decimal system is base 10, represented by the numbers 0 through 9. In hex color, to get the extra six digits, you continue coding with letters A through F.

After you define a new color, you may want to add it to the Color Swatches panel so that you can use it again. (For more information about the Color Swatches panel, see "Creating Color Sets" later in this chapter.)

To add a color to the Color Swatches panel:

1. Use any of the techniques described earlier in this section to define a new color in the Color Mixer panel.

2. From the Color Mixer panel's Options menu, choose Add Swatch.

   Flash appends the new color to the solid-colors section of the Color Swatches panel. (To access the Color Swatches panel if it is not open, choose Window > Design Panels > Color Swatches.)

✔ Tips

■ You can add new colors to the Color Swatches panel even if it is closed. But if you want to get the feedback when you add a swatch, open the Color Swatches panel in its own window. Resize the panel so that a bit of space appears below the existing swatches. You'll see the new swatch come in.

■ If the Color Swatches panel is open, you can add your newly defined color with a single click. Position the pointer over the gray area at the bottom of the set of swatches in the Color Swatches panel. The pointer changes to the paint-bucket tool. Click anywhere in the gray area, and Flash adds the new color swatch (**Figure 3.84**).

■ You can also delete swatches from the Color Swatches panel. Select the swatch you want to delete. From the Color Mixer panel's Options menu, choose Delete Swatch.

Creating New Gradients

In addition to solid colors, Flash works with gradients—bands of color that blend into each other. Gradients can be linear (parallel bars of color) or radial (concentric rings of color). Gradients can create interesting visual effects and are useful for adding shading—to make a circle look like a sphere, for example.

Flash defines each gradient with a set of markers, called gradient pointers, that indicate which color goes where in the lineup of color bands. You define the color for each pointer. By positioning the pointers on the gradient-definition bar, you control how wide each band of color is. Each gradient can contain as many as eight colors.

You define new gradients in the Color Mixer panel.

To create a three-color linear gradient:

1. Open the Color Mixer panel.

2. From the Color Mixer panel's Fill Style menu, choose Linear (**Figure 3.85**).

   The tools for defining gradients—a color-proxy box (a set of swatches for setting a gradient pointer's color) and a gradient-definition bar—appear.

3. If the panel is collapsed, click the triangle in the bottom-right corner of the panel.

   The Color Picker and gradient- preview window appear (**Figure 3.86**).

4. Position the pointer on or below the gradient-definition bar.

   Flash adds a plus sign to the pointer, indicating that you can add a new gradient pointer in this area.

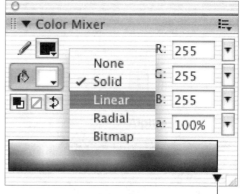

Click to expand or collapse panel

Figure 3.85 Choose Linear from the Fill Style menu to access the tools for defining linear gradients.

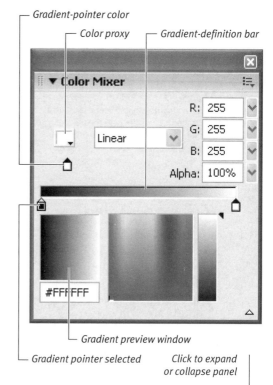

Gradient-pointer color

Color proxy — *Gradient-definition bar*

Gradient preview window

Gradient pointer selected   *Click to expand or collapse panel*

Figure 3.86 The expanded Color Mixer panel displays the gradient-preview window and Color Picker.

Gradient starts with white and blends first to gray and then to black; black fills out the gradient

#666666

Move pointers in to increase width of outside bands

#000000

Click to add pointers

#333333

Figure 3.87 Choose a color for each gradient pointer. The colors and positions of the pointers on the bar define a gradient's color transitions.

5. To add a new pointer, click anywhere along the gradient-definition bar.

Flash adds a new gradient pointer containing the color currently specified in the Color Mixer.

6. To change the leftmost pointer's color, select it and then *do one of the following:*

▲ Click the color-proxy box in the top half of the Color Mixer panel, and choose a color from the set of swatches that appears.

▲ Enter new values in the Alpha and/or RGB or HSB fields.

▲ Choose a new color in the Color Picker.

▲ Enter a new value in the Hex field.

7. Repeat step 6 for the middle and rightmost pointers.

8. Drag the pointers to position them on the gradient-definition bar (**Figure 3.87**).

Place pointers closer together to make the transition between colors more abrupt; place them farther apart to spread the transition out over more space.

As you modify the gradient, your changes appear in the Toolbar's fill-color box. The new gradient also appears in the Property Inspector for any tools that create a fill— say, the oval tool. Those tools are now loaded and ready to create shapes using that gradient.

✔ Tips

■ During each work session, the first time you define a gradient fill, the default two-color gradient appears in the Color Mixer panel: black on the left, blending to white on the right. You can add up to six additional colors.

■ To reduce the number of colors in a gradient, with the gradient selected in the Color Mixer, drag one or more gradient pointers downward, away from the gradient-definition bar. The pointer disappears as you drag. The gradient changes to blend the colors in the remaining gradient pointers.

■ When a gradient pointer is set to black, the Color Picker's Luminosity setting gets set to 0% (for white, Luminosity gets set to 100%). That setting means that the color-proxy window is going to show a solid black (or solid white) square even if you enter new RGB values or use the crosshair cursor to choose a new color. To change the color of a pointer that's set to black (or white), you must choose a new color from the color-proxy window's pop-up swatch set, reposition the Luminosity slider (on the right side of the Color Picker window), or enter a new Brightness value.

■ To reverse the direction of a gradient's color transition, drag one gradient pointer over another. In a white-to-black gradient (a white pointer on the left and a black pointer on the right), drag the white pointer to the right past the black one. Your gradient goes from black to white.

CREATING NEW GRADIENTS

About Bitmap Fills

In addition to solid fills and gradients, Flash lets you import bitmap images and use them as fills. They work similarly to the way gradient fills work. You might use a bitmap fill to create a tiling repeating image) for the background of a Web page. To learn about working with bitmaps and bitmap fills, see Chapter 14.

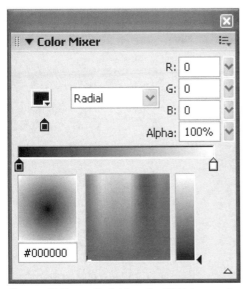

Figure 3.88 Choose Radial from the Fill Style menu to create a circular gradient. The preview window translates the horizontal gradient-definition bar into the appropriate circular color transitions.

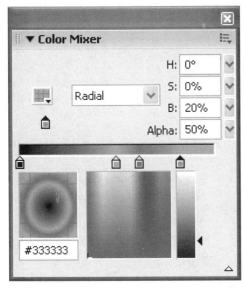

Figure 3.89 When transparent colors make up part of a gradient, grid lines appear in the gradient pointer, the color-proxy window, and the gradient-preview window.

To create a new radial gradient:

1. Open the Color Mixer panel.

2. From the Fill Style menu, choose Radial.

   The tools for defining circular gradients appear. The gradient-definition bar looks the same as it does for linear gradients, but the preview shows your gradient as a set of concentric circles (**Figure 3.88**). The leftmost pointer defines the inner ring; the rightmost pointer defines the outer ring.

3. Follow steps 4 through 8 of "To create a three-color linear gradient" earlier in this chapter to define the color transitions in the radial gradient.

✔ Tips

- To modify an existing gradient, choose it in the Color Swatches panel. Flash switches the Color Mixer panel to gradient mode and displays the selected gradient. Now you can make any changes you need.

- Gradients can have transparency. You simply use a transparent color in one or more gradient pointers (see "To define a color's transparency" earlier in this chapter). If a gradient has transparency, a grid shows up in the gradient pointer, in the color-proxy box, and in the transparent part of the gradient in the preview window (**Figure 3.89**).

- Each pointer in a gradient can have a different alpha setting. To create fade effects, try creating a gradient that blends from a fully opaque color to a transparent one.

CREATING NEW GRADIENTS

You can save a new gradient by adding it to the Color Swatches panel.

To add a gradient to the Color Swatches panel:

1. Create a new gradient, using any of the techniques outlined in the preceding sections.

2. In the Color Mixer panel, *do one of the following:*

▲ From the Options menu, choose Add Swatch.

▲ Position the pointer over the blank area of the Color Swatches panel, and when the paint-bucket icon appears, click.

Flash adds the new gradient to the gradients section of the Color Swatches panel.

✔ Tips

■ If the gradients section of the Color Swatches panel is so full you can't see the latest swatches you added, resize the section by dragging upward on the bar dividing the gradient swatches from the solid color swatches. You may need to resize the whole panel so there is room to drag upward.

■ If the swatches in the Color Swatches panel are too small for you, resize the panel. The swatches grow bigger as the window grows wider.

■ To create a new gradient swatch based on an existing one, in the Color Swatches panel, select the swatch you want to tweak. Position the pointer over the gray area below the swatch set. When the paint-bucket tool appears, click to add a copy of the selected swatch. Select the copy in the Color Swatches panel, and it loads into the Color Mixer panel, ready for you to modify.

Gradients Add Overhead

Gradients are lovely, but they do increase file sizes and thereby slow the loading of published movies. Each area of gradient fill requires an extra 50 bytes of data that a solid fill doesn't need.

In addition, gradients take processor power. If you use too many, you may see slower frame rates, or slower animations, in your finished movie.

CREATING NEW GRADIENTS

Click for Options menu

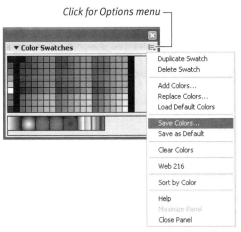

Figure 3.90 The Options menu in the Color Swatches panel offers commands for working with color sets.

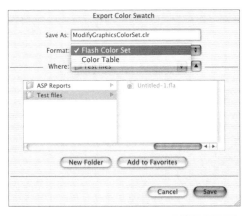

Figure 3.91 To save a set of colors for reuse, in the Export Color Swatch dialog choose Flash Color Set from the Save As menu (Mac, top) or Save As Type menu (Windows, bottom).

Creating Color Sets

Flash stores a default set of colors and gradients in the system color file, but it stores the colors and gradients used in each document with that document. Flash lets you define what colors and gradients make up the default set. In addition, you can create and save other color sets and load them into the Color Swatches panel. This practice makes it easy to maintain a consistent color palette when you are creating several documents for use in a single movie or on a single Web site.

To access the Color Swatches panel:

◆ If the Color Swatches panel is not open, from the Window menu, choose Design Panels > Color Swatches or press ⌘-F9 (Mac) or Ctrl-F9 (Windows).

The Color Swatches panel appears.

To define a new set of colors:

1. Define all the colors and gradients you want to use in your special color set (see the "Creating Solid Colors" and "Creating New Gradients" sections earlier in this chapter).

   You don't need to define all your colors at the same time, but after you have a set that you want to save, move on to step 2.

2. From the Color Swatches panel's Options menu, choose Save Colors (**Figure 3.90**).

   The Export Color Swatch dialog appears (**Figure 3.91**).

3. Navigate to the folder where you want to store your color set.

4. Enter a name for your color-set file in the Save As (Mac), or File Name field (Windows).

continues on next page

CREATING COLOR SETS

5. From the Format (Mac) or Save As Type (Windows) pop-up menu, *choose one of two formats:*

▲ To save colors and gradients in Flash's proprietary Flash Color Set (CLR) format, choose Flash Color Set.

▲ To save the colors in Color Table (ACT) format, choose Color Table.

The ACT format saves only colors (not gradients) but allows you to share color sets with other programs, such as Adobe Photoshop and Macromedia Fireworks.

6. Click Save.

To load a set of colors:

1. From the Options menu in the Color Swatches panel, *choose one of the following:*

▲ To add to the color set currently displayed in the Color Swatches panel, choose Add Colors.

▲ To replace the entire set currently displayed in the Color Swatches panel, choose Replace Colors.

The Import Color Swatch dialog appears (**Figure 3.92**).

2. To determine what types of files to display, from the Show pop-up menu (Mac) or Files of Type (Windows) pop-up menu, *choose one of the following:*

▲ All Formats, which displays CLR, ACT, and GIF files.

▲ Flash Color Set, which displays only CLR files.

▲ Color Table, which displays only ACT files.

▲ GIF, which displays only GIF files.

▲ All Files, which displays files of any format.

Note that the Color Table and Gif formats are for color import only; these formats do not handle gradients. Flash Color Set handles both colors and gradients.

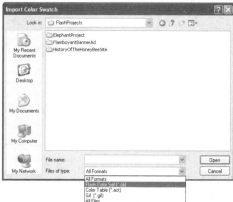

Figure 3.92 To reload a saved set of colors, in the Import Color Swatch dialog, choose Flash Color Set from the Show menu (Mac, top) or Files of Type menu (Windows, bottom).

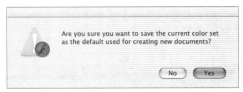

Figure 3.93 This warning dialog gives you a chance to change your mind after you've chosen Save As Default from the Options menu in the Color Swatches panel. You can't undo this operation.

3. Navigate to the file you want to import.

4. Click Open.

To define the default set of colors:

1. From the Options menu in the Color Swatches panel, choose Save As Default.

A warning dialog appears, giving you the chance to cancel the operation at this point (**Figure 3.93**).

2. *Do one of the following:*

▲ To cancel the operation, click No.

▲ To go ahead and create the new default color set, click Yes.

✔ Tips

■ The Options menu in the Color Swatches panel also offers some handy shortcuts for dealing with color sets. To reload the default color set, choose Load Default Colors. To remove all color swatches from the current panel window, choose Clear Colors. To load the standard Web-safe colors, choose Web 216. To arrange colors by hue, choose Sort by Color. (Note that you cannot undo the color sorting. So be sure to save your current set of colors if there's any chance that you'll want to restore the unsorted order.)

■ You can also use the Color Swatches panel to select colors for fills and strokes. The key is first to tell Flash where to apply the new color. You do that by clicking the stroke or fill icon in the Colors section of the Toolbar or in the Color Mixer panel. Then select a color in the Color Swatches panel. Flash puts that color in every fill-color or stroke-color box. In the Colors section of the Toolbar, for example, click the paint-bucket icon and then select blue in the Color Swatches panel. Blue now appears in the fill-color box in the Toolbar, in the Color Mixer panel, and in the Property Inspector.

CREATING COLOR SETS

Putting Gradients to Work

In "Creating New Gradients" earlier in this chapter, you learned how to create color blends. Flash treats gradients just like any other fill. You use the paint-bucket tool to fill outline shapes with a gradient and the brush tool to create freeform swashes of gradient color.

To fill a shape (or replace a solid fill) with a gradient:

1. In the Toolbar, select the paint-bucket icon.

2. In the Color Mixer panel, define a new gradient.

   or

   From the Color Swatches panel, or the fill-color box in the Toolbar or Property Inspector, choose an existing linear gradient (**Figure 3.94**) or radial gradient (**Figure 3.95**).

3. Click the paint bucket's hot spot (the tip of the drip of paint) somewhere inside the outline shape or within the existing fill.

   The shape fills with the gradient currently displayed in the fill-color boxes.

✔ Tips

- You can also change any fills that are currently selected on the Stage to gradient fills. Once the fills are selected, you just select the desired gradient from any fill-color box or from a swatch in the Color Swatches panel. The selected fills update with the gradient fill.

- For radial, unlocked gradients, click with the paint bucket's hot spot where you want the center of the gradient to appear.

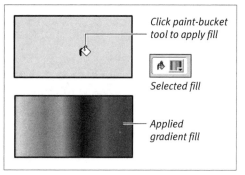

Click paint-bucket tool to apply fill

Selected fill

Applied gradient fill

Figure 3.94 You can use the paint-bucket tool to apply a linear-gradient fill.

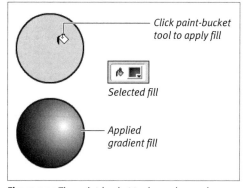

Click paint-bucket tool to apply fill

Selected fill

Applied gradient fill

Figure 3.95 The paint-bucket tool can also apply a radial-gradient fill.

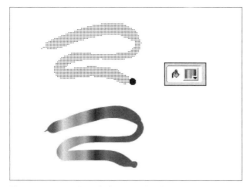

Lock Fill

Figure 3.96 Deselect the Lock Fill modifier to paint with an unlocked gradient.

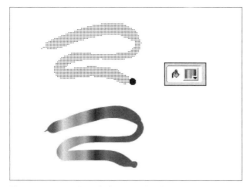

Figure 3.97 A painted shape with a linear-gradient fill.

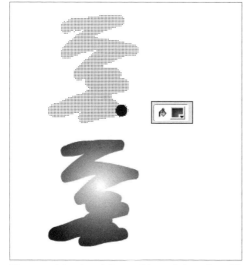

Figure 3.98 A painted shape with a radial-gradient fill.

To paint with an unlocked gradient:

1. In the Toolbar, select the brush tool.

2. Make sure that the Lock Fill modifier is deselected (**Figure 3.96**).

3. Using one of the methods described in the preceding exercises, choose a gradient.

4. Paint with the brush as described in Chapter 2.

Flash cannot preview the shape you paint with the gradient you chose, as it can do with solid-color fills. The preview shape has a black-and-white pattern.

5. When you finish your brush stroke, release the mouse button.

Flash redraws the painted shape, using the gradient currently selected in the fill-color box. Flash fills the shape's bounding box (an invisible rectangle that's just the right size to enclose the shape) with the gradient. The painted shape reveals portions of that gradient pattern (**Figure 3.97** and **Figure 3.98**).

✔ Tip

■ You can also create a single underlying gradient for several shapes on the Stage by using the Lock Fill modifier. With the paint-bucket tool selected, choose a gradient fill. Then click the Lock Fill modifier. Flash creates an underlying hidden rectangle—the same size as the Stage—filled with the locked gradient. Wherever you paint with the locked gradient by using the brush tool (or apply the locked fill to a shape by using the paint-bucket tool), Flash reveals that hidden gradient.

Modifying Applied Gradients

You can use Flash's fill-transform tool to modify a gradient fill. You can rotate the fill or change its size and center point.

To move a gradient fill's center point:

1. In the Toolbar, select the fill-transform tool (**Figure 3.99**).

   The pointer changes to the fill-transform-pointer.

2. Position the pointer over the graphic element whose gradient you want to modify.

3. Click.

   Handles for manipulating the element appear (**Figure 3.100**).

4. Drag the center-point handle to reposition the center point of the gradient (**Figure 3.101**).

Figure 3.99 The fill-transform tool (left) and the pointer with which you manipulate gradients (right).

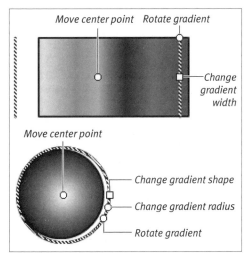

Figure 3.100 Handles for transforming fills appear when you click the fill with the fill transform pointer.

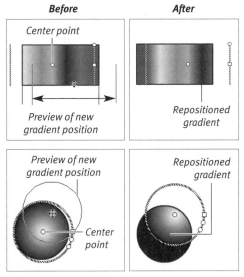

Figure 3.101 Drag the center-point handle to reposition the center of the gradient within your shape.

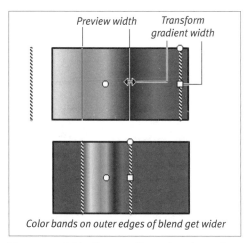

Preview width   Transform gradient width

Color bands on outer edges of blend get wider

Figure 3.102 With a linear gradient selected, use the fill-transform tool to drag the square handle inward and create a narrower rectangle for a gradient.

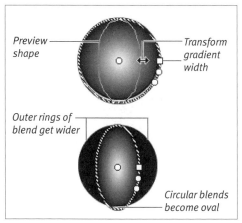

Preview shape   Transform gradient width

Outer rings of blend get wider

Circular blends become oval

Figure 3.103 With a radial gradient selected, use the fill-transform tool to drag the square handle inward to create a narrower oval for a gradient.

To resize a gradient fill:

1. With the fill-transform tool selected in the Toolbar, click the graphic element that contains the gradient you want to modify.

2. To change the width of a linear gradient, drag the square handle (**Figure 3.102**).

   The pointer changes to a double-headed arrow. Dragging toward the center of your shape squeezes the blend into a narrower space; dragging away from the center of your shape spreads the blend over a wider space.

3. To change the shape of a radial gradient, drag the square handle (**Figure 3.103**).

   The pointer changes to a double-headed arrow. Dragging toward the center of your shape creates a narrower oval space for the blend; dragging away from the center of your shape creates a wider oval space.

continues on next page

4. To change the radius of a radial gradient, drag the circular handle next to the square handle (**Figure 3.104**).

The pointer changes to a double-headed arrow within a circle. Dragging toward the center of your shape squeezes the blend into a smaller circular space; dragging away from the center of your shape spreads the blend over a larger circular space.

To rotate a gradient fill:

1. With the fill-transform tool selected in the Toolbar, click the graphic element with the gradient you want to modify.

2. To rotate the gradient, *do one of the following:*

- ▲ To rotate a linear gradient, drag the round handle (**Figure 3.105**).

- ▲ To rotate a radial gradient, drag the round handle farthest from the square handle.

The pointer changes to a circular arrow. You can rotate the gradient clockwise or counterclockwise.

✔ Tips

- You can click and drag with the paint-bucket tool to rotate the gradient as you apply it. To constrain the gradient angle to vertical, horizontal, or 45-degree angles, hold down the Shift key as you drag.

- When you rotate a gradient interactively with the paint-bucket tool, the fill-color box continues to display the gradient in its vertical position but the rotation persists for some tools. If you switch to the brush or paint bucket tool, they will use the rotated gradient. (The oval and rectangle tools will use the original unrotated gradient.) To remove the angle modification, use the paint-bucket tool to modify the gradient again or choose another fill and then choose the gradient again.

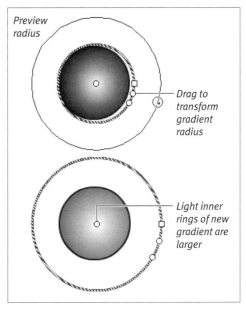

Figure 3.104 With a radial gradient, drag the first round handle outward to create a larger radius.

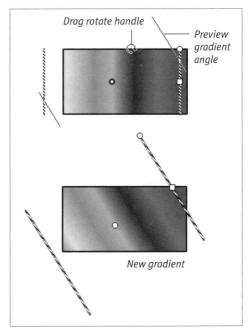

Figure 3.105 As you drag the gradient's rotate handle with the fill-transform tool, you spin the gradient around its center point.

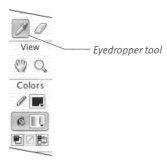

Eyedropper tool

Figure 3.106 Select the eyedropper tool to copy fills and strokes. On the Stage, click a fill or stroke. Flash copies the clicked element's attributes to the Property Inspector, then loads the paint bucket tool for fills or the ink bottle tool for strokes. You're ready to click another graphic to apply the copied attribute.

Applying Attributes of One Graphic Element to Another

To save time, you can copy the fill and stroke attributes of one element and apply them to another element.

To copy attributes between graphic elements:

1. In the Toolbar, select the eyedropper tool, or press I (**Figure 3.106**).

2. Move the pointer over the Stage.

   The pointer changes to an eyedropper.

3. To copy the attribute, *do one of the following:*

   ▲ To copy a fill color or gradient, position the eyedropper over a fill.

   ▲ To copy stroke attributes, position the eyedropper over a line or stroke.

4. Click the fill or stroke.

   Flash switches tools; the paint bucket appears for fills, the ink bottle for strokes. The selected attributes appear in all related panels, for example, the Property Inspector, Color Mixer, and Toolbar for fills.

5. Using the paint-bucket or ink bottle tool, click a different graphic element.

   Flash applies the new attributes to that element (see "Modifying Fill Colors" and "Modifying Strokes," earlier in this chapter).

✔ Tip

■ To pick up the color of a stroke or fill and use it for both strokes and fills, Shift-click with the eyedropper tool. Flash loads the selected color into the fill- and stroke-color boxes in the Toolbar, the Color Mixer panel, and the Property Inspectors relevant to the selected color.

APPLYING ATTRIBUTES OF GRAPHIC ELEMENTS

Converting Lines to Fills

Flash lets you convert lines and outlines (strokes) to fills, which you can then edit or fill with gradients. You can expand or contract a shape by a user-specified amount. And you can create soft-edged graphic elements. These conversions increase the number of curves that Flash creates and therefore may increase file size.

To convert a line to a fill:

1. In the Toolbar, select the pencil tool.

2. Draw a simple line on the Stage.

3. Change to the selection tool, and click the line to select it.

4. From the Modify menu, choose Shape > Convert Lines to Fills (**Figure 3.107**).

   Flash converts the line to a fill shape that looks exactly like the line. You can now edit the "line's" outline (or apply a gradient) as though you were working with a fill created with the brush tool (**Figure 3.108**).

To expand a fill:

1. In the Toolbar, select the oval tool with no stroke.

2. On the Stage, draw an oval shape.

3. Change to the selection tool, and click the shape to select it.

4. From the Modify menu, choose Shape > Expand Fill.

   The Expand Fill dialog appears (**Figure 3.109**).

Figure 3.107 Choose Modify > Shape > Convert Lines to Fills to transform strokes into fills.

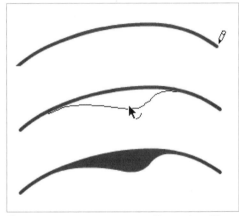

Figure 3.108 You can convert an outline, such as this line drawn with the pencil tool (top), to a fill. The fill then has its own editable outlines (middle and bottom).

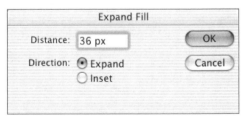

Figure 3.109 The Expand Fill dialog presents options for resizing a selected fill.

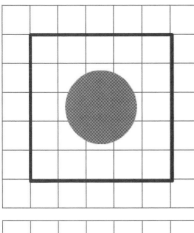

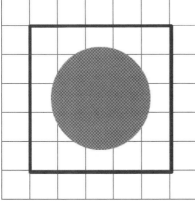

Figure 3.110 Using the Expand Fill command on the selected fill (top) causes its outlines to expand. The grid here is set to 36 pixels.

5. Enter a value in the Distance field.

6. Choose a Direction option.

Expand makes the shape larger. Inset makes the shape smaller.

7. Click OK.

Flash blows the fill shape up like a balloon or shrinks it (**Figure 3.110**).

To soften the edges of a fill:

1. In the Toolbar, select the oval tool with no stroke.

2. On the Stage, draw an oval shape.

3. Change to the selection tool, and click the shape to select it.

4. From the Modify menu, choose Shape > Soften Fill Edges.

The Soften Fill Edges dialog appears (**Figure 3.111**).

5. Enter values for Distance and Number of Steps.

6. Choose a Direction option.

Expand makes the shape larger; Inset makes the shape smaller.

continues on next page

Figure 3.111 Enter values in the Soften Fill Edges dialog to create a softer-looking edge for a selected shape.

7. Click OK.

Flash divides the expansion or inset value by the number of steps you specified and creates a series of concentric shapes that outline your original shape. The new shapes get progressively lighter in color as they approach the outer edge of the softened shape (**Figure 3.112**).

✔ Tips

■ The Expand Fill and Soften Fill Edges commands work best on plain fill shapes (fills without strokes). Small shapes and shapes with convoluted outlines take a longer time to convert, and the result may not be what you expect.

■ Using the Modify > Shape commands on fills that also have strokes around them will have some odd results. If you select just the fill and not the stroke, the stroke doesn't expand or shrink to match the expansion or inset. If you expand the fill, it will eat into—or cover over—the stroke. If you inset the fill, you wind up with a gap between the fill and the stroke. If you do select the stroke, the Modify > Shape commands will make the stroke disappear entirely!

■ The multiple bands created by the Soften Fill Edges command will consume processor power during playback. Used too often, or on complex shapes, the soft-edged effect will slow your final published movie's frame rate.

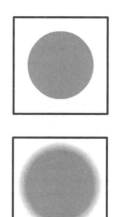

 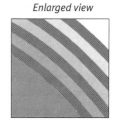

Enlarged view   *Enlarged view*

Figure 3.112 The Soften Fill Edges command creates a purposeful banding effect to give fill shapes a soft edge. The selected circle (top) gets a soft edge in eight steps (middle). Enlarged views show the banding more clearly (bottom left); you can select individual steps of the softened edge (bottom right).

COMPLEX GRAPHICS ON A SINGLE LAYER

In Chapters 2 and 3, you learned to make simple individual shapes from lines (strokes) and fills by using Macromedia Flash MX 2004's drawing tools. You learned to make a single oval and a lone rectangle, for example. In your movies, you'll want to use many shapes together, and you'll need to combine strokes and fills in complex ways. You might combine several ovals and rectangles to create a robot character, for example. To work effectively with complex graphics, you need to understand how Flash shapes interact when they are on the same layer or on different layers. In this chapter, you learn how to work with multiple shapes on one layer in a Flash Document. To learn more about the concept of layers, see Chapter 5.

Two of Flash's drawing tools—the brush tool and the eraser—offer special modes for use with multiple fills and strokes on a single layer. In this chapter, unless you are specifically requested to do otherwise, leave both tools at their default settings of Paint Normal (for the brush tool) and Erase Normal (for the eraser).

When Lines and Shapes Interact

You can think of each frame in a Flash movie as being a stack of transparent acetate sheets. In Flash terms, each "sheet" is a layer. Objects on different layers have a depth relationship: Objects on higher layers block your view of those on lower layers, just as a drawing on the top sheet of acetate would obscure drawings on lower sheets.

Imagine that you have two layers in your movie. If you draw a little yellow square on the bottom layer and then switch to the top layer and draw a big red square directly over the yellow one, the little square remains intact. You simply can't see it while the big red square on the top layer is in the way.

On a single layer in Flash, however, objects actually interact with one another, almost as though you were painting with wet finger paint. Here's a quick run down of how lines (strokes) and shapes (fills) interact within a single layer.

When Lines Intersect Lines

Intersecting lines drawn on the same layer affect one another. Draw one line, then draw a second line that intersects the first. The second line cuts— or, in Flash terminology, *segments*—the first. Segmentation happens whether the lines are the same color or different colors, but it's easiest to see with contrasting colors (**Figure 4.1**).

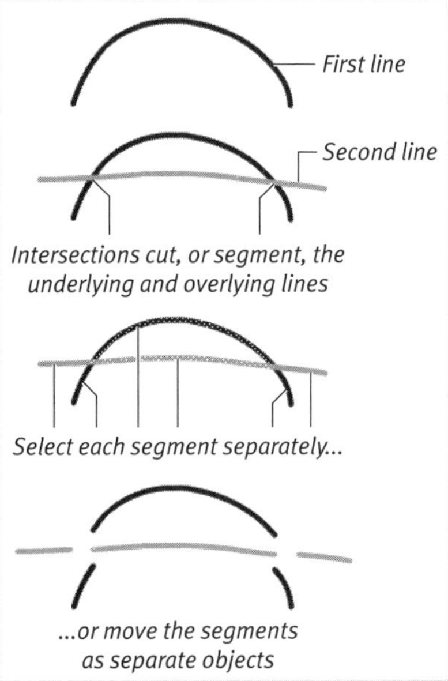

You might expect that the second line you drew would wind up on top of the first, but sometimes, that's not the case. Start with a red line, then draw a blue line across it; the blue line jumps *behind* the red one when you release the mouse button. Flash creates a stacking order for lines based on the hex-color value of the line's stroke-color setting. The higher the hex value of the stroke color, the higher the line sits in a stack of lines drawn on the Stage. A line whose stroke color is set to a hex value of 663399 always winds up on top of a stroke whose color is set to 333399.

continues on next page

First line

Second line

Intersections cut, or segment, the underlying and overlying lines

Select each segment separately...

...or move the segments as separate objects

Figure 4.1 When you draw one line across another, every intersection creates a separate segment.

When Lines and Shapes Interact *continued*

When Lines and Fills Intersect

Even the invisible outlines that describe painted brush-stroke fills can cut other lines. This means that when you draw lines over fills, you can wind up with lots of little segments. Try drawing lines with the pencil tool and the brush tool. If you paint a brush stroke that intersects a line, the brush stroke remains one solid object, but the line gets segmented (**Figure 4.2**). If you draw a line that intersects a brush stroke, the line cuts the brush stroke and the invisible outline of the brush stroke cuts the line (**Figure 4.3**).

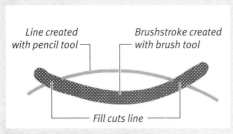

Figure 4.2 When a fill overlays a line, the fill segments the line. As the selection highlighting shows, the fill remains one solid object.

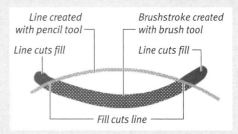

Figure 4.3 When a line overlays a fill, the line cuts the fill, and the fill's invisible outline cuts the line.

When Shapes/Fills Intersect

When intersecting fills are the same color, the newer fill simply adds to the shape (**Figure 4.4**).

When fills of different colors interact, the newer fill replaces the older one (**Figure 4.5**). If the new fill only intersects the old, it still replaces the part where the two overlap.

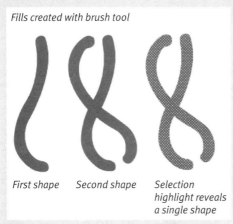

Figure 4.4 When you draw overlapping fills in the same color, Flash puts the two shapes together to create a single shape. (Compare this figure with the overlapping lines in Figure 4.1 that cut one another.)

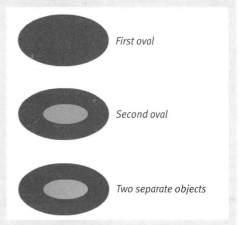

Figure 4.5 When one fill overlaps another of a different color, the fills don't meld but remain separate. The second oval here replaces the first where they overlap.

Understanding Grouping

Flash does give you ways to force its paint to "dry." When you turn objects into groups (or symbols), they are no longer immediately editable, and they stop interacting with other objects. (You can still edit the contents of groups and symbols, but you must invoke special editing modes to modify them.) If you put several groups (or symbols) on the same layer, they merely stack up, one on top of another. (To learn more about symbols, see Chapter 6.)

To create a group:

1. Select one or more objects on the Stage, using any of the methods discussed in Chapter 3 (**Figure 4.6**).

2. From the Modify menu, choose Group, or press ⌘-G (Mac) or Ctrl-G (Windows) (**Figure 4.7**).

   Flash groups the items, placing them within a bounding box (**Figure 4.8**). The visible bounding box lets you know that the group is selected. When the group is not selected, the bounding box is hidden.

To return objects to ungrouped status:

1. Select the group that you want to return to ungrouped status.

2. From the Modify menu, choose Ungroup, or press Shift-⌘-G (Mac) or Ctrl-Shift-G (Windows).

   Flash removes the bounding box and selects all the items.

✔ Tips

- If you prefer using a two-key shortcut rather than a three-key shortcut, the command for breaking apart symbols also works to ungroup groups. That command is ⌘-B (Mac) or Ctrl-B (Windows).

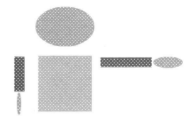

Figure 4.6 The first step in grouping is selecting the objects you want to use in the group.

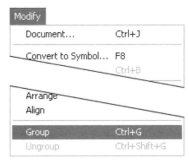

Figure 4.7 Choose Modify > Group to unite several selected objects as a group.

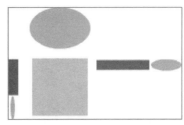

Figure 4.8 When you select the group, a highlighted bounding box appears, surrounding the grouped objects.

- Interactions between lines and fills occur not only when you draw a shape, but also when you place a copy of a shape or move a shape. Be careful when placing live shapes and lines on a single layer. You can inadvertently add to or delete part of an underlying shape.

UNDERSTANDING GROUPING

Figure 4.9 The oval before grouping.

Figure 4.10 The oval after grouping.

Figure 4.11 Draw a second oval on top of the grouped oval.

Figure 4.12 The ungrouped oval stacks beneath the grouped oval.

Figure 4.13 Drag the grouped oval to make the ungrouped oval visible.

Working with Grouped Elements

Grouping is a useful way to prevent shapes from interacting and to keep shapes together as you work with the elements on the Stage.

To prevent interaction between objects on the same layer:

1. In the Toolbar, choose the oval tool.

2. Set the stroke color to no color and the fill color to red.

3. On the Stage, draw a fairly large oval (**Figure 4.9**).

4. In the Toolbar, switch to the selection tool, and select the oval you just drew.

5. To make the oval a grouped element, from the Modify menu, choose Group (**Figure 4.10**).

6. Back in the Toolbar, choose the oval tool and a different fill color.

7. On the Stage, draw a smaller oval in the middle of your first oval (**Figure 4.11**).

   When you finish drawing the new oval, it immediately disappears behind the grouped oval (**Figure 4.12**). That's because grouped objects always stack on top of ungrouped objects (see the sidebar "Understanding the Stacking Order of Grouped Shapes" later in this chapter).

8. Switch to the selection tool, and reposition the large oval so that you can see the small one (**Figure 4.13**).

continues on next page

WORKING WITH GROUPED ELEMENTS

9. Deselect the large oval, and select the small oval (**Figure 4.14**).

10. To make the small oval a grouped element, from the Modify menu, choose Group.

Flash puts the small oval in a bounding box and brings it to the top of the stack (**Figure 4.15**). Flash always places the most recently created group on the top of the stack. Now you can reposition the two ovals however you like, and they will not interact.

Figure 4.14 Select the small oval.

Figure 4.15 After grouping, the small oval—the most recently created group—pops to the top of the stack.

✔ Tips

■ You can group several shapes so that you can manipulate them as a group but keep them in the same relationship to one another. You might, for example, make the eyes and eyebrows in a face a single group. That would allow you to create new facial expressions simply by repositioning the eye elements, or changing their size.

■ You can group grouped objects. If you want to position several items on top of one another, group them as individuals first. Position them as you like. Then group all the items to preserve their relationship.

■ You can lock groups so that you don't accidentally move or modify them. Select the group that you want to lock. Then, from the Modify menu, choose Arrange > Lock, or press Opt-⌘-L (Mac) or Ctrl-Alt-L (Windows). You can no longer select the item. To make it available again, choose Modify > Arrange > Unlock All from the Modify menu, or press Opt-Shift-⌘-L (Mac) or Ctrl-Alt-Shift-L (Windows). You cannot unlock locked items selectively.

Controlling the Stacking Order

You can change the stacking order of groups via the Modify > Arrange menu. Notice that the stacking order doesn't require that you actually stack objects on top of one another. If you have two groups on opposite sides of the Stage, their stacking order is not visible, but as soon as you drag the objects so that one overlaps the other, the order becomes apparent.

Each grouped object sits on its own sublayer. You can move objects up or down in the stacking order one level at a time, or you can bring an object forward or send it backward through the stack of sublayers. The sublayer containing the live, editable objects is always at the bottom; groups and symbols stack on top of ungrouped elements.

Understanding the Stacking Order of Grouped Shapes

Editable shapes on a single layer always stay on the same layer, cutting one another whenever they inhabit the same space on the Stage. Grouped items (and symbols), however, stack on top of one another. By default, Flash stacks each group that you create on top of the preceding one; the last group created winds up on top of all the others (**Figure 4.16**). A higher-level group obscures any groups that lie directly beneath it.

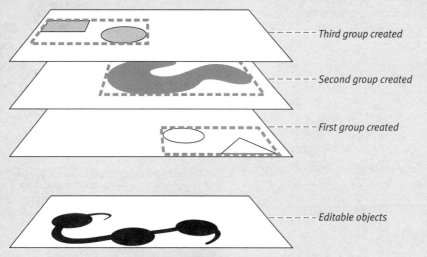

Third group created

Second group created

First group created

Editable objects

Figure 4.16 This schematic shows Flash's default stacking order for grouped items. The most recently created group is on top. Editable shapes are always on the bottom.

To change position in the stack by one level:

1. On the Stage, create at least three grouped objects.

2. Select one group.

3. From the Modify > Arrange menu, *choose one of the following:*

   ▲ To move the selected item up one level, choose Bring Forward, or press ⌘-up arrow (Mac) or Ctrl-up arrow (Windows).

   ▲ To move the selected item down one level, choose Send Backward, or press ⌘-down arrow (Mac) or Ctrl-down arrow (Windows).

   Flash moves the selected item up (or down) one sublayer in the stacking order (**Figure 4.17**).

To move an element to the top or bottom of the stack:

1. On the Stage, select one of the grouped objects you created in the previous task.

2. From the Modify > Arrange menu, *choose one of the following:*

   ▲ To bring the item to the top of the stack, choose Bring to Front, or press Option-Shift-up arrow (Mac) or Ctrl-Shift-up arrow (Windows).

   ▲ To move the item to the bottom of the stack, choose Send to Back, or press Option-Shift-down arrow (Mac) or Ctrl-Shift-down arrow (Windows).

   Flash places the selected item at the top (or bottom) of the heap.

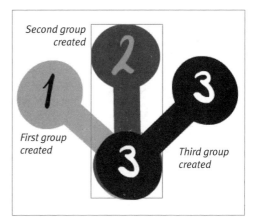

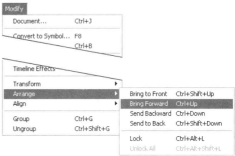

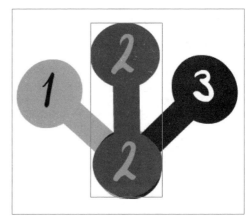

Figure 4.17 Each dumbbell here is a separate group (top). Choose Modify > Arrange > Bring Forward (middle) to move a selected group up one level in the stacking order (bottom).

Document-editing mode

Click Back button to return to document-editing mode   *Group-editing mode*

Grayed shapes do not belong to the group that's being edited

Double-click away from the group to return to document-editing mode

Figure 4.18 These eyes and eyebrows are a selected group (top). In group-editing mode (bottom), the other objects on the Stage are grayed out to indicate that you can't edit them.

Editing Groups

Although you can transform a group as a whole (scale, rotate, and skew it), you can't directly edit the individual shapes within the group, the way that you can edit an ungrouped shape. To edit the shapes within a group, you must use the Edit Selected command.

To edit the contents of a group:

1. In the Toolbar, select the selection tool.

2. On the Stage, select the group you want to edit.

3. From the Edit menu, choose Edit Selected.

   Flash enters group-editing mode (**Figure 4.18**). The Edit Bar just above the Stage Timeline changes to indicate that you are in group-editing mode. The bounding box for the selected group disappears, and Flash dims all the items on the Stage that are not part of the selected group. These dimmed items are not editable; they merely provide context for editing the selected group.

✔ Tips

- With the selection tool selected, you can enter group-editing mode quickly by double-clicking a grouped item on the Stage.

- When you have the Property Inspector open, you can see—and change—the height, width, and x and y coordinates of the bounding box of a selected group (**Figure 4.19**).

- You can also enter group-editing mode by choosing Edit > Edit in Place. When you edit groups, there is no difference between this command and Edit > Edit Selected. There is a difference when you use these commands to edit symbols. You'll learn about symbols in Chapter 6.

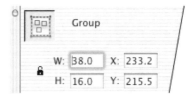

Figure 4.19 The Property Inspector displays the height, width, and x and y coordinates for the bounding box of a group that you've selected on the Stage. Enter new values to change any of those parameters.

EDITING GROUPS

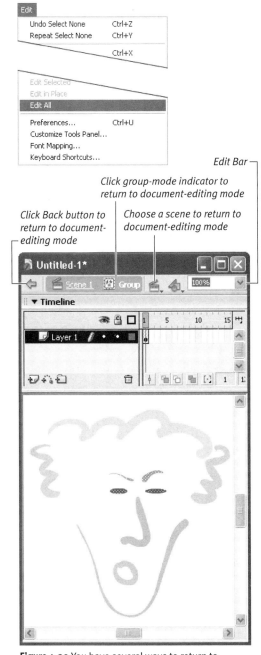

Figure 4.20 You have several ways to return to document-editing mode when you are editing a group. From the Edit menu, choose Edit All or Edit Document. Or you can click items in the Edit Bar: The Back button, the scene name, and the Scene pop-up menu all let you resume editing the movie.

To return to document-editing mode:

Do one of the following:

◆ From the Edit menu, choose Edit All (**Figure 4.20**).

◆ Double-click the Stage or the work area away from the shapes in the group you're editing.

◆ Click the current scene name in the Edit Bar.

◆ Click the Back button in the Edit Bar.

✔ Tips

■ When you are editing a group nested within another group, clicking the Back button moves you up one level in the nesting hierarchy.

■ If in addition to returning to document-editing mode, you want to work on a different scene, you can simply choose it from the pop-up menu of scenes in the Edit Bar. Flash takes you to the new scene in document-editing mode. (To learn more about scenes, see Chapter 10.)

EDITING GROUPS

Aligning Elements

As you get into the process of animation, you'll discover how important alignment can be. Flash's grids, guides, and Snap features (see Chapter 1) help you align objects on the Stage manually. Flash also offers automated alignment through the Align panel. You can line up selected objects by their top, bottom, left, or right edges or by their centers (**Figure 4.21**). You can align the objects to each other or align them to the Stage—for example, you can place the top edge of all selected objects at the top edge of the Stage. Flash can also resize one object to match the dimensions of another—making them the same width, for example.

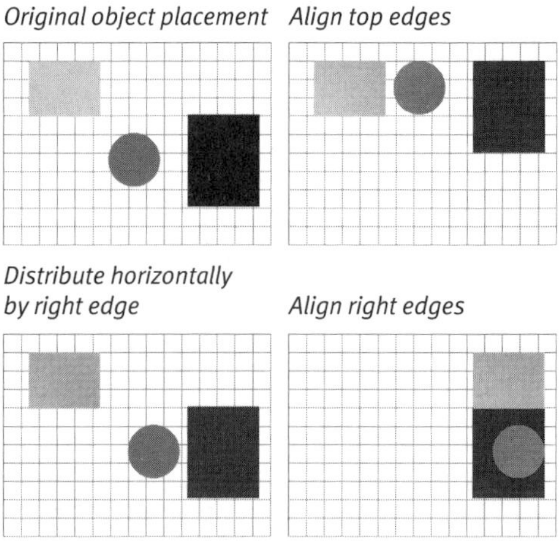

To access alignment options:

◆ From the Window menu, choose Design Panels > Align, or press ⌘-K (Mac) or Ctrl-K (Windows) (**Figure 4.22**).

The Align panel appears (**Figure 4.23**). You can apply any of the alignment options to selected objects on the Stage.

Original object placement   *Align top edges*

Distribute horizontally by right edge

Align right edges

Figure 4.21 Flash's Align panel can line up selected objects in various ways. Here are a few alignment choices used on the same set of objects.

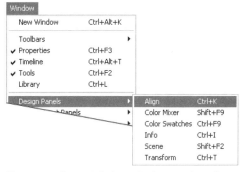

Figure 4.22 Choose Window > Design Panels > Align to open the Align panel.

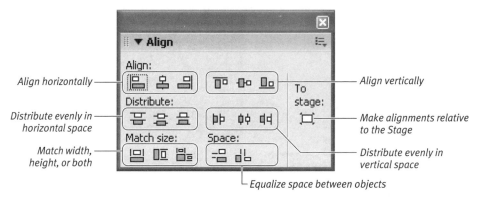

Figure 4.23 The Align panel offers options for aligning objects horizontally and vertically, distributing objects evenly in horizontal or vertical space, forcing objects to match each other (or the Stage) in width and height, and creating even spacing between objects.

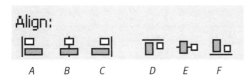

Figure 4.24 You can align objects horizontally by their left edges (A), centers (B), or right edges (C). You can align objects vertically by their top edges (D), centers (E), or bottom edges (F).

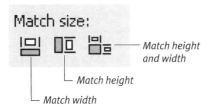

Original items

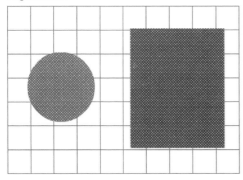

Items after matching height

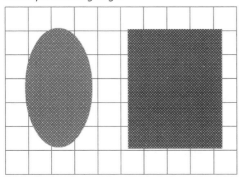

Figure 4.25 Choosing the Match Height option in the Match Size section of the Align panel (top) changes all selected items (middle) to be the same height (bottom). Flash makes shorter items grow to match the tallest selected item.

To align items:

1. On the Stage, select the items that you want to align.

2. In the Align section of the Align panel (**Figure 4.24**), *choose one of the following options:*
   ▲ Align left edge
   ▲ Align horizontal center
   ▲ Align right edge
   ▲ Align top edge
   ▲ Align vertical center
   ▲ Align bottom edge

   Flash rearranges the selected objects.

To match dimensions of items:

1. On the Stage, select the items that you want to change.

2. In the Match Size section of the Align panel (**Figure 4.25**), *do one of the following:*
   ▲ To expand all items to be the same width as the widest item, choose Match Width.
   ▲ To expand all items to be the same height as the tallest item, choose Match Height.
   ▲ To perform both of the preceding actions, choose Match Width and Height.

ALIGNING ELEMENTS

✔ Tips

■ You can make your alignment adjustments relative to the edges of the Stage by clicking the To Stage button. For example, with To Stage selected, choosing Align Bottom Edge puts the bottom edges of all the selected elements at the bottom of the Stage. Choosing Match size makes selected elements as tall as the Stage.

■ In addition to aligning items horizontally and vertically, you can create equal horizontal or vertical space among three or more items. The buttons in the Distribute section of the Align panel let you equalize the horizontal space between selected elements' left edges, centers, or right edges or equalize the vertical space between selected items' top edges, centers, or bottom edges.

■ Use the Align panel's Space options to create equal horizontal or vertical space between items' inside edges.

Figure 4.26
The Brush Mode menu lets you choose the way new brushstrokes interact with existing fills and strokes.

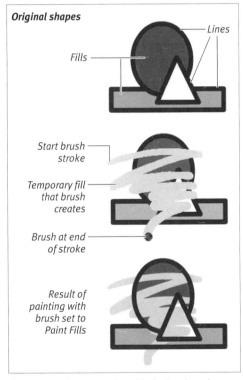

Figure 4.27 When you paint with the brush tool set to Paint Fills, Flash lets you paint over lines without affecting them. Lines pop to the front of the image when you release the mouse button.

Using the Complex Paint Modes with the Brush

In Chapter 3, you learned about using the brush in Normal mode, in which every stroke with the brush lays down a new fill. Flash offers four special brush modes that restrict the way the new brush strokes interact with existing editable lines (strokes) and fills. You can set the brush to paint over lines without affecting them (the fill winds up behind the lines instead of covering them), to paint only in blank areas of the Stage (existing lines and fills repel the paint), to paint only within a selection (if the brush slips outside the selection, nothing happens), or to paint only within the area where you started your brush stroke (all other areas repel the paint).

To leave lines intact when painting:

1. Create several shapes on the Stage.
   Use a variety of lines, fills, and colors.

2. In the Toolbar, select the brush tool.

3. Click the fill-color box (in the Toolbar or in the Brush Tool Property Inspector); from the pop-up swatch set, choose a color you haven't used in creating the fills and lines on the Stage.
   Testing the brush modes in a new color makes it easy to see what's happening.

4. From the Brush Mode menu, choose Paint Fills (**Figure 4.26**).

5. Start painting; paint over blank areas of the Stage as well as over the items you created.
   When you release the mouse button, Flash creates the new fill without affecting any lines you may have overlapped. (**Figure 4.27**).

To leave existing lines and fills intact when painting:

1. With a variety of lines and fills already on the Stage, select the brush tool in the Toolbar.

2. From the Brush Mode menu, choose Paint Behind.

3. Start painting; paint over blank areas of the Stage as well as over the elements you created.

   When you release the mouse button, Flash creates the new fill only in blank areas of the Stage (**Figure 4.28**).

✔ Tip

- The term *Paint Behind* is a bit misleading. You do not actually create fills that lie behind other fills. Rather, Flash allows existing lines and fills to repel, or cut away, any overlapping portions of the new fill you're creating. When you release the mouse button after painting a new fill, that fill appears to sink down behind the other fills on the Stage. When you use this mode, be sure to remember that any existing lines and fills will segment the new fill you create.

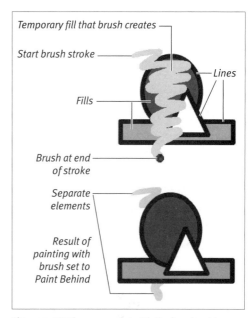

Figure 4.28 When you paint with the brush set to Paint Behind, Flash lets you paint over lines and fills without affecting them. Existing lines and fills pop to the front of the image when you release the mouse button.

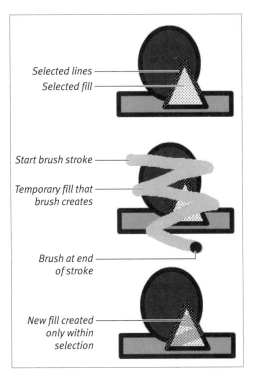

Selected lines
Selected fill

Start brush stroke

Temporary fill that
brush creates

Brush at end
of stroke

New fill created
only within
selection

Figure 4.29 When you paint with the brush set to Paint Selection, Flash ignores any brushstrokes you make outside the selection. In this mode, you cannot affect lines, and any unselected fills you accidentally paint over reappear when you release the mouse button.

To restrict paint to selected fills:

1. With a variety of lines and fills already on the Stage, select one or more of the fills but leave some fills unselected.

2. In the Toolbar, select the brush.

3. From the Brush Mode menu, choose Paint Selection.

4. Start painting; paint over blank areas of the Stage as well as over the elements you've created.

   When you release the mouse button, Flash creates the new fill only in areas of the Stage you had highlighted as a selection. Your new brushstroke has no effect on selected lines or on lines and fills that lie outside the selection (**Figure 4.29**).

How Can You Tell What You're Painting or Erasing?

Flash cannot accurately preview the fills you create in complex paint and erase modes the way it can in Normal mode. In complex painting modes, as you hold down the mouse button and paint with the brush tool, Flash displays a temporary fill that lies on top of every object it overlaps on the Stage and obscures any fills and lines that lie beneath it. When you release the mouse button, Flash calculates and redraws the new fill according to the paint mode you've selected in the Toolbar. Similarly, with the eraser tool, Flash temporarily obliterates everything the eraser touches while the mouse button is held. When you release the mouse button, Flash redraws the erasure according to the Erase mode selected in the Toolbar.

USING THE COMPLEX PAINT MODES WITH THE BRUSH

To restrict paint to one area:

1. With a variety of lines and fills already on the Stage, in the Toolbar, select the brush tool.

2. From the Brush Mode menu, choose Paint Inside.

3. Start painting from within one shape, extending your brush strokes to paint outside the shape where you began.

   When you release the mouse button, Flash creates the fill only inside the shape where you first clicked with the brush to begin painting (**Figure 4.30**).

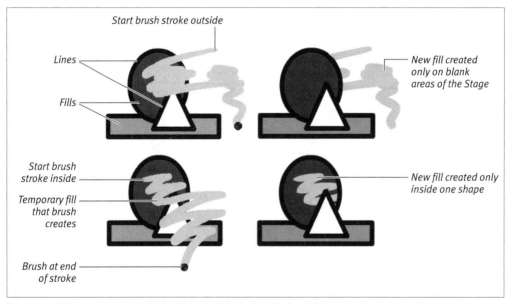

Figure 4.30 When you paint with the brush set to Paint Inside, Flash confines the creation of new brush strokes to the area where you started painting. Painting over lines has no effect, and if your brush slips outside the area in which you started, Flash simply ignores it.

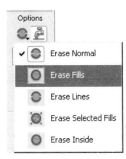

Figure 4.31 Choose an option from the Eraser Mode pop-up menu to determine how the eraser interacts with lines and fills.

Using the Eraser Tool with Multiple Shapes

Just as the brush has complex modes for interacting with live fills and lines, the eraser tool offers complex interaction modes. (For a review of the eraser's normal mode, see Chapter 3.)

Flash's eraser has four special modes that let you select what to erase; in each mode, the eraser interacts differently with lines and fills. In Erase Fills mode, the tool ignores any lines you drag over. In Erase Lines mode, the reverse occurs: The tool ignores fills and removes only lines. Erase Selected Fills mode ignores lines but also ignores any areas of fill you haven't selected. Erase Inside restricts you to erasing within a single fill: the one where you started erasing.

To restrict what the eraser removes:

1. Create several shapes on the Stage, using both lines and fills and a variety of colors.

2. In the Toolbar, select the eraser.

3. From the Eraser Shape pop-up menu, choose a shape for your eraser.

4. From the Eraser Mode pop-up menu (**Figure 4.31**), *choose one of the following modes:*
   ▲ Erase Fills
   ▲ Erase Lines
   ▲ Erase Selected Fills
   ▲ Erase Inside

5. Click and drag over the objects on the Stage.
   A preview erasure obliterates everything as you drag.

continues on next page

6. Release the mouse button.

Flash erases fills and strokes according to the mode you selected (**Figure 4.32**).

Erase Fills: Flash removes only the erased fills. Any lines that you dragged over and "erased" reappear.

Erase Lines: Flash removes only the erased lines. Any fills you "erased" pop back up.

Erase Selected Fills: Flash removes fills only from areas you highlighted as a selection. The eraser has no effect on selected lines or on lines and fills that lie outside the selection.

Erase Inside: Flash erases only inside the shape where you first clicked with the tool to begin erasing.

✔ Tip

■ Although the eraser set to Erase Selected Fills is not supposed to affect strokes, it does occasionally leave a gap in strokes with a stroke-height setting greater than 1 pixel. If this happens to you, undo your erasure and try it again. Try not to touch the exact same spot in the stroke that left a gap before.

Original Shapes

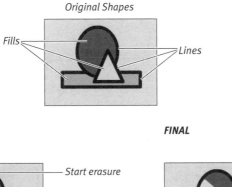

Fills ⟍ ⟍ ⟍ ⟋ *Lines*

PREVIEW   **FINAL**

Erase Fills

— Start erasure

— Temporary erasure

— End erasure

Erase Lines

— Start erasure

— Temporary erasure

— End erasure

Erase Selected Fills

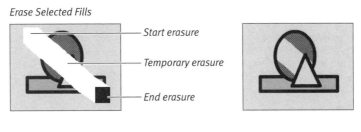

— Start erasure

— Temporary erasure

— End erasure

Erase Inside

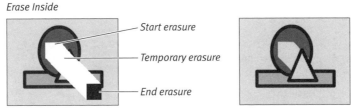

— Start erasure

— Temporary erasure

— End erasure

Figure 4.32 The Eraser tool's Erase modes restrict the way the eraser interacts with lines and fills on the Stage. The preview of your erasure looks like it removes everything you drag over—even restricted areas. The "erased" lines and fills reappear when you release the mouse button. Here the document's background color is set to light gray to make the eraser preview easier to see.

Applying Gradients to Multipart Shapes

As the characters and elements in your animations get more complex, you may wind up creating graphics made up of numerous parts. When applying gradients to multipart graphics, you have the choice of filling each part with its own separate gradient (as you learned to do in Chapter 3) or selecting several parts and applying one gradient to all of them.

To apply one gradient separately to multiple fills:

1. On the Stage, create a graphic made of several fills.

2. Select the fills to which you want to apply the same gradient.

3. To choose a gradient fill, *do one of the following:*

   ▲ Click any fill-color box (in the Toolbar, the Property Inspector, or the Color Mixer panel), and from the pop-up swatch set, select a gradient.

   ▲ In the Color Swatches panel, select a gradient.

   Flash applies the fill to each selected shape separately (**Figure 4.33**). The full range of the gradient appears within each shape.

✔ Tip

■ You can also use the paint-bucket tool to apply separate gradients to *unselected* shapes. Make sure that the Lock Fill modifier is deselected, choose the gradient you want, and then click the shapes to which you want to apply the gradient fills.

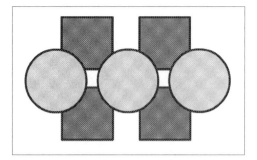

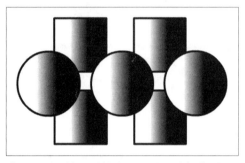

Figure 4.33 With several shapes selected (top), when you choose a gradient from a fill-color box or from the Color Swatches panel, Flash applies the gradient to each shape separately (bottom). The full range of the gradient fits within each shape.

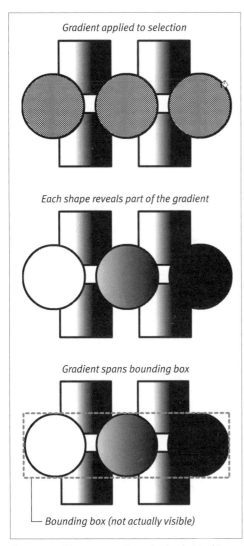

Gradient applied to selection

Each shape reveals part of the gradient

Gradient spans bounding box

Bounding box (not actually visible)

Figure 4.34 When you use the paint-bucket tool to apply a gradient to multiple selected shapes, none of the selected objects contains the entire color range of the gradient. Each object opens a window onto part of the gradient within a behind-the-scenes bounding box that contains a single gradient.

To spread one gradient across multiple fills:

1. On the Stage, create an object made of several fills.

2. On the Stage, select the fills to which you want to apply the gradient.

3. In the Toolbar, select the paint bucket.

4. Deselect the Lock Fill modifier.

5. Choose a gradient fill.

   Flash applies the gradient to each shape separately.

6. On the Stage, use the paint bucket to click any of the selected fills.

   Flash spreads a single gradient across all the selected fills (**Figure 4.34**).

✔ Tip

■ You can also spread a single gradient across unselected fills using the paint-bucket tool. In the Toolbar, select the paint bucket's Lock Fill modifier. Click each unselected fill on the Stage. Flash spreads the gradient across the entire Stage). Each shape you click reveals the portion of the gradient that corresponds to that location in the frame.

Graphics on Multiple Layers

In Flash MX 2004, you create an illusion of three-dimensional depth by overlapping objects. As you learned in Chapter 4, you can create this overlapping effect on one layer by stacking groups and symbols. The more elements the layer contains, however, the more difficult it becomes to manipulate and keep track of their stacking order. Layers help you to bring that task under control.

You could think of a Flash Document as being a stack of film: a sheaf of long, clear acetate strips divided into frames. Each filmstrip is analogous to a Flash layer. Shapes painted on the top filmstrip obscure shapes on lower strips; where the top filmstrip is blank, elements from lower strips show through.

When you place items on separate layers, it's easy to control and rearrange the way the items stack up. You can make shapes appear to be closer to the viewer by putting them in a higher layer. Additionally, raw shapes on different layers do not interact, so you don't need to worry about grouping the items or having one shape inadvertently delete another. You can also see and label each layer in the Timeline.

Touring the Timeline's Layer Features

Flash graphically represents each layer as one horizontal section of the Timeline and provides several controls for viewing and manipulating these graphic representations. Flash offers several features that make it easier to work with graphics on layers, such as viewing the items on layers as outlines and assigning different colors to those outlines so you can easily see which items are on which layers. You can lock layers so you don't edit their contents accidentally, and you can hide layers to make it easier to work with individual graphics in a welter of other graphics. You can create special guide layers for help in positioning elements, masks for hiding and revealing layers selectively, and guides for animating motion along a path. (You learn more about motion paths in Chapter 8.)

Flash also lets you create layer folders for organizing the layers in a movie. Complex movies contain dozens of layers. Viewing and navigating such hefty Timelines can get tedious and confusing. Layer folders keep the Timeline organized. You might want to keep all the layers related to one character or element together in one folder, for example. Flash considers a folder to be another type of layer, and the methods for adding and deleting layer folders are similar to those for adding and deleting layers. Layer folders do not by themselves hold graphic content, however, and folders have no keyframes in the Timeline.

Figure 5.1 offers a road map to the salient layer features in the Timeline.

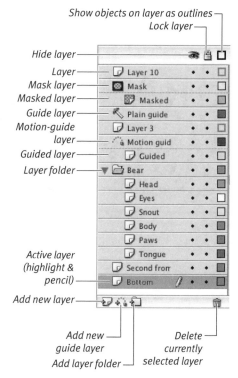

Figure 5.1 The Timeline provides a graphic representation of all the layers in a Flash movie. Layer folders let you organize layers in a complex movie. You can do much of the work of creating and manipulating layers and folders by clicking buttons in the Timeline.

Figure 5.2 Choose Insert > Timeline > Layer to add a new layer to the Timeline.

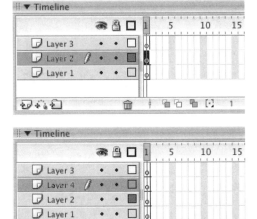

Figure 5.3 Select the layer that you want to wind up beneath the new layer (top); Flash inserts a new layer directly above the selected layer and gives the new layer a default name (bottom).

Creating and Deleting Layers and Folders

You can add new layers and layer folders as you need them while creating the ingredients of a particular scene in your movie.

To add a layers and folders:

1. In the Timeline, select a layer or folder layer.

   Flash always adds the new layer or folder directly above the one you selected, so be sure to choose the layer or folder that you want to wind up directly beneath the new one. If you want to add a layer or folder beneath the current bottom layer, create the layer first, then click and drag it to reposition it at the bottom of the stack.

2. To add a layer, *do one of the following:*

   ▲ From the Insert menu, choose Timeline > Layer. (**Figure 5.2**).

   ▲ In the Timeline, click the Insert Layer button.

   Flash adds a new layer and gives it a default name—for example, *Layer 4* (**Figure 5.3**).

   continues on next page

3. To add a folder, *do one of the following*:

▲ From the Insert menu, choose Timeline > Layer Folder.

▲ In the Timeline, click the Insert Layer Folder button.

Flash adds a new layer folder and gives it a default name—for example, *Folder 1* or *Folder 2* (**Figure 5.4**).

Flash bases the number in the default names on the number of layers or folders already created in the active scene of the document, not on the number of layers and folders that currently exist. Unlike the previous version of Flash, MX 2004 tracks layer and folder number separately; the first folder you insert among numerous layers gets the name *Folder 1*.

To delete a layer or folder:

1. In the Timeline, select the layer or folder you want to delete.

2. Click the Trash icon (**Figure 5.5**).

Flash removes that layer (and all its frames) or that folder (and all the layers it contains) from the Timeline.

✔ Tip

■ The contextual menu for layers offers some choices that otherwise are available only via buttons in the Timeline—for example, the Delete Layer and Delete Folder commands (**Figure 5.6**). To access this menu, Control-click a layer on the Mac or right-click it in Windows.

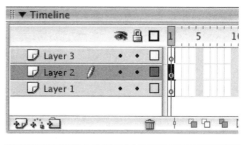

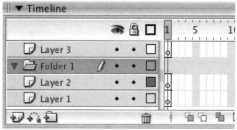

Figure 5.4 Select the layer that should be below the new folder (top). Flash creates a new folder above the layer you selected (bottom). Flash names new folders based on the number of folders that have been created in the current scene of the movie.

Delete layer or folder

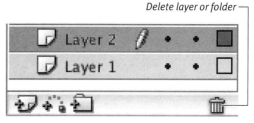

Figure 5.5 Click the Trash icon to delete a selected layer or folder.

Figure 5.6 The contextual menu for layers gives you easy access to layer commands, including some that you can otherwise access only via buttons—for example, Delete Layer. To access the contextual menu for layers, Control-click (Mac) or right-click (Windows) the icon of the layer you want to work with.

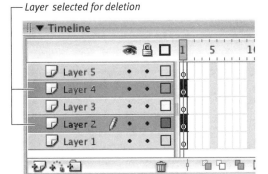

Layer selected for deletion

After deletion

Figure 5.7 To delete noncontiguous layers, ⌘-click (Mac) or Ctrl-click (Windows) the layers you want to add to your selection; then click the Trash icon.

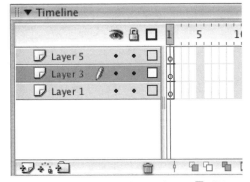

To delete multiple layers and/or folders:

1. In the Timeline, select the first layer or folder you want to remove.

2. ⌘-click (Mac) or Ctrl-click (Windows) every layer or folder you want to remove. This method of selection allows you to choose multiple layers that are not contiguous (**Figure 5.7**).

3. Click the Trash icon.

   Flash removes the selected layers (and their frames) from the Timeline.

   If your selection includes folders with content, a dialog appears, warning that deleting the layer folder will also delete all the layers it contains.

4. To delete the folder and its layers, click Yes.

   or

   To cancel the delete operation, click No.

✔ Tips

- You can also ⌘-click (Mac) or Ctrl-click (Windows) selected layers or folders to bring up the context menu, which contains commands for deleting layers and folders.

- To select a range of layers, click the lowest layer you want to delete; then Shift-click the highest layer you want to delete. Flash selects it and all the layers in between.

- You can drag selected layers to the Trash icon to delete them instead of selecting and clicking the Trash icon in two steps.

- You cannot delete all the layers in the Timeline. If you select all the layers and folders and click the Trash icon, Flash keeps the bottom layer and deletes the rest. Even if the bottom layer is nested in a folder, Flash keeps it and promotes it to regular layer status.

Controlling Layers and Folders

Layer properties are the parameters that define the look and function of a layer. Remember that layer folders are also a type of layer in Flash. You can name layers and folders. You can hide or show layers and folders, lock them to prevent any editing of their contents, and view them in outline form. Flash generally gives you two ways to control the properties of a selected layer or folder: set the property in the Layer Properties dialog or set the property via button controls located in the Timeline.

To work with the Layer Properties dialog:

1. In the Timeline, select the layer whose properties you want to define or change.

2. From the Modify menu, choose Timeline > Layer Properties.

   The Layer Properties dialog appears (**Figure 5.8**).

3. Name the layer or set other layer properties, or both, as described in the following sections.

4. Click OK.

   Flash applies all the selected settings to the current layer.

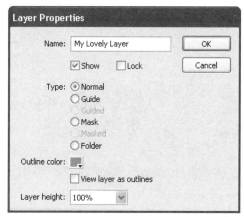

Figure 5.8 You can define a layer's type and other features in the Layer Properties dialog.

Layer Properties Dialog versus Timeline-Based Layer Controls

If you just want to set layer visibility, lock layer contents, or view layer elements as outlines, it makes no difference whether you call up the Layer Properties dialog to do so or click the various layer-property controls in the Timeline. Selecting a property in the dialog offers no more permanence than setting that property in the Timeline.

The Layer Properties dialog does offer functions that lack button equivalents: creating plain guide layers, changing the height of a layer in Timeline view, choosing an outline color, and changing an existing layer from one type to another.

The Timeline offers the capability to create motion guides, whereas the Layer Properties dialog does not.

Figure 5.9 There are six types of layers in Flash. You can set four of them via the Layer Properties dialog. Guided or masked layers must be set in the Timeline or via the contextual menu for layers.

To define the layer type:

1. Select a layer, and open the Layer Properties dialog.

2. Select one of the following radio buttons (**Figure 5.9**):
   - ▲ Normal
   - ▲ Guide
   - ▲ Guided
   - ▲ Mask
   - ▲ Masked
   - ▲ Folder

For a description of layer types, see the sidebar "Layer Types Defined."

✔ Tip

- You can change a folder into a regular layer by changing its layer type to Normal, but because layer folders have no frames in the Timeline, the first frame of the resulting layer winds up without a keyframe. If you try to draw on the layer right away, you'll get an error message. To make the layer usable, you need to add a keyframe to Frame 1. (For more information on working with keyframes, see Chapter 8.)

To name a layer or folder:

◆ In the Name field of the Layer Properties dialog, type a new name for the layer or folder.

When you call up the dialog, the Name field is selected; just start typing (**Figure 5.10**).

Although Flash numbers layers and folders, renaming them is a good idea. A movie may have dozens of layers and folders, and you'll never remember that *Layer 12* contains your company's name and *Folder 4* contains the elements that make up its logo.

✔ **Tip**

■ Double-clicking the folded-page icon or folder icon in the Timeline opens the Layer Properties dialog for that layer or folder.

Name: My Lovely Layer

Figure 5.10 You can rename a layer or folder by typing a new name in the Name field of the Layer Properties dialog.

Layer Types Defined

Flash creates six types of layers:

Normal: The default layer type is normal; all the items in a normal layer appear in your final movie.

Guide: Flash creates two types of guide layers: guides and motion guides. Lines or shapes on plain guide layers serve as reference points for placing and aligning objects on the Stage. A line drawn on a motion-guide layer becomes a path that an animated object can follow (see Chapter 8). You cannot define motion-guide layers directly from the Layer Properties dialog, you must set them from the Timeline or from the contextual menu for layers. Items on guide layers do not appear in the final movie.

Guided: Guided layers contain the objects that will animate by following the path on a guide layer. You must link the guided layer to the motion-guide layer.

Mask: A mask layer hides and reveals portions of linked layers that lie directly beneath the mask layer.

Masked: Masked layers contain elements that can be hidden or revealed by a mask layer.

Folder: Folder layers allow you to organize layers hierarchically. Setting the layer properties of a folder automatically sets the properties for all the layers within that folder. Collapsing (or expanding) folders hides (or reveals) the frames for all the layers within that folder in the Timeline.

Figure 5.11 You can set a layer or folder's visibility by selecting or deselecting Show in the Layer Properties dialog.

Figure 5.12 You can make the contents of a selected layer or folder uneditable by choosing Lock in the Layer Properties dialog. Locking a layer folder automatically locks all the layers within that folder.

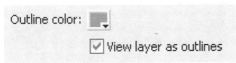

Figure 5.13 Click the View Layer As Outlines box to display the layer or folder's contents on the Stage in outline mode.

To set the visibility of layer or folder contents:

◆ In the Layer Properties dialog, check the Show check box (**Figure 5.11**).

When the check box is selected, the contents of the layer, or of all the layers contained in the folder, are visible on the Stage. When the check box is deselected, the contents of the layer or folder are hidden during authoring; the content will appear in your final published movie.

To prevent changes in contents of a layer or folder:

◆ In the Layer Properties dialog, check the Lock check box (**Figure 5.12**).

When the check box is selected, the layer or folder is locked. Although you can see the elements in that layer, or in all the layers contained in the folder, you can't select or edit those items. When the check box is deselected, the contents of the layer or folder are available for editing.

To view the contents of a layer as outlines:

1. In the Layer Properties dialog, click the View Layer As Outlines check box (**Figure 5.13**).

When the check box is checked, Flash displays the contents of the layer, or of all the layers contained in the folder, as outlines during authoring.

Using different colors for outlines on different layers makes it easier to edit graphics when you have many layers. Flash assigns default colors to each layer, but you can choose your own.

continues on next page

CONTROLLING LAYERS AND FOLDERS

2. From the Outline Color pop-up swatch set, choose a color for the outlines on the active layer (**Figure 5.14**).

Flash changes the color swatch to your selected color.

3. Click OK.

Flash displays the graphics on this layer as outlines, using the color you selected.

✔ Tips

■ When you select the View Layer As Outlines check box for a layer folder, Flash displays the contents of all the layers contained in the folder as outlines. Although you can specify an outline color for a layer folder, the color has no effect on what you see on the Stage. When you turn on outline view for the folder, each layer within the folder displays its contents in the outline color set for that layer.

■ You can tell Flash to use the layer-outline color for the bounding box that highlights selected objects. Doing so helps you keep track of the fact that selections are on different layers. Open the Preferences dialog—from the Flash menu (Mac) or Edit menu (windows), choose Preferences—then click the Use Layer Color button in the Color Highlight section of the General tab.

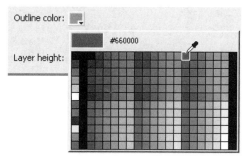

Figure 5.14 Select the color for displaying the outlines of a layer's objects from the pop-up swatch set in the Layer Properties dialog.

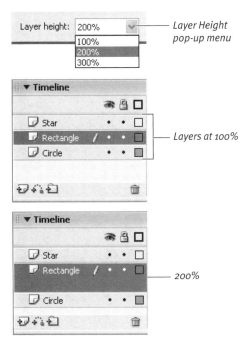

Layer Height pop-up menu

Layers at 100%

200%

Figure 5.15 Choose a larger percentage from the Layer Height pop-up menu in the Layer Properties dialog to increase the height of a selected layer.

To change the height at which layers or folders display in the Timeline:

◆ In the Layer Properties dialog, choose a percentage from the Layer Height pop-up menu (**Figure 5.15**).

Flash offers two enlarged layer views. The larger layers in the Timeline are especially useful for working with sounds. The waveform of each sound appears in the layer preview in the Timeline, and some sounds are difficult to see at the 100% setting. (You learn more about sounds in Chapter 15).

✔ Tip

■ You can change the size of the graphic representation of all the layers in the Timeline by choosing a size from the Frame View pop-up menu, located in the top-right corner of the Timeline. The Preview and Preview in Context options display thumbnails of the contents of each frame in the layers.

Setting Layer Properties via the Timeline

The Timeline represents each layer or layer folder as a horizontal field containing a name and three buttons for controlling the way the layer or folder's contents look on the Stage. You can hide a layer or folder (making all the elements on that layer or within that folder temporarily invisible), lock a layer or folder (making the contents visible but uneditable), and view the items on the layer or within the folder as outlines. These controls are helpful when you are editing numerous items on several layers.

To rename a layer or folder:

1. In the Timeline, double-click the layer or folder name.

Flash activates the name's text-entry field.

2. Type a new name.

3. Press Enter or click anywhere outside the name field.

To hide the contents of a layer or folder:

◆ In the Timeline for the layer or folder that you want to hide, click the bullet in the column below the eye icon (**Figure 5.16**).

Flash replaces the bullet with a red *X*, indicating that the contents of the layer or folder no longer appear on the Stage. The invisible setting does not affect the final movie. When you publish a movie (see Chapter 17), Flash includes all the contents of hidden layers and folders.

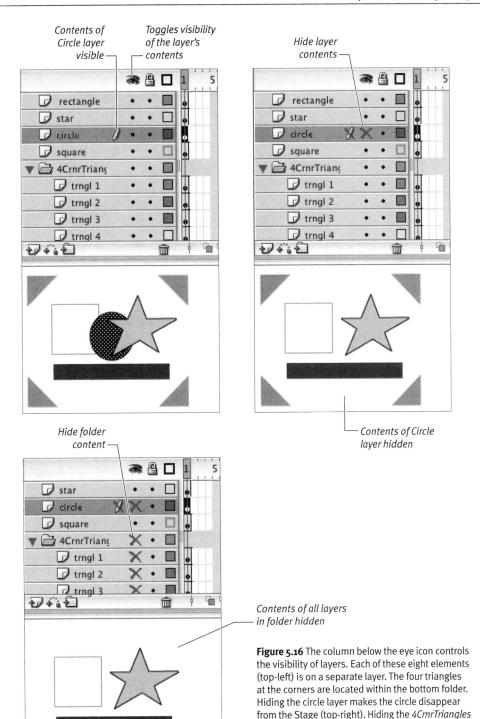

Contents of Circle layer visible — Toggles visibility of the layer's contents

Hide layer contents —

Hide folder content —

Contents of Circle layer hidden

Contents of all layers in folder hidden

Figure 5.16 The column below the eye icon controls the visibility of layers. Each of these eight elements (top-left) is on a separate layer. The four triangles at the corners are located within the bottom folder. Hiding the circle layer makes the circle disappear from the Stage (top-right). Hiding the *4CrnrTriangles* folder makes the four triangles disappear as well (bottom-left).

To show the hidden contents of a layer or folder:

◆ In the Timeline for the layer or folder that you want to show, click the red *X* in the column below the eye icon.

Flash replaces the *X* with a bullet and displays the contents of the layer or folder.

To lock a layer or folder:

◆ In the Timeline for the layer or folder that you want to lock, click the bullet in the column below the padlock icon (**Figure 5.17**).

Flash replaces the bullet with a padlock icon. The contents of the layer or folder appear on the Stage, but you can't edit them. Locking a layer or folder does not affect the final movie.

To unlock a layer or folder:

◆ In the Timeline for the layer or folder that you want to unlock, click the padlock icon.

Flash replaces the padlock with a bullet and makes the contents of the layer or folder editable.

To view the contents of a layer or folder as outlines:

◆ In the Timeline for the layer or folder that you want to view as outlines, click the solid square in the column below the square icon (**Figure 5.18**).

Flash replaces the solid square with a hollow square, indicating that the layer or folder is in outline mode. The contents of a layer appear on the Stage as outlines in the color that the square indicates. The elements on each layer within a folder appear in the outline color associated with their own layer, not in the outline color of the folder. Placing a layer or folder in outline mode does not affect the final movie.

SETTING LAYER PROPERTIES VIA THE TIMELINE

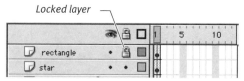

Locked layer

Figure 5.17 The padlock icon indicates that a layer is locked. The contents of a locked layer appear on the Stage, but you can't edit them.

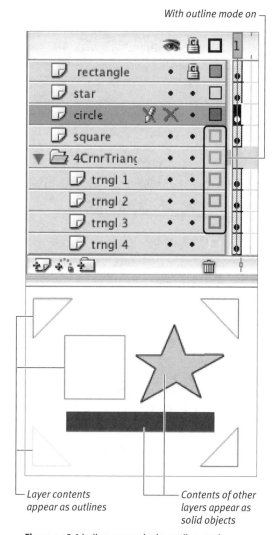

With outline mode on

Layer contents appear as outlines

Contents of other layers appear as solid objects

Figure 5.18 A hollow square in the outline-mode column indicates that objects on that layer appear as outlines. Setting a folder to outline mode automatically changes all the layers within it to outline mode.

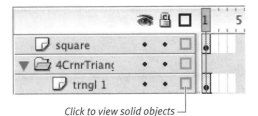

Click to view solid objects

Figure 5.19 Clicking the hollow square in the outline-mode column returns you to viewing the contents of that layer or folder as solid objects.

To view the contents of a layer or folder as solid objects:

◆ In the Timeline for the layer or folder whose contents you want to view as solid, click the hollow square (**Figure 5.19**).

Flash replaces the hollow square with a solid square, indicating that the layer or folder is no longer in outline mode. The contents of the layer or folder appear on the Stage as solid objects.

Working with Layer-View Columns

Flash provides several shortcuts for working with the three layer-view columns in the Timeline. The following tips describe hiding and showing layer or folder content; the controls in the Timeline for locking and unlocking layer contents and for viewing layer contents as outlines work the same way.

◆ To hide the contents of several layers or folders quickly, click the bullet in the column below the eye icon and drag through all the layers or folders you want to hide. As the pointer passes over each bullet, Flash changes it to a red *X*.

◆ To show numerous layers or folders quickly, click a red *X* in the eye column and drag through all the layers or folders whose contents you want to show.

◆ To hide the contents of all layers or folders but one, Option-click (Mac) or Alt-click (Windows) the bullet in the eye column of the layer or folder you want to see. Flash puts an *X* in that column for all the other layers or folders.

◆ To hide the contents of all the layers and folders, ⌘-click (Mac) or Ctrl-click (Windows) the eye column of any layer or folder, or click the eye icon in the column header. Flash puts an *X* in that column for all the layers. To show the contents of all the layers and folders, simply ⌘-click or Ctrl-click an *X* or click the eye icon again.

Controlling Layer Visibility in the Timeline

In addition to controlling the visibility and editability of the contents of a layer or folder, when you organize layers in folders, you gain control of which layers appear in the Timeline. When you close a folder, layers within it disappear from the Timeline; making it much easier to view and navigate. Closing the layer folder has no effect on the contents of each layer within it, however. All the elements on those layers continue to display on the Stage in whatever mode you chose for them before closing the folder.

When you create new layer folders, they are open by default.

To close layer folders in the Timeline:

◆ In the Timeline, click the triangle to the left of the open folder icon (**Figure 5.20**).

The triangle rotates to the closed position, and the icon changes to a closed folder. Flash hides all the layers contained within the layer folder in the Timeline.

To open layer folders in the Timeline:

◆ In the Timeline, click the triangle to the left of the closed folder icon.

The triangle rotates to the open position, and the icon changes to an open folder. Flash displays all the layers contained within the layer folder.

✔ Tip

■ You can open or close all the folders in a movie at the same time via the contextual menu. Access the menu by Control-clicking (Mac) or right-clicking (Windows) any Timeline layer. Then choose Expand All Folders or Collapse All Folders (**Figure 5.21**).

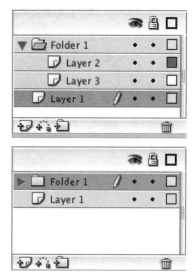

Figure 5.20 Clicking the triangle to the left of the folder icon toggles between open (top) and closed (bottom) folder views.

Figure 5.21 To open all folders at the same time, Control-click (Mac) or right-click (Windows) any layer to access the contextual menu for layers. Then choose Expand All Folders.

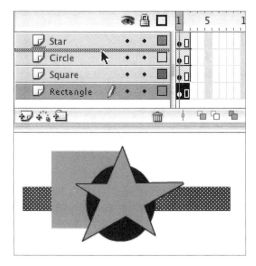

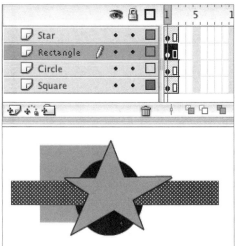

Figure 5.22 The gray line (top) represents the new location for the *Rectangle* layer you are dragging. Release the mouse button to drop the layer into its new position. Flash selects the layer and its contents (bottom).

Controlling the Stacking Order of Layers

As you add more layers to your document, you may need to rearrange them so that the objects that should appear in the foreground actually cover objects that appear in the background.

Layers make it easy to change the stacking order of numerous elements at the same time. You can, for example, bring all the elements on one layer to the top of the stack simply by dragging that layer to the top of the list in the Timeline. Doing so brings those elements to the front of the Stage (overlapping any items on other layers) in every frame of the movie.

To reorder layers:

1. Create a document with several layers.

2. In the Timeline, position the mouse pointer over the layer you want to move.

3. Click and drag the layer.

   Flash previews the layer's new location with a thick gray line.

4. Position the preview line in the layer order you want (**Figure 5.22**).

5. Release the mouse button.

   Flash moves the layer to the new location and selects it in the Timeline.

Organizing Layers in Folders

After you have created folders, you can drag existing layers into the folders to organize the Timeline. Repositioning a folder in the Timeline changes the stacking order of all the layers within that folder.

To move existing layers into folders:

1. In a document with several layers and folders, in the Timeline, position the mouse pointer over the layer you want to place in a folder.

2. Click and drag the layer over the folder where you want to place it.

   As you drag, Flash previews the layer's new location with a thick gray line; when you position the mouse directly over a folder, the preview line disappears and the folder highlights, turning gray (**Figure 5.23**).

3. Release the mouse button.

   Flash moves the layer into the folder, indents the layer name in the Timeline, selects the layer in the Timeline, and selects the layer's contents on the Stage.

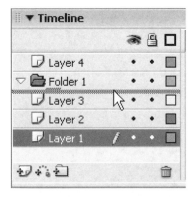

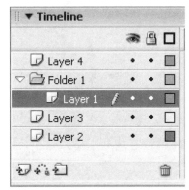

Figure 5.23 When you drag a layer over a folder layer, the folder icon turns gray (top). Release the mouse button to drop the layer into that folder. Flash selects the layer and its contents (bottom).

Drag right to position inside folder —

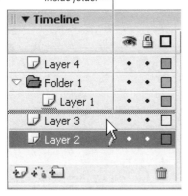

Drag left to position — outside folder

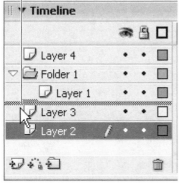

Figure 5.24 When you position layers at the bottom of a folder, you need to let Flash know whether you want the layers to wind up inside or outside the folder. The bump on top of the preview bar for the layer indicates where the layer will go.

✔ Tips

■ After you've added layers to a folder, you no longer need to drag new layers directly on top of the folder layer. Positioning a layer's preview line beneath any of the layers in a folder (the indented ones) places the layer you are repositioning in that folder, in the highlighted location.

■ Dragging a layer to a closed folder positions the layer at the top of the stack inside the folder.

■ Positioning layers beneath an open folder containing layers is a bit tricky. When you position a layer's preview line after the last layer in the folder, Flash defaults to adding the layer to the folder. You can close the folder to prevent putting the layer inside the folder. Or, with the folder open, watch the layer's preview line carefully as you drag. With the layer in position beneath the last layer in the folder, drag slightly to the left. The gray bump on the top of the preview bar moves over to the left (**Figure 5.24**). Release the mouse button, and the layer winds up outside the folder.

■ If you drag a layer whose contents are visible into a folder that's set to hide elements (a red *X* appears above the folder's eye column), the contents of the newly included layer remain visible (a bullet appears in that layer's eye column).

ORGANIZING LAYERS IN FOLDERS

To change folder order:

1. In a document with layers and folders, in the Timeline, click and drag a folder you want to move.

   Flash previews the folder's new location with a thick gray line.

2. Position the preview line where you want the folder to reside in the Timeline (**Figure 5.25**).

3. Release the mouse button.

   Flash moves the folder to the new location and selects the folder layer in the Timeline. The contents of the layers in the folder are not selected on the Stage.

To create a nested folder:

◆ Using the steps in the preceding exercise, drag one existing folder into another.

   or

   In the Timeline, select a layer within a folder and, *do one of the following:*

   ▲ Choose Insert > Timeline > Layer Folder.

   ▲ In the Timeline, click the Insert Layer Folder button.

   Flash adds a new indented layer folder.

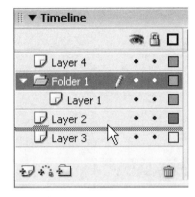

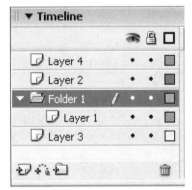

Figure 5.25 You reposition folder layers the same way you reposition other layers. Drag the folder, preview the location (top), and release the mouse button to place the folder (bottom).

Active layer

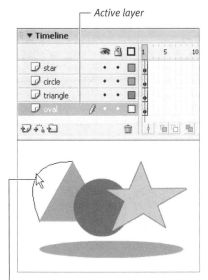

Use selection tool to modify shape on inactive layer

No change in active layer

Flash redraws shape

Figure 5.26 Selecting the oval makes the *Oval* layer the active layer. You can still edit objects on inactive layers by reshaping their outlines with the selection tool.

Working with Graphics on Different Layers

Unless you lock shapes, or lock or hide layers, the graphics on all layers are available for editing.

To edit shape outlines on inactive layers:

1. Create a document that has four layers.

2. Place a different shape on each layer.

   For this example, place a triangle on *Layer 1*, a circle on *Layer 2*, an oval on *Layer 3*, and a star on *Layer 4*.

3. In the Toolbar, select the selection tool.

4. On the Stage, click the oval.

   Flash selects the oval and makes its layer active (the pencil icon appears to the right of the layer name in the Timeline).

5. Click a blank area of the Stage.

   Flash deselects the oval but keeps its layer active.

6. On the Stage, position the pointer over the outline of the triangle.

   The curve or corner-point icon appears.

7. Drag the triangle's outline to reshape it.

8. Release the mouse button.

   Flash redraws the shape (**Figure 5.26**). Oval is still the active layer. Flash switches active layers only if you select a shape.

To edit fills across layers:

1. Continuing with the document that you created for the preceding task, make sure that the current layer is still the oval layer.

2. In the Toolbar, select the paint-bucket tool.

3. Click the fill-color box (in the Toolbar, Color Mixer panel, or Property Inspector), and choose a color you haven't used for any of the shapes on the Stage.

4. Position the paint bucket over the star shape, and click.

   Flash fills the star with the new color (**Figure 5.27**), but the *Oval* layer remains the active layer.

✔ Tip

■ To be safe, get into the habit of putting each graphic you create on a separate layer. That way, if you need to tweak the stacking order, you can. Having more layers doesn't increase the file size of your final movie significantly.

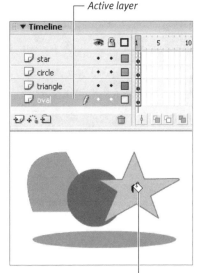

Active layer

Use paint bucket to modify fill on inactive layer

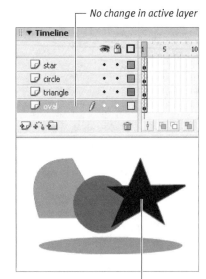

No change in active layer

Flash fills shape with new color

Figure 5.27 Use the paint-bucket tool to change a fill color on an inactive layer.

Active layer

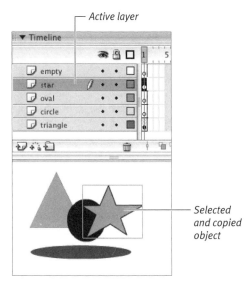

Selected
and copied
object

Select new active layer

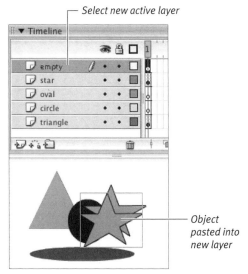

Object
pasted into
new layer

Figure 5.28 Copying a shape from one layer to another involves selecting the shape (top), copying it, selecting the target layer, and then pasting the copy there. The Paste in Center command (middle) positions the pasted shape in the center of the window (bottom).

Cutting and Pasting Between Layers

Flash allows you to create and place graphics only on the active layer of a document. But you can copy, cut, or delete elements from any visible, unlocked layer. You can select items on several layers, cut them, and then paste them all into a single layer. Or you can cut items individually from one layer and redistribute them to separate layers.

To paste across layers:

1. Create a document that contains several layers.

2. Place at least one element on all but one layer.

   Make a document with five layers, for example. Put a triangle on one layer, an oval on another, a circle on a third, a star on a fourth, and leave the fifth layer empty. To make the items easier to work with, group each one.

3. Name each layer according to its contents.

   Adding the names *Star, Circle, Triangle,* and so on makes it easier to remember which layer contains which items. It also makes it easier for you to see what's going on as you practice moving items across layers in this exercise.

4. On the Stage, select the star.

   Notice that Flash highlights the *star's* layer in the Timeline.

5. From the Edit menu, choose Copy.

6. In the Timeline, select the *empty* layer.

7. From the Edit menu, choose Paste in Center.

   Flash pastes the copy of the star in the *empty* layer, in the middle of the window (**Figure 5.28**). Now you can move the star to a new position, if you want.

To use the Paste in Place command across layers:

1. Using the document that you created in the preceding exercise, select the triangle.

2. Using the techniques that you learned in Chapter 3, add the oval and the circle to your selection.

3. From the Edit menu, choose Cut.

   Flash removes the three selected shapes (**Figure 5.29**).

4. In the Timeline, select the *empty* layer.

5. From the Edit menu, choose Paste in Place (**Figure 5.30**).

   Flash pastes all three shapes back into their original locations on the Stage but on a different layer (**Figure 5.31**). Try hiding the *empty* layer temporarily; you should no longer see those three objects.

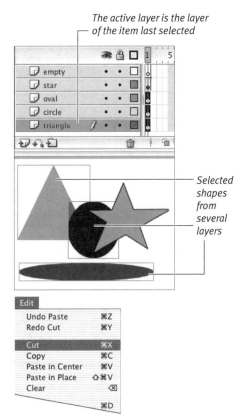

The active layer is the layer of the item last selected

Selected shapes from several layers

After cutting the objects

Where Do Pasted Objects Go?

A Flash document can have only one layer active at a time. Any new shapes you create wind up on the currently selected, or active, layer. The same is true of placing copies of shapes or instances of symbols; if you copy and paste an element, Flash pastes the copy on the active layer. When you drag a symbol instance from the Library window, it winds up on the active layer.

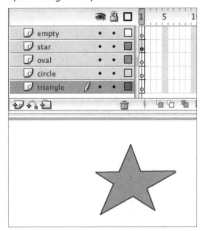

Figure 5.29 The first step in consolidating items from several layers on a single new layer involves selecting all the items and cutting them. Later, you'll paste them into the new active layer.

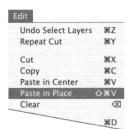

Figure 5.30 Choose Edit > Paste in Place to paste items back into their original positions, but on a new layer.

Objects after pasting in place

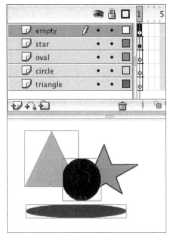

Click to hide layer

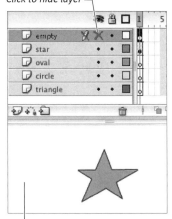

— *Layer containing the objects is now hidden*

Figure 5.31 The Paste in Place command positions the pasted items in the new layer. Each shape occupies the same coordinates it had on its former layer, but now all the shapes are together in the new layer. Hide the new layer to make sure that you did move the elements from their old layers.

✔ Tips

■ You've already learned that selecting an object on the Stage causes Flash to select that object's layer in the Timeline. As you move objects between layers, it helps to know that selections work the other way around, too. When you select a layer in the Timeline, Flash selects all the elements for that layer on the Stage.

■ The process of cutting elements and using the Paste in Place command is, obviously, time-consuming, because you have to keep selecting new layers as you place the elements. To automate the process, use the Distribute to Layers command (see "Distributing Graphic Elements to Layers," later in this chapter).

Two Ways to Paste

Flash offers two pasting modes: Paste in Center and Paste in Place. Paste in Center puts elements in the center of the open Flash window. (Note that the center of the window may not necessarily be the center of the Stage; if you want to paste to the center of the Stage, you must center the Stage in the open window.) Paste in Place puts an element at the same x and y coordinates it had when you cut or copied it. Paste in Place is useful for preserving the precise relationships of all elements in a scene as you move items from one layer to another.

Distributing Graphic Elements to Layers

As you draw elements for your movie, you may not always remember to create a new layer for each one. Using the Cut and Paste in Place commands can get tedious. Flash's Distribute to Layers feature automates the process, putting each element of a selection on a separate layer. This feature comes in handy when you start creating a type of animation called *motion tweening,* in which each element being animated must be on its own layer. (You'll learn more about motion tweening in Chapter 8.)

To place selected elements on individual layers:

1. Open a new file, and on the Stage, create several separate shapes on a single layer.

2. Choose Edit > Select All.

   Flash highlights all the shapes.

3. From the Modify menu, choose Timeline > Distribute to Layers, or press Shift-⌘-D (Mac) or Ctrl-Shift-D (Windows) (**Figure 5.32**).

   Flash creates a layer for each shape and adds the new layers to the bottom of the Timeline. Each shape winds up in the same location on the Stage, but on a separate layer.

✔ Tips

■ Distribute to Layers works with selected groups and symbols as well as with selected raw shapes. (You learn about symbols in Chapter 6.) Flash distributes each selected group or symbol to its own layer; the various elements of the group or symbol remain joined.

■ When you use Distribute to Layers, any unselected elements remain on their original layer. Only the selected shapes move to new layers.

Layers set to preview in context

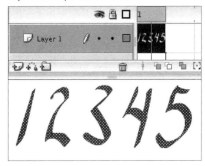

After Distribute to Layers

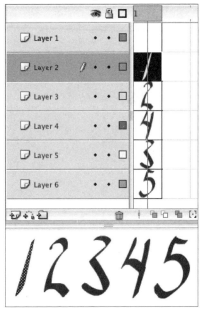

Figure 5.32 Selecting elements on the Stage and choosing Modify > Timeline > Distribute to Layers automatically cuts each element and pastes it in place in a new layer. The new layers follow the order in which you placed the elements on the Stage originally. In this series of numbers, the numeral 1 was drawn first, so it winds up at the top of the section of new layers.

Figure 5.33
Select Guide as the layer type in the Layer Properties dialog to change a normal layer to a guide layer.

— Layer to define as guide
— Motion-guide layer

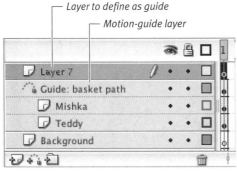

— Guide layer
— Motion-guide layer

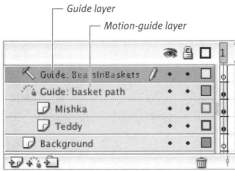

Figure 5.34 Select a layer (top) and define it as a guide layer. In the Timeline, Flash identifies the guide layer with a T-square icon; compare that with the icon for the motion-guide layer (bottom).

Working with Guide Layers

Flash offers two types of guide layers: guides and motion guides. Plain old guides can contain any kind of content: lines, shapes, or symbols. The contents of a regular guide layer merely serve as a point of reference to help you position items on the Stage. Flash doesn't include such guide layers in the final exported movie.

Motion guides, however, do make up part of the final movie. Motion-guide layers contain a single line that directs the movement of an animated object along a path. (To learn more about creating and animating with motion guides, see Chapter 8.) Another distinction to remember is that Flash creates motion guides by adding a new layer directly to the Timeline. To create plain guides, you must redefine an existing layer as a guide layer.

To create a plain guide layer:

1. *Do one of the following:*

    ▲ Create a new layer in the Timeline (for example, by clicking the Insert Layer button). Flash selects the new layer.

    ▲ Select a layer that already exists.

2. From the Modify menu, choose Timeline > Layer Properties to display the Layer Properties dialog.

3. In the Type section, click Guide (**Figure 5.33**).

    You can rename the layer to identify it as a guide, if you want.

4. Click OK.

    Flash turns the selected layer into a guide layer and places a little T-square icon before the layer name (**Figure 5.34**).

continues on next page

5. To make guide objects easier to use, *do any of the following:*

▲ From the View menu, choose Snapping > Snap to Objects (**Figure 5.35**).

Flash forces items that you draw or drag to snap to lines or shapes.

▲ From the View menu, choose Snapping > Snap Align. (This setting is on by default.)

Flash displays alignment guides as you drag objects near to other objects. Now you can more easily align items to the elements on your guide layers.

✔ Tips

■ You can create a guide layer quickly by Control-clicking (Mac) or right-clicking (Windows) the layer you want to define as a guide. Choose Guide from the pop-up contextual menu that appears.

■ When you've placed guide elements where you need them for a certain scene, lock the guide layer so that you don't move the guides accidentally as you draw on other layers.

■ The Snap to Guide feature sounds like it might help you snap to items on a guide layer, but it doesn't. The guides in this mode are the guide lines you drag out from rulers (see Chapter 1).

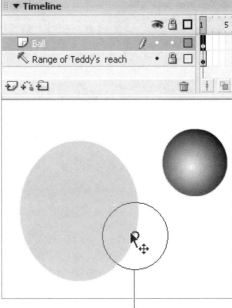

Center point snaps to an item on the guide layer as you drag

Figure 5.35 Choose View > Guides > Snap to Objects (top) to force items that you draw on other layers to snap to the lines or shapes on a guide layer (bottom).

WORKING WITH GUIDE LAYERS

Figure 5.36 Select Mask as the layer type in the Layer Properties dialog to define a layer as a mask.

Figure 5.37 The mask-layer icon imitates the masking effect with a dark mask shape over a checkerboard pattern.

Working with Mask Layers

Mask layers are special layers that allow you to hide and show elements on underlying layers. In the final movie, shapes on the Mask layer become holes that allow items on linked layers to show through.

To create a mask layer:

1. *Do one of the following:*

   ▲ Create a new layer in the Timeline (for example, by clicking the Insert Layer button). Flash selects the new layer.

   ▲ Select a layer that already exists.

   In general, you should create (or select) a layer directly above the layer containing content you want to mask, although you can always create the mask separately and link the masked layers to it later.

2. From the Modify menu, choose Timeline > Layer Properties to display the Layer Properties dialog.

3. In the Type section, click Mask (**Figure 5.36**).

   You can also rename the layer to identify it as a mask, if you want.

4. Click OK.

   Flash turns the selected layer into a mask layer and places a mask icon before the layer name (**Figure 5.37**).

To link layers to the mask:

1. In the Timeline, select the layer directly below the mask layer.

2. From the Modify menu, choose Timeline > Layer Properties to display the Layer Properties dialog.

3. In the Type section, click Masked.

You can rename the layer to identify it as a masked layer, if you want. If you accidentally select a layer that's not located directly below the mask layer, the Masked button will be disabled.

4. Click OK.

Flash links the selected layer to the mask layer directly above it and places a masked icon before the name (**Figure 5.38**). Flash indents the icon and layer name to indicate that the mask above this layer controls it.

5. Repeat steps 1 through 4 to create more linked layers.

One mask can affect many linked layers.

✔ Tips

■ To link existing layers to a mask layer quickly, simply drag them in the Timeline so that they sit directly below the mask itself or one of its linked layers.

■ Once you have linked a layer to the mask, you can create additional new linked layers for that mask quickly. Select the linked (masked) layer; then follow the steps for creating a new layer. Flash adds the new layers as masked layers directly above the selected layer.

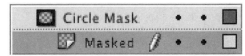

Figure 5.38 Set the Masked layer type in the Layer Properties dialog (top). The checkerboard pattern on the layer icon in the Timeline indicates that the layer is masked (bottom).

■ Positioning a layer beneath a list of masked layers can be tricky. When you position a layer's preview line after the last layer in the masked set, you have the choice of adding the layer to the masked set or placing it at the main level of the Timeline. Use the preview line's subtle clues to place the layer where you want it. Position the layer directly beneath the last masked layer. To add the layer to the masked set, drag slightly to the right; the bump on the top of the preview bar moves over to the right. To add the layer to the main level of the Timeline drag slightly to the left; the bump follows suit.

To create the mask:

1. Create one or more layers containing graphic elements you want to reveal only through a mask.

2. Create a mask layer above your masked-content layers, and make sure that it's selected, visible, and unlocked.

The layer should be highlighted in the Timeline, and the eye and padlock columns should contain bullets (not *X* or padlock icons).

3. Use the paintbrush or one of the geometric shape tools to create one or more fill shapes on the mask layer (**Figure 5.39**).

continues on next page

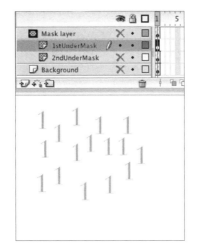

When you define this layer as a mask...

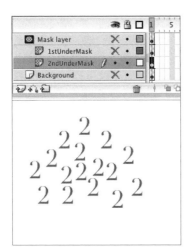

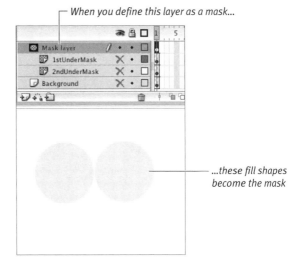

...these fill shapes become the mask

Figure 5.39 The content for the layers that the mask will reveal is just like any other content. You create the holes in the mask from filled shapes. All the mask elements must be on the same sublevel of the layer. In other words, you must either use only editable shapes or combine all your shapes into a single group or symbol.

Flash uses only fills to create the mask and ignores any lines on the mask layer. The mask may consist of several shapes on the mask layer, but they must all be on the same sublayer. (For more information on how sublayers within a layer work, see Chapter 4.)

You can use several editable shapes, or you can create one group or symbol that contains all the shapes. If you combine editable shapes and a group or symbol, Flash uses just the editable shapes to create the mask. If you have two or more groups or symbols, Flash uses just the bottom-most group or symbol. (For more details on stacking order for groups and symbols, see Chapter 4.)

✔ Tip

■ To convert a particular layer into a mask and link the layer beneath it in one step, use the contextual layer menu. Control-click (Mac) or right-click (Windows) the layer you want to be the mask. From the pop-up contextual menu, choose Mask. Flash automatically defines the layer as a mask, links the layer beneath the selected layer to the mask, and locks both layers so that masking is in effect.

Figure 5.40 The Show Masking command in the contextual menu for layers locks all layers linked to the selected mask.

To see the mask's effect:

◆ Lock the mask layer and all linked layers.

or

1. Control-click (Mac) or right-click (Windows) a mask (or masked) layer.

2. From the contextual menu, choose Show Masking (**Figure 5.40**).

 Flash automatically locks the mask layer and all the layers linked to it.

 In document-editing mode, you must lock the mask layer and any masked layers beneath it to see the mask effect (**Figure 5.41**). You can see the effect without locking the layers in one of Flash's test modes (see Chapter 11).

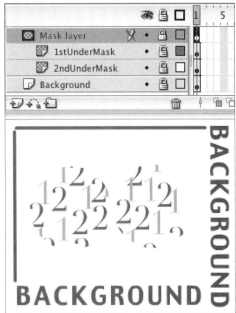

Transparent fill helps you see what mask will reveal

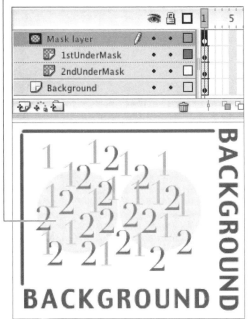

Masking not on

Masking turned on

Figure 5.41 After defining the mask and masked layers, you must lock them to see the mask in effect in document-editing mode.

WORKING WITH MASK LAYERS

To edit a mask:

1. In the Timeline, select the mask layer.

2. Make sure that the layer is visible and unlocked.

3. Use any of the techniques you learned in preceding chapters to create and edit fills.

✔ Tips

■ If you want to break the connection between a mask and its linked layers, you can simply redefine the layer type for the masked layer in the Layer Properties dialog.

■ If you delete a mask layer, Flash redefines all the layers linked to it as normal layers.

■ Keep in mind that masks use processor power. Using too many masks can slow the frame rate in your final movie.

The Mystery of Masks

A mask layer is like a window envelope (the ones you get your bills in). There may be whole sheaves of papers covered with numbers inside that envelope, but the outside presents a blank white front with just a little window that lets you see the portion of the bill showing your name and address. The mask layer is the window envelope, and the linked, or masked, layers are the papers inside.

In Flash, you create the window in the envelope by drawing and painting on a mask layer. (As you'll learn in Chapter 10, you can animate that window to create special effects.) Any filled shape on the mask layer becomes a window in the final movie. That window reveals whatever lies on the linked (or masked) layers inside the envelope. Within that envelope, you can have several layers that act just like any other Flash layers.

Here's where it gets a bit tricky. Any areas of the envelope (the mask layer) that you leave blank hide the corresponding areas of all the layers inside the envelope (the masked layers). But the same blank areas of the envelope allow all *unlinked* layers outside and below the envelope to show through.

SAVING AND REUSING GRAPHIC ELEMENTS

In the previous chapters, you learned to create and edit static graphics. Ultimately, you'll want to animate those graphics, and you're likely to want to use the same graphic over and over again. You may want an element to appear several times in one movie, or you may want to use the same element in several movies. Macromedia Flash MX 2004 provides a container for storing graphics that makes it easy to do both. This container is called a *library*.

Every Flash Document has its own library, where you can store the elements that go into a movie: text, sounds, video clips, animations, rollover buttons, bitmapped graphics, and vector graphics.

Flash's shared libraries let you share assets (including fonts) among movies. Sharing assets helps reduce the amount of material that must be downloaded to a user's system for viewing your Flash movies.

In this chapter, you learn to work with libraries and to create symbols that are static graphics. You also learn about shared libraries and font symbols. In later chapters, you learn about creating animated symbols and buttons (see Chapters 10 and 11), working with bitmapped graphics (see Chapter 14), and adding sounds and video (see Chapters 15 and 16).

Library Terminology

The general term for an item stored in a Flash library is an *asset*. More specifically, graphics created with Flash's drawing tools and stored in a library are called *symbols;* fonts stored in a library are called *font symbols;* and sounds, video clips, and bitmaps (which are always stored in a library) are just called *sounds, video clips,* and *bitmaps*. Flash refers to each copy of a library asset that you actually use in a movie as an *instance* of that asset.

Understanding the Library Window

The Library window offers several ways to view a library's contents and allows you to organize your symbols, sounds, video clips, fonts, and bitmaps in folders. The Library window provides information about when an item was last modified, what type of item it is, and how many times the movie uses it. The Library window also contains shortcut buttons and menus for working with symbols. Flash has shortcuts for creating new folders, for renaming elements, and for deleting items quickly.

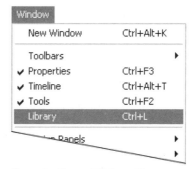

Figure 6.1 Choose Window > Library to open the library of the current Flash Document.

To open the library of the current movie:

◆ From the Window menu, choose Library, or press F11 or press ⌘-L (Mac) or Ctrl-L (Windows) (**Figure 6.1**).

The Library window appears on the desktop (**Figure 6.2**).

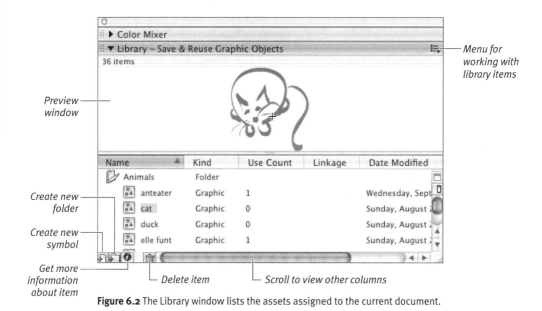

Figure 6.2 The Library window lists the assets assigned to the current document.

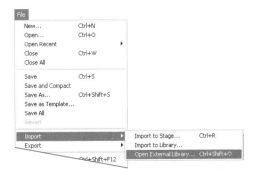

Figure 6.3 Choose File > Import > Open External Library to access symbols from the library of another file.

To open the library of another movie:

1. From the File menu, choose Import > Open External Library, or press Shift-⌘-O (Mac) or Ctrl-Shift-O (Windows) (**Figure 6.3**).

   The Open As Library dialog appears.

2. Navigate to the file whose library you want to open, select it, and click Open.

   The Library window appears on the desktop making those symbols available for use in other movies (see "Copying Symbols Between Movies" later in this chapter).

   When you open another file as a library following these steps, you cannot add to or modify the contents of that library. In Windows, Flash grays out the library background. On a Mac, the change is subtler; the names of library assets are gray, but the background remains white. In addition, in the library of an external file, the shortcut icons, and most of the Options-menu choices are disabled.

✔ Tips

- A word of warning: With multiple libraries open, it's easy to get confused about which library you are working with. When you open the library of an external file, Flash prevents you from making changes to the library assets. But if you have several documents and their libraries open simultaneously, it is possible to make changes to the library of an inactive document. The background (Windows) or asset names (Mac) appear in gray in the library of the inactive document, but some of the shortcut icons and Options menu commands still work. For example, you can delete an asset from the library of a document that is open but not currently active. If you try to add a new symbol, Flash brings the inactive document forward and makes it the current document.

continues on next page

UNDERSTANDING THE LIBRARY WINDOW

■ The variety of menus from which you can open a library of some sort can be daunting at first. Here's the short run-down. To open a library window for the current movie, use Window > Library; to open the library of another file, use File > Import > Open External Library; to open a library from your library of libraries, choose Window > Other Panels > Common Libraries (see the sidebar "What Are Common Libraries?").

■ You can use a common library to keep all the symbols, sounds, video clips, and bitmaps for a project accessible from the menu bar. As you create symbols or import sounds, video clips, and bitmaps, add a copy of each item to a special file, call it something like MyCurrentWork. Make the file one of your common libraries. When you choose MyCurrentWork from the Window > Other Panels > Common Libraries menu, Flash opens the library containing all your project's items.

What Are Common Libraries?

Flash makes a set of libraries available from the menu bar—a sort of library of libraries. Flash MX 2004 ships with three libraries, but you can add your own to the list. The Common Libraries menu makes it easy for you to access libraries of symbols, sounds, and bitmaps. The libraries in the Common Libraries menu are simply Flash files that live in the Libraries folder. (The Libraries folder is one of the folders in the Configuration folder. For details about the location of the Configuration folder, see the sidebar in Chapter 10.) Any files you add to the Libraries folder appear in the Common Libraries menu when you restart the application (**Figure 6.4**). Choosing an item from the Common Libraries menu opens only the library, not the file itself.

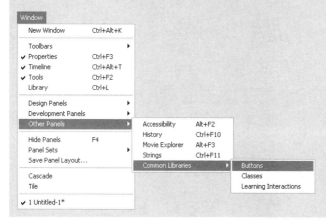

Figure 6.4 The Common Libraries menu gives you quick access to the libraries of Flash Documents located inside the Libraries folder.

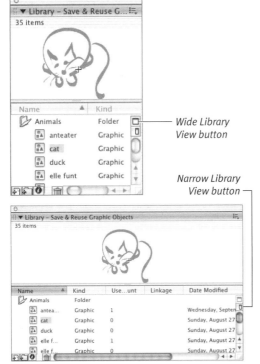

Wide Library View button

Narrow Library View button

Figure 6.5 Click the Wide Library View button to open a wide Library window. Click the Narrow Library View button to open a narrow one.

Understanding Library-Window Views

You can resize the Library window as you would any window, or toggle wide and narrow window views. In its wide state, the Library window displays up to five columns of information about each asset (its name, what kind of object it is, how many times it appears in the movie, whether it's exported or imported as a shared asset, and the last modification date).

To view the wide Library window:

◆ In the open Library window, click the Wide Library View button (**Figure 6.5**).

Flash widens the window to accommodate all columns.

To view the narrow Library window:

◆ In the open Library window, click the Narrow Library View button.

Flash narrows the window to accommodate just the first column.

To resize Library columns:

1. In the Library window, position the pointer over a column-head divider.

   The pointer changes to a double-arrow divider-moving icon.

2. Click and drag the divider (**Figure 6.6**).

✔ Tips

- You can't change the order of the columns in the Library window, but you can hide any middle column you don't need to see. Try hiding the Kind column to save space. (The icon preceding each item indicates what type of asset it is.) Drag the divider on the right side of the Kind header until it's almost on top of the left divider. To reveal the column again, drag the divider back to the right.

- Flash tracks how many times you use a symbol instance, but the Use Count column doesn't display the latest number automatically. To change that setting, from the Library window's Options menu, choose Keep Use Counts Updated. (This setting can slow Flash.) To update use counts periodically, choose Update Use Counts Now as needed.

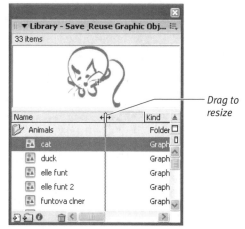

Drag to resize

Figure 6.6 Drag the divider between column headers to resize a column.

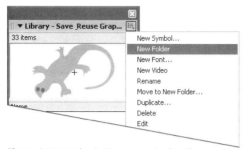

Figure 6.7 From the Options menu in the Library window, choose New Folder to create a library folder.

Select root-level item   To add root-level folder

New Folder button   Enter folder name

Select item within a folder   To add subfolder

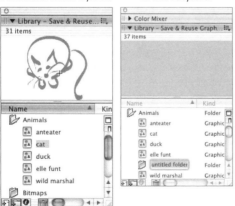

Figure 6.8 To create new folders and subfolders, click the New Folder button.

Understanding Library Hierarchy

Flash lets you store library elements hierarchically within folders, which makes it easy to organize the elements of movies that contain numerous reused elements. To further aid you in organizing the Library window, Flash allows you to sort items by column.

To create a library folder:

1. Open the Library window.

2. To select a location, *do one of the following*:
   ▲ To add a root-level folder, select an item at the root level.
   ▲ To add a subfolder, select an item within the folder where you want to add the new subfolder.

3. To create the new folder, *do one of the following*:
   ▲ From the pop-up Options menu in the top-right corner of the window, choose New Folder (**Figure 6.7**).
   ▲ At the bottom of the window, click the New Folder button (**Figure 6.8**).
   Flash creates a new folder, selects it, and activates the text entry field.

4. Type a name for your folder.

5. Press Enter.

To open one library folder:

1. In the Library window, select a closed folder.

2. To open the folder, *do one of the following:*

   ▲ Double-click the folder icon.

   ▲ From the Library window's Options menu, choose Expand Folder.

   The folder's contents appear in the Library window (**Figure 6.9**).

To close one library folder:

1. In the Library window, select an open folder.

2. To close the folder, *do one of the following:*

   ▲ Double-click the folder icon.

   ▲ From the Library window's Options menu, choose Collapse Folder.

✔ Tip

■ To open all library folders at the same time, from the Library window's Options menu, choose Expand All Folders. To close all folders, choose Collapse All Folders.

Figure 6.9 Open folders in the Library window to display their contents.

Click to display reverse alphanumeric order

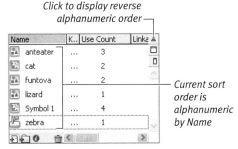

Current sort order is alphanumeric by Name

Windows

Click to display alphanumeric order

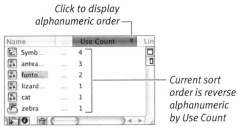

Current sort order is reverse alphanumeric by Use Count

Mac

Figure 6.10 In Windows (top), click the Sort button to change the sort order for the selected column. On a Mac (bottom), click the head of a selected column to change the sort order.

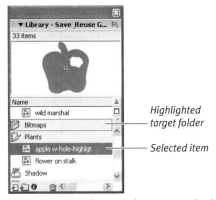

Highlighted target folder

Selected item

Figure 6.11 In the Library window, you can simply drag items between folders. The target folder highlights when it's ready to receive the dragged item.

To sort library items:

◆ In the Library window, click the heading of the column you want to sort by.

To sort items by name, for example, click the Name column header. Flash highlights the chosen column header and sorts the Library window by the items in that column.

✔ Tip

■ To change the sort order, in Windows, click the Sort button, which toggles between alphanumeric and reverse alphanumeric order (**Figure 6.10**). On a Mac, the selected column displays a small triangle indicating sort order. Clicking a selected column head toggles the sort order.

To move items between library folders:

1. In the open Library window, select the item you want to move.

2. Drag the selected item over the icon of the destination folder.

Flash highlights the target folder (**Figure 6.11**).

3. Release the mouse button.

Flash moves the item into the new folder.

✔ Tip

■ To move an item to a new folder quickly, from the Library window's Options menu, choose Move to New Folder. A dialog for naming the new folder appears. Enter a name and press Enter. Flash creates the folder and places the selected item in the folder in one step.

UNDERSTANDING LIBRARY HIERARCHY

243

Converting Graphics to Symbols

Not all graphics in a Flash movie are symbols; you need to take special steps to define the items you create as symbols. You can turn graphic elements you've already created into symbols, or you can create a symbol from scratch in the symbol editor. After you do, the symbol resides in the library of the document in which you created the symbol. You can copy a symbol from one document to another or from one library to another; the symbol then resides separately in each document's library. (You can also define shared symbols that reside in shared libraries; see "Creating Shared Libraries" later in this chapter.)

The standard library of a Flash Document contains all the symbols used in that document; it can also contain unused symbols and pointers to symbols in shared libraries.

The following exercise covers creating static graphic symbols. But you can also turn graphics into symbols that are animations (see Chapter 10) or buttons (see Chapter 11).

What Is Symbol Behavior?

In Flash, you must specify a behavior for each symbol. You have three choices: graphic, button, and movie clip.

Graphics are, as you might expect, graphic elements, but they can also be animated graphic elements. The feature that distinguishes one symbol behavior from another is the way the symbol interacts with the Timeline of the movie in which it appears. Graphic symbols operate in step with the Timeline of the movie in which they appear. If you have a static graphic symbol, it takes up one frame of the movie in which you place it (just as any graphic element would). A three-frame animated graphic symbol takes up three frames of the movie (see Chapter 10).

Buttons have their own four-frame Timeline; a button sits in a single frame of a movie but displays its four frames as a user's mouse interacts with it (see Chapter 11).

Movie clips have their own multiframe Timeline that plays independently of the main movie's Timeline (see Chapter 10).

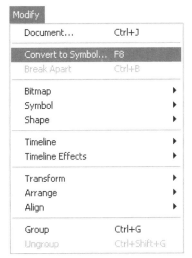

Figure 6.12 Choose Modify > Convert to Symbol to turn a selected existing graphic into a symbol.

To turn an existing graphic into a symbol:

1. On the Stage, select the graphic elements you want to convert to a symbol.

   Flash highlights the graphic elements.

2. From the Modify menu, choose Convert to Symbol (**Figure 6.12**), or press F8 on the keyboard.

   The Convert to Symbol dialog appears (**Figure 6.13**). Flash gives the symbol a default name—for example, Symbol 16—based on the number of symbols created for the library.

3. If you don't want to use the default, type a name for your symbol.

4. Choose Graphic as the behavior for your symbol.

continues on next page

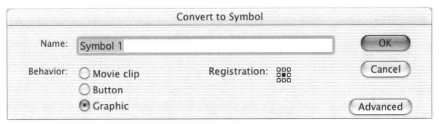

Figure 6.13 The Convert to Symbol dialog lets you name your symbol, define its behavior, and set its registration point. Click the Advanced button to expand the box to set linkages for sharing and import/export.

CONVERTING GRAPHICS TO SYMBOLS

5. To set the symbol's registration mark (see the sidebar, "Registration Mark Versus Transformation Point"), click one of the squares in the registration model.

By default, Flash registers a symbol by the upper-left corner of its bounding box. Click a different square on the registration model—another corner, the center, or the middle of a side—to make Flash register the symbol by the corresponding point on the symbol's bounding box.

6. Click OK.

Flash adds the symbol to the library. The selected graphic elements on the Stage become an instance of the symbol. The selection highlight no longer appears directly over the elements themselves, but on the symbol's bounding box. A crosshair appears, indicating the location of the registration mark; a circle, known as the transformation point, indicates the center of the symbol (**Figure 6.14**). You can no longer edit the item directly on the Stage; you must open it in one of Flash's symbol-editing modes.

Selected object

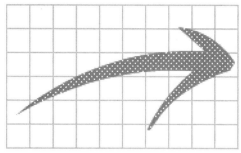

Converted to a symbol

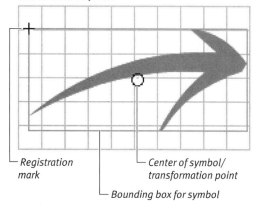

Registration mark

Center of symbol/ transformation point

Bounding box for symbol

Figure 6.14 A selected raw shape on the Stage is highlighted with dots. When you convert that shape to a symbol, the bounding box is the only item that gets highlighted. A crosshair indicates where the symbol's registration mark is. A circle indicates the symbol's center or transformation point.

✔ Tips

- A graphic symbol can consist of one raw shape, multiple raw shapes, grouped shapes—you name it. Once you learn to create symbols, you can even include symbols within symbols. Whatever is selected on the Stage when you choose Convert to Symbol becomes part of the symbol.

- To convert graphic elements to a symbol quickly, select the elements on the Stage and drag the selection to the lower half of the movie's Library window. The Convert to Symbol dialog appears. Name and define your symbol as described in the preceding exercise.

- The registration model is a rather elusive feature. It appears only in the Convert to Symbol dialog. That means you get only once chance to simply select a point on the symbol's bounding box or at its center and make that the registration point. You can, however, always go into symbol-editing mode and reposition the graphic elements in relation to the registration mark (see "Editing Master Symbols," later in this chapter).

Registration Mark Versus Transformation Point

The symbol's registration mark (the small crosshair) is the point that Flash considers to be the 0,0 point for the symbol. Flash uses that point to *register* the symbol—that is, to locate it via coordinates on the Stage, either during authoring (for example when you enter coordinates for a symbol in the Info panel) or during playback (for example, when you use ActionScript to move a symbol in response to user input). The registration mark stays the same for all instances of the symbol.

The transformation point (the small circle) is the point that you can use for snapping operations. It is the stable reference point Flash uses for transforming the symbol. When you rotate a symbol by using the free-transform tool in Rotate and Skew mode, for example, the transformation point is the pivot around which the symbol spins. Flash places the transformation point in the center of the master symbol, but you can redefine the transformation point of individual symbol instances by using the free-transform tool.

Creating New Symbols from Scratch

You can avoid the conversion process described in the preceding section by creating graphics directly in symbol-editing mode. This practice makes all the tools, frames, and layers of the Flash editor available, but Flash defines the element you are creating as a symbol from the start.

To create a new symbol:

1. To enter symbol-editing mode, *do one of the following:*

   ▲ From the Insert menu, choose New Symbol, or press ⌘-F8 (Mac) or Ctrl-F8 (Windows).

   ▲ From the Library window's Options menu, choose New Symbol (**Figure 6.15**).

   ▲ In the bottom-left corner of the Library window, click the New Symbol button (**Figure 6.16**).

   The Create New Symbol dialog appears.

2. Type a name for your symbol.

3. Choose Graphic as the behavior for your symbol.

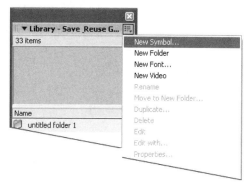

Figure 6.15 From the Library window's Options menu, choose New Symbol to create a symbol from scratch.

New Symbol button

Figure 6.16 Click the Library window's New Symbol button to create a symbol from scratch.

4. Click OK.

Flash enters symbol-editing mode. Flash displays the name of the symbol you are creating in the Edit Bar and places a crosshair in the center of the Stage (**Figure 6.17**). The crosshair indicates the symbol's registration mark.

5. Create your graphic on the Stage of the symbol editor as you would in the regular editing environment.

continues on next page

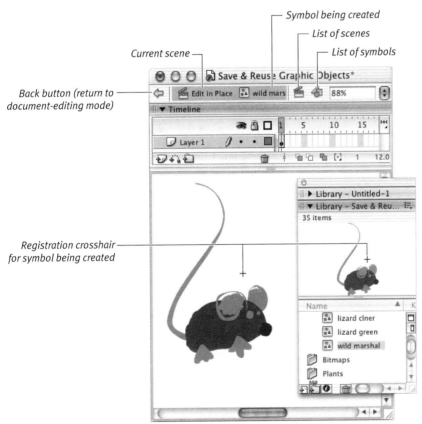

Current scene ─

Symbol being created ─

List of scenes ─

List of symbols ─

Back button (return to ─
document-editing mode)

Registration crosshair ─
for symbol being created

Figure 6.17 In symbol-editing mode, the name of the symbol being worked on appears in the Edit Bar just above the Stage.

CREATING NEW SYMBOLS FROM SCRATCH

6. To return to document-editing mode, *do one of the following:*

▲ From the Edit menu, choose Edit Document. Flash returns you to the current scene.

▲ In the Edit Bar, click the Back button or the Current Scene link (**Figure 6.18**). Flash returns you to the current scene.

▲ From the Edit Scene pop-up menu in the Edit Bar, choose a scene (**Figure 6.19**). Flash takes you to that scene.

✔ Tips

■ When creating new symbols, be sure to consider how the registration mark should work with your finished symbol so you can place your graphic elements appropriately in relation to the registration crosshair. Will you want to align this symbol by its center? Then position your elements evenly around the crosshair. Will you want to align this symbol along an outer edge or corner? Then position your elements accordingly.

■ When you enter symbol-editing mode, the registration crosshair may be outside the current viewing area. To bring the registration mark to the center of your window, choose View > Magnification > Show Frame.

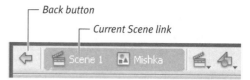

Figure 6.18 Click the Back button or the Current Scene button to return to document-editing mode.

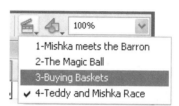

Figure 6.19 Choose a scene from the Edit Scene pop-up menu to return to document-editing mode.

Where Am I?

When you edit symbols in a Flash Document, the current window simply switches to symbol-editing mode. It's easy to get confused about whether you're editing the main document or a symbol. Learn to recognize the following subtle visual cues; they are the only indication that you are in symbol-editing mode.

In symbol-editing mode, a Flash Document displays the name of the scene and symbol you are editing in the Edit Bar and activates the Back button. Also, a small crosshair, which acts as a registration point for the symbol, appears on the Stage and the gray work area that surrounds the Stage disappears. If you entered symbol-editing mode via the Edit in Place command, any elements on the Stage that are not being edited appear in a ghostly form. Apart from these changes, the Timeline, the Stage, and the tools all appear and work just as they do in document-editing mode.

Preview location of symbol on the Stage

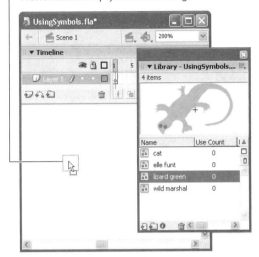

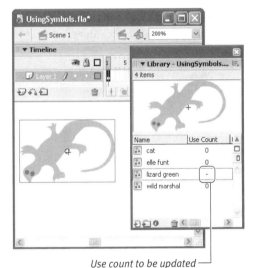

Use count to be updated

Figure 6.20 When you drag a symbol from the Library window to the Stage (top), Flash places the symbol on the Stage, selects it, and updates that symbol's use count internally (bottom). When you are not keeping use counts updated constantly, the dash in the Use Count column indicates a change. To see the actual figure, choose Update Use Counts Now from the Library window's Options menu.

Using Symbol Instances

A *symbol instance* is a pointer to the full description of the symbol. Symbols help keep file sizes small. If you converted a graphic on the Stage to a symbol, you have one symbol instance on the Stage. To use the symbol again, or if you created your symbol in symbol-editing mode, you'll need to get a copy out of the library and onto the Stage.

To place a symbol instance in your movie:

1. In the Timeline, select the layer and keyframe where you want the graphic symbol to appear.

   Flash can place symbols only in keyframes. If you select an in-between frame, Flash places the symbol in the preceding keyframe. (To learn more about keyframes, see Chapter 7.)

2. Open the library containing the symbol.

3. In the Library window, navigate to the symbol you want; click it to select it.

   Flash highlights the chosen symbol and displays it in the preview window.

4. Position your pointer over the preview window.

5. Click and drag a copy of the symbol onto the Stage.

   Flash previews the symbol's location on the Stage with a rectangular outline as you drag (**Figure 6.20**).

6. Release the mouse button.

   Flash places the symbol on the Stage and selects it.

✔ Tip

■ To place a symbol instance quickly, you can drag the symbol name directly from the Library window to the Stage without using the previewed image.

Why Use Symbols?

Symbols help you keep file sizes small. You've already learned how Flash uses vectors to hold down file size: Each vector shape is really just a set of instructions— a recipe for creating the shape. So you could duplicate a vector graphic that you want to reuse, and it would be smaller than a bitmapped version of the same graphic. But symbols are even more efficient than duplicate vector shapes.

A symbol is a master recipe. Imagine a busy restaurant that serves three kinds of soup—chicken noodle, cream of chicken rice, and chicken with garden vegetables—and each pot of soup has its own cook. The head chef could go over with each cook all the steps required to make chicken broth, but that would involve a lot of repetition and take a lot of time. If the restaurant has a master recipe for chicken broth, the chef can simply tell all the cooks to make a pot of chicken broth and then tell each cook just those additional steps that distinguish each dish—add noodles for chicken noodle; add rice and cream for cream of chicken rice; and add potatoes, carrots, and peas for garden vegetable.

Symbols act the same way in Flash. The full recipe is in the library. Each instance on the Stage contains just the instructions that say which recipe to start with and how to modify it—for example, use the recipe for the red rectangle but make it twice as large, change the color to blue, and rotate it 45 degrees clockwise. Because symbols can themselves contain other symbols, it really pays to break your graphic elements into their lowest-common-denominator parts, make each individual part a symbol, and then combine the parts into larger symbols or graphics.

Figure 6.21 Select a symbol instance on the Stage, and the Property Inspector becomes the gateway to modifying that symbol instance. You can alter the height, width, location, and behavior of the selected symbol by entering new values in the corresponding fields. You can apply color effects from the inspector's Color menu.

Figure 6.22 Choose Brightness from the Property Inspector's Color menu to change the intensity of a symbol instance. Enter a high value to make the symbol instance lighter; a low value to make it darker.

Modifying Symbol Instances

You can change the appearance of individual symbol instances without changing the master symbol itself. As with any other element, you can resize and reposition an instance (for example, scale and rotate it) by using Toolbar tools, panels, and the Property Inspector (see Chapter 3).

You can also change a symbol instance's color and transparency, but the method differs from that for assigning colors to raw shapes. You modify the color, intensity, and transparency of a symbol instance via the Color menu in the Property Inspector.

To access the Property Inspector:

◆ If the Property Inspector is not currently open, from the Window menu, choose Properties.

The Property Inspector opens (**Figure 6.21**).

To change an instance's brightness:

1. On the Stage, select the symbol instance you want to modify.

2. From the Property Inspector's Color menu, choose Brightness.

A field for entering a new brightness percentage appears (**Figure 6.22**).

continues on next page

3. Enter a value in the Brightness field.

A value of –100 makes the symbol black; a value of 0 leaves the symbol at its original brightness; a value of 100 makes the symbol white (**Figure 6.23**).

4. Press Enter.

Flash applies the brightness setting to the selected symbol on the Stage.

To change the instance's color:

1. On the Stage, select the symbol instance you want to modify.

2. From the Property Inspector's Color menu, choose Tint.

Tint-modification parameters appear (**Figure 6.24**).

3. To choose a new color, *do one of the following:*

▲ In the Red, Green, and Blue fields, enter new RGB values.

▲ Click the tint-color box, and choose a color from the pop-up swatch set.

4. Type a percentage in the Tint Amount field.

The tint percentage indicates how much of the new color to blend with the existing colors. Applying a tint of 100 percent changes all the lines and fills in the symbol to the new color. Applying a lesser percentage mixes some of the new color with the existing colors in the symbol. It's almost like placing a transparent film of the new color over the symbol.

5. Press Enter.

Flash applies the tint settings to the selected symbol on the Stage.

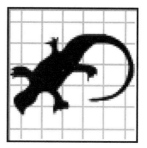

–100 percent brightness setting

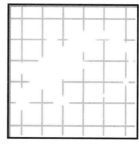

100 percent brightness setting

Figure 6.23 At its extremes, the Brightness setting lets you turn a symbol instance completely black or completely white.

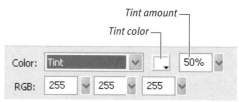

Tint amount
Tint color

Figure 6.24 Use the Tint settings in the Property Inspector to change the color of a symbol instance.

Figure 6.25 Use the Alpha settings in the Property Inspector's Color section to change the transparency of a symbol instance.

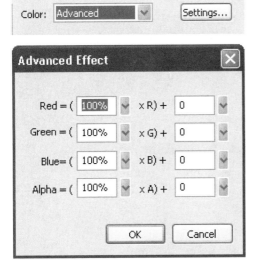

Figure 6.26 Click the Advanced Settings button in the Property Inspector (top) to access the Advanced Effect dialog (bottom). Enter new values to change the color and transparency of a symbol instance.

To change the instance's transparency:

1. On the Stage, select the symbol instance you want to modify.

2. From the Property Inspector's Color menu, choose Alpha (**Figure 6.25**).

3. Enter a new value in the Alpha field.

    A value of 0 makes the symbol completely transparent; a value of 100 makes the symbol completely opaque.

4. Press Enter.

    Flash applies the alpha setting to the selected symbol on the Stage.

To change the instance's tint and alpha simultaneously:

1. On the Stage, select the symbol instance you want to modify.

2. From the Property Inspector's Color menu, choose Advanced.

    A Settings button appears to the right of the menu in the Property Inspector.

3. Click the Settings button.

    The Advanced Effect dialog appears (**Figure 6.26**). This dialog contains sliders and text boxes for changing red, green, blue, and alpha values.

4. Adjust the values to fine-tune the color and transparency of the symbol instance.

5. To apply the color effect, click OK.

MODIFYING SYMBOL INSTANCES

✔ Tips

- Instead of pressing Enter to confirm a value you enter in one of the Property Inspector's fields, you can just click elsewhere in the Property Inspector or click the Stage.

- To preview new color values interactively, click and drag the triangle to the right of an entry field. Flash updates the symbol on the Stage as you drag the slider lever. When you release the slider, Flash confirms the change; you don't need to press Enter.

- You can change the transformation point of individual symbol instances. Using the free-transform tool, click the small white circle in the middle of the symbol instance. Drag the circle to a new location. Flash uses the transformation point for rotating and scaling the object.

The Mystery of Advanced Effect Settings

The Advanced Effect settings allow you to change the RGB values and alpha values for a symbol instance simultaneously. The sliders in the left-hand column control what percentage of the RGB and alpha values that make up the colors in the original symbol will appear in the symbol instance. The sliders on the right add to or subtract from the red, green, blue, and alpha values of the original colors.

Imagine a symbol with three ovals. One is pure red, one is pure green, and one is pure blue. The alpha setting is 50 percent. Changing the red slider in the left-hand column (the percentage of the current red value) affects only the red oval. The green and blue ovals contain 0 percent red; doubling it makes no visible change. Moving the right-hand slider upwards adds red to everything, including the green and blue ovals. These ovals start to change color when you increase the red value. (Of course if you move the right-hand slider downwards, decreasing the red value, you'll see no difference in the green and blue ovals where there was no red to start with.)

Creating Static Symbols via Timeline Effects

Flash MX 2004 comes with eight *Timeline Effects*—commands that help you perform common graphics tasks within the authoring environment. To get the hang of working with Timeline Effects, start with a simple one—like Drop Shadow.

To create a Drop Shadow effect:

1. Open a new Flash Document.

   Working in a new document makes it easier to see what items Flash adds to the library when it creates the effect.

2. Using the text tool create some text on the Stage, for example type the word *Parasol*.

continues on next page

The Mystery of Timeline Effects

Timeline effects accomplish their task by converting selected objects on the Stage into a symbol, then manipulating instances of that symbol. The Drop Shadow command, for example, places duplicate symbol instances on the Stage and modifies one of them according to user input about how the shadow should look. You can apply Timeline Effects to raw shapes, text, grouped shapes, and symbols.

Three of Flash's Timeline Effects—Copy to Grid, Distributed Duplicate, and Drop Shadow—can create static graphic symbols similar to the ones you've been learning about in this chapter. (Other Timeline Effects create animated graphic symbols and movie clip symbols, you'll learn more about these types of symbols in Chapter 10.) Exactly what Flash creates when it applies Timeline Effects is a little complex, as you'll learn later in this chapter. Moreover, the symbols created by Timeline Effects do not behave precisely the same way as symbols you create yourself. There are some peculiarities you'll need to watch out for.

3. Using the selection tool, select the text and turn it into a symbol.

It's a good idea to convert raw shapes or text to a graphic symbol before applying an effect (see "Converting Graphics to Symbols," earlier in this chapter). Give the symbol meaningful name, such as Parasol_forDropShadow. Making the text a symbol gives you a permanent copy that you can reuse should you need to re-create your finished effect or make new, slightly different versions later on. It also simplifies the process of making future modifications, to correct a typo in your drop-shadow text, for example (see "Modifying Timeline Effects," later in this chapter).

4. With your text symbol selected, from the Insert menu, choose Timeline Effects > Effects > Drop Shadow (**Figure 6.27**).

The Effect Setting dialog appears; the dialog bears the name of the effect you are creating, in this case, Drop Shadow (**Figure 6.28**).

5. To adjust the shadow's color, click the Color box and from the pop-up color swatch set, choose a new color.

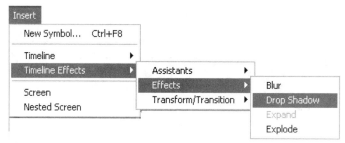

Figure 6.27 Choose Insert > Timeline Effects > Effects > Drop Shadow to add an offset shadow beneath selected text or shapes on the Stage.

6. To adjust how solid the shadow looks, *do one of the following:*

   ▲ Select the value in the Alpha Transparency field, then enter a percentage between 0 and 100.

   ▲ Click and drag the pointer in the transparency slider

7. To adjust shadow placement, select the values in the *x* and/or *y* fields for Shadow Offset, then enter a new value.

8. To view your changes before finalizing the effect, click the Update Preview button.

   You can make repeated adjustments, by repeating steps 5 through 8, until the shadow looks the way you want it.

continues on next page

Set shadow position

Set shadow color

Set shadow transparency

Click to preview current settings

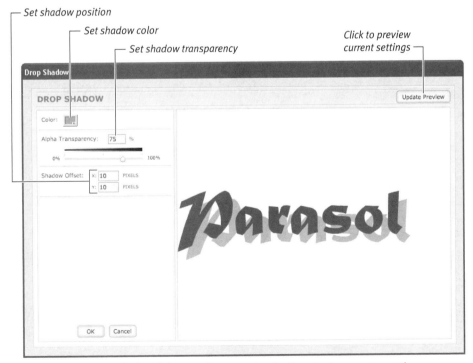

Figure 6.28 The Drop Shadow dialog contains parameters for the color, transparency, and placement of the shadow. To preview changes to your settings click the Update Preview button.

CREATING STATIC SYMBOLS VIA TIMELINE EFFECTS

9. To finalize the effect, click OK.

Flash creates two symbols: One is your original object turned into an effect symbol (a graphic symbol that becomes the building block from which Flash creates the effect); the other is the finished-effect symbol (a graphic symbol that displays the effect you chose). Flash replaces your original object on the Stage with an

instance of the finished-effect symbol and renames the layer containing that instance in the Timeline (**Figure 6.29**). (For a detailed breakdown of the changes Flash makes to your document when creating a Timeline Effect, see the sidebar "Dissecting a Drop Shadow," later in this chapter.)

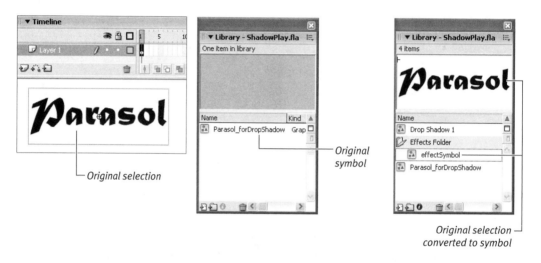

Original selection

Original symbol

Original selection converted to symbol

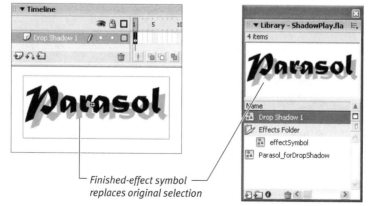

Finished-effect symbol replaces original selection

Figure 6.29 When you apply an effect to a selected object on the Stage (top), Flash replaces your original selection with an instance of the finished-effect symbol (bottom).

✔ Tips

- If you have a layer containing several items and you apply a Timeline Effect to just one, Flash moves the selected item to a new layer, directly below the original layer. Flash renames this new layer with the default effect name. The original layer keeps its name and all the unselected items remain on that layer. To retain control over the stacking order of your effect, always place the element that will receive the effect on its own layer to begin with and position it where you want it in the Timeline.

- It can be helpful to put the layer containing the object to which you will apply an effect into its own folder layer in the Timeline. Flash renames the layer containing the finished-effect symbol, but leaves any overlying folder name untouched. Give the folder a name that has meaning to you and your colleagues, such as CompanyNameRed_DropShadow. The named-folder technique becomes especially useful should you ever modify the Effect Setting for this symbol, because Flash will rename the layer again (see "Modifying Timeline Effects," later in this chapter).

- Macintosh users take note: The Macintosh OS allows you to name your hard drive using any characters you like (Windows systems are more restrictive). The drive name, however, may interfere with creating Timeline Effects. Flash must navigate your hard drive to find information that it needs to create an effect; Flash relies on JavaScript to carry out this search. That can create problems if the hard drive name contains characters that have a specific meaning in JavaScript. Some higher-level ASCII characters (such as apostrophe and question mark) can interfere with Flash's ability to create previews of effects. If you are getting JavaScript errors when you use Timeline Effects, try renaming your hard drive to remove such characters.

Effect Setting Warning: Don't Backspace!

Be careful how you enter numeric values into the fields of the Effect Setting dialog. These fields insist on displaying a number at all times. If you backspace in the field to delete the default value, Flash automatically adds the number 0 to the *right* of the insertion point. This ensures that Flash always has a number with which to perform its calculations. Unfortunately, it also means that when you enter a new value this way, Flash automatically multiplies it by 10! Always select the default value by dragging or double-clicking in the entry field, then typing your own value to replace the selection.

CREATING STATIC SYMBOLS VIA TIMELINE EFFECTS

Timeline Effects Warning: Using Multiple Instances

Should you use more than one instance of a finished-effect symbol? The answer is unclear. Macromedia seems to have intended Timeline Effects to be a quick-and-dirty way to create effects for one-shot use: add an effect to a selected object and use it once in your movie, end of story. But you can use multiple instances of a finished-effect symbol if you are careful and you understand the limitations and pitfalls of doing so. Here are some things to keep in mind.

Will you ever want to change the Effect Setting?

If you select the instance of the finished-effect symbol that Flash places on the Stage when you create a Timeline Effect, you'll see that an Edit button (a link to the Effect Setting dialog) appears in the Property Inspector. This button lets you make changes to the effect in the future (see "Modifying Timeline Effects," later in this chapter). But if you drag an instance from the library and select it, the Property Inspector does *not* display the Edit button, nor does the Edit button appear if you duplicate or copy the symbol instance on the Stage. To simplify your ability to make future updates to the effect, use the finished-effect symbol one time only. If you want to re-create the same effect elsewhere in the movie, start with your original symbol and apply the effect again to create a new finished-effect symbol. If you know the effect looks just how you want it, however, you could use multiple instances. Alternatively, if you don't mind giving up the ability to modify the symbol by using the Effect Setting dialog (you will need to go into the symbol to make future adjustments yourself) you can also feel free to use additional instances.

Will you ever want to remove the effect completely?

If you use only the original instance of a finished-effect symbol, you can easily remove all traces of it from the Stage and the library with the Remove Effect command. If you place multiple instances of the finished-effect symbol in your movie (either by duplicating or by dragging an instance from the library), Flash will be unable to completely remove them (see the "Removing Timeline Effects and Their Master Symbols" sidebar, later in this chapter).

Dissecting a Drop Shadow

In the process of creating Timeline Effects, Flash places symbols and folders in the current document's Library and renames the active layer in the Timeline. If you use Timeline Effects with multiple objects in one document, Flash's default names for effects symbols become repetitive, and the way Flash numbers these items adds to the confusion. For some symbols, numbering starts over with each new document; for others, numbers continue consecutively throughout your work session. The following rundown describes creating the first Timeline Effect in a work session.

When you select a symbol (or raw shape) and choose Insert > Timeline Effects > Effects > Drop Shadow, Flash does the following:

◆ Renames the layer containing the symbol (or shape) Drop Shadow 1.

◆ Creates a folder, named *Effects Folder*, in the document's library.

◆ Creates a graphic symbol from your original symbol (or shape), names the symbol effectSymbol, and places it in *Effects Folder*.

◆ Creates a graphic symbol that contains your graphic with its drop shadow, names the symbol Drop Shadow 1 (this symbol consists of two instances of effectSymbol, one acts as the top shape and the other—with altered tint, alpha, and position—acts as the shadow).

Flash creates just one *Effects Folder* per document. If you apply Timeline Effects to multiple graphics, the symbols made from the original graphics all wind up in *Effects Folder*. Within one document Flash names these symbols with the default names effectSymbol, effectSymbol_1, effectSymbol_2, and so on. Unfortunately, numbering for the finished-effect symbols works a bit differently. For these symbols, numbering continues consecutively throughout your work session. To add to the confusion, while the first symbol in the *Effects Folder* has no number attached (in essence it's 0), the finished-effect symbol—the symbol made from effectSymbol—does get a number, it's called Drop Shadow 1 (the next symbol pair will be effectSymbol_1 and Drop Shadow 2).

continues on next page

CREATING STATIC SYMBOLS VIA TIMELINE EFFECTS

Dissecting a Drop Shadow *continued*

Set the Movie Explorer panel to display symbols and definitions, to see exactly what Flash creates when you apply a Timeline Effect (**Figure 6.30**). You'll learn more about using the Movie Explorer in Chapter 13.

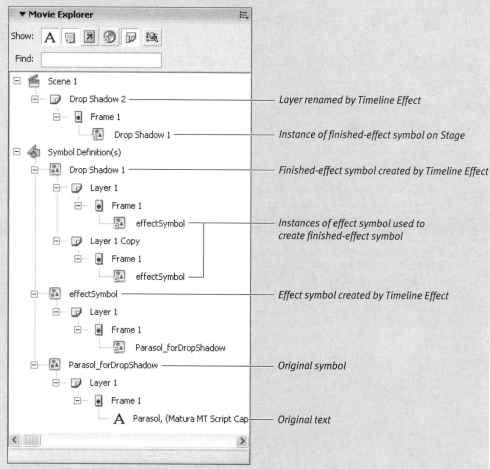

Figure 6.30 The Movie Explorer panel shows a breakdown of the symbols that make up the symbol created by the Drop Shadow Timeline Effect. (To access the panel, choose Windows > Other Panels > Movie Explorer.) Here you can see that Flash placed the original text into the symbol called effectSymbol, the symbol called Drop Shadow contains two instances of effectSymbol. And the movie contains one instance of Drop Shadow.

CREATING STATIC SYMBOLS VIA TIMELINE EFFECTS

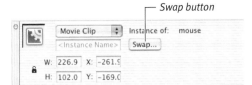

Figure 6.31 The Swap button in the Property Inspector lets you replace a selected symbol instance with an instance of a different symbol from the same document. (Choose Window > Properties to access the inspector if it is not already open.)

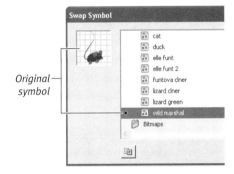

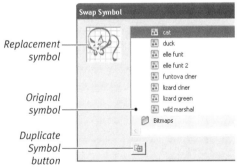

Figure 6.32 Select a replacement symbol from the list in the Swap Symbol dialog, and click OK to exchange one symbol for another.

Swapping One Symbol Instance for Another

Flash allows you to replace one symbol instance with another while retaining all the modifications you've made in the symbol instance. If, for example, you want to change the look of a logo in certain places in your site but not everywhere, you can create the new logo as a separate symbol and swap it in as needed. (If you want to change the look for every instance, you could edit the master logo symbol directly, as you learn to do in "Editing Master Symbols," later in the chapter.) You perform symbol swapping in the Property Inspector (**Figure 6.31**).

To switch symbols:

1. On the Stage, select the symbol instance you want to change.

2. In the Property Inspector, click the Swap Symbol button.

   The Swap Symbol dialog appears, listing all the symbols in the current document's library (**Figure 6.32**). In the Windows operating systems, Flash highlights the name of the symbol you're modifying and places a bullet next to its name in the Symbol list.

3. From the Symbol list, select the replacement symbol.

   The original symbol remains bulleted; Flash highlights the new symbol and places it in the preview window.

   continues on next page

4. Click OK.

Flash places the new symbol on the Stage, locating the new object where the old one was located and applying any modifications you previously made for that instance (**Figure 6.33**).

✔ Tips

- To swap symbols quickly, double-click the new symbol in the Swap Symbol dialog. Flash replaces it and closes the dialog.

- The Duplicate Symbol button in the Swap Symbol dialog allows you to make a copy of whatever symbol is selected in the list. If you know you need to tweak the master version of the replacement symbol for this instance but also want to keep the current version, create a duplicate and select it as the replacement. You can edit the duplicate's master symbol later.

Unmodified instance of mouse

Unmodified instance of cat

Instance of mouse scaled and rotated before swapping

After swapping: scaling and rotation applied to cat

Figure 6.33 When you swap symbols, any modifications you have made for the selected instance you're swapping apply to the replacement instance.

SWAPPING ONE SYMBOL INSTANCE FOR ANOTHER

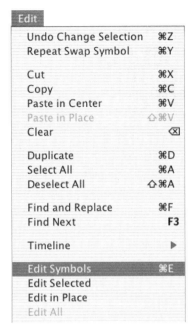

Figure 6.34 Choosing Edit > Edit Symbols takes you from document-editing mode to symbol-editing mode. If you have selected a symbol on the Stage, choosing Edit > Edit Selected also takes you to symbol-editing mode.

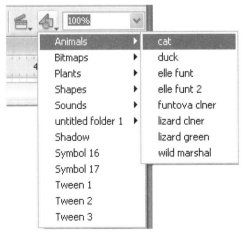

Figure 6.35 Choosing a symbol from this pop-up list of symbols in the Edit Bar takes you into symbol-editing mode.

Editing Master Symbols

After you create a symbol, you can refine and modify it in symbol-editing mode. Unlike modifications of a symbol instance, which affect just that instance on the Stage, leaving the master symbol in the library unchanged, modifications made in symbol-editing mode affect the master symbol and all instances of that symbol in your movie.

You can enter symbol-editing mode in several ways.

To enter symbol-editing mode from the Stage:

1. On the Stage, select the symbol you want to edit.

2. To open the symbol editor, *do one of the following:*

   ▲ From the Edit menu, choose Edit Symbols, or press ⌘-E (Mac) or Ctrl-E (Windows) (**Figure 6.34**).

   ▲ From the Edit menu, choose Edit Selected.

   ▲ From the pop-up list of symbols in the Edit Bar, choose the symbol you want to edit (**Figure 6.35**).

Flash opens the symbol editor in the current window.

To enter symbol-editing mode from the Library window:

1. In the Library window, select the symbol you want to edit.

2. To bring up the symbol editor, *do one of the following:*

   ▲ From the Options menu, choose Edit.

   ▲ Double-click the icon next to the selected symbol name.

   ▲ Double-click the symbol in the preview window.

Flash opens the symbol editor in the main window of the current movie (**Figure 6.36**).

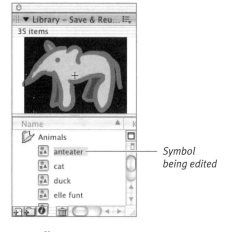

Symbol being edited

Choose a scene to return to main window and document-editing mode

Symbol being edited

Symbol-editing window

Figure 6.36 Double-clicking a symbol in the Library window (top) opens that symbol in symbol-editing mode in the main window of the active document (bottom).

Symbol being edited

Figure 6.37 The Edit in Place command allows you to see your symbol instance in context with other items on the stage. The symbol instance appears in full color; the other elements on the Stage are grayed out. In this mode, changes made to the instance affect the master symbol and all the instances in the movie.

✔ Tips

- After you've placed an instance of a symbol on the Stage, you may want to change the master symbol to make it fit with the items around it. The Edit in Place command allows you to edit your master symbol in context on the Stage with all other items grayed out (**Figure 6.37**). To evoke the Edit in Place command, choose Edit > Edit in Place. Or Control-click (Mac) or right-click (Windows) the symbol instance you want to edit, and from the contextual menu that appears, choose Edit in Place. Any changes you make affect all instances of that symbol.

- You can also enter Edit in Place mode quickly, by double-clicking a symbol instance on the Stage.

- You can edit a symbol in a separate window from your movie. Select an instance of the symbol on the Stage; Control-click (Mac) or right-click (Windows) to access the contextual menu; and choose Edit in New Window. To return to document-editing mode, close the window.

Modifying Timeline Effects

You can modify symbols made from Timeline Effects using the tools you've learned about in this chapter, but there are some important pitfalls to watch out for. Timeline Effects rely on symbols nested within symbols; that means you must pay special attention to which ones you are changing to avoid accidentally deleting a symbol that's the basis of a finished-effect symbol. Using the Drop Shadow 1 symbol you created in "Creating Static Symbols via Timeline Effects," earlier in this chapter, let's take a look at those caveats and pitfalls. The key lies in knowing what you want to modify: one instance of the finished-effect symbol (the text with its drop shadow) on the Stage; the parameters of the effect (the opacity of the shadow, for example); or the original element (in this case, the word *Parasol*).

To change one instance of the finished-effect symbol:

1. Follow the steps in "Creating Static Symbols via Timeline Effects," earlier in this chapter.

This task creates a symbol named Drop Shadow 1 containing the word *Parasol* with a drop shadow. To ensure that the default name of your symbols matches what's listed here, restart Flash and open a new document before creating the symbol.

2. Select the original instance of Drop Shadow 1 on the Stage.

3. To change the instance's size, placement on the stage, rotation, and/or skew, use the selection tool, free-transform tool, Transform panel, and Info panel, as described in Chapter 3.

4. To change the brightness, color, and/or transparency of the instance, use the techniques you learned in "Modifying Symbol Instances," earlier in this chapter.

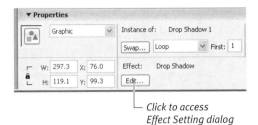

Click to access
Effect Setting dialog

Figure 6.38 When you select the original instance of a finished-effect symbol, the Edit button appears in the Effects section of the Property Inspector. Click the button to access the Effect Setting dialog.

To change the effect's appearance:

1. Follow steps 1 and 2 of the preceding exercise.

   This technique does not work with instances of the symbol dragged from the library (see the sidebar "Timeline Effects Warning: Using Multiple Instances," earlier in this chapter).

2. To access the Effect Setting dialog, *do one of the following:*

   ▲ In the Effect section of the Property Inspector, click the Edit button (**Figure 6.38**).

   ▲ From the Modify Menu choose Timeline Effects > Edit Effect.

   The Effect Setting dialog appears. In this case the dialog's name is Drop Shadow.

3. To modify the way the shadow looks, adjust the Color, Alpha Transparency, and Shadow Offset parameters.

   You can modify these parameters and preview your changes just as you did when you first created the effect (see "To create a drop shadow effect," earlier in this chapter).

4. To accept your changes, click OK.

   Flash creates a new version of the Drop Shadow symbol. CAUTION: Because it creates another finished-effect symbol, Flash renames the finished-effect symbol in the library and renames the layer containing that symbol in your document. There is no change to the original effect symbol.

✔ Tip

■ You can access the Effect Setting dialog by Ctrl-clicking (Mac) or right-clicking (Windows) the original instance of the Drop Shadow symbol on the Stage. From the contextual menu choose Timeline Effects > Edit Effect. This technique works only on the original symbol instance.

MODIFYING TIMELINE EFFECTS

To edit the original graphic underlying an effect:

1. Continuing with the same document from the preceding exercise, open the Library window.

2. Select the symbol to which you applied the Timeline Effect originally (**Figure 6.39**).

   Now you see how useful it is to create your Timeline Effect from a symbol instead of a raw shape, and the reason for giving it a meaningful name. In the preceding tasks this symbol is named `Parasol_forDropShadow`.

3. To access symbol-editing mode, *do one of the following:*

   ▲ From the Options menu in the upper-right corner of the Library window, choose Edit.

   ▲ Double-click the icon for `Parasol_forDropShadow`.

   Flash opens the symbol in symbol-editing mode.

4. Modify the symbol, for example, change the text from *Parasol* to *Umbrella*.

5. Return to document-editing mode, for example, by choosing Edit > Document.

   Your changes to the original symbol appear in the `effectSymbol` and `Drop Shadow` symbols in the library, and in the instance of `Drop Shadow` on the stage. This is the power of editing nested symbols.

Figure 6.39 Select `effectSymbol` in the Effects Folder then choose Edit from the Options menu to edit both the effect and the shape underlying it.

✔ **Tip**

■ If you apply a Timeline Effect to a raw shape or raw text, you can still edit that underlying shape. Just be careful to select the correct symbol to modify. In the library, open the Effects Folder and select the `effectSymbol` that Flash created from your original text (or shape). If you have several effects, it may be difficult to match up the `effectSymbol` name with the name of the finished-effect symbol. Use the library preview window to help you. Once you've selected the right `effectSymbol`, follow steps 4 through 6 in the preceding exercise.

Editing Finished-Effects in Context

You cannot edit a finished-effect symbol directly, the way you can edit symbols you create yourself. If you attempt to enter symbol-editing mode by double-clicking the original instance of **Drop Shadow** on the Stage, nothing happens. If you double-click the symbol's name (**Drop Shadow**) in the library, a dialog appears warning you that the symbol has an effect applied to it and that editing it will break the link to the Effect Setting dialog (**Figure 6.40**). If you want to make adjustments with the various pieces in place (for example, you want to position the shadow by dragging instead of specifying offsets and previewing each change), or you want to see the symbol in context with other elements on the Stage, you can override the warning and make all adjustments to the effect yourself. Just know that future assistance from the Effect Setting dialog will be unavailable to you. You'll have to edit the symbol manually from now on.

There are two cases in which Flash allows you to edit your symbol and still keep the link to the Effect Setting dialog. When you choose the finished-effect symbol from the Edit Symbols menu in the Edit Bar, or when you select the finished-effect symbol by name in the Library window, then double-click its image in the Preview window. Just be aware that the Effect Setting dialog does not recognize any changes you make while using these edit modes. In the future, when you select the finished-effect symbol on Stage and then click the Edit button in the Property Inspector, the Effect Setting dialog will display the symbol with the settings it had before you edited it.

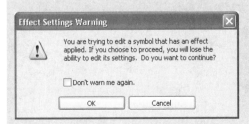

Figure 6.40 If you attempt to edit a finished-effect symbol by double-clicking its name in the library, Flash warns you that you are about to edit an effect symbol. To preserve the ability to modify the symbol using the Effect Setting dialog, click cancel. To go ahead and break the link to Effect Setting, click OK. You must edit this symbol manually from now on.

Duplicating Master Symbols

Although you can always modify the instances of a symbol on the Stage, if you need to use one variation of a symbol over and over, you can duplicate the original master symbol and then modify the duplicate to create a new master symbol with those variations.

To create a duplicate symbol:

1. In the Library window, select the symbol you want to duplicate.

2. From the Options menu, choose Duplicate (**Figure 6.41**).

   Flash opens the Duplicate Symbol dialog, giving the duplicate symbol a default name (**Figure 6.42**).

3. If you want, type a new name for your symbol.

4. Choose Graphic as the behavior for your symbol.

5. Click OK.

   Flash adds the new symbol to the library at the same level in the hierarchy as the original (**Figure 6.43**). The duplicate doesn't link to the original symbol in any way. You can change the duplicate without changing the original, and vice versa.

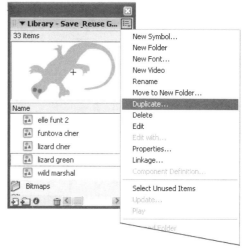

Figure 6.41 From the Library window's Options pop-up menu, choose Duplicate to make a copy of the selected symbol.

Figure 6.42 The default duplicate name for a symbol in the Duplicate Symbol dialog is the original name plus the word copy.

Figure 6.43 Flash puts duplicated symbols at the same library level as the original.

Timeline Effects Warning: Do Not Duplicate!

Although Flash allows you to duplicate finished-effect symbols by choosing Duplicate in the library's Options menu, you should never do so. If you make any changes to the original copy of the finished-effects symbol, the contents of the duplicate symbol disappear entirely. If you want to create a new version of the effect based on the same graphic, drag an instance of your original graphic symbol to the Stage and apply the Timeline Effect anew, using whatever parameters you want. If you originally applied the effect to a raw shape or text, drag an instance of the effectSymbol containing that shape or text from the *Effects Folder* to the Stage, select that instance, break it apart (Choose Modify > Break Apart), and then apply the new Timeline Effect.

DUPLICATING MASTER SYMBOLS

 — *Delete selected item*

Figure 6.44 Click the trash can icon to delete a selected library item.

Figure 6.45 You can also choose Delete from the Library window's Options menu to remove selected symbols from the active document.

Figure 6.46 The dialog that appears when you elect to delete Library items gives you a chance to cancel the operation. You can, however, undo library deletions in Flash MX 2004.

Deleting Master Symbols

Deleting symbols can be a little trickier than deleting raw shapes or grouped shapes on the Stage. Deleting one instance of a symbol from its place on the Stage is easy; just use the methods for cutting or deleting graphics discussed in Chapter 3. Deleting symbols from the Library is not difficult but does require some thought, because instances of the symbol may still be in use in your movie.

To delete one symbol from the library:

1. In the Library window, select the symbol you want to remove.

2. To delete the symbol, *do one of the following*:

   ▲ At the bottom of the window, click the Delete button (the trash-can icon) (**Figure 6.44**).

   ▲ From the pop-up Options menu in the top-right corner of the window, choose Delete (**Figure 6.45**).

   Flash displays a dialog asking you to confirm your deletion (**Figure 6.46**).

3. To delete all instances of the symbol from the movie completely, click Yes.

   or

   To cancel the deletion, click No.

✔ Tip

■ In previous versions of Flash, deleting symbols from the library was a permanent operation. Flash even warned you of that fact when you chose to delete master symbols from the library. With Flash MX 2004's revised Undo function and History panel, however, you can restore a deletion even from a library.

DELETING MASTER SYMBOLS

To delete a folder of symbols from the library:

1. Select the folder you want to remove.

2. Follow steps 2 and 3 of the preceding exercise.

   Flash removes the folder and all the symbols it contains from the library.

✔ Tip

■ Always check the usage numbers before you delete library items. You don't want to delete a symbol that you're currently using in a movie, which is especially easy to do if you've nested symbols within symbols. Some earlier versions of Flash would warn you when you tried to delete an item that was in use in a movie. Flash MX 2004 does not.

Removing Timeline Effects and Their Master Symbols

When you delete a finished-effect symbol from the library, using the steps outlined in this section, Flash removes the finished-effect symbol from the library and all its instances from the Stage. The *Effects Folder,* and the effectSymbol that Flash made from your original graphic, however, remain in the library.

You can restore your original graphic and remove all the symbols related to the finished effect from the library with one command, provided that you have not made any copies of the symbol and have not moved the symbol into a folder. Select your original instance on the Stage. From the Modify menu, choose Timeline Effects > Remove Effect (**Figure 6.47**). Flash converts the symbol back to the symbol or graphic you started with when you applied the effect. Flash removes all the related effect symbols in the library.

If you've made copies of the finished-effect symbol or its underlying effect symbol, or you've placed the finished-effect symbol in a separate folder within the Library, Flash simply breaks apart the finished-effect symbols on the Stage reducing them to instances of the effectSymbol.

Figure 6.47 Choose Modify > Timeline Effects > Remove Effect to convert a Finished Effect symbol on the Stage into instances of its effectSymbol. The Remove Effect command also deletes the master Finished Effect symbol from the library.

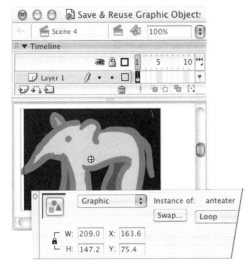

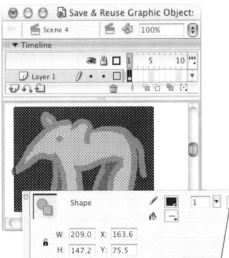

Figure 6.48 The Property Inspector reveals that the selected graphic is a symbol instance (top). To break the link with its master symbol, choose Modify > Break Apart. The Property Inspector reveals that the selection now consists of shapes; it's no longer a symbol instance (bottom).

Converting Symbol Instances to Graphics

At times, you'll want to break the link between a placed instance of a symbol and the master symbol. You may want to redraw the shape in a specific instance but not in every instance, for example. To convert a symbol back to an independent shape or set of shapes, break it apart, just as you break apart grouped shapes (see Chapter 4).

To break the symbol link:

1. On the Stage, select the symbol instance whose link you want to break.

2. From the Modify menu, choose Break Apart, or press ⌘-B (Mac) or Ctrl-B (Windows) (**Figure 6.48**).

   Flash breaks the link to the symbol in the library and selects the symbol's elements. The Property Inspector no longer displays information about the instance of the symbol; it displays information about the selected shapes, groups, and/or symbols.

   If you grouped any of the original elements, they remain grouped after you break the link; ungrouped elements stay ungrouped. Any symbols that existed within the original symbol remain as instances of their respective master symbols. Any finished-effect symbol becomes instances of its effectSymbol. Now you can edit these elements as you learned to do in previous chapters.

Copying Symbols Between Movies

It's easy to reuse symbols. You can transfer symbols via the Clipboard, copying or cutting symbols from one movie and using one of the paste commands to place them in another movie. You can transfer symbols by dragging them from one movie or library to another.

To transfer symbols to another movie:

1. Open the destination file (the movie in which you would like to reuse existing symbols), or create a new file.

2. Open the source file (the movie containing symbols that you want to reuse).

3. Open the Library window for each file.

   Be sure to size and position the movie-editing and Library windows so that all four are visible on your screen at the same time.

4. To transfer a symbol, *do one of the following:*

   ▲ On the Stage of the source file, select a symbol and drag it to the Stage of the destination file (**Figure 6.49**).

   ▲ In the Library of the source file, select a symbol and drag it to the Stage of the destination file.

   ▲ In the Library of the source file, select a symbol and drag it to the lower portion of the Library window of the destination file.

   When you drag a symbol to the Stage, Flash places the symbol at the root level of the library hierarchy. You can also drag the symbol directly into a library folder.

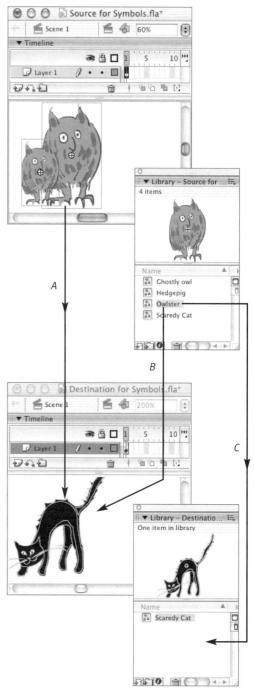

Figure 6.49 Flash lets you drag and drop symbols from Stage to Stage (A), Library window to Stage (B), or Library window to Library window (C).

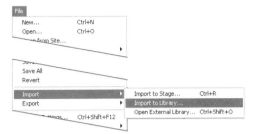

Figure 6.50 Flash allows you to resolve symbol conflicts when you attempt to import or drag in a symbol with the same name as an existing symbol.

✔ Tips

■ If you drag a symbol to the Stage, and a symbol with that name already exists in the root level of the destination file's library (or if you try to place that "duplicate" symbol in a folder containing a symbol with that name), Flash displays a warning dialog (**Figure 6.50**). The dialog allows you to cancel the transfer, replace the existing symbol with the one you are transferring, or disallow the replacement. If you choose not to replace the existing symbol, Flash places a new instance of the existing symbol on the Stage where you placed the one you were dragging. If you cancel the operation, you can rename the one of the conflicting symbols and repeat the operation of dragging in the source symbol. If you want to keep the original name of both symbols in their home files and rename the duplicate only in the destination file, create a new folder in your destination library, drag the conflicting symbol directly to that folder, then rename that symbol in your destination file.

■ You don't have to open the source file to drag symbols from its library. Choose File > Import > Open External Library to open just the Library window. Select a symbol and drag it to the destination Stage or Library window.

■ You can use the File > Import > Import to Library command to bring other individual asset files—such as video clips, sounds, and bitmaps—into your movie as well. (You'll learn more about importing non-Flash graphics in Chapter 14; Chapter 15 covers importing sounds; and Chapter 16, video.)

COPYING SYMBOLS BETWEEN MOVIES

Creating Shared Libraries

Flash provides two ways to share library assets. In *author-time sharing*, Flash authors can grab symbols (or other assets) from centralized source files and use those symbols in the movies they are creating. In *run-time sharing*, symbols (and other assets) used in one or more movies reside in a central location, from which the Flash Player downloads the symbols for playback.

For the following exercises, create two movies. Name them for their functions—for example, `ItemsToShare.fla` and `UsingSharedItems.fla`. In the file `ItemsToShare`, create one symbol named `Square` and another named `Rectangle`, and place an instance of each symbol on the Stage. In the file `UsingSharedItems`, create one symbol named `Circle` and another named `Oval`, and place an instance of each symbol on the Stage. Save both files in the same folder; call it *SharingTest*.

To access a shared symbol while authoring:

1. In the destination file (`UsingShared Items.fla`), select the symbol named `Circle` in the Library window.

2. From the Options menu in the top-right corner of the Library window, choose Properties.

   The Symbol Properties dialog appears (**Figure 6.51**).

3. If the dialog appears in its collapsed (Basic) mode, click the Advanced button to expand the dialog and make all its options visible.

4. In the Source section of the dialog, click the Browse button.

   The Locate Macromedia Flash Document File dialog appears.

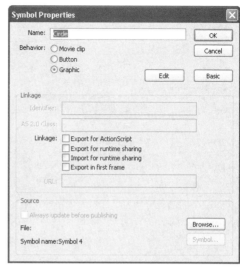

Figure 6.51 The expanded Symbol Properties dialog contains all the advanced symbol properties, such as linkage to source files for authoring and export/import of symbols for run-time sharing.

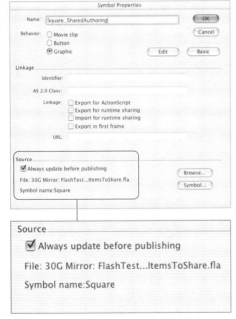

Figure 6.52 In the Select Source Symbol dialog, select a "super" master symbol to be shared while authoring a destination file (top). Flash automatically enters the pathway to the source file in the Source section of the Symbol Properties dialog (bottom).

Figure 6.53 With author-time shared symbols you can simply bring a shared symbol into your destination file; and create no further link to the source file; or you can create a link, so that changes made to the shared symbol in its source file also get made in the destination file when it's published. Check the Always Update Before Publishing check box if you want to incorporate new changes into the source symbol when you publish your movie.

5. Navigate to the source file (`ItemsTo Share.fla`), select it, and click Open.

The Select Source Symbol dialog appears, listing the symbols in the source file (**Figure 6.52**).

6. Select the symbol named `Square`.

7. Click OK.

Flash returns you to the Symbol Properties dialog. The Source section now lists the symbol name and the path to the source file.

8. In the Name field, enter a new name for the symbol, such as `Square_SharedAuthoring`.

Flash makes no obvious indication in either the source or destination library that a symbol is linked. For your own tracking, you may want to alter the names of linked symbols to remind you of that fact.

9. To create a permanent link to the shared symbol, in the Source section of the dialog, check the Always Update Before Publishing check box (**Figure 6.53**).

When you choose this setting, Flash takes the content of the latest version of the symbol from the source file and uses it to update the linked symbol in the destination file any time you publish or test the destination movie.

continues on next page

10. Click OK.

In the library of the destination movie (`UsingSharedItems.fla`), Flash replaces the content of the master symbol named `Circle` with the content of the source symbol named `Square`. Any instances of `Circle` in use in the destination movie get updated as well (**Figure 6.54**). All instances retain their individual positioning, sizing, and color effects.

Now any changes you make in the `Square` symbol in the source file get incorporated into the destination file when you publish the destination file.

✔ Tip

■ Earlier in this chapter, you learned to swap symbols within a single movie while retaining individual instance modifications. You can use author-time sharing as a sort of super symbol swap, bringing in a symbol that's not currently part of your document. Follow the steps in the preceding exercise, but omit step 9. Flash replaces the content of your selected symbol just once; future changes to the symbol in the source file will not affect the destination file.

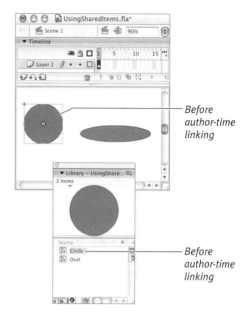

Before author-time linking

Before author-time linking

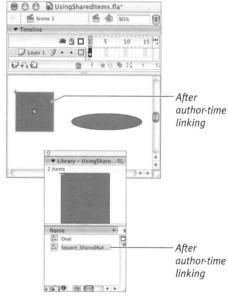

After author-time linking

After author-time linking

Figure 6.54 When you link the symbol named `Circle` to the author-time shared symbol named `Square` (top), Flash replaces the circle with the square. Unless you've renamed the `Circle` symbol, it's still called `Circle` in the destination file. You can give the symbol a name that indicates it's linked to another symbol (bottom).

Figure 6.55 Choose Linkage from the Library window's Options menu to define a shared symbol.

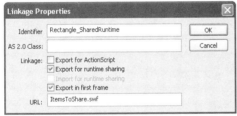

Figure 6.56 In the Linkage Properties dialog, select Export for Runtime Sharing to make a symbol available for sharing in other Flash movies (top). Fill in the identifier and URL for the symbol (bottom). Flash uses that information to locate and control the symbol. (The identifier must not contain any spaces. The URL is the pathway to the location of the source movie's Player file.)

To define symbols as shared for run time:

1. Open the source file (ItemsToShare.fla).

2. Open the Library window.

3. From the list of symbols, select the symbol to be shared: Rectangle.

4. From the Options menu in the top-right corner of the Library window, choose Linkage (**Figure 6.55**).
   The Linkage Properties dialog appears.

5. From the list of linkage options, select Export for Runtime Sharing (**Figure 6.56**).
   The name of the selected symbol appears in the Identifier field.

6. Enter an identifier for this shared symbol, such as Rectangle_SharedRuntime.
   Do not include spaces in the identifier.

7. In the URL field enter the pathname for the published version of the source file. For this exercise, enter ItemsToShare.swf.
   Because for this exercise, the source and destination files live in the same folder—and their Player (.swf) files will live there too (see the following exercise)—you can simply enter the name of the source Player (.swf) file. In real life, you will need to enter the path to the location where you will post the .swf file of shared symbols.

8. Click OK.

9. Save the file.

✔ Tip

■ You can define a symbol's linkage as Export for Runtime Sharing when you create the symbol. When you choose Insert > New Symbol or Modify > Convert to Symbol, the Symbol Properties dialog appears. The Linkage options are available in the expanded view of the dialog. Click the Advanced button if those options are not visible.

CREATING SHARED LIBRARIES

283

To make shared symbols available to other movies during playback:

1. Open the source file from the preceding exercises (ItemsToShare.fla).

   After creating and saving shared symbols in the Flash (.fla) file, you must create a Player (.swf) version of the file to make the shared items available for use in other movies.

2. From the File menu, choose Publish Settings.

   The Publish Settings dialog appears.

3. Click the Formats tab.

4. Check the Flash (.swf) check box (**Figure 6.57**).

   For the purpose of creating shared libraries, this check box is the only one that must be checked. Leave all other settings at their defaults. To learn more about the various publishing options and settings, see Chapter 17.

5. Click the Publish button.

   Flash exports the movie to a Flash Player file (ItemsToShare.swf) that contains the shared library. By default, the .swf file winds up in the same folder as the original file (*SharingTest*). (To learn to specify a different folder, see Chapter 17.)

6. Click OK.

✔ Tip

- To create a Flash Player file quickly, without going through the publishing process, all you need to do is test your movie. Choose Control > Test Movie. Flash creates a Player file, using default settings, and puts it in the same location as the .fla file.

Figure 6.57 In the Publish Settings dialog, check the Flash (.swf) check box to publish a .swf file that contains the shared library items.

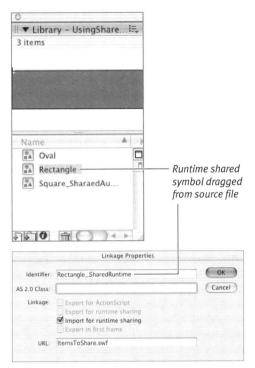

Runtime shared symbol dragged from source file

Figure 6.58 Dragging a run-time shared symbol into a destination file (top) creates the appropriate linkage automatically. Access the Linkage Properties dialog, and you can see that Flash has filled in the identifier and URL for the shared symbol automatically (bottom).

To add shared run-time symbols to your movie:

1. Open both the source file (ItemsToShare.fla) and the destination file (UsingSharedItems.fla) from the preceding exercises.

2. Open the Library window for each file.

3. Drag the Rectangle symbol from the source's Library window to the lower portion of the Library window of the open destination document.

   The shared symbol becomes part of the destination document's library. Because you set the symbol's linkage properties to Export for Runtime Sharing in the source file, Flash automatically sets the symbol's linkage properties to Import for Runtime Sharing in the destination file when you drag the symbol to the library. Flash enters the same identifier and URL that you entered when you originally made the symbol available for export as a shared symbol.

✔ Tips

- To verify that the shared symbol made it into the document with the correct links, open the library for the destination file. Select the symbol. From the Library window's Options menu, choose Linkage. In the Linkage Properties dialog, the symbol name should already appear, and the Import for Runtime Sharing check box should already be checked (**Figure 6.58**).

- You don't actually have to open the source file itself. You can use the File > Import > Open External Library command to open the source's library and then drag the symbol(s) you need to your destination library.

CREATING SHARED LIBRARIES

285

To link existing symbols in destination files to shared run-time symbols in source files:

1. With the destination file (UsingSharedItems.fla) active, open the Library window.

2. Select the symbol named Oval (or any symbol that you want to replace with a shared run-time symbol).

3. From the Options menu in the Library window, choose Properties.

   The Symbol Properties dialog appears.

4. In the Linkage section of the dialog, select Import for Runtime Sharing.

   If Linkage is not visible in the dialog, click the Advanced button to expand the dialog.

5. In the Identifier field, enter the identifier of the symbol you want to use—in this case, Rectangle_SharedRuntime.

   You create the link to a shared symbol by entering the identifier you used when you set linkage properties in the source file.

6. In the URL field, enter the pathname to the published Player file for the source symbol: ItemsToShare.swf.

   This step completes the link for playback.

7. Click OK (**Figure 6.59**).

8. Choose Control > Test Movie.

   Flash publishes the movie and opens the .swf file in the Player. You should now see the linked shared rectangle in the place where the oval symbol was originally.

✔ Tip

■ You can define a symbol's linkage as Import for Runtime Sharing when you create the symbol. When you choose Insert > New Symbol or Modify > Convert to Symbol, the dialog that appears contains the Linkage options. Click the Advanced button if those options are not visible.

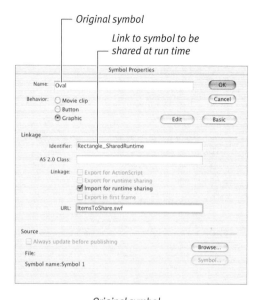

Original symbol

Link to symbol to be shared at run time

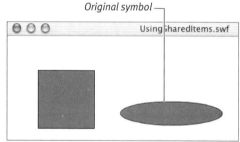

Original symbol

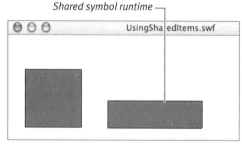

Shared symbol runtime

Figure 6.59 To define run-time symbol linkage manually from within a destination file, select the master symbol in the destination file's library, access the Linkage Properties dialog, specify Import for Runtime Sharing, and enter the identifier and URL for the run-time symbol in the source file. When you publish your movie, the linked symbol appears.

They'll Thank You for Sharing

Why use sharing? First, author-time sharing can help you control the consistency of elements and ensure that the most up-to-date versions of elements wind up in your finished movie. This practice is especially important when several people work on the same project. Imagine a project with five designers. If you create centralized files with the latest approved versions of all the graphic elements needed for the project, anyone working on the project can grab their symbols from the shared file. As updates get made—when the client wants to change the logo from red to blue, for example—the changes need to be made only in the shared source file. At publication time, Flash automatically updates all the instances of that shared logo symbol in all the files that linked to it.

You can think of author-time shared assets as being super symbols; the library of the shared source document becomes, in a sense, the library for all the documents containing symbols linked to it. Just as for individual .fla files, changes to a master symbol in a library update instances of that symbol in that movie; changes to shared symbols in a source file's library update instances of those symbols in all the movies containing links to those symbols. In both cases, the individual instances retain whatever color effects, positioning, or resizing you (or your colleagues) applied to them.

For regular libraries and their symbols, the updates take place immediately. For linked shared symbols, the updates take place on publication. But when you update the shared file, you update all the documents using instances of that symbol.

Note that the actual assets for a symbol linked for authoring purposes reside in each individual library file, whereas all the assets for symbols linked for run time stay in the one source file.

Symbols that are linked for sharing at run time can streamline movie playback/download for the end users who view your movies. These shared symbols are associated with a Flash Player file posted at a specific location accessible to the end user. Any number of published movies (.swf files) can then retrieve the linked symbols from that location.

For run-time sharing, you must create symbol links in two directions. In the file that acts as the source of shared symbols, you must give Flash permission to export the symbol at run time; in the file that links to those shared symbols, you must give Flash permission to import the symbol at run time. In both cases, you must specify the URL (the pathway to the source file's location) and the identifier for the symbol you want to use.

Using Font Symbols

Normally, Flash embeds the fonts you use within each published Flash movie. To avoid embedding the same font in multiple movies, you can create a special type of shared library element: the *font symbol*. Shared font symbols help you keep movie files smaller and make download times faster for your users.

The first step in setting up a shared font is creating a font symbol in a library; then you set the symbol's linkage properties just as you would for any other shared asset.

To create a font symbol:

1. Open the file containing symbols that you defined as shared in the preceding exercises (ItemsToShare.fla).

2. Open the file's Library window (choose Window > Library).

   The Library—ItemsToShare.fla window opens.

3. From the Options menu in the top-right corner of the Library window, choose New Font (**Figure 6.60**).

   The Font Symbol Properties dialog appears. Flash gives the symbol a default name—for example, Font 1 (**Figure 6.61**).

4. Enter a new name for the font if you want.

5. To specify which font is to be shared, *do one of the following:*

   ▲ In the Font field, enter the name of the font you want to be able to share.

   ▲ Click the triangle to the right of the field and choose a font from the drop-down menu.

6. Click OK.

Figure 6.60 From the Library window of the file where you are defining shared assets, choose Options > New Font to create a new font symbol.

Figure 6.61 Flash assigns a default name to Font symbols in the Font Symbol Properties dialog (top). You rename the font symbol and select a font for it (bottom).

Figure 6.62 To use a font symbol in a movie, choose it from the Font menu in the Property Inspector. The asterisk following a name in the font list indicates that the font is a font symbol.

To define a font symbol as a shared asset:

1. Open the source movie containing the font symbol you want to use (`ItemsToShare.fla`).

2. To set linkage properties for a font symbol, follow steps 2 through 9 in "To define symbols as shared for run time" earlier in this chapter, using the font symbol as your selected symbol.

3. To publish the library in a .swf file, follow the steps in "To make shared symbols available to other movies during playback" earlier in this chapter.

To use a font symbol in another movie:

1. Follow steps 1 through 3 in "To add shared run-time symbols to your movie" earlier in this chapter, using the font symbol as your selected symbol.

2. Make the destination file (`UsingSharedItems.fla`) the active movie.

3. In the Toolbar, select the Text tool.

4. Access the Text Tool Property Inspector.

   If the Property Inspector is not open, choose Window > Properties.

5. From the inspector's Font menu, choose the name of the shared font symbol (**Figure 6.62**).

   In font lists, an asterisk follows the name of a font symbol.

6. On the Stage, using the Text tool, create new text in the shared font.

FRAME-BY-FRAME ANIMATIONS

Frame-by-frame animation was the traditional form of animation used before the days of computers. Live-action movies are really a form of frame-by-frame animation. The movie camera captures motion by snapping a picture every so often. Animation simulates motion by showing drawings of objects at several stages of a motion.

Traditional animators, such as those who worked for the early Walt Disney or Warner Bros. studios from the 1930s through the 1960s, had to create hundreds of images, each one slightly different from the next, to achieve every movement of each character or element in the cartoon. To turn those drawings into animations, they captured the images on film, putting a different image in each frame of the movie.

Traditional animators painted individual characters (or parts of characters) and objects on transparent sheets called *cels*. They stacked the cels up to create the entire image for the frame. The cel technique allowed animators to save time by reusing parts of an image that stayed the same in more than one frame.

In Macromedia Flash MX 2004, you, too, can make frame-by-frame animations by placing different content in different frames. Flash calls the frames that hold new content *keyframes*.

Using the Timeline

In the Timeline, you have five size options for viewing frames and two options for previewing thumbnails of frame contents. A Flash movie may contain hundreds of frames; the Timeline's scroll bars enable you to access frames not currently visible in the Timeline window. You can also undock the Timeline so that it floats as a separate window and resize it to show more or fewer frames.

Figure 7.1 shows the Timeline for a movie with one layer and 15 defined frames.

To resize the Timeline's area:

1. Open a new Flash Document.

   The default Timeline appears.

2. Click the textured area on the left side of the title bar at the top of the Timeline, and drag away from the document window.

   A gray outline represents the Timeline window's new position.

3. With the Timeline in its new location, release the mouse button.

   The Timeline turns into a separate resizable window.

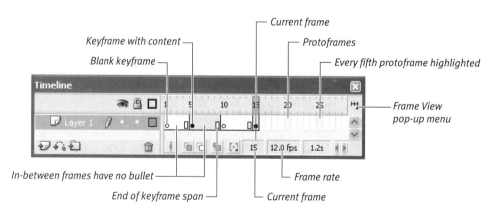

Figure 7.1 Similar to an interactive outline, the Timeline represents each frame of your movie. Click any frame, and Flash displays its contents on the Stage.

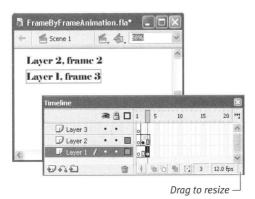

Drag to resize

Figure 7.2 After undocking the Timeline, you can resize it to show more frames.

4. Drag the bottom-right corner of the Timeline window to resize it as you would any other window (**Figure 7.2**).

You can make the Timeline wider than your open window showing the Stage to make more frames available without scrolling.

✔ Tips

- To redock the Timeline, reverse the procedure. Click inside the title bar at the top of the Timeline window, and drag toward the top of the document window. Position the Timeline at the top of the document window or over the Edit Bar at the top of the Stage, and release the mouse button. The Timeline redocks.

- For those who like a floating Timeline window, it can be a challenge not to redock the Timeline accidentally as you move windows around on your desktop. You can force the Timeline to stay undocked. Choose Edit > Preferences (Windows) or Flash > Preferences (Mac) to open the Preferences dialog; in the General tab, select Disable Timeline Docking.

The Mystery of Timeline Display

When you create a new Flash document, the Timeline displays a single layer with hundreds of little boxes. The first box has a solid black outline and contains a hollow bullet; the rest of the boxes are gray outlines. Every fifth box is solid gray. The box with the black outline and hollow bullet is a *keyframe;* the gray boxes are placeholder frames, or *protoframes*.

When you define a range of live frames by adding keyframes (see "Creating Keyframes" later in this chapter), the outline for the range of frames changes to black in the Timeline.

For a blank a keyframe (one that has no content on the Stage), the Timeline displays a hollow bullet. For a keyframe that has content, the Timeline displays a solid bullet.

Any in-between frames that follow a keyframe that has content display that content on the Stage. In the Timeline, the last in-between frame of a span contains a hollow rectangle. If you've set Frame View to Tinted Frames (the default), the in-between frames with content also have a tinted highlight in the Timeline.

To view frames in the Timeline at various sizes:

◆ In the Timeline, from the Frame View menu, choose a display option (**Figure 7.3**).

Flash resizes the frame representations in the Timeline to reflect your choice. **Figure 7.4** shows some of the frame views available.

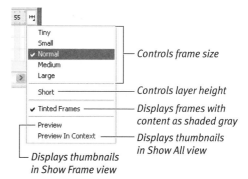

Controls frame size

Controls layer height

Displays frames with content as shaded gray

Displays thumbnails in Show All view

Displays thumbnails in Show Frame view

Figure 7.3 The Timeline's Frame View pop-up menu lets you control the display of frames in the Timeline.

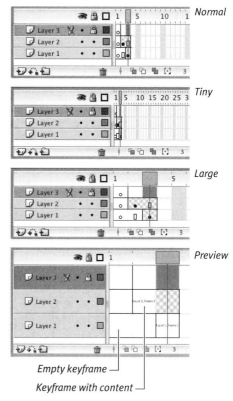

Normal

Tiny

Large

Preview

Empty keyframe —

Keyframe with content —

Figure 7.4 Flash can display the frames in the Timeline in a variety of sizes, from Tiny to Large. You can also preview the contents of each frame in the Timeline.

Selected frame

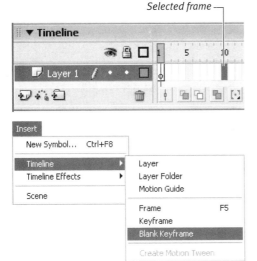

Last frame where content
from Keyframe 1 is visible

Figure 7.5 Select a frame in the Timeline (top) and then choose Insert > Timeline > Blank Keyframe (middle) to add a new blank keyframe (bottom).

Creating Keyframes

Flash offers two commands for creating keyframes. Insert > Timeline > Blank Keyframe defines a keyframe that's empty, and Insert > Timeline > Keyframe defines a keyframe that duplicates the content of the preceding keyframe in that layer. Use the Insert > Timeline > Blank Keyframe command when you want to change the contents of the Stage completely. Use Insert > Timeline > Keyframe when you want to duplicate the content of the preceding keyframe.

✔ Tip

■ The following tasks access frame-related commands from the main menu bar, but all the relevant commands for working with frames are available from the contextual frame menu as well. You can Control-click (Mac) or right-click (Windows) a frame in the Timeline to bring up the contextual frame menu.

To add a blank keyframe to the end of your movie:

1. Create a new Flash Document.

The new document by default has one layer and one blank keyframe at Frame 1.

2. In the Timeline, click the protoframe for Frame 10 to select it.

3. From the Insert menu, choose Timeline > Blank Keyframe (**Figure 7.5**).

Flash revises the Timeline to give you information about the frames you've defined. A hollow rectangle appears in Frame 9, and a black line separates Frame 9 from Frame 10. This line indicates where the content for one keyframe span ends and the content for the next keyframe begins. Flash replaces the gray bars separating protoframes 2 through 9 with gray tick marks and removes the gray highlight that appeared in every fifth frame of the undefined frames.

To create a blank keyframe in the middle of your movie:

1. Follow the steps in the preceding section to create a single-layer, 10-frame movie.

2. In the Timeline, click Frame 1 to select it.

3. Place an object on the Stage (use the drawing tools to create something new, copy something from another document, or bring in an instance of a symbol from a library).

   Flash updates the Timeline, adding a solid bullet to Frame 1 (**Figure 7.6**).

   With Tinted Frames selected in the Frame View menu (Flash's default setting), Flash shades Frames 1 through 9 with gray. The shading indicates that Keyframe 1 has content that remains visible until Frame 10 in this layer. A hollow rectangle appears in Frame 9, indicating the end of the span of in-between frames that displays the content of Keyframe 1.

   Frame 10 still contains a hollow bullet, meaning that it has no content. (Try clicking Frame 10 to see that the Stage is blank.)

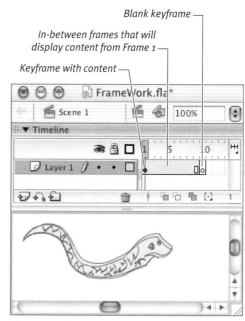

Blank keyframe

In-between frames that will display content from Frame 1

Keyframe with content

Figure 7.6 When you place content in a keyframe, Flash displays that frame in the Timeline with a solid bullet. The gray tint on the frames between keyframes indicates that content from the preceding keyframe appears during these frames. The hollow square indicates the end of the span of in-between frames displaying the same content.

Current frame ⎯

Display content from
preceding keyframe ⎯

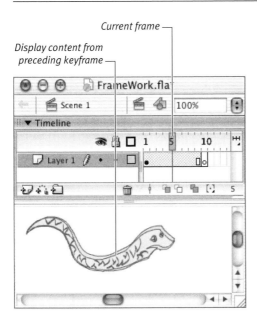

4. In the Timeline, click the number 5 or drag the playhead to position it in Frame 5.

Flash displays Frame 5 on the Stage. Notice that this in-between frame continues to display the content of the preceding keyframe, Frame 1.

5. From the Insert menu, choose Blank Keyframe.

Flash converts the selected in-between frame to a keyframe and removes all content from the Stage in that frame (**Figure 7.7**).

Blank keyframe inserted ⎯

Stage is empty ⎯

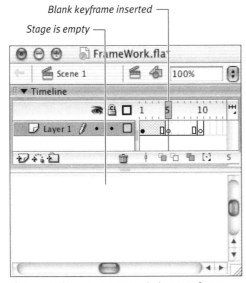

Figure 7.7 When you convert an in-between frame that displays content to a blank keyframe, Flash removes content from the Stage for that frame. Frames 6 through 9 are tinted when they display the content of Frame 1 (top). When you add a blank keyframe at Frame 5 (bottom), the tint disappears, because these frames now display the content of the most recent keyframe, Frame 5, which is empty.

To duplicate the contents of the preceding keyframe:

1. Open a new Flash Document.

2. Place some content in Frame 1.

3. In the Timeline, position the playhead in Frame 3.

4. From the Insert menu, choose Timeline > Keyframe.

   Flash creates a new keyframe, duplicates the contents of Frame 1 in Frame 3, and places a solid bullet in the Timeline at Frame 3 and a hollow rectangle in Frame 4 (**Figure 7.8**). The content of Frames 1 and 3 is totally separate. Try selecting Frame 1 and making changes—move the graphic or delete it. Now select Frame 3 again; it remains unchanged.

✔ Tips

■ The word *insert* used in connection with keyframes is a bit misleading. When you choose Insert > Timeline > Keyframe, Flash *adds* frames to your movie only if you've selected a protoframe. If you select an existing in-between frame, Insert > Timeline > Keyframe converts the selected frame to a keyframe and leaves the length of the movie as it was. The Insert > Timeline > Frame command, however, always adds frames to your movie.

■ The fact that Flash doesn't truly insert keyframes means that you cannot add a keyframe between two back-to-back keyframes. If you have keyframes in frames 5 and 6, and you select Frame 5 and choose Insert > Timeline > Blank Keyframe, Flash moves the playhead to Frame 6; Flash doesn't add a new blank keyframe. With Frame 5 selected, you must first choose Insert > Timeline > Frame. Flash creates an in-between frame at Frame 6. Now you can select Frame 5 or Frame 6 and choose Insert > Timeline > Blank Keyframe; Flash converts Frame 6 to a keyframe.

Current frame

Content of first keyframe

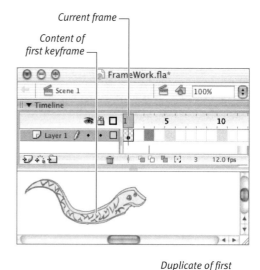

Duplicate of first keyframe

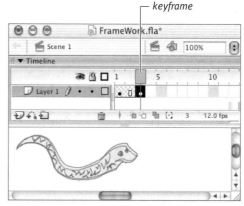

Figure 7.8 The Insert > Timeline > Keyframe command creates a keyframe that duplicates the contents of the preceding keyframe in that layer.

Keyframe Mysteries: Insert versus Convert

In addition to the Insert > Timeline > Keyframe and Insert > Timeline > Blank Keyframe commands, Flash offers commands for converting frames to keyframes. Choose Modify > Timeline > Convert to Keyframes (or press F6) or choose Modify > Timeline> Convert to Blank Keyframes (or press F7). These conversion commands are also found in the contextual menu for frames—Control-click (Mac) or right-click (Windows) a frame in the Timeline to access the menu.

Whether you should insert or convert keyframes depends on how many frames you have selected when you issue the command and how many frames you want to create. The Insert commands create a single keyframe regardless of how many frames you have selected; the Modify commands create multiple keyframes, one for each selected frame.

With a single frame selected, the Insert > Timeline > Keyframe command and the Modify > Timeline> Convert to Keyframe command work identically. If you select one protoframe or in-between frame, both commands transform that frame to a keyframe and duplicate the content of the preceding keyframe (if there is one). If you select a keyframe that is followed by an in-between frame or protoframe, both commands transform that following frame to a keyframe with the same content as the selected frame. Neither command has any effect on a selected keyframe that is followed by another keyframe.

With multiple protoframes or in-between frames selected, the Insert > Timeline > Keyframe command creates a single keyframe, usually in the same frame as the playhead (if you select frames at the end of your movie, the playhead can't actually move beyond the last defined frame, but Flash places the new keyframe in the last selected frame). The remaining selected frames become in-between frames.

With multiple protoframes or in-between frames selected, the Modify > Timeline> Convert to Keyframes command creates a keyframe in every selected frame.

The commands for blank keyframes work similarly. Insert > Timeline > Blank Keyframe creates one keyframe in the same frame as the playhead; the remaining frames become in-between frames. Modify > Timeline> Convert to Blank Keyframe creates a blank keyframe in all the selected frames.

Creating In-Between Frames

The frames that appear between keyframes are in a sense tied to the keyframe that precedes them. They display its content and allow you a space in which to create tweened animation (see Chapters 8 and 9). Flash makes the connections between these frames clear by highlighting them and placing a hollow rectangle at the end of the keyframe span.

To add in-between frames:

1. Create a new Flash Document with keyframes and content in Frame 1 and Frame 2.

2. In the Timeline, position the playhead in Frame 1.

3. From the Insert menu, choose Timeline > Frame, or press F5 on the keyboard (**Figure 7.9**).

   Flash adds an in-between frame (**Figure 7.10**). Your movie now contains a keyframe at Frame 1, an in-between frame at Frame 2, and another keyframe at Frame 3.

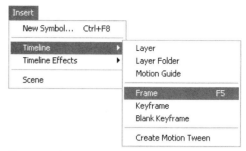

Figure 7.9 Choose Insert > Timeline > Frame to add in-between frames to the Timeline.

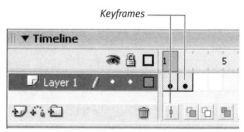

Timeline before evoking Insert > Timeline > Frame

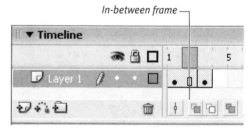

Timeline after evoking Insert > Timeline > Frame

Figure 7.10 The Insert > Timeline > Frame command adds an in-between frame after the selected frame. Unlike Insert > Timeline > Keyframe and Insert > Timeline > Blank Keyframe, which merely convert a selected in-between frame or protoframe to a keyframe, the Insert > Timeline > Frame command actually adds a new frame to your movie.

What Are Keyframes and In-Between Frames?

In the early days of animation, it took veritable armies of artists to create the enormous number of drawings that frame-by-frame animation requires. To keep costs down, the studios broke the work into various categories based on the artistic skill required and the pay provided. The work might start with creating spec sheets for each character. Then came storyboards that outlined the action over the course of the animation. Eventually, individual artists drew and painted hundreds of cels, each slightly different, to bring the animation to life.

To make the process manageable, animators broke each movement into a series of the most crucial frames that define a movement, called *keyframes,* and frames that incorporate the incremental changes necessary to simulate the movement, called *in-between frames*.

Keyframes define a significant change to a character or object. Imagine a 25-frame sequence in which Bugs Bunny starts out facing the audience and then turns to his right to look at Daffy Duck. This scene requires two keyframes—Bugs in a face-on view and Bugs in profile—and 23 in-between frames.

In the early days, some artists specialized in creating keyframes. Other artists—usually lower-paid—had the job of creating the frames that fell in between the keyframes. These in-betweeners (or tweeners, for short) copied the drawings in the keyframes, making just the slight adjustments necessary to create the intended movement in the desired number of frames while retaining the continuity of the character. In Chapters 8 and 9, you learn how to turn Flash into your own personal wage slave. The program takes on the drudgery of in-betweening for certain types of animation.

In Flash, you must use keyframes to define any change in the content or image, no matter how large or small the change. Flash doesn't use the term *in-between frames;* it simply uses the term *frame* for any frames that are not defined as keyframes. For clarity, the exercises in this book use the term *in-between frames* to refer to any defined frames that are not keyframes.

CREATING IN-BETWEEN FRAMES

Selecting Frames

Flash MX offers two styles for selecting frames in the Timeline. The default selection style, frame-based selection, treats every frame as an individual. The span-based style treats frames as members of a *keyframe span*—the keyframe plus any in-between frames that follow it and display its content. In the span-based selection style, clicking one frame in the middle of a span selects the entire span. When you understand the way each style works, you can choose one style (or change between styles) to take advantage of the different selection capabilities.

Except where noted, the examples in this book use Flash's default selection style, frame-based selection.

To choose a selection style:

1. From the Edit menu (Windows) or from the Flash application menu (Mac), choose Preferences.

The Preferences dialog appears.

2. Click the General tab (**Figure 7.11**).

3. In the Timeline Options section, *do one of the following:*

▲ To manipulate individual frames in the Timeline, uncheck the Span Based Selection check box.

▲ To manipulate keyframe spans in the Timeline, check the Span Based Selection check box.

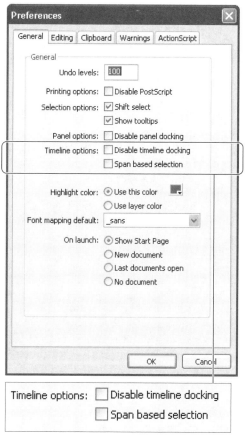

Figure 7.11 Choose the way frame selection works in the Timeline from the General tab of the Preferences dialog.

To work in frame-based selection mode:

In the Timeline, *do one of the following:*

◆ To select one protoframe, click it.

◆ To select two protoframes and all the frames between them, Shift-click the two protoframes.

◆ To select a keyframe, click it.

◆ To select the last frame in a keyframe span, click it.

◆ To select just a middle frame in a keyframe span, click that frame.

◆ To select an entire keyframe span, double-click a middle frame in the keyframe span.

◆ To add frames to your selection, Shift-click the frames. Flash selects all the frames between the playhead and the frame you Shift-click.

◆ To select a range of frames, click and drag through the frames.

To work in span-based selection mode:

In the Timeline, *do one of the following:*

◆ To select one protoframe, click it.

◆ To select two protoframes and all the frames between them, Shift-click the two protoframes.

◆ To select a keyframe, click it.

◆ To select the last frame in keyframe span, click it.

continues on next page

SELECTING FRAMES

- To select one in-between frame, ⌘-click (Mac) or Ctrl-click (Windows) that frame.

- To select an entire keyframe span, click a middle frame in the keyframe span.

- To select an entire keyframe span, Shift-click the first or last frame in the span.

- To add other spans to your selection, Shift-click the spans. The selection can include noncontiguous spans (**Figure 7.12**).

- To select a range of frames in the Windows operating system, Ctrl-drag through the frames.

✔ Tips

- In both selection styles, you can select all the frames in a layer by clicking the layer name. In span-base selection style, you can also select all the frames in a layer by double-clicking any frame.

- In both selection styles, you can select noncontiguous frames by ⌘-clicking (Mac) or Ctrl-clicking (Windows) each frame that you want to include.

- Can't remember what selection style you've got set in the Preferences dialog? Here's an easy way to check. In span-based selection style, when hovering over a keyframe or the last frame of a span, the pointer is a double-headed arrow. Over an in-between frame, the pointer is an arrow with a small square. In individual-frame selection style, when hovering over a keyframe or end-of-span frame, the pointer is an arrow with a square; over an in-between frame, the pointer is just an arrow (**Figure 7.13**).

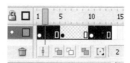

Figure 7.12 With Flash's span-based frame-selection style, you can Shift-click to select keyframe spans that are not contiguous.

Span-based

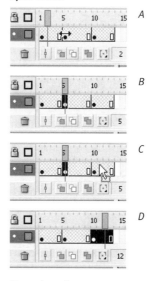

Frame-based

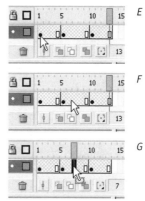

Figure 7.13 In span-based selection style, the pointer becomes a double-headed arrow when it's over a keyframe or end-of-span frame (A). Clicking selects that frame individually (B). Over an in-between frame, the pointer changes to an arrow with a square (C); clicking selects the whole keyframe span (D). In frame-based selection style, the pointer is the plain arrow when it's over a keyframe (E) or end-of-span frame; clicking selects that frame. Over an in-between frame, the pointer is a plain arrow (F); clicking selects just that frame (G).

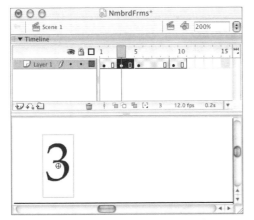

Figure 7.14 To practice moving frames around, create a document with keyframes at frames 1, 3, 5, and 9. Each keyframe contains a text box with the number of the frame.

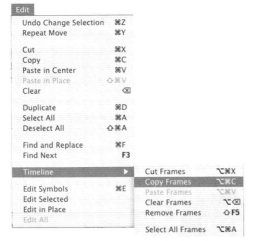

Figure 7.15 Flash's Edit menu provides special commands for copying and pasting frames in the Timeline.

Manipulating Frames in One Layer

You cannot copy or paste frames by using the standard Copy and Paste commands that you use for graphic elements. Flash's Edit menu provides special commands for copying and pasting frames. Flash also lets you drag selected frames to new locations in the Timeline.

For the following exercises, open a new Flash Document. Create a 10-frame movie with keyframes at frames 1, 3, 5, and 9. Using the text tool, place a text box in each keyframe, and enter the number of the frame in the text box; this technique makes it easy to tell what frame winds up where as you practice. Your document should look like **Figure 7.14**.

To copy and paste a single frame:

1. In the Timeline, select Frame 3.

2. From the Edit menu, choose Timeline > Copy Frames, or press Option-⌘-C (Mac) or Ctrl-Alt-C (Windows) (**Figure 7.15**).

   Flash copies the selected frame to the Clipboard.

   continues on next page

3. In the Timeline, click Frame 4 to select it as the location for pasting the copied frame.

4. From the Edit menu, choose Timeline > Paste Frames, or press Option-⌘-V (Mac) or Ctrl-Alt-V (Windows).

Flash pastes the copied frame into Frame 4 (**Figure 7.16**).

5. Paste another copy into Frame 5 (**Figure 7.17**).

Flash replaces the contents of Keyframe 5 with the content of Keyframe 3.

6. Paste another copy into Protoframe 12.

Flash extends the movie to accommodate the pasted frame.

Copy Keyframe 3

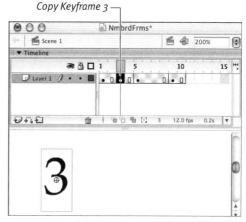

Selected Frame 4 for pasting

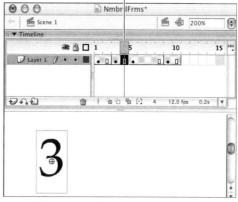

Flash pastes copied Keyframe 3 into Frame

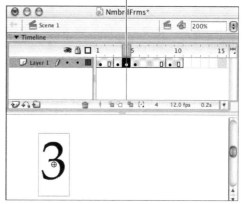

Figure 7.16 When you paste a frame with new content into an in-between frame, Flash converts the frame to a keyframe.

Flash replaces content of Keyframe 5...

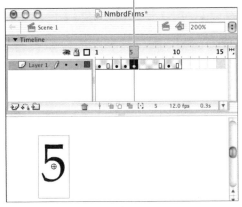

...with pasted Keyframe 3

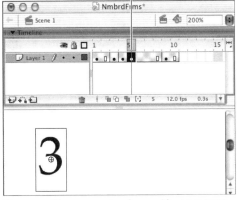

Figure 7.17 When you paste a frame with new content into a keyframe, Flash replaces the keyframe's content.

✔ Tips

- You can copy and paste multiple frames; in step 1 of the preceding exercise, select a range of frames.

- To copy and paste the content of a keyframe, you can also copy an in-between frame that displays that content. When you paste, Flash creates a new keyframe.

- Warning: Flash always replaces the content of the selected frame with the pasted frame (or, for multiple-frame pastes, with the first pasted frame). If you're not careful, you might eat up the content of keyframes you intended to keep. To be safe, always paste frames into in-between frames or blank keyframes. You can always delete an unwanted keyframe separately.

- You cannot paste frames between back-to-back keyframes in a single step. You must first create an in-between frame (press F5) between the two, select the new frame, and paste the copied frames into the new frame.

To move frames using drag and drop:

1. In the Timeline of your practice document, select the keyframe span that starts with Frame 5 and ends with Frame 8.

2. Position the pointer over the selected frames.

   The pointer changes to an arrow with a square.

3. Click and drag the selected frames.

   Flash further highlights the selection with a rectangle of hatched lines. Flash uses this rectangle to preview the new location for the selected frames as you drag in the Timeline.

4. To move the selected frames to the end of your movie, drag the rectangle past the last defined frame and into the area of protoframes, and release the mouse button.

   Flash adds frames to the end of the movie; these frames display the content from Frame 5. In frame-based selection style, Flash completely removes the content from frames 5 through 8 and adds those frames to the preceding span. In span-based selection style, Flash removes the content but keeps a keyframe at Frame 5 (**Figure 7.18**).

5. To move the selected frames to the beginning of your movie, drag the selected frames to Frame 1 and release the mouse button.

   The dragged frames replace the content of Frames 1 through 4.

Select and drag: either selection style

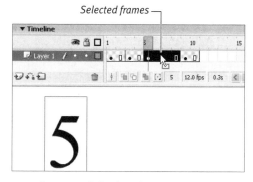

After drop: frame-based selection style

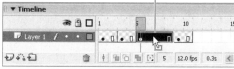

After drop: span-based selection style

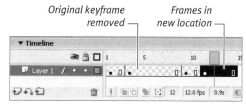

Figure 7.18 The process of dragging and dropping frames in the Timeline to relocate them is the same in Flash's two frame-selection styles (top). The results, however, are quite different (bottom). The frame-based selection style removes selected keyframes from their original location, leaving only in-between frames. The span-based style retains the original keyframes but removes their content.

The Trick to Extending Keyframe Spans

In span-based selection style, the pointer becomes a double-headed arrow when it hovers over a keyframe or an end-of-span frame. Use this pointer to drag that frame to the right or the left to increase or decrease the length of the span.

Resizing a span in the middle of other spans gets a bit tricky. Flash won't let your expanding span eat up the content of other keyframes. Your expansion can reduce the length of a neighboring span, however. In your practice document, for example, using span-based selection, position the pointer over the end of the span that runs from Frame 3 to Frame 4. With the double-headed arrow pointer, drag Frame 4 to the right. When you get to Frame 7, you can drag no further. Release the mouse button. The span that starts at Frame 3 now extends through Frame 7. The content that was originally in Keyframe 5 still exists, but Flash has pushed it into Frame 8.

To increase the length of a span without affecting the length of neighboring spans, select the span or any frame within it; then choose Insert > Timeline > Frame or press F5. Flash adds an in-between frame to the selected span and pushes all subsequent spans to the right in the Timeline.

When you reduce the size of a span by dragging, Flash creates blank keyframe spans to cover any gaps between the end of the span you are resizing and the beginning of the neighboring span.

✔ Tips

- To drag a copy of selected frames in the Timeline, hold down Option (Mac) or Alt (Windows) as you drag.

- In span-based selection mode, if you select a span that consists of a keyframe and one in-between frame, you never get the arrow-with-square pointer; you only get the double-headed arrow. That means you can't drag the span to move it. To move such spans, switch to frame-based selection, or Option-drag (Mac) or Alt-drag (Windows) a copy of the span; then remove the original.

- No matter which frame-selection style you use, pressing the ⌘ key (Mac) or Ctrl key (Windows) lets you access some of the functionality of the other style temporarily. In frame-based selection, the modifier lets you access the double-headed arrow pointer for extending keyframe spans. In span-based mode, the modifier gives you the arrow pointer for selecting individual frames.

- If you make a mistake in modifying the frames in the Timeline, you can undo your steps by choosing Edit > Undo. Operations such as dragging frames to move them or to extend spans may require repeated Undo commands, since some of the steps involved are things Flash does behind the scenes. To see the full set of steps, open the History Panel (see Chapter 13).

MANIPULATING FRAMES IN ONE LAYER

Removing Frames

Just as Flash has two kinds of frames and separate commands for creating each type, it has two commands for removing frames: Clear Keyframe and Remove Frames. The commands can be a little confusing at first. To choose the correct command, ask yourself in what sense you want to remove a frame. Do you want to eliminate it and reduce the length of the movie or just remove its status as a keyframe, keeping the same total number of frames?

Flash's Clear Keyframe command removes keyframe status from a selected frame or range of frames. Clear Keyframe changes keyframes into in-between frames and deletes the keyframes' content from the movie. Clear Keyframe has no effect on the number of frames in the movie.

Remove Frames removes frames (and their content, if they are keyframes) from the movie. Remove Frames reduces the number of frames in the movie.

For the following exercises, use the same practice document you created for working with the exercises in "Manipulating Frames in One Layer."

To remove keyframe status from a frame:

1. In the Timeline, select Keyframe 5.

2. From the Modify menu, choose Timeline > Clear Keyframe, or press Shift-F6 on the keyboard.

   Flash removes the bullet from Frame 5 in the Timeline (indicating that the frame is no longer a keyframe) and removes the graphic element it contained. Frame 5 becomes an in-between frame, displaying the contents of the keyframe at Frame 3 (**Figure 7.19**). The total number of frames in the movie remains the same.

Before clearing the keyframe

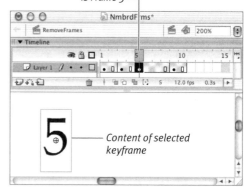

After clearing the keyframe

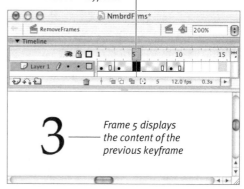

Figure 7.19 The Modify > Timeline > Clear Keyframe command removes the contents of the selected keyframe from the Stage and converts the keyframe to an in-between frame. The Clear Keyframe command doesn't change the overall length of the movie.

The Indelible Keyframe

The Remove Frames command appears to go haywire sometimes. This happens when you try to delete a keyframe without deleting the in-between frames that make up the whole keyframe span and when the content of the keyframe you are trying to remove differs from the content of the preceding keyframe.

In-between frames don't really have content, but Flash gives them virtual content because they show the graphic elements of the preceding keyframe. Any change in content requires a keyframe. If you try to delete a keyframe without deleting its associated in-between frames, a change in content seems to occur because of the leftover in-between frames. After removing the selected keyframe, Flash deals with the seeming change in content by transforming the next frame (originally, an in-between frame) into a keyframe using the virtual content. You wind up reducing the span by one frame, but the span still starts with a keyframe displaying the content you were trying to remove (**Figure 7.20**).

To avoid the problem, *do one of the following:*

◆   Select all associated in-between frames with any keyframes you want to delete.

◆   With the keyframe selected, delete the entire contents of the Stage before using the Remove Frames command.

◆   Use the Clear Keyframe command and then the Remove Frames command to reduce the number of in-between frames.

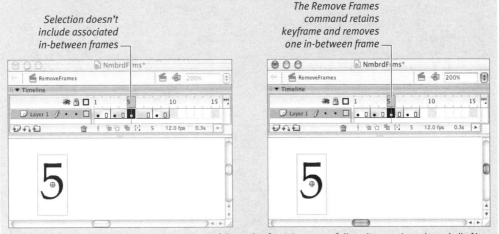

Selection doesn't include associated in-between frames

The Remove Frames command retains keyframe and removes one in-between frame

Figure 7.20 The Remove Frames command won't delete a keyframe's content fully unless you've selected all of its associated in-between frames.

To delete a single frame from a movie:

1. With your practice file in its original state (keyframes at 1, 3, 5, and 9), select Frame 4 in the Timeline.

   Frame 4 is an in-between frame associated with the keyframe in Frame 3.

2. From the Edit menu, choose Timeline > Remove Frames, or press Shift-F5 on the keyboard.

   Flash deletes Frame 4, reducing the overall length of the movie by one frame (**Figure 7.21**).

3. Now select the keyframe at Frame 3 and choose Edit > Timeline > Remove Frames again.

   Flash deletes the selected keyframe and its content, and reduces the length of the movie by one frame.

✔ Tip

- Flash doesn't allow you to use Clear Keyframe to remove keyframe status from the first frame of a movie, but you can delete it. If you select all the frames in the movie and choose Edit > Timeline > Remove Frames, Flash removes all the defined frames in the Timeline, leaving only protoframes. You must add back a keyframe at Frame 1 to place any content in the movie.

Selected in-between frame

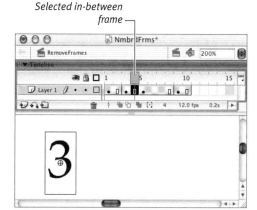

After deleting

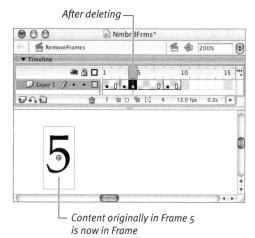

Content originally in Frame 5 is now in Frame

Figure 7.21 The Edit > Timeline > Remove Frames command removes frames from the movie and reduces its length.

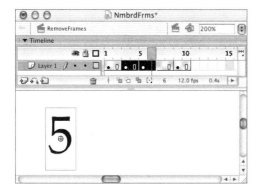

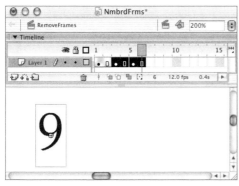

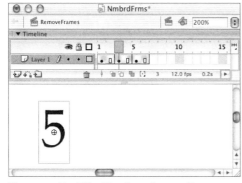

Figure 7.22 The Edit > Timeline > Remove Frames command can delete a selected range of frames. Because an entire keyframe span (frames 3 and 4) is included in the selection (top), Flash not only reduces the number of frames, but also removes the content of that keyframe span (middle). Where only part of a span is selected, the span gets shorter, but the content remains the same (bottom).

To delete a range of frames:

1. Using your practice file, in the Timeline, select frames 3 through 6.

2. From the Edit menu, choose Timeline > Remove Frames.

   Flash removes all the selected frames (**Figure 7.22**).

✔ Tip

- With frame-based selection style active, you can replace the contents of one keyframe with those of another quickly. Select an in-between frame that displays the contents you want to copy. Drag that source frame over the keyframe whose contents you want to replace. Flash copies the contents of the target keyframe with the contents of the source keyframe.

Making a Simple Frame-by-Frame Animation

In traditional cel animation or flip-book animation, you create the illusion of movement by showing a series of images, each slightly different from the rest, simulating snapshots of the movement. When you create each of these drawings and place them in a series of keyframes, that process is called *frame-by-frame animation*. When you create only the most crucial snapshots and allow Flash to interpolate the minor changes that take place between those snapshots, you're creating *tweened animation*. You learn more about tweening in Chapters 8 and 9.

A classic example of frame-by-frame animation is a bouncing ball. You can create a crude bouncing ball in just three frames.

To set up the initial keyframe:

1. Create a new Flash Document, and name it something like Frame-by-Frame Bounce.

   By default, Flash creates a document with one layer and a keyframe at Frame 1. Choose View > Grid > Show Grid to help you reposition your graphics in this exercise.

2. In the Timeline, select Frame 1.

   Use the Frame View pop-up menu to set the Timeline to Preview in Context mode. This setting makes it easy to keep track of what you do in the example.

3. In the Toolbar, select the oval tool.

4. Set stroke color to No Color.

5. Near the top of the Stage, draw a circle (**Figure 7.23**).

   This circle will be your ball. Make it fairly large.

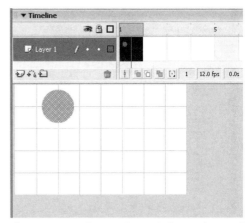

Figure 7.23 In Keyframe 1, draw a circle near the top of the Stage. This circle will become a bouncing ball.

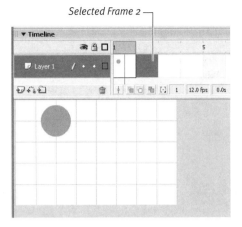

Selected Frame 2

To create the second keyframe:

1. In the Timeline, select Frame 2.

2. Choose Insert > Timeline > Keyframe.

   Flash creates a keyframe in Frame 2 that duplicates your ball from Frame 1.

3. In Frame 2, select the ball and reposition it at the bottom of the Stage (**Figure 7.24**).

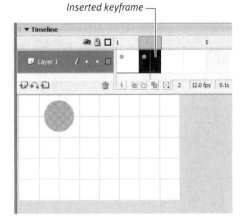

Inserted keyframe

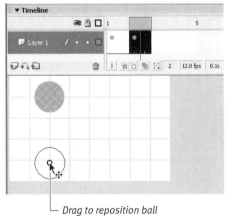

Drag to reposition ball

Figure 7.24 Use the Insert > Timeline > Keyframe command to duplicate the ball from Frame 1 in Frame 2. Then you can drag the ball to reposition it.

To create the third keyframe:

1. In the Timeline, select Frame 3.

2. Choose Insert > Timeline > Keyframe. Flash creates a keyframe in Frame 3 that duplicates your ball from Frame 2.

3. In Frame 3, select the ball and reposition it in the middle of the Stage (**Figure 7.25**).

That's it. Believe it or not, you have just created all the content you need to animate a bouncing ball. To see how it works, in the Timeline, click Frames 1, 2, and 3 in turn. As Flash changes the content of the Stage at each click, you see a very crude animation.

Selected Frame 3

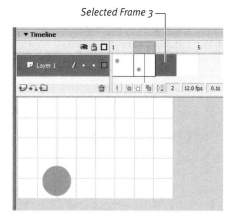

Inserted keyframe

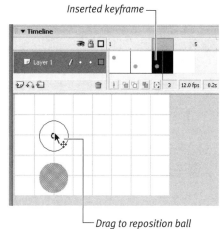

Drag to reposition ball

Figure 7.25 Use the Insert > Timeline > Keyframe command to duplicate the ball from Frame 2 in Frame 3. Drag the ball to reposition it again.

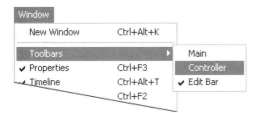

Figure 7.26 To access the Controller, from the Window menu choose Toolbars > Controller.

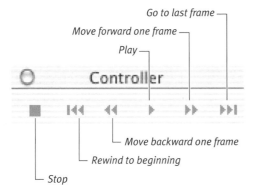

Figure 7.27 The Controller window contains VCR-style buttons for controlling playback of Flash movies.

Previewing the Action

Though you can click each frame to preview a movie, Flash provides more sophisticated ways to see your animation. The Controller window offers VCR-style playback buttons. The Control menu has commands for playback. You can also have Flash export the file and open it for you in Flash Player via the Test Movie command. (For more details about Test Movie, see Chapter 11.)

To use the controller:

1. From the Window menu, choose Toolbars > Controller (**Figure 7.26**).

Flash opens a window containing standard VCR-style buttons.

2. In the Controller window, click the button for the command you want to use (**Figure 7.27**).

✔ Tip

■ For those who prefer not to clutter the desktop with more floating windows, the Control menu in the main menu bar duplicates the Controller's functions.

To step sequentially through frames:

1. In the Timeline, select Frame 1.

2. From the Control menu (**Figure 7.28**), choose Step Forward One Frame, or press the period (.) key.
Flash moves to the following frame.

3. From the Control menu, choose Step Backward One Frame, or press the comma (,) key.
Flash moves to the preceding frame.

✔ Tip

■ You can *scrub* (scroll quickly back and forth) through the movie. Drag the playhead backward or forward through the frames in the Timeline. Flash displays the content of each frame as the playhead moves through it.

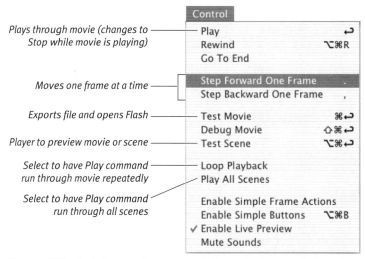

Figure 7.28 The Control menu offers commands for previewing your Flash movie.

Figure 7.29 Choosing Control > Loop Playback sets Flash to show your movie repeatedly when you subsequently issue a play command from the Controller, the Control menu, or the keyboard.

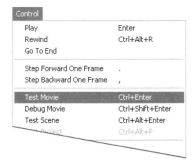

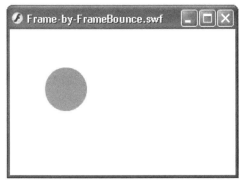

Figure 7.30 Choose Control > Test Movie (top) to see your movie in action in Flash Player (bottom).

To play through all frames in the Flash editor:

◆ To play through the frames once, from the Control menu choose Play, or press Enter.

Flash displays each frame in turn, starting with the current frame and running through the end of the movie. The Play command in the Control menu changes to a Stop command, which you can use to stop playback at any time.

✔ Tip

■ To play through the frames repeatedly, from the Control menu, choose Loop Playback (**Figure 7.29**). Now whenever you issue a Play command, Flash plays the movie repeatedly until you issue a Stop command.

To play frames in Flash Player:

◆ Choose Control > Test Movie (**Figure 7.30**).

Flash exports your movie to a Flash Player (.swf) file and opens it in Flash Player. Flash stores the .swf file at the same hierarchical level of your system as the original Flash file. The .swf file has the same name as the original, except that Flash appends the .swf extension.

✔ Tip

■ Warning: When you choose Control > Test Movie, Flash doesn't ask whether you want to replace an earlier version of the file that has the same name; it just replaces the file. The downside to that convention is that Flash may replace a file you don't intend it to replace. When you export a Flash movie yourself, it's tempting just to add the .swf extension to the original file name. Unfortunately, the Test Movie command will replace that file if it's in the same folder as the original movie. To be safe, always change the name of your movie when you export it yourself.

Smoothing the Animation by Adding Keyframes

The three-frame bouncing ball you created in the preceding exercise is crude; it's herky-jerky and much too fast. To smooth out the movement, you need to create more snapshots that define the ball's position in the air as it moves up and down. This means adding more keyframes and repositioning the ball slightly in each one.

In the preceding exercise, the ball moves from the top of the stage to the bottom in one step. In the following exercise, you expand that first bounce movement to three steps.

To add keyframes within an existing animation:

1. In the Timeline of the three-frame bouncing ball animation, select Frame 1.

2. Choose Insert > Timeline > Frame; then choose Insert > Timeline > Frame again.

   Flash creates new in-between frames at frames 2 and 3, and relocates the keyframes that show the ball at the bottom and middle of the stage to frames 4 and 5 (**Figure 7.31**).

3. In the Timeline, select frames 2 and 3.

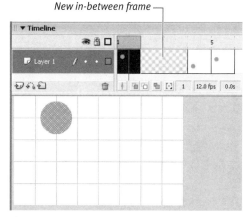

New in-between frame

Figure 7.31 With Frame 1 selected, invoking the Insert > Timeline > Frame command twice inserts two new in-between frames after the first frame and pushes the original Keyframe 2 (the ball at the bottom of the Stage) to Frame 4.

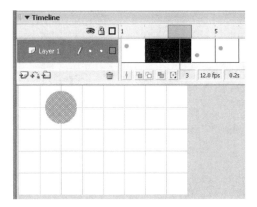

4. Choose Modify > Timeline > Convert to Keyframes.

Flash converts the in-between frames to keyframes that duplicate the content of Keyframe 1 (**Figure 7.32**).

5. In the Timeline, select Frame 2 and reposition the ball on the Stage.

You can use the grid line to help you visualize where to place the ball; you want to position it about a third of the distance between the top and bottom of the Stage.

continues on next page

Duplicates of Keyframe 1 —

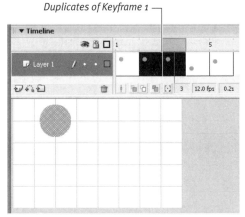

Figure 7.32 Modify > Timeline > Convert to Keyframes changes the selected in-between frames to keyframes containing the content of the preceding keyframe.

SMOOTHING THE ANIMATION BY ADDING KEYFRAMES

6. In the Timeline, select Frame 3 and reposition the ball on the Stage (**Figure 7.33**).

Position the ball about two-thirds of the distance between the top and bottom of the Stage.

7. Preview the animation, using any of the methods described in the preceding section.

The initial bounce movement is smoother. You can repeat these steps to add even more frames with incremental movement to the first half of the bounce. You can also add frames to make the second half of the bounce smoother.

Frames previewed in context

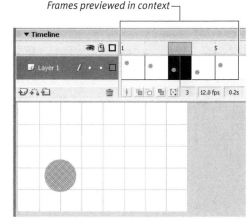

Figure 7.33 You can reposition the ball in keyframes 2 and 3 to make the first bounce smoother.

The Pitfall of Frame-by-Frame Animation

With frame-by-frame animation, the more frames you add, the smaller you can make the differences between frames and the smoother the action will be. Adding keyframes, however, also adds to your final movie's file size, which in turn affects the download time for people viewing your movie over the Web. Your goal is to strike a happy medium.

Turns on Onion Skin mode   *Onion skin markers*

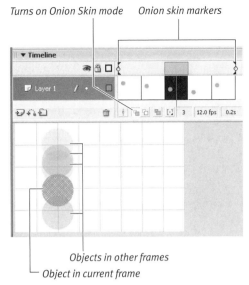

Objects in other frames

Object in current frame

Figure 7.34 In Onion Skin mode, Flash displays the content of multiple frames but dims everything that's not on the current frame. The onion skin markers in the Timeline indicate how many frames appear at the same time.

Using Onion Skinning

In the preceding section, you repositioned a circle to try to create smooth incremental movement for a bouncing ball. To make this task easier, Flash's onion skinning feature lets you see the circle in context with the circles in surrounding frames.

Onion skinning displays dimmed or outline versions of the content of surrounding frames. You determine how many of the surrounding frames Flash displays. The buttons for turning on and off the various types of onion skinning appear at the bottom of the Timeline, in the Timeline's Status bar.

To turn on onion skinning:

◆ In the Status bar of the Timeline, click the Onion Skin button.

The content of all the frames included in the onion skin markers appears in a dimmed form (**Figure 7.34**). You cannot edit the dimmed objects—only the full-color graphics in the current frame.

To turn on outline onion skinning:

◆ In the Status bar of the Timeline, click the Onion Skin Outlines button.

The content of all the frames included in the onion skin markers appears in outline form (**Figure 7.35**). You cannot edit the outline graphics—only the solid graphics that appear in the current frame.

To adjust the number of frames included in onion skinning:

1. In the Timeline, click the Modify Onion Markers button.

A pop-up menu appears, containing commands for setting the way the onion skin markers work (**Figure 7.36**).

2. To see frames on either side of the current frame, *do one of the following:*

   ▲ To see two frames on either side of the current frame, choose Onion 2.

   ▲ To see five frames on either side of the current frame, choose Onion 5.

   ▲ To see all the frames in the movie, choose Onion All.

Flash moves the onion skin markers around in the Timeline as you move the playhead. Flash always includes onion skins (either solid or outline) for objects in the selected number of frames before the current frame and after it.

✔ Tip

■ You can drag onion markers in the Timeline to include more frames or fewer frames in the onion skin view.

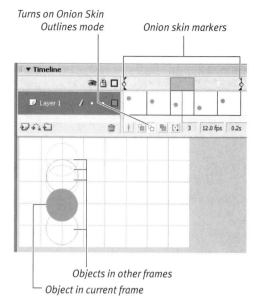

Turns on Onion Skin Outlines mode

Onion skin markers

Objects in other frames

Object in current frame

Figure 7.35 In Onion Skin Outlines mode, Flash displays the content of multiple frames, but it uses outlines for everything that's not in the current frame. Notice that two of the outlines appear very close together in this example of the bouncing ball. Using that visual cue, you can reposition the ball in Frame 4 to make the spacing (and, thereby, the movement) more even.

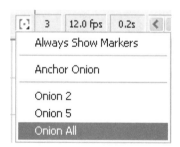

Figure 7.36 The Modify Onion Markers pop-up menu gives you control over the number of frames that appear as onion skins.

Anchored onion skin markers

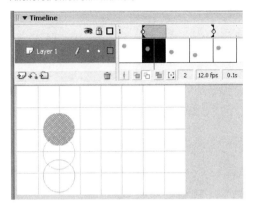

Moving playhead doesn't change markers

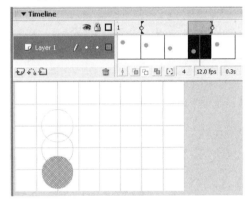

Figure 7.37 When you select Anchor Onion, Flash keeps the onion skin markers in place instead of moving them to follow the playhead. You can select any frame within the marked set and see the same set of onion skinned elements.

To display onion skins for a fixed set of frames:

◆ From the Modify Onion Markers menu, choose Anchor Onion.

Flash stops moving the onion skin markers when you move the playhead and simply displays as onion skins the frames currently within the markers. As long as you keep the playhead inside the anchored range, that set of frames stays in onion skin mode (**Figure 7.37**). This feature lets you work on frames within the set without constantly repositioning the onion skin markers.

Editing Multiple Frames

If you decide to change the location of an animated element, you must change the element's location in every keyframe in which it appears. Repositioning the items one frame at a time is not only tedious, but also dangerous. You might forget one frame, and you could easily get the animated elements out of alignment. Flash solves this problem by letting you move elements in multiple frames simultaneously. The same markers that indicate the frames to include in onion skinning indicate the frames you are allowed to edit simultaneously in Edit Multiple Frames mode.

To relocate animated graphics on the Stage:

1. Open your frame-by-frame animation of a bouncing ball.

2. In the Status bar, choose Edit Multiple Frames (**Figure 7.38**).

   Flash displays all graphics in all frames within the onion skin markers and makes them editable.

3. From the Modify Onion Markers menu, choose Onion All.

   Now you can see the ball at each stage of its bounce, and you can edit each of these stages.

4. In the Toolbar, select the selection tool.

5. Draw a selection rectangle that includes all the visible balls on the Stage (**Figure 7.39**).

   Flash selects them all.

Frames available for editing ⌐   *Current frame* ⌐

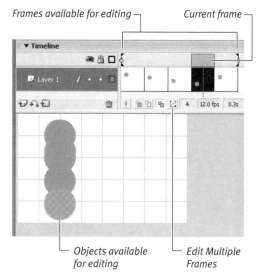

Objects available for editing —   *Edit Multiple Frames*

Figure 7.38 In Edit Multiple Frames mode, Flash displays and makes editable all the graphics in the frames that the onion skin markers indicate. This feature makes it possible to move an animated graphic to a new location in every keyframe at the same time.

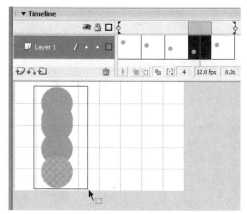

Figure 7.39 In Edit Multiple Frames mode, you can use a selection rectangle to select graphics in any of the frames enclosed in the onion skin markers.

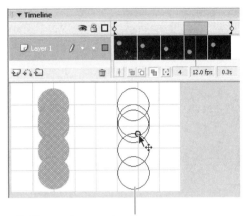

Outline previews new location as you drag selected objects

Figure 7.40 In Edit Multiple Frames mode, you can relocate an animated graphic completely, moving it in every keyframe with one action.

Outline-mode toggle

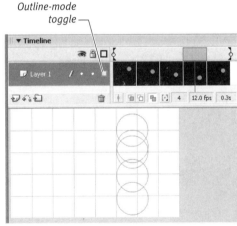

Figure 7.41 Select Outline mode to make it easier to work with graphics in multiple frames.

6. Drag the selection to the opposite side of the Stage (**Figure 7.40**).

With just a few steps, you've relocated the bouncing ball. (Imagine how much more work it would have been to select each frame separately, move the circle for that frame, select the next frame, line the circles up precisely in the new location, and so on.)

✔ Tip

■ When you select Edit Multiple Frames, Flash no longer displays onion skinning. If you find it confusing to view solid objects in multiple frames, turn on Outline view in the layer-properties section of the Timeline (**Figure 7.41**).

Understanding Frame Rate

The illusion of animation relies on the human brain's ability to fill in gaps in continuity. When we see a series of images in very quick succession, our brain perceives a continuous moving image. In animation, you must display the sequence of images fast enough to convince the brain that it's looking at a single image.

Frame rate controls how fast Flash delivers the images. If the images come too fast, the movie turns into a blur. Slow delivery too much, and your viewers start perceiving each frame as a separate image; then the movement seems jerky. In addition, when you're working in Flash, you're most likely planning to deliver the movie over the Web, and you may not be able to get the precise control you'd like to have to deliver a fast frame rate. The standard rate for film is 24 frames per second (fps). For animation that's going out over the Web, 12 fps is a good setting.

In Flash, you can set only one frame rate for the entire movie. You set the frame rate in the Document Properties dialog.

To set the frame rate:

1. To access the Document Properties dialog, *do one of the following*:

   ▲ From the Modify menu, choose Document, or press ⌘-J (Mac) or Ctrl-J (Windows).

   ▲ In the Timeline's Status bar, double-click the frame-rate number (**Figure 7.42**).

2. In the Document Properties dialog, enter a value in the Frame Rate field (**Figure 7.43**).

3. Click OK.

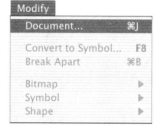

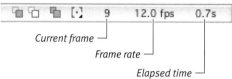

Current frame ⏐
Frame rate ⏐
Elapsed time ⏐

Figure 7.42 To call up the Document Properties dialog, choose Modify > Document (top) or double-click the frame-rate number in the Timeline's Status bar (bottom).

Frame rate ⏐

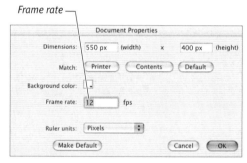

Figure 7.43 Enter a new value in the Frame Rate field. Flash's default frame rate is 12 fps.

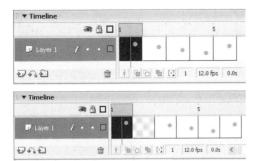

Figure 7.44 Select a frame and press F5 (top); Flash inserts an in-between frame directly after the selected frame.

Varying the Speed of Animations

Though the frame rate for a movie is constant, you can make any particular bit of animation go faster or slower by changing the number of frames it takes to complete the action. You can lengthen a portion of an animation by adding more keyframes or by adding in-between frames. In the bouncing-ball example, the ball might drop down slowly (say, over five frames) but rebound more quickly (over three frames). The smoothest frame-by-frame animation, has many keyframes each showing the ball in a slightly different position. Adding keyframes, however, increases file size. Sometimes, you can get away with simply adding in-between frames to slow the action. In-between frames add little to the exported movie's file size.

To add in-between frames:

1. Open (or create) a five-frame bouncing-ball movie.

   Frame 1 is a keyframe showing the ball at the top of the Stage, frames 2 and 3 are keyframes showing the ball at two places in its descent, Frame 4 shows the ball at the bottom of the Stage, and Frame 5 shows the ball bouncing halfway back up. (For step-by-step instructions, see the exercises in "Smoothing the Animation by Adding Keyframes" earlier in this chapter.)

2. From the File menu, choose Save As, and make a copy of the file.

   Give the file a distinguishing name, such as Bounce Slower.

3. In the copy's Timeline, select Frame 1.

4. From the Insert menu, choose Timeline > Frame (or press F5 on the keyboard).

   Flash inserts an in-between frame at Frame 2 and pushes the keyframe that was there to Frame 3 (**Figure 7.44**).

continues on next page

VARYING THE SPEED OF ANIMATIONS

5. Repeat steps 3 and 4 for the second and third keyframes in the movie.

You wind up with keyframes in Frames 1, 3, 5, 7, and 8 (**Figure 7.45**).

6. From the Control menu, choose Test Movie.

Flash exports the movie to a .swf file and opens it in Flash Player. Play through the regular 5-frame bouncing ball, then play through the one you just created (the one named Bounce Slower). You can see that the action in the movie with added in-between frames feels different from the action in the one in which one keyframe directly follows another.

Figure 7.45 With in-between frames separating the initial keyframes, the first part of the animation moves at a slower pace than the second.

✔ **Tip**

■ Keep in mind that this example serves to illustrate a process. In most animations, you would not want to overuse this technique. If you simply add many in-between frames, you'll slow the action too much and destroy the illusion of movement.

ANIMATION WITH MOTION TWEENING

8

Frame-by-frame animation has two drawbacks: First, it's labor-intensive; second, it creates large files. Macromedia Flash MX 2004 offers a way to mitigate both problems with a process called *tweening*. In Chapter 7, you created a three-frame animation of a bouncing ball by changing the position of the ball graphic in each of the three keyframes. Then you learned how to stretch out the animation by adding in-between frames that simply repeated the contents of the preceding keyframe. With tweening, you create similar keyframes, but Flash breaks the keyframe changes into multiple steps and displays them in the in-between frames.

To tween a graphic, Flash creates a series of incremental changes to that graphic; these changes are simple enough that Flash can describe them mathematically. Flash performs two types of tweening: motion tweening and shape tweening. This chapter covers motion tweening; Chapter 9 covers shape tweening.

Both types of tweening follow the same basic pattern. You give Flash the beginning and end of the sequence by placing graphic elements in keyframes. Then you tell Flash to spread the change out over a certain number of steps by placing that number of frames between the keyframes. Flash creates a series of images with incremental changes that accomplish the action in the desired number of frames.

Creating a Bouncing Ball with Motion Tweening

To have a working motion tween, you need three things: a beginning keyframe containing a group or a symbol, in-between frames defined as motion tweens, and an ending keyframe containing the same group or symbol to which you've made some kind of change. To create a motion tween you must place the appropriate type of content in the beginning and ending keyframes and then define the frame sequence as a motion tween in the Frame Property Inspector. You can get assistance in making motions tweens from the Create Motion Tween command, which you'll learn about later in this chapter. Some Timeline Effects also use motion tweening, you'll learn more about them in Chapter 10.

To access the Frame Property Inspector:

◆ With the Property Inspector open, select a Frame in the Timeline.

The Property Inspector displays information about the selected frame (**Figure 8.1**). (If the Frame Property Inspector is not open, choose Window > Properties.)

You can use motion tweening to create the same bouncing ball you made in Chapter 7, but in a slightly different way.

To prepare keyframes for motion tweening:

1. Create a new Flash Document, and name it something like Motion Tween Bounce.

   By default, Flash creates a document with one layer and a keyframe at Frame 1.

2. In the Timeline, select Frame 1.

3. In the Toolbar, choose the oval tool, and set the stroke to No Color.

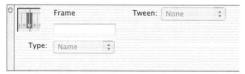

Protoframe selected in Timeline

Keyframe selected in Timeline

Figure 8.1 When you select a frame in the Timeline, the Property Inspector displays information about that frame.

Keyframes

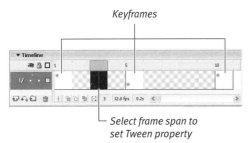

Select frame span to set Tween property

Figure 8.2 The initial keyframes for a motion tween are similar to those of a frame-by-frame animation. The difference is that you must use a symbol or a grouped object and define the keyframe span's Tween property.

Which Frames Contain Tweening?

As your road map of the movie, the Timeline provides visual cues about which frames contain tweens. Flash draws an arrow across a series of frames to indicate that those frames contain a tween.

Flash color-codes frames in the Timeline to distinguish motion tweens from shape tweens. With Tinted Frames active (choose it from the Frame View pop-up menu at the right end of the Timeline), Flash applies a light bluish-purple shade to the frames that contain a motion tween. If Tinted Frames is inactive, the frames are white (Mac) or cross-hatched (Windows), and Flash changes the arrow that indicates the presence of a tween from black to red. Flash indicates shape tweens by tinting frames light green (if Tinted Frames is active) or by changing the tweening arrow to light green (if Tinted Frames is inactive).

Frames containing a dotted line are set to contain a tween (either Motion or Shape), but something is wrong and Flash cannot complete the tween. Such tweens are called *broken* tweens.

4. Near the top of the Stage, draw a circle. This circle will be the ball. Make it fairly large.

5. Select the circle, and from the Modify menu, choose Convert to Symbol.

The Convert to Symbol dialog appears. Flash can make motion tweens only from symbols or groups. Using a symbol is the most efficient practice. Symbols help to keep final file sizes small; you can name the symbols, reuse them, find them in the library to modify, and so on.

6. Enter a name for your symbol—for example, `Ball`—and click OK.

7. In the Timeline, select Frame 5, and choose Insert > Timeline > Keyframe.

The Insert > Timeline > Keyframe command makes a new keyframe that contains the same elements as the preceding keyframe.

8. Select Frame 10, and choose Insert > Timeline > Keyframe.

9. Select Frame 5, and drag the ball to the bottom of the Stage.

You have just set up a frame-by-frame animation quite like the one you did in Chapter 7. In Frame 1, the ball is at the top of its bounce; in Frame 5, the ball is at the bottom of its bounce; and in Frame 10, the ball is back up at the top (**Figure 8.2**). To create a tweened animation, you must set the tween property for the in-between frames in each sequence.

CREATING A MOTION TWEEN

To set the span's property to Motion Tween:

1. To define a motion tween for the first half of the ball's bounce, in the Timeline, select any of the frames in the first keyframe span (1, 2, 3, or 4).

   Note that Flash automatically selects the ball symbol. When you define a motion tween, the item to be tweened must be selected.

2. From the Frame Property Inspector's Tween pop-up menu, choose Motion.

   The parameters for the motion tween appear (**Figure 8.3**). You learn more about using these parameters in the following exercises.

   Flash defines frames 1 through 4 as a motion tween, updating the Timeline to give you information about the tween (see the sidebar "Which Frames Contain Tweening?") (**Figure 8.4**). These in-between frames are still "empty," in the sense that there is nothing on the Stage that you can edit if you select one. They no longer display the content of the preceding keyframe, but they display the incrementally changed content that Flash creates.

3. To define the motion tween for the second half of the ball's bounce, in the Timeline, select any of the frames in the second keyframe span (5, 6, 7, 8, or 9).

4. Repeat step 2.

   Flash creates the second half of the ball's bounce with another motion tween (**Figure 8.5**).

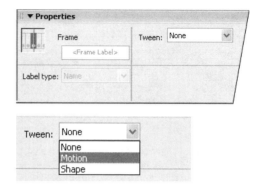

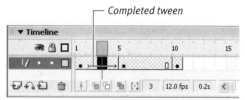

Figure 8.3 Choose Motion from the Frame Property Inspector's Tween pop-up menu to access the parameters for motion tweens.

Completed tween

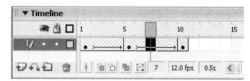

Figure 8.4 Flash adds information to the Timeline to indicate when frames contain motion tweens. Here, a blue tint and an arrow mean a completed motion tween.

Figure 8.5 With two motion-tween sequences, you can create a bouncing ball: One sequence shows the downward motion, the other shows the rebound.

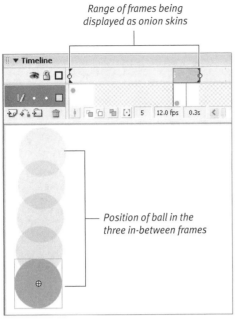

Range of frames being displayed as onion skins

Position of ball in the three in-between frames

Figure 8.6 Turn on onion skinning to preview the positions of a tweened object on the Stage.

✔ Tips

■ When you choose Preview or Preview in Context from the Frame View pop-up menu (at the right end of the Timeline), you can't see the incremental steps Flash creates for the tween. But if you turn on onion skinning, you can see all the in-between frames in position on the Stage (**Figure 8.6**).

■ Here's another way to select the proper frames for defining a motion tween. Position the playhead within the keyframe span that you want to tween; then, with the selection tool, select the symbol or grouped graphic on the Stage. Flash selects the keyframe span in the Timeline as well.

Motion Tweening or Shape Tweening?

The key to deciding whether to use motion tweening or shape tweening is to ask yourself whether you could make this change via a dialog, Property Inspector, or another panel. If the answer is yes, Flash can make the change with motion tweening. If the answer is no—if the change requires redrawing the object to be animated—Flash must use shape tweening.

Another important distinction between motion tweening and shape tweening is that motion tweening works only on symbols and groups, whereas shape tweening works only on editable shapes. Though you can sometimes arrive at the same tweening effect with either a motion tween or a shape tween, it's best to reserve shape tweens for the shape-changing animations that you can't achieve with motion tweens.

If you want to tween a multipart graphic— say, a robot constructed of many shapes—and you don't want to tween each shape separately, you'll need to make that graphic a symbol or group. When the graphic is a symbol, you can tween it only with motion tweening. If you want to create morphing effects—transforming a pumpkin into a magic coach, for example—you must use shape tweening. In addition, if you want Flash to move a tweened graphic around the Stage along a curving path (as opposed to a straight line), you must use motion tweening.

Adding Keyframes to Motion Tweens

After you have set up a motion tween, Flash creates new keyframes for you when you reposition a tweened object in an in-between frame. You can also add new keyframes by choosing Insert > Timeline > Keyframe.

To add keyframes by repositioning a tweened object:

1. Create a 10-frame motion tween of a bouncing ball, following the steps in the preceding exercise.

2. In the Timeline, select Frame 3.

   On the Stage, you see the ball symbol in one of the in-between positions Flash created.

3. In the Toolbar, select the selection tool.

4. Drag the ball to a new position—slightly to the right of its current position, for example.

   Flash inserts a new keyframe at Frame 3 and splits the preceding five-frame tween into separate tweens (**Figure 8.7**). The new keyframe contains another instance of the ball symbol. As you drag the ball symbol, the Timeline displays the broken-tween dotted line. Once you release the mouse, the completed-tween arrow appears in the new tween sequence.

To add keyframes by command:

1. Continuing with the document from the preceding exercise, select Frame 7 in the Timeline.

2. Choose Insert > Timeline > Keyframe.

   Flash creates a new keyframe in Frame 7. A new instance of your symbol appears on the Stage in the in-between position Flash created for it in that frame. You can now reposition the symbol.

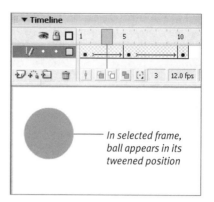

In selected frame, ball appears in its tweened position

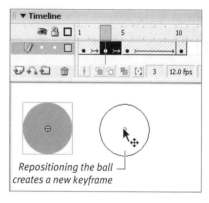

Repositioning the ball creates a new keyframe

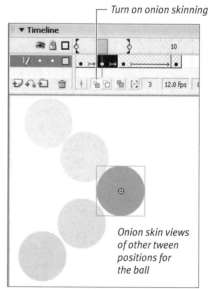

Turn on onion skinning

Onion skin views of other tween positions for the ball

Figure 8.7 Repositioning the ball in an in-between frame that's part of a tween creates a new keyframe and a revision of the tweened frames.

ADDING KEYFRAMES TO MOTION TWEENS

Figure 8.8 You can change the color of a symbol rather than its position in a motion tween. Flash creates transitional colors for each in-between frame.

Animating Color Effects

Tweening is not just about changing the position of an item on the Stage. You can also tween changes in the color of symbol instances.

To change a symbol's color over time:

1. Create a new Flash document.

2. On the Stage, place a symbol in Frame 1.

3. In the Timeline, select Frame 5, and choose Insert > Timeline > Keyframe.

   Flash duplicates the contents of Frame 1 in a new keyframe.

4. With Frame 5 as the current frame, select the symbol and change its color.

   (To change the color of a selected symbol, set new parameters in the Color section of the Property Inspector. For detailed instructions on editing symbols, see Chapter 6.)

5. Select any of the frames in the first keyframe span (1, 2, 3, or 4).

6. From the Property Inspector's Tween pop-up menu, choose Motion.

   Flash recolors the object in three transitional steps—one for each in-between frame (**Figure 8.8**).

✔ Tip

■ You can tween a change in an object's transparency to make that object appear to fade in or out.

Animating Graphics That Change Size

Flash can tween changes in the size of a graphic. To tween graphics that grow or shrink, you must check the Scale check box in the Frame Property Inspector.

To tween a growing and shrinking graphic:

1. Create a new Flash document.

2. On the Stage, place a symbol instance in Frame 1.

   To review creation and use of symbols, see Chapter 6.

3. To create a keyframe that defines the end of a growing sequence, in the Timeline, select Frame 5; then choose Insert > Timeline > Keyframe.

   Flash duplicates the symbol from Frame 1 in the new keyframe.

4. Select any of the frames in the keyframe span (1, 2, 3, or 4).

5. Set the Tween property for the span to Motion.

   To set the property, from the Property Inspector's Tween pop-up menu, choose Motion. The motion-tween arrow and color coding now appear in frames 2 through 4.

6. With the playhead in Frame 5, select your graphic and make it bigger.

   (For detailed instructions on resizing graphics, see Chapter 3.)

7. In the Timeline, select any of the frames in the first keyframe span (1, 2, 3, or 4).

8. In the Property Inspector, check the Scale check box.

   Flash increases the size of your graphic in equal steps from Frame 1 to Frame 5 (**Figure 8.9**).

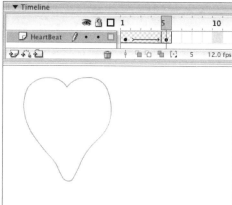

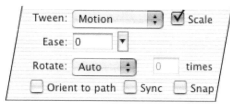

Figure 8.9 To tween a growing graphic, the graphic in the first keyframe of the sequence (top) must be smaller than the graphic in the end keyframe of the sequence (middle). To make the graphic grow in equal steps, set the Tween property of the frames in the tweened span to Motion, and choose the Scale property. You set the properties for a selected frame in the Frame Property Inspector (bottom).

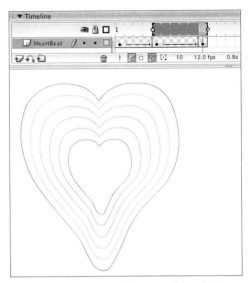

Figure 8.10 To tween a shrinking graphic, make it smaller in the end keyframe of the sequence. Turn on Onion Skin mode to see the size of the graphic Flash creates for each in-between frame.

To tween a shrinking graphic:

1. To add an ending keyframe for a shrinking sequence, in the Timeline, select Frame 10; then press F6.

Flash duplicates the symbol from Frame 5 in the new keyframe.

2. Select any of the frames in the keyframe span (5, 6, 7, 8, or 9).

3. Set the Tween property for the span to Motion (see step 5 of the preceding exercise).

The motion-tween arrow and color coding now appear in frames 6 through 9. The Scale property is already selected.

4. With the playhead in Frame 10, select your graphic and make it smaller.

Flash creates a tween that shrinks your graphic in five equal steps (**Figure 8.10**).

✔ Tip

■ As long as you don't change the settings in the Frame Property Inspector, the Scale check box remains checked, and Flash updates the tween any time you change the content in one of the keyframes in this series. You don't even have to have the Frame Property Inspector open to fine-tune the size of your scaling graphic.

ANIMATING GRAPHICS THAT CHANGE SIZE

Rotating and Spinning Graphics

You cannot create tweens of rotating and spinning graphics quite as simply as you create the types of tweens presented in the preceding exercises, because you can't describe rotation accurately with just two keyframes.

Imagine, for example, trying to rotate the pointer of a compass 180 degrees so that it turns from pointing north to pointing south. The initial keyframe contains the pointer pointing up; the ending keyframe contains the pointer pointing down. But how should the pointer move to reach that position?

Flash gives you three choices: rotate the pointer clockwise, rotate it counterclockwise, or simply flip it upside down. Trying to describe the pointer spinning all the way around the compass in just two keyframes would be even less informative, because the beginning and ending keyframes would be identical.

To clarify the motion, you could create a series of keyframes, rotating the pointer a few degrees in each one. That method is tedious, however, and adds to the file size of the final exported movie. Fortunately, Flash's Frame Property Inspector lets you provide extra information about tweens so that Flash can create rotational tweens with just two keyframes.

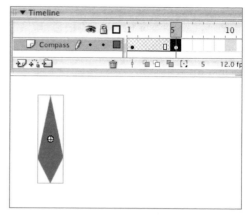

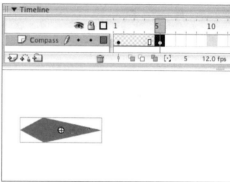

Figure 8.11 To prepare a rotational tween, in the keyframe that ends the tween, rotate the item to its ending position.

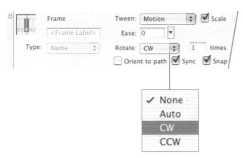

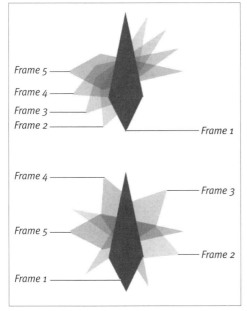

Figure 8.12 The Rotate menu in the Frame Property Inspector lets you tell Flash the direction in which to rotate a tweened object.

Figure 8.13 To create a tween that involves rotation, you can specify the direction of the rotation as clockwise or counterclockwise. You can also let Flash pick the direction that involves the smallest change, which allows Flash to create the smoothest motion. Compare the degree of change in each frame between rotating an arrow clockwise from 12 o'clock to 3 o'clock (top) versus rotating the arrow counterclockwise to reach the same position (bottom).

To rotate a graphic less than 360 degrees:

1. Create a new Flash document.

2. On the Stage, in Frame 1, create a new graphic (or place a symbol instance).

   Be sure to use something that will look different at various stages of its rotation (for example, a triangle or arrow).

3. If you've created a new graphic, select it and then choose Insert > Convert to Symbol or Modify > Group.

   Flash can create motion tweens only from grouped items or from symbols.

4. In the Timeline, select Frame 5, and choose Insert > Timeline > Keyframe.

   Flash duplicates the symbol from Frame 1 in the new keyframe.

5. On the Stage, in Frame 5, rotate your graphic 90 degrees clockwise (**Figure 8.11**).

   (For detailed instructions on rotating objects, see Chapter 3.)

6. In the Timeline, select any of the frames in the first keyframe span (1, 2, 3, or 4).

7. From the Frame Property Inspector's Tween pop-up menu, choose Motion.

   The parameters for motion tweening appear in the panel.

8. From the Rotate menu (**Figure 8.12**), *choose one of the following options:*

   ▲ To rotate the graphic in the direction that requires the smallest movement, choose Auto (**Figure 8.13**).

   ▲ To rotate the graphic clockwise, choose CW.

   ▲ To rotate the graphic counterclockwise, choose CCW.

   Flash tweens the graphic so that it rotates around its transformation point. Each in-between frame shows the graphic rotated a little more.

To spin a graphic 360 degrees:

1. Follow steps 1 through 4 of the preceding exercise to create a five-frame movie with identical keyframes in Frame 1 and Frame 5.

   You don't need to reposition your graphic, because the beginning frame and ending frame of a 360-degree spin should look exactly the same.

2. In the Timeline, select any of the frames in the first keyframe span (1, 2, 3, or 4).

3. From the Frame Property Inspector's Tween pop-up menu, choose Motion.

   The parameters for motion tweening appear in the panel.

4. From the Rotate menu, choose a direction of rotation.

5. In the Rotate field, to the right of the Rotate menu, enter the number of rotations that you want to use (**Figure 8.14**).

   The value that you enter in the Rotate field determines how Flash tweens the graphic. Flash creates new positions for the graphic to rotate it completely in the given number of in-between frames. Flash tweens the graphic differently depending on the number of rotations you choose (**Figure 8.15**).

   Flash tweens the item so that it spins the number of times you indicated over the span of frames that you defined as the motion tween.

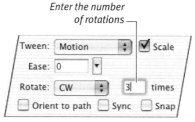

Enter the number of rotations

Figure 8.14 In the Frame Property Inspector, you can set the number of times a tweened item should spin.

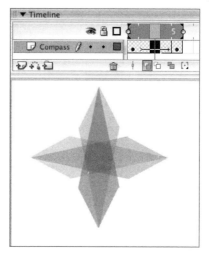

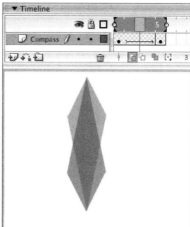

Figure 8.15 Compare a single rotation (top) with a double rotation (bottom) in the same number of frames.

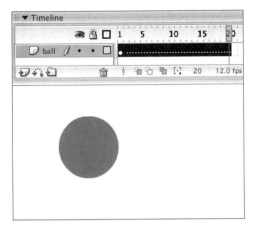

Figure 8.16 The dotted line in the Timeline indicates that these 20 frames contain a motion tween, but a broken one. The final keyframe is missing.

Moving Graphics in Straight Lines

In the preceding exercises, you created a well-behaved bouncing ball—one that moves up and down. To make one that bounces around like a crazy Ping-Pong ball, just add more keyframes and position the ball in various locations. The ball moves in a straight line from one position to the next, but the whole effect is livelier. To get frenetic bouncing, move the ball a great distance in a small number of in-between frames. To slow the action, move the ball a short distance or use a larger number of in-between frames.

To move an item from point to point:

1. Create a new Flash Document.

2. On the Stage, in Frame 1, place an instance of symbol containing a graphic of a ball.

   To review symbol creation, see Chapter 6, or follow steps 2 through 6 in "To prepare keyframes for motion tweening," earlier in this chapter.

3. In the Timeline, select Frame 20, and choose Insert >Timeline > Frame.

   Flash creates 19 in-between frames.

4. In the Timeline, select any frame in the keyframe span (frames 1 through 20).

5. From the Frame Property Inspector's Tween pop-up menu, choose Motion.

   Flash defines frames 1 through 20 as a motion tween but with a dotted line in the Timeline, indicating that the tween is not yet complete (**Figure 8.16**). You need to create keyframes that describe the ball's motion.

continues on next page

6. In the Timeline, position the playhead in Frame 5 (**Figure 8.17**).

7. On the Stage, drag the ball to a new position.

Try moving the ball a fair distance. Flash creates a new keyframe in Frame 5 and completes a tween for frames 1 through 5.

8. In the Timeline, position the playhead in Frame 10.

9. On the Stage, drag the ball to a new position.

Flash creates a new keyframe in Frame 10 and completes a tween for frames 5 through 10.

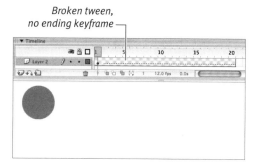

Broken tween, no ending keyframe

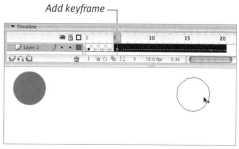

Add keyframe

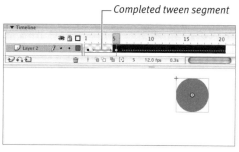

— Completed tween segment

Figure 8.17 As you move the ball to new positions in different frames within the motion tween, Flash creates keyframes and completes the tween between one keyframe and the next.

MOVING GRAPHICS IN STRAIGHT LINES

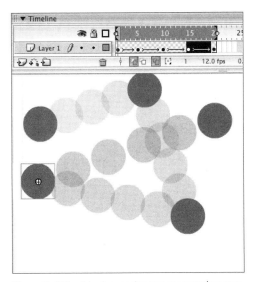

Figure 8.18 By stringing motion tweens together, you can animate an object that moves from point to point.

10. Repeat this repositioning process for frames 15 and 20.

You now have a ball that bounces around wildly (**Figure 8.18**).

11. To add more frames, select Frame 30 or Frame 40 and then choose Insert > Timeline > Frame.

Flash extends the motion tween, and you can add keyframes by following the procedure described earlier in this exercise. Just be sure to make the last frame in the series a keyframe.

12. To end the tween, select the last keyframe in the series.

13. From the Frame Property Inspector's pop-up tween menu, choose None.

If you do not change the last frame's Tween property to None, any frames that you add after that will also be set to Motion Tween, which may create unexpected results.

MOVING GRAPHICS IN STRAIGHT LINES

Moving Graphics Along a Path

The preceding exercise showed how you can make graphics move all over the Stage in short, point-to-point hops. For a ball that bounces off the walls, ceiling, and floor, that's appropriate. But for other things, you want movements that are softer—trajectories that are arcs, not straight lines. You could achieve this effect by stringing together many point-to-point keyframes, but Flash offers a more efficient method: the motion guide. You can even have several items following the same path, but you need to put them on separate layers linked to the same motion-guide layer. If you want different items to follow different paths, you need to create multiple motion-guide layers, each with its own set of guided layers.

To add a motion-guide layer:

1. Create a new Flash Document containing a 10-frame motion tween.

   In the first frame, place the graphic to be tweened (it must be a symbol or group) in the top-left corner of the Stage. In the last frame, place the graphic in the bottom-right corner of the Stage. Your document should resemble **Figure 8.19**.

2. Select the layer that contains the graphic you want to move along a path.

3. At the bottom of the Timeline, click the Add Motion Guide button.

   Flash adds the motion-guide layer directly above the layer you selected and gives it a default name of Guide, followed by the name of the layer you selected (**Figure 8.20**). The motion-guide icon appears next to the layer name. Flash also indents the layer linked to the motion-guide layer.

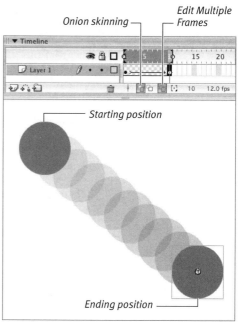

Onion skinning — Edit Multiple Frames

Starting position

Ending position

Figure 8.19 The first step in creating a tweened graphic that follows a path is defining a motion tween with the graphic in the beginning and ending positions you want to use. Here, the graphic moves from the beginning to the end in a straight line. (Onion Skin mode and Edit Multiple Frames are selected to show all the tween's components.)

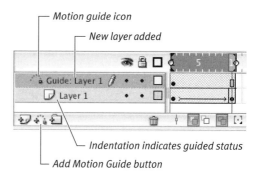

Motion guide icon
New layer added
Indentation indicates guided status
Add Motion Guide button

Figure 8.20 The Add Motion Guide button inserts a new layer, defined as a *motion-guide* layer, above the selected layer in the Timeline. The default name for the motion-guide layer includes the name of the layer selected when you created the motion-guide layer. The layer containing the tweened graphic is indented and linked to the motion-guide layer. Flash defines the linked layer as a *guided layer*.

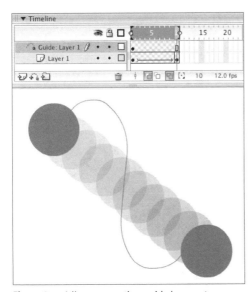

Figure 8.21 A line on a motion-guide layer acts as a path for the tweened graphic on a linked layer to follow.

4. With the motion-guide layer selected, use the pencil tool to draw a line on the Stage showing the path you want the graphic to take (**Figure 8.21**).

5. From the View menu, choose Snapping > Snap to Objects.

For Flash to move an item along a motion path, the transformation point of the item (a small white circle within the symbol or group) must be centered on the path. The Snap to Objects setting will help you position the tween graphic correctly.

6. In Frame 1, drag the tween graphic by its transformation point to position it directly over the beginning of the motion path.

As you drag, the snapping ring enlarges slightly when it approaches any snapping elements you have set. For example, with Snap to Objects active, the ring grows larger when the point you are dragging is centered over the motion guide.

continues on next page

The Mystery of Motion Guides

A *motion guide* is a graphic you create on a special separate layer. The motion guide defines the path for a linked, tweened graphic to follow. One motion-guide layer can control items on several layers. The motion-guide layer governs any layers linked to it. The linked layers are defined as guided layers in the Layer Properties dialog.

If you want different elements to follow different paths, you can create several motion-guide layers within a single Flash document. Each motion guide governs the actions of objects on its own set of linked layers.

MOVING GRAPHICS ALONG A PATH

7. In Frame 10, drag the tween graphic to position its transformation point directly over the end of the motion path.

Flash redraws the in-between frames so that the graphic follows the motion path (**Figure 8.22**). Flash centers the tweened graphic over the motion path in each in-between frame. In the final movie, Flash hides the path.

✔ Tips

■ After you draw the motion path, lock the motion-guide layer to prevent yourself from editing the path accidentally as you snap the graphic to the path.

■ In the Frame Property Inspector for the keyframes containing the tweened graphics, check the Snap check box to have Flash assist you in centering keyframe graphics over the end of the guide line.

■ You can use any of Flash's drawing tools—line, pencil, pen, oval, rectangle, polygon, polystar, and brush—to create a motion path.

■ In many graphics, the transformation point (indicated by a small white circle) and registration mark (indicated by a small crosshair) are in the same spot. It's possible to move the transformation point to a different location by using the free-transform tool. If you do, it's still the transformation point circle that you must snap to the motion guide.

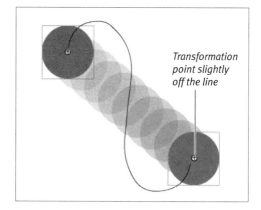

Transformation point slightly off the line

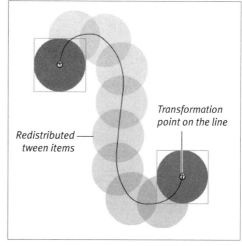

Redistributed tween items

Transformation point on the line

Figure 8.22 To follow the path, tweened items must have their transformation point (indicated by a small white circle within the selected graphic) sitting directly on the line.

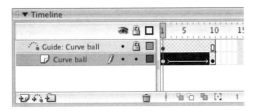

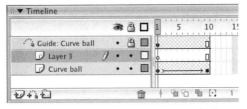

Figure 8.23 When a guided layer is selected (top), clicking the Insert Layer button creates another guided layer below the motion-guide layer (bottom).

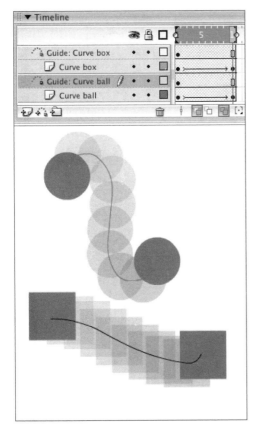

Figure 8.24 Add multiple guide layers to move objects along separate paths simultaneously.

To create a second guided layer:

1. In the Flash Document you created in the preceding exercise, select the guided layer (the one containing the circle).

2. To add a new layer, *do one of the following:*

   ▲ From the Insert menu, choose Timeline > Layer.

   ▲ In the Timeline, click the Insert Layer button.

   Flash adds a new indented (guided) layer above the selected layer (**Figure 8.23**). Tweened items on this layer follow the motion guide when you position them correctly.

To add a second motion-guide layer:

1. Create a Flash Document with at least one normal layer containing a motion tween, and one motion-guide layer with a linked guided layer containing a motion tween.

2. In the Timeline, create or select the normal layer containing the motion tween.

3. Click the Add Motion Guide button.

   Flash adds a motion-guide layer above the selected layer and links the selected layer to it. Follow the steps in the preceding exercises to draw the motion path and position the tweened item.

4. Play the movie.

   The two tweened graphics follow their own motion paths simultaneously (**Figure 8.24**).

✔ Tip

■ To convert an existing layer to a guided layer quickly, drag it below the motion-guide layer or any of its linked layers.

Orienting Graphics to a Motion Path

As a default, tweened graphics keep a fixed orientation (they do not rotate) even when they follow a motion path. To create more natural movement, you can force a tweened graphic to rotate to preserve its orientation to the path in each frame of a tween.

To orient a graphic to the path:

1. Create a 10-frame motion tween of an item that follows a motion guide, using the steps in the first exercise in "Moving Graphics Along a Path" earlier in this chapter.

   This time, however, don't use a circle; draw an arrow or triangle or an animal.

2. Turn on onion skinning to see how the item moves along the path without orientation.

3. In the Timeline, in the layer containing the tweened graphic, select Frame 1.

4. In the Frame Property Inspector, check the Orient to Path check box (**Figure 8.25**).

   Flash redraws the tween. In the in-between frames, Flash rotates the tweened item to align it with the path more naturally (**Figure 8.26**).

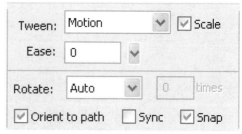

Figure 8.25 With Motion tweening selected in the Frame Property Inspector, check Orient to Path to make Flash rotate a tweened item to "face" the direction of movement.

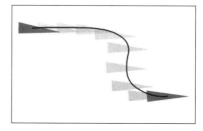

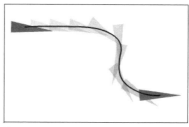

Figure 8.26 The arrow in the top tween is not oriented to the path; it stays parallel to the bottom of the Stage and moves to various points along the path. The bottom tween is oriented to the path. The arrow rotates to align better with the path.

Why Orient to Path?

Imagine a waiter carrying a full tray through a crowded room, raising and lowering the tray to avoid various obstacles but always keeping the tray level to avoid spilling anything. That's how tweened animation works if you don't orient the tweened graphic to the motion guide. The transformation point of the tweened graphic snaps to a new spot on the motion guide in each frame, but the graphic never rotates. With a ball, that procedure may result in natural-looking motion, but with other objects, the result is often unnatural. Orienting the graphic to the motion path forces a tweened graphic to rotate as the motion path curves. This rotation creates the illusion that object is always "facing" the direction it's going along the path.

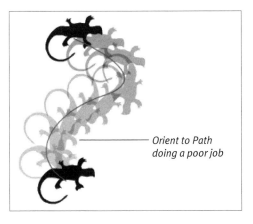

Orient to Path
doing a poor job

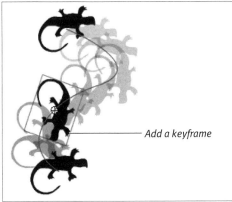

Add a keyframe

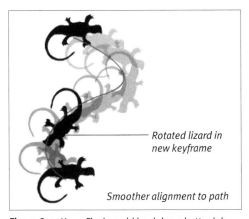

Rotated lizard in
new keyframe

Smoother alignment to path

Figure 8.27 Here, Flash could be doing a better job of aligning this lizard with the path (top). Creating a new keyframe and rotating the lizard manually in the seventh frame (middle) helps the Orient to Path feature do its job (bottom). (Tweaking the orientation of the lizard in the first and last keyframes would further improve this tween.)

✔ Tips

■ The Orient to Path option does not always create the most natural positions for your graphic. Step through the tween one frame at a time. When you get to a frame where Flash positions the graphic poorly, you can fix it. In the Timeline, select the in-between frame, and choose Insert > Timeline > Keyframe. In the new keyframe that Flash creates, select the graphic and rotate it manually to align it with the motion guide. Flash redraws the in-between frames (**Figure 8.27**).

■ Turn on onion skinning as you follow the preceding tip. That way, you can see how your adjustments affect the orientation of your graphic in each frame of the tween.

■ Sometimes, moving the transformation point of your graphic will help it orient to the path in a more lifelike manner. The default transformation point of the lizard in Figure 8.27 is at the center of the graphic's bounding box. Because the lizard has a huge curved tail, that point is not even inside the lizard body. Moving the transformation point to the middle of the lizard's body lets the Orient to Path setting create more lifelike movement. (You can use the free-transform tool to reposition the transformation point of a grouped graphic or a symbol instance.)

ORIENTING GRAPHICS TO A MOTION PATH

Changing Tween Speed

In Chapter 7, you learned to make an animated item appear to move slowly or quickly by adjusting the number of in-between frames. When you create an animation with tweening, that method no longer works, because Flash distributes the motion evenly over however many in-between frames you create. You can, however, make an animation slower at the beginning or end of a tween sequence by setting an Ease value in the Frame Property Inspector.

To make the animation start slowly and accelerate (ease in):

1. Create a 10-frame motion tween of a graphic that follows a motion guide, using the steps in the first exercise in "Moving Graphics Along a Path," earlier in this chapter.

2. In the Timeline, select any of the frames in the keyframe span (Frames 1 through 9).

3. In the Frame Property Inspector, enter a negative number in the Ease field (**Figure 8.28**).

4. Press Enter.

   The word *In* appears next to the field. Easing in makes the animation start slow and speed up toward the end. The lower the Ease value, the greater the rate of acceleration.

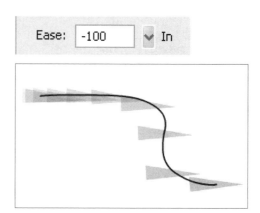

Figure 8.28 A negative Ease value (top), makes changes in the initial frames of the tween smaller and changes toward the end larger (bottom). The animation seems to start slowly and then speed up.

Why Use Easing?

Easing can create a more natural looking motion for objects that gravity affects. In an animation of a bouncing ball, for example, you might want the bouncing to start quickly but slow toward the end to simulate the way that entropy in the real world slows the ball's movement.

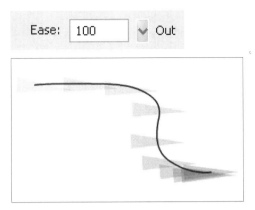

Figure 8.29 A positive Ease value (top), makes changes at the end of the animation smaller and changes in the initial frames larger (bottom). The animation seems to start quickly and then slow down.

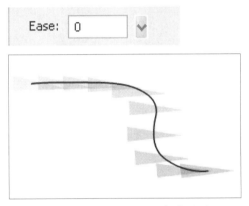

Figure 8.30 With an Ease value of o (top), Flash distributes the tweening changes evenly across the in-between frames (bottom). The effect is that of animation at a constant rate.

To make the animation start quickly and decelerate (ease out):

1. Follow steps 1 and 2 of the preceding exercise.

2. In the Frame Property Inspector, enter a positive number in the Ease field.

3. Press Enter.

   The word *Out* appears next to the field. Easing out makes the animation start quickly and slow toward the end (**Figure 8.29**). The higher the Ease value, the greater the rate of deceleration.

✔ Tips

- An Ease value of 0 causes Flash to display the whole animation at a constant rate (**Figure 8.30**).

- For easy entry of Ease values, click the triangle to the right of the Ease field. A slider pops open. Drag the slider's lever to choose a value between –100 and 100. Click away from the slider in the panel or on the Stage to confirm your entry.

- For even quicker changes, click and drag the slider triangle. When you release the slider's lever, Flash confirms the new Ease value; you don't need to click anywhere.

CHANGING TWEEN SPEED

Getting Help with Motion Tweens

Flash MX 2004 provides two types of assistance for making motion tweens: The Create Motion Tween command and certain of the Timeline Effects. When you define a motion tween as you learned to do in the preceding exercise, you must convert any raw shapes to a symbol or group and set the Tween property of the frames involved. Flash's Create Motion Tween command takes care of these tasks for you and helps ensure that your tween sequence is set up correctly.

The Transform effect (Insert > Timeline Effects > Transform) is one of the effects that automates creation of simple motion tweens. Transform makes motion tweens very similar to the ones you've learned in this chapter, in which an object moves in a single direction, in a straight line, with changes in rotation, color, size, transparency, and speed (easing). You'll learn about using the Transform Effect in Chapter 10.

To use the Create Motion Tween command:

1. Open a new Flash Document.

   The document has one layer and one keyframe by default.

2. Using the drawing tools, create a raw shape on the Stage.

   The shape winds up in Frame 1 of Layer 1.

3. In the Timeline, select Frame 1.

4. From the Insert menu, choose Timeline > Create Motion Tween.

   Flash selects your shape and converts it to a symbol, giving it a default name. Flash sets the Tween property of Frame 1 to Motion in the Property Inspector.

Figure 8.31 Adding frames to the motion tween results in a temporarily broken tween, indicated by the dotted line in the Timeline.

Figure 8.32 After you create a motion tween over a range of frames, reposition the frame's content in the last frame to convert that frame to a keyframe and complete the tween.

5. In the Timeline, select Frame 10.

6. Choose Insert > Timeline > Frame.

Flash adds frames containing a dotted line, indicating a broken tween (**Figure 8.31**). The tween sequence requires an ending keyframe.

7. In Frame 10, reposition the graphic on the Stage.

Flash creates a keyframe in Frame 10, with the symbol in its new position. The tween arrow now appears in the keyframe span (**Figure 8.32**). Note that Frame 10's Tween property is set to Motion in the Property Inspector. If you want subsequent frames to be tween frames, leave the property as is, otherwise you must change it.

8. To end the tweening sequence, select Frame 10.

9. In the Property Inspector, from the Tween pop-up menu, choose None.

✔ Tips

■ If you choose Insert > Timeline > Keyframe in step 6 of the preceding exercise, you will not see the broken-tween line in the Timeline, because that command duplicates the content of the preceding keyframe. Flash considers the tween to be complete when it finds an ending keyframe with content. Nevertheless, your tween will still seem to be broken (it won't actually *do* anything) until you go into the ending keyframe of the sequence and make a change to its content, for example to reposition it or change its color or size.

■ If the Property Inspector is not active, you can remove tweening status from a select frame by choosing Insert > Timeline > Remove Tween.

Dissecting Flash-Created Motion Tweens

When you choose Insert > Timeline > Create Motion Tween, Flash selects all the graphics in the active layer. Multiple shapes become one big symbol. Flash gives the new symbol a default name based on the number of tweening graphics already created in the movie (**Figure 8.33**). You can rename the tween symbol using the techniques described in Chapter 6. If the layer contains a symbol, not a raw shape, the Create Motion Tween command sets the Tween property for the keyframe span, but does not rename the symbol or make a new copy in the library.

Additionally the Create Motion Tween command sets the Tween property of frames in the currently selected keyframe span to Motion in the Property Inspector.

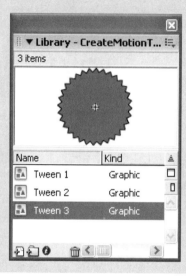

Figure 8.33 The Create Motion tween command turns an editable shape on the Stage in the selected frame into a symbol and names the symbol Tween 1, Tween 2, and so on.

ANIMATION WITH SHAPE TWEENING

In shape tweening, as in motion tweening, you define the beginning and ending graphics in keyframes. Macromedia Flash MX 2004 creates the in-between frames, redrawing the graphic with incremental changes that transform it. The important difference between motion tweening and shape tweening is that motion tweening works on symbols and groups, and shape tweening requires editable graphics.

Shape tweening doesn't restrict you to changing the graphic's shape. You can change any of the graphic's properties—size, color, location, and so on. Though it's possible to shape-tween graphics that move in straight lines, you can't make shapes follow a motion path as they tween. The other automated-motion features are also not available. You cannot instruct Flash to rotate a shape-tweened item 2 times clockwise, for example.

Flash can shape-tween more than one graphic on a layer, but the results can be unpredictable. When you have several shapes on a layer, there is no way to tell Flash which starting shape goes with which ending shape. By limiting yourself to a single shape tween on each layer, you tell Flash exactly what to change.

You define shape tweens by setting the tweening parameters in the Frame Property Inspector. For the exercises in this chapter, keep the Frame Property Inspector open.

Creating a Bouncing Ball with Shape Tweening

Although shape tweens can animate changes in many properties of graphics—color, size, location—the distinguishing function of shape tweening is to transform one shape into another. You could use a shape tween to replicate the simple bouncing-ball animation you created in chapters 7 and 8, but the beauty of shape tweening is that it allows you to change the shape of the ball. A better use of shape tweening for a bouncing ball would be to flatten the ball as it strikes the ground, for example.

To define shape tweens via the Frame Property Inspector:

1. Create a new Flash Document.

   The document has one layer and a keyframe at Frame 1.

2. In the Timeline, position the playhead in Frame 1.

3. In the Toolbar, choose the oval tool.

4. Set the stroke to No Color.

5. Near the top of the Stage, draw a circle.

   This circle will be the ball. Make it fairly large.

6. In the Timeline, select Frame 5, and choose Insert > Timeline > Keyframe.

   The Insert > Timeline > Keyframe command makes a new keyframe that contains the same elements as the preceding keyframe.

7. Select Frame 10, and choose Insert > Timeline > Keyframe.

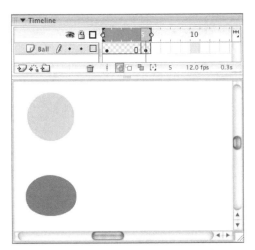

Figure 9.1 Changing the shape of the ball graphic in the keyframe representing the bottom of the bounce makes the movement appear more natural. The ball seems to respond to gravity by flattening on contact with something solid, say, the floor.

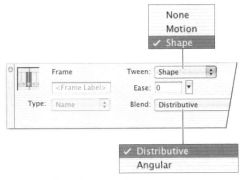

Figure 9.2 Choosing Shape from the Tween pop-up menu in the Frame Property Inspector displays the shape-tween parameters.

8. In Frame 5, select the ball, and drag it to the bottom of the Stage.

Now you have the keyframes necessary to make a simple bouncing ball like the one in the motion-tween exercise. In Frame 1, the ball is at the top of its bounce; in Frame 5, the ball is at the bottom of its bounce; and in Frame 10, the ball is back up at the top.

9. Use the drawing tools to reshape the oval in Frame 5, flattening the bottom and elongating it a bit sideways (**Figure 9.1**).

By changing the shape at the bottom of the bounce, you make it look like the ball really contacts something solid, such as a floor.

10. To define the shape tween for the first half of the ball's bounce, in the Timeline, select any of the frames in the first keyframe span (1, 2, 3, or 4).

Note that the ball is selected automatically. When you define a shape tween, the element to be tweened must be selected.

11. From the Frame Property Inspector's Tween pop-up menu, choose Shape.

The parameters for the shape tween appear (**Figure 9.2**).

Flash creates a shape tween in frames 1 through 4 and color-codes those frames in the Timeline. With Tinted Frames active (choose it from the Frame View pop-up menu at the end of the Edit Bar), Flash applies a light green shade to the frames containing a shape tween. If Tinted Frames is inactive, the frames are white (Mac) or cross-hatched (Windows), but Flash changes the arrow that indicates the presence of a tween from blue to green.

continues on next page

SHAPE TWEENING A BOUNCING BALL

12. In the Ease field, *do one of the following:*

▲ To make the bounce start slowly and speed up, enter a negative value.

▲ To make the bounce start quickly and slow down, enter a positive value.

▲ To keep the bounce constant, enter 0.

13. From the Blend menu, *choose one of the following options:*

▲ To preserve sharp corners and straight lines as one shape transforms into another, choose Angular.

▲ To smooth out the in-between shapes, choose Distributive.

14. To define the shape tween for the second half of the ball's bounce, in the Timeline, select any of the frames in the second keyframe span (5, 6, 7, 8, or 9).

15. Repeat steps 10 through 12.

Flash creates the second half of the ball's bounce with another shape tween (**Figure 9.3**).

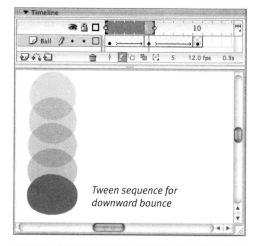

Tween sequence for downward bounce

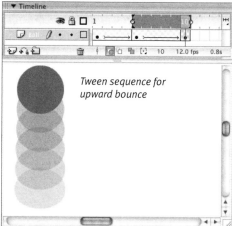

Tween sequence for upward bounce

Figure 9.3 With onion skinning turned on, you can see the in-between frames Flash creates for the shape tween. This animation looks similar to the bouncing ball created with a motion tween. In this case, the change in the object's shape creates the illusion of impact.

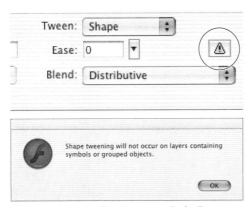

Figure 9.4 A warning button appears in the Frame Property Inspector when there are groups or symbols in frames you are defining as shape tweens (top). Click the exclamation-sign button to see the warning dialog (bottom).

✔ **Tip**

■ Flash doesn't prevent you from defining shape tweens for frames that contain grouped shapes or symbols. Flash does warn you by placing the broken-tween dotted line in the relevant frames in the Timeline. When you select such frames, a warning button appears in the Frame Property Inspector (**Figure 9.4**). When you see these warnings, go back to the Stage and reevaluate what's there. If the item you want to tween is a group or symbol, you could use motion tweening. Or, to use shape tweening, you could break the group or symbol apart (select the shape or symbol and then choose Modify > Break Apart). If there's a symbol or group on the same layer as the editable shape you want to tween, move the extra item to its own layer (select it and choose Modify > Timeline > Distribute to Layers).

Shape-Tween Requirements

To have a working shape tween, you need three things: a beginning keyframe containing one or more editable shapes, in-between frames defined as shape tweens, and an ending keyframe containing the new editable shape.

For motion tweens, the Create Motion Tween command can help you combine those ingredients correctly. No equivalent command is available for shape tweens. You must create all shape tweens manually by setting up the beginning and ending keyframes and then defining the in-between frames as shape tweens in the Frame Property Inspector.

Morphing Simple Lines and Fills

Flash can transform both fill shapes and lines (strokes). In this section, you try some shape-changing exercises with both types of shapes.

To transform an oval into a rectangle:

1. Create a new Flash Document.

2. On the Stage, in Frame 1, draw an outline oval (**Figure 9.5**).

3. In the Timeline, select Frame 5, and choose Insert > Timeline > Blank Keyframe.

   Flash creates a keyframe but removes all content from the Stage.

4. On the Stage, in Frame 5, draw an outline rectangle (**Figure 9.6**).

   Don't worry about placing the rectangle in exactly the same location on the Stage as the oval; you'll adjust the position later.

   In the Timeline, select any of the frames in the Keyframe span (1, 2, 3, or 4).

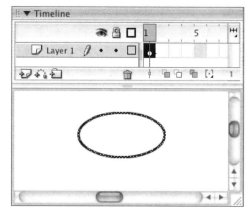

Figure 9.5 Draw an oval in the first keyframe of your shape tween.

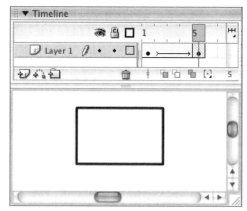

Figure 9.6 Draw a rectangle in the second keyframe of your shape tween.

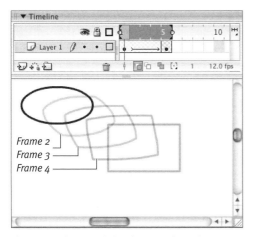

Figure 9.7 When you define frames 1 through 4 as shape tweens, Flash creates the three intermediate shapes that transform the oval into a square. Turn on onion skinning to see the shapes for the in-between frames.

5. From the Frame Property Inspector's Tween pop-up menu, choose Shape.

   Flash transforms the oval into the rectangle in three equal steps—one for each in-between frame (**Figure 9.7**).

6. To align the oval and rectangle, in the Timeline status bar, click the Onion Skin or Onion Skin Outlines button.

   Flash displays all the in-between frames.

7. In the Timeline, position the playhead in Frame 1.

8. On the Stage, select and reposition the oval so that it aligns with the rectangle (**Figure 9.8**).

   The oval transforms into a rectangle, remaining in one spot on the Stage.

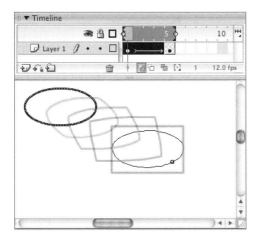

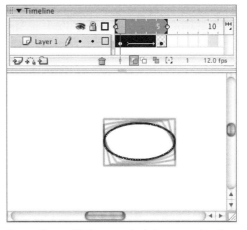

Figure 9.8 Use onion skinning to help position your keyframe shapes. Here, with Frame 1 selected, you can drag the oval to center it within the rectangle (left). That makes the oval grow into a rectangle without moving anywhere else on the Stage (right).

MORPHING SIMPLE LINES AND FILLS

To transform a rectangle into a freeform shape:

1. Create a new Flash Document.

2. On the Stage, in Frame 1, draw a rectangular fill.

3. In the Timeline, select Frame 5, and choose Insert > Timeline > Blank Keyframe.

4. On the Stage, in Frame 5, use the brush tool to paint a free-form fill.

   Don't make the fill too complex—just a blob or brush stroke with gentle curves.

5. In the Timeline, select any of the frames in the Keyframe span (1, 2, 3, or 4).

6. From the Frame Property Inspector's Tween pop-up menu, choose Shape.

   Flash transforms the rectangle into the fill in three equal steps—one for each in-between frame (**Figure 9.9**).

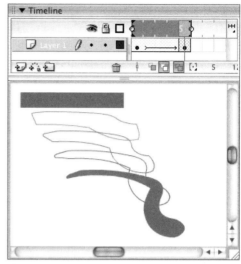

Figure 9.9 Flash transforms a rectangle into a freeform brush stroke with shape tweening.

Shape-Tweening Multiple Shapes

In motion tweening, Flash limits you to one item per tween, meaning just one item per layer. In shape tweening, however, Flash can handle more than one shape on a layer. The drawback is that you may get some very strange results if you try to tween several shapes on a layer. The simpler and fewer the shapes you use, the more reliable your multishape tweens will be. For the most predictable results, limit yourself to one shape per layer.

You may want to keep both shapes on the same layer for a fill with an outline (stroke), however. As long as the transformation is not too complicated, Flash can handle the two together.

When Multiple Shape Tweens on a Single Layer Go Bad

If you are shape-tweening stationary objects, you probably can get away with having several on the same layer. But if the objects move around much, Flash can get confused about which shape goes where. Though you may intend the paths of two shapes to cross, Flash creates the most direct route between the starting object and the ending object. **Figure 9.10** illustrates the problem.

All objects on one layer

All objects on one layer

Light circle and arrow on one layer

Dark circle and arrow on another layer

Figure 9.10 Tweening multiple shapes whose paths don't cross in a single layer works fine. In the left-hand image, both objects are on the same layer, and the light circle transforms into the light arrow without a hitch. In the middle image, both objects are on the same layer, but Flash transforms the light circle into the dark arrow and the dark circle into the light arrow because that's the most direct path. If you want to create diagonal paths that cross, you must put each object on its own layer, as in the right-hand image.

To shape-tween fills with strokes (outlines):

1. Follow the steps in the preceding exercises to create a shape tween of an outline oval transforming into a rectangle.

2. Fill each shape with a different color. Flash tweens the fill and the stroke together and tweens the change in color (**Figure 9.11**).

✔ Tips

■ You can tween a disappearing act: make a shape (or a stroke) get gradually lighter and lighter, till it finally disappears. Make the color of the final shape (or stroke) in the tween match the color of the background, or give it a fully transparent color (one with an alpha setting of 0%).

■ To ensure that the object in the preceding tip does fully disappear (some low-color monitors may not display tint and alpha changes accurately), select the frame following the last keyframe of the tween sequence. Choose Insert > Timeline > Keyframe to duplicate the previous keyframe; now actually delete your disappearing shape.

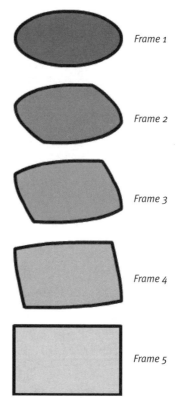

Frame 1

Frame 2

Frame 3

Frame 4

Frame 5

Figure 9.11 Here, Flash transforms a shape with a stroke in five frames. The shape tween changes not only the graphic's shape, but also its color (from dark to light).

Transforming a Simple Shape into a Complex Shape

The more complex the shape you tween, the more difficult it is for Flash to create the expected result. That's because Flash changes the shapes by changing the mathematical description of the graphic. Flash does not understand how the forces of gravity, light, and so on affect the ways humans see; therefore, it doesn't always choose to make a change in a way that preserves the illusion you want. You can help Flash tween better by using *shape hints*—markers that allow you to identify points on the original shape's outline that correspond to points on the final shape's outline.

To shape-tween a more complex shape:

1. Create a new Flash Document.

2. On the Stage, in Frame 1, draw an oval with no stroke.

3. In the Timeline, select Frame 5, and choose Insert > Timeline > Keyframe.

   Flash duplicates the contents of Keyframe 1 in Keyframe 5.

4. In the Timeline, select any of the frames in the Keyframe span (1, 2, 3, or 4).

5. From the Frame Property Inspector's Tween pop-up menu, choose Shape.

6. In the Timeline, position the playhead in Frame 5.

continues on next page

7. Using the selection tool or the pen and subselection tools, drag four corner points in toward the center of the oval to create a flower shape.

   For more detailed instructions on editing shapes, see Chapter 3.

8. Play the movie to see the shape tween.

   Flash handles the tweening for this change well (**Figure 9.12**). It's fairly obvious what points of the oval should move in to create the petal shapes. If you modify the shape further, however, it gets harder for Flash to know how to create the new shape. That's when you need to use shape hints.

To use shape hints:

1. Using the animation you created in the preceding exercise, in the Timeline, select Frame 10, and choose Insert > Timeline > Keyframe.

   Flash duplicates the flower shape in a new keyframe.

2. In Frame 10, edit the flower to add a stem.

   Reshape the outline with the selection tool or the pen and subselection tools, or add a stem with a brush stroke in the same color as the flower.

3. Define a shape tween for frames 5 through 9.

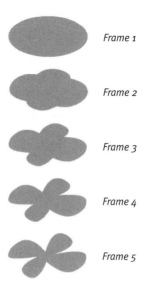

Frame 1

Frame 2

Frame 3

Frame 4

Frame 5

Figure 9.12 Flash handles the tween from an oval to a simple flower shape without requiring shape hints.

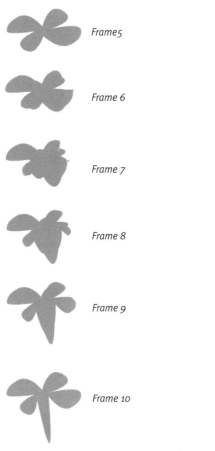

Frame 5

Frame 6

Frame 7

Frame 8

Frame 9

Frame 10

Figure 9.13 The addition of a stem to the flower overloads Flash's capability to create a smooth shape tween. Frames 7 and 8 are particularly bad.

Figure 9.14 Choose Modify > Shape > Add Shape Hint to activate markers that help Flash make connections between the original shape and the final shape of the tween.

4. Play the movie.

The addition of the stem to the flower makes it hard for Flash to create a smooth tween that looks right (**Figure 9.13**).

5. To begin adding shape hints, position the playhead in Frame 5 (the initial keyframe of this tweening sequence).

6. From the Modify menu, choose Shape > Add Shape Hint, or press Shift-⌘-H (Mac) or Ctrl-Shift-H (Windows) (**Figure 9.14**).

Flash places a shape hint—a small red circle labeled with a letter, starting with *a*—in the center of the object in the current frame. You need to reposition the shape hint to place it on a problem point on the shape's outline.

7. With the selection tool, drag the shape hint to a problem point on the edge of the shape.

Don't worry about getting the shape hint in exactly the right spot; you can fine-tune it later.

continues on next page

8. Repeat steps 6 and 7 until you have placed shape hints on all the problem points of your shape in Frame 5 (**Figure 9.15**).

   Each time you add a shape hint, you get another small red circle labeled with a letter. You cannot place the hints at random; you must place them so that they go in alphabetical order around the edge of the shape. (Flash does the best job when you place shape hints in counterclockwise order, but you can also place them in clockwise order.)

9. In the Timeline, position the playhead in Frame 10.

   Flash has already added shape hints to this frame; they all stack up in the center of the shape.

10. With the selection tool, drag each shape hint to its position on the new shape.

    Keep them in the same order (counterclockwise or clockwise) you chose in step 8 (**Figure 9.16**).

11. To evaluate the improvement in tweening, play the movie.

Areas of change

Figure 9.15 Start adding shape hints in the first keyframe of a tween sequence. Flash places the hints in the center of the tweened object (top). You must drag the hints into position (middle). Distribute the hints in alphabetical order around the outline of the object, placing them on crucial points of change (bottom). Here, the three points with hints a, b, and c define the points from which the stem of the flower will grow.

Figure 9.16 To complete the placement of shape hints, select the second keyframe of your tween sequence. Flash stacks up hints corresponding to the ones you placed in the preceding keyframe (top). You must drag them into the correct final position (bottom).

SIMPLE SHAPES INTO A COMPLEX SHAPE

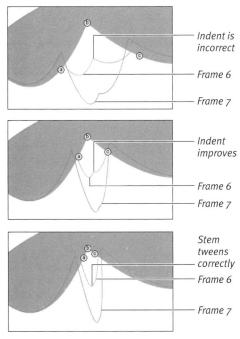

Indent is
incorrect

Frame 6

Frame 7

Indent
improves

Frame 6

Frame 7

Stem
tweens
correctly

Frame 6

Frame 7

Figure 9.17 It can be difficult to match up points in the two keyframes exactly when you first place the shape hints. When you've positioned the hints in the beginning and ending keyframes of a sequence, turn on onion skinning to see where you need to adjust the placement of your hints. With the initial placement, Flash starts the stem growing with an indent at the bottom (top). Moving the points closer together improves the tween (middle). When the onion skins reveal a smooth tween, you're done (bottom).

12. To fine-tune the shape hints' positions, select one of the tween's keyframes, and turn on Onion Skin mode.

Set the onion markers to include all the frames of the tween. Where the onion skins reveal rough spots in the tween, you may need to match the hint position better from the first keyframe to the last one (**Figure 9.17**). Repositioning the shape hints changes the in-between frames. You may need to adjust the shape hints in both keyframes. If you still can't get a smooth tween, try adding more shape hints.

✔ Tips

■ To remove a single shape hint, make the initial keyframe the current frame. Select the shape hint you want to remove, and drag it completely out of the document window. Or you can ⌘-click (Mac) or Ctrl-click (Windows) the shape hint and choose Remove Hint.

■ To remove all the hints at the same time, with the initial keyframe current, choose Modify > Shape > Remove All Hints. Or you can ⌘-click (Mac) or Ctrl-click (Windows) any shape hint and choose Remove All Hints.

■ Onion skins don't always update correctly when you reposition shape hints. Clicking a blank area of the Stage forces Flash to redraw them.

■ If you can't create a smooth tween using shape hints alone, break the tween into smaller pieces by adding keyframes where the morphing gets off track. Then redraw the shapes for those frames yourself.

SIMPLE SHAPES INTO A COMPLEX SHAPE

Creating Shapes That Move As They Change

You cannot create shape tweens that follow a path, but you can move shapes around the Stage in straight lines. You simply reposition the elements on the Stage from one keyframe to the next.

To shape-tween a moving graphic:

1. Create a new Flash Document.

2. On the Stage, select Frame 20, and choose Insert > Timeline > Frame.

    Flash adds a blank keyframe at Frame 20 and blank in-between frames at frames 2 through 20.

3. In the Timeline, select any frame in the keyframe span (frames 1 to 20).

    Note that you must click the frame to select it; you cannot just position the playhead in the frame.

4. From the Frame Property Inspector's Tween pop-up menu, choose Shape.

    Even though you have no shapes on the Stage to tween yet, Flash gives the frames the shape-tween property. In the Timeline, the frames contain a dotted line, indicating that the tween is incomplete (**Figure 9.18**). Now you can add keyframes and shapes.

5. In the Timeline, insert a blank keyframe at frames 5, 10, 15, and 20.

    Flash creates four shape-tween sequences (**Figure 9.19**).

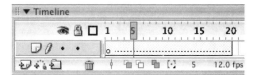

Figure 9.18 To save yourself numerous trips to the Frame Property Inspector's Tween pop-up menu, you can assign the shape-tween property to a range of frames and add keyframes and shapes later. Flash defines a shape tween even though there's no content to tween yet.

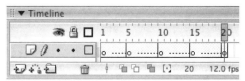

Figure 9.19 When you insert keyframes into a long tween sequence, Flash breaks it into smaller tween sequences. Until you place content in the keyframes, the Timeline will display the dotted line in each span to indicate a broken tween.

Onion skinning on — Edit Multiple
First half of the full — Frames
tween sequence

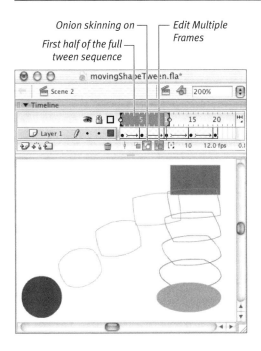

Second half of the full tween sequence —

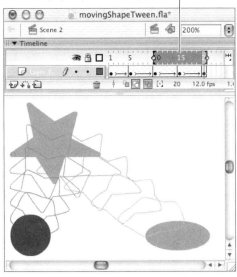

Figure 9.20 Place a different shape in a different location in each keyframe. Flash creates the intermediate steps necessary to transform the shapes and move them across the Stage. Play through the movie or turn on onion skinning to examine the motion and shape changes on the in-between frames. (Here, Edit Multiple Frames is also on, making it easy to see the keyframe shapes.)

6. In each keyframe, draw a different shape; place each one in a different corner of the Stage.

In Frame 1, for example, draw a circular fill in the bottom-left corner of the Stage. In Frame 5, draw a rectangular fill in the top-right corner of the Stage. In Frame 10, draw a flattened oval in the bottom-right corner of the Stage. In Frame 15, draw a star in the top-left corner of the Stage. And in Frame 20, duplicate Frame 1's circle in the bottom-left corner of the Stage. For extra variety, give each object a different color. As you add content to keyframe, Flash fills in the spans in the Timeline with tween arrows.

7. Play the movie.

You see a graphic that bounces around the Stage, morphing from one shape to the next (**Figure 9.20**).

✔ Tip

■ Although shape-tweened objects cannot follow a path the way motion-tweened objects can, you can make Flash do the work of creating the separate keyframes you need to animate shape tweens that move on curved paths. First, create your shape tween. In the Timeline, select the full range of frames in the tween sequence. From the Modify menu, choose Frames > Convert to Keyframes. Flash converts each in-between frame (with its transitional content) into a keyframe. Now you can position each keyframe object anywhere you like. To simulate a motion guide, create a regular guide layer, and draw the path you want your morphing shape to follow. Choose View > Guides > Snap to Objects. Reposition the shape in each keyframe. When you drag a shape close to the line on the guide layer, Flash snaps the shape to the line.

MORE-COMPLEX ANIMATION TASKS

10

So far, you've learned to manipulate shapes and animate them one at a time, in a single layer. In some cases, those techniques are all you need, but Macromedia Flash MX 2004 is capable of handling much more complicated animation tasks. To create complex animated movies, you're going to need to work with multiple shapes and multiple layers. You may even want to use multiple scenes to organize long animations. In this chapter, you learn to work with multiple layers in the Timeline, stack animations on the various layers to create more-complex movement, and save animations as reusable elements for easy manipulation—either as animated graphic symbols or as movie-clip symbols. With these techniques, you can really start to bring your animations to life.

Understanding Scenes

If the Timeline is the table of contents for the "book" of your movie, scenes are the chapters. A Flash project requiring lots of animation may run to hundreds of frames. You can break the animation into smaller chunks by creating scenes. When you publish a movie from a regular Flash Document, the scenes play back in order unless you use the interactivity features to provide instructions for playing the scenes in a different order. (To learn more about interactivity in Flash movies, see Chapters 11 and 12.) Flash's Scene panel makes it easy to see what scenes exist in your movie, create new scenes, delete scenes, and reorganize them.

To access the Scene panel:

◆ If the Scene panel is not open, from the Window menu, choose Design Panels > Scene.

The Scene panel appears. In a new Flash document, the Scene panel lists only the default Scene 1. When you add scenes to a movie, the Scene panel lists all the movie's scenes in order (**Figure 10.1**).

To add a scene:

Do one of the following:

◆ From the Insert menu, choose Scene (**Figure 10.2**).

◆ In the Scene panel, click the Add Scene button.

Flash adds another scene, giving it the default name Scene 2.

✔ Tip

■ Flash bases default scene names on the number of scenes you have ever added, not on the number of scenes currently in the movie. If you add Scenes 2 and 3 and then delete Scene 2, Flash names the next scene that you add Scene 4.

Duplicate scene ⎯
Add scene ⎯
Delete scene ⎯

Figure 10.1 The Scene panel lists all the scenes in a movie. It also provides buttons for adding, duplicating, and deleting scenes.

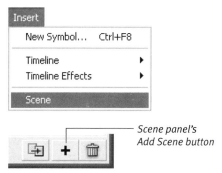

Scene panel's
Add Scene button

Figure 10.2 To add a new scene to your Flash document, choose Insert > Scene (top) or, in the Scene panel, click the Add Scene button (bottom).

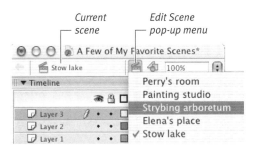

Figure 10.3 The Edit Bar displays the name of the current scene. Choose a scene from the Edit Scene pop-up menu to switch scenes quickly.

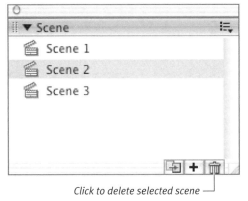

Click to delete selected scene

Figure 10.4 When you delete a scene (top), Flash asks you to confirm the deletion (bottom).

To select a scene to edit:

Do one of the following:

◆ Click the Edit Scene button in the Edit Bar above the Timeline.

A pop-up menu of scenes appears; select a scene from the list.

◆ From the scrolling list in the Scene panel, select a scene.

Flash displays the selected scene on the Stage, puts the scene name in the current-scene box in the Edit Bar, and places a check next to that scene's name in the Edit Scene pop-up menu (**Figure 10.3**).

To delete a selected scene:

1. In the Scene panel, click the Delete Scene button.

A dialog appears, asking you to confirm that you want to delete the selected scene (**Figure 10.4**).

2. Click OK.

Flash deletes the scene, removing it from the Edit Scene pop-up menu in the Timeline as well as from the scrolling list in the Scene panel.

✔ Tips

■ If you don't want to see the warning dialog when you delete a scene, ⌘-click (Mac) or Ctrl-click (Windows) the Delete Scene button in the Scene panel.

■ Though Flash wants you to confirm scene deletions, in MX 2004 (unlike previous versions), you can undo the deletion; press ⌘-Z (Mac) or Ctrl-Z (Windows).

UNDERSTANDING SCENES

To change scene order:

◆ In the Scene panel, drag a selected scene name up or down in the list.

Flash moves the clapper icon and scene name. In Windows, a highlighted line previews the new location for the scene (**Figure 10.5**).

To rename a scene:

1. In the Scene panel, double-click the name of the scene that you want to rename.

The Name field activates for entering text.

2. Type the new name in the Name field.

3. Press Enter.

or

Click outside the text-entry field.

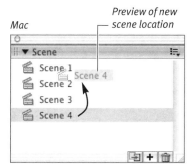

Mac

Preview of new scene location

Drag to reposition scene

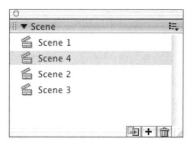

Reordered scenes

Windows

Preview of new scene location

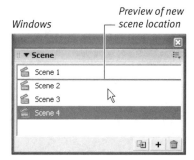

Figure 10.5 As you drag a selected scene, the clapper icon and scene name come along for the ride. Position the scene icon and name just above the scene that should follow the selected scene; release the mouse button. In Windows, a horizontal bar previews the new location for the scene.

The Pitfalls of Using Scenes

In Flash, each scene is like a self-contained movie. The fact that each scene is, in a sense, a new beginning can make it difficult to keep the continuity of actions between scenes. For some types of movies—ones with interactivity that requires variables, or preloading—scenes are inappropriate. In such cases, you may need to stick to a single long movie or use separate movies or separate movie clips within one movie to organize your animation.

UNDERSTANDING SCENES

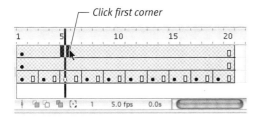

Click first corner

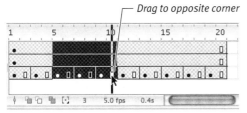

Drag to opposite corner

Figure 10.6 In frame-based selection style, click and drag across frames and layers (top) to select frames in those layers (bottom).

Manipulating Frames in Multiple Layers

As your animation gets more complex, you will need to add layers to your document. You can perform editing operations on selected frames and layers, for example, by copying, cutting, and pasting frames across multiple layers. You can also insert frames, keyframes, and blank keyframes into selected frames and layers.

To select and copy frames in several layers:

1. Open a new Flash Document.

2. Add two layers—for a total of three layers in the document—and insert 20 frames into each layer.

    Place content in the layers to help you see what's going on as you work with the various frames and layers. Use the text tool, for example, to place the frame number in every other frame of Layer 1 and to place a text block with the name of the layer in layers 2 and 3.

3. In the Timeline in Layer 3 in frame-based selections mode, click and drag as though you were drawing a selection rectangle around frames 5 through 10 in all three layers. In span-based selection mode, ⌘-click (Mac) or Ctrl-click (Windows) and drag to select a range of frames.

    Flash highlights the selected frames (**Figure 10.6**).

4. From the Edit menu, Choose Timeline > Copy Frames.

    Flash copies the frames and layer information to the Clipboard.

✔ Tip

■ To select a block of frames that spans several layers without dragging, in frame-based selection style, click a frame at one of the four corners of the block. Then Shift-click the frame at the opposite corner. Flash selects all the frames in the rectangle that you've defined (**Figure 10.7**). In span-based selection style, ⌘-click (Mac) or Ctrl-click (Windows) one corner and then Shift-⌘-click (Mac) or Ctrl-Shift-click (Windows) the opposite corner to make your selection.

To replace the content of frames with a multilayer selection:

1. Using the document that you created in the preceding exercise, select frames 15 through 20 on all three layers.

2. From the Edit menu, choose Timeline > Paste Frames.

   Flash pastes the copied frames 5 through 10 into frames 15 through 20 in each of the three layers. The numbers on the Stage in Layer 1 now start over with 5 at Frame 15, 7 at Frame 17, and 9 at Frame 19.

To paste a multiple-layer selection into blank frames:

1. Using the document that you created in the preceding exercise, select Frame 21 on all three layers.

2. From the Edit menu, choose Timeline > Paste Frames.

   Flash pastes the copied frames 5 through 10 into protoframes 21 through 26 in each of the three layers (**Figure 10.8**). Layer 1 now displays the number 5 at Frame 21, 7 at Frame 23, and 9 at Frame 25.

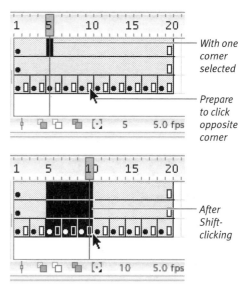

With one corner selected

Prepare to click opposite corner

After Shift-clicking

Figure 10.7 To select a block of frames, in frame-based selection style, click one corner of the block; then Shift-click the opposite corner to define the block. In span-based selection style, ⌘-click (Mac) or Ctrl-click (Windows) the first corner and then Shift-⌘-click (Mac) or Ctrl-Shift-click (Windows) the opposite corner of your selection block.

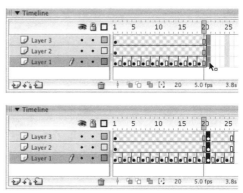

Figure 10.8 Pasting a multiple-layer, multiple-frame selection at the end of a set of defined frames (top) extends the Timeline to accommodate the new frames and layers (bottom).

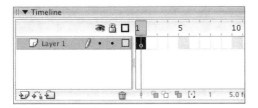

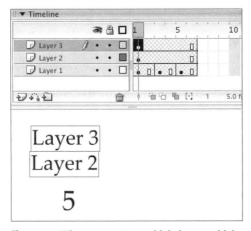

Figure 10.9 When you paste a multiple-layer, multiple-frame selection into the first frame of a new scene (top), Flash creates new layers and frames to hold the contents of the Clipboard (bottom).

To paste a multiple-layer selection into a new scene:

1. Using the document that you created in the preceding exercise, insert a new scene, following the instructions in the first section in this chapter.

   By default, the new scene has one layer and one frame.

2. Select Frame 1.

3. From the Edit menu, choose Timeline > Paste Frames.

   Flash pastes the copied selection from the first scene (frames 5 through 10 on layers 1 through 3) into the new scene. Flash adds layers 2 and 3 and creates frames 1 through 6 in each layer (**Figure 10.9**). Layer 1 now displays the number 5 at Frame 1, 7 at Frame 3, and 9 at Frame 5.

Animating Multiple Motion Tweens

As you learned in Chapter 8, Flash can motion-tween only one item per layer. You can tween multiple items simultaneously; you just have to put each one on a separate layer. You can use Onion Skin and Edit Multiple Frame modes to make sure that all the elements line up in the right place at the right time. To get a feel for tweening multiple items, try combining three simple motion tweens to create a game of Ping-Pong. One layer contains the ball; the other layers each contain a paddle.

To set up the three graphics in separate layers:

1. Open a new Flash Document, and add two new layers.

2. Rename the layers.

   Name the top layer *Ball,* the next layer *1st Paddle,* and the bottom layer *2nd Paddle.* Naming the layers helps you keep track of the elements and their locations.

3. Create the graphics.

   On the Stage, in the *Ball* layer, use the oval tool to create a ball; in the layer named *1st Paddle,* use the rectangle tool to create a paddle; and then copy the paddle and paste the copy into the layer named *2nd Paddle.* Give each shape a different color. Your file should look something like **Figure 10.10**.

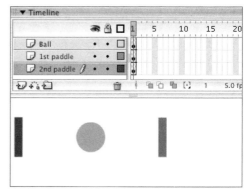

Figure 10.10 To have several graphics motion-tween simultaneously, you must place each one on a separate layer. Here, each item is on a separate layer. The descriptive layer names help you keep track of what goes where.

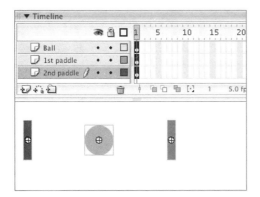

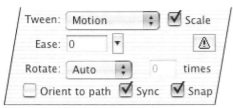

Figure 10.11 By using the Create Motion Tween command with frames selected on all three layers (top), you create three motion tweens with one command. The Frame Property Inspector reveals their status as motion tweens (bottom).

To set up the tween in all layers with one command:

1. Using the document that you created in the preceding task, in the Timeline, select Frame 1 in all three layers.

2. From the Insert menu, choose Timeline > Create Motion Tween.

Flash turns each shape into a symbol (naming the symbols Tween 1, Tween 2, and Tween 3) and gives all the frames the motion-tween property (**Figure 10.11**). It's a good idea to rename your tween symbols in the library.

3. In the Timeline, select Frame 20 in all three layers.

4. From the Insert menu, choose Timeline > Frame.

Flash extends the motion tween through Frame 20 on all three layers, placing a dotted line across the frames to indicate that they are part of an incomplete motion tween. You need to reposition the symbols and create keyframes to complete the tweens.

✔ Tip

■ You can also create the ball and paddle graphics as symbols from the very beginning, placing instances of each symbol in the appropriate layer in step 3 of the first exercise in this section. If you set up your tween with symbols initially, you can use either the Create Motion Tween command in step 2, or you can simply set the frame property to Motion in the Property Inspector (see Chapter 8).

ANIMATING MULTIPLE MOTION TWEENS

383

To adjust the positions of the tweened items:

1. Using the document that you created in the preceding task, in the Timeline, position the playhead in Frame 5.

2. On the Stage, drag the ball to the approximate location where it should connect with one of the paddles for the first hit.

   Flash makes *Ball* the active layer and creates a keyframe (in Frame 5) for the ball in its new location (**Figure 10.12**). Flash completes the motion tween between Frame 1 and Frame 5 of the *Ball* layer and leaves the broken-tween line in all the other frames.

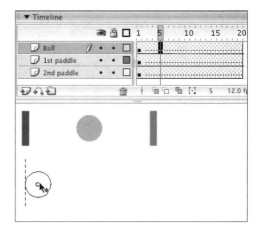

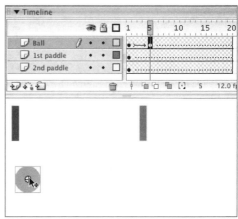

Figure 10.12 Moving a graphic in a frame that's defined as part of a motion tween causes Flash to make the layer containing the graphic the active layer (top). Flash creates a keyframe in that layer for the graphic's new position, completing one tween sequence (bottom).

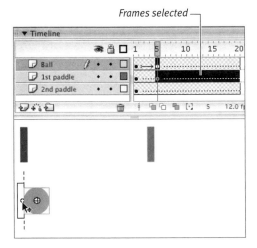

Frames selected

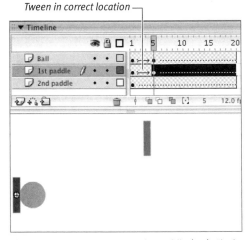

Tween in correct location

Figure 10.13 As you reposition the paddle (top), Flash appears to be selecting the wrong set of frames, but when you release the mouse button, Flash correctly tweens frames 1 through 4 (bottom).

3. On the Stage, reposition the first paddle graphic so that the paddle connects with the ball for the first hit.

Flash makes *1st Paddle* the active layer and creates a keyframe (in Frame 5) for the paddle in its new location (**Figure 10.13**).

4. In the Timeline, position the playhead in Frame 10.

5. On the Stage, drag the ball to the approximate location where you want it to connect with a paddle for the second hit.

Flash makes *Ball* the active layer and creates a keyframe (in Frame 10) for the ball in its new location. Flash completes the motion tween between Frame 5 and Frame 10 of the *Ball* layer.

continues on next page

ANIMATING MULTIPLE MOTION TWEENS

6. On the Stage, reposition the second paddle so that it connects with the ball for the second hit.

Flash makes *2nd Paddle* the active layer and creates a keyframe (in Frame 10) for the paddle in its new location (**Figure 10.14**).

7. Repeat steps 1 through 6, using keyframes 15 and 20, to make the ball connect with each paddle one more time.

8. Play the movie to see the animation in action.

9. Select Onion Skin Outlines and Edit Multiple Frames, and reposition objects as necessary to fine-tune the motion (**Figure 10.15**).

✔ Tips

■ After you define a set of frames as tweens, any slight change you make to an object causes Flash to create a new keyframe. Even simply clicking and holding long enough to select an object causes Flash to insert a keyframe. So that you don't change objects' positions or create new keyframes accidentally, lock or hide the layers that you're not working on.

■ To position items on the Stage with greater precision than dragging allows, select an item and use the Property Inspector or the Info panel to set the item's *x* and *y* coordinates.

■ If you like to use Snap Align, Flash's default setting, to help you position items, you'll notice that sometimes in the preceding exercise, the snapping guides don't appear as you drag graphic elements in in-between frames whose Tween property is set to Motion. These guides work best when all objects involved are in keyframes. If the guides are not appearing for you, just approximate locations by dragging initially. Once Flash has created the new keyframes, you can drag your elements and the guidelines will appear.

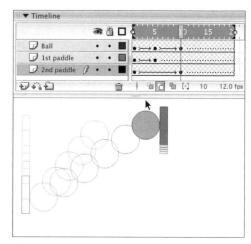

Figure 10.14 Moving an element in another frame creates another tween. Here, the paddle on the right side appears to move more slowly than the paddle on the left side, because Flash is creating a 10-frame tween for the right paddle, while the left paddle tweens in 5 frames.

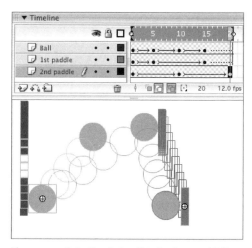

Figure 10.15 Selecting Onion Skin Outlines and Edit Multiple Frames makes fine-tuning the location of objects easier. Here, the paddle on the right doesn't move in a straight line. If you want it to do so, reposition the paddle graphics in the first and final frames so that one lies directly above the other; then reposition the ball so that it comes into contact with both paddles.

Motion-Tweening Text

You can use the multiple-motion tween idea to animate individual characters within a piece of text. After you create the text that you want to animate, select it and choose Modify > Break Apart. That command places each character in its own text box. Next, with each character of the text selected, choose Modify > Timeline > Distribute to Layers. Each character winds up on its own layer. Now use any of the animating techniques you learned in Chapters 8 and 9, or in earlier exercises in this chapter, to animate the individual text characters (**Figure 10.16**).

If you want to transform the shapes of the letters, you need to use shape tweening. That means converting the letters from editable text elements to editable graphics. Select one or more text boxes containing individual letters and choose Modify > Break Apart. The letterforms look the same, but now they are raw shapes that you can modify with the drawing tools and use in shape tweens.

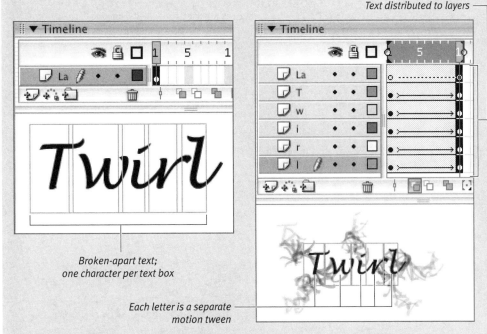

Text distributed to layers

*Broken-apart text;
one character per text box*

*Each letter is a separate
motion tween*

Figure 10.16 Using Flash's Modify > Break Apart command in conjunction with the Modify > Timeline > Distribute to Layers command, you can set up tweens quickly to animate individual text characters. Each letter in this animated text is a motion tween.

ANIMATING MULTIPLE MOTION TWEENS

Animating Shape Tweens in Multiple-Shape Graphics

An important thing to remember about complex shape tweens is that Flash deals most reliably with a single shape tween on a layer. In the following exercises, you create a multipart, multilayer graphic and shape-tween the whole package simultaneously.

To create shape tweens on separate layers:

1. Open a new Flash Document, and add two new layers.

2. Rename the layers *Top Flame, Middle Flame,* and *Bottom Flame.*

   Naming the layers helps you keep track of the objects and their locations.

3. Create the shapes.

   On the Stage, use the oval tool to create three concentric oval shapes. In the *Bottom Flame* layer, create a large oval; in the *Middle Flame* layer, create a medium oval (center it over the first oval); in the *Top Flame* layer, create a small oval (center it over the medium oval). Give each oval a different color. Your file should look something like **Figure 10.17**.

4. Select Frame 5 in all three layers.

5. From the Insert menu, choose Timeline > Keyframe.

   Flash creates a keyframe with the same content as Frame 1 for each layer.

6. In the Timeline, select any of the frames in the Keyframe 1 span (1, 2, 3, or 4) in all three layers.

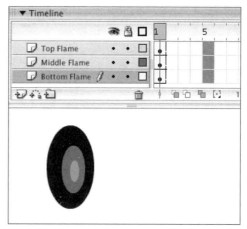

Figure 10.17 Create each part of a multiple-element shape tween on a separate layer. Name the layers to help you track what goes where.

When Should One Element Span Several Layers?

Often, an element that you think of as a single entity actually consists of several shapes in Flash. A candle flame is a good example. To simulate the flickering of a lighted candle, you might create a flame with three shades of orange and then animate changes in the flame shape and colors.

One natural way to do this is to draw each flame segment in the same layer so that you can see the interaction of the shapes immediately. Unfortunately, Flash has trouble tweening shapes that you create that way. You'll be better off creating a rough version of each segment in a separate layer and then fine-tuning that version. Or create your shapes in one layer, but then select them and choose Insert > Timeline > Distribute to Layers to place them on separate layers. That way, Flash has to tween only one shape per layer, and the result will be cleaner.

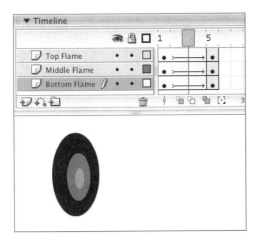

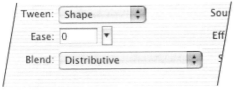

Figure 10.18 When you select multiple frames, you can set the tweening property for those frames simultaneously by choosing a property from the Tween pop-up menu in the Property Inspector.

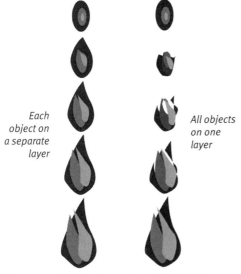

Each object on a separate layer

All objects on one layer

Figure 10.19 With the three colors of flames on separate layers (left), Flash does a reasonable job of tweening even when you don't add shape hints. With the three flame shapes on a single layer (right), Flash has great difficulty creating the tweens.

7. From the Frame Property Inspector's Tween menu, choose Shape.

Flash gives the shape-tween property to frames 1 through 4 on all three layers (**Figure 10.18**). To create flickering flames, you need to reshape the ovals in Frame 5.

8. In the Timeline, position the playhead in Frame 5.

9. On the Stage, edit the ovals to create flame shapes.

10. Play the movie to see the animation in action.

Flash handles the shape-tweening of each layer separately. For comparison, try creating the oval and flame shapes on a single layer and then shape-tweening them (**Figure 10.19**).

11. Select Onion Skin Outlines and Edit Multiple Frames; then reposition the flame objects as necessary to fine-tune the motion.

SHAPE TWEENING MULTIPLE-SHAPE GRAPHICS

Reversing Frames

Sometimes, you can save work by creating just half the animation that you need and letting Flash do the rest of the work. Think of the candle flame that you created in the preceding section. You might want the flame to grow larger and then shrink back to its original size. The shrinking phase is really just the reverse of the growing phase. You can make a copy of the growing-flame animation and then have Flash reverse the order of the frames.

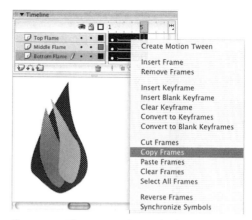

Figure 10.20 The contextual menu for frames lets you copy all selected frames with a single command.

To reverse the order of frames:

1. Open the document that you created in the preceding section.

   This movie spans five frames on three layers. The first keyframe shows the flame as three concentric oval shapes; the final keyframe shows the flame in a taller, flickering configuration.

2. In the Timeline, select all five frames on all three layers.

3. In one of the selected frames, Control-click (Mac) or right-click (Windows) to access the frame-editing contextual menu; then Choose Copy Frames (**Figure 10.20**).

4. In the Timeline, select Frame 6 in all three layers.

5. In one of the selected frames, Control-click (Mac) or right-click (Windows) to access the frame-editing contextual menu, and choose Paste Frames.

   Your movie now contains two back-to-back animation sequences of the growing flame (**Figure 10.21**).

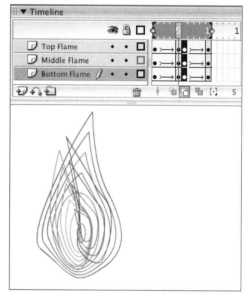

Figure 10.21 After you paste the copied selection, you have two tween sequences ending with the tall, flickering flame.

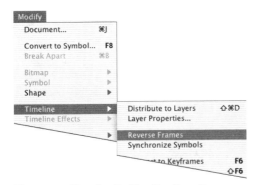

Figure 10.22 Choosing Modify > Timeline > Reverse Frames rearranges the order of selected frames. Use this command to make a selected tween run backward.

6. In the Timeline, select frames 6 through 10 on all three layers.

7. From the Modify menu, choose Timeline > Reverse Frames (**Figure 10.22**).

Flash reverses the tween in the second sequence so that the flame starts out tall and flickery, and winds up in its original oval configuration in the final keyframe (**Figure 10.23**).

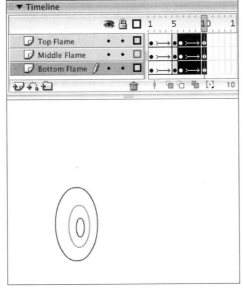

Figure 10.23 After you reverse the frames, the second tween sequence ends with the oval flame.

REVERSING FRAMES

Combining Tweening with Frame-by-Frame Techniques

Especially with shape tweening, you cannot rely on Flash to create the in-between frames that capture the exact movement you want. You can combine Flash's tweening with your own frame-by-frame efforts, however, letting Flash do the work whenever it can. Or let Flash create the broad outlines of your animation and then add keyframes to refine the movement. Flash helps with the process by allowing you to convert those intangible in-between frames to keyframes that you can edit and refine yourself.

In the preceding section, you created a crude version of a flickering flame. In the following exercises, you refine it.

To convert in-between frames to keyframes:

1. Open the Flash Document that you created in the preceding section.

2. In the Timeline, position the playhead in Frame 2.

   The first step in this tween is not particularly effective: The central flame portion seems to be a bit too far to the side (**Figure 10.24**). Because Frame 2 is an in-between frame, however, you can't edit it. You can try to improve the motion by adding shape hints, or you can create a new keyframe to refine the animation.

3. To convert the in-between frame to a keyframe, in the Timeline, select Frame 2 in all three layers.

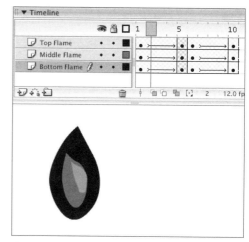

Figure 10.24 Flash's shape tween in Frame 2 leaves something to be desired.

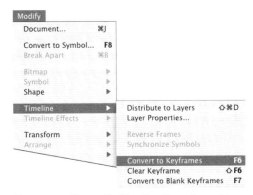

Figure 10.25 Choose Modify > Timeline > Convert to Keyframes to add a keyframe for adjusting your multilayer tween.

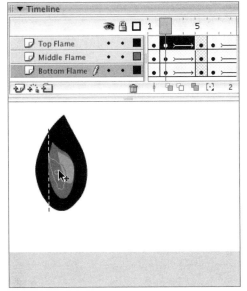

Figure 10.26 After you convert Frame 2 from an in-between frame (part of a tween) to a keyframe, you can edit the flame objects.

4. From the Modify menu, choose Timeline > Convert to Keyframes, or press F6 (**Figure 10.25**).

Flash converts Frame 2 from an in-between frame to a keyframe; then it creates the contents of Keyframe 2 from the transitional shapes that it created for the shape tween at that frame. Now you are free to edit the contents to improve the tweening action (**Figure 10.26**). If you want to create a smoother motion, expand the tween between Keyframe 1 and Keyframe 2.

5. To add more in-between frames, position the playhead in Frame 1.

6. From the Insert menu, choose Timeline > Frame, or press F5.

Flash adds new in-between frames in all layers. You can repeat the Insert > Timeline > Frame command to add as many frames as you like. These frames inherit the shape-tween property that you defined for Frame 1. Now you can examine Flash's tweening for the new frames and repeat the process of converting any awkward tween frames to keyframes and editing them.

✔ Tips

■ You can convert multiple in-between frames of a shape or motion tween by selecting them and then choosing Modify > Timeline > Convert to Keyframes.

■ Flash limits you to one color change per tween sequence. To speed the process of making several color changes, set up one long tween (either motion or shape) that goes from the initial color to the final color. Then selectively convert in-between frames to keyframes so that you can make additional color changes.

COMBINING TWEENING WITH FRAME-BY-FRAME

Saving Animations As Graphic Symbols

In Chapter 6, you learned to save work for reuse and keep file sizes small by using symbols. Flash lets you do the same thing with entire multiple-frame, multiple-layer animation sequences. You can save such sequences either as an animated graphic symbol or as a movie-clip symbol. You can use these symbols repeatedly with a much smaller hit on file size than if you simply re-create the animation by using graphic-symbol instances within separate animations. Additionally, for complex animations, symbols help keep down the number of frames and layers that you have to deal with at any time.

To convert an animation to a graphic symbol:

1. Open the document that you created to make the Ping-Pong animation in "Animating Multiple Motion Tweens" earlier in this chapter, or create your own multiple-layer animation.

   The Ping-Pong animation is a three-layer, 20-frame animation.

2. In the Timeline, select all 20 frames in all three layers.

3. From the Edit menu, Choose Timeline > Copy Frames.

4. From the Insert menu, choose New Symbol, or press ⌘-F8 (Mac) or Ctrl-F8 (Windows).

   The Create New Symbol dialog appears (**Figure 10.27**).

5. In the Create New Symbol dialog, type a name for your symbol (for example, Ping-Pong Animation).

Figure 10.27 You set a new symbol's behavior in the Create New Symbol dialog. Movie clips operate from their own independent Timeline. Animated graphic symbols play in sync with the main movie that contains them. One frame in the main movie's Timeline displays one frame of the symbol's Timeline.

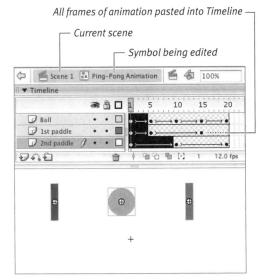

All frames of animation pasted into Timeline —

Current scene

Symbol being edited

Figure 10.28 When you create a new symbol, Flash switches to symbol-editing mode, making the new symbol's Timeline available for editing. You must paste all the frames of your animation into the symbol's Timeline to create the animated symbol.

Symbols Reduce Layer Buildup

In general, for tweened animations, you need to place each shape on a separate layer. To animate a person, for example, create separate layers for the head, the torso, each arm, and each leg. For complex motion, you might even create separate layers for eyes, mouth, fingers, and toes. Add some other elements to this character's environment, and you wind up dealing with many layers.

Turning an animation sequence into a symbol in effect collapses all those layers into one object. The process is a bit like grouping. On the Stage, the symbol exists on a single layer, but that layer contains all the layers of the original animation.

6. Choose Graphic as the behavior type.

In Flash, a symbol's behavior identifies what kind of symbol it is: graphic, button, or movie clip.

7. Click OK.

Flash creates a new symbol in the library and switches you to symbol-editing mode for that symbol.

The name of your symbol appears in the Edit Bar above the Timeline. The default Timeline for your new symbol consists of just one layer and a blank keyframe at Frame 1.

8. In the symbol Timeline, select Frame 1, and choose Edit > Timeline > Paste Frames.

Flash pastes the 20 frames and three layers that you copied from the original Ping-Pong movie into the Timeline for the Ping-Pong Animation symbol (**Figure 10.28**). If you want to make any adjustments in the animation sequence, you can do so at this point.

9. To return to document-editing mode, choose Edit > Edit Document.

✔ Tips

- In the list of symbols in the Library window, an animated graphic symbol looks the same as a static graphic symbol; both have the same icon, and both are listed as Graphic in the Kind column. An animated graphic symbol, however, has Play and Stop buttons in the top-right corner of the Library window; a static graphic symbol does not (**Figure 10.29**). You can preview an animated symbol by clicking the Play button.

- When you paste multiple frames and layers into the Timeline in symbol-editing mode, the registration crosshair may be in a strange position for the symbol as a whole. To reposition the items making up the symbol, in the Status bar, select the Edit Multiple Frames button; from the Modify Onion Markers pop-up menu, choose Onion All; finally, choose Edit > Select All to select the contents of each keyframe in each layer. Now you can position the symbol as a whole in relation to the crosshair.

Animated graphic symbol

Stop and Play buttons

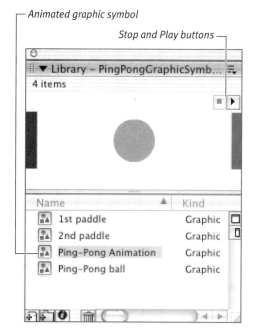

Static graphic symbol

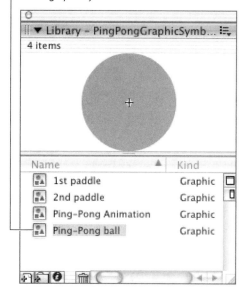

Figure 10.29 An animated graphic symbol (top) in the Library window has Stop and Play buttons as part of its preview; otherwise, it's indistinguishable from a static graphic symbol (bottom).

How Do Animated Graphic Symbols Differ from Movie-Clip Symbols?

Flash provides for two kinds of animated symbols: graphic symbols and movie clips. The difference is a bit subtle and hard to grasp at first. An animated graphic symbol is tied to the Timeline of any movie in which you place the symbol, whereas a movie-clip symbol runs on its own independent Timeline. A rule of thumb is to remember that when the playhead stops moving in the main Timeline, an animated graphic symbol stops playing, but a movie-clip symbol continues to play.

You can think of animated graphic symbols as being a slide show. Each frame of the symbol is a separate slide. When you move to the next frame in the animated graphic symbol, you must move to another frame in the hosting movie. Also, there's no sound track. Even if you have sounds or interactivity functions in a movie, when you convert it to a graphic symbol, you lose those features.

A movie-clip symbol is like a film loop. You can project all its frames one after another, over and over, in a single frame of the hosting movie. Movie clips do have a sound track and do retain their interactivity. (To learn more about sound, see Chapter 15. For interactivity, see Chapters 11 and 12.)

One more thing to know about the two symbol types is that movie clips, because they run on their own Timeline, do not appear as animations in the Flash authoring environment. You see only the first frame of the movie as a static object on the Stage. Animated graphic symbols, which use the same Timeline as the main movie, do display their animation in the authoring environment.

Using Animated Graphic Symbols

To put an animated graphic symbol to work, you must place an instance of it in your main movie. The layer containing the movie must have enough frames to display the frames of the symbol. You can use instances of an animated graphic symbol just as you would any other symbol—combine it with other graphics on a layer; motion-tween it; modify its color, size, and rotation; and so on.

To place an instance of an animated graphic symbol:

1. Using the movie and symbol that you created in the preceding section, from the Insert menu, choose Scene to create a new scene.

   Flash displays the new scene's Timeline—a single layer with a blank keyframe in Frame 1. The Stage is empty.

   Adding a new scene gives you a blank Stage to work with and makes it easy to compare the two animations: the original (created directly in the main movie) and the instance of the graphic symbol placed in the movie.

2. Access the Library window.

   If it's not open, choose Window > Library.

3. In the Library window for your document, select the Ping-Pong Animation symbol.

   The first frame of the animation appears in the preview window.

4. Drag a copy of the selected symbol to the Stage.

   Flash places the symbol in Keyframe 1. At this point, you can see only the first frame of the animation (**Figure 10.30**). The animation is 20 frames long, so you need to add least 20 frames to view the symbol in its entirety.

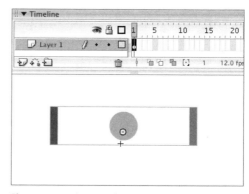

Figure 10.30 When you drag an instance of the animated graphic to the Stage, you see the symbol's first frame with its graphics selected. You must add frames to allow the full animation of the symbol to play in the main movie.

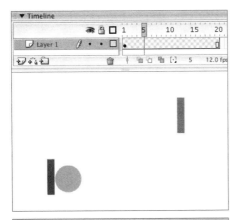

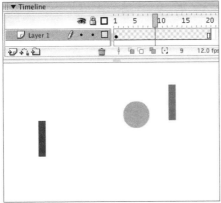

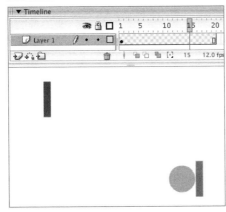

Figure 10.31 Frames 1 through 20 have a tweening property of None, but they still display animation. Flash displays the 20 tween frames of the graphic symbol that you placed in Keyframe 1. It's as though the symbol is a tray of slides, and Flash is projecting one image per frame in the main movie. If the main movie is longer than the slide show, Flash just starts the slide show over.

5. In the Timeline, select Frame 20, and choose Insert > Timeline > Frame.

Flash adds in-between frames 2 through 20.

6. Play the movie.

Now Flash can display each frame of the animated graphic symbol in a frame of the movie. Frame 2 of the symbol appears in Frame 2 of the movie, Frame 5 of the symbol appears in Frame 5 of the movie, and so on (**Figure 10.31**). If you place fewer than 20 frames in the movie, Flash truncates the symbol and displays only as many frames of the symbol as there are frames in the movie. If you place more than 20 frames, Flash starts playing the graphic symbol over again in Frame 21.

✔ Tip

■ To create complex motion, you can use animated graphic symbols in motion tweens in your main movie. You can create, for example, an animated graphic symbol of a bug whose legs move to simulate walking. Place an instance of the bug symbol in keyframes at frames 1 and 5. You can motion-tween the bug symbol in your main movie and add a motion guide layer to make the walking bug follow a path.

USING ANIMATED GRAPHIC SYMBOLS

Creating Animated Graphic Symbols with Timeline Effects

Flash MX 2004 provides several Timeline Effects that create a variation on animated graphic symbols. These effects symbols are tied to the Timeline of the movie in which they are placed, but their presence in that Timeline is not fully under your control. Animated Timeline Effects have the same pitfalls as static effects (see Chapter 6), plus a few new ones (see the sidebar, "Dissecting a Transformation," later in this section). To learn more about the way Timeline Effects create animated graphic symbols, look at the Transform effect. Transform automates the procedure of creating a single-layer motion tween where the object changes position, size, rotation, and/or color.

To apply the Transform Timeline Effect:

1. Open a new Flash Document.

   Working in a new document makes it easier to see what items Flash adds to the library when it creates the effect.

2. Create a graphic symbol containing the object that you would like to animate.

   For example, use the text tool to create a static text box containing the word *Motion*. (For details about working with text, see Chapter 2; for details about creating symbols, see Chapter 6.) Give the symbol a meaningful name, such as, `Motion_forTransform`.

   Although Timeline Effects work on raw shapes and text, applying an effect to a symbol gives you more options should you need to re-create your finished effect or make new, slightly different versions. You can use your original symbol to make future modifications, to correct a typo in your animated text, for example.

Figure 10.32 The Transform effect is hidden deep in the nested menus below Insert.

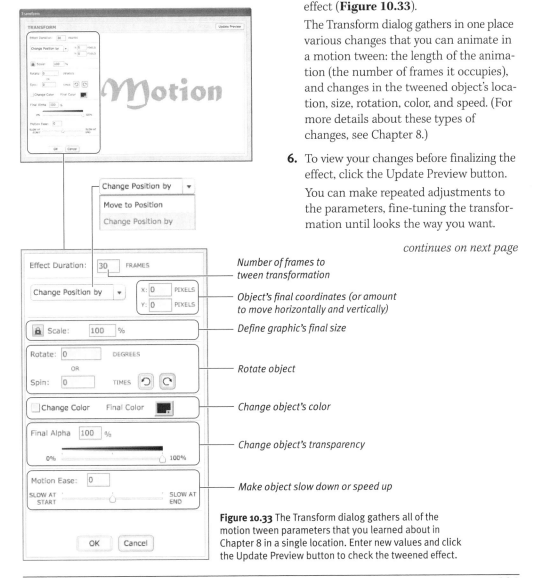

Number of frames to tween transformation

Object's final coordinates (or amount to move horizontally and vertically)

Define graphic's final size

Rotate object

Change object's color

Change object's transparency

Make object slow down or speed up

Figure 10.33 The Transform dialog gathers all of the motion tween parameters that you learned about in Chapter 8 in a single location. Enter new values and click the Update Preview button to check the tweened effect.

3. Place an instance of the symbol on the Stage and select the symbol.

4. From the Insert menu, choose Timeline Effects > Transform/Transition > Transform (**Figure 10.32**).

   The Effects Settings dialog appears; the dialog bears the name of the effect you are creating, in this case, Transform.

5. Set the parameters of the Transform effect (**Figure 10.33**).

   The Transform dialog gathers in one place various changes that you can animate in a motion tween: the length of the animation (the number of frames it occupies), and changes in the tweened object's location, size, rotation, color, and speed. (For more details about these types of changes, see Chapter 8.)

6. To view your changes before finalizing the effect, click the Update Preview button.

   You can make repeated adjustments to the parameters, fine-tuning the transformation until looks the way you want.

continues on next page

GRAPHIC SYMBOLS WITH TIMELINE EFFECTS

7. To finalize the effect, click OK.

Flash replaces your original symbol on the Stage with the finished-effect symbol (using it to create the beginning and ending keyframes of a motion tween), renames the layer containing that instance in the Timeline, and adds or removes frames as necessary to display the number of frames you specified for the duration of the effect.

✔ Tip

■ The instructions (and cautions) for using and modifying static Timeline Effects also apply to animated Timeline Effects, such as Transform. See Chapter 6 for more details.

Dissecting a Transformation

The numbering and naming conventions for Flash's animated Timeline Effects are similar to those for static effects (see the sidebar "Dissecting a Drop Shadow," in Chapter 6).

Here's what happens when you apply the Transform effect to an object. (Note that symbol numbering will vary depending on whether you've created effects before in this document or work session.)

◆ Flash creates a new library folder called *Effects Folder* (or uses the existing one if you've already created effects in this document).

◆ Flash creates two new symbols:

effectSymbol, is your original object (or symbol) turned into a graphic symbol. The effectSymbol—the building block from which Flash creates the finished effect—lives in the *Effects Folder*.

Transform 1, is an animated graphic symbol from which Flash creates a motion tween using the parameters you specify.

◆ Flash replaces your original object (or symbol) on the Stage with one instance of Transform 1.

◆ Flash renames the layer containing that instance and adds (or removes) in-between frames to display the full length of the transformation (**Figure 10.34**).

Figure 10.34 The Movie Explorer reveals all the symbols created by the Transform Timeline Effect. The default Transform effect takes 30 frames. The tinted frames contain the content of the animated graphic symbol created by the effect.

Regular Symbols versus Symbols Created by Timeline Effects

For the most part, animated graphic symbols created by the Timeline Effect commands work the same way as symbols you create from scratch. But there are a few differences.

When you place an instance of a regular animated graphic symbol on the Stage, it sits in a keyframe and displays its first frame. You're in charge of adding enough in-between frames in the layer containing the symbol to display the rest of the animation. Generally, the number of in-between frames in the main Timeline should match the number of frames in the symbol itself. Define fewer frames than the symbol has, and you chop off the end of the animation; define more frames, and the animation starts over again. You can always add and delete frames in the Timeline to adjust that playback.

When creating a Timeline Effect, Flash automatically defines enough in-between frames in the main Timeline to display the effect (using the Duration value in the Effect Settings dialog). These in-between frames become a unit. They act as if you are using the span-based selection style even if you have chosen frame-based selection style. (For more information about frame-selection styles, see Chapter 7.) You can drag the effect span to reposition it in a layer; but you can't add frames to the span directly in the Timeline without breaking the link to the Effects Settings dialog. Generally, if you try to add frames (or keyframes) before the span, within it, or after it, a dialog appears warning that this symbol has an effect applied to it; if you edit it normally, you will "lose the ability to edit its settings." If your document contains other layers that have more frames than the layer with the effect, however, you can add in-between frames to the end of the effect. The effect starts over again, just as a regular animated graphic symbol would.

If this sounds confusing—it is! You may find it easiest to limit the way you work with effects; for example, always create an object to which you will apply an effect in its own layer; to reposition it in the Timeline, drag its span; to lengthen or shorten it, change the Duration parameter in the Effects Settings dialog (select the effect Symbol, then click the Edit button in the Effect section of the Property Inspector to access the dialog). Or, you can think of the Timeline Effect commands as an initial helper that automates creating all the parts of an effect. After that's done, if you need to make changes, go ahead and edit the Timeline (or the effect itself) as you would normally. When you get that scary warning dialog telling you that you will lose the ability to edit settings, just go ahead and click OK. Remember that what you lose is the ability to use the Effects Settings dialog to change the symbol's parameters. You can still edit the symbol as you would any other (for details about editing symbols, see Chapter 6).

Saving Animations As Movie-Clip Symbols

The procedure that you use to save an animation as a movie-clip symbol is the same as for saving an animated graphic symbol, except that you define the symbol as a movie clip in the Create New Symbol dialog.

To convert an animation to a movie-clip symbol:

1. Open the document that you created to make the Ping-Pong animation in "Animating Multiple Motion Tweens" earlier in this chapter.

   The Ping-Pong animation is a three-layer, 20-frame animation.

2. In the Timeline, select all 20 frames in all three layers.

3. From the Edit menu, Choose Timeline > Copy Frames.

4. From the Insert menu, choose New Symbol, or press ⌘-F8 (Mac) or Ctrl-F8 (Windows).

   The Create New Symbol dialog appears.

5. In the Name field, type a name for your symbol—for example, Ping-Pong Clip.

   Flash remembers what behavior you selected for the last symbol you created and selects that behavior for you again when you choose Insert > New Symbol.

6. Select Movie Clip as the behavior for your symbol (**Figure 10.35**).

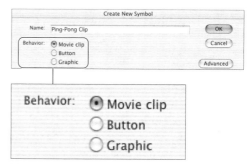

Figure 10.35 Selecting Movie Clip in the Behavior section of the Create New Symbol dialog defines a symbol that has an independent Timeline. The entire movie-clip symbol runs in a single frame of the main movie that contains that symbol.

Turning Timeline Effects into Movie Clip Symbols

If you apply a Timeline Effect to a raw shape or a graphic symbol, Flash creates a graphic symbol for the finished effect, whether the effect is static or animated. If you would prefer to have the effect animation take place within a movie clip, simply start with a movie clip symbol as your original object. (Create a raw shape or text, select it, choose Insert > Convert to Symbol, assign it Movie Clip behavior, click OK.) Flash nests your movie clip inside a graphic symbol to create the effectSymbol building block in the *Effects Folder*, but Flash assigns the finished-effect symbol movie clip behavior.

Placing an effect symbol in a layer, even a single-frame movie clip effect, limits the ways that you can work with the frames in that layer (see "Regular Symbols versus Symbols Created by Timeline Effects," earlier in this chapter).

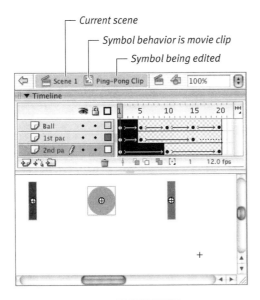

Current scene

Symbol behavior is movie clip

Symbol being edited

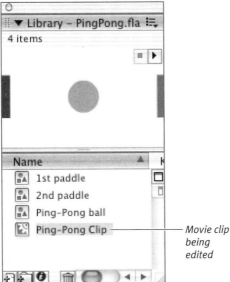

Movie clip being edited

Figure 10.36 After you name the symbol and define its behavior in the Create New Symbol dialog, Flash switches to symbol-editing mode. The icon that precedes the name of the symbol indicates that this symbol has movie-clip behavior. Now you can paste the animation frames into the symbol's Timeline.

7. Click OK.

   Flash creates a new symbol in the Library window and switches you to symbol-editing mode, with that symbol selected.

   The name of your symbol appears in the Edit Bar. The default Timeline for your new symbol consists of just one layer and a blank keyframe at Frame 1.

8. In the symbol Timeline, select Frame 1, and choose Edit > Timeline > Paste Frames.

   Flash pastes all 20 frames and three layers that you copied from the original Ping-Pong animation into the Timeline for the Ping-Pong Clip symbol (**Figure 10.36**). If you want to make any adjustments in the animation sequence, you can do so at this point.

9. To return to document-editing mode, click the current scene name in the Edit Bar.

✔ Tip

■ If you want to make a movie clip that contains exactly the same frames as an existing animated graphic symbol (as you did in the preceding exercise), you can duplicate that symbol and change its behavior. Select the animated graphic symbol in the Library window. From the Library window's Options menu, choose Duplicate. The Duplicate Symbol dialog appears, allowing you to rename the symbol and give it Movie Clip behavior.

SAVING ANIMATIONS AS MOVIE-CLIP SYMBOLS

Using Movie-Clip Symbols

You put movie-clip symbols to work by placing an instance of the symbol on the Stage in your Flash document. Unlike animated graphic symbols, movie-clip symbols have their own Timeline. A movie clip plays continuously, like a little film loop, in a single frame of the main movie. As long as the movie contains no other instructions that stop the clip from playing—a blank keyframe in the Timeline for the layer containing the movie clip, for example—the clip continues to loop.

As you work on your Flash document, you can see only the first frame of a movie clip. To view the animation of the movie-clip symbol in context with all the other elements of your movie, you must export the movie (by choosing one of the test modes, for example). You can preview the animation of the movie-clip symbol by itself in the Library window.

To place an instance of a movie clip:

1. With the movie that you created in the preceding exercises open, from the Insert menu, choose Scene.

   Flash creates a new scene and displays in its Timeline a single layer with a blank keyframe in Frame 1. The Stage is empty.

2. Access the Library window.

   If it's not open, choose Window > Library.

3. Select the Ping-Pong Clip symbol.

   The first frame of the animation appears in the preview window.

4. Drag a copy of the selected symbol to the Stage.

   Flash places the symbol in Keyframe 1 (**Figure 10.37**). You don't need to add any more frames to accommodate the animation, but you must export the movie to see the animation.

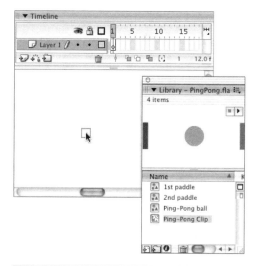

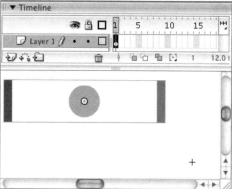

Figure 10.37 Drag an instance of your movie clip from the Library window to the Stage (top). Flash places the instance in Keyframe 1 (bottom).

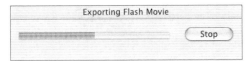

Figure 10.38 Choose Control > Test Scene to preview the animation of just one scene in a movie.

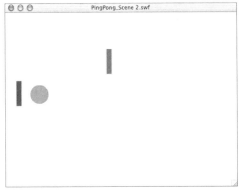

Figure 10.39 The Exporting Flash Movie dialog contains a progress bar and a button for canceling the export.

Figure 10.40 Flash Player displays your movie in a regular window. To exit the Player, close the window.

To view movie-clip animation in context:

1. Continuing with the movie that you created in the preceding exercise, from the Control menu, choose Test Scene (**Figure 10.38**).

   Flash exports the movie to a Flash Player format file, adding the .swf extension to the filename and using the current publishing settings for all the export options. (For more information on using the Publish Settings dialog, see Chapter 17.) During export, Flash displays the Exporting Flash Movie dialog, which contains a progress bar and a Stop (Mac) or Cancel (Windows) button for canceling the operation (**Figure 10.39**).

   When it finishes exporting the movie, Flash opens the .swf file in Flash Player so that you can see the movie in action (**Figure 10.40**).

2. When you have seen enough of the movie in test mode, click the movie window's Close box (Windows) or Close button (Mac) to exit Flash Player.

   Flash returns you to the authoring environment.

Using Animated Masks

In Chapter 5, you learned about Flash's capability to create mask layers that hide and reveal objects on lower layers. Sometimes, the best way to create the illusion of movement is to animate a mask so that it gradually hides or reveals objects.

Imagine a line that starts at the left edge of the Stage and goes all the way to the right edge. If you create a mask that reveals the line bit by bit, you create the illusion of a line that draws itself. Reverse the process, and you have a line that gradually erases itself.

Creating rotating and shape-tweened mask graphics can give you some interesting effects. The more familiar you are with using animated masks to reveal stationary items, the better sense you'll have of when to use this technique. For practice, try animating a mask that creates a growing rainbow.

To create a stationary graphic and a moving mask that reveals it:

1. Open a new Flash Document, and add a second layer.

2. In the Timeline, rename the bottom layer *Rainbow,* and rename the top layer *Rotating Rectangle.*

3. In Frame 1 of the *Rainbow* layer, on the Stage, use the oval tool to draw a perfect circle with a radial-gradient fill.

   To create a rainbow effect, use a gradient that has distinct bands of color.

4. Erase the bottom half of the circle (**Figure 10.41**).

   What's left is your rainbow shape. For safety, convert the rainbow to a symbol (select the rainbow on the Stage, choose Modify > Convert to Symbol, choose Graphic behavior, name the symbol, and click OK) so that you'll have a copy of the rainbow in case you accidentally delete the original.

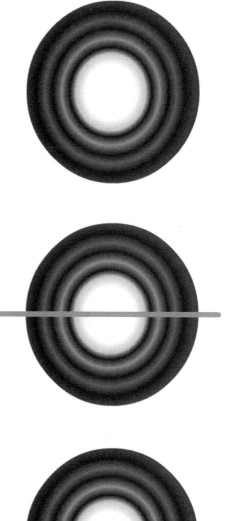

Figure 10.41 An easy way to create a rainbow object is to fill a circle with a multiple-color radial gradient and then delete the bottom half of the circle. Here, bisecting the circle by drawing a line through it (middle) makes deletion easy; just select the line and the bottom half of the circle (bottom), and press Delete.

Figure 10.42 When you create a mask layer, Flash automatically links the layer directly below the mask layer in the Timeline and locks both layers.

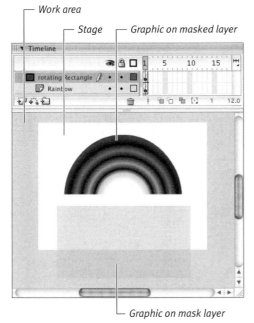

Figure 10.43 To create a mask that reveals the entire rainbow, draw a rectangle that's wider and taller than the rainbow. Positioning the rectangle below the rainbow hides the rainbow completely.

5. In the Timeline, Control-click (Mac) or right-click (Windows) the *Rotating Rectangle* layer.

The contextual menu for layers appears.

6. Choose Mask.

Flash converts the layer to a mask, links the *Rainbow* layer to the mask, and locks both layers (**Figure 10.42**).

7. In the Timeline, click the padlock icons in the *Rotating Rectangle* and *Rainbow* layers to unlock them.

8. On the Stage, in Frame 1 of the *Rotating Rectangle* layer, use the rectangle tool to draw a rectangle just below the bottom of the rainbow (**Figure 10.43**).

The rectangle is your mask. Any items that lie below the rectangle on a linked layer appear; everything else is hidden.

Make the rectangle a bit larger than the rainbow so that the mask can cover the whole rainbow. Using a transparent fill color lets you see the rainbow through the mask rectangle and helps you verify the mask's position. (To make the rectangle's fill color transparent, select it and then, in the Color Mixer panel, assign it a low Alpha percentage.)

✔ Tip

■ You can use any of the three types of animation on a mask layer: frame-by-frame, motion tweening, or shape tweening. Advanced ActionScripters can also use ActionScript to tell one movie clip symbol to mask another.

To prepare the mask for rotational animation:

1. Select the rectangle, and choose Modify > Convert to Symbol.

   Because you want to create rotational animation, you must use a motion tween for the mask, which means that the mask graphic must be a symbol or a grouped element.

   The Convert to Symbol dialog appears.

2. In the Name field, enter a name for the symbol; then click OK.

3. Using the free-transform tool, select the rectangle on the Stage, and position the pointer over the white circle that indicates the transformation point of the object.

   A small white circle appears next to the arrow pointer, indicating that you can move the selected object's transformation point.

4. Drag the transformation-point circle straight up until it rests in the middle of the top edge of the rectangle (**Figure 10.44**).

   Now you can rotate the rectangle so that it swings up and over the rainbow.

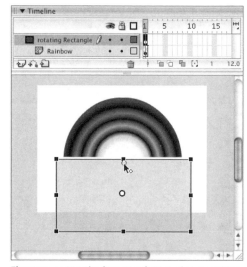

Figure 10.44 Use the free-transform tool to reposition the point around which a symbol (or grouped item) rotates. Drag the circle that indicates the transformation point to a new position. A small circle previews the new transformation-point location.

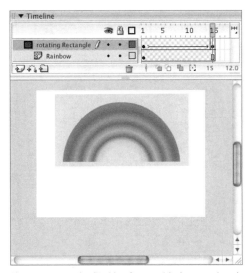

Figure 10.45 In the final keyframe with the completed motion tween for the mask object, the mask covers the rainbow. Giving the mask a transparent fill lets you see the objects to be revealed through it as you work. The transparency of objects on the mask layer doesn't appear in the final movie.

To complete the rotating-mask animation:

1. In the Timeline, in the Rainbow layer, select Frame 15, and choose Insert > Timeline > Frame.

2. In the Timeline, in the Rotating Rectangle layer, select Frame 15, and choose Insert > Timeline > Keyframe.

3. In Frame 15, with the rectangle selected on the Stage, use the Rotate and Skew modifier of the free-transform tool to reposition the rectangle; click and drag the bottom-left corner of the rectangle and rotate it so that the rectangle completely covers the rainbow.

   The mask that covers the rainbow in authoring mode will reveal the rainbow in the final movie.

4. In the Timeline, in the Rotating Rectangle layer, select any of the frames in the Keyframe 1 span (frames 1 through 14).

5. From the Frame Property Inspector's Tween pop-up menu, choose Motion.

6. From the Rotate pop-up menu, choose CW.

7. Enter 0 in the Times field.

   This step sets up the motion tween that rotates the rectangle180 degrees, swinging it up and over the rainbow until it fully covers the rainbow (**Figure 10.45**).

USING ANIMATED MASKS

To preview the animation:

◆ Choose Control > Test Movie or
Control > Test Scene.

or

◆ In the Timeline, click the lock icon to lock
both layers to see the masked rainbow;
then play the movie to see the mask
reveal the rainbow.

If the rainbow is not fully revealed during
the tween, you may need to enlarge or
reposition the rectangle. Unlock both
layers, and move the playhead through
the movie to see where the rectangle is in
each in-between frame (**Figure 10.46**).

✔ Tips

■ A quick way to lock a mask and its
masked layers is to ⌘-click (Mac) or
Ctrl-click (Windows) the mask layer or
any of the masked layers.

■ To make the rainbow appear to fade in
gradually, tween a change in its transparency. Select Frame 15 of the Rainbow
layer and press F6, duplicating the rainbow symbol instance in a new keyframe.
In Frame 1, select the rainbow symbol
instance; in the Property Inspector, from
the Color menu, choose Alpha; in the
Value field, enter a low percentage; from
the Tween pop-up menu, choose Motion.

■ The Timeline Effect named Transition uses
a motion tween mask to create wipes
and fades. In a practice document, make
a few Transition effects with different
parameter settings. In the Library, double-click one of the finished-effect symbols (Transition 1, Transition 2, and so
on). A dialog appears warning that if you
edit the symbol you lose the ability to
edit the effect via the Transition dialog.
Click OK. You'll lose Flash's ability to help
modify the effect but gain a chance to
see how it's put together.

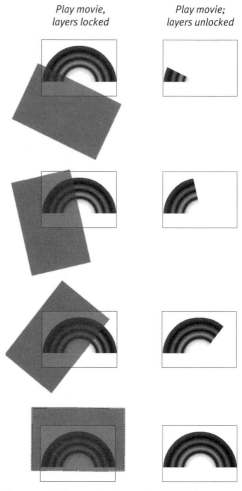

*Play movie,
layers locked*

*Play movie;
layers unlocked*

Figure 10.46 As you play the movie with the layers
unlocked (left), you can see the in-between positions
of the mask graphic. When you lock the layers (right),
you see the masking as it will appear in the final
exported movie.

BUILDING
BUTTONS FOR
INTERACTIVITY

After you master the drawing and animating tools in Flash MX 20004, you can create movies that play from beginning to end. But Flash is more than a tool for making animated movies. You can use it to create interactive environments that transform viewers into users. To move your Flash movie into the realm of interactive experience, you need to create user interface elements that allow users to control and interact with your application. The most common interface element is a button. Buttons have two levels of interactivity: First, a button can respond to a user with visual feedback, for example changing color when the pointer enters the button area; second, the button can carry out tasks, for example, switching to a new scene when the user clicks the button.

Flash comes with a number of predefined interface elements, including button symbols and button components. For these elements, built-in coding takes care of the first level of button interactivity, responding to mouse movements with visual feedback. For example when a user positions the pointer over a button symbol or component's hot spot, built-in coding tells Flash to change the pointer to the hand cursor and change the look of the button.

In this chapter, you learn to set up the first level of interactivity by working with button symbols and button components. You also learn to set up a movie clip symbol that can act as a visually responsive button.

To achieve the second level of interactivity, you must attach scripts to individual button instances to make buttons respond in new ways and carry out tasks. You'll learn some simple ways to do that in Chapter 12.

The Mystery of Button Symbols

In Flash, you can create a button by creating a symbol and then assigning it button behavior. Buttons are actually short—four frames, to be precise—interactive movies. When you select button behavior for a symbol, Flash sets up a Timeline with four keyframes. You create graphics for the first three keyframes to display the button in three common states: Up, Over, and Down. The fourth keyframe (never shown to the viewer) defines the active area of the button.

In the Up state, you create a graphic that looks like a static, unused button. This graphic appears whenever the pointer lies outside the active area of the button. In the Over state, create the graphic as it should look when the pointer rolls over the button. Flash automatically changes the pointer to the hand cursor for the Over state, but often, you want additional visual changes to alert your viewer that the pointer is now on a live button. In the Down state, create the graphic as it should look when someone clicks the button. In the fourth frame, the Hit frame, create a graphic that defines the boundary of the button. Any filled shape in this frame becomes a place where mouse movements trigger the button during movie playback.

Any changes you make in the appearance of the graphic elements in the keyframes create the illusion of movement. In other Flash animation sequences, changes occur over time as the playhead moves through the frames. In button symbols, however, changes occur when the user moves the pointer over a specific area of the screen.

You can include movie clips within each frame of a button to create buttons that are fully animated, and you can attach actions to buttons to give your viewers more control of the movie.

Figure 11.1 Choosing Insert > New Symbol is the first step in creating a button.

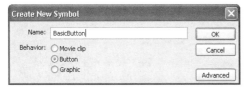

Figure 11.2 To make a button, you must create a new symbol and assign it button behavior in the Create New Symbol dialog. You can also name the button there.

Figure 11.3 The Timeline for every button symbol contains just four frames: Up, Over, Down, and Hit. Flash automatically puts a keyframe in the Up frame of a new button symbol.

Creating a Basic Button Symbol

A button is really just a Flash movie clip with different frames to represent the button in all its possible states. The button symbol offers three frames for button state—Up, Over, Down—plus one frame that defines the active button area. To create the most basic button symbol, choose a simple shape and use it for each frame; change its color or add or modify internal elements for the various states. When you complete all four frames, your button is ready to use. Return to document-editing mode, and drag a copy of the button symbol from the Library window to the Stage.

To create a button symbol:

1. Open a new Flash Document, or open an existing document to which you want to add buttons.

2. From the Insert menu, choose New Symbol, or press ⌘-F8 (Mac) or Ctrl-F8 (Windows) (**Figure 11.1**).

   The Create New Symbol dialog appears.

3. Type a name in the Name field (for example, MyBasicButton), choose Button in the Behavior section, and click OK (**Figure 11.2**).

   Flash creates a new symbol in the Library window and returns you to the Timeline and Stage in symbol-editing mode. The Timeline for a button symbol contains the four frames that you need to define the button: Up, Over, Down, and Hit.

   By default, the Up frame contains a keyframe (**Figure 11.3**). You must add keyframes to the Over, Down, and Hit frames, and place the graphic elements in each frame of the button. To give users feedback about the button—so that they can tell when they're on a live button and sense the difference when they actually click it—use a different graphic in each frame.

415

To create the Up state:

1. Using the file from the preceding exercise, in the Timeline, select the Up frame.

2. On the Stage, create a new graphic or place a graphic symbol (**Figure 11.4**).

   This graphic element becomes the button as it's just sitting onstage in your movie, waiting for someone to click it. The crosshair in the middle of the Stage in symbol-editing mode will become both the center point of the symbol and the point for registering the symbol in document-editing mode.

To create the Over state:

1. Using the file from the preceding exercise, in the Timeline, select the Over frame.

2. From the Insert menu, choose Timeline > Keyframe.

   Flash inserts a keyframe that duplicates the contents of the Up keyframe. Now you can make minor changes in the Up graphic to convert it to an Over graphic. You might enlarge an element within the button, for example (**Figure 11.5**). Duplicating the preceding keyframe makes it easy to align all your button elements so that they don't appear to jump around as they change states.

Registration crosshair marks the center of the symbol's Stage —

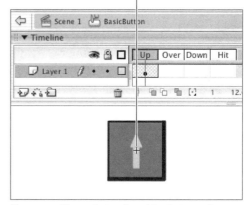

Figure 11.4 When a button is waiting for your viewer to notice and interact with it, Flash displays the contents of the Up frame.

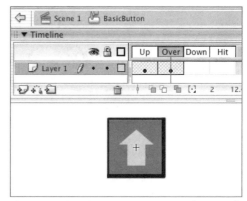

Figure 11.5 When the viewer's pointer rolls (or pauses) over the button, Flash displays the contents of the Over frame.

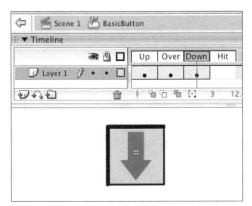

Figure 11.6 When the viewer clicks the button, Flash displays the contents of the Down frame.

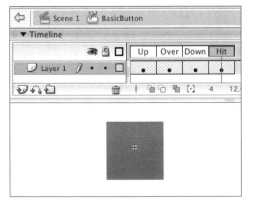

Figure 11.7 The Hit-frame graphic doesn't need to be a fully detailed image of the button in any state; it just needs to be a silhouette of the button shape. Flash uses that shape to define the active button area. This Hit frame contains a copy of the Down frame that has been filled with dark gray.

To create the Down state:

1. Using the file from the preceding exercise, in the Timeline, select the Down frame.

2. From the Insert menu, choose Timeline > Keyframe.

Flash inserts a keyframe that duplicates the contents of the Over keyframe. Now you can make minor changes to convert the Over graphic to a Down graphic. You might change the button color, for example, and reverse the shadow effect so that the button looks indented (**Figure 11.6**).

After you create graphics for the three states of your button, you need to define the active area of the button.

To create the Hit state:

1. Using the file from the preceding exercise, in the Timeline, select the Hit frame.

2. From the Insert menu, choose Timeline > Keyframe to duplicate the contents of the Down keyframe.

When you use a graphic with the same shape and size for all three phases of your button, you can safely use a copy of any previous frame as the Hit-frame graphic.

3. If you want, use the paint bucket and ink bottle tools to fill the Hit-frame graphic with a single color (**Figure 11.7**).

This step is not required, but it helps remind you that this graphic is not the one that viewers of your movie will actually see.

continues on next page

4. From the Edit menu, choose Edit
Document, or click the Back button
in the Edit Bar.

Flash returns you to the main Timeline.
Now you can use the button symbol in
your movie just as you would use any
other symbol.

✔ Tip

- If you use a copy of the Up, Over, or Down
graphic in the Hit frame, try enlarging
that copy slightly. Using a larger image
ensures that users activate the button
easily as soon as they get near it. To
enlarge the graphic by a small amount
quickly, select the graphic. From the
Modify menu, choose Shape > Expand
Fill. In the Expand Fill dialog, enter a
small value (say, 2 pixels). Choose Expand.
Click OK. You're done.

The Mystery of Hit-Frame Graphics

Though it never appears in a Flash movie, the Hit frame's graphic content is vital to a button's
operation. The sole purpose of the Hit-frame graphic is to define the button's boundaries. This
graphic doesn't need to be detailed; it's just a silhouette that defines the button shape. Any
fill or line in the Hit frame becomes an active part of the button. During playback, when the
viewer moves the pointer into that area, the Over frame of the button appears; when the user
clicks that area, the Down frame appears.

For the clearest, most user-friendly buttons, make sure that your Hit-frame graphic is large
enough to cover all the graphics in the first three frames of the button. To be safe, make your
Hit-frame graphic a little larger than the other graphics.

If your button is something delicate, such as a piece of type or a line drawing, make your Hit-
frame graphic a geometric shape —say, a filled rectangle or oval—that completely covers the
Up, Over, and Down graphics. That way, your viewers will have no trouble finding and clicking the button.

To place the newly created button in your movie:

◆ Continuing with the file from the preceding exercise, drag an instance of the button MyButton from the Library window to the Stage.

You can modify the instance to change its size, rotation, and color. (For more information on modifying symbol instances, see Chapter 6.)

✔ Tips

■ To create a consistent look on a Web site, you might want to use a set of buttons over and over. You can even reuse buttons in several projects with only slight changes. To save time, try devoting one whole document to buttons and always create your button symbols there. Then you can copy a button from this master button file to your current Flash Document and tweak the button there. You can also create a shared library of buttons (see Chapter 6).

■ Always fill your Hit-frame silhouette with the same color—say, light gray or neon blue. That way, the silhouette becomes another visual cue that you are in the Hit frame of a button, in symbol-editing mode.

■ You can preview the Up, Over, and Down states of your button by selecting it in the Library window and then clicking the Play button in the preview window. Flash displays each frame in turn.

■ Choose Control > Enable Simple Buttons to evoke the different states for a button instance on the Stage in authoring mode. Flash displays the Up, Over, and Down states as you move the pointer over the button and click. Remember, with buttons enabled, you can't select them or work with them. To turn off Enable Simple Button mode, choose Control > Enable Simple Buttons again.

Creating Shape-Changing Button Symbols

Now that you have a feel for creating simple button symbols, it's time to explore ways to make fancier ones, something more exotic than the simple geometric shapes you'd find on a telephone or calculator. Button graphics can emulate real-world switches or toggles. You can disguise buttons as part of a movie's scenery—making the blinking eye of a character a button, for example. That situation often happens in games; finding the hot spots or buttons is part of the fun. When the Up, Over, and Down frames of your button symbol contain graphics of different shapes and sizes, however, creating an effective Hit-frame graphic can be a bit tricky. You need to create a graphic for the Hit state that covers all of the other states.

To create Up, Over, and Down states with various graphics:

1. Open a new Flash Document, or open an existing Flash Document to which you want to add buttons.

2. From the Insert menu, choose New Symbol.

   The Create New Symbol dialog appears.

3. Enter a name in the Name field (for example, `AnimatedBtn`), choose Button in the Behavior section, and click OK.

   Flash creates a new symbol in the Library window and returns you to the Timeline and Stage in symbol-editing mode. The Timeline for a button symbol contains the four frames necessary for defining the button: Up, Over, Down, and Hit.

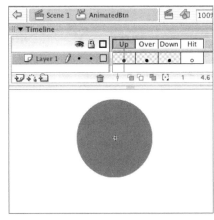

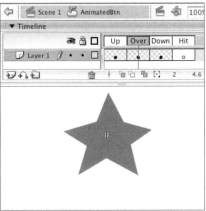

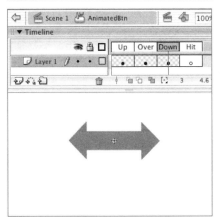

Figure 11.8 You can create fanciful buttons that change shape when a user rolls over or clicks them. In this example, the inactive button is a simple circle (top). When the pointer rolls over the button, the circle changes to a star (middle). When the user clicks the button, it changes to a double-headed arrow (bottom).

4. In the Timeline, select the Over, Down, and Hit frames.

5. From the Modify menu, choose Timeline > Convert to Blank Keyframes.

Now you have a blank keyframe in every frame of your button, and you're ready to place various graphics in each frame.

6. With the Up frame selected in the Timeline, on the Stage, create a new graphic, or place the graphic symbol that you want to use for the button's Up state.

7. Repeat step 6 for the Over and Down frames.

For this exercise, use graphics that have different shapes—a circle, a star, and a double-headed arrow, for example (**Figure 11.8**).

To create the Hit state for graphics of various shapes:

1. Using the file that you created in the preceding exercise, in the Timeline, select the Hit frame.

2. To create the Hit-frame graphic, *do one of the following:*

   ▲ Draw a simple geometric shape large enough to cover all areas of the button. Turn on onion skinning so that you can see exactly what you need to cover (**Figure 11.9**).

   ▲ Use Flash's Edit > Copy and Edit > Paste in Place commands to copy the graphic elements from the first three frames of the button and paste them into the Hit frame of the button one by one.

   ▲ The graphics stack up in the Hit frame, occupying the exact area needed to cover the button in any phase of its operation (**Figure 11.10**).

✔ Tips

- When you use the copy-and-paste-in-place technique to create your Hit-frame graphic, itís a good idea to expand the resulting graphic slightly—by using the Modify > Shape > Expand Fill command, for example. Making the Hit graphic slop over the edges of the active button areas ensures that your viewers will easily activate the button.

- Use a transparent color (one with an alpha value less than 100 percent) for your Hit-frame graphic. The other graphics will show through the Hit-frame graphic in onion-skin mode, making it easy to see how to position or size the Hit-frame graphic to cover the graphics in the other frames.

Onion-skin outlines ⌐

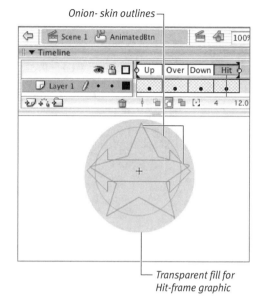

Transparent fill for Hit-frame graphic

Figure 11.9 The Hit-frame silhouette needs to encompass all possible button areas in all three button modes. If, for example, you duplicate only the circle as your Hit frame for this button, you exclude the tips of the star. A user who clicks those tips in the Over phase will be unable to activate the button. If you duplicate only the star, the user could roll over several areas of the circle and never discover that it's a button.

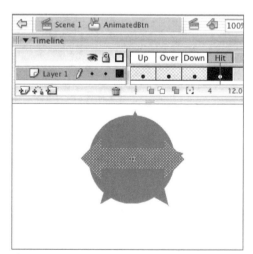

Figure 11.10 By copying the graphic in each of the button states and using the Paste in Place command to place them in the Hit frame, you wind up with a perfectly positioned silhouette that incorporates all the possible button areas.

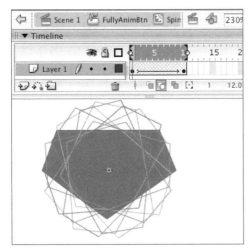

Figure 11.11 Onion skinning reveals all the frames of the spinning pentagon (a motion tween) that appear when the fully animated button is in the Up state.

Figure 11.12 The Preview mode of the Timeline shows the animation of the clip that appears when the pointer rolls or rests over the button area.

Creating Fully Animated Button Symbols

The button symbols that you created in the preceding exercises are animated in the sense that they change as the user interacts with them. Flash also allows you to create button symbols that are fully animated—a glowing light bulb, for example, or a little ladybug that jumps up and down, saying, "Click me!" The trick to making fully animated buttons is placing movie clips in the frames of your button. Because the movie clips play in their own Timeline, animated buttons remain animated even when you pause the movie.

To animate a rollover button:

1. Create a new Flash Document, or open an existing Flash Document to which you want to add buttons.

2. Choose Insert > New Symbol.

   The Create New Symbol dialog appears.

3. Name your button (for example, `FullyAnimBtn`), choose Button in the Behavior section, and click OK.

4. In the Timeline, select the Over, Down, and Hit frames of the button, and choose Modify > Timeline > Convert to Blank Keyframes.

   Flash creates blank keyframes for the button's Over, Down, and Hit frames.

5. In the Timeline, select the Up frame, and create a movie-clip symbol or import one from another file.

   For this example, the Up-frame clip contains a spinning pentagon (**Figure 11.11**).

6. In the Timeline, select the Over frame, and create a movie-clip symbol or import one from another file.

   In this example, the Over-frame clip contains a pentagon that turns into a star (**Figure 11.12**).

   continues on next page

7. In the Timeline, select the Down frame, and create a movie-clip symbol or import one from another file.

For this example, the Down-frame clip contains a star that flies apart (**Figure 11.13**).

8. In the Timeline, select the Hit frame, and create a graphic that covers all the button areas for the three button states (Up, Over, and Down).

A large oval works well for this purpose (**Figure 11.14**). This graphic creates an active button area that's larger than the spinning pentagon. As your viewer's pointer nears the spinning graphic during playback, the button switches to Over mode. In Over mode, the oval is big enough to encompass all points of the star, and in Down mode, the user can let the pointer drift a fair amount and still be within the confines of the button.

9. Return to document-editing mode by clicking the name of the current scene in the Edit Bar at the top of the Stage.

10. Drag a copy of the FullyAnimBtn symbol from the Library window to the Stage.

✔ Tips

- You can place a movie clip in the Hit frame of your button, but only the visible graphic from the clip's first frame determines the hit area.

- With buttons enabled, in document-editing mode, Flash previews the Up, Over, and Down frames of your button symbol but not its complete animation. For each frame, you see only the first frame of the movie clip. To view the fully animated button, you must export the movie and view it in Flash Player (by choosing Control > Test Movie, for example).

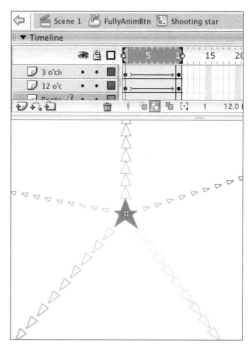

Figure 11.13 Onion skinning reveals the animation of the clip that appears when the viewer clicks inside the button area.

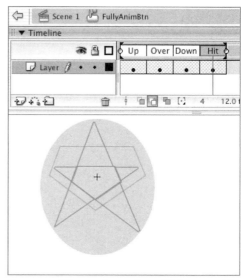

Figure 11.14 When you're creating a Hit-frame graphic, use onion skinning to see the first frame of the movie clip in each button frame. Here, the Hit-frame graphic is a transparent fill, which also helps you position the graphic to cover the graphics in the other frames.

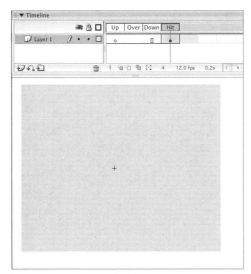

Figure 11.15 To make an invisible button, create a button symbol that has nothing in the Up, Over, and Down frames. Here, the Hit frame contains a filled rectangle large enough to cover the Stage.

Creating Invisible Button Symbols

You don't actually have to place a graphic in every frame of a button. The only frame that must have content is the Hit frame, because it describes the active button area. Buttons without content in the Up, Over, and Down frames are invisible in the final movie. An invisible button with a Hit-frame graphic that covers the whole Stage allows users to click anywhere in the frame to trigger whatever actions you script the button to carry out.

To create an invisible button:

1. Create a new Flash Document, or open an existing one to which you want to add an invisible button.

2. Choose Insert > New Symbol.

   The Create New Symbol dialog appears.

3. Name your button (for example, HiddenButton), choose Button in the Behavior section, and click OK.

4. In symbol-editing mode, in the Timeline, select the Hit frame of the button, and choose Insert > Timeline > Blank Keyframe.

   Flash creates a blank keyframe for the button's Hit frame.

5. On the Stage, create a graphic element to represent the active button area.

   To create an invisible button that allows users to click anywhere in the frame to trigger an action, use the rectangle tool to draw a filled rectangle large enough to cover the entire Stage (**Figure 11.15**). The solid rectangle turns the whole Stage into an active button, but because no graphics are associated with the button, it will be invisible to the user.

   continues on next page

6. Return to document-editing mode, and drag a copy of the `HiddenButton` symbol to the Stage.

Flash shows a transparent object that previews the hot-spot area (**Figure 11.16**). If necessary, you can reposition (or resize) the button so that it covers the Stage fully.

✔ Tip

■ In symbol-editing mode, the Stage is a fixed size (20 inches by 20 inches), and it's not necessarily the same size as the Stage in your current movie. If you want the Hit-frame rectangle of an invisible button to cover the whole Stage, select the rectangle, then in the Info panel or Property Inspector, enter values in the Width and Height fields, that are slightly larger than the dimensions of your document.

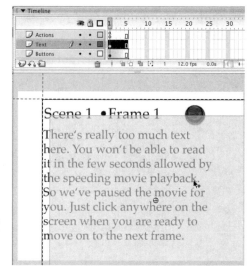

Figure 11.16 When the Up frame of a symbol is empty, Flash displays a transparent version of the Hit-frame graphic to help you position your invisible button in document-editing mode.

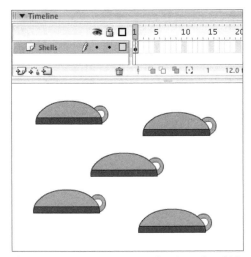

Figure 11.17 On the Stage, create the picture for which you want to activate multiple hot spots. Here, five cups are part of a shell game. One cup hides an item; the others are empty. You can use one button with multiple hot spots to display the same message when the user clicks any of the empty cups.

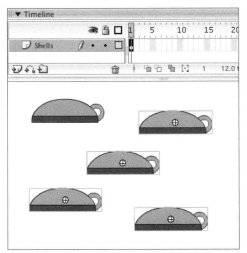

Figure 11.18 Select the empty cups on the Stage and copy them as preparation for creating a hit frame for a button with multiple hot spots.

Creating Button Symbols with Multiple Hot Spots

Part of the fun of buttons is that you can use them for anything. You don't have to simulate buttons or switches. Flash buttons are versatile in part because each frame of a button can have quite different content. The Hit-frame graphic, for example, need not coincide with any of the graphics of the previous frames: It can be a separate graphic that creates hot spots in various areas of the Stage.

Imagine an animated shell game in which your viewer must determine which cup is hiding a bean. You could create a separate button that displays the message "Nope, guess again!" for each empty cup, or you could create one button that displays the message and put a graphic for each empty cup in the Hit frame of that button.

To create multiple hot spots for a single button:

1. Create a new Flash document with a simple illustration of five cups in Frame 1 (**Figure 11.17**).

2. On the Stage, use the selection tool to select four of the cups, and choose Edit > Copy (**Figure 11.18**).

3. Choose Insert > New Symbol.
   The Create New Symbol dialog appears.

continues on next page

4. Type a name (for example, MultipleButton), choose Button in the Behavior section, click OK.

5. In symbol-editing mode, in the Timeline for your button, select the Hit frame.

6. Choose Insert > Timeline > Blank Keyframe.

7. Choose Edit > Paste in Center.

Flash pastes copies of the four cups in the center of the Stage (**Figure 11.19**). You can fill these graphics with a solid color if you want to remind yourself that users will not see them.

8. In the Timeline, select the Down frame.

9. Choose Insert > Timeline > Blank Keyframe.

10. On the Stage, create the message that you want people to see when they click an empty cup (**Figure 11.20**).

11. Return to document-editing mode, and drag a copy of the MultipleButton symbol to the Stage.

Flash shows transparent previews of the hot-spot area.

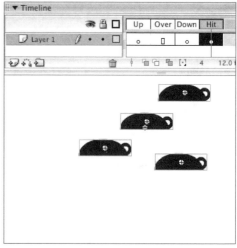

Figure 11.19 In symbol-editing mode, paste the Clipboard contents (the empty cups) into the Hit frame of your invisible button.

Figure 11.20 Whatever you place in the Down frame appears whenever someone clicks one of the hot-spot areas that you created for the Hit-frame graphic. Here, onion skinning is turned on to help with positioning the message text.

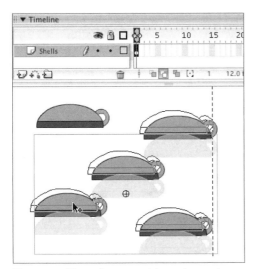

Figure 11.21 When a button contains no images in the Up frame, Flash displays a transparent version of the Hit-frame graphic. You can use the selection tool or the arrow keys to position the button so that the preview graphics precisely cover the graphic elements on the Stage.

12. Use the selection tool or the arrow keys to reposition the hot-spot cups to coincide with the cups in Frame 1 of your movie (**Figure 11.21**).

You're ready to see the button in action.

13. Choose Control > Test Movie.

Flash exports the movie and opens it in Flash Player. When you click one of the four empty cups, Flash displays the message that you created for the Down frame of your button.

✔ Tip

■ If you were creating a real game, you'd want to be sure to create another, separate button to place over the fifth cup. Not only might you want to display a winner's message (or start an animation or jump to another frame) when someone clicks this cup, but you also would want to be sure that the pointer would change to the pointing finger consistently, so as not to give the game away.

Using Button Components

Button symbols handle the scripting necessary for displaying the common button states, but allow you to define the graphic look of a button. Using button symbols you can create infinite interface looks for your projects. Flash also provides a different type of button—the button component—that has a predefined graphic look. A component is actually a special type of movie clip, called a *.swc file,* or compiled clip. While it is possible to change the graphic elements of a component, the techniques for doing so are beyond the scope of this book (see "The Mystery of Components" sidebar, later in this chapter). Each component does have certain parameters that you can modify via the Component Inspector panel or the Property Inspector. To put a component to use, you place an instance of it in your Flash Document.

To place an instance of the button component:

1. Open a new Flash Document.

2. Access the Components panel, Components Inspector, Property Inspector, and the Library window.

   To open the Components panel, choose Window > Development Panels > Components; to open the Component Inspector, choose Window > Development Panels > Component Inspector; to open the Property Inspector, choose Window > Properties; to open the library, choose Window > Library.

3. If necessary, in the Components panel, expand the list of user interface components (**Figure 11.22**).

   Click the triangle (Mac) or plus sign (Windows) to the left of the name UI Components to toggle between the expanded and collapsed views of the list.

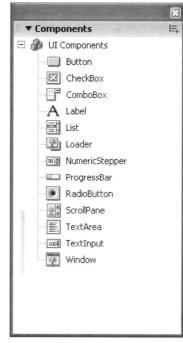

Figure 11.22 The Components panel lists all of the default components that come with Flash. You can expand or collapse the list by clicking the plus sign (Windows) or triangle (Mac) to the left of the title UI Components.

Figure 11.23 A button component is actually a special form of movie clip. When you drag a component from the Components panel to your document, the component symbol appears in the Library window of that document, with its Kind listed as Compiled Clip.

Figure 11.24 You can rename a compiled-clip symbol in the Library window. Renaming doesn't change the button's text, however. To do that you must modify the component's Label parameter.

4. Drag an instance of the Button component to the Stage.

Flash adds the Button component to the document's library as a compiled-clip symbol (**Figure 11.23**). In many ways, compiled clips work just like other library assets (for more about working with library assets, see Chapter 6). You can, for example, rename compiled clips and drag new instances directly from the Library window.

5. In the Library window, double-click the compiled clip's name (Button) to activate the text field, and type a new name, MyBtnComponent.

6. Press Enter.

Look at the symbol's preview in the Library Window; you have changed the name of the master compiled-clip symbol, but the symbol itself still bears the label "Button" (**Figure 11.24**). To change the label, you must modify the component instance. One big difference between compiled-clip symbols and regular movie-clip symbols is that you cannot edit a compiled-clip symbol directly as you can a movie-clip symbol (see "The Mystery of Components" sidebar). Each component has certain editable parameters, which you can modify, on an instance-by-instance basis, via the Component Inspector and/or the Property Inspector.

To preview the component instance:

◆ To view a limited component preview during authoring, choose Control > Enable Live Preview (**Figure 11.25**).

As a default, the Enable Live Preview setting is active. If you are working with many components, this setting can slow things down a bit and you may prefer to turn it off for a time. While the Enable Simple Buttons setting allows you to preview a button symbols Up, Over, and Down states; Enable Live Preview basically reveals the button's parameter settings in the Up state. To view a fully enabled button component, you must view it in Flash Player. When Enable Live Preview is inactive, Flash previews component instances as simple outline rectangles on the Stage.

◆ To view all the parameters and button states of a component, choose Control > Test Movie.

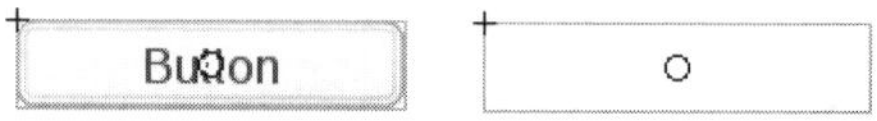

Figure 11.25 With Enable Live Preview active (Flash's default setting) you can see the parameters for component instances on the Stage while authoring (left). With Enable Live Preview inactive, Flash previews components with simple rectangular outlines that give no hint about what kind of element they represent (right).

Figure 11.26 To change the dimensions of a button component instance, access the Properties tab of the Property Inspector and enter new values in the Width and Height fields.

Figure 11.27 You can change the rectangular Button component to a square by entering the same value for width and height.

Modifying Button Components

You can change a button component's dimensions, change its label text, add an icon to customize the button, set the button's visibility, and set the button to act as a toggle.

To modify button-component dimensions:

1. Continuing with the file you created in the preceding exercise, on the Stage, select the instance of MyBtnComponent.

2. In the Property Inspector, click the Properties tab to access the Button component's properties.

3. In the W and H fields, enter new values for width and height (**Figure 11.26**).

   For this exercise, enter **100** pixels in the Height field to match the button's width of 100 pixels and create a large, square button.

4. Press Enter to confirm the new value(s).

   The button's dimensions change according to the value(s) you enter (**Figure 11.27**). The bounding box of the button defines the active area of the button. As you change the dimensions, Flash automatically changes the hit area for the button component to match.

✔ Tips

■ To force Flash to keep the button's aspect ratio (the ratio of width to height) the same as you increase or decrease the button components dimensions, click the small lock icon to the left of the W and H fields before you enter new values.

■ Another way to resize the button component is by using the Transform panel or the free-transform tool. You can also rotate or skew the component with these methods, however doing so makes the button's label text disappear.

■ You can position your button precisely by entering values in the Property Inspector's *x* and *y* coordinate fields.

■ Don't be confused by the minHeight and minWidth parameters in the Component Inspector. These extra parameters are not functional in Flash MX 2004. They will allow Macromedia to expand the way the button component works in the future.

To modify button-component labels:

1. Continuing with the file you created in the preceding exercise, on the Stage, select the instance of `MyBtnComponent`.

2. Access the Component Inspector.

   The panel displays a two-column table (**Figure 11.28**). The first column contains the parameter name; the second column contains the value for each parameter.

3. To modify the text that appears on the button, in the row for "label," click the name *Button*.

   Flash activates the text field and selects the name; you can enter a new name, such as `testComponent` (**Figure 11.29**).

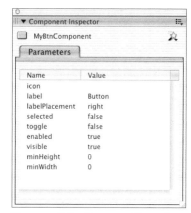

Figure 11.28 The Component Inspector displays all of the parameters of the Button component that you can modify during authoring.

Figure 11.29 Click the value field in the Label row to activate text entry. Type your new label text. Press enter to confirm the new label.

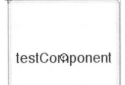

Figure 11.30 With Live Preview Enabled active, Flash previews your new label text in the button instance on the Stage.

4. Press Enter, or click outside the active text field.

With Flash's default settings, the new label text appears within the button-component instance (**Figure 11.30**).

If you do not see the new text, choose Control > Enable Live Preview. Be forewarned, if your text is wider than the button instance, Flash will truncate the text to make it fit within the visible button area.

✔ Tip

■ You can also modify most of the button component's parameters from within the Property Inspector. With an instance of the Button component selected on the Stage, access the Property Inspector and click the Parameters tab to display parameter fields for the Button component.

The Mystery of Components

The Button is just one element in Flash's set of User Interface Components. These components contain built-in coding that makes them easy to use. Macromedia designed them to work together to give an application or Web site a consistent look and feel.

Components are basically sophisticated, scripted movie clip symbols whose scripts have been compiled to save time during publishing. Compiled symbols (also called .swc files) are not directly editable within the authoring environment the way other symbols are. Each component does have its own editable parameters, however. Flash assists you in modifying these attributes through the Component Inspector panel.

More experienced Flash authors can change the look of components by editing the underlying theme, style, and skin files on which components are based. Advanced scripters can change the look of components during playback via ActionScript. These modification techniques are beyond the scope of this book.

While many of the advantages of components belong to advanced Flash authors who can use ActionScript to make components communicate with one another and to change them on the fly at runtime, even someone unfamiliar with scripting can use simple components to add interactivity to a project.

All the components that come with Flash appear in the Components panel. One of the beauties of components is that advanced scripters can create their own components and share them with other Flash authors. One source for new components is the Macromedia Exchange portion of the Macromedia Web site. As third-party components become available, you will be able to add them to your Components panel for easy access.

To create icons for button components:

1. Continuing with the file you created in the preceding exercise, choose Insert > New Symbol.

   The Create New Symbol dialog appears. A button component icon is really just a graphic or movie-clip symbol. You cannot edit the graphic elements of a button component directly, therefore, you cannot simply place the icon symbol within the component graphics yourself. But ActionScript can do that during playback. The icon parameter sets up behind-the-scenes scripting that displays a symbol within the button component at runtime.

2. In the dialog, enter a name, BtnIcon, and choose Movie Clip or Graphic as the Behavior.

3. In the Linkage section, click Export for ActionScript.

   Flash puts the symbol name in the Linkage Identifier field (**Figure 11.31**). You could type in a new identifier to match your own naming scheme, but for this exercise, use the default name. (If you do not see the Linkage section, click the Advanced button to expand the dialog.)

4. Click OK.

   Flash closes the dialog and returns you to the document in symbol-editing mode.

5. Use the drawing tools to create a graphic element on the Stage.

   You might, for example, draw a star with the polystar tool.

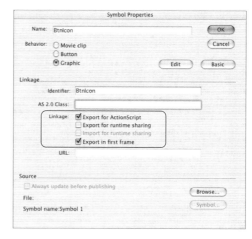

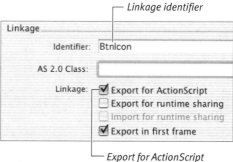

Figure 11.31 Select Export for ActionScript to make a movie clip or graphic symbol available as an icon for a button component. The default Linkage identifier is the name of the symbol.

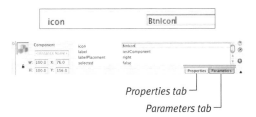

Properties tab

Parameters tab

Figure 11.32 Click the Property Inspector's Parameters tab, then enter your symbol's linkage identifier as the value for the Icon parameter. This value tells Flash which symbol to display within the button component.

6. Select the graphic element on the Stage, and enter **0,0** as its *X,Y* coordinates in the Property Inspector.

   The coordinates **0,0** set the symbol's registration point to the upper left corner of the bounding box. At runtime, Flash aligns the upper-left corner of the symbol with the upper-left corner of the button component, assuring that the symbol appears to be inside the button. If the symbol is larger than the button, however, it will slop over the button component's edges.

7. Return to document-editing mode, for example, by choosing Edit > Document.

To add an icon to the button component:

1. Continue with the file from the preceding exercise.

2. Select the component instance on the Stage.

3. In the in the Parameters tab of the Property Inspector (or in the Component Inspector), click anywhere in the row labeled "icon."

   The text field for the icon parameter's value activates.

4. Enter the linkage identifier for the symbol you created in the preceding exercise (**BtnIcon**) in the Value field for the icon parameter (**Figure 11.32**).

5. Press Enter.

   Flash places a small gray square in the component instance on the Stage. This square is a placeholder indicating the icon's position relative to the button's label. You can change the position, by changing the labelPlacement parameter.

   continues on next page

6. In the Component Inspector, or in the Parameters tab of the Property Inspector, click anywhere in the row labeled "labelPlacement."

The field for the labelPlacement value activates as a pop-up menu. To view possible values, click the value field again.

7. From the menu, select a relative position for the text; for this exercise, choose bottom.

Flash repositions the icon placeholder and the button label in the instance on the Stage (**Figure 11.33**). You are ready to preview the button component in action.

8. To see your button component in all its glory, choose Control > Test Movie.

Flash exports the movie and opens it in Flash Player. The button component displays your icon above the new label text. As you move the pointer over the button, its edges highlight with a light glowing green. Click the button and it fills with green to indicate the down state. All of this interactivity is built into the button component.

✔ Tip

- Live Preview can cause Flash to bog down during authoring. If you are using lots of components, you may want to deactivate it (choose Control > Enable Live Preview).

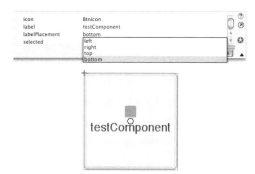

Figure 11.33 By choosing Bottom as the labelPosition value (top), you tell Flash to position the icon above the button component's text (bottom).

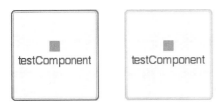

Figure 11.34 When the Button component instance has a Toggle value of True, it acts as a toggle button. Here the button component instances are viewed on the Stage with live preview enabled. The button on the left is selected, the one on the right is deselected.

To set the button to act as a toggle:

1. Select an instance of a button component on the Stage.

2. In the Component Inspector, or the Parameters tab of the Property Inspector, set the Toggle value to True. Click anywhere in the row labeled "toggle," to activate the value pop-up menu. Click the value field and select True. The button now acts as a toggle, so that repeated clicks turn the button on and off (**Figure 11.34**).

✔ Tip

■ The Property Inspector and Component Inspector also contain a field for the button component's Selected value (the choices are True or False). The Selected value should determine the toggle button's initial state, with True setting the button to be selected initially and False setting the button to be deselected initially. Unfortunately, toggling button components whose properties are set via the Component Inspector always appear deselected at first. To show the selected state initially, you must use more advanced ActionScript techniques.

MODIFYING BUTTON COMPONENTS

Creating Movie-Clip Buttons

Flash's button symbols and button components have built-in rules about how the button displays its four states in response to the user's mouse movements. You can take control of that functionality yourself, and also create a button that has more than three states, by making your own movie-clip button. In the following exercises, you learn to assemble artwork in the Timeline of the movie-clip to create a button with four states: Up, Over, Down, and Disabled. To give the movie-clip button even the first level of interactivity, to make the movie clip respond to mouse movements by displaying different states, you must attach ActionScript. You learn to do that in Chapter 12.

To create the button states:

1. Open a new Flash Document.

2. Choose Insert > New Symbol.
   The Create New Symbol dialog appears.

3. Type a name for your symbol, MovieClipBtn; choose Movie Clip behavior; and click OK.
   Flash switches to symbol-editing mode. In the Timeline you see one layer, with a keyframe in Frame 1.

4. Add two new layers to the Timeline, for a total of three layers.
   Each layer will hold a different type of information for your button. The top layer will hold ActionScript that tells the movie-clip button what to do; name this layer *Actions*. The second layer will hold text that identifying each keyframe that represents a button state; name this layer *Labels*. The bottom layer will hold the graphic elements that give the button its look in each state; name this layer *ButtonGraphics*.

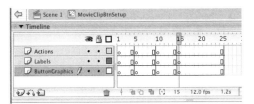

Figure 11.35 Your movie clip button needs a keyframe for each button state. It's a good idea to create a separate layer for the actions, text, and graphic elements in the movie-clip's Timeline.

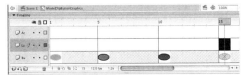

Figure 11.36 With Preview in Context turned on in the Timeline, you can see all the button-state graphics you've placed in the keyframes of the movie-clip button symbol. Use shades of gray for the graphics in the frame that represents the disabled state. (For clarity, since this book can't show you colors, the disabled-state graphic also contains an *X*.)

5. In the Timeline, for all three layers, insert keyframes in frames 5, 10, and 15 (**Figure 11.35**).

The layers that you added already had keyframes at frame 1. You need to add three more keyframes to accommodate all four button states: Up, Over, Down, and Disabled. Spacing the keyframes every five frames makes them a bit easier to deal with and allows you to view the frame labels that you create in the following task.

6. In the *ButtonGraphics* layer, select Keyframe 1 and using the oval tool, draw an oval centered over the registration mark on the Stage.

This graphic represents the button's Up state. Give the oval a red fill and a black stroke. Make the stroke fairly wide to make the graphic look more button like.

7. Select the oval and choose Edit > Copy.

8. Select Keyframe 5 in the *ButtonGraphics* layer, choose Edit > Paste in Place.

This graphic represents the button's Over state. Change the fill color to green.

9. Repeat step 8 for keyframes 10 and 15.

In Keyframe 10, change the oval fill to blue to represent the Down state. In Keyframe 15, change the fill to a light gray and the stroke to a dark gray to represent the button in its Disabled state (**Figure 11.36**).

✔ Tip

■ There is no need to create a Hit-state keyframe for a movie-clip button. When you add the appropriate ActionScript (see Chapter 12), Flash automatically defines the hit area as the graphic element(s) in the first frame of your movie clip.

To assign frames labels to button-state keyframes:

1. Continuing with the file you created in the preceding exercise, access the Property Inspector.

    If the Property Inspector is not open, choose Window > Properties.

2. In the Labels layer of the Timeline, select Keyframe 1.

3. Click in the Frame Label field of the Property Inspector to activate the field and type the name of this button state: Up (**Figure 11.37**).

    Flash places a red flag icon in any keyframe that has a label. If there's enough room in that keyframe span, Flash also displays the label name.

4. Repeat steps 2 and 3 for keyframes 5, 10, and 15, entering the names Over, Down, and Disabled (**Figure 11.38**).

    There are two reasons to assign labels to keyframes: First, the label reminds you what is in the keyframe; second, and more important, you can use ActionScript to find a frame with a particular label name and then display that frame. You'll use this technique to create the button's visual feedback in response to mouse movements.

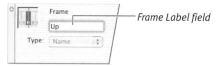

Figure 11.37 You enter a label for a selected keyframe in the Frame Label field of the Property Inspector.

Figure 11.38 A red flag in a keyframe indicates that the frame has a label. If there are enough in-between frames following the keyframe, Flash displays the frame label as well as the flag. The labeled keyframes in this movie-clip symbol indicate which button state the keyframe represents.

The Mystery of Frame Label Naming

Flash is sensitive about names. Frame Label names actually become part of target paths in ActionScripting, therefore, certain characters that have special meaning in scripting, such as slashes equal signs, plus signs, and so on, are off limits for labeling frames. To be safe, use only letters, numbers, and underscore characters; don't even use spaces to make word divisions in frame labels. Use capitalization and the underscore character instead.

5. Return to document-editing mode, for example, by clicking the Back button in the Edit Bar.

If you'd like to check out your button states, click the Play button in the symbol preview in the Library window.

6. Drag an instance of the `MovieClipBtn` symbol to the Stage.

This movie clip is ready to be scripted to act like a button and to carry out whatever tasks you set for it with ActionScript. You'll learn to complete the button's interactivity in Chapter 12.

7. Save this document for use in Chapter 12. Call it `MyOwnBtn.fla`.

✔ Tips

■ Another way to add a reminder about what a keyframe does is to add a comment. To enter a frame comment, select the keyframe; in the Frame Label field in the Property Inspector, type two slashes (//) followed by your comment text. Frame labels and frame comments are mutually exclusive, each keyframe can have just one or the other. You can work around that limitation by adding separate layers for comments and labels. Place keyframes in both layers, then add comments to one layer and labels to the other, as needed.

■ Because ActionScript may use frame labels to create interactivity, Flash exports frame-label text with the other movie data when you publish a Flash Player file. Keeping frame labels short helps keep files sizes small. Comments do not get exported with the final movie. You can make comments as long as you like, but remember that the next keyframe in the layer will cut off the comment text. Size your comments to fit the span containing them.

Why Make Movie Clip Buttons?

Flash's button symbols make it easy to create buttons quickly, but they limit you to just three states: Up, Over, and Down. Sometimes you'd like a button to have more states than that. Think of a typical slide show, for example, that has one button for moving to the next slide and another button for returning to the previous slide. The best interface designs use elements consistently. That way users know what options are available to them and always know where to find the interface elements for carrying out a task. Still, on the last page of a slide show, there's no next slide to go to. In that case, it's common to display the Next button in a state indicating that the button doesn't function right now. When you make your own movie-clip buttons, you can create as many states as you like.

BASIC
INTERACTIVITY
USING BEHAVIORS

By default, Macromedia Flash MX 2004 plays the scenes and frames of a movie created from a Flash Document sequentially. The movie opens with Scene 1, plays all those frames in order, moves to Scene 2, plays all those frames, and so on. Sometimes, that's appropriate; sometimes you want to be able to make a movie jump around during playback, move to scenes and frames in any order you choose. You can achieve that goal by creating scripts in Flash's scripting language, ActionScript. A script is a series of commands, or *statements*, that you string together to make Flash perform certain tasks at runtime, that is, when your published Flash file (a .swf file) runs in Flash Player for viewing by your end users (see Chapter 17). You might create a script that replays Scene 2 at the end of every other scene, or that repeatedly displays the first five frames of a movie until all the other frames in the movie have loaded. ActionScripting can add efficiency and a degree of intelligence or interactivity to your movie.

In this chapter, you'll use Behaviors (which generate scripts for common interactivity tasks) to assign actions to buttons for controlling and interacting with movies as they play.

Touring the Actions Panel

The Actions panel is a whole scripting environment in a box. It has three separate work areas: the Script pane, the Actions Toolbox, and the Script Navigator.

The *Script pane* is a text window where you assemble your scripts. You can enter actions into the pane manually, it acts like a text editor; you can also add actions from the Actions Toolbox or the Add pop-up menu. You can import scripts or pieces of script from an external file, such as one created with a stand-alone text editor. When you use Behaviors, Flash adds the script directly to the Script pane of the Actions panel.

The Mystery of ActionScripting

Flash provides a full-fledged scripting language called ActionScript for adding actions to movies. Flash MX 2004 introduces a new version of that language, ActionScript 2.0. You can create ActionScripts in the Actions panel; create them in an external editor and copy them into the Flash authoring environment; or create the script in an external file and have Flash pull the scripting in when you publish or export the movie.

In previous versions of Flash, using the Actions panel in Normal mode provided a great deal of assistance for anyone who was just starting to work with scripting or who preferred not to delve deeply into it. In Flash MX 2004, this assisted mode no longer exists. You will find some assistance for creating simple interactivities through a new feature, called *Behaviors*. To use a Behavior, select an object on the Stage or a keyframe in the Timeline, then choose a command from the Behaviors panel; Flash creates a script for you.

Even using Behaviors, however, you still need to familiarize yourself with the scripting environment to a certain degree. And in the end, Behaviors can only take you so far. Teaching scripting with ActionScript is beyond the scope of a Visual QuickStart Guide. In this chapter and the next, you will learn to navigate the scripting environment and use Behaviors to put together scripts that carry out basic interactive tasks.

The *Actions Toolbox* contains most of the "words" (actions) that make up the Action-Script language; these pieces of code appear in lists that are arranged hierarchically under folder-like category icons. Double-clicking an action adds it to the script pane. You can also drag items from the Actions Toolbox to the Script pane. (The list of ActionScript actions also appears in the Add menu. To access the menu, click the plus sign located above the Script pane. Selecting an action adds it to the Script pane.)

The *Script Navigator* helps you to locate and maneuver through the scripts in your movie.

Figure 12.1 shows the various elements of the Actions panel.

Add

Search

Replace

Enter target path

Check syntax

Auto format

Display code hints

Reference

Debug options

View options

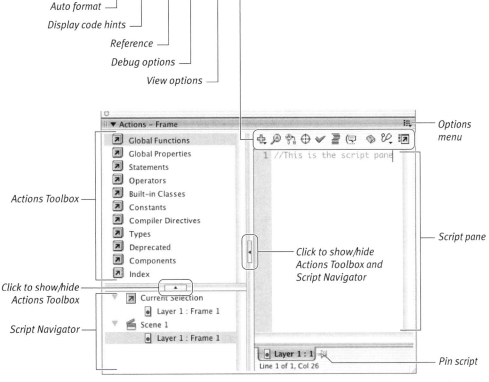

Options menu

Actions Toolbox

Click to show/hide Actions Toolbox and Script Navigator

Script pane

Click to show/hide Actions Toolbox

Script Navigator

Pin script

Figure 12.1 The Actions panel has three main areas: the Actions Toolbox, where you can choose actions; the Script pane, where Flash assembles the ActionScript; and the Script Navigator, where Flash displays the elements in your movie that have scripts attached.

To access the Actions panel:

If the Actions panel is not active, *do one of the following:*

◆ From the Window menu, choose Development Panels > Actions (**Figure 12.2**).

◆ Press F9.

The Actions-Frame panel opens.

✔ Tips

■ The Actions panel's title bar generally reveals what type of item the script you are creating will attach to: a frame, movie clip, or button. If, however, you select a button component, the panel just says "Actions."

■ While working on a script for a keyframe, it's easy to click a movie clip or button on the Stage accidentally; the title bar changes and you'll be entering script for that object. To return to the Actions panel for frames, click the keyframe in the Timeline, or click an empty area of the Stage or work area.

To close the Actions panel:

◆ Repeat any of the actions in the preceding exercise.

or

◆ Click the Actions panel's close box (Windows) or close button (Mac).

or

◆ From the Options menu, choose Close Panel.

Figure 12.2 Choose Window > Development Panels > Actions to access the Actions panel. When you select a keyframe in the Timeline, the panel's title bar indicates that you are creating a script for a selected frame.

Customizing the Actions Panel

The Actions panel takes up a good deal of room on your screen. You can resize the panel and its panes, even collapse panes completely. You can customize the way that scripts appear in the Script pane to make them appear in the smallest typeface you can read, for example (or, if you've spent long hours staring at tiny onscreen type, you can make scripts display in nice large letters). You can choose settings for font and type size; you can set Flash to highlight different types of script elements in different colors; you can control the number of spaces Flash uses to indent with each tab you type; and you can turn on or off code hints.

Two Types of Actions

Flash uses two basic types of scripts: scripts that attach to keyframes and scripts that attach to objects. You can create both types of scripts directly in the Script pane of the Actions panel, or by using Behaviors. Before entering the script or choosing the Behavior, you must first select the keyframe or object to which the script belongs.

Frame-based scripts are sets of actions attached to a keyframe. In the final exported movie, when the playhead reaches a keyframe that contains a script, Flash carries out the script's instructions. More advanced ActionScripters can create frame-based scripts that respond to object-based events, for example, carrying out a task when a user clicks a button.

Object-based scripts are sets of actions attached to buttons, movie clips, or components (compiled clips). Actions attached to buttons usually require input from someone who is viewing the movie. In a text-heavy frame, for example, you could make the movie pause until the user clicks a button that instructs Flash to resume playback.

Actions attached to movie clips and components can also respond to user input. More advanced scripters can use ActionScript to trigger movie-clip actions without user intervention, for example, to make all sounds stop playing when a movie clip first appears.

In addition, advanced ActionScripters can create scripts that target text fields, performing operations that modify them or retrieve information from them. Text fields on their own, however, cannot have attached scripts.

To set preferences for the Actions panel:

1. From the Edit menu (Windows) or from the Flash application menu (Mac), choose Preferences.

   or

   From the Options menu in the top-right corner of the Actions panel, choose Preferences.

   The Preferences dialog appears.

2. Click the ActionScript tab.

   The various settings for working with statements in the Script pane of the Actions panel appear (**Figure 12.3**).

3. To get scripting help from code hints, in the Editing Options section, check the Code Hints check box.

   Move the lever of the Delay slider to set the amount of time your pointer must hover over an item before Flash displays the hint.

4. To choose the font for writing scripts, in the Text section, *do the following:*

   ▲ From the pop-up menu of installed fonts, choose a font.

   ▲ From the pop-up menu of sizes, choose a type size.

   The Actions panel can display scripts in text as small as 8 points and as large as 72 points.

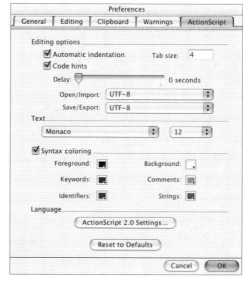

Figure 12.3 In the Preferences dialog, the ActionScript tab contains settings for customizing the way Flash displays your scripts.

Figure 12.4 Set syntax coloring in the Preferences dialog. Change the colors to make more of a distinction between scripting "words" to begin getting a feel for ActionScript's parts of speech.

5. To color-code script items, check the Syntax Coloring check box (**Figure 12.4**).

From the pop-up sets of color swatches, *choose new colors for the following:*

▲ Foreground. The basic text color for your scripts.

▲ Keywords. Words reserved for special purposes in ActionScript.

▲ Identifiers. The names of things, such as the names of objects, variables, and functions.

▲ Background. The color against which your script displays in the Script pane.

▲ Comments. Text that Flash ignores when it reads the script; used to make notes about what's going on in the script.

▲ Strings. Series of characters (letters, numbers, and punctuation marks).

6. Click OK.

Flash applies your preferences settings immediately.

✔ Tips

■ Flash's default settings for keywords, identifiers, and strings are all similar shades of blue. Try setting them to wildly different colors—say, pink, orange, and brown. This technique will help you learn to recognize these different parts of ActionScript speech as they are used in the script you'll create using Behaviors.

■ You may want to color-code only certain parts of your scripts. If, for example, you want your comments to appear in a different color but nothing else, set the color boxes for Keywords, Identifiers, and Strings to match the color you choose for Foreground.

CUSTOMIZING THE ACTIONS PANEL

The Mystery of Code Hints

Code hints work like tool tips within the Actions panel, displaying information about ActionScript statements. With code hints turned on, you can make the Actions panel display certain types of scripting information in a tool-tip-type box or drop-down menu. Position the insertion point to the right of a dot (a period character) or an opening parenthesis in the Script pane, then click the Show Code Hints button. If you enable Code Hints, the hints appear automatically whenever you type a period or opening parenthesis.

To get the greatest use from code hints, you must use the use the proper suffixes when you name an object. Using the proper suffix insures that you'll be able to see all the code hints relevant to that object when it appears in a script. The suffix `_btn`, for example, tells Flash that the object so named is a button symbol. When more advanced scripters name a button-symbol instance with the `_btn` suffix, they can view code hints that list the properties, methods, functions, and events appropriate to button symbols.

Taming the Unwieldy ActionScript Panel

The Actions panel is quite large. You can resize and collapse the entire the panel as you would any other panel and dock it with other panels—or, in the Windows world, dock it to the application window. You can also resize or hide certain portions of the panel to keep the window more manageable. Try these techniques:

Move the Vertical Divider. Position the pointer over the divider to the left of the Script pane. The pointer changes to the resize icon (a double-headed arrow). Click and drag to the left to make the Script pane larger; click and drag to the right to make the Script pane smaller.

Move the Horizontal Divider. Position the pointer between the Actions Toolbox and the Script Navigator panes. The pointer changes to the resize icon. Click and drag upwards to make the Script Navigator pane larger; click and drag downwards to make the Actions Toolbox pane larger.

Hide/show the Panes. Click the left-pointing triangle in the middle of the vertical divider to hide the Actions Toolbox and Script Navigator panes completely. The triangle on the divider now points to the right; click the triangle again to restore the previous position. The triangle in the middle of the horizontal divider works similarly to hide and show the Actions Toolbox.

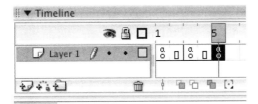

Figure 12.5 Keyframes that contain actions display the letter *a* in the Timeline.

Organizing Frame Actions

A little letter *a* in the Timeline indicates a keyframe that has actions attached (**Figure 12.5**). Can you imagine scrolling through dozens—or hundreds—of layers, looking for little letter *a*'s when you want to edit the actions in your document? That's a recipe for eyestrain. And more than that, it's a recipe for disaster if you (or someone else) needs to come back into your document and fix or change your ActionScript at a later date when you have no immediate memory of where the actions might be lurking.

The best practice is to centralize all scripts. Ideally that means creating one large script, in a single keyframe, that directs everything. This involves a fairly high level of abstract thinking and sophisticated scripting ability. Beginning scripters can start to work towards this goal by creating a separate layer just for frame actions. You'll may still spend time scrolling the length of the Timeline looking for keyframes with *a*'s, but you won't have to hunt through multiple layers as well. Restricting frame actions to their own layer also prevents you from accidentally putting actions in keyframes in two different layers for the same frame number, which could cause problems if you reorder the layers at some point.

To create a separate layer for actions:

1. Open a new Flash Document.

2. In the Timeline, add a new layer.
   (For detailed instructions on adding layers, see Chapter 5.)

3. Rename the layer *Actions*.

4. Drag the layer to the top or bottom of the Timeline.

   With a separate *Actions* layer as the top or bottom layer, you'll always know where to find the keyframes that contain actions when you need to modify or add to them (**Figure 12.6**).

✔ Tip

■ To prevent yourself from adding any graphic elements to the Actions layer accidentally, lock it (by clicking the bullet in the padlock column). Locking keeps you from making changes in the elements on the Stage for that layer, but it doesn't prevent you from adding actions to keyframes.

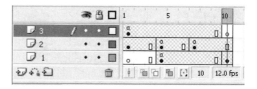

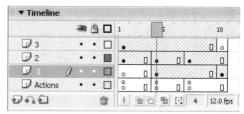

Figure 12.6 When you assign actions to many layers (top), it's harder to find them, and you might accidentally assign actions to the same frame number on different layers. Adding a separate layer just for actions (bottom) makes it easy to find them all and to see whether a certain frame does contain an action.

The Pitfall of Placing Actions on Multiple Layers

At each point in the Timeline, Flash implements the actions in the highest-level keyframe that contains an action. Imagine a three-layer movie. Frame 2 of the top layer contains no actions. In Frame 2 of the middle layer, a keyframe contains an action telling Flash to skip to Frame 5. In Frame 2 of the bottom layer, a keyframe contains an action telling Flash to skip to Frame 10. When you play this movie, and the playhead hits Frame 2, Flash looks in the top layer for actions and finds none. Flash moves to the next layer down. There, it finds an instruction and follows it. Flash whisks you away to Frame 5; it never has a chance to get to the instruction in the bottom layer. But if you reorder the layers so that the bottom layer is on top, Flash whisks you to Frame 10 instead of Frame 5! This situation could cause havoc with your movie.

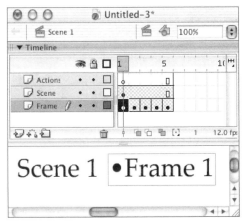

Figure 12.7 To test frame actions, ones that instruct Flash to move to a specific frame or to start and stop playback, it's useful to have a document that identifies each frame. That way you can see the results of your scripts easily.

Adding Frame Actions

Some of the most basic scripting tasks involve controlling movie playback: making your movie stop and start and jump from place to place. Because the movie begins running at playback by default, your first scripting task is to tell the playhead to stop in a specific frame. For most tasks in this book you'll use Behaviors to create scripts. While you could use the Goto and Stop Behavior to achieve the desired result (stopping the playhead in a specified frame), the `goto` part is really beside the point (you'll use this Behavior more appropriately later in this chapter). Plus, adding a `stop` action to a keyframe is easy to do it yourself and you'll get a taste of working in the Script pane.

To make your first script in Flash, set up a multiframe document that has identifying text in each frame. Then add a `stop` action to Keyframe 1, to make the movie start out paused at playback. As you create other scripts to navigate the movie, you can easily see their results. Save this file as a template for use in other scripting exercises.

To set up a document for testing frame actions:

1. Open a new Flash Document, and create three layers: *Actions, Scene,* and *Frames*.

2. In the *Scene* layer, create a keyframe in Frame 1 and in-between frames in frames 2 through 5.

3. On the Stage, for Keyframe 1, create text that identifies the scene (Scene 1).

4. In the *Frames* layer, create keyframes in frames 1 through 5.

5. On the Stage, for each keyframe, add text that identifies the frame number (Frame 1, Frame 2, and so on).

   Your document should look like **Figure 12.7**.

To start scripting by adding comments:

1. Continuing with the document you created in the preceding exercise, in the *Actions* layer, select Keyframe 1.

2. Access the Actions panel.

   The name Actions-Frame appears in the title bar of the Actions panel. If the panel is not open, choose Window > Development Panels > Actions.

3. From the Actions panel's Options (or View Options) menu, in the upper right corner, choose View Line Numbers (**Figure 12.8**).

   Visible line numbers make it easier to keep your place as you script.

4. From the Actions panel's Options menu, choose Word Wrap.

   Word Wrap forces the lines of your script to break to fit within the script pane. Note that such line breaks are not really meaningful in the script itself, the ActionScript syntax tells Flash where the meaningful divisions in script text occur (see the sidebar "The Mystery of ActionScript Syntax").

5. Click within the Script pane.

   A blinking insertion point appears in the Script pane. (In Windows, Flash also highlights the line-number area.) You are ready to enter comments.

6. In Line 1, type two slashes (//) to begin your comments.

   The double slash is known as a *comment delimiter;* the delimiter sets the boundaries of a comment within a script. Flash ignores any text between the two slashes and the next paragraph return for the purposes of scripting. When compiling the script for playback, Flash leaves that text out of the final file. It's a good idea to write notes about your script to remind yourself what you intend the script to do. Comments will also help anyone who might need to modify your script later.

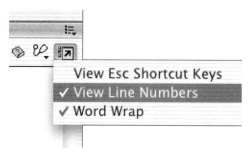

Figure 12.8 Use the Options or View Options menu in the Actions panel to turn on line numbering and word wrap in the Script pane. Visible line numbers make it easier to keep your place while scripting; word wrap makes it easier to view the scripts as it forces them to stay within the open pane area.

Figure 12.9 The two slashes indicate the beginning of a comment. When you turn on the Script pane's View Line Numbers and Word Wrap features, the comment text breaks and moves to a new line as needed to fit within the width of the pane. New line number appears only where you create a line break by pressing Return.

7. Type Pause the movie on frame 1 at runtime (**Figure 12.9**).

If you like, continue typing comments to get a feel for working in the Script pane. Because you turned on word wrap in Step 4, you need not worry about line breaks. When you finish typing, press Enter to start the next line of the script.

✔ Tips

■ When you are typing comments with word wrap turned off, you can press Enter to break lines to keep the comment visible in the Script pane. If you do, however, remember to type two slashes at the start of each new comment line.

■ For really long comments, Flash provides a second type of comment delimiter. Begin your comment with /* and end the comment with */. Flash excludes everything in between the opening and closing delimiters from the script.

■ When you are testing long scripts or trying out various ways to achieve your scripting task, it can be useful to temporarily remove a part of the script to see what happens. Comment delimiters let you do this quickly without actually removing your work. Just place the double slashes at the front of a line or two of the script. If you have a large section of the script that you want to block out, use the /* and */ delimiters.

To set the movie to pause at playback:

1. Continuing with the document you created in the preceding exercise, press Return to start a new line.

2. Type stop();.
   Your script should look like **Figure 12.10**.

3. Save the document as a template for future use; name it FrameActionsTemplate.
   (For detailed instructions about saving documents as templates, see Chapter 1.)

4. Close the document.
   You do not want to inadvertently make more changes to your master template document, so close it at this point.

✔ Tips

- Instead of typing the script, you could let the Add menu in the Actions panel help you. Click the plus sign located just above the line numbers in the Script pane to view the menu. Choose Global Functions > Timeline Control > stop. Flash adds stop(); to your script.

- Another way to add the stop(); script is to access the Actions Toolbox; click the book icon for the category Global Functions (once) to view its subcategories. Click the book icon for the subcategory Timeline Control to access the relevant ActionScript statements.

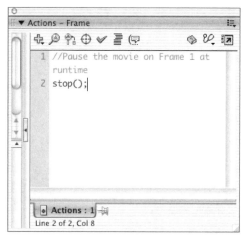

Figure 12.10 Enter the script, the stop action, below the comment text.

The Mystery of ActionScript Syntax

ActionScript has its own rules, which are analogous to the rules of grammar and spelling in English. These rules, called *syntax*, govern such things as word order, capitalization, and punctuation of action statements. When you use Behaviors, Flash handles all the details of syntax for you. When you start moving toward more independent scripting, you need to handle these details yourself. The following list briefly describes five crucial ActionScript punctuation marks that you'll see in those scripts.

Dot (.). ActionScript uses *dot syntax*, meaning that periods act as links between objects and the *properties* (characteristics) and *methods* (behaviors) applied to them. In the statement

```
clone_mc_duplicateMovieClip
```

the dot (the period) links the object (a movie clip named clone_mc) with the method that creates a copy of the movie clip.

ActionScript also uses the dot to indicate the hierarchy of files and folders in path names for targeting objects (such as movie-clip symbols) within one Flash file, similar to the way that HTML syntax uses a slash. (Note that Flash 3 and 4 used slashes to indicate these types of path names. Flash MX 2004 and Player 7 still recognize this *slash syntax*, but ActionScript 2.0 does not). Macromedia recommends using dot syntax unless you are creating files for playback in Flash 3 or 4, and that's what you'll find in the scripts created by Behaviors.

Semicolon (;). A semicolon indicates the end of a statement. The semicolon is not required—Flash interprets the end of the line of statements correctly without it—but including it is good scripting practice. The semicolon also acts as a separator in some action statements.

Braces ({}). Braces set off ActionScript statements that belong together. A set of actions that take place after on (release), for example, must be set off by braces.

Note that the action statements within braces can require their own beginning and ending braces. The opening and closing braces must pair up evenly. When you use Behaviors to enter multiple actions in a script, Flash handles positioning of braces; ensuring that the pairs match. When you enter multiple actions, you must pay attention to where you are adding statements and braces within the Script pane, however, to ensure that you group the actions as you intend.

Parentheses (). Parentheses group the arguments that apply to a particular statement—defining the scene and frame in a goto action, for example. Parentheses also allow you to group operations, such as mathematical calculations, so that they take place in the right order.

Adding Event Handlers via Behaviors

As you learned in the previous chapter, Flash's button symbols and button components have certain actions built in. By default, when you move the mouse into the button area, Flash jumps to the Over frame; when you click the button, Flash takes you to the Down frame. To make the button actually carry out a task or to refine the way a button responds to a user's mouse movements, you attach ActionScripts to an instance of a button. Flash MX 2004 comes with a set of Behaviors that automate the process of creating scripts for certain common actions. Behaviors are a quick way to get started scripting your buttons.

To prepare a document for testing button scripts:

1. Open a new copy of the `FrameActionsTemplate` that you created earlier in this chapter.

   This is a five-frame document, with identifying text for each frame, and a `stop` action in frame 1.

2. In the Timeline, add a new layer anywhere below the Actions layer; name the new layer *Buttons*.

   Frame 1 of the new layer is a keyframe; frames 2 through 5 are in-between frames. Any items you place on this layer will be visible throughout the 5-frame movie.

The Mystery of Instance Names

The exercises in this section suggest that you end the name of a button instance with the suffix _btn. This practice has two purposes. First, it reminds you what type of object you're looking at; if you name objects consistently with Flash's suffixes, when you read through your scripts you'll be able to see what type of objects are involved. Additionally, the code-hint feature of the Actions panel can provide more information about scripting objects if the object type is identified by the proper suffix.

Because instance names may wind up as part of an ActionScript, you must avoid using instance names that include characters that have special meaning in ActionScript, for example, slashes, or the equals sign. To be safe, use only letters, numbers, and underscore characters.

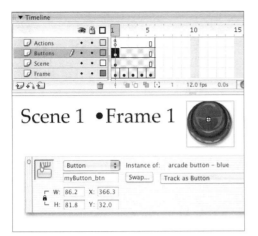

Figure 12.11 Place a button in Keyframe 1 on its own layer. Because the in-between frames in the Buttons layer extend to the match the length of the other layers, the button will be visible throughout the movie.

3. With the *Buttons* layer selected, place an instance of a button symbol on the Stage.

Follow the steps in the preceding exercise to create a new button, or use one from the Common Library of buttons. To access this library of button symbols that comes with Flash, choose Window > Other Panels > Common Libraries > Buttons). You can drag an instance of a button from the Buttons library to your document.

4. To name the button instance, access the Property Inspector and type a name in the Instance name field (**Figure 12.11**).

It's a good idea to get into the habit of naming each instance of a symbol in your document. For ActionScript to be able to control a symbol, the symbol must have a unique instance name.

5. Save your document as a template for use throughout this chapter, and name it ObjectActionsTemplate.

(For detailed instructions about saving documents as templates, see Chapter 1.)

6. Close the document.

Choosing Save As doesn't close the file you're in. To avoid making further changes to the master template document, you must close it at this point.

ADDING EVENT HANDLERS VIA BEHAVIORS

To add an action to a button-symbol instance using Behaviors:

1. Open a new copy of the `ObjectActions Template` that you created in the preceding exercise.

   This is a five-frame document with identifying text, one button instance, and a `stop` action in Keyframe 1.

2. Access the Behaviors panel.

   If the panel is not open, choose Window > Development Panels > Behaviors.

3. Access the Actions panel.

   If the panel is not open, choose Window > Development Panels > Actions.

4. On the Stage, select the button instance.

   The Actions panel name changes to Actions - Button. The Behaviors panel displays a button icon and the name of the selected button (**Figure 12.12**).

5. From the Add Behavior menu (the plus sign in the upper-left corner of the Behaviors panel), choose a Behavior (for this exercise, choose Movieclip > Goto and Stop at Frame or Label) (**Figure 12.13**).

   The Goto and Stop at Frame or Label dialog appears. This dialog presents choices for you to make to fill in the parameters of the `goto` action.

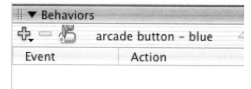

Figure 12.12 The Actions panel (top) and Behaviors panel (bottom) both bear labels indicating what type of element you are scripting.

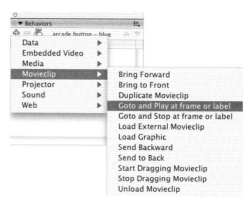

Figure 12.13 Flash comes with a number of Behaviors that assist you with creating scripts for common functions. Behaviors that control Timelines, for example, stopping playback of a movie or jumping to a new frame or scene, live under the Movieclip category in the Add Behavior menu.

6. To script the button to send the playhead to Frame 3 and then stop movie
playback, *do the following:*

▲ For pathname style, select Relative.
A relative pathname identifies the
target Timeline in terms of its "relative" position within the hierarchy of
Timelines in your movie: for example,
saying start where I am, the target is
one level above me, or the target is
within me one level down. An absolute
pathname describes the location more
specifically, always starting with the
top-level Timeline and working its
way down to the target movie.

▲ In the target movie clip pane, select
the clip named _root.

▲ This pane lists the movie clips in
your document. Flash refers to the
main document as a "movie clip"
named _root. To instruct Flash to
move around in the main Timeline,
choose _root as your target movie
clip. Flash then translates that target
to the appropriate ActionScript
statement using the selected pathname style, in this case, this, and
puts it in the target path field.

▲ For the frame at which to stop playing, type 3 (**Figure 12.14**).

continues on next page

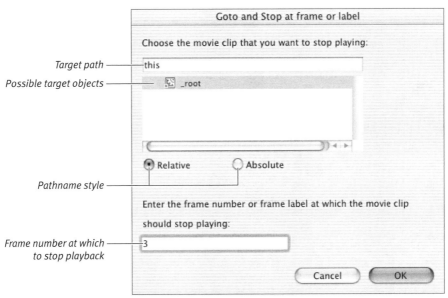

Target path ── this
Possible target objects ── _root

Relative   Absolute

Pathname style ──

Frame number at which ── 3
to stop playback

Figure 12.14 Flash uses the parameters in the Goto and Stop dialog to create the script for the Behavior
that takes the playhead to a specific frame and stops playback.

7. Click OK.

Flash adds the Behavior to the Behaviors panel and adds comments and code to the Script pane of the Actions panel (**Figure 12.15**). You're ready to test your button, see "Previewing Actions at Work," later in this chapter.

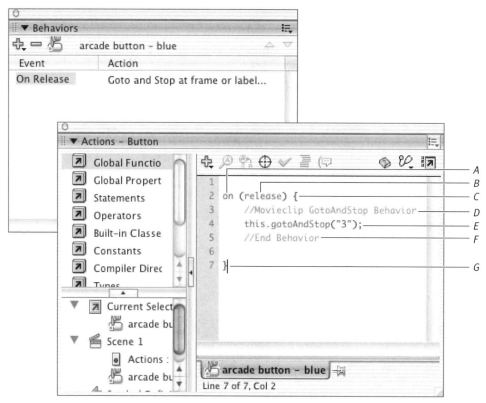

Figure 12.15 Flash lists all Behaviors for a selected Object (or frame) in the Behaviors panel (top). The script created by choosing Behavior > Movieclip > Goto and Stop instructs Flash to move to Frame 3 and then pause playback (bottom). The script contains the following elements: A) an event handler; B) the event parameter (the triggering event); C) a curly brace marking the beginning of actions that take place in response to the event; D) a comment noting the beginning of the code specific to this behavior; E) a set of actions triggered by clicking and releasing the mouse button inside the active button area (in the main Timeline, go to frame 3 and pause); F) a comment noting the end of the code specific to this behavior; and G) a curly brace marking the end of the actions that take place in response to the event.

The Mystery of Target Paths

You can use the Goto and Stop (or Goto and Play) at Frame or Label Behavior with both button symbols and button components. The fact that a button component is a actually a type of movie clip, and thus has its own independent Timeline, affects the way Flash creates target pathnames, however. Place a button component and a button symbol in the same Flash document and apply a Behavior to each to jump to a specific frame in the main Timeline. The Absolute pathname that Flash creates for both button elements is _root. For the button symbol targeting the main Timeline, Flash creates the Relative pathname this; for the button component targeting the main Timeline, Flash creates the Relative pathname this._parent. What's going on? Flash considers the button symbol to be controlled by the main Timeline. Hence the pathname this. You can think of translating "this" as "me" or "my." The target Timeline is "my Timeline." The button component has its own Timeline, so its pathname basically translates to "my parent Timeline."

✔ Tips

■ In the preceding exercise, you made the playhead move to a specific frame and stop playback. You can also make the playhead jump to a new frame and resume playback from there. Select your button instance on the Stage. In the Behaviors panel, choose Movieclip > Goto and Play at Frame or Label. The parameters for the Goto and Play Behavior are the same as for Goto and Stop. You must specify a pathname style, target movie clip, and frame number in the Goto and Play dialog. Click OK, and the Behavior creates the script.

■ When you use Behaviors to create a script, Flash leaves Line 1 of the script blank. You can use that line to add your own comments. Each Behavior adds its own comments, but they are fairly cryptic and are just a general note about which Behavior the script is for, for example, //Movieclip GotoAndStop Behavior. A comment like //Go to the Company Address page might be more meaningful to your project.

To add an action to a button component instance using Behaviors:

1. Continuing with the copy of ObjectActionsTemplate that you created in the preceding exercise, access the Components panel.

2. Drag an instance of the button component to the stage.

3. On the Stage, select the button-component instance.

   The Actions panel name changes to just plain Actions. The Behaviors panel displays a button icon and the name of the selected button component.

4. From the Add Behavior menu choose Movieclip > Goto and Stop at Frame or Label.

   Note that for button components, you have only two choices for Movieclip Behavior: Goto and Play and Goto and Stop.

5. In the Goto and Stop dialog, to script the button to send the playhead to Frame 4 and then stop movie playback, *do the following*:

   ▲ For pathname style, select Relative.

   ▲ In the target movie-clip pane, select _root. Flash creates the pathname in the target path field (**Figure 12.16**). Notice the difference from the preceding exercise. In both cases, you select _root (the main Timeline) as the target movie clip, but the relative target pathname is slightly different for each. When you add the Behavior to a button symbol, the relative target pathname is this. When you add the Behavior to a button component the relative target pathname is this._parent (see the sidebar "The Mystery of Target Paths").

   ▲ For the frame at which to stop playing, type 4.

Figure 12.16 When you add a Goto Behavior to a button component, you are asking Flash to control a nested Timeline. The pathname this._parent reflects that hierarchy.

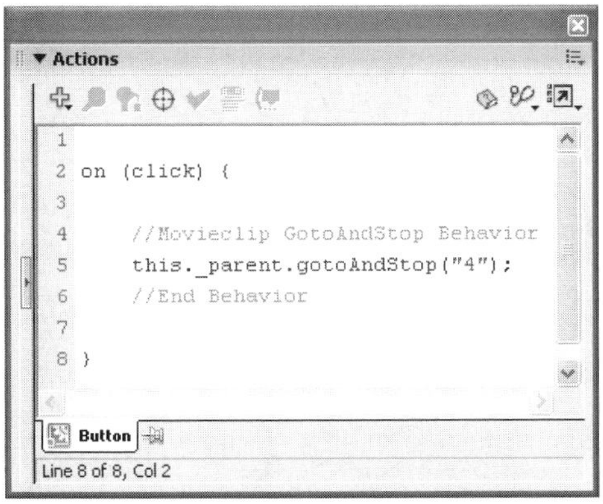

Figure 12.17 The button component contains behind-the-scenes scripting that tells it how to respond to mouse movements to display button states. Button components have just one event possibility—`click`.

6. Click OK.

Flash adds the appropriate script to the Script pane (**Figure 12.17**). Button components take their own special event, `click`.

The Mystery of Event Handlers

Scripts attached to buttons and movie clips start with a special action statement that tells Flash to make the scripted object respond to mouse movements. That statement is called an *event handler* because it responds to things that happen (events) and uses that incoming information to decide (handle) when and how to run a chunk of ActionScript. When you use Behaviors to attach a script to an object, Flash uses the event handler on().

What follows the handler in parentheses—(`release`), for example—indicates the condition under which the handler tells the script to run (in this example, when the user clicks and releases the pointer over a button's hot spot or within the graphic area of a movie clip. The statement inside the parentheses is the *event*. Using Behaviors, you can select which mouse-related event *(mouseEvent)* or keyboard-related event *(keypress)* will trigger the script created by the Behavior.

By default, Behaviors use the `release` event for buttons and movie clips You can change the triggering event by selecting a new one in the Behaviors panel or by deleting `release` and typing a new event directly in the Script pane of the Actions panel.

Behaviors use the `click` event for button components. This is the only triggering event for this type of object.

The other items that your script requires when you set up event handlers are curly braces.

{ indicates the beginning of the list of actions that are to be triggered by the specified event.

} indicates the end of the list of the actions that are to be triggered by the specified event.

All actions between the two braces take place when the triggering event occurs.

Previewing Actions at Work

To see the results of any script, you must view the movie in Flash Player. You can do this by publishing the movie (see Chapter 17) or by using one of the test modes. Flash's test mode is the only place in the authoring environment where you can check the full interactivity of buttons, movie clips, components, and scripts. Test mode is really just an abbreviated form of publishing a movie.

To test fully enabled elements:

1. Open the Flash document containing the elements you want to test.

2. From the Control menu, choose Test Movie or Test Scene (**Figure 12.18**).

   Flash exports the movie or scene to a Flash Player file, adding the .swf extension to the filename and using the parameters currently assigned in the Publish Settings dialog. (For more information on Publish Settings, see Chapter 17.) During export, Flash displays the Exporting Flash Movie dialog, which contains a progress bar and a button for canceling the operation (**Figure 12.19**).

   When it finishes exporting the movie, Flash opens the .swf file in Flash Player so that you see the movie in action. The buttons and movie clips in the test window are all live, so you can see how they interact with mouse actions by the viewer. Any scripts you have created will run.

3. When you finish testing, click the movie window's close box (Windows) or close button (Mac) to exit the Player.

   Flash returns you to the document-editing environment.

Figure 12.18 To test the full animation and interactivity of buttons, you must export your movie, for example, by choosing Control > Test Movie or Control >Test Scene.

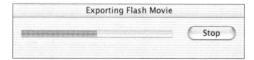

Figure 12.19 The Exporting Flash Movie dialog appears during export. Click Stop to cancel the export.

✔ Tips

■ In previous versions of Flash you could choose to test a simple button script within document-editing mode by choosing Control > Enable Simple Buttons. In Flash MX 2004, that setting allows you to see only the various button states; clicking the button reveals its Down state but doesn't perform any actions.

■ Warning: When you choose Control > Test Movie, Flash creates a test Player file and appends .swf to the file's name. Flash doesn't ask whether you want to replace earlier versions of the file that have the same name; it just assumes that you do. The downside of that convention, however, is that Flash may replace a file that you don't intend to replace. When you export a Flash movie yourself, it's tempting to use the filename and just add the .swf extension to differentiate your original Flash file from your exported .swf file. Unfortunately, Flash can't tell the difference between .swf files that you create and .swf files that it creates in test mode. As a result, the Test Movie command replaces your file. To be safe, always change the name of your movie when you export it yourself.

■ When you choose Control > Test Scene, Flash appends the name of the scene to the file, as well as .swf, when it creates the Player file. This situation can make the file name exceed the number of allowable characters. If Test Movie worked fine with your file, but Test Scene brings up the warning dialog. Try shortening the scene name.

Changing Event Handlers via Behaviors

When you preview the three states of a basic button symbol during authoring (choose Enable Simple Buttons), pressing the mouse button down is what actually triggers Flash to display the Down frame. You can use ActionScript to override a button's built-in actions. When you use Behaviors to attach actions to a button-symbol instance, Flash automatically adds the default event handler, on (release), to the Script pane. That code makes the release of the mouse button trigger the actions attached to the button. You can select different triggering events in the Behaviors panel.

To choose the triggering mouse event:

1. Open a new copy of ObjectActions Template, which you created earlier in this chapter.

2. On the Stage, select the button-symbol instance and duplicate it.

   Choose Edit > Duplicate or copy and paste to create a duplicate. To help you remember which button is which, place identifying text near each button. Label the original button Release; label the duplicate Press.

3. Select the button labeled Press.

   The script created by the Goto and Stop Behavior appears in the Script pane in the Actions panel.

4. In the Behaviors panel, click the first line in the Event column (the words *On Release*).

   Flash activates a menu of events (**Figure 12.20**).

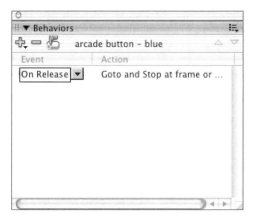

Figure 12.20 Click the entry in the Event column for a Behavior to activate a list of events (top). Click the active field or the triangle to its right to expand the list (bottom).

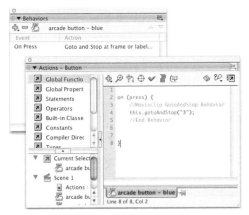

Figure 12.21 Choose a new event to modify the selected Behavior. Flash updates the script in the Actions panel accordingly. The on Press event makes a button carry out its task as soon as the user presses down on the mouse button.

5. To view the event choices, click the triangle to the right of the words *On Release*. A list of events appears.

6. From the list of events, select On Press.

Flash changes the value in the Events column of the Behaviors panel to on Press and updates the script in the Actions panel (**Figure 12.21**).

7. Choose Control Test Movie to see these buttons in action.

Position the pointer over the original button (labeled Release); click and hold for a second or two, and then let go of the mouse button. Flash moves to Frame 3 only after you release the mouse button. Now return to the first frame where your buttons are (choose Control > Rewind). Position the pointer over the button labeled Press. Click and hold; Flash takes you to Frame 3 immediately, you don't need to release to activate the script.

The Mystery of Mouse Events

For button symbols and movie clips, the event handler on() can respond to eight different events. Because most of these events involve user input with a mouse (or equivalent device), they are often called *mouse events*. You can choose which mouse event triggers your button or movie clip's script.

◆ Press refers to the downward part of a click when the pointer is located within the hit area of a button.

◆ Release refers to the upward part of a click (the user presses and then releases the mouse button) when the pointer is located within the hit area of a button. A Release event lets users click and then change their minds—and avoid activating the button— by dragging away before releasing the mouse button. This is the way most buttons in professional programs work.

◆ Release Outside happens when the user clicks inside the button area, holds down the mouse button, and moves the mouse outside the active button area before releasing the mouse button.

◆ Key Press happens any time the user presses the specified keyboard key while the Flash button is present. The user doesn't have to use the mouse to interact with the button for this event to trigger an action.

◆ Roll Over occurs any time the pointer rolls into the button's hit area when the mouse button has not been pressed.

◆ Roll Out happens any time the pointer rolls out of the button's hit area when the mouse button has not been pressed.

◆ Drag Over works in a slightly unexpected way. A Drag Over event occurs when the user clicks and holds down the mouse button within the button's hit area, rolls the pointer outside the hit area, and then rolls the pointer back into the hit area.

◆ Drag Out happens when the user clicks within the button's hit area, holds down the mouse button, and rolls the pointer out of the hit area.

◆ For button components, the handler responds to one event, click, which is the equivalent of Release.

Working with Multiple Behaviors

Flash's Behaviors panel doesn't limit you to a single action for each button script. You can combine Behaviors to make a button carry out several tasks in response to one event.

To add multiple Behaviors to a button instance:

1. Open a new copy of the `ObjectActions Template` that you created earlier in this chapter.

   This movie has five keyframes, a `stop` action in Keyframe 1, and a button instance in Keyframe 1.

2. Select the button in Keyframe 1.

3. In the Behaviors panel, from the Add Behavior menu, choose Movieclip > Goto and Stop at Frame or Label.

4. In the Goto and Stop dialog, *do the following:*

   ▲ In the target movie-clip pane, select `_root`.

   ▲ For style of pathname, select Relative.

   ▲ For the frame at which to stop playing, type 3.

5. Click OK.

   Flash adds comments and code to the Script pane of the Actions panel.

6. With the button selected, from the Add Behavior menu in the Behaviors panel, choose Web > Go to Web Page.

   The Go to URL dialog appears. Leave the default settings for this dialog. It will open the user's browser in a separate window and display the default URL.

   continues on next page

7. Click OK.

The Behaviors panel now shows that there are two Behaviors attached to this button (**Figure 12.22**). The Script pane contains code telling Flash to open a browser window and display the Macromedia Web site, then move to frame 3 in the movie (**Figure 12.23**).

✔ Tips

■ As you add Behaviors to the same object, Flash puts the code for each addition at the head of the existing script. In the preceding exercise, if you wanted the movie to go to frame 3 first and then open a browser window, you could assign the Behavior to open the browser first and then assign the Goto and Stop Behavior. You can also use the Move Up and Move Down buttons, the triangle icons in the upper-right corner of the Behaviors panel, to move a selected Behavior to a new place in the list.

■ Once you get a feel for working with scripts and are more familiar with ActionScript syntax, you can cut and paste or drag and drop sections of code to reorganize a Behavior-created script to make actions occur in any order you want. Extensive manual alterations to the code created by the Behavior (or introduction of syntax errors) may prevent Flash from recognizing the script as a Behavior, however. In that case, you will not be able to use the Behaviors panel to modify or delete it.

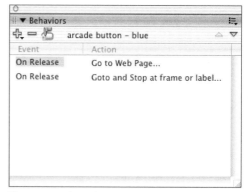

Figure 12.22 The Behaviors panel lists all of the Behaviors you have applied to the button. With two On Release events, clicking the button carries out each task in turn.

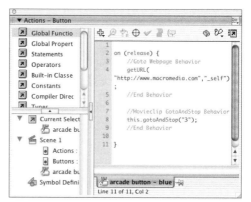

Figure 12.23 When you select multiple Behaviors for one button, Flash creates the script necessary to carry out both tasks, placing the action statements correctly within the curly braces of the event handler. The Behavior-created script carries out the actions in the reverse order of assignment. This script is the result of choosing Go to Web Page second.

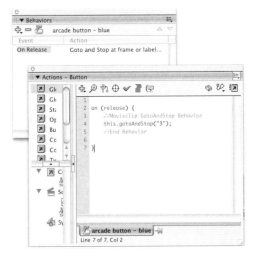

Figure 12.24 Click the Delete Behaviors button in the Behaviors panel to remove selected items (here, the Go to Web Page Behavior was selected for deletion). Flash removes the appropriate code in the Action panel's Script pane, provided that you have not significantly altered the Behavior code in the Script pane yourself.

To delete Behaviors:

1. Continuing with the file you created in the preceding exercise, access the Behaviors panel.

2. In the Action column of the Behaviors panel, select Go to Web Page.

Flash selects the row. In the Macintosh OS, the Event column for the selected Behavior is highlighted; on Windows both the Event and Action columns highlight.

3. To remove the selected Behavior, click the Delete Behavior button (the minus sign at the top of the panel).

Flash removes the Behavior from the panel and removes its associated script and comments from the Script pane (**Figure 12.24**).

✔ Tips

■ If you accidentally click the Event column entry, thereby activating the event list, the Delete Behavior button will not work. The whole line must be selected before you click the delete button. In Windows, the whole line highlights when it's selected; on Macs, only the Event column highlights.

■ When you attach a script to a frame (or object) by using a Behavior, Flash starts the script with a blank line. If you use the Delete Behavior button to remove the script, Flash fails to delete that first blank line from the Script pane. That means that the little letter a remains in the keyframe in the Timeline. To avoid confusion, always manually delete the blank line too.

■ Once you become comfortable working in ActionScript, you can also delete behaviors directly in the Script pane. You just need to be careful to select and delete only the parts of the Behavior-created script that you want to eliminate.

Using Multiple Handlers for One Button

You can make a single button respond differently to different mouse events by placing several handlers in the button's script. You could, for example, create one action set that jumps Flash to the next frame when the user clicks and then releases the mouse button within the active button area. You could create a second action set that opens a new movie with help information in a separate window if the user clicks within the button area but then drags the pointer out of the button area before releasing the mouse button. And you could deliver yet another action if the user presses a key on the keyboard, such as jumping to a frame that displays the message "You must click the button to move to the next question." You can add multiple event handlers via Behaviors.

To vary a button's response to different mouse events:

1. Open a new copy of the `ObjectActionsTemplate` that you created earlier in this chapter.

2. Access the Behaviors and Actions panels.

3. Select the button on the Stage.

Button Symbols and Timeline Effects

You can apply Flash's Timeline Effects to button symbols. The process works like that described in Chapter 6 for creating static graphic symbols with Timeline Effects. There's just one little twist to be aware of. When you apply a Timeline Effect to a button symbol, Flash creates a movie-clip symbol for the finished-effect symbol (as opposed to a graphic symbol or button symbol). This fact has implications for applying a Behavior to a finished effect created from a button. A movie clip has its own Timeline nested within the Timeline of the main document. When you apply a Goto Behavior to a nested movie clip, you will see the finished-effect clip in the target movie-clip pane of the parameters dialog, whereas a plain button would not appear there. Do not select the finished-effect "button." To control the main Timeline choose the movie clip named `_root`.

Figure 12.25 The Event column in the Behaviors panel reflects the mouse event you have chosen for the Behavior.

4. From the Add Behavior menu, choose Movieclip > Goto and Stop at Frame or Label.

The Goto and Stop at Frame or Label dialog appears.

5. To script the button, *do the following:*

▲ In the target movie clip pane, select _root.

▲ For style of pathname, select Relative.

▲ For the frame at which to stop playing, type 4.

6. Click OK.

Flash lists the Goto and Stop Behavior in the Behaviors panel and adds the appropriate comments and script to the Script pane in the Actions panel.

7. In the Event column of the Behaviors panel, click the words *On Release* to activate the list of events.

8. Click the triangle or the active field to open the menu of event choices and select On Roll Out.

Flash changes the Behaviors panel and Script pane of the Actions panel to reflect the new event (**Figure 12.25**).

9. Repeat steps 3 through 6, this time in step 5, type **5** as the target frame.

continues on next page

USING MULTIPLE HANDLERS FOR ONE BUTTON

10. In the first row of the Behaviors panel, in the Event column, double-click the words *On Release*.

Flash opens the list of events.

11. Select On Drag Out.

Flash changes the Behaviors panel and Script pane in the Actions panel to reflect the new event. Note that when you use Behaviors, Flash automatically handles the syntax and placement of the two scripts in relation to one another (**Figure 12.26**).

12. Choose Control > Test Movie.

Move the pointer so that it rolls into and then out of the button area without pressing the mouse button; you jump to frame 4. Click the movie button, then drag out of the button area without releasing the mouse button; you jump to frame 5. When you are done viewing the movie in test mode, close the Flash Player window.

13. Save your file for use in an upcoming exercise, name it `MultiEventBtn.fla`.

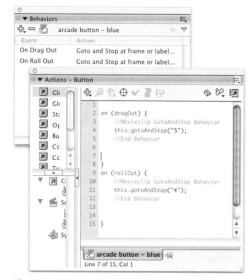

Figure 12.26 Flash handles placement of the scripts for multiple event handlers. Note how this script contrasts with the one you created earlier in Figure 12.23 to carry out multiple separate actions. In that script, multiple action statements appear within one set of curly braces. In this script, multiple sets of curly braces appear, each containing one action.

USING MULTIPLE HANDLERS FOR ONE BUTTON

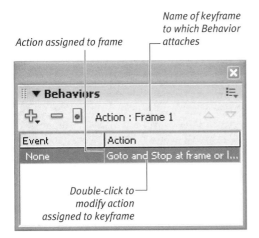

Action assigned to frame

Name of keyframe
to which Behavior
attaches

Double-click to
modify action
assigned to keyframe

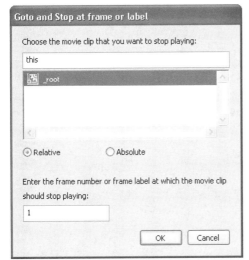

Figure 12.27 The stop action for the first frame of this movie was created with a Behavior (note the keyframe icon at the top of the panel). To modify the Behavior, double-click the action name in the Action column (top). The dialog containing parameters for that action appears (bottom). Changes you make to these parameters appear in the Script pane after you close the dialog.

Modifying a Behavior's Action

In the preceding exercise you used the Behaviors panel to modify the triggering event for the Behavior. You can also modify the other Behavior parameters through the Behaviors panel. When you become more familiar with scripting, you can also edit the Behavior's script directly in the Actions panel. If you alter the script significantly, however, you will break the link to the Behaviors panel.

To change an action via the Behaviors panel:

1. Open a document containing an object or keyframe with an attached Behavior.

2. Access the Behaviors and Actions panels.

3. Select the object (or keyframe) whose Behavior you want to modify.

   The Behaviors panel displays the Behavior assigned to the object (or keyframe); the script for this Behavior appears in the Script pane of the Actions panel.

4. In the Action column of the Behaviors panel, double-click the action you want to change.

   The dialog containing the parameters for the Behavior appears. You can change any of the parameters. In a Goto and Stop at Frame or Label action, for example, you can change the target movie clip, the pathname style, and/or the frame number (**Figure 12.27**).

Triggering Actions from the Keyboard

The keyPress mouse event allows users to trigger actions from the keyboard by pressing a specified key. Although you assign it to a button (or a movie clip), on (keyPress) affects the entire range of frames in which that button resides. A button symbol's Hit-frame graphic need not cover the whole Stage, and the user need not position the pointer over the button before pressing the specified key. Whenever the button is in the currently displayed frame, pressing the specified key triggers the assigned actions.

To set up an action triggered by a key press:

1. Open a new copy of the ObjectActionsTemplate that you created earlier in this chapter.

2. Access the Behaviors and Actions panels.

3. Select the button on the Stage.

4. From the Add Behavior menu, choose Movieclip > Goto and Stop at Frame or Label.
   The Goto and Stop at Frame or Label dialog appears.

5. In the dialog, *do the following:*
   ▲ In the target movie-clip pane, select _root.
   ▲ For pathname style, select Relative.
   ▲ For the frame at which to stop playing, type 3.

6. Click OK.

7. In the Event column of the Behaviors panel, double-click On Release, to view the list of events.

8. Choose On Key Press.
   The Keypress dialog appears (**Figure 12.28**).

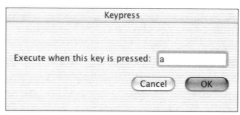

Figure 12.28 The keyPress event allows users to trigger a script by pressing keyboard keys. Enter the triggering character in the Keypress dialog.

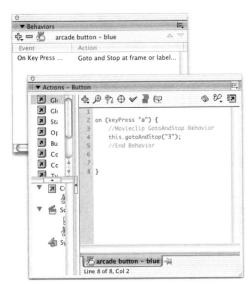

Figure 12.29 Flash adds the appropriate script for using the letter *a* as a trigger for actions whenever the button appears on screen.

9. In dialog's text-entry field, type the letter *a*.

In the Script pane, the event handler changes to on (keyPress "a") (**Figure 12.29**).

10. Click OK.

You're ready to test the movie. During playback, no matter where the pointer is in relation to the button, when the button is on-screen and you press *a* on the keyboard, Flash jumps to frame 3 of the movie.

11. Save your file for use in the next exercise; name it KeyPressBtn.fla.

✔ Tips

■ In some situations, assigned key-press actions fail to work in a published movie. (Browsers, for example, often intercept all key presses, assuming that the user wants to enter a new URL.) When a user clicks a button in a Flash movie, Flash grabs the key-press focus—the capability to intercept all key presses—for itself.

To ensure that your key-press actions always work, include a button for users to click before they can enter a part of the movie that uses key presses.

■ As you test the movie in the preceding exercise, note that pressing the button does absolutely nothing. If a button's sole purpose is to hold a script that triggers actions from the keyboard, you can use an invisible button (one that has graphics only in the Hit-frame graphic).

■ If the triggering key is also a keyboard shortcut in Test Movie mode, such as the Enter key, choose Control > Disable Keyboard Shortcuts when you test your movie. Otherwise, Flash will just interpret the keypress in its normal way.

TRIGGERING ACTIONS FROM THE KEYBOARD

Adding Actions to Movie-Clips

All of the preceding exercises for scripting button symbols also work for scripting movie clips. When you add the on (mouseEvent) handler to a movie clip, Flash creates a hit area for you from the graphic elements in the currently displayed frame of the movie clip. When a user positions the pointer over the scripted movie clip, Flash changes the pointer to the pointing hand cursor, indicating that this movie clip can respond to mouse movements.

To add actions to make a movie clip duplicate itself:

1. Open a new Flash Document and open the Behaviors and Actions panels.

2. Place an instance of a movie-clip symbol on the Stage.

   Create a new movie clip symbol (see Chapter 10) or bring one in from an existing document.

3. Select the movie-clip instance.

   The Actions panel name changes to Actions - Movie Clip. The Behaviors panel displays a movie-clip icon and the name of the selected movie clip.

4. In the Behaviors panel, from the Add Behavior menu (click the plus sign to access the menu), choose Movieclip > Duplicate Movieclip.

   The Duplicate Movieclip dialog appears. This dialog helps you to supply values for the required parameters of the duplicate MovieClip action (**Figure 12.30**).

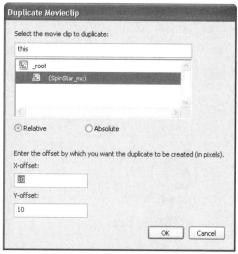

Figure 12.30 The Duplicate Movieclip dialog contains the parameters required for letting users make copies of movie clips by clicking a button symbol or movie clip. The offset values define the location of the duplicate.

5. In the dialog, *do the following*:

▲ In the target movie-clip pane, select the movie clip that you want to duplicate. Note that you cannot duplicate the main movie, so do not select _root. You movie-clip instance will appear indented beneath _root. If you haven't named the instances the movie-clip name appears in parentheses.

▲ For pathname style, select Relative.

▲ Enter values for X-offset and Y-offset. These tell Flash where to position the movie clip copy in relation to the original. To make the duplicate appear far away from its original, enter large values.

6. Click OK.

Flash adds the Behavior to the Behaviors panel and adds comments and code to the Script pane of the Actions panel (**Figure 12.31**).

You're ready to try out the movie clip that responds to mouse movements. During playback, as you move the pointer over the movie clip, the pointing-hand cursor appears. When you click and release within the movie-clip area, Flash makes a copy of the clip. Click the original or the copy to make another duplicate.

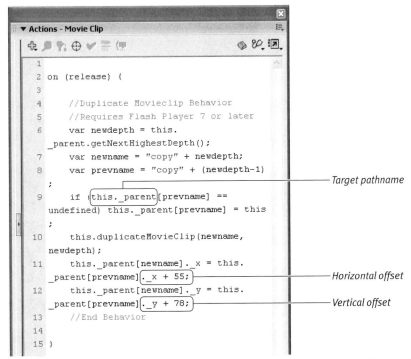

Figure 12.31 The script for the Duplicate Movieclip Behavior gives you some idea of the complexity of advanced ActionScripting. This script must account for naming each duplicate movie-clip instance and placing it on its own sub layer (or *level*) of the frame to ensure that all instances appear correctly and don't interfere with one another. Still, the basic parameters you set up in the dialog are there.

Adding Actions to Movie-Clip Buttons

In Chapter 11, you created artwork for a movie clip with four keyframes, each representing a different button state. The procedure for turning this movie clip into a responsive button element is basically the same as the one you learned earlier in this chapter for making a button symbol respond to different mouse events. In this case, different mouse events will trigger the display of different button-state frames in the movie clip. To start, you must make the movie-clip button pause on the first frame. Next, use Behaviors, to assign the actions.

To pause the movie-clip button:

1. Open a new copy of the FrameActionsTemplate that you created earlier in this chapter.

2. In the Timeline, add a new layer beneath the *Actions* layer, name it *mcButtons,* and place an instance of a movie-clip button on the Stage.

   The movie clip should contain four labeled keyframes for the Up, Over, Down, and Disabled states. Open the library of the file MyOwnBtn.fla, which you created for the exercise "Creating Movie-Clip buttons," in Chapter 11 and drag an instance of the movie-clip button symbol (MovieClipBtn_mc) to the Stage, or create a new movie-clip symbol that contains those button states. For instructions for opening external library files, see Chapter 6.

Tips for Naming Instances

A movie clip's instance name may wind up being part of the pathname in a script. Therefore, you must be careful how you name the instances of buttons and movie clips. Use letters and numbers; feel free to use the underscore character or capitalization to act as word dividers. Do not use spaces or other punctuation marks as these may have special meanings in ActionScript and will create errors in scripting.

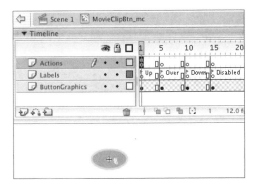

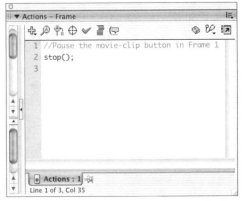

Figure 12.32 To pause the movie-clip button, edit the movie-clip master symbol to add a stop action to the first keyframe. The letter *a* (indicating the presence of an action) appears in the Timeline (top); the script should look like the figure at the bottom.

3. Access the Behaviors and Actions panels.

4. Using the techniques you learned in "Adding Frame Actions," earlier in this chapter, edit the master button-style movie-clip symbol to add a `stop` action in Keyframe 1.

   Your symbol and its script should look something like **Figure 12.32**. For more details about editing master symbols, see Chapter 6.

To add the mouseEvent handler that displays the Over state:

1. Continuing with the file from the preceding exercise, select the instance of `MovieClipBtn_mc` on the Stage.

   The Actions panel's title bar changes to Actions-Movie Clip.

2. From the Behaviors panel's Add Behavior menu, choose Movieclip > Goto and Stop at Frame or Label.

continues on next page

Why Target Frame Labels?

In setting up the target-frame parameter for the `Goto` Behavior for a movie-clip button, you could enter a frame number instead of a frame label. But there's an advantage to using frame labels. If you ever add or remove frames from the movie-clip button, the frame numbers for the various states could change. If they do, you must go back into the Behaviors panel or Script to update the frame numbers. It's a hassle, and you must *remember* that you need to do it. If you target the frame by label, you need never update the script to accommodate changes to frame numbers.

---

3. In the Goto and Stop dialog that appears, *do the following:*

▲ In the target movie-clip pane, select your movie-clip instance; it's the clip located directly below _root (**Figure 12.33**). If you have not given the symbol instance an instance name in the Property Inspector, the master symbol name appears in parentheses, in this example, it's (MovieClipBtn_mc).

▲ For pathname style, select Relative.

▲ For the target frame (the frame at which to stop playing), type Over. This parameter tells Flash which frame to jump to. You can specify a frame number, or as in this exercise a frame label.

4. Click OK.

Flash places the default event handler on (release) in the Script pane (**Figure 12.34**).

The default event tells Flash to implement the ActionScript as soon as the user clicks and releases mouse button while the pointer is within the image area of the movie clip. As you did for button symbols earlier in this chapter, you can change the event parameter of the handler so that other mouse actions or keyboard input will trigger the movie-clip button's script.

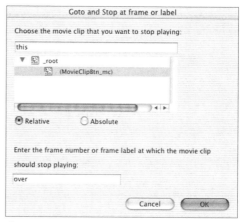

Figure 12.33 To apply the gotoAndStop action to the movie clip itself (not to the main Timeline), choose the movie clip in the target movie-clip pane. A symbol instance that has no instance name appears in parentheses in the target movie-clip pane.

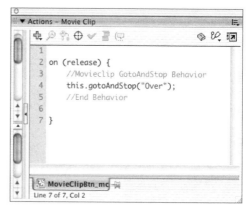

Figure 12.34 When you apply the Goto and Stop Behavior to a movie clip, Flash creates the script using the default handler and event on (Release). The Release event responds only to mouse clicks, and only when they occur directly over the movie clip itself. To make the movie clip notice when the mouse enters the movie-clip area, you must change the event.

Figure 12.35 Changing the event to On Roll Over in the Behaviors panel, updates the script to on (rollOver) in the Script pane.

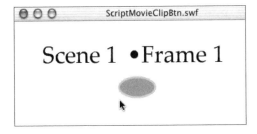

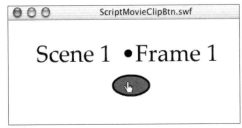

Figure 12.36 During playback, when the pointer is outside the graphic area of the movie-clip button scripted to respond to on (rollOver) (top), the graphic from the Up frame appears. When the pointer enters the graphic area of the movie clip, the pointer changes to the pointing-hand cursor and the graphic from the Over frame appears. Unless you do additional scripting, once the Over frame appears, it remains the visible frame.

5. In the Behaviors panel, change the event to On Roll Over.

Double-click the first line in the Event column to view the list of events and select On Roll Over. Flash changes the value in the Event column of the Behaviors panel to on (rollOver) and updates the script in the Actions panel (**Figure 12.35**). This script tells Flash to display the Over frame of the movie-clip whenever the pointer enters the movie clip's graphic area.

6. Choose Control > Test Movie to try out the first phase of your button-style movie clip.

In the Flash Player window, position the pointer over various areas of the Stage. Upon moving into the image area of the movie clip, the pointer changes from an arrow to a pointing hand, and the graphic for the Over state appears (**Figure 12.36**). Once that Over-state graphic appears, however, it doesn't change. To get the movie clip to work like a button symbol, you must tell it to display the Up graphic when the pointer rolls out of the movie-clip area, as well has how to handle all the other states.

To add the mouseEvent handlers that display the Up and Down states:

1. Continuing in the same file, with the movie-clip instance selected on the Stage, choose Movieclip > Goto and Stop at Frame or Label from the Behaviors panel's Add Behavior menu.

2. In the Goto and Stop dialog, for the target frame, type Up.

   The other parameter settings in the dialog should remain the same: (MovieClipBtn_mc) is the target object. The pathname style is Relative.

3. Click OK.

   Flash places the default event handler on (release) in the Script pane.

   You need to change the handler's event parameter so that moving the pointer out of the movie-clip's graphic area triggers the script to display the Up frame of the movie clip.

4. In the Behaviors panel, change the event to On Roll Out (**Figure 12.37**).

5. Repeat steps 1 through 4 above.

   This time change the event parameter of the handler so that pressing the mouse button down triggers the script to display the Down frame of the movie clip. In step 2, change the target frame to Down; in step 4, change the event to On Press.

6. Repeat steps 1 through 4 above.

   This time in step 2, change the target frame to Up; in step 4, change the event parameter of the handler to On Release Outside. If the user clicks the button, and then has a change of heart and moves the pointer away before releasing the mouse button, you want the button to reset itself to its waiting state.

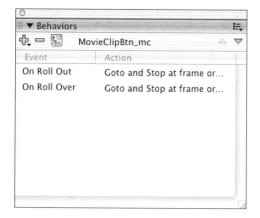

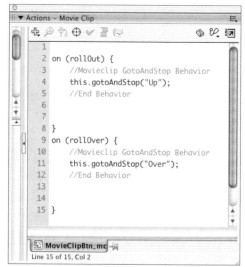

Figure 12.37 When you add the On Roll Over and On Roll Out Behaviors (top) to your movie-clip button, Flash creates a script (bottom) that gives the movie-clip symbol the rollover responsiveness that's built into a button symbol.

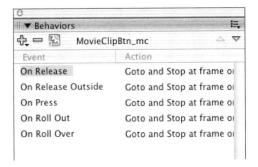

```
1
2  on (release) {
3      //Movieclip GotoAndStop Behavior
4      this.gotoAndStop("Up");
5      //End Behavior
6
7  }
8  on (releaseOutside) {
9      //Movieclip GotoAndStop Behavior
10     this.gotoAndStop("Up");
11     //End Behavior
12
13 }
14 on (press) {
15     //Movieclip GotoAndStop Behavior
16     this.gotoAndStop("Down");
17     //End Behavior
18
19 }
20 on (rollOut) {
21     //Movieclip GotoAndStop Behavior
22     this.gotoAndStop("Up");
23     //End Behavior
24
25 }
26 on (rollOver) {
27     //Movieclip GotoAndStop Behavior
28     this.gotoAndStop("Over");
29     //End Behavior
30
31 }
```

MovieClipBtn_mc

Line 29 of 31, Col 16

Figure 12.38 The full set of behaviors (top) covers the important mouse interactions with the movie clip: when the mouse moves into the movie-clip button area, when it moves out, when the mouse button goes down, and so on. The completed script (bottom) has separate handlers and associated actions for each Behavior.

7. Repeat steps 1 through 4 above.

This time in step 2, change the target frame to Up; in step 4, there's no need to change the event parameter of the handler. When the user releases the mouse button, you want the button to reset itself to its waiting state. The script is complete (**Figure 12.38**).

You are ready to test your button movie clip. During playback, as you interact with the button, you can see that your movie-clip button now acts just like Flash's built-in button symbol.

8. Save this file for use in the following exercise; name it ScriptAClipBtn.fla.

✔ Tips

■ To make the button actually do something, you need to script it to perform another task on release, for example, moving to another frame. To try that out, add one more Goto and Stop Behavior to the movie-clip button. Repeat steps 2 and 3 of the preceding exercise. In step 2, select the main Timeline (_root) as the target movie clip; change the target frame to 3. There is no need to change the event parameter, you want Flash to carry out the task when the user releases the mouse button within the movie-clip button area.

■ The preceding exercise scripts a single instance of a movie-clip button. To save that work for reuse, select the scripted symbol instance on the Stage; choose Modify > Convert to Symbol (you're making a symbol within a symbol); name the symbol something meaningful, for example, mcBtnScripted_mc. Now drag an instance of mcBtnScripted_mc to the Stage and choose Modify > Break Apart. The movie clip is already scripted to show its button states. You're ready to select the clip and add new Behaviors.

Making Movie-Clip Buttons Display Additional States

The preceding exercise works with the standard button states (up, over, and down), but makes no use of the movie-clip button's disabled state. While you might want some additional states to appear in response to user interaction (for example, a previously selected state that indicates the user has clicked that button before), you probably want the Disabled state to appear only in certain frames of your movie. Imagine using your movie-clip button as a Previous button, one that takes users to the previous page. In the first frame of your application, the button should be disabled. You can use a frame action to achieve this goal.

To add frame actions to display the disabled state:

1. Open the file you created in the preceding exercise, `ScriptAClipBtn.fla`.

   This is a document containing four five-frame layers: *Actions*, *mcButtons*, *Scene*, and *Frame*.

2. Access the Property Inspector and the Behaviors and Actions panels.

3. Select the movie-clip instance on the Stage.

4. In the Property Inspector's Instance Name field, type a name for this instance, for example, `mcBtnScripted1_mc`.

Ready to insert new script

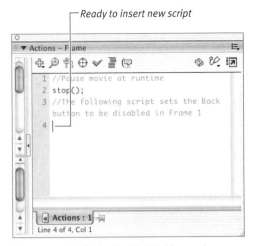

Figure 12.39 To display the Disabled frame of your movie-clip button, you must add to the script for Frame 1 of the main Timeline. Place the insertion point in the line below the stop action that you created in the original file; the Behavior adds to the script at that point.

5. In the Script pane of the Actions panel, select all the text and delete it.

Since this button has no meaningful function in this frame, you need to delete all of the script that makes this movie clip respond to the user's mouse movements. The Script pane works just like a text editor, you can press ⌘-A (Mac) or Ctrl-A (Windows) to select all the text then backspace to delete it.

6. Select Keyframe 1 in the *Actions* layer.

The Actions panel title changes to Actions-Frame.

7. Click Line 3 in the Script pane of the Actions panel and enter a comment.

Line 3 is the first blank line following the script you created for the original document

//Pause movie at runtime
stop();

8. Type two slashes followed by a new comment.

Enter a comment describing the new script's task, for example, //The following script sets the Back button to be disabled in Frame 1. Press return to end your comment (**Figure 12.39**).

9. In the Behaviors panel, from the Add Behaviors menu, select Goto and Stop at Frame or Label.

continues on next page

10. In the Goto and Stop dialog that appears, *set the following parameters:*

▲ Choose the movie-clip button named `mcBtnScripted1_mc` in the target movie-clip pane.

▲ Leave the pathname style as Relative.

▲ Type `Disabled` in the target-frame field.

11. Click OK.

Flash adds the Behavior to the Behaviors panel and updates script in the Script pane (**Figure 12.40**). You are ready to test the movie-clip button in Flash Player. The grayed out version of the button appears when playback starts; when you roll over the button or click it, nothing happens.

Figure 12.40 The script attached to Frame 1 of the main Timeline basically tells Flash "in me, in the movie-clip instance named mcBtnScripted1_mc, go to the frame labeled Disabled, and stop the playhead."

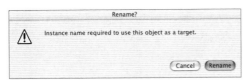

Figure 12.41 When you want to set up a button that controls playback of a movie clip, the target movie clip must have an instance name. Flash warns you if you select an instance that lacks an instance name.

Using Buttons to Control Movie Clips

Most Flash projects will employ a mixture of interface objects: button symbols, button components, and movie clips. More advanced ActionScripters can add script to control any type of object. Behaviors are not quite as open ended, but they will allow you to control the playback of movie clips, by adding scripts to button symbols, button components, movie clips, and frames. You could script a button to start and stop a movie clip, or script a button component to jump to a specific frame in a movie clip. The key is to specify the correct target path. When you use Flash's Goto Behavior, for example, you must select the target movie clip in the Goto parameters dialog. Flash specifies the appropriate pathname in ActionScript.

To make a button (symbol or component) stop movie-clip playback:

1. Open a new Flash Document and open the Actions and Behaviors panels.

2. Place one instance of a button symbol, a button component, and an animated movie-clip symbol (for example, one containing a simple motion tween) on the Stage.

3. Select the button-symbol instance.

4. From the Add menu in the Behaviors panel, select Goto and Stop at Frame or Label. The Goto and Stop dialog appears.

5. In the target movie-clip pane, select the movie clip instance.

    For one object to control another, the object that is being controlled must have an instance name. Since you did not name the movie clip instance name in Step 2, a warning dialog appears (**Figure 12.41**).

continues on next page

USING BUTTONS TO CONTROL MOVIE CLIPS

6. In the Rename? dialog, click the Rename button.

The Instance Name dialog appears.

7. Enter an instance name for your movie clip, for example, `ControlledClip_mc` (**Figure 12.42**).

8. Click OK.

Flash returns you to the Goto and Stop dialog. Leave the other parameters at their default settings: Relative pathname, with frame 1 as the target frame on which to stop playback.

9. In the Goto and Stop dialog, click OK.

10. On the Stage, select the button-component instance.

11. Repeat steps 4 and 5 only this time, in the Behaviors panel, select Goto and Play at Frame or Label.

Flash opens the Goto and Play dialog. (Because you already named the movie-clip instance, the Rename warning dialog does not appear.)

12. In the Goto and Play dialog, *set the following parameters.*

▲ Select `ControlledClip_mc` as the target movie clip.

▲ Select Relative as the pathname style.

▲ Type 1 in the target-frame field (**Figure 12.43**).

13. Click OK.

You're ready to test your buttons in Flash Player. When you click the button symbol, the animated movie clip stops playing. Click the button component and the movie clip resumes playing.

Figure 12.42 The Instance Name dialog allows you to name an instance while you are setting parameters in the Goto dialog. Otherwise, you would have to return to the Stage, select the instance, and enter a name for it in the Property Inspector.

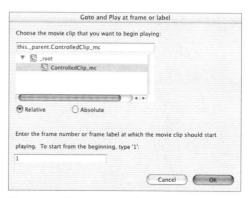

Figure 12.43 The parameters for Goto and Play are just like those for Goto and Stop. When you opt to control a movie clip with a button, the target frame is the frame in the movie clip that you want to jump to. To simply stop the movie clip at the beginning, choose frame 1.

Using the Script Navigator

The Script Navigator is a separate pane of the Actions panel that shows all of the items in your document that have scripts attached. Clicking on an item in the Script Navigator list selects that item in the document, and, unless you have pinned a script, shows that item's script in the Script pane.

To select and view scripts via the Script Navigator:

1. Open the document named MultiEventBtn.fla, which you created in "Using Multiple Handlers for one Button," earlier in this chapter.

2. On the Stage, select and copy the button that responds differently to different mouse events. You can close this document now if you wish.

   When you copy a button instance that has script attached, you also copy that script.

3. Open the document named KeyPressBtn.fla, which you created and saved in the exercise "Triggering Actions from the Keyboard," earlier in this chapter.

4. In the Timeline, in the Buttons layer, select Frame 3 and insert a blank keyframe (press F7).

5. Paste the button you copied in step 2.

6. Access the Scenes panel and click the Duplicate Scene button.

   If the panel is not open, choose Window > Design Panels > Scene.

7. Access the Actions panel.

   If the panel is not open, choose Window > Development Panels > Actions.

continues on next page

USING THE SCRIPT NAVIGATOR

8. Resize the horizontal and vertical dividers of the Actions panel as needed to view the Script Navigator pane in the lower-left corner of the panel.

For this exercise you can close the Actions toolbox completely (see "Touring the Actions Panel," earlier in this chapter). The Script Navigator displays a list of items divided by category: Current selection, Scene, Symbol Definition(s). These are the frames and objects in this document that have scripts attached (**Figure 12.44**).

9. In the Script Navigator, Under Scene 1, select the first item: `Actions: Frame 1`.

Flash selects Frame 1 of the Actions layer and displays the associated script in the Script pane of the Actions panel. In this case the script is a single line with the action `stop();` (**Figure 12.45**).

10. In the Script Navigator, Under Scene 1, select the second item.

Flash displays that scene in the Timeline, moves the playhead to Frame 1, selects the button instance on the Stage, and displays the associated script in the Script pane of the Actions panel.

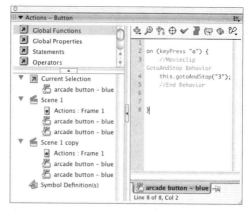

Figure 12.44 The Script Navigator pane of the Actions panel displays a hierarchical listing of all the elements in the current movie that have scripts attached.

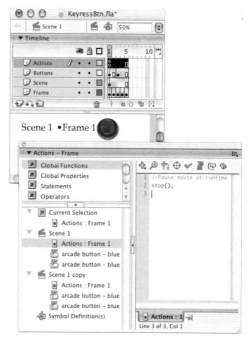

Figure 12.45 Choosing Frame 1 of Scene 1 in the Script Navigator displays the script for that frame in the Script pane of the Actions Panel.

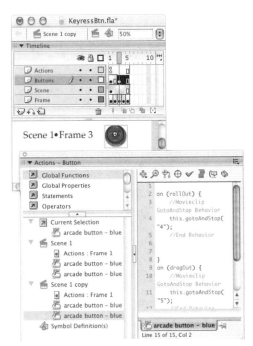

Figure 12.46 Choosing an element in another scene causes Flash to move the playhead to the scene and frame that contain that element.

11. In the Script Navigator, Under Scene 1 copy, select the third item.

Flash displays that scene in the Timeline, moves the playhead to frame 3, and selects the button. The button script appears in the Script pane (**Figure 12.46**). Continue checking out the scripts in this document by choosing items in the Script Navigator. In more complex documents with more elements and scripts, you may need to expand or collapse sections of the Navigator to find the precise script you want. To do so, click the plus (or minus) signs (Windows) or triangles (Mac) to the left of the items in the list.

✔ **Tips**

■ Double-clicking an item in the Script Navigator pins it in the Script pane. For more details about pinning scripts, see the sidebar "The Mystery of Pinned Scripts."

■ If you'd like to examine a file with more complicated ActionScript, try opening a copy of one of the Quiz templates that come with Flash. These documents contain a number of scripted elements.

The Mystery of Pinned Scripts

To prevent Flash from displaying or starting a different script as you select various items on the stage, you can *pin* a script. Pinning forces Flash to continue displaying the same script even if you select a different frame in the Timeline or object on the Stage. Pinning allows you to examine a variety of elements and situations without losing your place in the script you are creating. To pin the script currently displayed in the Script pane, click the pushpin icon below the pane; the icon changes to a more upright version of a pushpin. You can pin multiple scripts. To display a new script to pin, select an item in the Script Navigator. Double-clicking the item pins its script. Flash adds tabs for pinned scripts to the area below the script pane.

The item currently selected on the Stage or in the Timeline, always appears in the leftmost tab below the Script pane. The tab for a pinned script currently on display is highlighted (in Windows, it's white, on the Mac it's blue); tabs for other pinned scripts are gray. Click a gray tab to select that script. To unpin a script, display that script, then click the upright-pushpin icon (**Figure 12.47**).

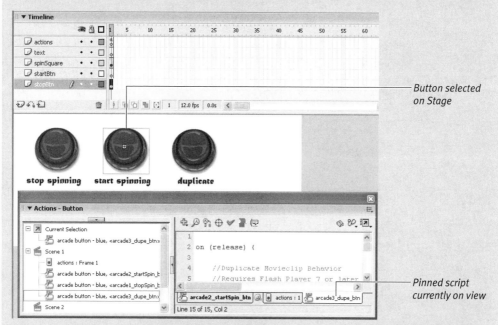

Button selected on Stage

Pinned script currently on view

Figure 12.47 The leftmost tab beneath the Script pane displays the name of the item currently selected in the document; the highlighted tab (blue on Macs, white in Windows) displays the name of the pinned script currently visible in the Script pane; the gray tabs indicate other pinned scripts. To select another pinned script, click its tab.

AUTHORING UTILITIES

As your Flash projects grow in size and scope, you'll find yourself doing a number of repetitive tasks, and performing a variety of housekeeping tasks: tracking elements, finding items to replace or update them, undoing mistakes, applying settings repeatedly, moving elements in repetitious ways, cleaning up spelling, and so on. Flash MX 2004 includes several utilities that help with these tasks: the Movie Explorer, the Spelling Checker, the Find and Replace panel, the History panel, and the Commands menu.

The Movie Explorer gives you a bird's eye view of an entire Flash document, with live links to each element so that you can use it to find items and navigate to them easily. The Spelling Checker verifies spellings in any type of text in your document (text boxes, scripts, labels, and so on). The Find and Replace panel works for text, fonts, symbols, colors, sound clips, and video clips. The History panel creates a roadmap of all the steps you've performed in a work session, making it possible to undo, redo, and repeat steps easily. The Commands menu enables you to transform History panel steps into a macro for reuse in any document, thereby streamlining some repetitive tasks.

Setting Movie Explorer Parameters

As you add text, graphic symbols, buttons, movie clips, and actions to your movies, the job of tracking where each element resides increases dramatically. The Movie Explorer is a powerful tool for tracking, finding, and modifying the elements in your movies. It also gives you an overview of the whole movie.

The Movie Explorer panel displays the various movie elements hierarchically in a *display list*. You determine which types of elements appear in the list. You can expand and collapse the list levels, similar to the way that you expand and collapse folders as you navigate your hard drive.

To access the Movie Explorer panel:

◆ If the Movie Explorer panel is not open, from the Window menu, choose Other Panels > Movie Explorer (**Figure 13.1**).

To determine the overall content of the display list:

From the Options menu in the Movie Explorer panel's top-right corner (**Figure 13.2**), *choose any of the following:*

◆ To display all the elements in the movie, choose Show Movie Elements.

◆ To display a list of all the symbols used in the movie (including a display list for the elements that make up each movie clip), choose Show Symbol Definitions.

◆ To display the contents of all the scenes of a movie—not just the current scene—choose Show All Scenes.

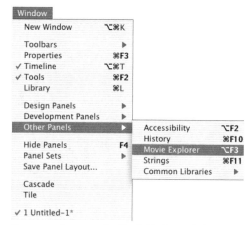

Figure 13.1 To access the Movie Explorer window, choose Window > Other Panels > Movie Explorer.

Figure 13.2 The Movie Explorer panel's Options menu lets you choose what elements of your movie appear in the panel's display list and offers commands for editing elements that you've selected in the display list.

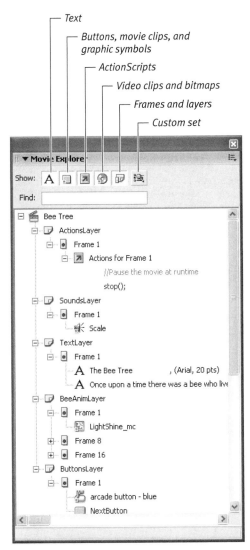

Text

Buttons, movie clips, and
graphic symbols

ActionScripts

Video clips and bitmaps

Frames and layers

Custom set

Figure 13.3 Click the buttons in the Show section of
the Movie Explorer window to specify which movie
elements to display.

To determine which types of elements appear in the display list:

In the Show section of the Movie Explorer
panel, *do any of the following*:

◆ To display text elements, click the first
button (**Figure 13.3**).

◆ To display buttons, movie clips, and
graphic elements, click the second button.

◆ To display ActionScripts, click the
third button.

◆ To display video clips, sounds, and
bitmapped graphics, click the fourth
button.

◆ To display frame and layer information,
click the fifth button.

◆ To create a custom set of elements to
display, click the sixth button, and select
elements in the Movie Explorer Settings
window that appears.

SETTING MOVIE EXPLORER PARAMETERS

501

Searching and Editing with Movie Explorer

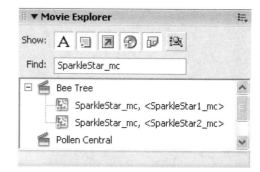

To find an element:

In the Find field of the Movie Explorer panel, enter text that identifies the element you want to find (**Figure 13.4**), *as in the following examples:*

◆ To find one instance of a symbol, enter the instance name.

◆ To find all instances of a symbol, enter the symbol name.

◆ To find all text boxes that use a certain font, enter the font name.

Figure 13.4 To find all instances of a movie-clip symbol, enter the symbol name in the Find field.

✔ Tips

■ You don't need to press Enter after typing in the Find field; Flash starts searching as soon as you enter any characters.

■ The Movie Explorer panel puts a big drain on your system, because it constantly checks for changes. Even when the panel is just sitting open on your desktop as you work on a file, Flash can slow to a crawl. Keep this panel closed until you're ready to use it.

To modify elements from the Movie Explorer panel:

1. In the display list, select the element you want to modify.

2. From the Options menu, *choose one of the following options:*

   ▲ To select the object on the Stage, choose Go to Location.

   ▲ To rename an element, choose Rename.

   ▲ To edit a symbol, choose Edit in Place or Edit in New Window.

Figure 13.5 Double-click a text item to edit it directly in the Movie Explorer window.

✔ Tips

- Double-click an element to modify it quickly. Double-click a scene or a text box, for example, to change the scene's name, or change the contents of the text box directly in the Movie Explorer window (**Figure 13.5**). Double-click a symbol to open it in symbol-editing mode. Double-click an ActionScript to open the Actions panel, where you can update the selected script.

- When you have a text box selected in the Movie Explorer panel, choosing Rename from the Options menu activates the text box for editing.

- Flash has its own spelling checker, which you'll learn to use later in this chapter. If you prefer to use one in a different text editor, for example, because it contains a specialized dictionary, you can. Just copy text from the Movie Explorer window, paste it into your preferred text editor, check and correct the spelling, and then reversing the process, copy and paste the corrected text into Flash.

To print a display list:

1. Set the display list to show the hierarchy levels and contents you want to print.

2. From the Options menu, choose Print.

Choosing Spelling Checker Options

Flash MX 2004 includes a full-fledged spelling checker. In previous versions, you had to export text to check the spelling and then re-import it. The checker comes with a number of built-in dictionaries and also allows you to create custom dictionaries. The spelling checker can locate, check, and correct text in text boxes, frame labels, symbol names, instance names, and ActionScript. You can check the spelling within all those elements, or just one or two, say just text boxes and layer names. Before running your first spelling check, you must set the spelling checker options.

To set options for spelling check:

1. Open a Flash Document containing text that needs to be checked.

2. From the Text menu, choose Spelling Setup (**Figure 13.6**).

   The Spelling Setup dialog appears. This dialog presents options for which text types to review, which dictionaries to use, and how to deal with individual words.

3. To choose the types of text to verify select any of the check boxes in the Document Options section of the Spelling Setup dialog (**Figure 13.7**).

   You can use these settings to refine the spelling check, for example, limiting it to just text boxes, or just symbol names. To make the search as broad as possible and check any element that involves text of any sort, select all the check boxes.

Figure 13.6 The first time you use the spelling checker, you should run Spelling Setup to customize it for the types of checks you want to do. Thereafter, you need to run Spelling Setup only when you want to change those options.

Figure 13.7 Choose the document options appropriate to your task. Frame labels, and symbol names, for example, are often not very English like. If your main goal is to check the text that appears on screen during playback, the spelling check will go faster if you leave out the text in other elements.

CHOOSING SPELLING CHECKER OPTIONS

Figure 13.8 Flash can use any combination of English or foreign-language dictionaries that come with the program to verify spellings and suggest changes. You can also create and edit personal dictionaries of special terms.

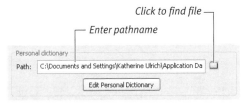

Figure 13.9 You specify a personal dictionary by entering its pathname or browsing to it.

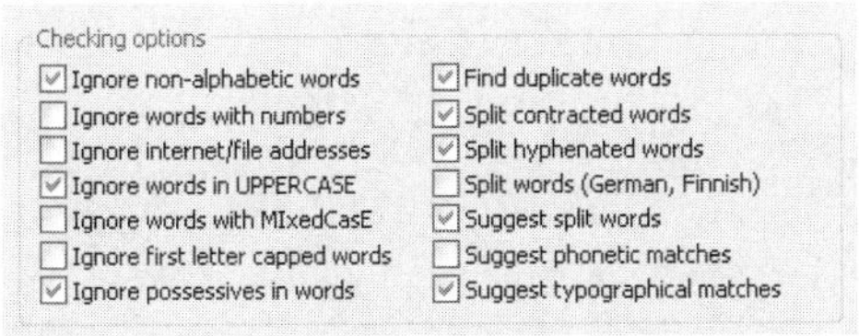

Figure 13.10 Flash allows you to determine how to deal with 14 common spelling conundrums, such as, words spelled with all capital letters, possessives, or duplicates. Click a setting to activate it during the next spelling check.

4. To choose which dictionaries Flash consults to determine correct spellings and suggest changes, select any of the dictionaries in the Dictionaries list (**Figure 13.8**).

Flash comes with 2 English dictionaries (one American, one British), 12 foreign-language dictionaries, 1 dictionary of special Macromedia terms, and 1 editable personal dictionary. You can create other personal dictionaries, as you'll learn later in this chapter.

5. To select a personal dictionary, in the Personal Dictionary section of the panel, *do one of the following:*

▲ Enter the pathname for the dictionary file in the Path field (**Figure 13.9**).

▲ Click the Browse button and navigate to the file that you want to use as a dictionary. Flash adds the pathname for the file you select to the Path field.

6. To set the rules for dealing with common spelling situations, select any of the check boxes in the Checking Options section (**Figure 13.10**).

✔ Tip

■ Most of the options in the Document Options and Checking Options sections are straightforward and you can figure them out by their names. A few are bit obscure, however. If you have activated Show Tool tips in the General tab of the Preferences dialog (see Chapter 1), you can position the pointer over an option to see more information about the option.

Working with Personal Dictionaries

Flash comes with one blank personal dictionary to which you can add new words either from within the Spelling Setup dialog or during a spelling check. You can create additional personal dictionaries, but you can only use one at a time. Personal dictionaries must be in the format .tlx or .txt (you can open .tlx files or create .txt files with any text editor).

To create a new text-only personal dictionary:

1. Using the text editor of your choice, create a new file.

2. Enter a list of words, each on its own line.

3. Save the file as text only, with the extension .txt.

   Give the file a meaningful name, for example, MyProjectTerms.txt.

4. Place the file in the Common folder along with Flash's built-in personal dictionary.

   Flash stores the default personal dictionary in a folder that's shared by all Macromedia MX 2004 applications. (That means entries added to the personal dictionary in, say, Dreamweaver MX 2004 get used to check spelling in Flash when you choose the default personal dictionary.)

   ▲ The full pathname on the Mac is *hardDriveName*:Users:*userName*: Library:Application Support: Macromedia:Common:Personal Dictionary MX.tlx.

Figure 13.11 The Edit Personal Dictionary window acts as a text editor, allowing you to add a large number of words to your personal dictionary at one go. You can also delete or edit any of the entries in your dictionary in this window.

▲ In Windows 2000 and XP, the path name is C:\Documents and Settings\ *userName*\Application Data\ Macromedia\Common\Personal Dictionary MX.tlx.

▲ In Windows 98, the pathname is C:\WINDOWS\Profiles*userName*\ Application Data\Macromedia\ Common\Personal Dictionary MX.tlx.

You can add other personal dictionaries to that folder, or create another location for them on your system.

You can now click the Browse button in the Spelling Setup dialog and select this dictionary just as you would the built-in personal dictionary.

To edit a personal dictionary from within Flash:

1. Open a Flash Document and choose Text > Spelling Setup.

   The Spelling Setup dialog appears.

2. In the Personal Dictionary section of the dialog, select the dictionary you want to modify.

3. Click the Edit Personal Dictionary button located beneath the Path field.

   The Edit Personal Dictionary window appears. This window works like a little text editor. When the blinking insertion point appears in the window, you can type new entries and correct or delete existing entries (**Figure 13.11**).

4. Click OK to confirm your changes to the dictionary file.

Running the Spelling Check

Once you have set up the appropriate options for your spelling check (see "Choosing Spelling Checker Options," earlier in this chapter), you're ready to correct the spellings in your Flash Document. You can check the text of a selected item, or of every item in the document (limited, of course to the types currently selected in the Spelling Setup dialog).

To check and correct spelling for a selected text box:

1. Open a Flash Document that contains at least one text box with spelling errors.

2. On the Stage, select the text box.

3. Choose Text > Check Spelling.

When it finds a word it doesn't recognize, Flash opens the Check Spelling dialog, which displays the unrecognized text and offers suggested changes (**Figure 13.12**). When the Spelling Setup dialog is set to Select During Spell Checking (the default setting), Flash also activates the Movie Explorer panel (bringing it to the front if it's already open; opening it if it's closed). As Flash examines an element in the document, that element appears selected in the Movie Explorer panel.

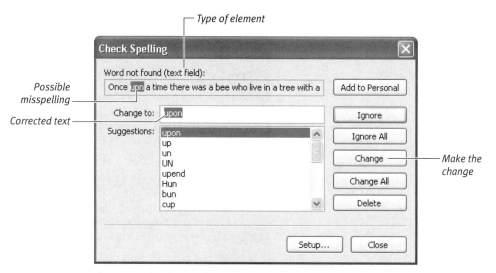

Figure 13.12 The Check Spelling dialog displays the text from a selected text box in the Word Not Found field, highlighting the suspect text. To make a correction, type new text into the Change To field or choose one of the words in the Suggestions list, then click the Change button.

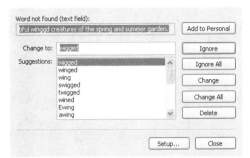

Figure 13.13 Selecting a word in the Suggestions list adds that word to the Change To field. Click the Change button to make the correction.

4. To resolve a suspected spelling problem, *do one of the following:*

   ▲ To leave the word as is, click Ignore. To have Flash skip other instances of this word, click Ignore All.

   ▲ To replace the word with one of the words in the Suggestions list, first click the word in the list, Flash highlights the selected word and displays it in the Change To field (**Figure 13.13**). Next, click Change. To have Flash change all instances of this word, click Change All.

   ▲ To remove the word, click Delete.

   ▲ To correct the spelling yourself, type the corrected word in the Change To field, then click Change.

   ▲ To add the word to a personal dictionary, click Add to Personal. Flash adds the word to the currently selected personal dictionary.

✔ Tips

■ If at any point during the spelling check you wish to alter the options for what's being checked or how to deal with it, or if you want to change the dictionaries that Flash is using, click the Setup button to open the Spelling Setup dialog.

■ If you want to end a spelling check before checking an entire selection or document, click the Close button in the Check Spelling dialog.

RUNNING THE SPELLING CHECK

509

Spelling Checker Quirks

In many ways Flash's spelling checker will seem familiar to anyone who's used a word processor. But Flash's spelling checker has a few eccentricities.

On the Mac, when you choose to change a spelling, the entire Check Spelling dialog closes down and disappears for second or two. Don't' be alarmed; the spelling checker will return. On the Windows side, the dialog doesn't close, but it sometimes blinks. If Select During Spell Checking is active (the default setting), the Check Spelling dialog dances a do-si-do with the Movie Explorer panel, which comes to the front briefly, for each change you make.

There are several ways to see some context for a suspect word during a spelling check but they can be a bit finicky. In the Check Spelling dialog itself, the Word Not Found field contains the entire text of a selected item. Unfortunately for anyone who uses lengthy text boxes, the field displays only 60 characters at a time and it doesn't scroll automatically to display the next suspect word. If Flash offers suggestions for a word you cannot see, press the right arrow key to scroll to the right in the field, press the left arrow key to scroll to the left, press the Home key to jump to the beginning of the field, or press the End key to jump to the end.

The Live Edit During Spell Checking option helps you to see words in context in text boxes. It selects the suspect word on the Stage, activating the word's text box, and entering symbol-editing mode if the text is located inside a symbol.

The Select During Spell Checking option works similarly to Live Edit, in addition it selects layer names when checking their text, and it opens up the Movie Explorer panel, selecting whatever element in the display list contains the text, text box, symbol, ActionScript, and so on.

When you use Live Edit During Spell Checking and Select During Spell Checking to check a word's context on Stage, you need to make sure that nothing obscures your view of the Stage. You can reposition the Check Spelling dialog on the screen if it gets in the way, but you cannot reposition any other panels that might be covering part of a text box that's being checked. Your best bet is to position all panels away from the Stage before beginning to check spelling.

The problem of panels obscuring your view of the Stage applies in particular to the Movie Explorer if you opt to Select During Spell Checking (that is, to track checked items in the Movie Explorer). The Movie Explorer remembers its last position on screen even after you close the panel. You may begin your spelling check with a clear view of the Stage only to find the view suddenly obstructed by the newly opened Movie Explorer panel.

Another complication for viewing words in context when you have chosen Select During Spell Checking, is the fact that the first time the spelling checker finds a suspect word in a text box it selects the text box, but doesn't activate it for editing until you deal with the first suspect word. To ensure that you can see that first word in context, activate the text box, for example, by double-clicking it using the selection tool, before you start the spelling check.

RUNNING THE SPELLING CHECK

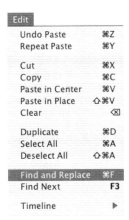

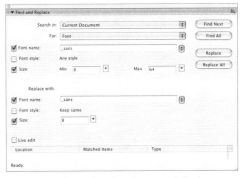

Figure 13.14 Choose Edit > Find and Replace to open a panel that allows you to search and replace text; change colors; and swap symbols, sound clips, and video clips, anywhere in your document.

Figure 13.15 The Find and Replace panel displays parameters appropriate to your search. The Search In and Replace With fields; the Live Edit check box; and the Location field all represent constant parameters, available for any type of search. The Find Next, Find All, Replace, and Replace All buttons allow you to control the search.

Dialog or Panel?

Macromedia's documentation refers to the window that opens when you choose Edit > Find and Replace as a *dialog box*. Except for the fact that you don't choose it under the Window menu, however, this item operates just like a panel. It expands and collapses, it docks, and it has an Options menu. The exercises in this book will refer to the Find and Replace *panel*.

Using Find and Replace

Like the Spelling Checker, the Find and Replace feature is a tool for working with your whole document, especially in its later stages when numerous elements are already in place and you need to modify them uniformly throughout. If your need to change the color scheme, or update a logo at the last minute, Find and Replace will make the task less arduous. The Find and Replace feature works not only for text elements, such as text boxes, symbol names, or script segments, but also works like a more powerful version of the Swap Symbol button (described in Chapter 6), allowing you to swap symbols, colors, fonts, pieces of text, video clips, sound clips, and bitmap graphics. The options for each type of search-and-replace operation vary, but certain parameters remain constant for all types.

To access the Find and Replace panel:

1. Open a Flash Document containing a variety of elements: text, symbols, graphic elements, sounds, video clips, and/or bitmaps.

   Make sure that some of the elements are used more than once in the document. That way you can practice finding and replacing multiple instances.

2. From the Edit menu, choose Find and Replace (**Figure 13.14**) or press ⌘-F (Mac) or (Ctrl-F Windows).

   Flash opens the Find and Replace panel (**Figure 13.15**). The panel displays a variety of search features; some are available for every type of search, others appropriate to specific types of searches appear only when that type of search is selected. Searches for text, for example, require more parameters than do searches for symbol instances.

511

To set the general search parameters:

1. Access the Find and Replace panel.

2. To determine the scenes to be searched, from the Search In menu, *select one of the following:*

   ▲ To search every scene in the document, select Current Document.

   ▲ To search one scene, select Current Scene. Flash searches only the scene currently displayed in the document.

3. From the For pop-up menu, choose the type of item to find.

   You have seven options: Text, Font, Color, Symbol, Sound, Video, and Bitmap (**Figure 13.16**).

4. To make Flash open a found item automatically, so that you can edit it in place in the document, select the Live Edit check box.

   With Live Edit active, as soon as it finds the first match for your search, Flash opens the element on the Stage in its editable form (if the item can be edited in place on the Stage). If you are dealing with a text string, for example, Flash selects the text tool in the Toolbar, selects and activates the text box containing the word on the Stage, and selects the word within the text box. If you are dealing with a symbol instance, Flash does the equivalent of double-clicking the symbol instance on the Stage, entering symbol-editing mode with that symbol selected and all other elements in place on the Stage, but dimmed.

✔ Tip

■ You can select a new scene while the Find and Replace panel is active. Position the panel so that you can access the Edit Scene menu in the document's Edit Bar, then select the scene to search from the menu.

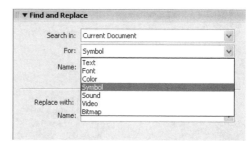

Figure 13.16 The Find and Replace panel can search for seven types of elements. Choose the search-target type from the For pop-up menu.

USING FIND AND REPLACE

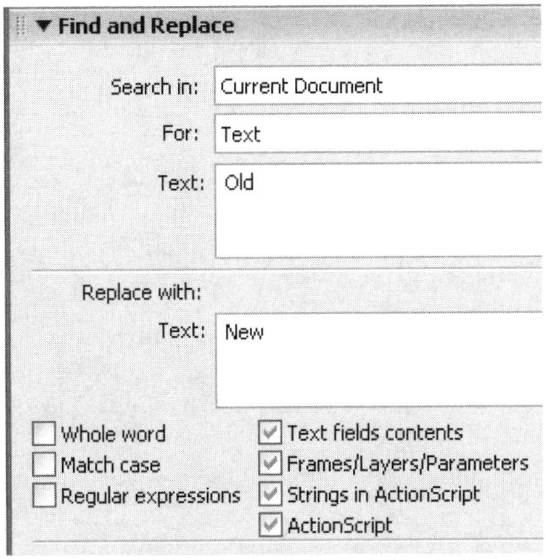

Figure 13.17 When you choose Text as the search-for type, seven search-filter check boxes appear in the Replace section of the panel. They refine the search process, allowing you, for example, to restrict the search to just text fields, or just ActionScript.

To set search parameters for text:

1. In the Find and Replace panel, select Text from the For pop-up menu.

   The panel displays the specific parameters for text searches (**Figure 13.17**).

2. Type the text string that you want to find (and/or modify) into the Text field in the Search In section (the upper portion of the panel).

3. Type the replacement text into the Text field in the Replace With section (the lower portion of the panel).

4. To refine your search, select any of the search-filter check boxes (see the sidebar "Search-Filter Rundown").

Search-Filter Rundown

When you search and replace text strings, you can set various filter options to make the search process more specific.

◆ To skip instances where the text string is part of a larger word, choose Whole Word.

◆ To skip instances where the text string is the same, but capitalization is different, choose Match Case.

◆ To perform wild-card searches, choose Regular Expressions. Regular Expressions are elaborate, specific wild cards developed for searching code. When you select the Regular Expressions option, certain special characters become wild cards. The most familiar expression is the asterisk. Typing at* as the search text with Regular Expressions selected, for example, finds the letters *at* in *cat, batty,* and *category.* The same search with Regular Expressions deselected finds none of those words, only the combo *at*.*

◆ To search in text boxes, choose Text Fields Contents.

◆ To search in frame labels and comments, layer names, and component parameters (for example, in the label of a button component), choose Frames/Layers/Parameters.

◆ To search in ActionScript strings (groups of characters within a piece of script that are interpreted as text, not code), choose Strings in ActionScript.

◆ To search in other ActionScript code, choose ActionScript.

To set search parameters for fonts:

1. In the Find and Replace panel, select Font from the For pop-up menu.

   Check boxes for three font parameters—Font Name, Font Style, and Font size—appear in both the Search In and Replace With sections of the panel (**Figure 13.18**).

2. To refine your search, *select any of the font-parameter check boxes:*

   ▲ To search for a specific font, select the Font Name check box. From the pop-up menu of fonts that appears, select the desired font.

   ▲ To search for a specific style (plain, bold, italic, bold ital), select the Style check box. From the pop-up menu of styles that appears, select the desired style.

   ▲ To search for a specific size, select the Size check box. Two fields—Min and Max—appear. Enter the smallest point size for your search into Min and the largest into Max; enter the same value into both to find a single font size.

   If you leave any check boxes deselected, Flash searches all fonts that meet the remaining criteria. If, for example, you select a font name, but leave the style and size deselected, Flash searches for all instances of that font, no matter what size or style they appear in.

3. To set the font-replacement parameters, repeat step 2 for the check boxes that appear in the Replace With section of the panel.

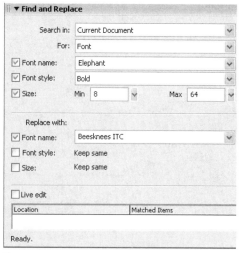

Figure 13.18 Select the Font Name, Font Style, and/or Size check box to restrict searches (or replacements) to a subset of the full font family.

✔ Tip

- When you select the Size parameter in the Replace With section of the Find and Replace dialog only one value-entry field appears. If you were searching for a range of sizes for the Font, and you want the replacement fonts to keep their original sizes, deselect the Size check box. The notation Keep Same appears.

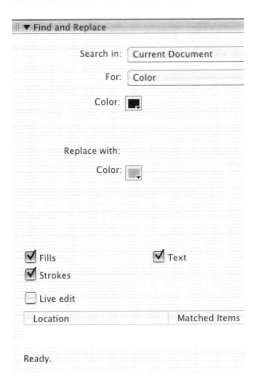

Figure 13.19 When you modify colors using the Find and Replace panel, Flash lets you choose the search color and the replacement color using the familiar color-swatch pop-up found in the Property Inspector and Color Mixer panel.

Figure 13.20 The check boxes in the Replace With section of the Find and Replace panel allow you to restrict your color modifications to just strokes, fills, or text, or any combination thereof.

To set search parameters for color:

1. In the Find and Replace panel, select Color from the For pop-up menu.

   A Color box appears in both the Search In and Replace With sections of the panel (**Figure 13.19**). Check boxes for Fills, Strokes, and Text appear in the Replace With section of the panel.

2. Click the Color box in the Search In Section.

   The pointer changes to an eyedropper, and a pop-up set of swatches appears.

3. Select the color you want to find.

   For detailed instructions on using pop-up swatch sets to choose colors, see Chapter 2.

4. To select a replacement color, repeat steps 2 and 3 using the Color box in the Replace With section.

5. To refine the selection and/or replacement, *do one of the following:*

   ▲ To modify fill colors, select the Fills check box.

   ▲ To modify the color of lines (strokes), select the Strokes check box.

   ▲ To modify the color of text in text boxes, select the Text check box (**Figure 13.20**).

✔ Tips

■ Although the Find and Replace feature will work on text within symbols, it does not work on colors within symbols unless you are editing the symbol itself.

■ Select all the check boxes to find and replace a color wherever it occurs in the current Timeline.

USING FIND AND REPLACE

To set search parameters for symbols, sounds, video clips, and bitmaps:

1. In the Find and Replace panel, from the For pop-up menu, select the type of element you want to find: Symbol, Sound, Video, or Bitmap.

   For these four element types, the only parameters you must specify are the name of the original item and the name of the replacement item.

2. Click the Name pop-up menu in the Search in section.

   This menu lists all the elements of the selected type that are contained in the library for this document.

3. Select the symbol (sound, video clip, or bitmap) that you want to find.

4. Repeat steps 2 and 3 in the Replace With section, this time selecting the replacement item (**Figure 13.21**).

✔ Tips

- Although you can choose Live Edit when you are searching for sounds, video clips, or bitmaps, there is no actual edit-in-place feature for these items. Flash will not highlight found sounds in the Timeline or video clips or bitmaps where they occur on the Stage. Examine the information in the Location, Matched Items, and Type fields of the matched-items table at the bottom of the panel to be sure you have the instance that you want.

- You cannot replace one element type with another; you cannot, for example, replace a video clip with a bitmap graphic. When you choose to modify symbols, however, the replacement symbol need not be the same symbol type as the original. You can, for example, replace a graphic symbol with a movie clip, or a movie clip with a button.

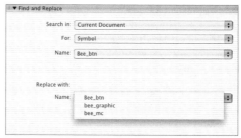

Figure 13.21 The only parameters required for finding and replacing symbols, sound clips, video clips, and bitmaps are the names of the original item and its replacement. The Name pop-up menu lists all the items of the selected type that exist in the library of the current document.

Figure 13.22 Click the buttons in the upper-right corner of the Find and Replace panel to initiate searches and replacements based on the parameters defined elsewhere in the panel.

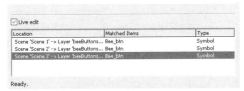

Figure 13.23 Each time you click the Find button, Flash adds the next matching instance to the table at the bottom of the Find and Replace panel. When you see the notation "Ready," in the lower-left corner of the panel, it means Flash has stopped searching. Click the Replace button to make your change, or click Find to skip this instance and find the next one.

Carrying Out a Find-and-Replace Operation

Once you have set the parameters describing what to search for and what to replace it with, you're ready to carry out the search-and-replace operation. You control the search process and the replacement process by clicking the buttons in the upper-right corner of the Find and Replace panel (**Figure 13.22**). You can find and/or replace items instance-by-instance, or you can find and/or replace all the instances at once.

To find/replace one matching item at a time:

1. Set the parameters for the search, as described in the preceding section.

2. Click the Find button.

   Flash begins searching your document, starting with the first frame of the first scene (or of the current scene if you've restricted the search to one scene). When it finds a match, Flash selects the item on the Stage and lists that item in the matched-items table at the bottom of the panel, showing the item's location (the scene, layer, and frame), its name, and the type of item it is (**Figure 13.23**).

   If Live Edit is active, Flash also opens the appropriate mode for editing that item. If the item is a symbol, for example, Flash opens the symbol in edit-in-place mode on the Stage.

3. To replace the selected item, click the Replace button.

   Flash makes the replacement and searches for the next match, adding it to the table of matched items.

   continues on next page

4. To skip the selected item, Click the Find button.

Flash searches for the next match and adds it to the table.

5. Repeat steps 3 and/or 4 as needed.

✔ Tip

■ If at any point you wish to stop moving instance-by-instance, you can make the replacement for all matching items in the document by clicking the Replace All button. Flash searches out and replaces all remaining matches.

To find/replace all matching items:

1. Set the parameters for the search, as described in the preceding section.

2. Click the Find All button.

Flash displays all of the items that meet the search criteria in the table of matched items (**Figure 13.24**). Note that when you use the Find All button, Flash doesn't select items on the Stage and even with Live Edit active, Flash doesn't enter editing mode for the found items.

3. To replace the first matching item, click the Replace button.

4. To replace all matching items, click the Replace All button.

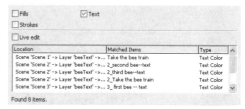

Figure 13.24 When you click the Find All button, Flash displays all the matching items in a table at the bottom of the Find and Replace panel. Here you see the results of a Color search restricted to text elements. The total number of finds appears in the lower left corner of the panel.

✔ Tips

■ Although the Live Edit mode doesn't work when you select Find All, you can use the table of matching items as the gateway to editing each match. When you select an item in the table, Flash selects that item in your document. When you double-click an item in the table, Flash puts that item into its appropriate edit mode in your document.

■ The table of matched items may not display all of the matches. Scroll bars appear when the table holds more items than it can display. Flash notes the total number of matches below the table.

■ You need not got through the process of finding items to replace them. Once the parameters are set in the Find and Replace panel, you can click the Replace button repeatedly to replace each matching item in turn, or click Replace All to swap all the matching items in one fell swoop. When Live Edit is active, and you click the Replace button, Flash opens the item in the appropriate editing mode to make the replacement; when you click the Replace All button, Flash simply makes the replacements.

■ With Live Edit active, when you replace individual symbol instances, it may temporarily appear that Flash is not making the replacement. The original symbol opens in edit-in-place mode, but the replacement symbol appears only after you return to document-editing mode. If you finish making replacements with the Find and Replace panel and your original symbol still appears in place on the Stage, you need to return to document-editing mode. Click the Back button in the document's Edit Bar; you return to document-editing mode and the new item appears in place on the Stage.

Using the History Panel

Flash has always tracked the steps you perform as you work in a document, allowing you to undo and redo operations, almost without limit. In previous versions of Flash, you could not undo some operations, even though Flash clearly retained the pertinent data. Previously, deleting items from the Library window, for example, was a permanent operation, although the data for the item remained in the library taking up file size until you saved the file with a new name. In Flash MX 2004, you can undo library deletions.

The History panel doesn't replace the Undo, Redo, and Repeat commands, you can still choose Edit > Undo, Edit > Redo, or Edit > Repeat; the History panel simply lists all the possible steps for doing and undoing. In addition, the History panel allows you to capture those steps for reuse within the current document, within other documents opened during the same work session, and even more permanently
as a menu command to apply to documents in future work sessions.

The Mystery of the History Undo

In previous versions, Flash tracked the steps you performed for different Timelines separately, that meant not only creating separate undo lists for each document, but also creating separate undo lists within one document for steps performed in the main Timeline and for steps performed in creating each symbol. In Flash MX 2004, there is just one long list of steps performed in the History panel. If you place a text box on the Stage, then create a new symbol, then return to editing your document and place a second text box, you cannot use the Edit > Undo command (or the Undo slider in the History panel) to delete both text boxes without passing through, and thereby demolishing the symbol you created.

While the History panel's single undo list may limit your use of the Undo feature with symbols, it allows the other features of the History panel and commands to work. If you find that you need to use the Undo command in a way that would destroy your work on a symbol, you should save the symbol in another document before starting the undo process. (You could also make a copy of the current document to hold the symbol temporarily.) Once you've finished undoing, you can drag a copy of the symbol back into your current document.

Touring the History Panel

The History panel lists the steps carried out in a single work session in a Flash Document. You can select a series of sequential (or non-sequential) steps and have Flash perform them again. The replay can be applied to new objects or new situations (including being applied within a different document) to streamline performance of some repetitive tasks. Repositioning the lever of the undo/redo slider effectively undoes all steps below the new "last step." A red *X* in the icon for a step indicates a step that cannot be saved or replayed (though it can be redone) (**Figure 13.25**).

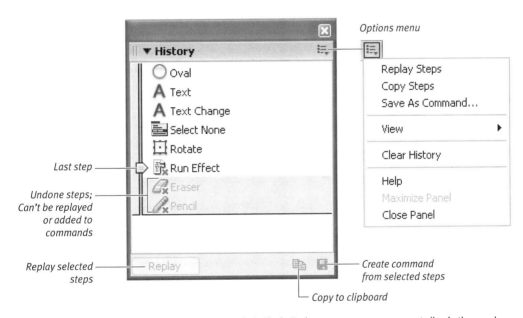

Figure 13.25 The History panel tracks everything you do in Flash. Each step appears on a separate line in the panel. You can use the panel to undo or redo steps or to repeat selected steps in a new context, for example, to modify a different object or a different document. You can also permanently record steps for replay from the Commands menu.

✔ Tips

- Just because there's a history panel, doesn't mean you have to give up the Undo and Repeat commands you're used to. Choosing Edit > Undo or pressing ⌘-Z (Mac) or Ctrl-Z (Windows) undoes steps in order. Choose Edit > Repeat or pressing ⌘-Y or Ctrl-Y redoes your undone steps. You can even see the name of the step that will be undone or redone if you choose the command from the Edit menu. The results of your Undo or Repeat commands appear within the History panel as the undo/redo slider moves in response to the menu commands you issue.

- Previous versions of Flash offered a Redo command instead of Repeat. Redo restores whatever you undo with the Undo command. After choosing Edit > Undo, choosing Edit > Repeat also restores your work. But Repeat also does more; it allows you to apply your previous step to another object. For example, if you have two ovals on the Stage, and you drag one to a new position, you can drag the other by the same amount by selecting the second oval, then choosing Edit > Repeat.

To access the history panel:

1. Open a Flash Document.

2. From the window menu, choose Other Panels > History or press ⌘-F10 (Mac) or Ctrl-F10 (Windows).

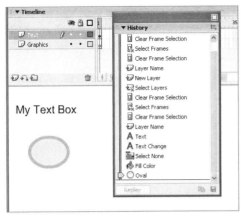

Figure 13.26 The first step you perform in a work session for a document appears at the top of the History panel, the last step appears at the bottom. The Oval step represents the creation of the oval graphic on the Stage.

Undoing/Redoing Steps via the History Panel

The History panel allows you to undo a series of steps in a single operation. Once you've undone them, you can just as easily redo them and restore the document to its previous state.

To undo a block of steps:

1. Open a Flash Document, and perform several simple operations.

   Add a layer so that the Timeline contains two layers; rename them Graphics and Text. Using the text tool, create a static text box on the Stage and type into it This is my text. Use the oval tool to create an oval shape; give it a different fill color and stroke color.

2. Access the History panel.

   The panel lists each of the steps you just performed (**Figure 13.26**). The steps appear in order from top (earliest) to bottom (most recent); a slider appears at the left side of the panel, with its lever pointing to the last step performed.

   continues on next page

3. In the History panel, to select the steps you wish to undo, *do one of the following:*

▲ Drag the undo/redo slider upwards until the lever points to the last step that you want to keep (**Figure 13.27**).

▲ Position the pointer in the gray area to the left of the last step that you want to keep. A tool tip appears with details about scripting for the step for that line in the panel. Click to make the slider's lever point to this step.

Flash grays out all the steps below the marked step, undoing each step in the document as it goes.

To redo a block of steps:

Continuing with the file from the preceding exercise, to select the steps you wish to redo, *do one of the following:*

◆ Drag the undo/redo slider lever downwards until it points to the last step that you want to redo.

◆ Position the pointer in the gray area to the left of the last step that you want to redo and click to make the slider's lever point to this step.

Flash removes the gray highlighting and redoes each step in your document as it goes.

Figure 13.27 To undo steps, drag the undo/redo slider upward in the History panel. Here undoing the Oval step removes the oval graphic from the Stage (top). Undoing more steps restores the default name to the layer that you added to the Timeline (bottom).

Replaying Steps via the History Panel

You can use the History panel's Replay feature both to redo steps that you've undone, and to perform repetitive actions multiple times. There are limits to which actions Flash can replay; any step listed in the History panel with a red X in its icon cannot be replayed (although it can be re*done* if you've undone it). The Replay procedure works well for step-and-repeat operations where you perform the same operation on copies of an object. For example, creating a sense of perspective by copying an object, offsetting the copy, and scaling it smaller each time.

To replay a set of steps:

1. Open a new Flash Document, and create an object that you want to use in a step-and-repeat operation.

   For this task, create a simple pine tree that you might add to a drawing of a road to create a sense of perspective. On the Stage, using the rectangle tool create a slender brown trunk; using the brush tool, add to it a green pine-tree top. Select the shapes and group them (choose Modify > Group).

2. Perform the repetitive operations.

   Select the grouped shapes. Choose Edit > Copy, then Edit > Paste in Place. To offset the copy, press Shift-up-arrow five times and Shift-right arrow five times. To scale the copy, access the Transform panel (if it's not open, choose Window > Design Panels > Transform), select Constrain, and in the Width (or Height) field enter 80 percent, press Return.

   continues on next page

3. Access the History panel and from its Options menu, choose View > Arguments in Panel.

All of the steps you just went through appear in the panel followed by the appropriate scripting arguments (**Figure 13.28**). Even if you know nothing about scripting, you may find it helpful to view the scripting arguments or JavaScript commands in the History panel because they give you a little more information about what each step is doing. If you prefer to see JavaScript, choose View > JavaScript in Panel.

4. To select the steps to replay, in the History panel, *do one of the following:*

▲ Click the Copy step, then Shift-click the Transform step.

▲ Shift click the Copy, Paste, Move, and Transform steps.

▲ Click and drag, starting with the Copy step and ending with the Transform step.

Flash highlights the selected steps in blue (**Figure 13.29**).

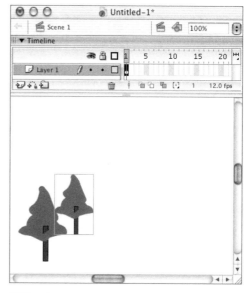

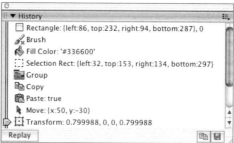

Figure 13.28 The steps you used to create, copy, and transform an object all appear in the History panel. You can select the Copy, Paste, Move, and Transform steps and replay them repeatedly.

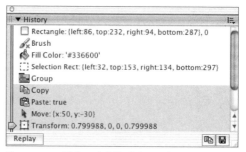

Figure 13.29 Click and shift-click to select a range of steps, or click and drag from the first step to the last step you want to select.

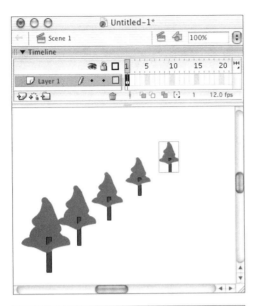

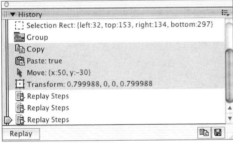

Figure 13.30 Replaying the steps to copy, paste, move, and scale-down a selected object creates a series of increasingly smaller versions of that object. Offsetting the objects up and over by a constant amount makes them appear to recede into the distance.

5. With the reduced copy of the pine tree selected on the Stage, click the Replay button in the History panel.

Flash applies all the steps to the selected object, copying it, offsetting it, and scaling it to 80 percent of its starting size. You can repeat the Replay a number of times to create a row of trees leading off into the distance (**Figure 13.30**).

✔ Tips

■ You can apply the same steps to a different object—use the drawing tools to create another tree, select that tree, and click the Replay button. You can even select multiple tree copies and press Replay to resize and offset them, thereby populating a whole forest with trees of different sizes.

■ You need not play an entire sequence of steps when you use Replay, you can skip steps. To select non-sequential steps, Shift-⌘-click (Mac) or Shift-Ctrl-click (Windows) the steps you want to include, then click the Replay button.

■ If you are performing many operations before you carry out the ones that you plan to replay, you can weed them out of the history panel. In the preceding exercise, for example, after you finish grouping the shapes for the pine tree, from the Options menu in the History panel, choose Clear History, a warning dialog appears notifying you that you can't undo *this* step. Click Yes to continue. Flash removes all previous steps from the History panel. Now it will be easy to find the step-and-repeat steps that you want to replay.

■ With all of the tracking that it does, the History panel consumes memory and disk space. You can also use the Options > Clear History command to make more memory and disk space available.

To replay steps in a different document:

1. Follow steps 1 through 4 in the preceding exercise.

   You have carried out several steps that you want to replay and selected them in the History panel.

2. To copy the steps, *do one of the following:*

   ▲ From the Options menu in the upper-right corner of the History panel, choose Copy Steps.

   ▲ Click the Copy Steps button in the lower-right corner of the panel.

3. Open another Flash Document.

   The History panel is blank; each document maintains its own history list.

4. Using the drawing tools, create a new graphic element on the Stage, for example, draw a simple oval.

5. Select the element.

6. To replay the steps you copied in step 2, choose Edit > Paste.

   Flash carries out the same copy, paste, move, and transform operations as in the preceding exercise. Note that the History panel for this document does not display a list of the steps you originally copied; it lists a single operation, Paste (**Figure 13.31**).

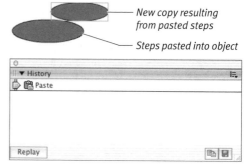

New copy resulting from pasted steps

Steps pasted into object

Figure 13.31 When you paste copied steps into an object in a new document, the History panel records a Paste operation, the panel does not re-list the steps originally copied.

✔ Tips

- When tracking the steps you made using the drawing and text tools, the History panel makes no record of the tools' attributes. If you replay such steps (or use them in a command, as in the following exercise), Flash simply uses the tool's current settings. For example, when you replay the steps for drawing an oval, Flash draws an oval with the original coordinates, but using the current fill color, stroke color, and stroke width settings. Always double-check a tool's attributes before replaying any steps using that tool.

- If you want to repeat the steps for drawing a shape with one of the geometric tools (oval, rectangle, or polystar) using specific fill and stroke attributes, first draw the shape using a fill or stroke you don't want. Then use the paint bucket and/or ink bottle tools to change the attributes. The History panel correctly records the drawing of the shape, and the application of the correct fill and stroke attributes. Now you can replay that whole sequence or save it as a command.

- When you click the Stage or work area to deselect everything, the History panel records a step Select None. If you click the Stage again, even though nothing is already selected, you record another Select None step.

Recording Steps with the History Panel

Copying and pasting steps from the History panel is one way to reuse your work, but when you close a document, Flash automatically clears all steps from the panel. To preserve steps for use in future work sessions, you need to save the history steps as a command. To get a feel for creating commands, try recording a simple repetitive task, such as creating and naming layers that you use often.

To save a set of steps as commands:

1. Open a new Flash Document and access the History panel.

The document contains one default layer, *Layer 1*.

2. With *Layer 1* selected, choose Modify > Timeline > Layer Properties.

3. In the Layer Properties dialog that appears, type Buttons in the Name field, and click OK.

4. Choose Insert > Timeline > Layer, to add a new layer and repeat steps 2 and 3 to rename this layer Text.

5. Repeat step 4 to create two more layers, renaming them Graphics and Actions.

The History panel should look like **Figure 13.32**.

6. Select all of the steps in the History panel. Click the first step, then Shift-click the last step to select them all.

7. To create the command, *do one of the following:*

▲ From the Options menu, choose Save as Command.

▲ Click the Save Selected Steps as Command button in the lower-right corner of the panel.

The Save As Command dialog appears.

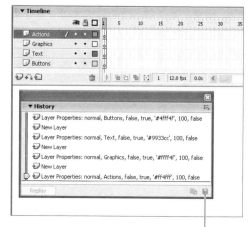

Save selected steps as command ⏤

Figure 13.32 This history panel shows the results of renaming and adding layers to a new Flash Document.

Figure 13.33 The Save As Command dialog allows you to name the command created from the steps highlighted in the History panel.

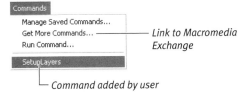

Figure 13.34 Any commands you create from the History panel appear in the Commands menu. This menu also provides a link to Macromedia's Flash Exchange area where you can download extensions created by other Flash authors.

8. In the Command Name field, type a name for your command.

For this example, type SetupLayers (**Figure 13.33**).

9. Click OK.

Flash adds your command to the Commands menu. The command will be available in any new documents you create.

To run a command:

1. Open a new Flash Document.

2. From the Commands menu, choose SetupLayers, the command you created in the preceding exercise (**Figure 13.34**). Flash replays the saved steps creating four layers in the document and naming them Buttons, Text, Graphics, and Actions.

✔ Tips

■ If at any point you want to get rid of commands that you've made, choose Commands > Manage Saved Commands. A dialog appears with options for renaming or deleting existing commands.

■ If you don't want to view arguments or JavaScript in the History panel itself, you can still view that information, as needed, in a tool tip. From the Options menu in the History panel, choose View > Arguments in Tool Tip (or View > JavaScript in Tool Tip). Now when you let the pointer hover over a step in the panel, you can view its arguments (or JavaScript commands). These tool tips appear regardless of whether or not you activate Show Tool tips in the General tab of the Preferences dialog.

The Quirks of Commands

Commands make use of Flash MX 2004's extensibility features. When you use the History panel to make a command, Flash translates the steps into JavaScript, creating a script that manipulates the Flash authoring environment. Although it's outside the scope of this book, anyone who knows JavaScript can edit those scripts, to make them work more effectively; JavaScript-savvy users can also create new scripts directly in JavaScript (see "The Mystery of Extensibility," in the Introduction).

Using the History panel alone to create commands can be a bit tricky. There are limitations to what you can do; many steps do not transfer directly into JavaScript via the History panel. (A red *X* in the icon of a step means that step cannot be replayed or saved as a command.) In addition, commands created via the History panel are literal-minded. Here's an example. If you make a selection by clicking an item, the History panel lists a step named Change Selection. You can replay that step, but Flash will make a selection only if there's something to select located at the exact coordinate where you clicked the first time. If you make a selection by choosing Edit > Select All, the History panel lists a step named Select All. You can replay that step, and Flash will select everything on the Stage, every time.

If you plan to replay steps, or turn them into a command, you need to think about how you perform them as you "record" them in the History panel. Still if you find yourself doing certain operations over and over again, it's worth examining the History panel to see if those steps make good candidates for commands.

USING
NON-FLASH GRAPHICS

Macromedia Flash MX 2004's drawing tools provide a lot of power, but that doesn't mean you have to abandon all other sources of graphic material. You may already be using another vector graphics program—Macromedia FreeHand or Adobe Illustrator, for example—and you may feel more comfortable with its tools or want to take advantage of some advanced features it offers. Or you may want to include scanned photos or other bitmaps in your Flash movie, or use a body of artwork that you created outside Flash. Don't despair; you can import those graphics into Flash.

Importing Non-Flash Graphics

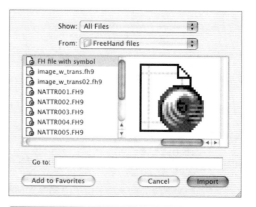

Flash imports vector art and bitmapped graphics either through the Clipboard or via the Import command. When you import graphics from FreeHand versions 7 through 10, and MX, you can also drag and drop elements directly between files.

If you use a program other than Flash to create a series of images that will be keyframes in a movie (a set of FreeHand files, for example), Flash can expedite the import process if the filenames end in a series of sequential numbers. (To learn more about keyframe animation, see Chapter 8.)

To import a FreeHand file to the Stage:

1. Open a Flash Document.

2. From the File menu, choose Import > Import to Stage.
   The Import dialog appears (**Figure 14.1**).

3. From the Show (Mac) or Files of Type (Windows) menu, choose the format of the file you want to import, FreeHand.

4. Navigate to the file on your system.

5. Select the file.

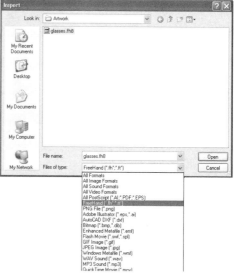

Figure 14.1 Bring graphics created in other applications into your Flash movie through the Import dialog: Mac (top), Windows (bottom).

IMPORTING NON-FLASH GRAPHICS

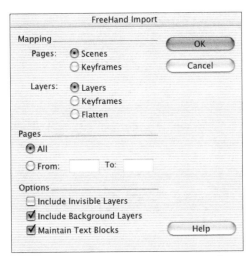

Figure 14.2 When you import files from FreeHand versions 7 through 10 and MX, you have control over how the elements appear in the Flash document.

The Flash/FreeHand Partnership

Although not all features of other vector programs translate directly into Flash, there are strong ties between Flash and Macromedia FreeHand versions 7 through 10 and MX. You can import the full FreeHand file, copy selected FreeHand content via the Clipboard and paste it on the Stage in Flash, and drag content from an open FreeHand file directly onto the Stage in Flash.

When you choose File > Import > Import to Stage, the FreeHand Import dialog appears, giving you a chance to control the way that content appears in the Flash document. In addition, if you are importing FreeHand 9, 10, or MX files that contain symbols, Flash automatically adds those symbols to the Flash document's library.

6. Click Import (Mac) or Open (Windows).

First, the Importing External File dialog appears, with a Stop button for canceling the operation. Then, the FreeHand Import dialog appears (**Figure 14.2**).

7. In the Mapping section, to convert the FreeHand file's pages and layers to Flash format, *do one of the following:*

▲ To create a new scene from each FreeHand page, in the Pages subsection, choose Scenes.

▲ To create a new keyframe from each FreeHand page, in the Pages subsection, choose Keyframes.

▲ To create a new layer from each FreeHand layer, in the Layers subsection, choose Layers.

▲ To create a new keyframe from each FreeHand layer, in the Layers subsection, choose Keyframes.

▲ To combine multiple FreeHand layers into one layer, in the Layers subsection, choose Flatten.

8. In the Pages section, to select the pages to import, *do one of the following:*

▲ To import the entire FreeHand file, choose All.

▲ To import a range of pages from the FreeHand file, choose From/To and then enter the first and last page number.

continues on next page

IMPORTING NON-FLASH GRAPHICS

9. In the Options section, *do one of the following:*

▲ To import any hidden layers from the FreeHand file, choose Include Invisible Layers.

▲ To import the background layer of the FreeHand file, choose Include Background Layers.

▲ To have Flash create editable text blocks from any FreeHand text blocks, choose Maintain Text Blocks. Otherwise, Flash imports the text characters as grouped shapes.

10. Click OK.

The Importing External File dialog appears, with a Stop button for canceling the operation. Flash imports the FreeHand graphics and places them on the Stage creating layers and/or keyframes in the main Timeline of your document according to the import options you selected (**Figure 14.3**).

✔ Tips

■ If your FreeHand file contains a set of overlapping objects on a single layer, those elements will segment themselves, just as they would in Flash. To keep objects distinct, be sure to place them on multiple layers in FreeHand; then when importing, choose Mapping: Layers: Layers in Flash's FreeHand Import dialog.

■ If you import a FreeHand file containing objects that have transparent lens fills, Flash sets the imported objects' transparency to re-create the transparent effect.

■ Flash supports only eight-color gradient fills. If you import FreeHand objects that have gradients with more colors, Flash adds clipping paths to simulate the gradient, which increases the file size. For best results, when creating FreeHand gradient fills, restrict yourself to eight color changes.

Imported layers

Figure 14.3 Flash imports files from FreeHand versions 7 through 10 and MX according to the settings in the FreeHand Import dialog. Here, the import options were set to include the background layer.

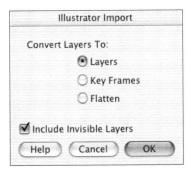

Figure 14.4 The Illustrator Import dialog offers options for dealing with the layers of an original .ai file created in Illustrator 8 or earlier.

To import Adobe Illustrator (.ai, version 8 or earlier), files to the Stage:

1. With your Flash Document open, from the File menu, choose Import > Import to Stage.

   The Import dialog appears.

2. From the Show (Mac) or Files of Type (Windows) menu, *choose one of the following:*

   ▲ All PostScript. This setting displays files with the extensions .ai, .pdf, and .eps.

   ▲ Adobe Illustrator. This setting displays files with the extensions .ai and .eps.

3. Navigate to the file, select it, and Click Import (Mac) or Open (Windows).

   The Illustrator Import dialog appears (**Figure 14.4**).

4. In the Convert Layers To section, *do one of the following:*

   ▲ To re-create the layers in the original file, choose Layers.

   ▲ To convert the layers to keyframes, choose Key Frames.

   ▲ To place all the graphics on one layer, choose Flatten.

5. To import any invisible layers, check the Include Invisible Layers check box.

6. Click OK.

To import Adobe Illustrator (.ai, version 9 or later), Portable Document Format (.pdf) or Encapsulated PostScript (.eps) files to the Stage:

1. Follow steps 1 through 3 in the preceding exercise.

   The Import Options dialog appears (**Figure 14.5**). Note that to view .pdf files, you should select All PostScript in step 3.

2. In the Convert Pages To section, *do one of the following:*

   ▲ To make each page a new scene, choose Scenes.

   ▲ To make each page a new keyframe, choose Keyframes.

3. In the Convert Layers To section, *do one of the following:*

   ▲ To re-create the layers in the original file, choose Layers.

   ▲ To convert the layers to keyframes, choose Keyframes.

   ▲ To place all the graphics on one layer, choose Flatten.

4. In the Which Pages to Import section, *do one of the following:*

   ▲ To import all pages, choose All.

   ▲ To import a selected page range, choose From/To and enter the first and last page number.

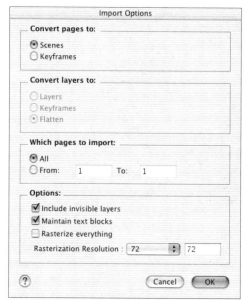

Figure 14.5 When you import an .ai (created in Illustrator 9 or later), .eps or .pdf file, you have more control over the import than with earlier .ai files, choosing how to handle pages, layers, invisible layers, and text blocks. You can also rasterize the imported text and graphic elements and set the resolution of the resulting images.

What Graphics Formats Does Flash Import?

Flash imports a variety of bitmapped and vector-graphic file formats. For bitmaps, Flash accepts files in GIF, animated GIF, PNG, JPEG, and BMP (Windows) formats. For vector graphics, Flash accepts files from FreeHand versions 7 through 10,and MX; Illustrator version 10.0 and earlier; .eps, and .pdf files in version 1.4 or earlier (Adobe Acrobat 5.0, for example, creates version 1.4 .pdf files). Flash also accepts files in PICT (Mac) and in WMF and EMF (Windows).

When Flash imports graphics in a format that includes transparency, Flash preserves the transparency. Transparent areas of a GIF image, for example, have an alpha value of 0 when imported into Flash. When it imports PICTs or PNGs with alpha channels, Flash correctly reads the transparency values of the alpha channel.

Flash can also import AutoCAD DXF files from version 10.

Flash works with Apple's QuickTime 4 (or a later version) to import additional file formats. Both Mac and Windows users who have the Flash MX/QuickTime 4 combination can import files in Photoshop, QuickTime Image, QuickTime Movie, Silicon Graphics Image, TGA, TIFF, and MacPaint formats. In addition, Windows users can import PICT files as bitmaps and Mac users can import BMP files.

5. In the Options section, *do one of the following:*

   ▲ To import any invisible layers, choose Include Invisible Layers.

   ▲ To import text into editable, static text boxes, choose Maintain Text Blocks.

   ▲ To convert all graphic and text elements into bitmaps, choose Rasterize Everything and enter the Rasterization Resolution, either by selecting a value from the pop-up menu, or by typing the value into the field.

6. Click OK.

✔ Tip

■ You can have Flash import a file directly to the library, creating a graphic symbol, instead of placing the graphic on the Stage. You simply choose File > Import > Import to Library. The import options for each file type are the same whether you import to the Stage or to the library. When you import a vector graphic to the library, however, Flash places the graphic within a symbol in the library and places nothing on the Stage. Any layers and keyframes that you request in the Import Options dialog appear in the symbol's Timeline not in the main Timeline.

IMPORTING NON-FLASH GRAPHICS

To import bitmapped graphics to the Stage:

◆ Follow steps 1 through 3 of the first exercise in this section, choosing the bitmap format of your choice in step 3.

There are no special import options for bitmaps, Flash imports the file you selected into your document, storing a master bitmap asset in the library and placing an instance of the bitmap on the Stage in the active layer (**Figure 14.6**).

✔ Tip

■ You can edit an imported bitmap in its creator program, if that program is installed on your system; or you can use any installed bitmap-editing program. Select the bitmap in the Library window, Control-click (Mac) or right-click (Windows) the bitmap icon, and choose Edit With from the contextual menu. (If the creator program is present, it will appear as a menu choice.) In the window that opens, navigate to an editing program and click Open to launch it. The selected bitmap opens in the external program. When you save the bitmap file, Flash updates the imported image in your library.

To import a series of graphics files to the Stage:

1. Follow steps 1 through 6 of the first exercise in this section. In step 3, choose the appropriate format and navigate to the first file in the series.

A dialog appears, asking whether you want to import what looks like a series of sequential images (**Figure 14.7**). Flash recognizes files that form a sequence if they are all within a single folder and have filenames that differ only in the number at the end of the filename—for example, bounce1, bounce2, and bounce3.

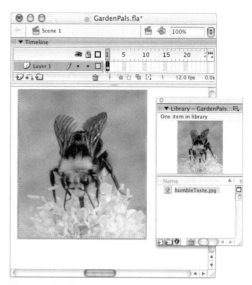

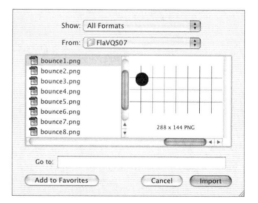

Figure 14.6 When you import a bitmap to the Stage, Flash also stores a master copy of the bitmap in the library.

Figure 14.7 When you import one file in a series of numbered files (top), Flash asks whether you want to import the whole series (bottom).

IMPORTING NON-FLASH GRAPHICS

Preview mode shows
images in keyframes

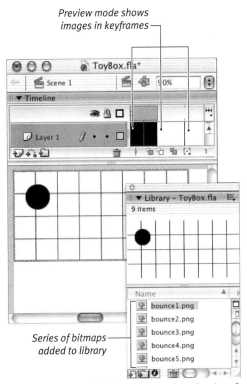

Series of bitmaps
added to library

Figure 14.8 When Flash imports a numbered series of files, it places each one in a separate keyframe in the Timeline of the current document.

2. In the dialog, click Yes.

Flash places each image in a separate keyframe in the active layer (**Figure 14.8**).

✔ Tips

- You can also bring bitmaps and vector graphics into Flash via the Clipboard. Open the original graphic and copy it, using the procedures appropriate to the creator application. Open your Flash document and choose Edit > Paste in Center. If the graphic is a bitmap, Flash pastes it on the Stage as a group; Flash also places it in the library. If the graphic is a vector, Flash places it on the Stage as a grouped element. When you import multiple items, Flash brings each one in as a separate group. Flash does not add imported vectors to the library.

- To preserve individual text boxes from FreeHand versions 7 through 10 and MX as editable text when importing through the Clipboard, choose Flash > Preferences (Mac) or Edit > Preferences (Windows); in the Preferences dialog, click the Clipboard tab; in the FreeHand Text section, choose Maintain Text As Blocks. Otherwise, Flash imports each character in a text block as a grouped shape and groups those groups.

- Copy and paste is not the most reliable process for importing graphics into Flash. Vector graphics in particular may lose something in translation when they go through the Clipboard. If you have trouble using the Clipboard with a particular item, try saving the file that contains the graphic in one of the formats that Flash imports and then bringing the whole file in with the Import command. You can always delete any portions of the file you don't want to use in Flash.

Turning Bitmaps into Vector Graphics

After you import a bitmap into a Flash file, you can trace the bitmap to turn it into a set of vector shapes that look like the bitmap. Flash offers several parameters to help you strike a balance between the accurate rendering of the various color areas in the bitmap and the creation of too many curves and small vectors within one object, which increases the file size.

To trace a bitmap:

1. Place a copy of the bitmap on the Stage.

2. Select the bitmap.

3. From the Modify menu, choose Bitmap > Trace Bitmap (**Figure 14.9**).

    The Trace Bitmap dialog appears (**Figure 14.10**).

4. Enter values for the four parameters in the dialog: Color Threshold, Minimum Area, Curve Fit, and Corner Threshold.

    The parameters in this dialog control how closely the vector image matches the bitmapped image. Flash creates the vectors by examining the pixels that make up the bitmap, lumping together contiguous pixels that are the same color and making a vector shape out of that clump.

    Color Threshold (a number between 1 and 500) tells Flash how to decide when one pixel is the same color as its neighbor. The higher the threshold, the broader the range of colors Flash lumps together. A sky made up of light and dark blue pixels in three slightly different shades, for example, might wind up as one vector shape if you set a high-enough threshold but might wind up as dozens of separate shapes if you set a low threshold.

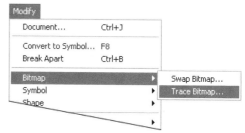

Figure 14.9 Choose Modify > Bitmap > Trace Bitmap to convert a bitmap to a group of vector shapes.

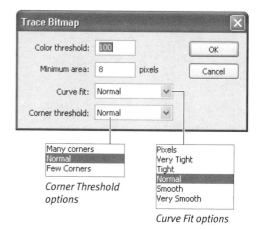

Figure 14.10 The Trace Bitmap dialog controls how Flash converts bitmaps to vectors.

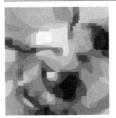

Figure 14.11 These tracings use different settings. The top one closely imitates the original bitmap; the bottom one has a posterized effect but ends up at a much smaller file size.

Minimum Area (a number between 1 and 1,000) determines how many neighbor pixels to include in calculating the color.

Curve Fit tells Flash how smoothly to draw the outlines around the vector shapes it creates.

Corner Threshold tells Flash whether to create sharp corners or smoother, more rounded ones.

5. Click OK.

The Tracing Bitmap dialog appears, with a progress bar and a Stop button. (To cancel the tracing process, click Stop.)

Flash replaces the bitmap with filled vector shapes that imitate the image (**Figure 14.11**).

✔ Tip

■ For tracing bitmaps that are scans of photographs, Macromedia recommends settings of 10 for Color Threshold, 1 for Minimum Area, Pixels for Curve Fit, and Many Corners for Corner Threshold. These settings can result in really huge files, however.

TURNING BITMAPS INTO VECTOR GRAPHICS

Editing Bitmaps with Flash's Tools

You can always edit bitmaps with an external bitmap editor, but Flash also lets you create a version of a bitmap that you can edit (to a certain degree) within Flash. First, you break the image apart; next, use the magic-wand tool to select a region of color within the image; and finally, use Flash's drawing tools to edit that region.

To create a bitmap that you can edit in Flash:

1. Create a new Flash Document.

2. Import a bitmapped graphic, using the procedures in "Importing Non-Flash Graphics" earlier in this chapter.

   An instance of the bitmap appears on the Stage, and Flash adds the bitmap to the library.

3. Select the bitmap instance on the Stage.

4. From the Modify menu, choose Break Apart (**Figure 14.12**).

   Flash converts the bitmap to a special type of graphic and selects it (**Figure 14.13**). Flash has no specific name for this type of graphic, but let's call it an *editable bitmap*. An editable bitmap is no longer a collection of individual pixels, each with its own color value; neither is it a collection of tiny vector shapes.

   A bitmap you've broken apart acts more or less like a single vector shape with a gradient fill. (Macromedia describes this state as being a number of discrete color areas.) If you click any area of the image now, you select the entire image.

   Try selecting the paint bucket tool and setting the fill color to solid red; click the image, and it becomes a red rectangle. Don't forget to undo your experiment.

Figure 14.12 The first step toward editing a bitmap with Flash's tools is to select an instance of bitmap on the Stage; then choose Modify > Break Apart.

Figure 14.13 The Break Apart command converts the bitmap instance to an editable bitmap. The editable bitmap acts like a gradient fill in that it's not a single color, but the various color areas are not vector shapes.

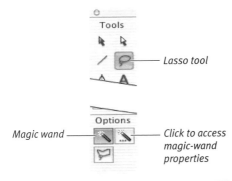

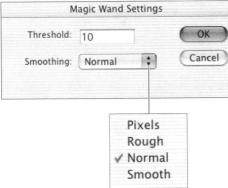

Figure 14.14 The Magic Wand modifier of the lasso tool allows you to select regions of color within an editable bitmap.

The Mystery of the Magic Wand

With the magic wand tool, clicking a pixel within a bitmap that's been broken apart selects that pixel and any pixels of the "same" color that touch it.

The magic wand's Threshold setting determines how different two colors can be and still have Flash consider them to be the same color.

After you've made a magic wand selection, you can fill that selection with a single color. The filled region becomes an editable vector shape.

To select a range of colors within an editable bitmap:

1. Following the steps in the preceding exercise, create an editable bitmap.

2. Deselect the editable bitmap.

3. In the Toolbar, select the lasso tool.

4. Select the Magic Wand Properties modifier (**Figure 14.14**).

   The Magic Wand Settings dialog appears.

5. In the dialog, enter the settings for Threshold and Smoothing.

   The Threshold setting works the same way as the Color Threshold setting in the Trace Bitmap dialog (described earlier in this chapter). Smoothing works similarly to the Curve Fit setting of the Trace Bitmap dialog; it determines how smooth a vector path Flash draws when the magic wand makes a selection.

6. Click OK.

7. Select Magic Wand mode in the Toolbar.

8. On the Stage, position the pointer over the editable bitmap.

   The pointer changes to a magic-wand icon. The tool's hot spot is the transparent area in the center of the starburst.

continues on next page

9. Click a pixel in the region you want to select.

Flash selects that pixel and all the surrounding pixels that fall within the threshold you chose (**Figure 14.15**).

✔ Tips

■ Once you've selected a region of similar colors, you can turn the selection into a solid fill shape. With the selection active in the editable bitmap, select a new fill color from any fill-color box, for example, the one on the Toolbar. The selection changes to the new color. This fill creates a solid vector shape that you can edit with Flash's tools.

■ If the magic wand fails to grab the full range of colors you wanted, change Threshold to a higher number and try again. You can also add to the selection by clicking (or Shift-clicking, depending on your Preferences setting) the missed pixels.

■ You can use the magic wand to reduce the number of colors in an editable bitmap. Keep selecting regions of similar colors and filling them with solid color until the entire bitmapped fill consists of vector shapes filled with solid colors. Use higher Threshold settings to gather more colors in each selection. If you were to select and convert all the color regions in the editable bitmap to vector shapes, the result would be something like tracing a bitmap.

■ If you select a broken apart bitmap with the eyedropper tool, to use it as a tiling fill, Flash still uses the original bitmap as the tiling fill. It brings the tiles in at full size, however. When you select the bitmap as a fill in the Color Mixer, the tiles are tiny.

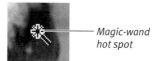

Magic-wand hot spot

Click to Select

Selection with threshold of 10

Selection with threshold of 55

Figure 14.15 Click with the magic wand's hot spot to select a region of color. The Threshold setting in the Magic Wand Settings dialog determines how large a color range the magic wand grabs.

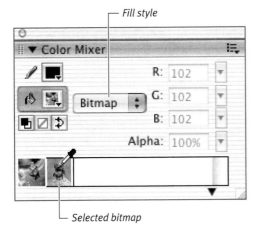

Fill style

Selected bitmap

Figure 14.16 Select Bitmap in the Fill Style menu of the Color Mixer panel to see bitmap thumbnails.

Using Bitmaps As Fills

You can create bitmap fills in two ways: by using the bitmaps that live in the library or by using editable bitmaps. When you select a bitmap as a fill, Flash turns it into a repeating, or *tiling*, pattern within the area it fills.

You can use bitmap fills with any of the drawing tools that create fills: the oval, rectangle, polystar, pen, paintbrush, and paint bucket tools.

To apply a bitmap fill from the Color Mixer:

1. Open a new Flash Document.

2. On the Stage, create a shape with a solid fill, using the oval, rectangle, polystar, pen, or paintbrush tool.

3. Access the Color Mixer panel.

   If the panel is not already open, choose Window > Design Panels > Color Mixer.

4. From the Fill Style menu, choose Bitmap.

   Flash replaces the panel's color-definition bar with a window displaying thumbnails of all the bitmaps in the current document's library. If the library contains no bitmaps, Flash opens the Import to Library dialog so that you can import one.

5. Position the pointer over one of the thumbnails.

   The pointer changes to the eyedropper tool (**Figure 14.16**).

6. Click the bitmap thumbnail you want to use.

   Flash makes the bitmap the current fill selection in all the fill-color boxes, for example, the one on the Toolbar. You are ready to use the bitmap fill as you would any other fill color.

   continues on next page

7. In the Toolbar, select the paint bucket; position the paint bucket over the shape you created in step 2; then click.

Flash fills your shape with a tiling pattern made from the bitmap you selected (**Figure 14.17**).

To apply an editable-bitmap as a fill:

1. On the Stage, create a shape with a solid fill using the oval, rectangle, polystar, pen, or paintbrush tool.

2. Create an editable bitmap, following the steps in "Editing Bitmaps with Flash's Tools" earlier in this chapter.

3. In the Toolbar, select the eyedropper tool.

4. Position the eyedropper over the editable bitmap on the Stage (**Figure 14.18**).

5. Click anywhere within the editable bitmap.

In the Toolbar, Flash makes the bitmap the current fill selection and selects the paint bucket tool.

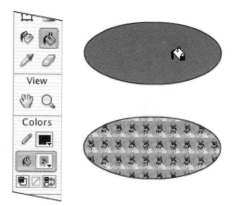

Figure 14.17 With the bitmap fill selected as the fill "color," click the item you want to fill with the bitmap pattern (top). Flash fills the shape with repeating tiles of the bitmap (bottom).

Figure 14.18 Use the eyedropper tool to pick up an editable bitmap as the fill "color."

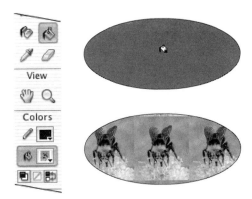

Figure 14.19 When you sample an editable bitmap with the eyedropper tool, Flash makes the bitmap the current fill color and selects the paint bucket tool. Click the item you want to fill with the bit-mapped pattern (top). Flash fills the shape with repeating tiles of the editable bitmap (bottom).

6. Position the paint bucket over the fill shape you created in step 1, then click.

Flash fills your shape with a tiling pattern made from the editable bitmap (**Figure 14.19**).

✔ Tip

■ Any of the tools that create fill shapes can create shapes with the bitmap fill as the chosen "color." Try, for example, selecting the paintbrush tool in the Toolbar, then select a bitmap as the fill following the steps in either of the preceding exercises. Paint a shape on the Stage. The brushstrokes you create fill with the tiling pattern. You can use the filled oval, rectangle, polystar, and pen tools this way, too.

Modifying Bitmap Fills

You can modify—scale, rotate, and skew—bitmap fills the same way you would modify gradient fills.

To move a bitmap fill's center point:

1. Following the steps in the preceding exercises, create a shape and assign a fill to it, either from the Color Mixer or by sampling an editable-bitmap.

2. In the Toolbar, select the fill-transform tool (**Figure 14.20**).

   The pointer changes to the fill-transform arrow.

3. Position the pointer over the shape with the bitmap fill you want to modify.

4. Click.

   Handles for manipulating the fill appear around one tile of the fill (**Figure 14.21**).

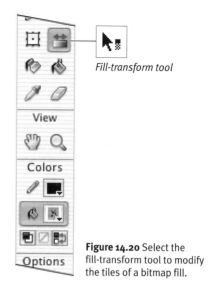

Fill-transform tool

Figure 14.20 Select the fill-transform tool to modify the tiles of a bitmap fill.

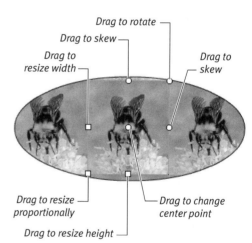

Drag to rotate
Drag to skew
Drag to resize width
Drag to skew
Drag to resize proportionally
Drag to change center point
Drag to resize height

Figure 14.21 Clicking the bitmap fill pattern with the fill-transform tool brings up handles for modifying the tiles.

Preview of tile's new position

Center point

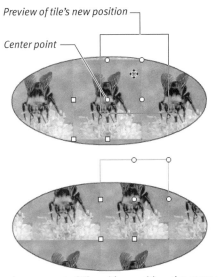

Arrangement of tiles with repositioned center point

Figure 14.22 Drag the center point of the selected tile to change the way the tiling pattern fits within the object.

Preview of new tile height

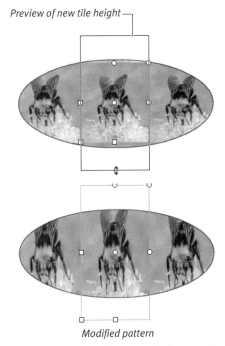

Modified pattern

Figure 14.23 Drag the handle on the bottom edge of the tile to make the tile taller or shorter.

5. Drag the center-point handle to reposition the center point of the fill (**Figure 14.22**).

Repositioning the center point changes the way the tiling pattern fits within your shape.

✔ Tip

■ When you choose a bitmap fill from the Color Mixer panel, the resulting tiles can be quite small. When you select one with the fill-transform tool, the transform handles stack up one on top of another, making it difficult to modify the tile. To make the handles more accessible, choose a larger magnification for viewing the Stage.

To resize a bitmap fill:

1. Follow steps 1 through 4 of the preceding exercise.

2. To change the height of the bitmap tiles, drag the square handle at the bottom edge of the tile (**Figure 14.23**).

The pointer changes to a double-headed arrow. Dragging toward the center of the tile makes all the tiles shorter; dragging away from the center of the tile makes all the tiles taller.

3. To change the width of the bitmap tiles, drag the square handle on the left side of the tile.

The pointer changes to a double-headed arrow. Dragging toward the center of the tile makes all the tiles narrower; dragging away from the center of the tile makes all the tiles wider.

continues on next page

4. To change the size of the bitmap tiles proportionally, drag the square handle at the bottom-left corner of the tile.

The pointer changes to a double-headed arrow. Dragging toward the center of the tile makes all the tiles smaller; dragging away from the center of the tile makes all the tiles larger.

✔ Tips

- You can also rotate and skew the bitmap tiles. With the fill-transform tool selected, click the shape whose bitmap fill you want to modify. The modification handles appear. To rotate the tiles, drag the round handle in the top-right corner. The pointer changes to a circular arrow. You can rotate the tiles clockwise or counterclockwise. To skew the tiles, drag the round handle on the right side or top edge .The pointer changes to a double-headed arrow indicating the direction of the skew.

- If you skew, scale, and/or rotate an editable bitmap (a bitmap that you've broken apart), instead of skewing and scaling tiles within the filled shape, you can save your modifications for later use. Select the modified bitmap; then choose Insert > Convert to Symbol. When you need that fill again, drag an instance of the symbol to the Stage, break it apart, and sample it again with the eyedropper tool. Flash makes that fill the active one in the fill-color box.

ADDING SOUND

It's amazing how much a classic silent film conveys with just moving pictures and text, but that era is history. Audio is a vital feature of today's Web sites. In Macromedia Flash, you can incorporate sound in your projects, either as an ongoing background element or as a synchronized element that matches a particular piece of action—say, a slapping sound that accompanies a pair of hands clapping.

Using Sounds in Flash

To add sound to Flash movies, you must import the sound clips to the library and then attach instances of the sound clips to keyframes. You access sounds and control synchronization of sounds via the Property Inspector that appears when you select a frame. You can also call up Flash's simple sound-editing tools through this Frame Property Inspector.

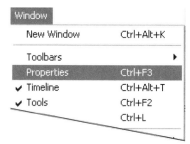

Figure 15.1 You access Flash's sound tools from the Property Inspector for frames. Select a frame in the Timeline, then choose Window > Properties to open the Property Inspector.

To access the Frame Property Inspector:

◆ If the Frame Property Inspector is not currently active, from the Window menu, choose Properties (**Figure 15.1**).

The Frame Property Inspector opens or comes to the front if other panels are on top of it (**Figure 15.2**).

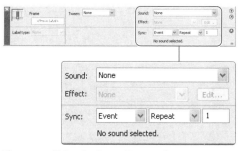

Figure 15.2 Using the Frame Property Inspector, you can attach sounds to keyframes, set synchronization, and perform simple sound-editing operations. Some sound tools are always visible on the right side of the panel. To view all the tools, click the triangle in the bottom-right corner of the panel to expand it.

Flash Sound Features

Flash deals only with *sampled* sounds—those that have been recorded digitally or converted to digital format. Flash imports AIFF-format files for the Mac OS, WAV-format files for Windows, and MP3-format files for both platforms. In addition, with the combination of Flash MX and QuickTime 4 (or later versions), users on both platforms can import QuickTime movies containing sounds and Sun AU files; Mac users can import WAV, Sound Designer II, and System 7 sounds; and Windows users can import AIFF sounds. Any sounds you import or copy into a Flash document reside in the file's library.

Flash offers a limited form of sound editing. You can clip the ends off a sound and adjust its volume, but you must do other kinds of sound editing outside Flash.

When you publish your finished movie, pay attention to the sampling rate and compression of sounds to balance sound quality with the file size of your finished movie. You learn more about these considerations in Chapter 17.

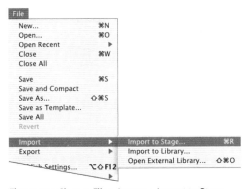

Figure 15.3 Choose File > Import > Import to Stage (or Import to Library) to bring sounds into your Flash Document.

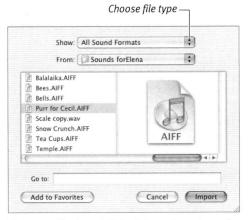

Choose file type

Figure 15.4 The Import dialog lets you import sound files into Flash. Choose the sound-file type that is appropriate for your platform from the pop-up menu of file types.

Importing Sounds

The procedure for importing sounds is just like the procedure for importing bitmaps or other artwork: You use the File > Import > Import to Stage or File > Import > Import to Library command. Flash brings the sound file into the library for the current document, and you drag a copy of the sound from the Library window into a specific keyframe.

To import a sound file:

1. Open the file to which you want to add sounds.

2. From the File menu, choose Import > Import to Stage or press ⌘-R (Mac) or Ctrl-R (Windows) (**Figure 15.3**).

   You can also choose File > Import > Import to Library. The standard file-import dialog appears (**Figure 15.4**).

3. From the Show pop-up menu (Mac) or the Files of Type pop-up menu (Windows), choose the format of the sound file that you want to import.

   Choose All Sound Formats to see files in any sound format.

   continues on next page

4. Navigate to the sound file on your system.

5. Select the file.

6. Click Import (Mac) or Open (Windows).

Flash imports the sound file that you selected, placing it in the library. The waveform of the sound appears in the Library preview window (**Figure 15.5**).

✔ Tips

- For imported graphics, the File > Import > Import to Stage command actually places an instance on the Stage in the selected keyframe. For sounds imported to Flash, that's not true, the imported sounds wind up in the Library; you must place them in the keyframe yourself.

- You can hear a sound without placing it in a movie. Select the sound in the Library window. Flash displays the waveform in the preview window. To hear the sound, click the Play button in the preview window.

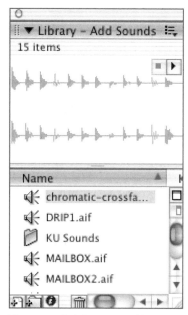

Figure 15.5 Flash keeps sound files in the library, giving each file a separate sound-file icon. You can see the waveform for a selected sound in the preview window. Click the Play button to hear the sound.

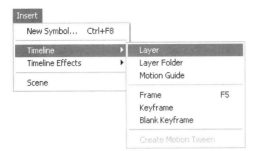

Figure 15.6 It's best to keep sounds in separate layers from the graphics and actions in your movie. To add a new layer, choose Insert > Timeline > Layer.

Organizing Sounds

Nothing prevents you from adding sounds in layers that contain other content, but your document will be easier to handle—and sounds will be easier to find for updating and editing—if you always put sounds in separate layers reserved just for your sound-track. Flash can handle up to eight sounds playing at one time.

To add a layer for sound:

1. Open a new Flash Document, or open an existing one to which you want to add sound.

2. In the Timeline, select a layer.

3. *Do one of the following:*

   ▲ From the Insert menu, choose Timeline > Layer (**Figure 15.6**).

   ▲ In the Timeline, click the Add Layer button.

   Flash always adds the new layer directly above the selected layer.

4. Drag the layer to the desired position in the layer stacking order.

   The position in the stacking order of layers has no effect on the playback of sounds in the movie, but you may find it helpful to place all your sound layers at either the bottom of the layers or at the top so that you can find them easily.

5. Rename the layer.

   For detailed instructions on working with layers, see Chapter 5.

ORGANIZING SOUNDS

✔ Tips

- After you've placed sounds in a layer, you can lock the layer—to prevent yourself from adding graphics to it accidentally—by clicking the bullet in the column below the padlock icon.

- If you will be working with numerous sound layers, add a layer folder, and name it *SoundTracks*. Drag every sound layer into the *SoundTracks* folder (**Figure 15.7**).

- The default layer height is 100 percent; increasing the height for sound layers makes it a bit easier to see the waveform (a graphic image of the sound) for that layer. From the Modify menu, choose Timeline > Layer (or double-click the layer icon of the selected layer) to access the Layer Properties dialog. From the Layer Height pop-up menu, choose 200% or 300% to make the layer taller. Click OK.

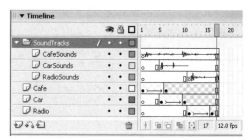

Figure 15.7 To organize multiple sound layers, place them in a separate layer folder.

ORGANIZING SOUNDS

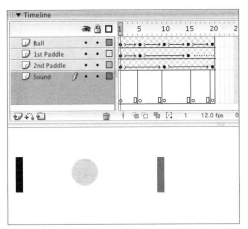

Figure 15.8 Create a separate layer for the sounds in your movie. In that layer, add a separate keyframe at each place where you want a sound to occur. Here, the keyframes in the *Sound* layer correspond to the keyframes in other layers where the ball makes contact with a paddle.

Adding Sounds to Frames

You can assign a sound to a keyframe the same way that you place a symbol or bitmap: by selecting the keyframe and then dragging a copy of the sound from an open Library window (either that document's or another's) to the Stage. You can also assign any sound that resides in a document's library to a selected keyframe in that document by choosing the sound from the Sound pop-up menu in the Frame Property Inspector.

To assign a sound to a keyframe:

1. Open a Flash Document to which you want to add sound.

   The Ping-Pong animation that you created in Chapter 10 makes a good practice file. The movie contains four keyframes in which a ball connects with a paddle. Adding sound can heighten the reality of that contact: You can make the sound realistic (say, a small *thwock*) or make it humorous, if the sound is unexpected (a *boing*, for example).

2. Add a new layer for the sounds in your document.

   For more detailed instructions, follow the steps in "Organizing Sounds" earlier in this chapter.

3. Name the layer *Sound*.

4. In the Timeline, select the *Sound* layer, and add keyframes at frames 5, 10, 15, and 20.

   These four keyframes match the keyframes in the animation in which the ball hits one of the paddles (**Figure 15.8**).

continues on next page

5. Import the sound you want to hear when the paddle connects with the ball.

For more detailed instructions, follow the steps in "Importing Sounds" earlier in this chapter. If you do not have your own stock of sound clips, you can download a sound clip named BallHit from the companion Web site for this book. (Click the *Files* link on *http://www.peachpit.com/vqs/flashmx2004/* to find the materials for this chapter.)

6. In the Timeline, select Keyframe 5 of the *Sound* layer.

This is the first frame in which the ball and paddle connect.

7. Access the Library window and select your sound (**Figure 15.9**).

Its waveform appears in the preview window.

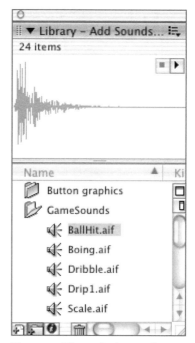

Figure 15.9 After you've imported a sound, it appears in the Library window. Select the sound to add it to a keyframe.

ADDING SOUNDS TO FRAMES

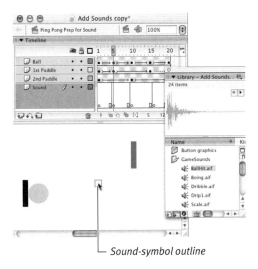

Sound-symbol outline

Waveform of sound
assigned to Keyframe 5

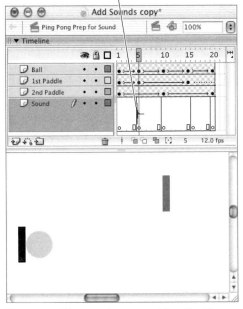

Figure 15.10 When you drag a sound from the Library window to the Stage, you see the symbol outline (top). A sound has no visible presence on the Stage, but Flash displays the sound's waveform in the Timeline (bottom).

8. Drag a copy of the sound from the Library window to the Stage.

Although sounds have no visible presence on the Stage, you must drag the sound copy to the Stage. As you drag the sound, you see the outline of a box on the Stage. When you release the mouse button, Flash puts the sound in the selected keyframe and displays the waveform in that keyframe and any in-between frames associated with it (**Figure 15.10**).

9. In the Timeline, select Keyframe 10 of the *Sound* layer.

This is the second frame in which the ball and paddle connect.

10. Access the Frame Property Inspector.

continues on next page

11. From the Sound pop-up menu, choose your sound.

All the sounds in the movie's library are available from the Frame Property Inspector's Sound pop-up menu (**Figure 15.11**). You don't have to drag a copy of the sound to the Stage each time you want to turn that sound on in a keyframe.

For now, leave the other settings in the Frame Property Inspector alone. You learn more about them in later tasks.

12. Repeat steps 7 and 8 (or 9, 10, and 11) for keyframes 15 and 20.

After adding the sound to the four keyframes, you are ready to play the movie and check out the sounds (**Figure 15.12**). As each paddle strikes the ball, Flash plays the assigned sound, adding a level of realism to your simple Ping-Pong animation.

✔ Tip

■ If you want to try adding sounds to your Flash projects, but don't have the equipment to record your own, there are lots of copyright-free sounds available. You can purchase CDs of sounds for use in projects; there are also online sites with downloadable sounds. Just make sure that the sounds are copyright free before you download them for use in your own project.

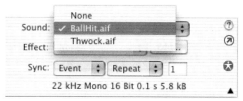

Figure 15.11 In the Frame Property Inspector, the Sound pop-up menu lists all the sounds that are in the library of the current document. From this menu, you can choose a sound that you want to assign to the keyframe that's selected in the Timeline.

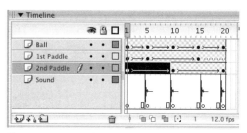

Figure 15.12 For each spot in the movie where a sound should occur, add a sound to a keyframe in the sound layer.

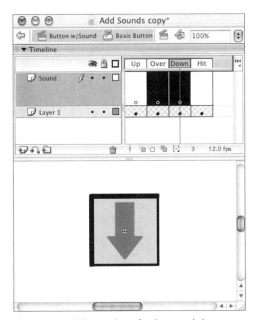

Figure 15.13 Add a new layer for the sounds in a button symbol, and create keyframes at the points where you plan to assign sounds.

Adding Sounds to Buttons

Auditory feedback helps people who view your Flash creation interact with buttons correctly. For buttons that look like real-world buttons, adding a click sound to the Down frame provides a more realistic feel. For more fanciful buttons or ones disguised as part of the scenery of your movie, adding sound to the Over frame lets users know that they've discovered a hot spot.

To enhance buttons with auditory feedback:

1. Open a Flash Document containing a button symbol to which you want to add sound.

   (To learn about working with button symbols, see Chapter 11.)

2. Open the file's Library window (choose Window > Library), and select the button symbol that you want to modify.

3. From the Options menu, choose Edit.

   Flash opens the button in symbol-editing mode.

4. In the Timeline, add a new layer (click the Add Layer button), and name it *Sound*.

5. In the *Sound* layer, select the Over and Down frames, and choose Modify > Timeline > Convert to Blank Keyframes (**Figure 15.13**).

   continues on next page

6. Using the techniques described in "Adding Sounds to Frames" earlier in this chapter, assign a sound to the Over frame and a different sound to the Down frame.

Flash displays as much of the waveform as possible in each frame. When you add sounds to buttons, it makes sense to increase the height of the layer that contains sounds (**Figure 15.14**).

7. Return to document-editing mode.

Every instance of the button symbol in the document now has sounds attached.

8. To hear the buttons in action, choose Control > Enable Simple Buttons.

When you move the pointer over the button, Flash plays the sound that you assigned to the Over frame. When you click the button, you hear the sound that you assigned to the Down frame.

✔ Tips

■ The most common frames to use for button feedback are the Over and Down frames, but you can add sounds to any of the button symbol's frames. Sounds added to the Up frame play when the pointer rolls out of the active button area. Sounds added to the Hit frame play when you release the mouse button within the active button area.

■ You can also add sounds to movie-clip buttons, such as those you learned about in Chapters 10 and 11. As in this exercise, you add a sound layer to the symbol, then add sounds to the relevant keyframes in the movie-clip symbol.

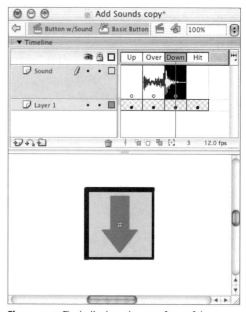

Figure 15.14 Flash displays the waveform of the assigned sound in the keyframe. Unlike movie Timelines, button symbol Timelines have no in-between frames that can contain part of the waveform. Increasing the layer height for a button symbol's *Sound* layer enlarges any waveforms in the button's frames, letting you see more detail.

Using Event Sounds

One of the sound parameters available in the Frame Property Inspector is Sync. The Sync setting determines the way that Flash synchronizes the sounds in your movie. Sync has four settings: Event, Start, Stop, and Stream. The default is Event.

Event sounds play independently of the main Timeline. Flash starts an event sound at a keyframe in a movie; the event sound plays until Flash reaches the end of the sound clip or encounters an instruction to stop playing that sound or all sounds. Long event sounds continue to play after the playhead reaches the last frame in the movie. If your movie loops, every time the playhead passes a frame with an event sound, Flash starts another instance of that sound playing.

To understand how synchronization works, it is helpful to work in a file that has identifying text in keyframes.

To set up a file for testing sounds:

1. Create a 20-frame, 3-layer Flash document.

2. Label the layers *Objects, Sound 1,* and *Sound 2.*

3. In all layers, insert keyframes into frames 1, 5, 10, 15, and 20.

4. In the *Objects* layer, place identifying text on the Stage for each keyframe.

5. Import several sounds of different lengths into the file's library.

   This example uses a 15.8-second sound clip of a musical-scale passage, a water drop sound, a melodic passage, and some rhythm sounds.

6. Save the document as a template for use throughout this chapter, and name it `SoundSyncTemplate`.

   For detailed instructions on saving documents as templates, see Chapter 1.

Independent Sounds Versus Synchronized Sounds

Unsynchronized sound clips play independently of the frames in a movie and can even continue playing after the playhead reaches the last frame in the movie. Flash starts these *event sounds* at a specific frame, but thereafter, event sounds play without relation to specific frames. On one viewer's computer, the sound may take 10 frames to play; on a slower setup, the sound may finish when only 5 frames have appeared.

Flash can also synchronize entire sound clips with specific frames. Flash breaks these *stream sounds* (or *streaming sounds*) into smaller pieces and attaches each piece to a specific frame. For streaming sounds, Flash forces the animation to keep up with the sounds. On slower setups, Flash draws fewer frames so that important actions and sounds stay together.

To make an assigned sound an event sound:

1. Open a new copy of SoundSyncTemplate, created in the preceding exercise.

2. In the Timeline, select Frame 5 of the *Sound 1* layer (**Figure 15.15**).

3. In the Frame Property Inspector, from the Sound pop-up menu, choose the sound named Scale (**Figure 15.16**).

4. From the Sync pop-up menu, choose Event (**Figure 15.17**).

   The Scale sound is assigned to Keyframe 5 of the *Sound 1* layer.

5. Position the playhead in Frame 1, and play your movie (choose Control > Play).

   In a movie that has a standard frame rate of 12 frames per second (fps), the 15.8-second Scale sound continues to play after the playhead reaches the last frame of the movie.

✔ Tip

- To understand better how Flash handles event sounds, choose Control > Loop Playback. Now play the movie again, and let it loop through a couple of times. Each time the playhead enters Frame 5, Flash starts another instance of the Scale sound, and you start to hear not one set of notes going up the scale, but a cacophony of bad harmonies. When you stop the playback, each sound instance plays out until its end—an effect sort of like people singing a round.

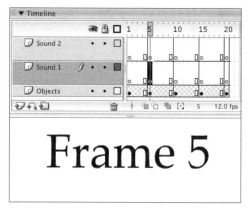

Figure 15.15 Select the keyframe to which you want to assign a sound. Settings that you create in the Frame Property Inspector get applied to the selected keyframe.

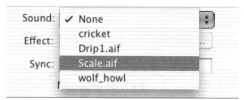

Figure 15.16 In the Frame Property Inspector, choose a sound from the Sound pop-up menu.

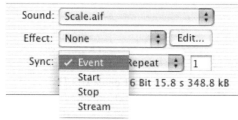

Figure 15.17 From the Sync pop-up menu, choose Event to make the assigned sound start in the selected keyframe and play to the end of the sound, without synchronizing to any subsequent frames of the movie.

USING EVENT SOUNDS

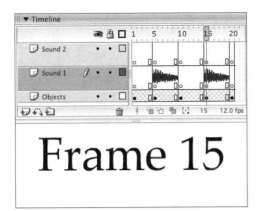

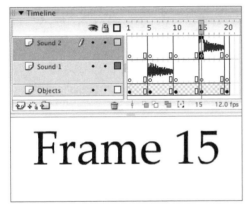

Figure 15.18 You can add a second instance of your sound and make it play on top of the first. Event sounds play independent of the main Timeline, so you're free to add the second sound to the same layer as the first (top). Alternatively, you can add the second sound to its own layer (bottom).

To play overlapping instances of the same sound:

1. Using the file that you created in the preceding exercise, to assign a sound to a later point in the movie's Timeline, *do one of the following:*

   ▲ Select Frame 15 of the *Sound 1* layer.

   ▲ Select Frame 15 of the *Sound 2* layer.

   Because Flash starts a new instance of an event sound, even if that sound is already playing, you have the choice of adding a second instance to the same layer as the first or adding it to a different layer.

2. In the Frame Property Inspector, from the Sound pop-up menu, choose the sound named Scale.

3. From the Sync pop-up menu, choose Event.

   The Scale sound is assigned to Keyframe 15 of whichever layer you chose (**Figure 15.18**).

4. Position the playhead in Frame 1, and play your movie one time.

   When the playhead reaches Frame 5, the Scale sound starts. When the playhead reaches Frame 15, another instance of the Scale sound starts, and the two sounds play together (you hear two voices). When the first instance ends, you again hear only one voice. Within a single layer, each frame can contain only one sound. To make Flash play multiple sounds at the same point in a movie, you must put the sounds in separate layers.

5. Save this file for use in a later exercise; name it OverlapSnds.fla.

To start different sounds simultaneously:

1. Open a new copy of the SoundSyncTemplate that you created earlier in this chapter.

2. In the Timeline, select Keyframe 5 of the *Sound 1* layer.

3. In the Frame Property Inspector, from the Sound pop-up menu, choose Scale.

4. From the Sync pop-up menu, choose Event.

5. In the Timeline, select Keyframe 5 of the *Sound 2* layer.

6. In the Frame Property Inspector, from the Sound pop-up menu, choose a different sound.

You could also import a new sound to your movie's library or open the Library window of another movie containing the sound you want to use and then drag a copy of the sound to the Stage. This example uses a sound named Melody.

Flash places the waveform for the second sound in Keyframe 5 of the *Sound 2* layer (**Figure 15.19**).

7. In the Frame Property Inspector, from the Sync pop-up menu, choose Event.

8. Position the playhead in Frame 1, and play your movie one time.

When the playhead reaches Frame 5, Flash starts playing the Scale and Melody sounds simultaneously.

✔ Tip

■ All the information required to play an event sound lives in the keyframe to which you assigned that sound. When you play the movie, Flash pauses at that keyframe until all the information has downloaded. It's best to reserve Event Syncing for short sound clips; otherwise, your movie may be interrupted by long pauses for downloading sounds.

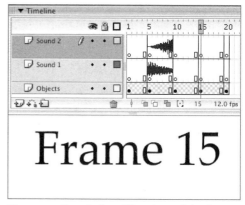

Figure 15.19 To make two different sounds begin playing simultaneously, you must put each sound in a different layer.

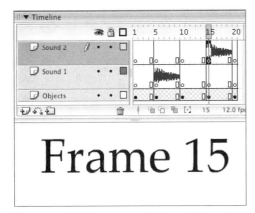

Frame 15

Figure 15.20 To change a sound's Sync setting, select the keyframe that contains the sound. Then, from the Frame Property Inspector's Sync pop-up menu, choose a new setting.

Figure 15.21 To prevent Flash from playing another instance of the sound, if that sound is already playing, choose Start from the Frame Property Inspector's Sync pop-up menu.

Using Start Sounds

Start sounds behave just like event sounds, with one important difference: Flash does not play a new instance of a start sound if that sound is already playing.

To set an assigned sound's Sync to Start:

1. Open OverlapSnds.fla, the file you created in "To play overlapping instances of the same sound" earlier in this chapter.

   You should have one instance of the Scale sound in Keyframe 5 and another in Keyframe 15. The second instance is in the *Sound 1* or *Sound 2* layer, depending on what you did in the earlier exercise.

2. In the Timeline, select the Keyframe 15 that contains the Scale sound (**Figure 15.20**).

3. In the Frame Property Inspector, from the Sync pop-up menu, choose Start (**Figure 15.21**).

4. Position the playhead in Frame 1, and play your movie one time.

   When the playhead reaches Frame 5, the Scale sound starts. When the playhead reaches Frame 15, nothing changes; you continue to hear just one voice as the Scale sound continues playing. When a sound is playing and Flash encounters another instance of the same sound, the Sync setting determines whether Flash plays that sound. When Sync is set to Start, Flash does not play another instance of the sound.

✔ Tip

- To avoid playing multiple instances of a sound when a movie loops, set the sound's Sync to Start. If the sound is still playing when Flash starts the movie again, Flash lets the sound play, adding nothing new. If the sound has finished, Flash starts the sound again when the playhead enters a keyframe containing the sound.

569

Using Stream Sounds

Stream sounds are specifically geared for playback over the Web. When Sync is set to Stream, Flash breaks a sound into smaller sound clips. Flash synchronizes these sub-clips with specific frames of the movie—as many frames as are required to play the sound. Flash stops streaming sounds when playback reaches a new keyframe or an instruction to stop playing either that specific sound or all sounds.

Unlike event sounds, which must download fully before they can play, stream sounds can start playing after a few frames have down-loaded. This situation makes streaming the best choice for long sounds, especially if you'll be delivering your movie over the Web.

To make an assigned sound a stream sound:

1. Open a new copy of the SoundSyncTemplate that you created earlier in this chapter.

2. In the Timeline, in the *Sound 1* layer, remove keyframe status from Frame 10 (select it and choose Modify > Timeline > Clear Keyframe).

3. In the Timeline, in the *Sound 1* layer, select Keyframe 5.

4. In the Frame Property Inspector, from the Sound pop-up menu, choose Scale.

5. From the Sync pop-up menu, choose Stream (**Figure 15.22**).

6. To see how the sound fits into the available time in your movie, in the Sound section of the Frame Property Inspector, click the Edit button.

   The Edit Envelope window appears.

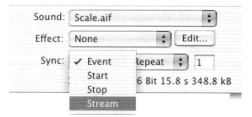

Figure 15.22 To make Flash force a sound to synchronize with specific frames of your movie, choose Stream from the Frame Property Inspector's Sync pop-up menu.

The Mystery of Streaming Sound

When you choose Stream as the Sync setting for a sound, Flash divides that sound clip into smaller subclips and embeds them in individual frames. The movie's frame rate determines the subclips' size. In a movie with a frame rate of 10 frames per second (fps), for example, Flash divides stream-ing sounds into subclips that are a tenth of a second long. For every 10 frames, Flash plays 1 second of the sound.

Flash synchronizes the start of each subclip with a specific frame of the movie. If the sound plays back faster than the computer can draw frames, Flash sacrifices some visuals (skips drawing some frames of the animation) so that sound and images match up as closely as possible. Setting a sound's Sync setting to Stream ensures, for example, that you hear the door slam when you see it swing shut—not a few seconds before. If the discrepancy between sound-playback speed and frame-drawing speed gets big enough, however, those dropped frames make the movie look jerky, just as it would if you set a low frame rate to begin with.

Edit button

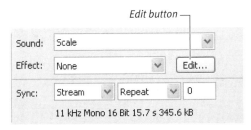

11 kHz Mono 16 Bit 15.7 s 345.6 kB

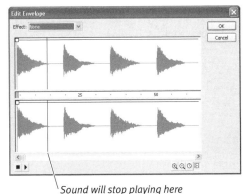

Sound will stop playing here

Figure 15.23 When you set a sound's Sync to Stream, you can check how much of the sound will play, given the number of in-between frames your movie has for the sound to play in. Click the Frame Property Inspector's Edit button (top) to open the Edit Envelope window (bottom). This window displays a sound's full waveform in relation to time or to frame numbers.

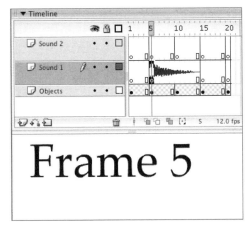

Figure 15.24 There is time enough in the 10 frames between Keyframe 5 and Keyframe 15 to play only the first note of the Scale sound. Flash displays just that much of the full 15.8-second waveform in the Timeline.

At 15.8 seconds, the Scale sound is too long to play completely in the frames between Keyframe 5 and Keyframe 15. When Sync is set to Stream, Flash plays only as much of the sound as can fit in the frames that are available to it—in this case, slightly less than a second. In the Edit Envelope window, a vertical line indicates where Flash truncates this instance of the sound (**Figure 15.23**).

7. To close the Edit Envelope window, click OK or Cancel.

The truncated waveform appears in frames 5 through 15 (**Figure 15.24**).

8. Position the playhead in Frame 1, and play your movie to hear the sound in action.

When the playhead reaches Frame 5, the Scale sound starts. When the playhead reaches Frame 15, the keyframe span ends, and Flash stops playback of the Scale sound.

9. Choose Control > Loop Playback, then play the movie to hear the sound in looping mode.

Flash simply repeats the same snippet of sound, stopping it each time the playhead reaches Frame 15.

✔ Tips

■ You can hear streaming sounds play as you drag the playhead through the Timeline (a technique called *scrubbing* in audio circles). As the playhead moves over the waveform, you can see how the images and sounds fit together. You can then add or delete frames to better synchronize the sounds with the images onscreen.

continues on next page

USING STREAM SOUNDS

- Try Shift-clicking the Timeline to take the playhead to a particular frame (or Shift-dragging the playhead to that frame). As long as you hold down the shift key and the mouse button, Flash repeats the portion of sound that synchronizes with the frame where the playhead is.

- If you find that your stream sound is getting cut off too soon, switch the units of measure in the Edit Envelope window to see how many frames you need to add to accommodate the sound (**Figure 15.25**).

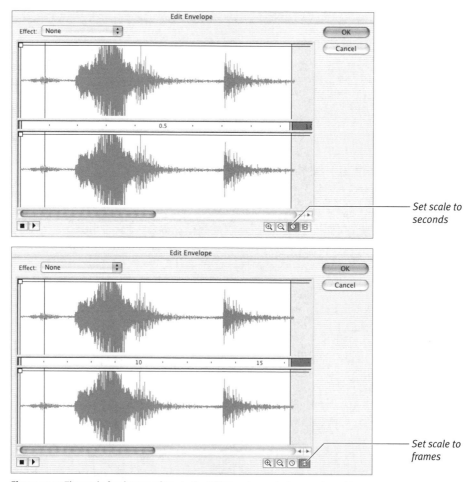

Set scale to seconds

Set scale to frames

Figure 15.25 The scale for the waveform in the Edit Envelope window can be set to seconds (top) or frames (bottom). If you set the scale to frames, you can see exactly how many frames you need to provide enough time for the major parts of the sound to finish. (For this sound, you would need 15 frames.) Usually, you want to make room for the segments of the wave that have the greatest amplitude.

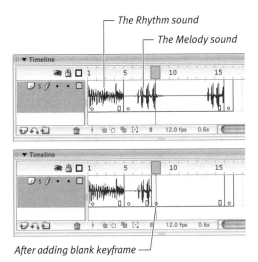

The Rhythm sound

The Melody sound

After adding blank keyframe

Figure 15.26 Inserting a new keyframe cuts off your view of the preceding sound's waveform in the Timeline. If the sound is an event sound, however, it continues playing even when the playhead moves past the keyframe.

Stopping Sounds

Although event sounds normally play to the end, you can force them to stop at a specific keyframe. To issue an instruction to stop a specific sound, you must set that sound's Sync parameter to Stop.

To stop playback of a sound:

1. Create a new 15-frame Flash document with two fairly long event sounds (at least 2 or 3 seconds each); place one sound in Keyframe 1 and the other in Keyframe 5.

(For more detailed instructions, see "Adding Sounds to Frames" earlier in this chapter.) In this example, Keyframe 1 contains the sound Rhythm, and Keyframe 5 contains the sound Melody.

2. In the Timeline, insert a new blank keyframe at Frame 8 (**Figure 15.26**).

Flash cuts off the waveform at Frame 8 because of the keyframe, but on playback, both event sounds continue to play after the playhead reaches Frame 8.

3. Select Keyframe 8.

4. In the Frame Property Inspector, from the Sound pop-up menu, choose Rhythm.

continues on next page

continues on next page

STOPPING SOUNDS

5. From the Sync pop-up menu, choose Stop (**Figure 15.27**).

Flash uses this instruction to stop playback of the Rhythm sound at Frame 8.

Flash places a small square in the middle of Keyframe 8 in the Timeline to indicate that the frame contains a stop-sound instruction (**Figure 15.28**).

6. Position the playhead in Frame 1, and play your movie to hear the sounds in action.

The Rhythm sound starts immediately; Melody kicks in at Frame 5. When the playhead reaches Frame 8, Rhythm cuts out, but Melody plays on, even after the playhead reaches the end of the movie.

✔ Tips

- The Stop setting and the sound that it stops can be in different layers. The Stop setting stops playback of all instances of the specified sound that are currently playing in any layer.

- If you want to stop only one instance of a sound, set the Sync parameter of that instance to Stream; then, in the layer containing that instance, put a blank keyframe in the frame where you want that instance of the sound to stop.

Figure 15.27 To stop a sound's playback at a specific point in a movie, create and then select the keyframe where the sound should stop. From the Frame Property Inspector's Sound pop-up menu, choose the sound you want to stop. From the Sync pop-up menu, choose Stop. Here, the Stop instruction refers to the Rhythm sound.

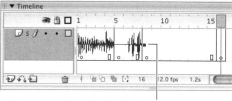

Sync is set to Stop for this keyframe

Figure 15.28 In the Timeline, a small square in the middle of a keyframe indicates the presence of the stop-sound instruction.

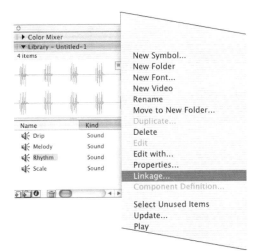

Figure 15.29 To prepare a sound to be targeted by ActionScript, you must set its Linkage properties. Select the sound in the Library, from the Options menu choose Linkage, to see a dialog with linkage settings.

Figure 15.30 When you select Export for ActionScript in the Linkage Properties dialog, Flash assigns a default identifier. You can change the ID if you wish.

Using Behaviors to Control Sounds

In the previous exercises, you control sound playback by adding and removing sound instances directly in the Timeline during authoring. ActionScript allows you to control sounds during playback—loading, playing, and stopping sounds as needed at runtime. Using the Sound Behaviors, you can attach ActionScript to button symbols, button components, or movie clips, setting them up to load and play a specific sound, to replay a loaded sound, or to stop all event sounds that are currently playing whether they were loaded with ActionScript or placed in the Timeline during authoring. In order to target a sound with a Behavior, you must set the sound's Linkage properties so that ActionScript can locate and work with the sound.

To set a sound's Linkage Properties:

1. Open a new copy of the SoundSyncTemplate you created earlier in this chapter.

   The document contains three Timeline layers (*Sound 1, Sound 2,* and *Objects*); identifying text in keyframes 1, 5, 10, 15, and 20; and several sounds in the library (Rhythm, Melody, Drip, and Scale).

2. Select Rhythm in the Library window.

3. From the Library window's Options menu, choose Linkage (**Figure 15.29**).

   The Linkage Properties dialog appears.

4. Select the Export for ActionScripting check box.

   Flash automatically enters the sound's name (here, Rhythm) as the default Identifier and selects the Export in First Frame check box. For this exercise, keep these default settings (**Figure 15.30**).

5. Repeat steps 1 through 4 for all the sounds that you plan to control with ActionScript.

For the following exercise, you need at least two sounds, Rhythm and Melody.

To load and play a sound with a button:

1. Continuing with the file you created in the preceding exercise, place an instance of the first sound (Rhythm) in Keyframe 1 of the *Sound 1* layer.

2. Give the sound a Sync setting of Event.

   With Keyframe 1 selected, in the Frame Property Inspector, choose Event from the Sync pop-up menu.

3. Insert a new layer in the Timeline, name it *Buttons*.

4. With Keyframe 1 of the *Buttons* layer selected, place an instance of a button symbol on the Stage.

   For more detailed instructions about using button symbols, see Chapter 11. To keep the button visible throughout the entire movie during playback, make sure the *Buttons* layer extends the whole length of the movie (if it doesn't, select Frame 20 in the *Button* layer and press F5 to insert in-between frames). Your document should look like **Figure 15.31**. It's a good idea to give the button an instance name, for example, Drum_btn.

5. Access the Behaviors and ActionScript panels.

   If the panels are not open, press Shift-F3 to open the Behaviors panel; press F9 to open the Actions panel.

6. Select the button-symbol instance on the Stage.

7. From the Add Behavior menu in the Behaviors panel, choose Sound > Load Sound from Library (**Figure 15.32**).

   The Load Sound from Library dialog appears.

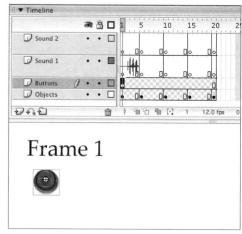

Figure 15.31 Open a copy of the SoundSynchTemplate you created; add a button symbol instance in its own layer. Now you can assign a Behavior to the button to load and play a sound.

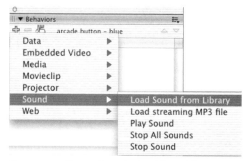

Figure 15.32 Choose Sound > Load Sound from Library to script a button that loads (and plays) a sound when a user clicks the button during playback of your movie.

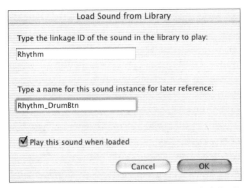

Figure 15.33 When the Play Sound when Loaded check box is selected, clicking the button during playback both loads and plays the sound. Deselect the check box if you want to load the sound now, but play it later. In that case, you'll need another triggering object and event to play the sound.

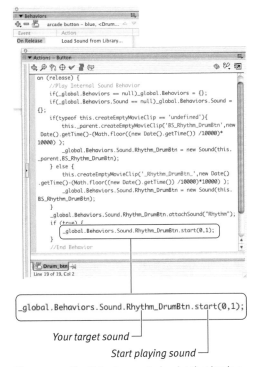

Figure 15.34 The Behavior-created script that loads a sound from the Library is quite complex. You can see that Flash is targeting the instance name you created for your sound, however, and issuing a command for it to start playing.

8. In the Load Sound from Library dialog, *do the following:*

▲ Type the linkage identifier in the first field. This is the name you assigned when you set the sound's Linkage property in the preceding exercise. The Linkage ID tells ActionScript which master sound to use. In the preceding exercise, you used the default linkage ID, Rhythm.

▲ Type an instance name in the second field; for this example, type Rhythm_DrumBtn. You can only assign instance names to sound instances via ActionScript. The Behavior will take care of the scripting for you, using the name you enter here.

▲ Leave the Play this Sound When Loaded check box selected (**Figure 15.33**). This setting tells Flash to load the sound and play it immediately when the user clicks the button during playback. To simply load a sound for future use, deselect this check box.

9. Click OK.

Flash adds the Behavior to the Behaviors panel and adds the appropriate ActionScript to the Script panel of the Actions panel (**Figure 15.34**).

continues on next page

10. Repeat steps 4 through 9 for a second button.

Set this button to load and play a different sound, for example, `Melody`. Give the button an instance name, for example, `Song_btn`. For clarity, add text boxes (to the *Button* layer or a separate *Text* layer) to indicate which button plays which sound.

11. Choose Control > Test Movie to try out your buttons.

The first time you click the `Drum_btn` button, Flash loads the `Rhythm` sound and starts it playing; click the `Song_btn` button and Flash loads and plays the `Melody` sound. On subsequent clicks, Flash merely starts each sound playing again, there's no need to reload it.

✔ Tips

- If you can't remember the Linkage ID for a sound, you can see it in the Library window. Linkage is the fourth column in the window and often gets hidden when you size panels to take up as little screen real estate as possible. Resize the window, or scroll to see the Linkage column.

- It's a good idea to add your own comments to a script created by a Behavior. In the Script pane of the Actions panel, click the first line (which the Behavior leaves blank). Type two slashes and your comment text, for example, `//This script makes the Drum button load and play the Rhythm sound`.

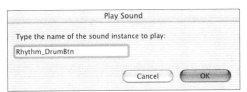

Figure 15.35 To replay a loaded sound, you need to tell Flash which precise sound instance to play. Use the instance name that you assigned when you set up the Behavior, Load Sound from Library.

To replay loaded sounds:

1. Continuing with the file from the preceding exercise, add a third button to keyframe 1 of the *Button* layer.

   You could add a text box to label this button Play Rhythm.

2. With the Play Rhythm button selected on the Stage, from the Add Behavior menu in the Behaviors panel, choose Sound > Play Sound.

   The Play Sound dialog appears.

3. Type the sound's instance name that you created in step 8 of the preceding exercise, Rhythm_DrumBtn (**Figure 15.35**).

4. Click OK.

5. Choose Control > Test Movie to try out your buttons.

   Click the Drum_btn and Song_btn buttons to load those sounds and start them playing. Now click the Play Rhythm button; Flash starts the Rhythm sound playing again.

To stop all sounds:

1. Open a new Flash Document and add layers, keyframes, and sounds.

   Place a few different sounds into different layers and keyframes. The sounds should be 1 or 2 seconds long so that you'll have time to click a button while they're still playing. Select each sound in its keyframe, and choose Event as the Sync setting in the Property Inspector.

2. Add a new layer for buttons, and place an instance of a button symbol in Keyframe 1 of that layer.

   Make sure the layer contains enough in-between frames to match length of the other layers. That way this button will be visible throughout the movie. To be very methodical, name the layer and give the button an instance name as well.

3. Select the button.

4. From the Add Behavior menu in the Behaviors panel, choose Sound > Stop All Sounds.

   The Stop All Sounds dialog appears. This dialog simply reminds you that this Behavior will cause all sounds to stop playing.

5. Click OK.

   Flash adds the Stop all Sounds to the Behaviors panel and creates a script in the Script pane of the Actions panel for your button (**Figure 15.36**).

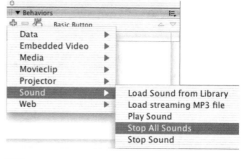

Figure 15.36 Choosing Add Behavior > Stop all Sounds (top) brings up a dialog explaining the Behavior's function (middle). The resulting script (bottom) is much simpler than the Behavior-created script for stopping a particular target sound.

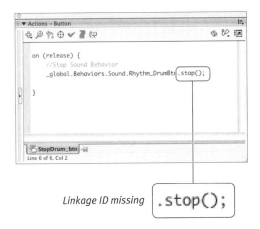

Linkage ID missing `.stop();`

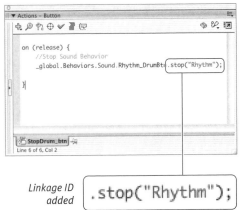

Linkage ID added `.stop("Rhythm");`

Figure 15.37 The script created by the Stop Sound Behavior (top) contains a flaw that makes it stop all sounds, not a specific target sound . To tweak the script so that it stops individual loaded sounds, you must add the sound's Linkage ID, within quote marks, between the parentheses of the stop () action (bottom).

6. Choose Control > Test Movie to test your button.

As the movie plays, the sounds you placed begin playing. When you click the button, all the sounds that are currently playing cease playing until the playhead reaches the next keyframe that contains a sound—for example, when the movie loops back to the beginning.

✔ Tips

■ For fun, try adding buttons that load and play sounds from the library to this file. You'll see that the stopAllSounds action stops these loaded sounds as well.

■ Flash also includes a Behavior (Sound > Stop Sound) that's designed to let you script buttons that stop the playback of individual loaded sounds. Unfortunately, a flaw in the script created by the Behavior makes it stop all sounds not just individual target sounds. To make the Behavior work as intended, follow the steps in "To replay a loaded sound," This time, in step 2, choose Sound > Stop Sound. When the Behavior has created the script, access the Actions panel, go into the Script pane, and add the Linkage ID as the parameter for the sound you want to stop as in **Figure 15.37**.

Repeating Sounds

Flash's sound-repeating parameter allows you to play a sound several times in a row without adding other instances of the sound to a frame. Type a value in the Repeat field in the sound area (the right side) of the Frame Property Inspector. Flash plays the sound the specified number of times. You can repeat event sounds and streaming sounds. The sound's Sync parameter applies to the whole set of repeated sounds. You can also set sounds to loop until further instruction.

To set a Repeat value:

1. Create a 5-frame Flash document with a short event sound in Keyframe 1.

   This exercise uses a sound called Drip.

2. In the Timeline, select Frame 1.

3. In the sound area of the Frame Property Inspector, from the Repeat pop-up menu, choose Repeat (the default setting).

4. Type 3 in the field to the right of the Repeat menu (**Figure 15.38**).

   Flash extends the sound's waveform by stringing together three copies of it. In the Timeline, Flash displays as much of the extended waveform as will fit in the available frames (**Figure 15.39**).

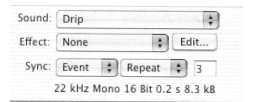

Figure 15.38 Typing a value in the Repeat field tells Flash how many times to play selected sound.

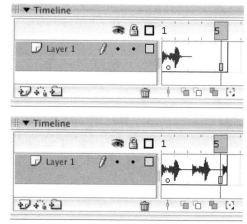

Figure 15.39 When Repeat is set to 0, Flash displays just the original waveform in the Timeline (top). When Repeat is set to 3, Flash displays as much of the repeated waveform as there is room for (bottom).

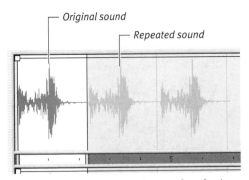

Original sound

Repeated sound

Figure 15.40 You can see a precise waveform for the repeated sound graphed against seconds or frames (shown here) of your movie in the Edit Envelope window. The grayed-out waveforms are the repeated portion of the sound.

✔ Tips

■ To make a sound repeat continuously until you issue an instruction to stop the sound, choose Loop from the Repeat menu.

■ Although you can use the Repeat parameter with sounds whose Sync parameter is Stream, doing so adds to the size of your exported file.

■ To see the extended waveform graphed against seconds or frames, click Edit in the Frame Property Inspector. The full sound appears in the Edit Envelope window (**Figure 15.40**).

■ Because Flash links the repeated sounds and displays them as a single sound in the Edit Envelope window, you can edit the repeating sound. You can change the volume so that the sound gets louder with each repetition, for example. You learn about editing sounds in the following section of this chapter.

Editing Sounds

Flash allows you to make limited changes in each instance of a sound in the Edit Envelope window. You can change the start and end point of the sound (that is, cut a piece off the beginning or end of the waveform) and adjust the sound's volume.

Flash offers six predefined volume edits: Left Channel, Right Channel, Fade Left to Right, Fade Right to Left, Fade In, and Fade Out. These sound-editing templates create common sound effects, such as making a sound grow gradually louder (Fade In) or softer (Fade Out), or (for stereo sounds) making the sound move from one speaker channel to the other.

In addition to changing a sound's volume, you can make a sound shorter by instructing Flash to remove sound data from the beginning, the end, or both.

To assign packaged volume effects:

1. Open the document that you created in the preceding exercise.

   This is a 5-frame movie with an event sound that loops three times in Frame 1.

2. In the Timeline, select Frame 1.

3. In the sound area of the Frame Property Inspector, click the Edit button.

   The Edit Envelope window appears (**Figure 15.41**).

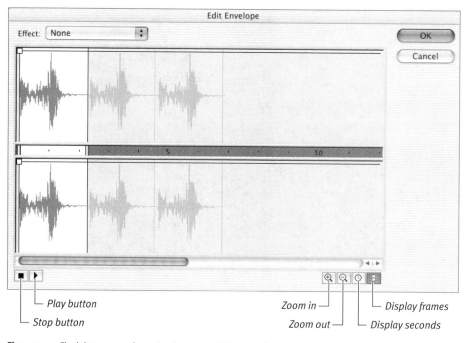

Figure 15.41 Flash lets you perform simple sound editing—for length and volume—in the Edit Envelope window.

EDITING SOUNDS

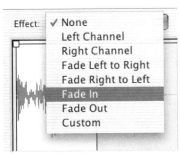

Figure 15.42 The Effect pop-up menu in the Edit Envelope window offers six templates for common sound effects that deal with volume. You can also choose Custom to create your own effect.

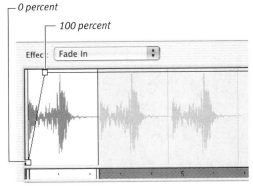

— 0 percent

— 100 percent

Figure 15.43 The Fade In effect brings the sound's envelope down to 0 percent (the bottom of the sound-editing window) at the start of the sound and quickly raises it to 100 percent (the top of the sound-editing window).

Figure 15.44 To edit the volume of a sound yourself, from the Effect pop-up menu in the Edit Envelope window, choose Custom.

4. From the Effect pop-up menu, choose Fade In (**Figure 15.42**).

Flash adjusts the sound envelope (**Figure 15.43**). When the envelope line is at the top of the window, Flash plays 100 percent of the available sound. When the envelope line is at the bottom of the window, Flash plays 0 percent of the available sound.

5. Click the Play button to hear the sound with its fade-in effect.

The first iteration of the sound starts soft and grows louder. The repetitions play at full volume.

6. Click OK.

Flash returns you to document-editing mode.

✔ Tip

■ If you don't need to look at your sound's waveform, you can bypass the Edit Envelope window. Just choose an effect from the Effect pop-up menu in the sound area of the Frame Property Inspector.

To customize volume effects:

1. Using the movie that you created in the preceding exercise, select Keyframe 1.

2. To access the Edit Envelope window, in the sound area of the Frame Property Inspector, click the Edit button.

3. From the Effect pop-up menu, choose Custom (**Figure 15.44**).

4. In the Edit Envelope window, drag the square envelope handles that appear at the 0-second mark in both channels down to 0 percent.

continues on next page

EDITING SOUNDS

5. In the right channel (the top section of the window), click the waveform at the 0.2-, 0.4-, and 0.45-second marks.

Flash adds new envelope handles to both channels.

6. In the right-channel window, at the 0.2-second mark, drag the handle up to the 50 percent volume level (**Figure 15.45**).

7. Repeat step 6 for the left channel.

8. In both channels, drag the 0.4-second mark handles to the 50 percent level and the 0.45-second mark handles to the 100 percent level (**Figure 15.46**).

You can add as many as eight handles to create a variety of volume changes within one sound.

9. Click the Play button to hear the sound with its fade-in effect.

Flash fades in the first iteration of the sound, plays the second iteration at half volume, and plays the third iteration at full volume.

10. Click OK.

✔ Tips

- To remove unwanted envelope handles, drag them out of the sound-editing window.

- When you add a handle to one channel, Flash automatically adds another to the same location in the other channel. To create different volumes from the two channels, however, you can drag the handle to a different level in each channel.

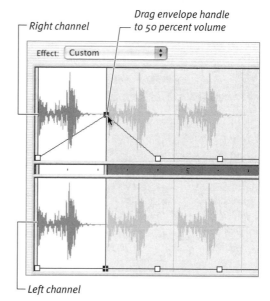

Figure 15.45 Click the waveform in the sound-editing window to add a handle. Drag the handle to adjust the sound envelope. You can make the sound envelope the same or different for both channels. For monaural sounds, both waveforms are identical.

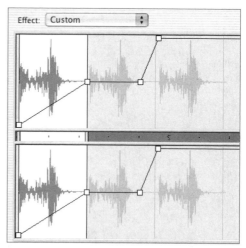

Figure 15.46 You can use up to eight handles to shape a sound's envelope. By using the zoom tools to view more of the sound in the Edit Envelope window, you can see the sound envelope for all three iterations of the sound. The first fades in, the second plays at 50 percent volume, and the third plays at full volume.

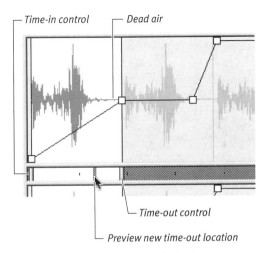

Time-in control — *Dead air* —

— *Time-out control*

— *Preview new time-out location*

Figure 15.47 Flash lets you trim the beginning and end of a sound in the Edit Envelope window. Here, dragging the time-out control clips off the end of the sound (which is just very soft sound or silence).

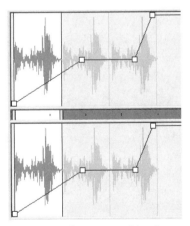

Figure 15.48 After you reposition the time-out control, the new, shorter waveform appears in the Edit Envelope window.

To edit sounds for length:

1. Using the movie that you created in the preceding exercise, select Frame 1.

2. To access the Edit Envelope window, in the Frame Property Inspector, click the Edit button.

3. In the Edit Envelope window, drag the time-out control to the 0.15-second mark (**Figure 15.47**).

   Flash shortens the sound in both channels (**Figure 15.48**).

continues on next page

4. Click OK.

Flash returns you to document-editing mode. Now all three iterations of the repeating sound are visible in the Timeline (**Figure 15.49**).

✔ Tip

■ Although you can change the start and end points of a sound in Flash, you still have the whole sound taking up room in your movie file. If you find yourself trimming many sounds in Flash, you should consider investing in a sound-editing program that allows you to leave the excess on the cutting-room floor rather than behind the curtains in Flash.

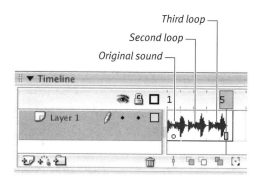

Third loop
Second loop
Original sound

Figure 15.49 After you shorten the sound, all three iterations fit into the 5-frame movie.

EDITING SOUNDS

16

ADDING VIDEO

Another way to bring realism to your Flash creations is to add video. Macromedia Flash MX 2004 allows you to embed video clips for playback directly in Flash Player. In addition, you have the option of linking video clips to your movie during authoring and then exporting the movie to QuickTime, where all the Flash animation takes place on a separate track from the video. And for advanced ActionScripters, there's the option to link to external Flash video (.flv) files during playback of your movie.

Sorenson Media's Spark codec, which is built into Flash, handles the compression of video for import into Flash's authoring environment and decompression of the video data during playback of the published movie. This system allows you to include short video clips in your Flash movies and still keep file sizes manageable.

Importing Video

Flash allows you to embed video clips for playback directly in Flash Player, or to create links to QuickTime video clips that play at runtime, when your end user views the published movie. Working with linked QuickTime files, however requires that you publish your Flash movie as a QuickTime file (for more details about publishing Flash movies, see Chapter 17). Publishing as QuickTime somewhat limits your ability to provide interactivity because QuickTime currently supports only those interactivity features available in Flash 4.

With embedded video, you can create movies that use all of Flash's animation and interactivity capabilities. In addition, anyone who has the Flash 7 (or 6) player can play embedded video; there's no need for QuickTime or other plug-ins.

The first step to using video with Flash is to import a video file, just as you would import artwork or sounds from other external sources.

What Video Formats Does Flash Accept?

Flash imports Macromedia Flash Video Format (.flv) files directly. There are three ways to create .flv files. One is to export video clips from within Flash itself; the second is to use Sorenson Media's Squeeze codec. (Squeeze is the professional version of Spark and offers more features for manipulating and compressing video.) And the third is to use Macromedia's FLV Export plug-in. (The FLV Export plug-in is available only to users of Macromedia Flash MX 2004 Professional. The exporter enables certain dedicated video-editing software to export .flv files directly.) To import other video formats, you need a codec or a program that acts as a translator installed on your system. With QuickTime 4 (or a later version) installed on Windows and Macintosh, you can import .mov, .mpg, .mpeg, .dv, and .avi files. On the Windows platform, you can also use DirectX 7 (or a later version) to import .wmv, .asf, .mpg, .mpeg, and .avi files.

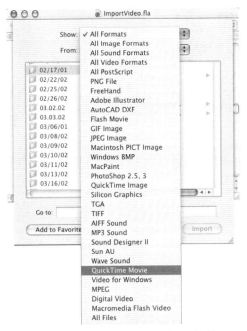

Figure 16.1 Choose QuickTime Movie from the Show (Mac) or Files of Type (Windows) pop-up menu in the Import dialog to locate QuickTime files for import.

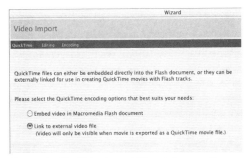

Figure 16.2 The Video Import Wizard gives you the choice of linking a QuickTime video clip or embedding it.

Figure 16.3 Flash can expand the selected keyframe span automatically to accommodate every frame in the video clip that you are importing.

To import links to QuickTime video clips:

1. Create a Flash Document in which to place the linked video, and select the keyframe in which you want the video to start.

2. From the File menu, choose Import > Import to Stage or press ⌘-R (Mac) or Ctrl-R (Windows).

   The standard file-import dialog appears.

3. From the Show pop-up menu (Mac) or the Files of Type pop-up menu (Windows), choose QuickTime Movie (**Figure 16.1**).

4. Navigate to a QuickTime file on your system, and select the file.

5. Click Open.

   The Video Import Wizard appears, displaying QuickTime options.

6. Choose Link to External Video File (**Figure 16.2**).

7. Click Next.

   If the keyframe span currently selected in the Timeline contains fewer frames than the linked video clip, a warning dialog appears, asking whether you want to add enough frames to display the entire linked clip (**Figure 16.3**).

continues on next page

8. To enlarge the keyframe span, click Yes.
Flash adds enough in-between frames to
the span to reveal the entire video clip.

or

To retain the current number of frames
in the keyframe span, click No. Flash
truncates the video clip to fit within the
existing frames.

Flash adds the linked video clip to the
active document's library and places an
instance of the linked video clip on the
Stage. The video images appear on the
Stage whenever the playhead is located
in the keyframe span.

Flash identifies linked video clips by a
special icon (a small movie camera with
a chain link attached) in the library and
lists them as Linked Video in the Kind
column (**Figure 16.4**).

✔ Tips

■ Tired of seeing that warning dialog about
insufficient frames? Check the Don't Show
Me This Message Again check box. Then
click Yes to have Flash always add sufficient frames to display the full video clip.
Click No to have Flash truncate imported
clips. To restore your choice in the matter,
reset the preference for showing or skip-
ping this warning in the Warnings tab of
the Preferences dialog. Choose Flash >
Preferences (Mac) or Edit > Preferences
(Windows) to open the dialog, then
select the Warnings tab.

■ Even when you refuse to allow Flash to
add frames when you place an instance
of a video clip on the Stage, the full clip
is there. You can add frames to the span
later to reveal more of the video clip.

■ To import the video without placing an
instance on the Stage, choose File >
Import > Import to Library.

Figure 16.4 Imported video clips live in the library of
the active Flash document. The Kind column indicates
whether a clip is linked or embedded.

Figure 16.5 To view all the video files available for import by Flash, choose All Video Formats from the Show (Mac) or Files of Type (Windows) pop-up menu in the Import dialog.

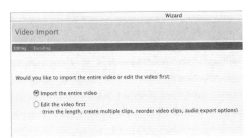

Figure 16.6 The Video Import Wizard allows you to import the entire video clip as is, or edit it, for example to shorten it, before importing.

To bring embedded video clips into a Flash movie:

1. Follow steps 1 and 2 of the preceding exercise.

2. From the Show pop-up menu (Mac) or the Files of Type pop-up menu (Windows), choose All Video Formats (**Figure 16.5**).

3. Navigate to and select the video file on your system.

4. Click Import (Mac) or Open (Windows). The Video Import Wizard appears.

   ▲ If you are importing a QuickTime file, the Wizard displays the QuickTime options to link or embed the file, as in the preceding exercise. Choose Embed Video in Macromedia Flash Document, and click Next. The Editing section of the Video Import Wizard appears.

   ▲ If you are importing a Flash video file (.flv), the video clip imports directly to the stage.

   ▲ For all other types of video files, the Editing section of the Video Import Wizard appears immediately (**Figure 16.6**).

5. In the Wizard, select *one of the following options:*

   ▲ To make simple modifications to the video before importing it, select Edit the Video First. Video-editing options appear in the Wizard. Make any desired changes, for example, set In and Out points once to trim the clip's beginning or ending. Click the Next button. The Encoding section of the Video Import Wizard appears.

   ▲ To embed the video clip as is, select Import the Entire Video. The Encoding section of the Video Import Wizard appears.

continues on next page

6. To optimize compression for the video clip from the Compression Profile pop-up menu, *do one of the following:*

▲ Choose one of the five preset Compression Profiles (**Figure 16.7**).

▲ To create your own Compression Profile, choose Create New Profile or, with one of the preset profiles selected, click the Edit button. The Compression Settings options appear. Make the desired modifications (see "To Create Custom Compression Profiles," later in this chapter).

7. To set additional encoding parameters, from the Advanced Settings pop-up menu, select Create New Profile (**Figure 16.8**).

The Advanced Settings options appear. Make the desired modifications (see "To create Advanced Settings Profiles," later in this chapter). Flash provides no preset advanced-encoding profiles, but once you create one, it appears in the pop-up menu.

8. Click Finish.

The Importing dialog appears, displaying a progress bar, Time Elapsed and Total Time counters, and a Stop button for canceling the import operation.

If the span for the selected keyframe contains fewer frames than the embedded video clip, a warning dialog appears, asking whether you want to add enough frames to display the entire clip.

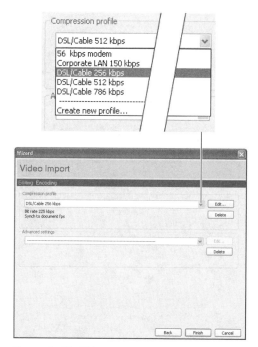

Figure 16.7 The Video Import Wizard is your interface with the Sorenson Spark codec. Spark encodes and compresses the video file on import. You can edit a Compression Profile to balance file size and quality.

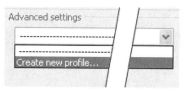

Figure 16.8 To further balance file size and quality, you can customize the advanced encoding parameters. Choose Create New Profile from the Advanced Settings pop-up menu.

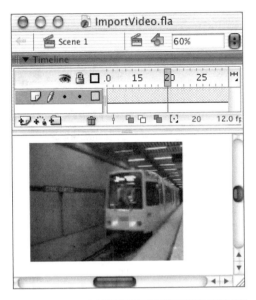

Figure 16.9 Unlike movie clips, which display only their first frame in document-editing mode, the changing frames of an imported video clip appear on the Stage in each frame of the span containing the clip.

9. To enlarge the keyframe span, click Yes. Flash adds enough frames to the span to reveal the entire video clip.

or

To retain the current number of frames in the keyframe span, click No.

Flash adds the embedded video clip to the active document's library and places an instance of it on the Stage. The video frames appear on the Stage when the playhead is located in the keyframe span (**Figure 16.9**).

Flash identifies embedded video clips with their own icon (a small movie camera) in the library and lists them as Embedded Video in the Kind column (**Figure 16.10**).

✔ Tip

■ If you use the video-editing features of the Wizard to create multiple clips, you can export them as separate video objects, or have Spark glue them back together into a single video clip. The latter effectively allows you to cut something from the middle of a clip instead of just trimming the beginning and ending.

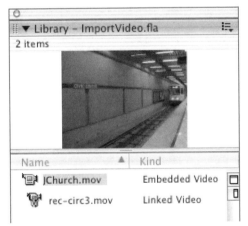

Figure 16.10 Video-clip symbols bear their own identifying icon. Check the Kind column in the Library window to see whether the video is linked or embedded.

To create custom Compression Profiles:

1. Follow steps 1 through 5 in the preceding exercise.

   The Encoding Section of the Video Import Wizard appears.

2. From the Compression Profile pop-up menu, *do one of the following:*

   ▲ Choose Create New Profile.

   ▲ Choose one of the preset profiles and click the Edit button.

   Compression Settings options appear (**Figure 16.11**). When you choose Create New Profile, all options are set to zero. When you choose a preset, those settings appear in the Wizard.

3. Set the compression options appropriate to your situation (see the sidebar, "The Mystery of Encoding: Compression Settings).

4. To save your settings, click Next.

   The Save Settings options appear (**Figure 16.12**).

5. Type a name and description for your profile.

6. Click Next.

7. You return to the Encoding (Compression Settings) section of the Wizard.

   If these are the only custom settings you wish to apply, continue by following steps 7 and 8 of the preceding exercise.

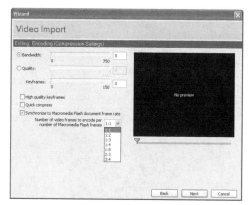

Figure 16.11 The Video Import Wizard lets you create custom Compression Profiles. The options in the Encoding (Compression Settings) section of the Wizard help you to balance file size, download speed, and video quality.

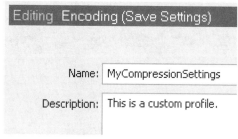

Figure 16.12 To save your custom profile, give it a name. It's also a good idea to type description of your settings.

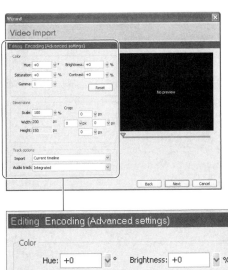

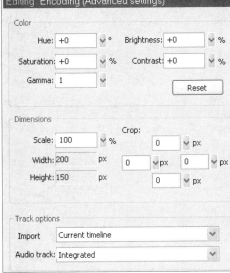

Figure 16.13 The advanced-encoding options allow you to make simple color corrections, change the dimensions of the video image, and choose how to deal with the soundtrack of the imported video clip.

To create Advanced Settings Profiles:

1. Follow steps 1 through 5 in the exercise named "To bring embedded video clips into a Flash movie" earlier in this section.

2. In the Encoding section of the Video Import Wizard, choose Create New Profile from the Advanced Settings pop-up menu.

   Advanced Settings options appear (**Figure 16.13**). Once you have created an Advanced Settings profile, it too appears in the pop-up menu; you can choose it, or use it as a base for further custom profiles.

3. Set the advanced-encoding options appropriate to your situation (see the sidebar, "The Mystery of Encoding: Advanced Settings).

4. Follow steps 4 through 7 in the preceding exercise.

The Mystery of Encoding: Compression Settings

The key to working with video in Flash is Sorenson Media's Spark codec. Spark carries out Flash's video-import functions by encoding and decoding (compressing and decompressing) the video data to bring clips into Flash and to take them back out again and present them to your audience. Your goal—the ever-present juggling act for Web developers—is to balance quality and file size. With video, that balance is particularly important because of the large amounts of data involved. Each pixel in a video image contains 24 bits of information, if the video image is a 100-by-100-pixel square, that's already 240,000 bits for each frame, and for video viewed over the Web, you usually want to display at least 10 frames every second to sustain the illusion of motion. Each second of uncompressed video can easily contain millions of bits of data. To bring those numbers down to a reasonable range for transmission over the Web, you need to eliminate and/or compress some of that data. Here's a quick overview of Spark's compression settings, with particular reference to settings that deal with the quality-size balance in your published (.swf) file. Spark's Bandwidth and Quality settings define two different ways that Spark can balance file size and quality; you must choose one setting or the other.

Bandwidth. Choose this setting when you want to maintain a uniform speed for downloading a .swf file containing video. The Bandwidth setting sacrifices some image quality to maintain a constant download speed. You might use it to insure that playback over slow connections, such as 56K modems, will not bog down. Although we often think of bandwidth as being how much information can be sent through the user's Internet connection, in the context of the Video Import Wizard, the Bandwidth setting refers to the amount of data that there is to send. By selecting a Bandwidth setting you tell Spark to compress (and decompress) the video to create a target *bit rate*. Bit rate refers to the amount of data used to re-create the video image. The smaller the bit rate, the less data Spark uses to define each frame of the video. A smaller bit rate results in a smaller .swf file. Compare two Bandwidth settings: 200 Kpbs and 400 Kpbs. At 400 Kbps, Spark uses twice the amount of data it would use at 200 Kbps; the result is a slower download, but a more faithful rendition of the video image. For most Web video, the 200 Kpbs setting is sufficient.

Quality. Choose this setting when image quality is more important to you than download speed. The Quality setting applies a uniform level of compression for all frames in a video clip, resulting in uniform image quality. By selecting a Quality setting, you tell Spark to allow the download speed to vary, for example, slowing down during a section of the video that contains lots of intricate motion and speeding up when there's little change from one frame to the next. Spark applies JPEG-like compression to the image data in imported video clips to achieve the Quality setting. A setting of 100 results in the most faithful rendition of the video information. A setting of 0 creates a highly pixelated rendition. Here, lower numbers translate into smaller file sizes for .swf files.

continues on next page

The Mystery of Encoding: Compression Settings *continued*

Keyframe. The term *keyframe* here refers not to the keyframes in the Timeline, but to a series of crucial frames created as Spark compresses the video clip. To reduce the amount of information in the clip, Spark does not usually encode all the data required to redraw a full-frame image for every frame in a video clip. Spark encodes the full-frame image only for crucial frames (keyframes). For the other frames, Spark encodes information about how the frame differs from the preceding keyframe and uses that data to redraw only the changed portions of the frame. The Keyframe Interval setting tells Spark how often to encode a full frame. It's a bit of a brain-twister, but higher numbers translate to smaller .swf files. A higher number means a larger interval between keyframes, which means fewer keyframes, which in turn means less data in the .swf. (To force Spark to encode every frame as a keyframe, enter 1 as the Keyframe Interval setting. With a setting of 0, Spark never encodes a full keyframe, always just redrawing the changes from one frame to the next.)

High Quality Keyframes. This setting overrides Spark's normal attempt to keep download speed constant when you choose a bandwidth setting. Checking High Quality Keyframes forces Spark to keep the image quality of keyframes high even if that means reducing download speed.

Quick compress. This setting speeds up the time it takes Spark to compress the video you import into a Flash document. It allows Spark to reduce image quality, if necessary, to accomplish that task.

Synchronize. Video and Flash animation are both frame-based media, but when the frame rate of an embedded video clip differs from the frame rate of the Flash movie containing it, you can wind up with a situation reminiscent of a goat and a giraffe walking together: For each step the giraffe takes, the goat must take several steps to keep up, or the giraffe must reduce its stride.

When you check the Synchronize Video to Macromedia Flash check box, Spark encodes the video in a way that forces Flash to preserve the original duration of the embedded video clip in all situations. If, for example, you have a 10-second, 10-frames-per-second (fps) clip, with the Synchronize Video to Macromedia Flash setting, the video lasts 10 seconds, no matter what the Flash movie's frame rate is. In a 5-fps Flash movie, Flash drops enough frames of the video clip so that the clip still takes just 10 seconds to play. In a 20-fps Flash movie, Flash duplicates video-clip frames so that the clip still takes a full 10 seconds to play.

If you uncheck the Synchronize check box, the frames go in lock step, but you get to control how the steps interlock by selecting the ratio of video frames to Flash frames. In the Number of Video Frames to Encode per Number of Macromedia Flash Frames section, you can choose from seven different ratios (1:1, 1:2, 1:3, 1:4, 1:8, 2:3, and 3:4). Take a look at importing the 10-second, 10-fps clip; uncheck the Synchronize check box and choose a frame-encoding ratio of 1:1 (one video frame for each Flash frame). Placed in a 5-fps Flash movie, the clip takes twice as long to play completely (20 seconds); in a 20-fps Flash movie, the clip takes just half as long (10 seconds).

The Mystery of Encoding: Advanced Settings

In addition to allowing you to set compression options for embedded video, the Video Import Wizard offers advanced settings for dealing with the content of your video. Most of the advanced settings have little effect on the size of your published (.swf) file.

Color. Hue, Saturation, Gamma, Brightness, and Contrast settings have no effect on the size of your .swf, but do allow you to make simple color corrections and optimize the look of your video for different situations.

Dimensions. The Scale setting (0 to 100 percent) allows you to reduce the dimensions of the video clip, while retaining the original aspect ratio (ratio of width to height) of your video clip (the Width and Height field show the new dimensions in pixels). Once again, smaller numbers equal smaller .swf files. You can also enter Crop values to reduce the dimensions of the video image. Cropping actually eliminates data from the embedded video, thereby reducing file size.

Track Options. Spark always creates a special video-clip asset in the library of the document into which you import video, but you can also tell Spark to place the video inside other symbols. Choosing Current Timeline brings the video frames into the main Timeline; choosing Movie Clip, brings them into a movie-clip symbol; and choosing Graphic Symbol brings them into an animated graphic symbol. If you choose File > Import > Import to Stage, Flash places an instance of the resulting movie-clip or graphic symbol into Frame 1 of the main Timeline. Placing the video clip within a symbol does not add to your final file size.

Audio Track. If your video clip contains audio that's sampled at 44.100Hz, 22.050Hz, 11.025Hz, or 5.50125Hz, you can import the audio together with the video. Audio sampled at other frequencies or created with other codecs may not import. To treat the audio as a separate sound asset that you can manipulate as you learned to do in Chapter 15, choose Separate. Separating the audio into a separate asset doesn't add to your file size. To keep the audio inside the video-clip symbol, choose Integrated. To eliminate the audio component, choose None; this setting reduces the file size of your final movie. If you import video containing audio sampled at an unsupported rate, Flash warns you that you cannot import the audio track.

Using Embedded Video Clips in Your Movie

Embedded video clips bear similarities to other symbols, yet they are a distinct and unique type of element. As with bitmaps, you can update video clips, bringing in a new copy of a file you edited with an external editor. Like graphic animation symbols, video clips play within—and must synchronize with—frames within the main movie Timeline. Like sound clips, video clips can contain audio, although if you import audio as an integrated track, you cannot see the sound's waveform in the Timeline. Placing video within a Flash movie-clip symbol, gives the video an independent Timeline, and you gain the full control over the video clip that you have over movie clips.

As with any symbol, you place an instance of a video clip by dragging a copy from the Library window to the Stage. You can modify a selected instance of a video clip in many (but not all) of the ways that you modify other objects in Flash. The Property Inspector gives you information about selected instances of embedded video clips.

More About Modifying and Animating Video Clips

You can modify the size, shape, and location of the video clip, and even use video clips for motion tweens; you can name the instance and target it with ActionScript. But you cannot change the color or transparency of the clip. To gain control of a video clip's brightness, tint, and alpha properties, you must place the embedded video clip within a movie-clip symbol. You can then manipulate that movie-clip instance to change its color, transparency, and so on. Flash places the imported video directly into a movie clip on import if you choose Import > Movie Clip under Track Options in the advanced-encoding section of the Video Import Wizard.

To place embedded video clips in your movie:

1. Open the Flash Document in which you want to use video clips.

2. Import the video clips as described in the preceding section.

3. In the Timeline, select the keyframe in which you want a video clip to start playing.

4. From the Library window, drag a copy of an embedded video clip to the Stage (**Figure 16.14**).

   Unlike movie clips, which play in their own independent Timeline, embedded video clips need to fit their frames into the frames of the Timeline of the movie or movie clip containing them. Each time you drag an instance of the video clip to the Stage, if the span for the selected keyframe contains fewer frames than the embedded video clip, a warning dialog appears, asking whether you want to add enough frames to display the entire clip.

5. To enlarge the keyframe span, click Yes.

   Flash adds enough frames to the span to reveal the entire video clip.

   or

   To retain the current number of frames in the keyframe span, click No.

   Flash places the video clip on the Stage, but restricts it to displaying the number of frames in the keyframe span in which you place it.

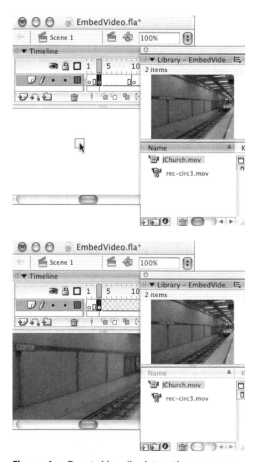

Figure 16.14 To put video clips into action, you must drag an instance from the Library window to the Stage.

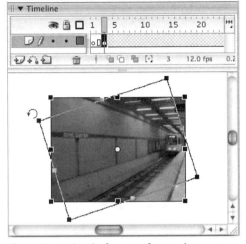

Figure 16.15 Using the free-transform tool, you can scale, rotate, and skew a video-clip instance. The free-transform tool's Distort and Envelope modifiers do not work with video clips.

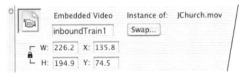

Figure 16.16 When you select an instance of an embedded video clip, the Embedded Video Property Inspector displays information about that clip. Changing values in the Width, Height, *x*, and/or *y* fields modifies the selected clip.

To modify video-clip instances:

1. On the Stage, select the instance of the video clip that you want to modify.

2. To modify the selected instance, *use any of the following methods:*

   ▲ With the selection tool, reposition the video-clip instance on the Stage.

   ▲ With the free-transform tool, scale, rotate, and/or skew the video-clip instance (**Figure 16.15**). The Distort and Envelope modifiers do not work on video-clip instances.

   ▲ In the Embedded Video Property Inspector, enter new height and width, and/or *x* and *y* values to change the dimensions and location of the video-clip instance (**Figure 16.16**).

   ▲ In the Info panel, enter new height and width and/or *x* and *y* values to change the dimensions and location of the video-clip instance.

   ▲ In the Transform panel, enter new values to scale, rotate, or skew the video-clip instance.

USING EMBEDDED VIDEO CLIPS IN YOUR MOVIE

Updating Video Clips

You cannot edit video clips directly in Flash, To update embedded video clips that you have edited with external video-editing software you must re-import them through the Video Import Wizard (unless they are Flash Video [.flv] files). You can update a linked video clip by giving it the correct path name to the updated QuickTime file. You can swap one embedded video clip for another embedded video clip, or swap one linked video clip for another linked video clip. You cannot, however, mix and match linked and embedded clips in a swap, nor can you swap a video clip for a movie clip or any other type of symbol.

To update linked video clips:

1. Open the Flash Document containing the linked video clip that needs to be updated.

2. In the Library window, select the linked video clip.

   If the window is not open, choose Window > Library.

3. From the Options pop-up menu in the top-right corner of the Library window, choose Properties, or double-click the selected clip's icon in the Library window (**Figure 16.17**).

   The Linked Video Properties dialog appears (**Figure 16.18**).

4. To change the clip's path name, click the Set Path button.

   The Open dialog appears.

5. Navigate to the updated QuickTime file, then click Open.

   Flash updates the path name for the linked clip in the library. The video clip in the library retains its original name, but its content switches to that of the updated file.

6. Click OK to dismiss the Linked Video Properties dialog.

Figure 16.17 The first step to updating a linked video clip's path is to access the clip's properties. Select the linked video clip in the Library window; then choose Properties from the Options pop-up menu.

Figure 16.18 To change the linked video clip's path name, so that it points to the latest version of the source file, click the Set Path button in the Linked Video Properties dialog.

UPDATING VIDEO CLIPS

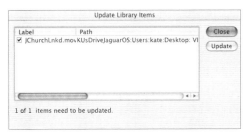

Figure 16.19 In the Update Library Items dialog, select the check box of any items you want Flash to update. Linked video clips update automatically each time you re-open the file containing them.

Previewing Video Clips in a Movie

Embedded and linked video clips display their images within the keyframe span that contains the clip during authoring. You can simply play the movie (choose Control > Play) or move the playhead through the Timeline to view the changing video frames. If the embedded audio has an audio track, however, you must use one of the test modes to preview the sound. (If you import the audio track as a separate sound asset and place an instance in the movie, you will hear the audio play when you drag the playhead through the Timeline or you choose Control > Play.)

For embedded clips, you can also use one of the test modes to see the video in context with interactive elements such as Flash movie clips and ActionScripting (choose Control > Test Scene or Control > Test Movie). You cannot preview linked video clips in test mode. To view linked clips in context with other interactive elements, you must publish the movie in QuickTime format (for details, see Chapter 17).

✔ Tips

■ If you follow the steps of the preceding exercise but select an embedded video clip in the library, the Embedded Video Properties dialog appears, sporting a different set of buttons. One, button, Update, might seem just the ticket for updating embedded video without going through the Video Import Wizard, however that option works only for Macromedia Flash Video (.flv) files. Unless you have the capacity to create and update .flv files externally (for example, you or a colleague use Sorenson Squeeze or Macromedia Flash MX 2004 Professional's Video Export plug-in), this option is not much help for updating embedded video clips. (The button does help you to update other types of externally edited media, though, for example, sound files.)

■ If you've modified the instance of an embedded video clip on the Stage, for example rotating it and changing its transparency, you can preserve those changes by importing the updated version of the clip with a slightly different name. Then use the Swap function, which you learn in the following exercise.

■ To update a linked video clip whose path name stays the same, select the clip in the Library window; from the Options pop-up menu in the top-right corner of the window, choose Update. A dialog appears in which you can select the video clip that needs updating (**Figure 16.19**). In addition, Flash automatically updates linked video each time you close and reopen the Flash file containing the linked clip.

To swap video clips:

1. Open a Flash Document containing video clips.

   You must have imported at least two video clips of the same type (embedded or linked) and placed an instance of at least one of them on the Stage.

2. On the Stage, select an instance of an embedded or linked video clip.

   You can replace one embedded clip with another embedded clip, or one linked clip with another linked clip. The procedure is the same; only the names of the Property Inspector and dialogs change to reflect the type of clip selected. This exercise uses an embedded clip. (Note that you cannot swap an embedded clip for a linked one.)

3. Access the Embedded Video Property Inspector.

   If the panel isn't open, choose Window > Properties.

4. Click the Swap button.

   The Swap Embedded Video dialog appears (**Figure 16.20**).

5. In the list of available video clips, select the replacement clip.

6. Click OK.

   Flash places an instance of the replacement clip on the Stage.

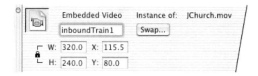

Figure 16.20 With a video clip selected on the Stage, clicking the Swap button in the Property Inspector lets you substitute a different clip. You can swap one embedded video clip for another embedded clip or one linked clip for another linked clip, but you can't mix and match.

Using Behaviors to Control Video Clips

You can use ActionScript to control the playback of video within your movie. Flash comes with seven Behaviors that create scripts for common video-control functions. By applying Behaviors to buttons, you can create video controllers that allow your end users to fast forward or rewind a video clip, pause or stop a clip's playback, resume or initiate playback from a paused or stopped state, and hide or show a video clip.

To pause video clips with buttons:

1. Open a new Flash Document and create two layers in the Timeline, name the top layer *Buttons* and the bottom layer *Video*.

Create in-between frames in both layers to give your video room to play, for example, select frame 25 in both layers and press F5.

2. Using the techniques offered in the preceding exercises, create an embedded video clip for your document.

Place the video clip in frame 1 of the *Video* layer.

3. Select the video clip on the Stage; in the Property Inspector, type an instance name for the clip.

To create scripts, Behaviors rely on each target video clip having an instance name. For this example, use the name MyVideo1. (If you forget to give the clip an instance name before choosing the Behavior, Flash allows you to name the instance when you apply the Behavior.)

continues on next page

4. With Keyframe 1 of the *Buttons* layer selected, place an instance of a button symbol on the Stage.

For more detailed instructions about using button symbols, see Chapters 11 and 12. It's a good idea to give the button an instance name, for example, `PauseMyVideo1_btn`. Your document should look like **Figure 16.21**.

5. Access the Behaviors and ActionScript panels.

If the panels are not open, press Shift-F3 to open the Behaviors panel; press F9 to open the Actions panel.

6. Select the button-symbol instance on the Stage.

7. From the Add Behavior menu in the Behaviors panel, choose Embedded Video > Pause (**Figure 16.22**).

The Pause Video dialog appears.

Figure 16.21 You can use Behaviors to script buttons that control playback of a video clip. The video clip must have an instance name.

Figure 16.22 The Embedded Video > Pause Behavior creates a script for pausing video playback.

Target video clips

Pathname

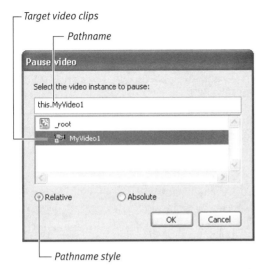

Pathname style

Figure 16.23 Select the video clip you want to control in the target video-clip pane of the Pause Video dialog. The clip must have an instance name.

Figure 16.24 The Pause Embedded Video Behavior creates a script for pausing playback of the target clip's parent Timeline.

8. In the dialog, *do the following:*

▲ In the target video-clip pane, choose the clip you want the button to control, for this example, MyVideo1. Flash enters the pathname for this clip in the target-path field (**Figure 16.23**).

▲ Leave the pathname style as Relative.

9. Click OK.

Flash adds the Behavior to the Behaviors panel and adds the appropriate ActionScript to the Script pane of the Actions panel (**Figure 16.24**). You can work with the Behavior using the techniques you learned in Chapter 12, for example, to change to the event that triggers the button to pause the video.

10. Choose Control > Test Movie to try out your button.

When you click the PauseMyVideo1_btn button, the video stops playing. The ActionScript created by Behavior > Embedded Video > Pause actually pauses playback of the main Timeline containing the target video clip. If you place more than one video clip in the main Timeline, clicking a button scripted to pause one of the clips stops them all.

✔ Tips

■ If you need to control multiple video clips individually, you must put them in independent Timelines, for example, place each one in a separate movie clip.

■ It's a good idea to add your own comments to a script created by a Behavior. In the Script pane of the Actions panel, click the first line (which the Behavior leaves blank). Type two slashes and your comment text, for example, `//This script makes the Timeline containing the clip MyVideo1 pause.`

■ If you want to make the video clip pause when someone clicks anywhere in its image area, you could place the video in a movie clip and apply the Behavior to the movie clip directly. If you select the video object on the Stage and choose the Behavior, Flash does the work of converting the video into a movie clip for you.

DELIVERING MOVIES TO YOUR AUDIENCE

17

When you finish creating graphics, animation, and interactivity in Macromedia Flash MX 2004, it's time to deliver the goods to your audience. You must export the Flash movie file to another format for playback. You have several formats to choose among. The one that guarantees viewers will see all your animations and take part in all your movie's interactivity is the Flash Player format. Player files end with the extension .swf.

Installing Flash MX 2004 also installs version 7 of the Flash Player application. You can view .swf files running directly in Flash Player on your computer. Other programs, such as Web browsers, can control Flash Player, too.

You can export movies as a series of images in either bitmap format (.GIF or .PNG files, for example) or vector format (such as Adobe Illustrator files). Another option for movie delivery is a self-playing file called a projector. Users double-click the projector file to open and play the movie. And you can print your entire movie or individual frames, should you want to give someone a hard-copy version of the movie (for storyboarding, for example).

Preparing Your Movie for Optimal Playback

When you create movies to show over the Web, you must face the issue of quality versus quantity. Higher quality (smoother animation and better sounds) increases file size. The larger the file, the longer the download time and the slower your movie will be. Things that add to your file's size include lots of bitmaps (especially animated bitmaps), video clips, sounds, lots of keyframes instead of tweening, multiple areas of animation at one time, embedded fonts, gradients, and separate graphic elements instead of symbols and groups.

To help you find out where your movie is bogging down, Flash offers simulated streaming. The Size Report and Bandwidth Profiler reveal which frames will cause hang-ups. You can then rethink or optimize the problem areas.

To use Bandwidth Profiler:

1. Open the Flash document that you want to test for playback over the Web.

2. From the Control menu, choose Test Movie (or Test Scene).

   Flash exports the movie and opens it in Flash Player.

3. From Flash Player's View menu, choose > Download Settings and select the download speed that you want to test.

   The menu lists eight speeds, all of which are customizable. To change them, choose View > Download Settings > Customize (**Figure 17.1**). By default, Flash lists five common connection speeds—14.4 Kbps, 28.8 Kbps, 56 Kbps, DSL, and T1—set to simulate real-world data-transfer rates in the Custom Download Settings dialog (**Figure 17.2**).

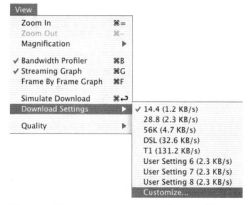

Figure 17.1 To create a custom connection speed for simulating playback over the Web, from the test environment's View menu, choose Download Settings > Customize.

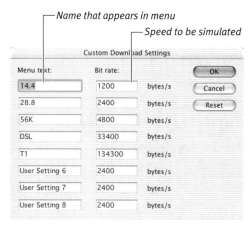

Figure 17.2 At its default setting, Flash offers choices for simulating four standard connection speeds. You can change the test names and rates in the Custom Download Settings dialog.

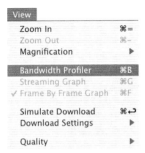

Figure 17.3 To view a graph of the amount of data in each frame, choose View > Bandwidth Profiler when a Flash Player window is open.

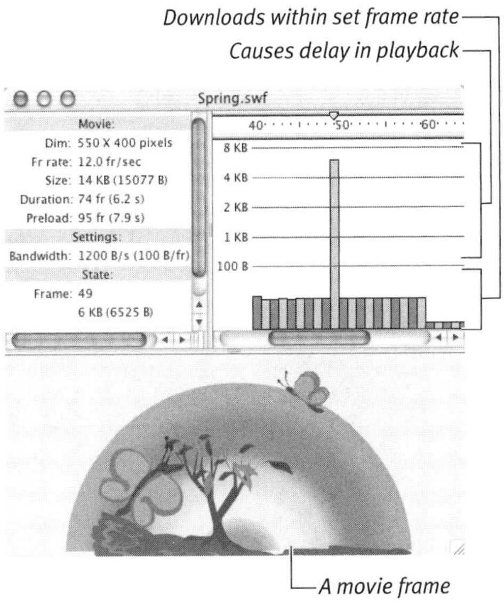

Downloads within set frame rate
Causes delay in playback

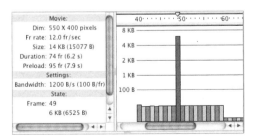

A movie frame

Figure 17.4 The Bandwidth Profiler graph at the top of the Flash Player window shows you how much data each movie frame contains and where the movie will pause to download data. Each bar in this version of the graph represents a frame of the movie.

4. From Flash Player's View menu, choose Bandwidth Profiler (**Figure 17.3**).

At the top of the Test Movie window, Flash graphs the amount of data that is being transmitted against the movie's Timeline (**Figure 17.4**). The bars represent the number of bytes of data per frame. The bottom line (highlighted in red) represents the amount of data that will safely download fast enough to keep up with the movie's frame rate. Any frame that contains a greater amount of data forces the movie to pause while the data downloads.

To view the contents of each frame separately:

1. From the View menu, choose Frame by Frame Graph, or press ⌘-F (Mac) or Ctrl-F (Windows).

Flash presents a single bar for each frame in the Bandwidth Profiler graph. The numbers along the top of the graph represent frames (**Figure 17.5**). The height of the bar represents the amount of data in that frame.

2. Select a bar.

Specifics about that frame and the movie in general appear in the profile window.

Figure 17.5 In Frame by Frame Graph mode, the height of each bar indicates how much data the frame holds. If the bar extends above the bottom line of the graph, the movie must pause to download the frame. In this movie, Frame 49 will cause a pause in playback.

To see how frames stream:

1. From the View menu, choose Streaming Graph, or press ⌘-G (Mac) or Ctrl-G (Windows).

   Flash displays the frames as alternating bars of light and dark gray, sized to reflect the time each one takes to download (**Figure 17.6**). The numbers along the top of the streaming graph represent frames as a unit of time based on the frame rate. (In a 12-fps movie, for example, each number represents 1/12 second.) For frames that contain very little data, you might see several bars in a single time unit in the graph. Frames that have lots of data stretch out over several time units.

2. Select a bar.

   Specifics about that frame and the movie in general appear in the left profile window.

To display a download-progress bar:

◆ With Bandwidth Profiler active, from Flash Player's View menu, choose Simulate Download, or press ⌘-Return (Mac) or Ctrl-Enter (Windows).

   As the animation plays in the test window, Flash highlights the numbers of the Timeline in green to show where you are in the download process.

To exit Bandwidth Profiler:

◆ From Flash Player's View menu, choose Bandwidth Profiler again.

✔ Tips

■ After you set up a test environment incorporating the Bandwidth Profiler, you can open any .swf file directly in test mode. Choose File > Open, navigate to the file that you want to test, and then click Open. Flash opens the movie in a Flash Player window, using the Bandwidth Profiler and other viewing options that you selected.

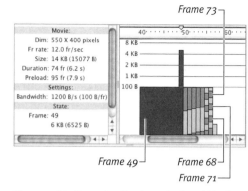

Frame 73

Frame 49 Frame 68
Frame 71

Figure 17.6 In Streaming Graph mode, the width of each bar indicates how long the frame takes to download at the given connection speed and frame rate. In this movie, Frame 49 contains 6KB of data and takes roughly 5 seconds to download at a frame rate of 12 fps over a 14.4 Kbps modem. Each number along the top of the graph is a frame, and at 12 fps, this equals 1/12 second.

■ You can get a printed version of the information about the amount of data in each frame. Choose the Generate Size Report option in the Export Flash Player dialog or the Flash tab of the Publish Settings dialog (for more information, see "Publishing and Exporting" later in this chapter). During the export or publishing process, Flash simultaneously creates a text file documenting how many bytes of information each frame of the movie contains.

A Note About Accessibility

As you think about the best ways to deliver Flash movies to your audience, you should also consider the fact that some members of that audience may have physical conditions that affect the way they interact with your site. As the Web has become more of a visual medium, it presents challenges to users with visual impairments who want to take advantage of the many resources available there.

Our society is becoming more sensitive to the ways in which activities and resources exclude people with disabilities. Web designers need to use Flash not only to make eye-catching Web sites that dazzle with artwork, animation, interactivity, sound, and video, but also to make sites that can convey information to a wide range of people. Remember that some of your users are unable to view or hear a site's content; some need to navigate and explore the site strictly through an input device, for example, by tabbing to each element in turn.

Flash addresses the issue of accessible Web sites by allowing you to make Flash content available to screen-reading software that uses Microsoft Active Accessibility (MSAA) technology. (At the time Flash MX 2004 was released, MSAA was available only for Windows.) Screen readers provide audio feedback about a variety of elements on a Web site, reading aloud the labels of buttons, for example, or reading the contents of text fields. Through Flash's accessibility features, you can create descriptions of objects for the screen reader; prevent the screen reader from attempting to describe certain objects (such as purely decorative movie clips); and also assign keyboard commands that let the user manipulate objects by pressing keyboard commands or tabbing through text fields, for example.

The considerations that go into making an effective, accessible site are too numerous and complex to cover in this book. But you can check out the tools for defining accessible objects in the Accessibility panel. Choose Window > Other Panels > Accessibility to open the panel, or click the Accessibility icon in the bottom-right quadrant of the Property Inspector (**Figure 17.7**). The accessibility parameters for selected objects appear in the panel.

Macromedia outlines some of the basic concepts of accessible Web design in the Help panel (see the topic Using Flash > Creating Accessible Content). More information is available on Macromedia's Accessibility page (*www.macromedia.com/macromedia/accessibility/*).

Figure 17.7 Clicking the Accessibility icon (left) in the Property Inspector opens the Accessibility panel (right). Use these settings to make selected objects in your movie available (or unavailable) to screen-reader software.

Publishing and Exporting

Flash's Publish function is geared toward presenting material on the Web. The Publish command can create the Flash Player (.swf) file and an HTML document that puts your Flash Player file in a browser window. The Publish command can also create alternate file formats—GIF, JPEG, PNG, and Quick-Time—and the HTML needed to display them in the browser window. Alternate formats let you make some of the animation and interactivity of your site available even to viewers who lack the Flash plug-in. Flash can also create stand-alone projector files.

Flash's Export Movie command exports a movie directly into a single format. In general, the options for exporting from Flash—GIF, JPEG, PNG, and QuickTime—are the same as those for publishing to those formats. The arrangement of some options differs between the export and publish dialogs, and some formats have more options in the Publish Settings dialog. In the Publish Settings dialog, for example, you have the choice to remove gradients from GIFs (to keep the file size small), whereas in the Export GIF dialog, you don't have that option. Another difference between publishing and exporting is that Flash stores the publish settings with the movie file for reuse.

Figure 17.8 To access the settings for publishing a movie, choose File > Publish Settings.

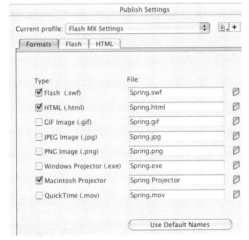

Figure 17.9 The Formats tab of the Publish Settings dialog allows you to publish your Flash movie in as many as seven formats at the same time. You also can create an HTML document for displaying the published files in a browser.

✔ Tip

■ If you have the Property Inspector open as you work on your Flash document, you can open the Publish Settings dialog quickly by clicking the Settings button in the Property Inspector.

To set a movie's publishing format:

1. Open the Flash Document that you want to publish.

2. From the File menu, choose Publish Settings, or press Option-Shift-F12 (Mac) or Ctrl-Shift-F12 (Windows) (**Figure 17.8**). The Publish Settings dialog appears. The top of the dialog displays a Current Profile and buttons for working with profiles. If you are working in a new document and have never created a profile, Default is your only option. If you open a file made with a previous version of Flash, the profile name reflects that version. A profile is the compilation of settings for the various publishing options. You can save settings in new profiles (see "Creating Publishing Profiles," later in this chapter). Leave the current profile in place.

3. Click the Formats tab (**Figure 17.9**).

4. Choose one of the eight format options. The formats available are Flash (.swf), HTML (.html), GIF Image (.gif), JPEG Image (.jpg), PNG Image (.png), Windows Projector, Macintosh Projector, and QuickTime (.mov).

5. To set the options for a selected format, choose the tab associated with that format (as outlined in separate exercises later in this chapter).

6. To save these settings with the current file, click OK.

   Flash uses these settings each time you choose the Publish or Publish Preview command for this document. Flash also uses a file's current publish settings when you enter test mode (by choosing Control > Test Movie or Control > Test Scene).

To publish a movie:

1. Open the Flash file that you want to publish.

2. To issue the Publish command, *do one of the following:*

   ▲ From the File menu, choose Publish Settings. The Publish Settings dialog appears. You can follow the steps in the preceding exercise to set new format options or accept the current settings. Then click the Publish button (**Figure 17.10**).

   ▲ From the File menu, choose Publish, or press Shift-F12. The Publishing dialog appears, displaying a progress bar and a button for canceling the procedure (**Figure 17.11**). Flash uses the publish settings that are stored with your Flash document.

   Flash creates a new file for each format that is selected in the Publish Settings dialog.

✔ Tips

■ By default, Flash places the published files in the same location as the original Flash file. You can choose a new location. In the formats tab of the Publish Settings dialog, click the folder icon to the right of the file name. The Select Publish Destination dialog appears, allowing you to select a new location for the file.

■ You can open your browser and preview a movie in one step. Choose File > Publish Preview. Flash offers a menu that contains all the formats selected in the Publish Settings dialog (**Figure 17.12**). Choose a format. Flash publishes the file in that format, using the current settings, and opens the movie in a browser window.

Figure 17.10 Click the Publish button in the Publish Settings dialog (top) or choose File > Publish (bottom) to publish your Flash files.

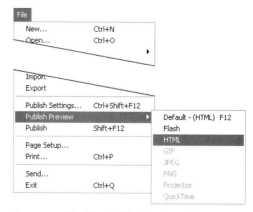

Figure 17.11 To cancel the publishing process, click the Stop (Mac) or Cancel (Windows) button in the Publishing dialog.

Figure 17.12 The File > Publish Preview submenu displays all the formats that are selected in the Publish Settings dialog. Flash publishes your movie in the selected format and opens it in your browser.

Figure 17.13 You can type your own filenames in the fields of the Publish Settings dialog box. Just be sure to end the name with the proper extension. To return to the default name, click the Use Default Names button.

- Flash makes one of the formats the default for Publish Preview. To publish in the default format, press Shift-F12. If you want to do lots of testing in a format other than SWF (if you want to test your animated GIF versions, for example), set your publish settings in only that format. Then that format will be the default, and you can choose it quickly by pressing Shift-F12.

- By default, Flash names the published files by adding the appropriate extension to the file name, adding .gif for a GIF file or .png for a PNG file, for example. You change the name by typing a different name in the name field in the Publish Settings dialog. To return to the default name, click the Use Default Names button (**Figure 17.13**).

- The Publish and Publish Preview commands do not give you a chance to name the published files; they take the names directly from the Publish Settings dialog. If you want to publish multiple versions of a movie, each with different settings, you must make sure that you don't overwrite the published file. Rename the published file, move that file to a new location, or type a different name in the Formats tab of the Publish Settings dialog.

Working with Flash Player Settings

The stand-alone Flash Player is an application file that installs with Flash. The Player opens when you double-click the icon of a file that has the .swf extension. (From within Flash Player, you can use the File > Open command to open and play .swf files.) To prepare a Flash movie for playing in the stand-alone Player, choose either the Export or Publish command in the Flash editor. The options are basically the same for both commands.

To publish a Flash Player (.swf) file:

1. In the Flash editor, open the Flash file that you want to publish.

2. From the File menu, choose Publish Settings.

   The Publish Settings dialog appears; choose a base publishing profile, or leave the current setting.

3. Click the Formats tab.

4. In the Type section, select Flash (.swf).

   If you wish, type a new name in the File field for the Flash (.swf) file. Be sure to include the .swf extension.

5. Select the Flash tab (**Figure 17.14**).

6. Set Flash options as described in the following exercises.

7. Click Publish.

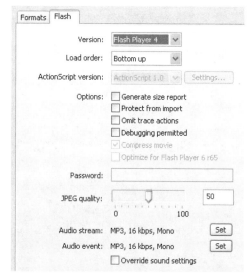

Figure 17.14 The Flash tab of the Publish Settings dialog offers options for publishing your Flash movie as a Flash Player (.swf) file.

Figure 17.15 The Load Order pop-up menu determines the order in which Flash draws the layers of the first frame of your movie.

To choose a Flash Player version:

◆ From the Version pop-up menu, choose one of the seven versions of Flash Player.

Your options are Flash Player 1 (formerly known as FutureSplash Animator) through 7. If you publish your file as a version earlier than Flash Player 7, you lose some features specific to Flash MX 2004.

✔ Tip

■ Before you start creating any ActionScripts, set the Flash export options in the Publish Settings dialog to the earliest version of Flash Player to which you plan to export. Any Flash MX 2004 actions that won't work in that version appear with yellow highlighting in the Actions Toolbox in the Actions panel.

To control how Flash draws the movie's first frame:

◆ From the Load Order pop-up menu, choose the order in which Flash loads a movie's layers for displaying the first frame of your movie (**Figure 17.15**).

When playback over the Web is slow, Flash starts displaying individual layers as they download. The Top Down setting tells Flash to send (and display) the top layer first and then work its way to the bottom layer. Bottom Up does just the opposite.

To choose the version of ActionScript used (Flash Player 6 and 7):

◆ From the pop-up menu, choose ActionScript version.1. 0 or ActionScript version 2.0 (**Figure 17.16**).

This setting tells Flash which version of the scripting language you've used in scripts in your document so the compiler treats the code appropriately. The menu becomes active only when you have chosen Player versions 6 or 7.

✔ Tip

■ The components found in Flash MX 2004's Components panel rely on ActionScript 2.0. If you've used any of those components in the current document, you must choose ActionScript 2.0.

To list the amount of data in the movie by frame:

◆ Check the Generate Size Report check box (**Figure 17.17**).

Flash creates a separate text file listing the frames of the movie and how much data each frame contains. This report helps you find frames that bog down the movie's playback. You can then optimize or eliminate some of the content in those frames.

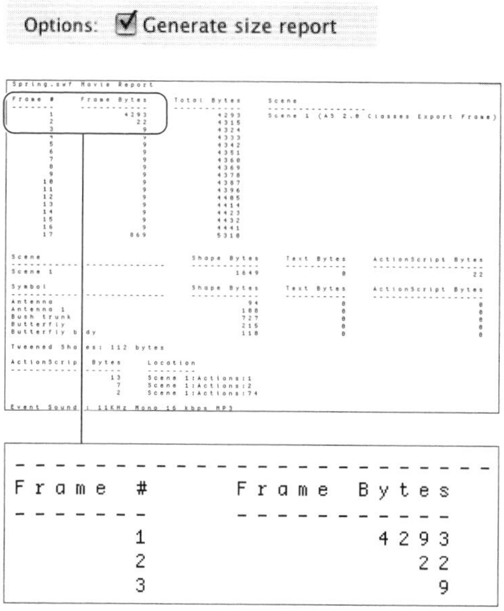

To protect your work:

◆ Check the Protect from Import check box.

This setting prevents viewers from obtaining the .swf file and converting it back to a Flash movie. This setting is especially important if you plan to make the file available for remote debugging.

✔ Tip

■ You can make the Protect from Import setting selective. Enter a password in the Password field. Any one who enters the correct password, can import the .swf file.

Figure 17.16 ActionScript 2.0 presents special tasks for the compiler when Flash publishes a .swf file. Be sure to select it if you use version 2.0 for scripting.

Figure 17.17 Choose Generate Size Report (top) to have Flash create a text file that lists the amount of data in your movie (bottom).

Figure 17.18 When you check the Debugging Permitted check box, you should also enter a password to protect movies that are open to remote debugging.

To set trace and debug options:

To tell Flash how to deal with **trace** actions and debugging (options that are useful for more advanced ActionScripters), *do any of the following:*

◆ To prevent **trace** actions from appearing in the Output window during debugging, check the Omit Trace Actions check box. This option strips the **trace** actions from the published movie, allowing you view only non-**trace** debugging items in the Output window. Omitting **trace** actions also reduces file size slightly if your scripts contain lots of trace actions.

◆ To allow remote debugging of ActionScripts check the Debugging Permitted check box. This option allows you or other users to debug a Flash Player (.swf) file as it plays over the Internet.

✔ Tip

■ When the Debugging Permitted option is selected, you should always enter a password in the Password field (**Figure 17.18**). This password prohibits unauthorized individuals from accessing your script but allows authorized personnel to debug the file remotely.

WORKING WITH FLASH PLAYER SETTINGS

To compress the .swf file (Flash Player 6 and 7):

1. Choose Flash Player 6 or 7 from the Version pop-up menu.

2. Check the Compress Movie option.

   The best reason to implement movie compression is for text-heavy movies. Movie compression works both on text that appears in the movie and text that's hidden in scripts. Compress Movie is an option only when you publish for Flash Player versions 6 or 7.

To target specific versions of Flash Player 6:

◆ Choose Flash Player 6 from the Version pop-up menu. Select Optimize for Flash Player 6 r65.

   Optimizing allows Flash to take advantage of performance improvements made to Flash Player 6 (these enhancements appear in release 65 and later of Flash Player 6). This option is active only when you have chosen Flash Player 6 from the Version menu.

To compress the bitmaps in your movie:

To set JPEG compression, *do one of the following:*

◆ Adjust the JPEG Quality slider.

◆ Enter a specific value in the JPEG Quality field (**Figure 17.19**).

   This setting controls how Flash applies JPEG compression as it exports the bitmaps in your movie. A setting of 0 provides the most compression (and the lowest quality, because that compression leads to loss of data).

Figure 17.19 To set JPEG compression for any bitmaps in your movie, type a value in the JPEG Quality field or use the slider. A setting of 0 results in the most compression (worst quality); 100 results in the least compression (best quality).

✔ Tip

■ Flash doesn't apply JPEG compression to GIF images that you've imported into your movie, because Flash defaults to using lossless compression for GIFs.

WORKING WITH FLASH PLAYER SETTINGS

Figure 17.20 You must set the sample rate and compression options for stream sounds and event sounds separately. Click the Set button to access the options for each type of sound.

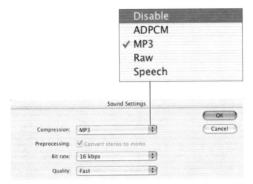

Figure 17.21 Choose a compression method from the Compression pop-up menu. Other options appropriate to the selected method appear. Choose Disable to turn off sound.

To control compression and sample rate for all movie sounds:

1. In the Audio Stream section (or the Audio Event section) of the Publish Settings dialog, click the Set button (**Figure 17.20**).

   The Sound Settings dialog appears. Flash divides sounds into two types: stream and event (for more details, see Chapter 15). You must set the compression for each type separately, but the process and options are the same for both.

2. To set compression parameters, from the Compression pop-up menu (**Figure 17.21**), *choose one of the following:*

   ▲ To make Flash omit sound from the published file, choose Disable.

   ▲ To set compression for movies containing mostly short event sounds, such as handclaps or button clicks, choose ADPCM. (Generally, you'll use this setting in the Audio Event section.) The ADPCM options appear. From the ADPCM Bits pop-up menu, choose 2-Bit for the greatest degree of compression (resulting in the lowest-quality sound); choose 5-Bit for the least compression (resulting in the highest-quality sound). With the ADPCM setting, you can also set a sample rate and convert stereo sound to mono sound.

continues on next page

Sample-Rate Rule of Thumb

Sample rates are measured in kHz or frequency. Recording for music CDs is done at 44 kHz. For multimedia CD-ROMs, 22 kHz is a standard rate. For music clips in Flash movies played on the Web, 11 kHz is often sufficient. For shorter sounds, including spoken words, you may be able to get away with even lower sampling rates.

▲ To set compression for movies containing mostly longer stream sounds, choose MP3. (Generally, you'll use this setting in the Audio Stream section.) The MP3 options appear. From the Bit Rate pop-up menu, choose one of 12 bit rates for the published sounds. At Bit Rate settings of less than 20 Kbps, Flash converts sounds from stereo to mono; at settings of 20 Kbps and above, you can publish stereo sounds or convert them to mono sounds. From the Quality pop-up menu, choose Fast for movies that will play back over the Web; Medium and Best provide better quality.

▲ To omit sound compression, choose Raw. Raw does allow you to control file size by choosing a sample rate and converting stereo sound to mono.

▲ To set compression for sounds consisting of spoken words, choose Speech. Choose a sample rate from the pop-up menu of options that appears.

Digitally Recorded Sounds

As motion pictures are to movement, digital recordings are to sound. Both media capture slices of a continuous event. By playing the captured slices back in order, you re-create the event. In a movie, the slices are frames of film; in a digital recording, they're slices of sound.

You can think of the recording process as capturing a sound wave by laying a grid over it and copying a piece of the wave at each intersection on the grid. The lines across the horizontal axis are the *sample rate*—how often you capture the sound. The lines up and down the vertical axis are the *bit rate*—how much of the sound wave's amplitude you capture. The greater the frequency and bit rate (the finer the mesh of your recording grid), the greater the realism of your recording during playback. Unfortunately, greater realism translates into larger files.

The sound options in the Publish Settings dialog give you the flexibility to create different versions of your movie with different sample rates and bit rates without actually changing the sounds embedded in the movie. You might allow yourself larger file sizes and higher-quality sounds for a version being delivered on CD-ROM than for a version being distributed on the Web. As you try different sound options, be sure to actually listen to your published sounds to determine the best balance between sound quality and file size.

Advanced Sound Handling

The sound-compression settings in the Publish Settings dialog apply to all the sounds in your movie unless you have specified sound settings for individual sounds in the library of the Flash Document. A more advanced method of dealing with sound compression is setting compression options and sample rates for sounds individually. Assigning the highest quality to selected sounds helps you keep file size reasonable but still have high-quality sound where you need it.

You set compression options for individual sounds via the Sound Properties dialog, which you access from the movie's Library window. Control-click (Mac) or right-click (Windows) a sound name in the Library window; then choose Properties from the contextual menu that appears. The Sound Properties dialog appears. Its Compression pop-up menu gives you access to the same sound-export settings as the Flash tab of the Publish Settings dialog.

If some sounds in a movie have individual sound-export settings, Flash uses those settings for those sounds when you choose Publish. Flash uses the sound options that you set in the Publish Settings dialog for all other sounds in that movie.

If you've used individual compression methods for some sounds in your movie, you can force Flash to ignore them and publish all sounds with the sound options you've chosen in the Publish Settings dialog. In the Flash tab of the Publish Settings dialog, choose Override Sound Settings. You might use this feature to make a lower-quality Web version of a movie that you created for CD-ROM.

Publishing HTML for Flash Player Files

An *HTML document* is a master set of instructions that tells a browser how to display Web content. The Publish function of Flash creates an HTML document that tells the browser how to display the published files for your document (these files can be in Flash, GIF, JPEG, PNG, and/or QuickTime format, whatever you choose in the Formats tab of the Publish Settings dialog).

The Publish command creates the required HTML by filling in blanks in a template document. Flash comes with nine templates; you can create your own templates.

To publish HTML for displaying a Flash file:

1. Open the Flash Document that you want to publish for the Web.

2. From the File menu, choose Publish Settings.

 The Publish Settings dialog appears; choose a new base publishing profile, or leave the current setting.

3. Click the Formats tab.

4. In the Type section, choose HTML (.html).

 When you choose HTML, Flash automatically selects Flash (.swf) as well.

5. Select the HTML tab (**Figure 17.22**).

 The options for displaying your Flash movie in the browser window appear in the dialog. When you publish the current file, Flash feeds your choices into the appropriate HTML tags and parameters in the template of your choice.

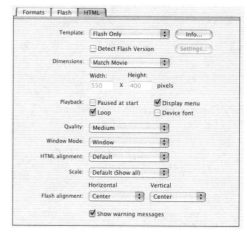

Figure 17.22 The HTML tab of the Publish Settings dialog displays options for displaying your Flash movie in the browser window.

PUBLISHING HTML FOR FLASH PLAYER FILES

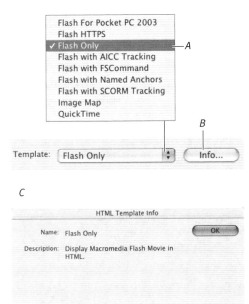

Figure 17.23 Choose Flash Only (A) as the template when you want to create HTML for displaying only a Flash movie, with no other options for alternate images. Click the Info button (B) to see a description of what the template does (C).

To create HTML for Flash only:

◆ From the Template pop-up menu, choose Flash Only (**Figure 17.23**).

This template is the simplest one. It uses the OBJECT and EMBED tags to display your Flash content for viewers who are properly equipped with the Flash Player version that you select in the Flash tab of the Publish Settings dialog. Other viewers will be unable to see your content. (Other template choices create HTML that displays alternate images or files when the viewer lacks the proper plug-in.)

✔ Tips

■ If you can't remember what one of the included HTML templates does, select it from the Template pop-up menu in the HTML tab of the Publish Settings dialog, then click the Info button next to the menu. Flash displays a brief description, including instructions about choosing alternate formats.

■ Although Flash's publishing features currently make use of HTML's OBJECT and EMBED tags, Microsoft is in the process of changing the way those tags work to display interactive content in the Microsoft Explorer browser. As this book goes to press, information about what these changes will be and how they will affect the way you need to structure HTML to work with Flash is just emerging. Check the Macromedia and/or Microsoft Web sites for continued updates to help you deal with the changing technology.

The Mystery of HTML Templates

The HTML codes (called *tags*) required for displaying a .swf file in a browser window are OBJECT for Internet Explorer (Windows) and EMBED for Netscape Navigator (Mac and Windows) and Internet Explorer (Mac). (In addition, Flash can use the IMG tag to display a file in another format, such as a JPEG image or an animated GIF. If you have created named anchors in your Flash movie and you choose the Flash with Named Anchors template, Flash can create anchor tags for browser navigation, as well.)

Flash's Publish command works hand in hand with HTML templates—which are fill-in-the-blank recipes—to define the parameters of those tags. These parameters include the width and height of the movie window, the quality of the images (the amount of antialiasing to provide), and the way the movie window aligns with the browser window.

Each option and parameter in the HTML tab of the Publish Settings dialog has an equivalent template variable. The template variable is a code word that starts with the dollar sign ($). When you choose an option in the Publish Settings dialog, Flash enters your choice as an HTML tag that replaces the variable in the template document. If you set the width of your movie as 500 pixels in the Publish Settings dialog for HTML, for example, Flash replaces the template variable for width ($WI) with the proper coding to display the movie in a window 500 pixels wide.

Flash's HTML templates contain coding not only for displaying your Flash movie, but also for showing the JPEG, GIF, or PNG versions of your movie that you want to make available to viewers who don't have the proper browser player to view Flash.

During the publishing process, Flash saves a copy of the HTML template for your movie, giving it the name of your movie file and adding whatever extension the template file has. (The template files that come with Flash use the extension .html, for example.) You can go into a template file as you would any other text file and modify the HTML coding.

You can extend the Publish command's capacity for creating HTML documents by setting up your own HTML templates. To be available to Flash's template menu, the HTML file must include a title (use the code $TT). The HTML file must be inside the HTML folder, which lives in the Configuration Folder. For more details on locating this folder, see the sidebar, "The Mystery of the Configuration Folder," in Chapter 1.

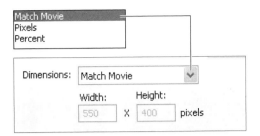

Figure 17.24 Choose a method for sizing the movie-display window (the window in which a browser displays your Flash movie).

Controlling Movie Placement in the Browser

When you publish HTML for displaying movies in a Web page, you need to think in terms of three windows:

◆ The *browser window* contains the entire Web page.

◆ Within the browser window is a *movie-display* window (created by the OBJECT, EMBED, and IMG tags), where the Flash plug-in displays a Flash movie.

◆ Inside the movie-display window is the actual *movie window*.

Each of the three windows has its own dimensions, and you need to tell Flash where to put the windows and how to handle them if their aspect ratios differ, for example, or when a user resizes the browser window. You instruct browsers on how to deal with these three windows by choosing settings in the HTML tab of the Publish Settings dialog. When you define a movie-display window with a different width or height from the original Flash movie, you must tell Flash how to scale the movie to fit in that window.

To set the dimensions of the movie-display window:

To set the width and height of the rectangle created by the OBJECT and EMBED tags for displaying your movie in the browser, from the Dimensions pop-up menu in the HTML tab of the Publish Settings dialog (**Figure 17.24**), *choose one of the following:*

◆ To use the movie's dimensions (specified in the Document Properties dialog), choose Match Movie.

continues on next page

- To specify the dimensions as a percentage of the browser window's dimensions, choose Percent, and type a value between 1 and 100 in the Width and Height fields.

- To specify new dimensions, choose Pixels, and type the new values in the Width and Height fields.

To scale the movie to fit a movie-display window:

From the Scale pop-up menu (**Figure 17.25**), *choose one of the following:*

- To keep the movie's original aspect ratio (width to height) and resize the movie so that it fits completely within the newly specified rectangle, choose Default (Show All) (**Figure 17.26**). (Be aware that the resized movie may not fill the new rectangle: Gaps may appear on the sides or at the top and bottom.)

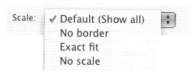

Figure 17.25 The scale method tells Flash how to fit the Flash movie inside the movie-display window that you define. You need to set the scale only if you define a movie-display window with different dimensions from those of the movie itself—as a percentage of the browser width and height, for example.

Dimensions: Match Movie; Scale: NA

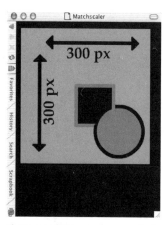

Dimensions: 100 by 50 pixels; Scale: No Border

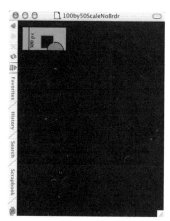

Dimensions: 100 by 50 pixels; Scale: Exact Fit

Figure 17.26 This 300-by-300–pixel movie looks quite different in the different dimension-and-scale combinations. The movie-display window's dimensions and the scale setting are identified in the examples above. (Here the browser background has been set to black to make the movie display window visible.)

CONTROLLING MOVIE PLACEMENT IN THE BROWSER

Horizontal: Right; Vertical: Center

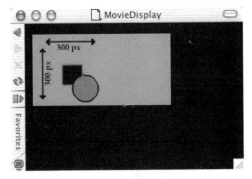

Horizontal: Left; Vertical: Center

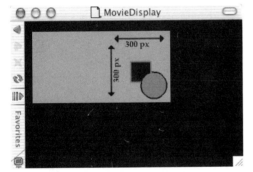

Figure 17.27 The Flash Alignment section's Horizontal and Vertical pop-up menus allow you to position your movie within the movie-display window when the dimensions of that window differ from those of the movie. Compare the results of two different settings for this 300-by-300–pixel movie set inside a 200-by-100–pixel display window. The light-gray rectangle is the display window, which automatically fills with the same color as your movie's background.

◆ To keep the movie's original aspect ratio and resize the movie so that the whole new rectangle is filled with the movie, choose No Border. (Some of the movie may slop over the edges and be cropped.)

◆ To change the movie's height and width to the new specifications, even if it involves changing the aspect ratio and distorting the image, choose Exact Fit.

◆ To keep the movie at a constant size, choose No Scale. Resizing the browser window can crop the image.

✔ Tip

■ If you define the movie-display window as 100 percent of the width and height of the browser window, in some browser versions, no matter how large your viewer makes the browser window, a scroll bar always appears. Setting the width and height to 95 percent (or lower) ensures that all viewers will be able to enlarge the browser window enough to eliminate the scroll bar.

To control placement of the movie window in the movie-display window:

To align the movie window within the movie-display window, in the Flash Alignment section of the HTML tab of the Publish Settings dialog, *do one of the following:*

◆ From the Horizontal pop-up menu, choose Left, Center, or Right.

◆ From the Vertical pop-up menu, choose Top, Center, or Bottom.

Flash positions the movie within the movie-display window (**Figure 17.27**).

To set playback options:

In the Playback section of the HTML tab of the Publish Settings dialog, *choose any of the following options:*

◆ To make users begin the movie manually (by clicking a button or by choosing Play from the contextual menu), choose Paused At Start.

◆ To create a contextual menu with playback options that are available to users, choose Display Menu.

◆ To make the movie start over when it reaches the last frame, choose Loop.

◆ To speed playback on Windows systems, choose Device Font. The Device Font option allows Windows systems to substitute aliased system fonts for fonts that are not installed on the user's system. This substitution takes place only in static text blocks where you have enabled device fonts during the authoring phase.

To control antialiasing and smoothing:

From the Quality pop-up menu in the HTML tab of the Publish Settings dialog (**Figure 17.28**), *choose one of the following options:*

◆ Low. Flash keeps antialiasing off.

◆ Auto Low. Flash starts playback with antialiasing off, but if it finds that the viewer's computer and connection can handle antialiasing while keeping the movie's specified frame rate, Flash turns antialiasing on.

◆ Auto High. Flash turns antialiasing on to start with and turns it off if playback drops below the movie's specified frame rate.

Figure 17.28 The Quality setting for publishing HTML balances image quality against playback speed in a published movie.

Figure 17.29 For viewers of your movie who use qualified browsers, you can create a transparency effect that reveals Web-page elements beneath any transparent areas of your Flash movie. In the HTML tab of the Publish Settings dialog, set Window Mode to Transparent Windowless.

- ◆ **Medium.** Taking the middle ground, Flash forgoes bitmap smoothing but does do some antialiasing.

- ◆ **High.** Flash uses antialiasing on everything, but smooths bitmaps only if there is no animation.

- ◆ **Best.** Flash keeps antialiasing on.

To control transparency:

From the Window Mode pop-up menu, *choose one of the following options:*

- ◆ To play the movie in its own window within the Web page, choose Window.

- ◆ To make the transparent areas of your movie block out the background and other elements of the Web page that lie below the Flash movie, choose Opaque Windowless.

- ◆ To allow those elements to show through in any transparent areas of your movie, choose Transparent Windowless (**Figure 17.29**). Only certain browsers support the ability to create transparent backgrounds for your published .swf content. On the Mac, for OS X 10.1.5 and 10.2, Internet Explorer (IE) 5.1 and 5.2 can handle this setting; in Windows, IE 5.0, 5.5, and 6.0 can; on both platforms, Netscape 7.0 (or later), Opera 6 (or later), Mozilla 1.0 (or later), and AOL/CompuServe can.

CONTROLLING MOVIE PLACEMENT IN THE BROWSER

To see warning about missing alternate content:

◆ At the bottom of the HTML tab of the Publish Settings dialog, check the Show Warning Messages check box if you want Flash to notify you if the currently selected template creates tags to display alternate content—a GIF file, for example—but you have neglected to select the appropriate format in the Formats tab of the Publish Settings dialog.

✔ Tip

■ The default HTML template automatically sets the background color of your Web page to the background color of your movie. If you want to use a different color, try creating a modified template (**Figure 17.30**). Open the default template, and save a copy with a new name. In the first line of code—$TTFlash Only—change the title to something like $TTFlash Only (BlackBackground), so that Flash recognizes and adds the template to the Template menu. In the tag <BODY bgcolor="$BG">, replace $BG with the HTML code for a specific hex color (000000 for a black background, for example). Be sure to place the new template in Flash's HTML folder inside the Configuration folder (for more details, see the sidebar "The Mystery of the Configuration Folder," in Chapter 1).

Title of template for menu

```
$TTFlash Only
$DS
Display Macromedia Flash Movie in HTML.
$DF
```

```
$CS
<TITLE>$TI</TITLE>
</HEAD>
<BODY bgcolor="$BG">
```

Background-color variable

New title of template for menu

```
$TTFlash Only (BlackBackground)
$DS
Display Macromedia Flash Movie in HTML.
$DF
```

```
$CS
<TITLE>$TI</TITLE>
</HEAD>
<BODY bgcolor="000000">
```

New background-color variable

Flash For Pocket PC 2003
Flash HTTPS
Flash Only
Flash Only (BlackBackground)
Flash with AICC Tracking
Flash with FSCommand
Flash with Named Anchors
Flash with SCORM Tracking
Image Map
QuickTime

Figure 17.30 The default HTML template picks up the movie's background color as the Web page's background color. You can modify a copy of the template (top). Change the Title tag, and set a specific background color (middle). The new title appears in the Template menu in the HTML tab of the Publish Settings dialog (bottom).

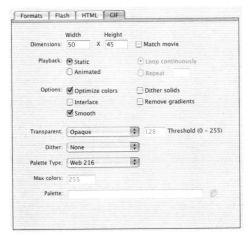

Figure 17.31 Click the GIF tab of the Publish Settings dialog to access the options for creating a static or animated GIF for your alternate image.

About the Image Map Template

If your Flash file contains button symbols linking to URLs, you can convert that content to an image map, a GIF (or PNG or JPEG) file containing hot spots that link to other sites. To have Flash create an image map whose hot spots coincide with your Flash button symbols, choose HTML as well as GIF (or PNG or JPEG) in the Formats tab of the Publish Settings dialog. From the Template pop-up menu in the HTML tab of the dialog, choose Image Map. Click Publish. Although Flash creates a .swf file whenever you publish HTML format files, the Image Map template creates an .html file that tells browsers to display the .gif (or .png or .jpg) file not the .swf. When the browser displays the image map, viewers see your graphic content, and the buttons seem live because they are active links. (Note that the Image Map template creates hot spots only from button symbols, not button components or movie clips acting as buttons).

Using Alternate Image Formats

Although most viewers have access to the Flash Player plug-in required to view your Flash content, some may not. You can make at least some of your site available to them by providing alternate image files for their browsers to display. If you're using Flash animation for a simple Web banner, for example, you could use an animated GIF to re-create that banner for viewers who lack the Flash plug-in. Flash can publish alternate GIF, JPEG, PNG, and QuickTime files. Of course, you need a file with the proper HTML coding to direct the viewer's browser to display the alternate file. The HTML Templates named Image Map and QuickTime can assist you in creating the necessary .html file, as can Flash's version-detection feature (see "Using Version Detection," later in this chapter).

Although each image format has its own set of publishing options, the basic methods for publishing all four alternate formats are the same. This exercise walks you though the settings for GIF files.

To publish GIF files:

1. Open the Flash Document and choose File > Publish Settings.

   The Publish Setting dialog appears; choose a new base publishing profile, or leave the current setting.

2. In the Formats tab of the dialog, choose GIF Image (.gif).

3. In the GIF tab of the dialog (**Figure 17.31**), set GIF options as described in the following exercises.

4. Click Publish.

To set the dimensions of the GIF image:

In the Dimensions section of the GIF tab of the Publish Settings dialog, *do one of the following:*

◆ To create a new size for the published GIF image, deselect Match Movie and enter values in the Width and Height fields.

◆ To keep the GIF images the same size as the original Flash movie, choose Match Movie (**Figure 17.32**).

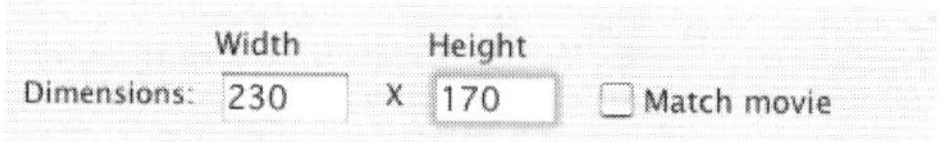

To make an animated GIF:

1. In the Playback section of the GIF tab of the Publish Settings dialog, choose Animated (**Figure 17.33**).

   The animation settings become active.

2. Choose Loop Continuously.

   You can also limit the number of times that the animation loops by choosing Repeat and typing a number. (Choosing Static makes Flash export only the first frame of the movie as a single GIF image.)

To balance size, download speed, and appearance:

In the Options section of the GIF tab of the Publish Settings dialog (**Figure 17.34**), *do one of the following:*

◆ To remove any unused colors from the GIF file's color table, choose Optimize Colors.

◆ To make the GIF appear quickly at low resolution and come into focus as the download continues, choose Interlace. (The Interlace option should be used only for static GIFs.)

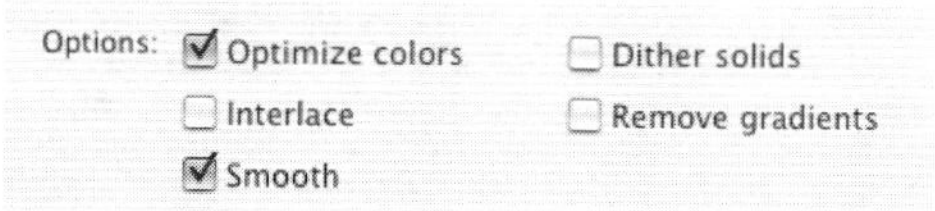

Figure 17.32 Deselect Match Movie to enter the dimensions you want the published GIF image to be, or choose Match Movie to use the movie's dimensions as the dimensions of your GIF image.

Figure 17.33 To preserve the motion of your Flash movie (though not the sound or interactivity) for viewers who lack the Flash plug-in, choose Animated in the GIF tab of the Publish Settings dialog.

Figure 17.34 The settings in the Options section of the GIF tab help you limit the amount of time that your viewers will spend looking at a blank screen, waiting for an image to appear. (The Remove Gradients option is available only in the Publish Settings dialog, not in the Export GIF dialog.)

About the QuickTime Template

If you want to convert your Flash content to a QuickTime movie, choose QuickTime and HTML in the Formats tab of the Publish Settings dialog. From the Template pop-up menu in the HTML tab of the dialog, choose QuickTime. Click Publish. The QuickTime template embeds the QuickTime version of your content within the .html file. Note that currently, the QuickTime player can only handle playback of Flash Player 4 (or earlier) content.

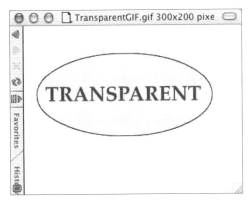

Figure 17.35 The Transparent setting (top) determines how the background of a published GIF appears. Choose Opaque to make the GIF's background a solid color (middle); choose Transparent to make the GIF's background invisible (bottom).

◆ To reduce the size of the file, deselect Smooth. (Select it if you want Flash to create smoothed bitmaps for your animated GIF.)

◆ To apply the dither method to solids as well as gradients and bitmapped images, choose Dither Solids (see "To control colors that are not in the current color palette" later in this chapter).

◆ To reduce file size by converting gradient fills to solid fills, choose Remove Gradients. (Flash uses the first color in the gradient as the solid fill color.)

To set a GIF's background transparency:

From the Transparent pop-up menu of the GIF tab of the Publish Settings dialog (**Figure 17.35**), *do one of the following:*

◆ To make background areas of the Flash movie opaque in the published GIF, choose Opaque.

◆ To make the background areas of the Flash movie transparent in the published GIF, choose Transparent.

To control transparency of Flash fill colors in GIFs:

◆ From the Transparent pop-up menu in the GIF tab of the Publish Settings dialog, choose Alpha.

The Alpha setting makes the GIF's background transparent and allows you to set a threshold below which partially transparent fills in Flash convert to full transparency in the published GIF. The threshold settings are values from 0 to 255 (the number of possible colors in a GIF image). The default threshold value is 128 (corresponding to an Alpha value of 50 percent in Flash).

✔ Tip

- The GIF Alpha transparency setting can have unexpected results, especially in animated GIFs. Full GIF transparency appears only where a filled graphic element sits directly on the background of the Flash movie. Wherever the graphic element overlaps (or moves over) another fill, the "invisible" graphic suddenly pops into view again (**Figure 17.36**).

To control colors that are not in the current color palette:

1. From the Dither pop-up menu of the GIF tab of the Publish Settings dialog (**Figure 17.37**), *choose one of the following options:*

   - ▲ To replace the missing color with the closest match from the current palette, choose None.

   - ▲ To simulate the missing color by applying a regular pattern of colors from the current palette, choose Ordered.

   - ▲ To simulate the missing color by applying a random pattern of colors from the Web 216 palette, choose Diffusion. (You must also choose Web 216 as your Palette Type in Step 2 for Diffusion to work.)

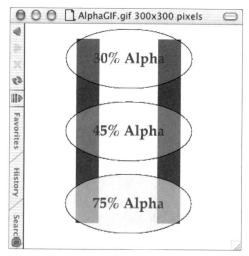

Figure 17.36 When you publish a movie as a GIF, you can make partially transparent graphic elements sitting on the background of the Flash movie look fully transparent in a browser window. Each oval here has the same color fill but a different Alpha value. For this GIF, the Transparent option is set to Alpha with a threshold of 128 (equal to 50 percent Alpha in Flash). The 30 percent and 45 percent ovals are fully transparent where only background lies below them. Where those ovals overlap other graphic elements, however, they are 30 percent and 45 percent transparent, respectively. The 75 percent oval (above the threshold value) retains its partial transparency even over the background.

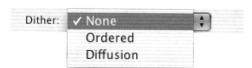

Figure 17.37 The GIF format has three options for dithering the colors that are not included in the current color table.

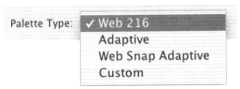

Figure 17.38 Choose a palette that optimizes colors for the published GIF image. You can create custom palettes or use the Web-safe or adaptive palettes provided by Flash.

Figure 17.39 When you choose Custom from the Palette Type pop-up menu, you must enter a filename in the Palette field. Click the Browse button (the folder icon) to open a dialog for locating the file.

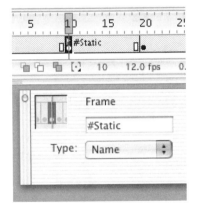

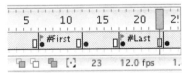

Figure 17.40 Assigning the frame label #Static tells Flash to use that frame for static GIF files (top). Assigning the frame labels #First and #Last allows you to limit the range of frames that Flash publishes as an animated GIF (bottom).

2. From the Palette Type pop-up menu, choose a color table for use with this GIF (**Figure 17.38**).

Your choices are Web 216 (the standard 216 Web-safe colors), Adaptive (only colors used in your document; 256 colors maximum), Web Snap Adaptive (a modified Adaptive palette, substituting Web-safe colors for any near matches to colors in the document that are not Web safe), and Custom (the color table specified in Step 4).

3. If you chose Adaptive or Web Snap Adaptive as the Palette Type, in the Max Colors field, type the number of colors that you want to use.

This option allows you to further limit the size of the color table available for the GIF and, thus, reduce file size.

4. If you chose Custom as the Palette Type, load the custom palette (**Figure 17.39**).

Click the Browse button (the folder icon). The file-import dialog appears; navigate to the custom palette, select it, and click Open.

✔ Tips

- By default, when creating a static GIF, Flash uses the first frame of your movie. To use another frame, create a keyframe at the desired frame number. Assign it the frame label #Static.

- When creating animated GIFs, you can tell Flash to publish a subset of the movie's frames. Assign the label #First to the first keyframe of the subset; assign the label #Last to the keyframe that ends the subset. Flash creates an animated GIF from that range of frames (**Figure 17.40**).

Using Version Detection

Version Detection is the process of verifying what version of Flash Player is running on your viewer's system. If the viewer has the player required to view your Flash content, the browser displays your regular content. If the Flash Player is missing, or the version number is too low, you can display a message; link to Macromedia's Web site to download the correct player; display one of the alternate image files you learned about in the preceding section; or display a completely different site.

To detect viewer's Flash Player version:

1. Open your Flash Document and choose File > Publish Settings.

   The Publish Settings dialog appears; choose a new base publishing profile, or leave the current setting.

2. In the Flash tab of the dialog, choose Flash version 4 or higher from the Version pop-up menu.

3. In the HTML tab, select the Detect Flash Version check box.

4. Click the Settings button.

   The Version Detection Settings dialog appears (**Figure 17.41**). When you select the detection option, Flash publishes three types of documents: The Detection File, a .swf file that becomes part of the EMBED tag and detects which version of Flash Player your viewer has. The Content File, an .html file, instructs the browser to display the .swf file created from your Flash document. The Alternate File (.html) instructs the browser to display a substitute for your .swf file. The default Alternate File displays a warning that this Web site requires a different version of Flash Player; it also contains a link to the

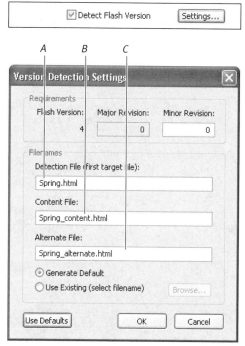

Figure 17.41 With Detect Flash Version selected (top), Flash creates three .html documents when you publish your file (bottom): One detects the viewer's Flash Player version (A); one directs the browser to play your .swf (B); and one directs the browser to play alternate content if the correct player version is missing (C).

Macromedia site, where viewers can download the latest player version.

5. To determine which specific files fulfill the three roles, *do one of the following:*

▲ To let Flash create its standard Detection and Alternate files, select Generate Default or click the Use Defaults button.

▲ To use your own alternate file, select Use Existing, then enter the pathname to the file in the Alternate File field. You can also select the field, click the Browse button (the folder icon to the right of the field), navigate to the appropriate file via the Open file dialog, select the file, and click Open; Flash enters the path name for you.

6. Click OK.

✔ Tip

■ Earlier in this chapter, you learned to create GIF, PNG, or JPEG files from your Flash content. To use one of those files—say a .gif file—as the Alternate File in Flash's Detect Flash Version feature, you must enter its pathname in the Alternate File field of the Version Detection Settings dialog. One way to accomplish that is to run the publishing procedure twice. First, follow the steps in "Using Alternate Image Formats" to create an alternate image file, for example, a .gif file. Second, follow the steps in the preceding exercise to create the version-detection files. In step 5, select Use Existing, click the Browse button to access the Open file dialog, navigate to the .gif file created during the first Publish operation, select the file, and click Open; Flash enters the pathname for you. Now click Publish. When viewers who lack the right Flash Player version go to your site, they get redirected to your .gif alternate.

Creating Projectors

Projectors are self-sufficient applications for playing Flash content. To play a projector file, you simply double-click the projector icon. Projectors are an excellent way to distribute movies directly to people, such as to e-mail a Flash-animated greeting card to a friend. Projectors are platform-specific, but you can make projectors for both the Mac and Windows platform, from either platform.

To create a projector:

1. Open the Flash Document from which you want to publish a projector.

2. Choose File > Publish Settings.

   The Publish Settings dialog appears; choose a new base publishing profile, or leave the current setting.

3. In the Formats tab (**Figure 17.42**), *choose one of the following options:*

   ▲ To create a projector that runs on a Mac, choose Macintosh Projector.

   ▲ To create a projector that runs in Windows, choose Windows Projector (.exe).

4. Click the Publish button.

   As it creates the projector files, Flash displays the Publishing dialog, which has a progress bar and a button for canceling the operation. Unless you choose a new location (via the file destination button), Flash places the projector files in the same location as the original Flash Document. A projector has a distinctive icon (**Figure 17.43**).

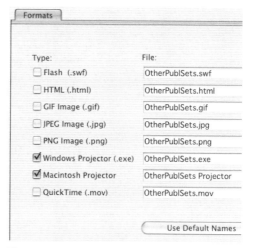

Figure 17.42 To create a run-time version of your movie, choose Windows Projector or Macintosh Projector in the Formats tab of the Publish Settings dialog. You have no other options for formatting projectors.

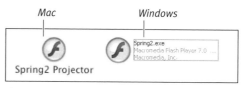

Figure 17.43 The projector is a stand-alone run-time file. Double-click the icon to launch the projector.

Playing Macintosh Projectors Created in Windows

When you publish a Macintosh projector on a computer running the Windows operating system, Flash gives the projector the extension .hqx. That extension indicates a file encoded in binhex format. Macintosh users need to translate the file by using a program such as BinHex or StuffIt Deluxe to play the projector on the Mac OS.

Delete current profile
Open Profile Properties dialog
Duplicate existing profile
Create new profile
Import/export custom profile

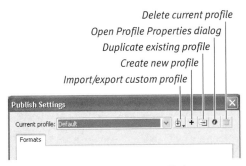

Figure 17.44 Click the Create New Profile button to begin the process of adding a new publishing profile to the current document.

Figure 17.45 Name your profile in the Create New Profile dialog.

Creating Publishing Profiles

Setting all the various publishing options can be tedious. If you use particular groups of settings repeatedly, you can save them as a publishing profile. The profile information gets stored with each document. This means that unlike for HTML Templates, there is no master menu of profiles available each time you call up the Publish Settings dialog. You can, however, import and export profiles to make them available to other documents. Another important difference is that a Publish Profile is not an immutable set of options that's always the same each time you choose it. When you click OK or Publish, all the current publishing options get incorporated into the profile that's selected in the Current Profile pop-up menu. Next time you open the Publish Settings dialog for that document, either in this work session or a later one, choosing a profile calls up the last settings you made with that profile selected in that document.

To save settings under a new profile name:

1. Open your Flash Document.

2. Choose File > Publish Settings.

3. In the Publish Settings dialog, click the Create New Profile button, the plus sign to the right of the Current Profile menu (**Figure 17.44**).

   The Create New Profile dialog appears (**Figure 17.45**).

4. Type a name for your profile in the Profile Name field, for example, MyPubSettings.

continues on next page

5. Click OK to accept the name in the Create New Profile dialog.

You return to the Publish Settings dialog, with your new profile selected in the Current Profile menu.

6. Set your desired publishing options, using any techniques learned earlier in this chapter.

7. Click Publish or OK.

Flash updates the current profile in the open document and publishes and/or closes the dialog. Flash incorporates the settings you made in Step 6 into the profile named `MyPubSettings`, and stores them with the current document. If you open a new document, that profile is not available. To make the profile available to other documents, you must export it.

✔ Tips

■ If you want to make small adjustments to an existing profile and save it as a new profile, start by duplicating the basic profile. Select the basic profile from the Current profile menu, then click the Duplicate Profile button. The Duplicate Profile dialog appears for naming the new profile. Now follow steps 4 through 7 in the preceding exercise.

■ To delete a profile from the current Flash Document, select the profile from the Current Profile menu and click the Delete Profile button (the Trash can icon). A Flash MX dialog appears asking you to verify the deletion. Click OK.

■ To rename a profile in the current Flash Document, select the profile from the Current Profile menu and click the Profile Properties Profile button (the *i* icon). The Profile Properties dialong appears. Type the profile's new name in the Profile Name field. Click OK.

Figure 17.46 You can export publishing profiles to make use of them in other documents.

Figure 17.47 Store exported profiles in the Publishing Profiles folder in the Configuration folder, or store them with your Flash documents.

To export a profile:

1. Follow steps 1 through 6 in the preceding exercise.

2. Click OK.

3. From the Import/Export pop-up menu to the right of the Current Profile field, select Export (**Figure 17.46**).

   The Export Profile dialog appears (**Figure 17.47**). This is basically a Save As dialog, with a different name. By default, Profile (.xml) is selected in the Show (Mac) or Files of Type (Windows) menu.

4. Navigate to the location where you want to save the profile file.

5. Enter a name for the file.

6. Click Save.

   Flash saves the profile as an .xml file in the specified location.

✔ Tip

■ The default location for storing profiles is in a folder named Publish Profiles in the Configuration Folder (see "The Mystery of the Configuration Folder," in Chapter 1). Since the profiles do not get pulled into new Flash documents automatically, however, there is no reason you must store them there.

CREATING PUBLISHING PROFILES

647

To import a profile:

1. Open a Flash Document in which you want to use the saved profile.

2. Choose File > Publish Settings.

3. From the Import/Export pop-up menu, select Import (**Figure 17.48**).

   The Import Profile dialog appears. This is basically a normal file-import dialog (**Figure 17.49**). By default, Profile (.xml) is selected in the Show (Mac) or Files of Type (Windows) menu.

4. Navigate to the saved the profile.

5. Click Open.

   The profile becomes available from the Current Profile menu in the Publish Settings dialog of the active Flash document.

Figure 17.48 To use a saved profile in a different document, you must import it. Select Import from the Import/Export Profile menu in the Publish Settings dialog.

Figure 17.49 Navigate to the saved profile via the Import Profile dialog, click Open, to make the profile available from the Current Profile menu in the Publish Settings dialog.

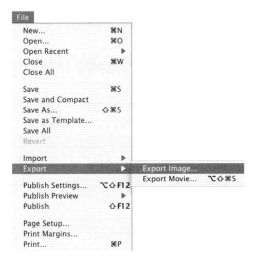

Figure 17.50 To export a single frame of your movie, choose File > Export > Export Image.

Figure 17.51 The Export Image dialog allows you to select an export format, name your file, and navigate to the location where you want to save the file.

Exporting Flash to Other Formats

When you export Flash movies, you can export the entire movie or just one frame. Flash exports to a variety of formats that are not included in the Publish Settings dialog: for both Mac and Windows, Adobe Illustrator, EPS, and DXF; for Mac only, PICT and QuickTime Video; and for Windows only, Enhanced Metafile (EMF), Windows Metafile (WMF), Windows AVI, and WAV. Although the options for the export formats differ, the basic process is always the same. The example used in the following sections exports to Illustrator format, which preserves the vector information from your Flash graphics.

To export a single frame to Illustrator format:

1. Open the Flash file that contains the frame that you want to export to another format.

2. In the Timeline, move the playhead to the frame that you want to export.

3. From the File menu, choose Export > Export Image (**Figure 17.50**).

   The Export Image dialog appears (**Figure 17.51**).

4. Navigate to the location where you want to save the file.

5. Enter a name in the Name (Mac) or Filename (Windows) field.

6. From the Format (Mac) or Save As Type (Windows) pop-up menu, choose Adobe Illustrator.

   Flash adds the proper extension, .ai, to your filename.

continues on next page

7. Click Save.

The Export Adobe Illustrator dialog appears (**Figure 17.52**).

Whenever your chosen export format requires you to set further parameters, Flash displays those parameters in a dialog after you click Save. For Illustrator format, the additional parameter is a version number.

8. Choose the version to which you want to export.

9. Click OK.

Flash displays the Exporting dialog, which contains a progress bar and a button for canceling the export process.

To export the entire movie to Illustrator format:

◆ Follow the instructions in the preceding exercise, but in step 3, from the File menu, choose Export > Export Movie, or press Option-Shift-⌘-S (Mac) or Ctrl-Alt-Shift-S (Windows) (**Figure 17.53**), and in step 6, choose Adobe Illustrator Sequence.

When you chose Export Movie, Flash creates a separate Illustrator file for each frame of the movie and numbers the files sequentially.

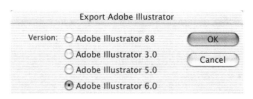

Figure 17.52 Whenever an export format requires additional settings, a dialog with format-specific options appears when you click Save in the Export Image dialog. You can export to four versions of Illustrator, for example.

Figure 17.53 To export all the frames of your movie, choose File > Export> Export Movie.

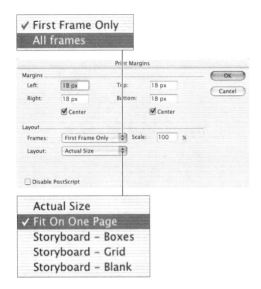

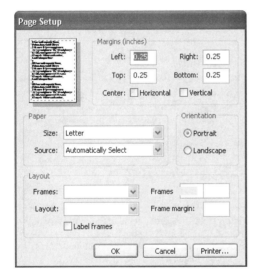

Figure 17.54 The options in the Print Margins (Mac, top) and Page Setup (Windows, bottom) dialogs enable you to print the frames of your movie as single pages or as storyboard layouts during authoring.

Printing from Flash

When you are editing a Flash document, you can print frames as individual pages or print several frames per page in a storyboard layout. You choose how many frames each row in the storyboard contains. Flash sizes the frames accordingly. Use the Print Margins (Mac) or Page Setup (Windows) command to choose layout options.

To print a single frame:

1. Open the Flash Document from which you want to print.

2. From the File menu, choose Print Margins (Mac) or Page Setup (Windows). The Print Margins or Page Setup dialog appears (**Figure 17.54**).

3. From the Frames pop-up menu, choose All Frames.

4. From the Layout pop-up menu, choose Fit on One Page.

5. Click OK.

6. From the File menu, choose Print. The Print dialog appears.

7. Enter the desired frame numbers in the From and To fields.

8. Click Print.

✔ Tip

■ If your Macintosh printer isn't capable of printing PostScript, be sure to check the Disable PostScript check box.

To print storyboard thumbnails:

1. Follow steps 1 through 3 of the preceding exercise.

2. From the Layout pop-up menu, *choose one of the following options:*

   ▲ To outline each movie-frame rectangle, choose Storyboard-Boxes.

   ▲ To print the frames in a grid, choose Storyboard-Grid.

   ▲ To print just the graphic elements of each movie frame, choose Storyboard-Blank.

   The layout parameters appear.

3. In the Frames Across field, enter the number of frames that you want to print across the page.

   Flash prints as many as 128 frames in a single storyboard row.

4. In the Story Margin (Mac) or Frame Margin (Windows) field, enter the amount of space that you want to use between frames in your layout.

5. Click OK.

6. From the File menu, choose Print.

   The Print dialog appears.

7. If you want to print only some pages of your thumbnails, type those page numbers in the From and To fields.

8. Click OK.

   Flash creates the thumbnails, using the options you specified (**Figure 17.55**).

✔ Tip

■ To print the scene and frame number below each frame in the layout, choose Label Frames in the Print Margins (Mac) or Page Setup (Windows) dialog.

Storyboard boxes

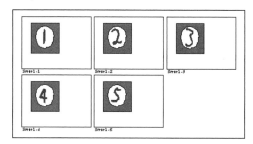

Storyboard grid

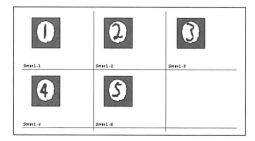

Storyboard blank

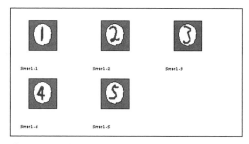

Figure 17.55 The Layout menu of the Print Margins (Mac) or Page Setup (Windows) dialog offers three storyboard options: movie frames outlined in a box, frames set inside a grid, or each frame alone.

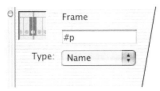

Figure 17.56 To define keyframes that print when viewers choose Print from Flash Player's contextual menu, select the keyframe and enter #p in the Label field of the Frame Property Inspector.

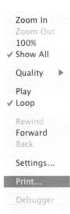

Figure 17.57 In your browser, Control-click (Mac) or right-click (Windows) to access Flash Player's contextual menu. Choosing Print outputs all the pages defined as printable.

Printing from Flash Player

Flash gives you the option of letting your viewers print some or all of a movie directly from Flash Player's contextual menu. By default, the contextual menu's Print command prints every frame in the movie. You restrict printing to certain frames by labeling them as printable in the original Flash Document. (Advanced ActionScripters can provide viewers with other options for printing Flash content.)

To set frames to print from the contextual menu:

1. Create a Flash Document with three keyframes.

   Place different content in each frame to make it easy to tell which frames you've actually printed. Add a `stop` action to each keyframe, and add buttons that take you from frame to frame in the published movie. Use Behaviors to add a `gotoAndPlay` action to each button; make the frame containing the button the target frame (for details on using buttons with Behaviors, see Chapter 12).

2. In the Timeline, select Keyframe 1.

3. Access the Frames Property Inspector.

4. To define the selected frame as printable, in the Label field, enter #p (**Figure 17.56**).

5. In the Timeline, select Keyframe 3.

6. Repeat Step 4.

7. Publish your Flash movie, and view the resulting Flash Player file in your browser.

8. To access the contextual menu, Control-click (Mac) or right-click (Windows) anywhere in the movie window.

   The contextual menu appears (**Figure 17.57**).

continues on next page

9. Choose Print.

Flash prints the frames you labeled as printable (frames 1 and 3) and skips the frame that doesn't contain the #p label (Frame 2).

✔ Tips

■ If there are no frames with the #p label in the movie, the contextual menu's Print command prints each frame in the movie.

■ If you define more than one frame as printable by labeling it #p, when you publish the movie, Flash displays a warning message in the Output window, letting you know that there are multiple frames with the same label name. If the only duplicates are #p labels, just ignore the warning.

To disable printing from Flash Player:

1. Open the Flash file for which you want to disable printing.

2. In the Timeline, select any frame.

3. Access the Frame Property Inspector.

4. In the Label field, enter !#p.

When you publish the file, the Print option is unavailable from Flash Player's contextual menu (**Figure 17.58**).

✔ Tip

■ You can remove the contextual menu from your published Flash Player file by unchecking the Display Menu check box in the Playback section of the HTML tab of the Publish Settings dialog (**Figure 17.59**).

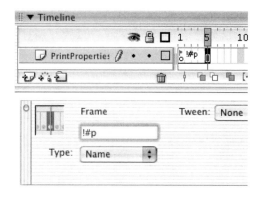

Figure 17.58 Attaching the label !#p to any frame in a movie (top) grays out the Print option in the contextual menu of Flash Player (bottom).

Figure 17.59 Deselecting the Display Menu check box in the HTML tab of the Publish Settings dialog (top) limits the functions of the contextual menu for your published movie and is one way to disable printing from within your movie (bottom). The browser's print functions will still be available, however.

INDEX

INDEX

INDEX

T

W

WAV files, 554
waveforms, 556, 564, 572, 582–588
Web
    accessibility issues, 615
    sound and, 626
    streaming sound over, 570–572
web browsers
    browser window, 631
    color in, 641
    HTML and, 629
    movies shown in, 631–636
    transparency and, 635
Web-safe colors, 641
Wide Library View button, 239
windows, 41. *See also* panels; *specific windows*
Windows platform
    Configuration folder, 11
    cross-platform issues, xiii
    installing Flash MX, 2–3
    projectors, 644
    system requirements, xxiv
WMF format, 539
.wmv files, 590
work area, 12
wrapping text, 91

X

x and y coordinates, 117–118

Z

Zoom Control field, 33–35
zoom tool, 34–35
zooming, 33–35